Handbook of Communication and Emotion

Research, Theory,
Applications, and Contexts

To the four most significant people in my life with whom I have shared every conceivable emotion: My wife, Dr. Janis Andersen; my daughter, Kirsten Andersen; and my parents, Alexander and Mildred Andersen
　　　—P. A. A.

To all those who have rocked my emotions and helped fill my life with more positive than negative affect, especially my husband, Vico; my parents, Bob and Carol; my sister, Cindy and her family; and my brother, Mark
　　　—L. K. G.

Handbook of Communication and Emotion

Research, Theory, Applications, and Contexts

Edited by

Peter A. Andersen
San Diego State University
San Diego, California

Laura K. Guerrero
Arizona State University
Tempe, Arizona

Academic Press
San Diego   London   Boston   New York
Sydney   Tokyo   Toronto

Copyright © 1998 by ACADEMIC PRESS

Academic Press
a division of Harcourt Brace & Company
525 B Street, Suite 1900, San Diego, California 92101-4495, USA
http://www.apnet.com

Academic Press Limited
24-28 Oval Road, London NW1 7DX, UK
http://www.hbuk.co.uk/ap/

Library of Congress Cataloging-in-Publication Data

Handbook of communication and emotion : research, theory,
   applications, and contexts / edited by Peter A. Andersen, Laura K.
   Guerrero.
       p.   cm.
   Includes index.
   ISBN 0-12-057770-4 (hardcover : alk. paper)
   1. Interpersonal communication.   2. Expression.   3. Emotions.
   I. Andersen, Peter A.   II. Guerrero, Laura K.
   BF637.C45H283   1997
   153.6--dc21   97-23315
                                                      CIP

PRINTED IN THE UNITED STATES OF AMERICA
97 98 99 00 01 02 BB 9 8 7 6 5 4 3 2 1

Contents

PART I

Introduction

3   Principles of Communication and Emotion in Social Interaction

Peter A. Andersen and Laura K. Guerrero

PART II

The "Dark Side" of Emotions

4   Strategic Embarrassment: The Culprit of Emotion

Lisa Bradford and Sandra Petronio

5   Guilt and Hurt: Similarities, Distinctions, and Conversational Strategies

Anita L. Vangelisti and Rhonda J. Sprague

6 *Jealousy Experience and Expression in Romantic Relationships*

Laura K. Guerrero and Peter A. Andersen

7 *The Experience and Expression of Anger in Interpersonal Settings*

Daniel J. Canary, Brian H. Spitzberg, and Beth A. Semic

8 *Interpersonal Communication Problems Associated with Depression and Loneliness*

Chris Segrin

PART III

The "Bright Side" of Emotions

12 *Loving and Liking*
Carolyn B. Taraban, Susan S. Hendrick, and Clyde Hendrick

13 *Communication and Sexual Desire*
Sandra Metts, Susan Sprecher, and Pamela C. Regan

PART IV

Applications and Contexts

14 *Emotional Expression in the Deception Process*
David B. Buller and Judee K. Burgoon

Contributors

Numbers in parentheses indicate the pages on which the authors' contributions begin.

Peter A. Andersen (3, 49, 155, 303)
School of Communication
San Diego State University
San Diego, California 92182

Anita Barbee (281)
Department of Psychology
University of Louisville
Louisville, Kentucky 40292

Lisa Bradford (99)
Department of Communication
University of Wisconsin, Milwaukee
Milwaukee, Wisconsin 53201

David B. Buller (381)
Department of Communication
University of Arizona
Tucson, Arizona 85721

Judee K. Burgoon (381)
Department of Communication
University of Arizona
Tucson, Arizona 85721

Brant R. Burleson (245)
Department of Communication
Purdue University
West Lafayette, Indiana 47907

Daniel J. Canary (189)
Department of Speech Communication
Pennsylvania State University
University Park, Pennsylvania 16802

Michael R. Cunningham (281)
Department of Psychology
University of Louisville
Louisville, Kentucky 40292

Judith A. Feeney (473)
School of Psychology
University of Queensland
St. Lucia, Queensland 4072
Australia

Stanley O. Gaines, Jr. (507)
Department of Psychology
Pomona College
Claremont, California 91711

Daena J. Goldsmith (245)
Department of Speech Communication
University of Illinois
Urbana, Illinois 61801

Laura K. Guerrero (3, 49, 155, 303)
Department of Communication
Arizona State University
Tempe, Arizona 85287

Clyde Hendrick (331)
Department of Psychology
Texas Tech University
Lubbock, Texas 79409

Susan S. Hendrick (331)
Department of Psychology
Texas Tech University
Lubbock, Texas 79409

Peter F. Jorgensen (403)
Department of Communication
Western Illinois University
Macomb, Illinois 61455

Sandra Metts (353)
Department of Communication
Illinois State University
Normal, Illinois 61790

Patricia Noller (473)
School of Psychology
University of Queensland
St. Lucia, Queensland 4072
Australia

Sandra Petronio (99)
Department of Communication
Arizona State University
Tempe, Arizona 85287

Sally Planalp (29)
Department of Communication Studies
University of Montana
Missoula, Montana 59812

Richard E. Porter (451)
Department of Communication Studies
California State University, Long Beach
Long Beach, California 90801

Pamela C. Regan (353)
Department of Psychology
California State University, Los Angeles
Los Angeles, California 90032

Nigel Roberts (473)
School of Psychology
University of Queensland
St. Lucia, Queensland 4072
Australia

Tammy L. Rowatt (281)
Department of Psychology
University of Louisville
Louisville, Kentucky 40292

Larry A. Samovar (451)
School of Communication
San Diego State University
San Diego, California 92182

Chris Segrin (215)
Department of Communication Studies
University of Kansas
Lawrence, Kansas 66045

Beth Semic (189)
Department of Speech Communication
Pennsylvania State University
University Park, Pennsylvania 16802

Stacy L. Smith (533)
Department of Communication
University of California, Santa Barbara
Santa Barbara, California 93106

Brian J. Spitzberg (189)
Department of Communication
San Diego State University
San Diego, California 92182

Rhonda J. Sprague (123)
Department of Speech Communication
University of Texas, Austin
Austin, Texas 78712

Susan Sprecher (353)
Department of Sociology
Illinois State University
Normal, Illinois 61790

Carolyn Taraban (331)
Department of Psychology
Texas Tech University
Lubbock, Texas 79409

Melanie R. Trost (3)
Department of Communication
Arizona State University
Tempe, Arizona 85287

Anita L. Vangelisti (123)
Department of Speech Communication
University of Texas, Austin
Austin, Texas 78712

Barbara J. Wilson (533)
Department of Communication
University of California, Santa Barbara
Santa Barbara, California 93106

Kim Witte (432)
Department of Communication
Michigan State University
East Lansing, Michigan 48824

Acknowledgments

This volume was made possible with the help of many people. Walid Afifi, Janis Andersen, Dan Canary, and Brian Spitzberg deserve special thanks for serving as special reviewers for the chapters we wrote. We are also grateful to all of the authors who contributed to this volume. It was pleasure to work with first-rate authors who were conscientious and prompt, and who contributed interesting and intellectually stimulating material. We are particularly indebted to Jim Dillard, who wrote the foreword for this book. Jim probably didn't know what he was getting into when we asked him to "read the book" and write some introductory comments. We would also like to acknowledge everyone at Academic Press who helped with this project, especially Nikki Levy and Eileen Favorite. Most of all, we thank everyone who helped keep our emotions happy and sane as we edited this volume.

Foreword

The Role of Affect in Communication, Biology, and Social Relationships

James Price Dillard
University of Wisconsin–Madison
Madison, Wisconsin

Is it mere tautology to assert that social beings communicate with one another? Perhaps so, but the questions that follow from that observation are anything but trivial. What forms might communication take and to what end? What other processes provide the scaffolding for interaction? How does communication tie those social beings together or propel them apart?

This book examines one of the essential aspects of the communication process: affect. I call it essential because it figures so prominently in virtually all of the questions that we might pose about communication. Although the individual chapters will make this case far more persuasively than my assertion, in the pages that follow I provide some foundation for the chapters themselves. My arguments depend heavily on a claim that is uncontroversial in most circles, that is, that human beings have evolved to meet adaptive challenges posed by the environment. I develop three points:

1. The primary function of affect is to guide behavior. Affect evolved because it enabled successful interaction with the environment.

2. For human beings, the important environment was the social environment. Affect evolved in the presence and service of social interaction.

3. For better or worse, human beings strategically manage their affective states. The relative utility of these efforts can be judged only by reference to the environment.

INTERACTING WITH THE ENVIRONMENT: BASIC PROCESSES

Organisms of all sorts strive to maintain inclusion in their respective gene pools (Mayr, 1982). From *Paramecium* to *Homo sapiens,* these organisms must acquire resources from the environment if they are to survive and reproduce. This entails two problems. For one, whenever some change in the environment takes place, the organism must discern its relevance and nature. Does it matter to me? And, if so, is it hostile or hospitable? This is the problem of appraisal. It can be simple and straightforward, as when someone wins the lottery, but often it is not. A curved stick may be mistaken for a snake, a water pistol for a genuine Smith & Wesson .357. Because of the ambiguous and polysemic nature of the environment, particularly the social environment, accurate appraisal of environmental changes is no simple task.

Then there is the problem of response. At base, the behavioral options and their corresponding motivations are only two: approach and withdrawal (Schneirla, 1959).[1] People seek sustenance and lovers, whereas they attack enemies. These are all forms of approach. Withdrawal can be seen in efforts to avoid toxins and boors.

Choosing[2] between the response strategies is often difficult because most of the elements in the environment are multivalenced. That is, they present consequences that are both desirable and undesirable. High fat foods, for instance, offer the gratification of flavor against the downside of weight gain and coronary threat. Further complications are introduced because the relative strength of the approach and withdrawal motivations change as a function of distance from the issue under consideration. When organisms are far from the stimulus, the approach motivation is relatively stronger than the withdrawal motivation. The relationship between the two motivations reverses itself when the organism is in close proximity to the stimulus (Miller, 1959).

Making the appropriate response to relevant elements in the environment is clearly important to any organism. It serves the long-range goal of inclusive fitness, the mid-range goal of survival, and the immediate goal of, for example, satiating one's hunger. But in addition to the complexities introduced by multivalenced elements and varying proximity to those elements, there is time pressure. Some environmental changes are imperative. They demand an immediate response. At the extreme, the contemplative organism is the dead organism.

Evolution has provided affect as a solution to the problems posed by interaction with the environment. The primary function of affect is to guide behavior. There are numerous lines that might be drawn within the conceptual domain of affect (see

---

[1]Of course, there are distinctly different forms of approach, ranging from nurturance to attack, and different forms of withdrawal, as seen in fright versus contempt. These are important distinctions, but space does not permit a thorough examination of them.

[2]As a matter of convenience, I will use the language of choice throughout this chapter. However, I do not mean to imply that people are necessarily aware of their options nor that they make considered judgments concerning the course of action that they pursue.

Guerrero, Andersen, & Trost, Chapter 1, this volume), but whether we are talking about moods, emotions, or other feeling states, the function is the same. Affect advises behavior.

I want to emphasize that it is not the environment itself that presents the adaptive problem, but rather the question of how to interact with it (Burleson & Goldsmith, Chapter 9, this volume; Lazarus, 1991). This point is vital because it reveals that the solution must be two-sided. On one side is the state of the environment and the *phasic* responses made to it. On the other side is the *tonic,* or preexisting, affective state that the organism brings to the interaction. Both require consideration.

Affect as Phasic

Environmental imperatives are dealt with by coarse programs that run very rapidly, that is, by emotions. The emotions can be likened to computer programs in that they accept certain forms of information, analyze that information, and then output instructions that shift the organism into a mode of operation suited to dealing with the change (Oatley, 1992). The alterations in mode of operation are both swift and global. They sweep through the physiological, cognitive, motivational, and expressive systems, mobilizing resources from each so as to yield a mode of operation suitable for dealing with the environmental change.

These programs must be considered coarse in that the input they accept is very limited and the range of values they output fairly small. Some writers take the position that the human emotional system has only a few basic output values. Oatley (1992), for example, contends that there are only five such states: happiness, sadness, fear, anger, and disgust. Each one has implications for some form of engagement or withdrawal depending on environmental conditions. However, there are compelling reasons to treat these emotions, and perhaps others, as conceptually and operationally distinct. Different affects are designed to accommodate different configurations of person–environment relations. These differences are reflected in the physiology (Ekman, Levenson, & Friesen, 1983; Sinha, Lovallo, & Parsons, 1992) and phenomenology of the emotions. There is more to emotion than *just* approach or withdrawal.

Affect as Tonic

If we view emotions as phasic responses to the environment, the other side of the solution is the tonic (baseline) state of the organism. Any decision as to the appropriate course of action (i.e., engagement versus withdrawal) must depend on the resources available to the organism at the time the action is required. The experiential aspect of moods can be thought of as a readout of the operating level of the organism's various biopsychological systems. When the individual is fatigued, malnourished, or overcaffeinated, these conditions are typically manifested in mood. Bad moods might warn of the depletion of resources and the inadvisability of engaging in some challenging interaction with the environment. Good moods, in contrast, signal a "full tank" and a corresponding potential for successful interaction (see Guerrero et al., Chapter 1, this volume).

A single continuum running from good to bad is probably not the best way to conceptualize mood. In fact, there is considerable evidence that two separate dimensions, one positive and one negative, provide a more theoretically precise and empirically valid conception of mood. Factor analytic work on mood consistently reveals a two-factor structure labeled positive and negative affect by Watson and Tellegen (1985) and energetic and tense arousal by Thayer (1989). These two affects are statistically independent of one another (Watson & Tellegen, 1985). Furthermore, there is evidence that their neural substrates are differentiated in the left and right hemispheres of the brain, respectively (Fox, 1991). The left hemisphere is the biological substrate of approach behavior and positive or energetic affect, whereas the right hemisphere contains the withdrawal or inhibition systems that generate the corresponding behaviors and negative or tense affect (Davidson, 1993; Gray, 1987).[3]

All of this suggests that one's tonic affective state is a function of the interaction of two systems. Any given individual might be high or low on both or either dimension. One's tonic state is determined by both the absolute values of the two systems and their activation levels relative to one another.

The Complexity of Affect in Practice

With the ideas of tonic and phasic affect in place, it is possible to see how interaction with the environment occurs. Emotions are evoked by environmental imperatives, but their type, intensity, and trigger points are shaped by the tonic state of the organism. An individual at full strength may respond to a threat with anger. At another time, suffering from depleted resources, he may experience fear upon exposure to the same threat. Yet the manner in which either emotion is instantiated as behavior is influenced by the environment. For example, fear is an emotion that one would normally associate with movement away from the threatening stimulus. However, fear can also provide the basis for defensive aggression, such as when an otherwise docile animal is cornered. The organism–environment interaction is a multifaceted process.

As an example, Jorgensen (Chapter 15, this volume) makes the point that the

---

[3]In the service of clarity, my discussion of this research glosses over a great many complexities and even some contradictions. For instance, it is not clear that mood and brain researchers would equate these systems to nearly the degree that I have done here.

study of persuasive communication must embrace both tonic and phasic conceptions of affect. Although we can and should devote attention to understanding emotional appeals, it is also important to recognize that persuasive messages are not processed in an affective vacuum. Current theorizing suggests that preexisting mood states may shape message processing through a variety of mechanisms. Positively valanced moods seem to discourage close scrutiny of the message, by reducing processing capacity, motivation to process, or both.

Because of the twin challenges to appraisal, ambiguity, and polysemy, we might expect that organisms frequently experience multiple emotions.[4] Given one interpretation of the environment, the corresponding emotional program is activated and run. Yet because multiple interpretations are possible and there is a need for accuracy, individuals may consider several alternatives, which in turn result in several emotions. In fact, studies report evidence of multiple emotional responses to discussions of politics (Dillard & Backhaus, 1997) and nuclear energy (Penner, 1996), to news of the Gulf War (Hoffner & Haefner, 1993; Kinder, 1994), and to AIDS-related public service announcements (Dillard, Plotnick, Godbold, Freimuth, & Edgar, 1996).

But if the presence of multiple emotions means the presence of multiple, and perhaps conflicting action tendencies, how then does one settle on the proper interpretation and the corresponding course of action? Planalp (Chapter 2, this volume) suggests an answer: individuals make use of multiple cues in multiple channels. Participants in her intriguing study were asked to monitor someone they knew well and, when they noticed that person experiencing an emotion, to keep a record of how they arrived at that conclusion. Her results revealed that the modal number of cues used to infer an emotion was four. Most often, the cues came from three or more different categories (e.g., vocal cues, verbal cues, facial cues). Of course, the meaning of these various cues and the weighting accorded them are surely shaped by developmental processes (Feeney, Noller, & Roberts, Chapter 18, this volume; Wilson & Smith, Chapter 20, this volume) and cultural experience (Porter & Samovar, Chapter 17, this volume).

Transition

Affect enables organisms to address the challenges posed by interaction with the environment. One fundamental problem is how to acquire the resources that enable survival and reproduction. Social life-forms have adopted a strategy for solving that problem, which depends on cooperation and role specialization. This strategy gives rise to a new problem, one of dividing acquired resources among members of the social group, the focus of the next section.

---

[4]I suspect that these are not blends, but oscillations. If emotions occur more rapidly than the procedures designed to measure them, they would appear as blends because they aggregated over too large a time unit to distinguish between them.

INTERACTION WITH THE ENVIRONMENT:
SOCIAL PROCESSES

It is no accident that humans are such social creatures. Much more so than the physical makeup of the environment, the social group constituted the selection environment for *Homo sapiens*. Throughout the development of the species, group life has had numerous advantages over more solitary modes of existence. Whereas individuals were easy targets for large predators, groups of humans could more successfully defend against attack. Individuals acting in concert could track and kill large prey—an unachievable end for the lone hunter. In addition, the division of labor into hunting and gathering could not be accomplished without sufficient numbers to form a group. But these are only problems of survival. Because evolution operates as a function of differential reproduction, not simply differential survival, there were other, probably more important, adaptive challenges that arose not from large predators but from the group itself.

Reproductive success is directly and indirectly enhanced by cooperation. The attraction and retention of a mate require a certain degree of cooperation between partners. During the lengthy period that human young are unable to care for themselves, two parents working collaboratively are better able to ensure the survival of the offspring than is one parent. And in groups other than mating dyads, the formation of intrasexual alliances (i.e., friendships and coalitions) has the potential to enhance inclusive fitness. Thus, the social, communicative environment in which humans evolved selected for adaptations such as cooperativeness, kindness, and fear of social exclusion (see Andersen & Guerrero, Chapter 3, this volume; Brewer & Caporael, 1990). The resulting networks of affiliation provide a mechanism for the distribution of resources.

Still, there are distinct limits to the advantages of cooperation. If all members of the group are striving for reproductive fitness, then they are, necessarily, in competition with one another. Scarce resources, ranging from food to breeding opportunities, must be allocated among members of the group. This problem of resource distribution is likely to be recurrent in that each time new food reaches the group, it must be distributed. Similarly, as the young move toward maturity and gain the ability to reproduce, they too become resources because members of sexually dimorphic species need mates to reproduce. It seems that such an environment would select for aggressiveness. Although this may in part be true, there is considerable risk to resolving every occurrence of a distribution problem through physical combat. A status hierarchy is one means of avoiding the need for constant renegotiation of resources. This hierarchy provides another means of resolving the distribution of resources problem.

In line with the reasoning outlined above, Hogan (1982) suggested that the challenges of social life are reducible to just two overarching issues: getting along and getting ahead. The human group creates status hierarchies and networks of affiliation that correspond to these two issues. Together they constitute social structure.

Locating oneself in this social structure is an essential element of human existence. In fact, Segrin (Chapter 8, this volume) reminds us that the absence of social ties is closely associated with emotional dysfunction.

Dominance and affiliation relations are efficient means of regulating resource distribution and arguably the defining ingredients in the human experience. The communication of emotion is central to the development, maintenance, and modification of these structures. Hogan's two challenges are worked out in social episodes, that is, thematically interwoven strings of behaviors produced by two or more persons. Individual actions or utterances convey the speaker's conception of the relationship (cf. Burgoon & Hale, 1984; Rogers-Miller & Millar, 1979). Over the course of one or more social episodes the interactants negotiate their relationship in terms of dominance and affiliation. Affect plays a pivotal role in such negotiations (Bailey, 1983).

Elsewhere, I have argued that affect in the communication process might be viewed from at least three, nonexclusive perspectives (Dillard, 1993; see also Buller & Burgoon, Chapter 14, this volume). First, affect might precede and serve as the basis for communication. Words driven by anger or anguish are instances of *emotion-motivated* communication. Second, communication is *emotion-manifesting* when it provides information about the internal state of the actor. This can occur explicitly as when one announces "I am sad" or inexplicitly, as when we wear our feelings on our sleeves. Finally, communication can be *emotion-inducing*. This occurs whenever one party elicits an affective response in the other. Whereas these distinctions are useful to researchers, all three perspectives are part of any interaction to varying degrees. The instance of the exasperated parent who shows his irritation and, in so doing, produces shame in the misbehaving teenager illustrates the point. Also inherent in the transaction is the reconstitution of social structure. The parent has reasserted his authority and the child has accepted, emotionally, that relational definition.

The set of relational definitions that emerge from interaction constitutes social structure. It consists of two aspects that are conceptually separable but remain behaviorally intertwined: the dominance hierarchy and the affiliative network. "Bright side" affects (to borrow a term from this volume) such as liking and loving are social adhesives insofar as they bind individuals together in friendships, coalitions, and mating pairs. In so doing, they contribute to the stability of the social structure. But feelings of liking, loving, and sexual desire are not fixed with regard to target or intensity. The instability of affiliative emotions is of considerable significance to the social group because relationships not only determine the distribution of resources, but are themselves resources. Mating relationships provide the mechanism for attaining inclusive fitness. Thus, shifts in affiliative relationships may ripple through the social network, causing destabilization and a host of other "dark side" affects such as anger (Canary, Spitzberg, & Semic, Chapter 7, this volume) and jealousy (Guerrero & Andersen, Chapter 6, this volume).

Dark side affects underlie threat and attack, two other means of acquiring resources. Rather than relying on physical assault, however, people typically rely on anger displays. Among the primates with higher brain-to-body ratios, status tends to be established via verbal and nonverbal communication (Mazur, 1973). We begin to get a glimmer that certain communication skills (e.g., impression management and argumentativeness) might enhance an individual's inclusive fitness. In line with this thinking, Canary et al. (Chapter 7, this volume) suggest that aggression is the strategy of last resort: individuals who suffer from deficits in argumentative skill are most likely to behave aggressively.

In short, it is convenient to group the affects into those associated with affiliation and solidarity and those associated with dominance and social control. Although the distinction will ultimately fail (in just a few pages), it is serviceable for the moment. It will allow us to examine the chapters of this volume in greater detail.

Affects Associated with Getting Along

There are specific affects associated with development and maintenance of various sorts of affiliative relationships. Friends like one another. These relationships are characterized by "relatively high levels of emotional (but not physical) intimacy" (Gaines et al., Chapter 19, this volume, p. 508). Romantic partners experience warmth and love for one another (Andersen & Guerrero, Chapter 11, this volume; Taraban, Hendrick, & Hendrick, Chapter 12, this volume). Such feelings contribute to the stability of the social network, by linking individuals to one another in ways that provide for sharing resources. These affects, warmth, liking, and loving, can be seen as relational analogues to tonic intrapersonal states. The parallel lies in their relative permanence. Relative to rapid emotions such as fear and anger, they are fairly enduring states. This is true as well of their counterparts, which include disliking and hating.

Still, these long-lasting affects are built from experiences that occur within particular social episodes. Relationships provide a forum where varying ranges of emotions are presented. Speaking of friendships, Gaines et al. (Chapter 19, this volume) note that "joy is likely to be expressed in a variety of friendships, whereas sadness is likely to be expressed only in the closest of relationships" (p. 511). Similarly, Burleson and Goldsmith (Chapter 9, this volume) point to a certain level of trust as requisite for the discussion of negative emotion. These observations have potentially interesting implications for the definition and investigation of personal relationships. In a field that typically defines intimacy in terms of the frequency and depth of interaction, perhaps there is an alternative. Is the real meaning of a relationship determined by the range and type of feelings that are discussed?

Metts, Sprecher, and Regan's contribution (Chapter 13, this volume) takes up the question of whether sexual desire should be considered an emotion. Their position stretches the envelope of lay definitions in certain respects, but sexual desire does seem to possess many of the defining features of affect. It is a subjective feeling state with motivational properties and clear implications for behavior. With regard to the framework developed in this chapter, it is clearly an affiliative affect. And in line with the previous paragraph, the expression of sexual desire is a signal event, a turning point, in relational definition.

Affects Associated with Getting (and Staying) Ahead

Anger is an approach emotion in that individuals move to engage the source of their anger. And the experience and expression of anger are intimately bound up with issues of social hierarchy and aggression.[5] As Canary et al. (Chapter 7, this volume) note, anger may arise from a variety of sources (e.g., aggression by others, perceptions of unfairness) and take a variety of forms ranging from rage to irritation. Despite this diversity, all the various interpersonal instigators of anger can be seen as perceived threats to one's notions of how social relations should be conducted. When individuals attempt to influence one another, their efforts vary in perceived dominance (Dillard & Harkness, 1992). They are saying, in varying degrees, that they intend to control the target and, by implication, that they are *not* status peers. Furthermore, it is the degree of perceived dominance that determines the extent to which anger is aroused in the target of those messages (Dillard & Kinney, 1994; Dillard, Kinney, & Cruz, 1996). Success in influencing another produces feelings of positive affect in the message source, whereas failure yields anger and guilt (Segrin & Dillard, 1991).

In line with the evolutionary logic on which this chapter builds, LoPreato (1984) defines power as the "capacity of an individual or group within a dominance order to impede the access to fitness-enhancing resources by others and to facilitate it for oneself" (p. 346). From here it is but a short step to see that a threat to one's mating relationship poses a danger to one's place in the gene pool.[6] As Guerrero and Anderson discuss (Chapter 6, this volume), potential disruption of a relationship may evoke that distinctive form of anger known as jealousy. This, in turn, activates a complex sequence of events including information acquisition (to deal with the appraisal problem), evaluation of one's options (to deal with the response problem), and action. A rich variety of communication behaviors are possible at each step of the sequence. As a whole, the sequence is oriented toward reestablishing accessibility to resources.

---

[5]Although I am classifying anger here as an approach emotion because it encourages movement toward the stimulus (i.e., attack), it can also be instantiated as a withdrawal tendency as in the case of "cold anger." While space does not permit an elaborate discussion of this point, I believe that most, if not all, emotions can underlie either approach or withdrawal depending on the circumstances in which they arise. For example, fear generally suggests movement away from the threat, but if escape is not possible it can produce defensive aggression (as when an animal or a person is cornered).

[6]Here again, I want to emphasize that I am not suggesting that individuals have inclusive fitness as their goal. Rather, that is the aim of genes. Individuals do not rise up in the morning with a fresh plan to propagate their genes on a daily basis. They do behave in ways that enhanced reproduction in an earlier era.

Earlier I reported research claiming that "higher" primates prefer communication to combat as a means of constructing status hierarchies and influencing one another (Mazur, 1973). Questions concerning the form and content of those messages were left unaddressed. Witte (Chapter 16, this volume) suggests some answers. Taking a position similar to the one I have advanced here, Witte argues that fear might encourage either approach or withdrawal depending on the relevance of the stimulus to the individual and his or her power to deal with the threat. The thrust of her argument is that individuals respond by engaging threats to their well-being when they are able to do so. But they tend to withdraw when they see their capacity to effect change as absent. Barbee, Lawrence, and Cunningham (Chapter 10, this volume) draw similar lines in their analysis of social support. They argue that coping behaviors can be examined in terms of two dimensions: approach–avoidance and problem-focused versus emotion-focused.

The Interplay between Status Hierarchies and Affiliative Networks

I have treated dominance and affiliation relationships as cleanly separable. However, studies of nonhuman species provide a clue that such distinctions are more convenient than real. For example, McKenna (1978) reported that aggressive interactions between langurs significantly increase the likelihood that grooming will occur. Similarly, de Waal and Roosmalen's (1979) work revealed that chimpanzees have a heightened tendency to make body contact with their opponent following an aggressive interaction. This contact usually takes the form of kissing. Both studies suggest that dominance and affiliation are intimately bound up with one another (de Waal, 1986). Following episodes in which dominance relations are negotiated, there is a tendency to repair or solidify the affiliative component of social structure.

Guilt is an emotion that clearly demonstrates the degree to which the issues of dominance and affiliation are intertwined. Vangelisti and Sprague (Chapter 5, this volume) report that guilt is most commonly elicited in the context of very close relationships, presumably as a result of failure to meet the role requirements of that relationship. Substantial numbers of people attempt to induce guilt in their conversational partners as a means of social influence. Although the evidence is limited to health-related persuasion attempts, there is some indication that such appeals have a dual effect (Rook, Thuras, & Lewis, 1990). While they are successful at inducing behavioral compliance, they also produce negative reactions such as anger that ultimately degrade tonic relational affects (see also Coulter & Pinto, 1995).

In Chapter 4 (this volume) Bradford and Petronio strike several fundamental themes. They argue that embarrassment is an inherently social emotion that arises from the perception that one is being judged by others. Although we have all committed some public blunder that left us feeling foolish, Bradford and Petronio focus on those instances in which one individual *deliberately* embarrasses another. Creation of the situation and the resulting emotion are often used to dispute the existing social hierarchy. One example that comes quickly to mind is the ceaseless efforts of

Republicans and Democrats to expose errors of judgment in members of the opposing party. However, as Bradford and Petronio note, some strategic embarrassment episodes are constructed by well-meaning others so that one individual has the opportunity to strengthen an affiliative bond with another. Here again, we get a glimpse of how emotions are used episodically to both challenge and stabilize social structure.

Another layer of complexity is added by the possibility of deception. In their review of Interpersonal Deception Theory, Buller and Burgoon (Chapter 14, this volume) point out that there is no necessary correspondence between felt emotions and expressed emotions. Individuals smile in desire and in deceit. Emotional deception is used for all the same ends as emotional truth-telling and, in fact, both can be conceived of simply as information management conducted with an eye toward the social environment. The capacity and propensity to prevaricate is surely a social adaptation for there is little gain in deceiving inanimate objects.

Transition

Social beings constantly juggle the opportunities and challenges posed by their associations with conspecifics. These relationships, in both their episodic and stable forms, address the interdependent issues of affiliation and dominance. And these relationships are accomplished through the exchange of affect. An already complex task is rendered even more formidable by the possibility of deception. At the evolutionary level, such pressures result in a "cognitive arms race" (Dawkins, 1976; Trivers, 1971) the physical manifestations of which can be seen in the rapid development (in evolutionary terms) of the frontal lobes. With the ability to reason came a recognition of the flaws and foibles of the affect system.

AFFECT MANAGEMENT

Human beings actively manage their feelings. Why? Is it simply that revenge (or pleasure) is its own reward? Perhaps there is a deeper reason. Evolutionary processes shape a species through the interaction of the environment and the gene pool. Features of an organism that enhance likelihood of reproduction are retained over generations, while those that diminish fitness are lost. This process of sifting and winnowing genes, generation after generation, yield species that are compilations of information-processing mechanisms, each of which is designed to solve particular adaptive problems. Moods and emotions are one such set of mechanisms.

Most of this gene–environment interaction took place between 2 million and 10 thousand years ago during the Pleistocene era (Tooby & Cosmides, 1989). Because of changes in the environment called human civilization, *Homo sapiens* are now in an unusual position. We are designed for an environment that no longer exists. "Humans are living fossils—collections of mechanisms produced by prior selection pressures operating on a long and unbroken line of ancestors" (Buss, 1995, p. 10). Affects are part of the human species because of the work they accomplished. The evolved mechanisms so well suited to the Pleistocene era may not lend quite the same benefits as they once did. They may be, at least slightly, obsolete.

One feature of affect is subjective experience. The phenomenological readout informs the cognitive apparatus as to the state of the organism and organism–environment relations. Positive affect signals propitious relations, whereas negative affect indicates that there is a problem to be solved. From an inclusive fitness standpoint, organisms that experienced positive states or resolved negative ones did so because of good or improved person–environment relationships. However, it is subjective experience that makes possible an inversion between the means and the end. At the genetic level, across generations, love operates in the service of inclusive fitness. But for the individual, the pursuit of happiness is a worthy goal in its own right. Affect, which developed as a means of enhancing reproductive success, can become an end in itself. This suggests that, for individuals, emotional regulation can be both functional and dysfunctional.

Functional and Dysfunctional Affect Management

The mechanisms of affect management are often social (Barbee et al., Chapter 10, this volume). We seek others to help us to induce positive states (Andersen & Guerrero, Chapter 11, this volume) and relieve negative ones (Burleson & Goldsmith, Chapter 9, this volume). But simply talking is insufficient. Burleson and Goldsmith (Chapter 9, this volume) consider in detail the ways in which one individual might discursively comfort another. They emphasize that it is not the objective state of the environment that matters so much as it is how the individual evaluates that environment. The effective comforter is able to assist another with the task of appraising and reappraising the person–environment relationship. The authors carefully and convincingly illustrate the complexity of that simple-sounding task through the lens of their appraisal perspective.

Segrin (Chapter 8, this volume) also provides perspective on the delicate complexity of the communication process in affect management. Individuals who suffer from depression are often deficient in the interactive skills required to manage social relationships. Relative to the nondepressed, they speak more slowly and more quietly, pause more frequently, and exhibit longer response latencies and less pitch variation. Others find interacting with the depressed unrewarding and, consequently, reject them. As with the Burleson and Goldsmith chapter, we see that there is a great deal more to effective social relationships than simply their number or the content of the talk.

Functional forms of affect regulation are not, however, restricted to social sources. As Wilson and Smith (Chapter 20, this volume) suggest, individuals who are bored often seek out exciting entertainment. Those who are upset may choose something calm or distracting. But these affect management processes are not so simple as tuning in a positive show when one is feeling blue. Wilson and Smith note that anxious individuals may consume arousing media in an effort to desensitize themselves. They apparently try to toughen themselves to frightening real-world events by exposing themselves to arousing programming.

Much of the foregoing illustrates the adaptive uses to which people put media and other people. But the potential for maladaptive responses looms large for two reasons that I've outlined already: our emotion systems are out of date relative to the current environment and, as individual organisms, we seek to alleviate negative affects and promote positive affects as ends in themselves. All of this suggests the possibility of "emotional mistakes." People may be drawn to certain forms of media because they present information well suited to an evolved mechanism (Malamuth, 1996). Sexual desire, for example, can be aroused by exposure to a potential sex partner or to images of the same. Pornography may be both effective and problematic because the information-processing mechanisms that produce erotic desire cannot themselves discriminate between fact and fantasy.

Paying close attention to violence probably contributed to one's longevity in the Pleistocene era. Knowledge of the identity of the instigator, the method of attack, and the circumstances surrounding it provided information concerning one's own relative capacity for offense or defense. However, as Wilson and Smith (Chapter 20, this volume) make plain, a steady diet of violent programming in contemporary times may result in a range of undesirable changes in beliefs and attitudes.

Comedy, sex, and violence readily lend themselves to evolutionary explanation. Feelings such as sadness seem to present more of a challenge. Among humanists, the question of why individuals would willingly expose themselves to narratives that induce sadness is known as the "paradox of tragedy." From an evolutionary perspective, it is important to recall that we are products of a reciprocal interaction with the environment: the environment acts on the person and the person on the environment. Individuals need not wait for the environment to come to them when they can seek out circumstances that engage the mechanisms of which they are constituted. It is quite possible that individuals pursue and evaluate media experiences on the basis of the variety of emotions that are induced and the meta-reactions that individuals make to those experiences. It is not sadness per se that is enjoyable, but the reaction to one's own sadness (Oliver, 1993). Much as people exercise their linguistic abilities with crossword puzzles, they may use media to exercise their affective systems. These efforts may be viewed as either functional or dysfunctional.

The Calibration of Affect Mechanisms

The fact that humans possess information-processing mechanisms that produce affect is a result of our evolutionary heritage. But the manner in which those mechanisms operate in any given individual is a function of interaction with the environment during the development of that individual. In humans, affect mechanisms are calibrated by the social relationships experienced during childhood.

In contrast to some species, human infants are helpless for an extended period. For the first several years of a child's life he or she is completely dependent on others to provide sustenance and care. According to attachment theory, those caregivers act as defining influences on the child's conception of relationships (Bowlby, 1969). The manner in which relationships themselves are defined is an issue that is addressed at several points in this volume (Andersen & Guerrero, Chapter 3, Chapter 11; Feeney et al., Chapter 18). Regardless of which of the several approaches to relational definition one takes, there is consensus that much of what is included there concerns emotional regulation. For example, there is evidence that avoidant infants learn to mask their negative feelings. When these babies are separated from their mothers, those classified as avoidant show physiological distress (indexed cardiovascularly), but less behavioral distress (indexed by negative vocalizations) than infants typed as secure. It has been suggested that masking protects the infant from rejection by the caregiver on whom he or she is so dependent (Bowlby, 1988). It would seem that the capacity for emotional deception comes very early in life (see Buller & Burgoon, Chapter 14, this volume).

The relational lessons learned as a child may be replayed in adulthood (Hazan & Shaver, 1994). Feeney et al. (Chapter 18, this volume) speak to this issue in their work on emotional expression in romantic dyads. Individuals assessed as secure prefer not to limit their expression of negative feelings, and they see this as aligned with the desires of their partner. In other words, they believe that their partners prefer that they not censor their bad feelings either. Avoidant adults show the opposite pattern. However, the authors go on to make the important point that negative affect is a broad category, one that encompasses some substantially disparate feelings. And dyad members report that they control anger more than sadness and sadness more than anxiety.

Conclusion

Emotions are the simple-minded servants of behavior. Recognizing this, individuals often endeavor to regulate their affective states. Functional efforts can be seen in the commiseration that follows a loss or when an individual puts him- or herself in a good mood prior to job interview. Alternatively, we may dampen our giddiness to deal with something serious or scare ourselves with knowledge of the consequences of a bad habit. Affect management can also be dysfunctional, as when we use television to distract us from a problem that really should be addressed. And the efforts of infants to negotiate emotional balance with their caregivers may entrain strategies that prove counterproductive in adult relationships. Whatever judgment one might render regarding the functionality of affect management, there can be little argument concerning its existence.

SUMMARY

My basic claim has been that the study of communication should be intimately engaged with the study of affect. Within the framework of concepts offered by evolutionary biology, I have tried to make a case by sketching the common origins of communication and affect in the demands of the social environment. Whereas my strokes have necessarily been broad, the chapters that follow explore these issues in detail. As a group, they offer an exciting and contemporary view of the vital relationship between communication and affect.

ACKNOWLEDGMENTS

I am grateful to Denise Solomon and Kyle Tusing for their comments on an early version of the manuscript.

REFERENCES

Bailey, F. G. (1983). *The tactical uses of passion: An essay on power, reason, and reality.* Ithaca, NY: Cornell Univ. Press.

Bowlby, J. (1969). *Attachment and loss: Vol. 1. Attachment.* New York: Basic Books.

Bowlby, J. (1988). *A secure base.* New York: Basic Books.

Brewer, M. B., & Caporael, L. R. (1990). Selfish genes versus selfish people: Sociobiology as an origin myth. *Motivation and Emotion,* **14,** 237–243.

Burgoon, J. K., & Hale, J. L. (1984). The fundamental topoi of relational communication. *Communication Monographs,* **51,** 193–214.

Buss, D. M. (1995). Evolutionary psychology: A new paradigm for psychological science. *Psychological Inquiry,* **6,** 1–30.

Coulter, R. B., & Pinto, M. B. (1995). Guilt appeals in advertising: What are their effects? *Journal of Applied Psychology,* **80,** 697–705.

Davidson, R. J. (1993). Parsing affective space: Perspectives from neuropsychology and psychophysiology. *Neuropsychology, 7,* 464–475.

Dawkins, R. (1976). *The selfish gene.* New York: Oxford University Press.

de Waal, F.B.M. (1986). The integration of dominance and social bonding in primates. *Quarterly Review of Biology,* **61,** 459–479.

de Waal, F.B.M., & van Roosmalen, A. (1979). Reconciliation and consolation among chimpanzees. *Behavioral Ecology and Sociobiology,* **5,** 55–66.

Dillard, J. P. (1993). Epilogue. *Journal of Language and Social Psychology,* **12,** 153–161.

Dillard, J. P., & Harkness, C. D. (1992). Exploring the affective impact of interpersonal influence messages. *Journal of Language and Social Psychology,* **11,** 179–191.

Dillard, J. P., & Kinney, T. A. (1994). Experiential and physiological responses to interpersonal influence. *Human Communication Research,* **20,** 502–528.

Dillard, J. P., Kinney, T. A., & Cruz, M. G. (1996). Influence, appraisal, and emotions in close relationships. *Communication Monographs,* **63,** 105–130.

Dillard, J. P., Plotnick, C. A., Godbold, L. C., Freimuth, V. S., & Edgar, T. (1996). The multiple affective consequences of AIDS PSAs: Fear appeals do more than scare people. *Communication Research,* **23,** 44–72.

Dillard, J. P., & Backhaus, S. J. (1997, May). *An exploration into civic deliberation, emotional response, and political involvement.* Paper presented at the annual meeting of the International Communication Association, Montreal.

Ekman, P., Levenson, R. W., & Friesen, W. V. (1983). Autonomic nervous activity differentiates the emotions. *Science,* **221,** 1208–1210.

Fox, N. A. (1991). If it's not left, it's right. *American Psychologist,* **46,** 863–872.

Gray, J. A. (1987). *The psychology of fear and stress.* 2nd ed. Cambridge, UK: Cambridge Univ. Press.

Hazan, C., & Shaver, P. R. (1994). Attachment as an organizational framework for research on close relationships. *Psychological Inquiry,* **5,** 1–22.

Hoffner, C., & Haefner, M. J. (1993). Children's affective responses to news coverage of the war. In B. S. Greenberg & W. Gantz (Eds.), *Desert Storm and the mass media* (pp. 364–380). Crosskill, NJ: Hampton Press.

Hogan, R. (1982). A socioanalytic theory of personality. In M. M. Page (Ed.), *Nebraska symposium on motivation* (pp. 55–89). Lincoln, NE: University of Nebraska Press.

Kinder, D. R. (1994). Reason and emotion in American political life. In R. C. Schank & E. Langer (Eds.), *Beliefs, reasoning, & decision-making* (pp. 277–314). Hillsdale, NJ: Lawrence Erlbaum.

Lazarus, R. S. (1991). *Emotion & adaptation.* New York: Oxford University Press.

LoPreato, J. (1984). Human nature and biocultural evolution. London: Allen & Unwin.

Malamuth, N. (1996). Sexually explicit media, gender differences, and evolutionary theory. *Journal of Communication,* **46,** 8–31.

Mayr, E. (1982). *The growth of biological thought: Diversity, evolution, and inheritance.* Cambridge, MA: Harvard Univ. Press.

Mazur, A. (1973). A cross-species comparison of status in small established groups. *American Sociological Review,* **38,** 513–527.

McKenna, J. (1978). Biosocial function of grooming behavior among the common langur monkey (*Presbytis entellus*). *American Journal of Physical Anthropology,* **48,** 503–510.

Miller, N. (1959). Liberalization of basic S-R concepts: Extensions to conflict behavior, motivation and social learning. In S. Koch (Ed.), *Psychology: A study of science, Study 1* (pp. 198–292). New York: McGraw-Hill.

Oatley, K. (1992). *Best laid schemes: The psychology of emotions.* Paris: Cambridge Univ. Press.

Oliver, M. B. (1993). Exploring the paradox of the enjoyment of sad films. *Human Communication Research,* **19,** 315–342.

Penner, A. (1996). *Nuclear professionals' views on communicating about nuclear power with the general public.* Unpublished manuscript, University of Wisconsin–Madison.

Rogers-Millar, L. E., & Millar, F. E. (1979). Domineeringness and dominance: A transactional view. *Human Communication Research,* **5,** 238–246.

Rook, K. S., Thuras, P. D., & Lewis, M. A. (1990). Social control, health risk taking, and psychological distress among the elderly. *Psychology and Aging,* **5,** 327–334.

Schneirla, T. C. (1959). An evolutionary and developmental theory of biphasic processes underlying approach and withdrawal. In M. R. Jones (Ed.), *Nebraska symposium and motivation* (vol. 6, pp. 1–42). Lincoln, NE: University of Nebraska Press.

Segrin, C., & Dillard, J. P. (1991). (Non)depressed persons' cognitive and affective reactions to (un)successful interpersonal influence. *Communication Monographs,* **58,** 115–134.

Sinha, R., Lovallo, W. R., & Parsons, O. A. (1992). Cardiovascular differentiation of emotions. *Psychosomatic Medicine,* **54,** 422–535.

Thayer, R. E. (1989). *The biopsychology of mood and arousal.* New York: Oxford Univ. Press.

Tooby, J., & Cosmides, L. (1989). Evolutionary psychology and the generation of culture, part I. *Ethology and Sociobiology,* **10,** 29–49.

Trivers, R. L. (1971). The evolution of reciprocals altruism. *Quarterly Review of Biology,* **46,** 35–57.

Watson, D., & Tellegen, A. (1985). Toward a consensual structure. *Psychological Bulletin,* **98,** 219–235.

PART I

Introduction

CHAPTER 1

Communication and Emotion: Basic Concepts and Approaches

Laura K. Guerrero

Arizona State University
Tempe, Arizona

Peter A. Andersen

San Diego State University
San Diego, California

Melanie R. Trost

Arizona State University
Tempe, Arizona

Dear Professor,

I find myself caught in the middle of a tug-o-war. My boyfriend and my best friend, who is also my roommate, hate each other. When I'm with each of them individually, everything is great. I'm deeply in love with my boyfriend and we have discussed getting married someday. My best friend and I have known each other since 10th grade and I love her like a sister. Each of them acts convinced that the other is "bad" for me, but I think that they may actually just be jealous of each other. I am trying to juggle my time between the two of them, but this is becoming increasingly difficult. Both of them make me feel guilty for spending time with the other. To make matters worse, I feel like I have no one to turn to about this problem because they are the two people I usually go to for advice and comfort and they just don't understand. It seems ironic that two people who make me so happy can also make me feel so miserable. Can you summarize some research that helps explain (and might help me get off) this emotional rollercoaster without having to choose between them?

Sincerely,

Caught in the Middle

This letter, which was written by one of our students as part of a class assignment, illustrates the powerful effect that emotions have on our interpersonal communication, our relationships, and our lives. Clearly, emotional experience and expression is part of a fabric of thoughts, feelings, and behaviors that blend together to characterize the tapestry of interpersonal interaction. Yet despite the relevance of emotion to our daily interaction, most contemporary books in communication and related disciplines treat emotion as a "stepchild" that stands at the periphery of scientific enterprise.

Although the worldwide scientific study of emotion dates back to the 19th century (see Darwin, 1872; James, 1884; Lange, 1885; Wundt, 1897), it is only within the past two decades that emotions have been studied extensively within social contexts. And it is only within the last few years that a handful of studies have begun examining communication as a primary antecedent of emotion. As Vangelisti (1994) lamented: "Although theorists and researchers have pointed to the general processes underlying the social elicitation of emotions, empirical work testing these processes is sparse" (p. 55). Campos (1995) similarly asserted that emotions such as embarrassment, guilt, jealousy, and pride "have always been the province of the poet and the novelist, but rarely of the social scientist" (p. ix). He also asked: "Why should emotions that are so prevalent, and so crucial for the human condition, be so elusive a phenomenon of scientific study?" (Campos, 1995, p. ix). Likewise, communication research has neglected communicative responses to emotion and the functions that emotions serve in everyday conversations. As Metts and Bowers (1994) stated, "mainstream communication [research] is rarely focused in the affective concerns that motivate and channelize most communication processes" (p. 508). This neglect is especially unfortunate given that the communication field has its roots in fundamental rhetorical concepts such as pathos.

Others argue that emotional communication represents an "obvious gap" in our knowledge about interpersonal communication (Planalp, 1993, p. 4) and that the study of communication and emotion is "poised for flight" (Dillard & Wilson, 1993, p. 644). Indeed, in recent years, scholars from communication, sociology, and anthropology have joined researchers from the psychological sciences in their quest to understand emotion. This multidisciplinary interest signals a shift from studying emotion as an internal, subjective experience, to emotions as a type of interpersonal and social phenomenon. White (1993) stated: "These developments suggest there is a potential for convergence of interest between cultural and linguistic-psychological approaches that view emotions as meaning-laden social processes" (p. 30).

Given the integral role interpersonal communication plays as both an elicitor of and a response to emotion (see Andersen & Guerrero, Chapter 3, this volume), communication researchers stand poised to contribute significantly to these multidisciplinary efforts. Over the past few years, significant strides have already been taken in this direction. For example, a 1993 issue of *Communication Research* was devoted to articles on communication and emotion, and communication research on many of the topics represented in this book (e.g., embarrassment; guilt and hurt) is beginning to build. Synthesizing and providing directions for this relatively new body of literature was a primary impetus for writing this book.

In this chapter, we provide a conceptual foundation for this volume by defining basic emotion terms and reviewing general approaches to the study of emotion. We begin by differentiating three related constructs—affect, emotion, and mood. Next, we differentiate between emotional experience and expression. We then discuss three prominent approaches to emotion that are discussed in the social psychology literature: the discrete emotions, dimensional, and prototype approaches.

AFFECT, EMOTION, AND MOOD

Although some researchers use the terms *affect, emotion,* and *mood* interchangeably, there is growing consensus that affect refers to the general valence of an emotional state, emotion refers to specific types or clusters of feelings that occur in response to particular events, and moods refer to relatively enduring and global states of pleasant or unpleasant feelings (see Batson, Shaw, & Olsen, 1992; Frijda, 1993). Each of these concepts is discussed next.

Affect

Affect is a more general term than *emotions* or *moods.* Clore, Schwarz, and Conway (1994) defined affect simply as the positive or negative valence of the emotional experience. Frijda (1993) defines affect as "the irreducible aspect" of emotion "that gives feelings their emotional, noncognitive character" (p. 383). Both dimensional (e.g., Daly, Lancee, & Polivy, 1983; Russell, 1978, 1980) and prototype (e.g., Fitness & Fletcher, 1993; Shaver, Schwartz, Kirson, & O'Connor, 1987) approaches to conceptualizing emotions include affect (positive vs. negative) as a central characteristic of emotional experience and expression. Similarly, mood is often conceptualized as an expectation about feeling positive or negative affect in the future (Batson et al., 1992) or feeling generally pleasant or unpleasant (Frijda, 1993). Researchers have argued that there is only one necessary condition for a state to be considered an emotion or for a predisposition to be considered a mood: An individual must make a cognitive appraisal of something as "good" or "bad" (Clore et al., 1994; Strongman, 1987; but see also Dillard, this volume).

Many researchers contend that affective valence is the most basic feature of emotion. Batson et al. (1992) argued that affect is more phylogenetically and ontogenetically primitive than emotion or mood. Dillard and Wilson (1993) noted that "absolutely every theoretical position accords a central role to valence" (p. 638). They also reported that valence typically accounts for approximately twice as much variance as discrete emotions. Thus, it is important for researchers to consider how affective valence influences the communication process.

Emotion

Defining *emotion* is a tricky proposition. Indeed, one may compare it to trying to define pornography. Instead of knowing it when you see it, with an emotion you know it when you feel it. Recent work, however, has helped social scientists clarify the properties that constitute an emotion. Ortony, Clore, and Foss (1987), for example, defined emotions as specific "internal mental states that are focused primarily on affect" (p. 325). Two key concepts guide this definition. First, emotions are internal rather than external. Second, emotions are affective states, rather than bodily, cognitive, or behavioral states. Clore et al. (1994) contend that words such as "abandoned" refer to external states. However, the internal affective states that result from being abandoned (e.g., fear, anxiety, sadness) are emotions. In this case, "being abandoned" is the emotion-eliciting event, whereas fear, anxiety, and sadness are the emotions. Similarly, Clore et al. discount bodily states (e.g., tiredness, pain), cognitive states (e.g., uncertainty, confusion), and behavioral states (e.g., timidity, aggressiveness) as emotional states. These bodily, cognitive, and behavioral states may contribute to the ways that emotions are experienced and expressed, but they are not emotions in their own right.

In another study, Clore and Ortony (1988) argued that the best examples of emotions are affect-laden in the context of both "feeling" and "being." For example, feeling abandoned and being abandoned are likely to conjure up different images, with more affect connected to the former. However, "feeling angry" and "being angry" are likely to produce similar images (Clore & Ortony, 1988). Thus, Clore and Ortony contend that anger is a better example of an emotion than is abandonment.

Other research has shown that laypeople's common sense definitions of emotion tend to fit these criteria. For example, Fehr and Russell (1984) asked people to list words that fit under the general category of "emotion." Seven emotions surfaced most frequently: happiness, anger, sadness, love, fear, hate, and joy. Shaver et al. (1987), who had respondents rate the prototypicality of 213 emotion words, found the following ten words to be identified as the clearest examples of emotions: love, anger, hate, depression, fear, jealousy, happiness, passion, affection, and sadness. Poor examples of emotions included: intelligence, deliberateness, practicality, carefulness, alertness, self-control, interest, and indecision. With the possible exception of affection, the words identified as good examplars fit Ortony et al.'s (1987) criteria for defining emotion terms. The words identified as poor examples tend to violate one or more criteria. For example, indecision is a cognitive state, alertness is a physiological state, and self-control is a behavioral state.

Despite the above findings (i.e., Fehr & Russell, 1984; Ortony et al., 1987), some scholars still do not consider love, hate, jealousy, passion, and affection to be emotions. For example, Ekman (1984, 1992) labeled love and jealousy as multiperson "plots" rather than emotions because they rely considerably on relationships and social contacts (i.e., love usually involves two people; jealousy usually involves three). However, we contend that "plots" are simply *social* (rather than purely intrapersonal) emotions (see also Shaver, Morgan, & Wu, 1996).

Emotions have also been conceptualized as multicomponential phenomena. Specifically, Scherer (1994) argued that emotions are characterized by four components. The *cognitive component* refers to the interpretation of the emotion-eliciting event or stimuli, and any resultant changes in perceptions or beliefs. *Action readiness* concerns increases or decreases in one's desire to take action. Frijda (1986) argued that action readiness can result in expressiveness or emotional control. The third component, *feelings,* references the valence of the emotion, including the pleasure/pain dimension. Finally, *physiological change* refers to increases or decreases in arousal level and physiological reactions such as sweaty palms and blushing. Thus, even though the best examples of emotion are heavily affect-laden, they still contain cognitive, behavioral, and physiological components. It should also be noted that the presence of a single component is usually insufficient for identifying an emotional experience. Burgoon (1993), for example, has argued that changes in physiological arousal are not synonymous with emotional experience (see also Buller & Burgoon, Chapter 14, this volume). Arousal changes can result from a number of nonemotional stimuli, including increased attention, physical exercise, or jet lag. The feelings component, because of its connection with affective valence, is probably the most central of Scherer's (1994) four components of emotion.

Mood

Although they are nonemotional stimuli, physical exercise, jet lag, and even a sunny or noisy environment can subtly influence our approach to the world on any given day by affecting our *mood.* The differences between moods and emotions have been contested, but one important distinction goes back to our definition of emotions as *specific,* internal mental states (from Ortony et al., 1987). Emotions are typically characterized as having an object or identifiable stimulus event, such as joy after having a child or anger at being jilted (Averill, 1980). In contrast, moods are frequently described as more diffuse and nonspecific (Clore et al., 1994; Frijda, 1986). One way of capturing the distinction is to think of two possible responses to the question, "Why are you so happy today?" When an immediate object comes to mind, "I'm happy because . . ." the affect is more likely due to an emotion. On the other hand, when you can think of no immediate cause or you "just feel good," then the positive affect is more likely due to an elevated mood. Moods are longer lasting feeling states that need not be about anything in particular (Clore et al., 1994). They are relatively mild, mundane affective experiences that are neither distracting nor disruptive, but do influence a variety of behaviors (Isen, 1987).

Moods are most often described by their valence—either positive or negative, happy or sad, good or bad or neutral (Fiske & Taylor, 1984; Isen, 1987). As opposed to those in neutral or bad moods, people in good moods are more cooperative (Carnevale & Isen, 1986), more helpful to others (Isen, Clark, & Schwartz, 1976), more likely to initiate conversations (Batson, Coke, Chard, Smith, & Taliaferro, 1979), more persuasive in producing counterattitudinal messages (Bohner & Schwarz, 1993), and more easily persuaded under some circumstances (Galizio &

Hendrick, 1972; Janis, Kaye, & Kirschner, 1965). They speak faster (Natale, 1977), take greater risks (Isen, Means, Patrick, & Nowicki, 1982), and report more satisfaction with their cars (Isen, Shalker, Clark, & Karp, 1978) and with their lives (Schwarz, Strack, Kommer, & Wagner, 1987). Negative moods are associated with greater pessimism, increased aggression, more controlled information-processing strategies, and less helping (Clark & Isen, 1982), although they sometimes lead to increased helping, as well (Kenrick, Baumann, & Cialdini, 1979). Intuitively, it might appear that mood valence should reflect mirror images of good and bad behaviors, but research indicates that positive and negative moods operate independently of affect behavior (Isen, 1984, 1987).

Since the early 1980s, most of the research into mood effects has examined how moods mediate information processing and memory retrieval. We will briefly describe several of the models here (Clore et al., 1994, provide a comprehensive review of the models and supporting research). The *resource allocation model* (Ellis & Ashbrook, 1988) proposes that emotional states regulate the amount of cognitive capacity an individual has available to deal with the task at hand. Evidence indicates that both disruptive moods, such as depression and sadness (Ellis & Ashbrook, 1988), and happy moods (Mackie & Worth, 1989, 1991) can decrease the amount of capacity available for processing information and stimuli. The *associative network model* (Bower, 1981; Isen, 1984) describes moods as memory-retrieval cues that activate other pieces of stored information with the same feeling-tone and lead to such effects as mood-congruent memory. For instance, when in a positive mood people remember more positive life events than when in a negative mood (for reviews, see Blaney, 1986; Singer & Salovey, 1988). Another perspective focuses on *feelings as information,* and argues that we use our feeling states as a heuristic in making judgments (Schwarz, 1990; Schwarz & Clore, 1988). For instance, when we simply "feel good," our positive mood generalizes to the task or judgment ("I feel good, therefore I must feel positive about what I'm doing or judging"). According to this model, moods lose their information value when they are irrelevant to the task or made less salient. For instance, being able to label one's mood as due to the weather (Schwarz & Clore, 1983) or to an unpleasant room (Schwarz et al., 1987) eliminated mood effects on judgments of general well-being. The *affect infusion model* (Forgas, 1995) integrates the previous models by identifying four judgmental strategies that vary in the extent to which they can be "infused" with affect. The four strategies include (a) direct access of a preexisting judgment; (b) motivated processing to meet a preexisting goal; (c) use of a simple heuristic; and (d) the substantive generation and computation of a new judgment. The first two, direct access and goal-directed processing, leave little room for the impact of affect on decision making (low-infusion strategies). On the other hand, using heuristics or generating new judgments both allow space for affect to influence judgments, either through primed associations (heuristics) or directly (information value; both are high-infusion strategies). Forgas (1995) attempted to lend some coherence to the various perspectives on mood effects by incorporating them into a single model that considers the role of the target, judge, and situational variables in determining processing strategy.

EMOTIONAL EXPERIENCE VERSUS EMOTIONAL EXPRESSION

Emotional Experience

In addition to distinguishing among affect, emotions, and mood, researchers have found it helpful to differentiate between emotional experience and emotional expression. Emotional experience refers to the intrapersonal, internal reaction one has to an emotion-eliciting stimulus. As such it can encompass affect, emotion, and moods. For example, if someone is in a cheerful mood and then receives disappointing news, both their good mood and their negative emotional reaction to the bad news would be part of their emotional experience.

Several components have been studied as part of emotional experience. Of these, the most dominant characteristic is affective valence. When people describe their emotional experiences, they often do so in terms of how much pleasure or displeasure they feel in response to a stimulus. Frijda (1986, 1993) discussed four main components, plus a corollary, that are often part of people's emotional experiences: (a) affect; (b) an awareness of the situational meaning structure and/or a cognitive appraisal of events; (c) a state of action readiness, which is defined as a felt tendency to exhibit or inhibit behavior; and (d) felt bodily change, which includes heartbeat, arousal changes, and responses to one's own facial expressions. Frijda (1993) also introduced the emotion's "significance" as a corollary to emotional experience. Significance refers to the "reflective judgment" of an emotion as "controllable or uncontrollable, desirable or undesirable, . . . acceptable or unacceptable" and so forth (Frijda, 1993, p. 383).

Emotional Expression

Emotions are inherently interpersonally expressive phenomena (see Andersen & Guerrero, Chapter 3, this volume). Although emotions can be experienced and not expressed, the natural condition of emotion is that they are interpersonally expressed. Emotional expression encompasses actions that occur in private (e.g., grimacing and swearing when hitting your hand with a hammer), spontaneous emotional expressions (e.g., automatically smiling back at someone), and strategic communication (e.g., telling someone you love them before criticizing them). Humans may also express (or not express) emotion by using display rules (see Andersen & Guerrero, Chapter 3, this volume; Saarni, 1993) that involve strategically altering their emotional expression in a manner consistent with their personal goals or with rules of social appropriateness. For example, hiding jealous feelings, pretending to be surprised when you're not, and smiling when you're sad, are all forms of emotional expression that often involve conscious, strategic communication processes.

A large body of literature shows that emotions are communicated both nonverbally and verbally. On the nonverbal side, emotions are typically accompanied by nonverbal expressions in the face (see Buck, 1984; Ekman & Friesen, 1975) and the voice (see Burgoon, Buller, & Woodall, 1996; Kappas, Hess, & Scherer, 1991; Scherer, Banse, Wallbott, & Goldbeck, 1991). Emotions are also expressed through verbal communication that implicitly or explicitly reveals the emotions that a person is experiencing. In fact, Rimé, Mesquita, Philippot, and Boca (1991) reported findings from six studies that show that most individuals verbally disclose emotional experiences to other people, and these findings obtain for all types of emotions. Research shows that emotions are one of the most common topics of talk (White, 1993).

GENERAL APPROACHES TO CONCEPTUALIZING EMOTION

The ways that various emotions are experienced and expressed help researchers and laypeople conceptualize emotions and differentiate among them. Three general approaches to conceptualizing emotion are most prominent in recent literature: the discrete (or basic) emotions approach, the dimensional approach, and the prototype approach. Although these approaches are not necessarily incompatible (Clore & Ortony, 1991), each provides a unique view of emotion and each has different implications for the study of communication and emotion.

The Discrete or Basic Emotions Approach

According to the discrete emotions approach, individuals experience basic emotions as distinct from one another. The major proponents of this view (Ekman, 1972, 1992; Izard, 1977; Tomkins, 1963) contend that basic emotions evolved because they had adaptive value. These emotions, which can be identified by their distinct biological and physiological elements, comprise a universal "prewired" emotion system (Ekman, Levenson, & Friesen, 1983; Panksepp, 1992). Other criteria utilized to distinguish basic from nonbasic emotions include (a) a distinct and universally recognized facial expression; (b) rapid, spontaneous onset and automatic appraisal; and (c) a unique feeling state (see Ekman, 1992; Izard, 1992). However, there is considerable disagreement regarding which emotions fit these criteria. Ekman (1972; Ekman, Friesen, & Ellsworth, 1972) made a case for happiness, sadness, fear, surprise, anger, and disgust/contempt. Tompkins (1962, 1963) forwarded a similar list, except that sadness is excluded, whereas interest, distress, and shame are added. Izard (1977) proposed the longest list of basic, universal emotions: interest, joy, surprise, sadness, anger, disgust, contempt, fear, shame, shyness, and guilt. The discrete emotions approach holds that nonbasic emotions are "blends" of the primary or basic emotions. Thus, rage may be a blend of anger and fear; disappointment may be a blend of surprise, sadness, and disgust; and jealousy may be a blend of fear, anger, and sadness.

Another approach to defining basic emotions rests on the identification of "semantic primitives." According to Johnson-Laird and Oatley (1989), semantic primitives have unique status because they defy definition (i.e., other words cannot define them). Johnson-Laird and Oatley classify happiness, sadness, anger, fear, and disgust as semantic primitives that represent the most basic-level emotions. They contend that second-level basic emotions are derivatives of the five semantic primitives. Love, for example, is viewed as a special case of happiness, whereas hate is viewed as a special case of anger.

Taken together, the above research suggests that whether scholars work from a universalist or a linguistic perspective, some emotions are regarded as basic. Furthermore, these basic emotions have a unique combination of properties that make them discrete from one another. The clearest examples of basic examples appear to be anger, happiness, sadness, and fear.

Most researchers also agree that emotions are influenced by both innate and cultural forces. For example, Ekman (1972) contended that although the basic emotions are innate, what elicits them and how they are expressed are at least partially dependent upon cultural factors. A snake may frighten a child from North America, but a child from certain parts of Africa may be filled with awe as snakes are considered to be mystical, sacred creatures. When it comes to expressing emotions, people apply rules of social appropriateness that they learned in their culture (see Andersen & Guerrero, Chapter 3, this volume; Porter & Samovar, Chapter 17, this volume).

A study by Scherer and Wallbott (1994) provided evidence for the influence of both universal and cultural factors. These researchers collected data from nearly 3000 participants in 37 different countries around the globe to determine the extent to which emotions are characterized by universal versus culturally relevant features. Seven emotions—joy, fear, anger, sadness, disgust, shame, and guilt—were studied. They concluded that there were "consistently strong effects for universal, emotion-specific effects and small to medium effects for country and the Emotion × Country interaction" (p. 324). Thus, their data are more supportive of a universalist perspective, but do not discount that culture has both direct and moderating effects on the feelings, physiological symptoms, and behaviors associated with various emotions.

Scherer and Wallbott (1994) also provided profiles of characteristics associated with the seven emotions they studied, including psychometric properties, physiological reactions, and behavioral expression. In terms of psychometric properties, they examined several factors including the duration, intensity, and interpersonal valence of the seven emotions. Results indicated that fear and disgust are generally short-term emotions, whereas sadness, joy, and guilt tend to be of longer duration. People reported feeling sadness, joy, fear, and anger more intensely than they felt disgust, shame, or guilt. When it came to the interpersonal valence of the seven emotions, anger, disgust, shame, and guilt were perceived to have the strongest negative impact on relationships, in that order. As would be expected, joy stood alone as the emotion having the most positive relational consequences.

The findings associated with physiological reactions and expressive behavior are shown in Table I. These profiles appear to generalize well across the 37 countries studied by Scherer and Wallbott. It is not surprising that specific facial expressions characterized and differentiated five out of the seven emotions, because research

TABLE I   Physiological Symptoms and Expressive Behaviors Associated with Some "Basic" Emotions[a]

Emotion	Physiological reactions	Expressive behaviors
Joy	Warm temperature Accelerated heartbeat	Laughing/smiling Approach behavior Long utterances Melody change in voice
Fear	Accelerated heart rate Tense muscles Breathing change Perspiration Cold temperature Lump in throat	Silence Facial expression
Anger	Accelerated heart rate Tense muscles Breathing changes Hot temperature	Facial expression General vocal changes Long utterances Aggression Tempo change
Sadness	Lump in throat Tense muscles	Silence Crying/sobbing[b] Avoidance behaviors Facial expression
Disgust	[No particular symptoms indicated]	Silence Facial expression
Shame	Hot temperature Accelerated heart rate	Silence Facial expression
Guilt	Lump in throat	Silence

[a]Adapted from Scherer and Wallbott's (1994) data.
[b]Crying/sobbing was classified as both a physiological reaction and an expressive behavior.

(Ekman, 1972; Ekman, Sorenson, & Friesen, 1969; Izard, 1971) has shown that facial expressions commonly associated with the basic emotions are encoded and de-
coded similarly by members of different cultures. It is also interesting that silence
was a fairly common response to these emotions. This illustrates the power that
emotion has to interrupt or inhibit communication, as well as to promote it. Finally, it is noteworthy that disgust, shame, and guilt, which are sometimes *not* identified as basic emotions, were characterized by less distinctive attributes than were the
other four emotions. Thus, the more "basic" an emotion is, the more likely it is to
be expressed similarly across different cultures and to be universally recognized.

Dimensional Approaches

Discrete emotion approaches focus on the characteristics that *distinguish* emotions
from one another. In contrast, dimensional approaches concentrate on identifying
emotions based on their *placement* on dimensions. Not surprisingly, most dimensional approaches for studying emotion include a valence (i.e., positive vs. negative
affect) dimension. Research suggests that dimensions such as activity (i.e.,
aroused–relaxed) and intensity (i.e., strong–weak) are also useful. In this section, we
examine three of the most popular dimensional models of emotions: Russell's
(1978, 1980) two-dimensional circumplex model, Daly et al.'s (1983) three-dimensional model, and Plutchik's (1983, 1984) multidimensional model.

The Circumplex Model

The circumplex model (Russell, 1978, 1980, 1983) has generated considerable research. A circumplex is a two-dimensional, circular structure. Two dimensions (valence and activation) cut the circular space into four quadrants (see Figure 1). Emotions are plotted on the circumplex based on their level of activity (i.e., passive vs.
active) and their valence (i.e., positive or negative). For example, delight is characterized by moderately high activity and positive affect, whereas sadness is characterized by moderately low activity and negative affect. Within the model, emotions
that are across the circle from one another (i.e., delight and sadness; annoyance and
contentment) correlate inversely. The closer two terms are to one another on the
circumference, the higher their positive correlation. Therefore, distress correlates
highly with both annoyance and frustration. Notice also that tiredness and sleepiness, as well as happiness and pleasure, are highly correlated even though they are
in different quadrants. This fact, and the circular configuration of the model, illustrate that emotions have a multifarious structure and share complex associations
with one another.

The circumplex model has at least three important strengths: structure, parsimony, and power. As Larsen and Diener (1992) stated, "by accounting for a majority of the variance in affect measures, [the model] suggests a simple yet powerful

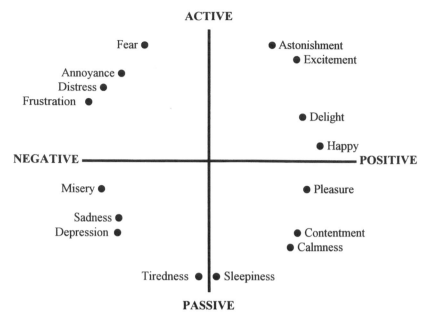

FIGURE 1   The circumplex model of emotions. (Adapted from Russell, 1989.)

way to organize facts about emotion" (p. 27). The model contains a clear structure that has implications for how emotions are experienced in terms of cognitive appraisals (i.e., as good or bad, desired or undesired) and physiological responses (i.e., levels of arousal and attention). The power of affective valence in distinguishing emotions and predicting outcomes was discussed previously in this chapter. The activity dimension has similar predictive power. For example, theories focusing on anger, deception, and intimacy exchange all feature physiological arousal as a predictor of behavior (see Andersen & Guerrero, Chapter 11, this volume; Buller & Burgoon, Chapter 14, this volume; Canary, Spitzberg, & Semic, Chapter 7, this volume).

The circumplex model has also been criticized. Larsen and Deiner (1992) argued that the model is too simplistic to capture the complexity of emotion. They use the relationship between anger and fear as an example. These two emotions are highly correlated within the circumplex model because that they are both high in activity and unpleasantness. Yet they are still distinctly different. Thus, two dimensions alone are inadequate descriptors of anger and fear. In addition, the circumplex model does not account for eliciting stimuli or cognitive labeling processes, and is based on largely intuitive, atheoretical reasoning (Larsen & Diener, 1992). Some scholars have also objected to some of the emotion terms described within the circumplex model. For example, according to most contemporary criteria, sleepiness and tiredness do not qualify as emotions. Shaver et al. (1987) suggested that these terms were utilized "to fill out the low-arousal portion of the circumplex," for which there are no true examples of emotions (p. 1064). Finally, Larsen and Diener (1992) criticized the circumplex model's activity dimension by claiming that intensity and arousal level (i.e., activity) are different, though related, dimensions. This issue leads us to examine Daly et al.'s (1983) three-dimensional model of emotions.

A Three-Dimensional Model

Daly et al. (1983) added emotional intensity to the dimensions of valence and activity. Their model is similar to Osgood, Suci, and Tannenbaum's (1957) evaluation, potency, and activity model. Intensity refers to how strong or weak an emotion is. At first glance, it may appear that intensity and activity are quite similar dimensions; however, they are distinctly different. Activity is concerned with deviation from one's normal physiological state, with *decreases* in this state representing low activity and *increases* representing high activity. Therefore, activity can be thought of as a dimension that moves from a central point either upwards or downwards. In contrast, intensity is concerned with the degree to which the emotional experience produces a change from a neutral, nonemotional state. The more change, the more intense the emotion is. Notice that this dimension operates in a unidirectional manner: Small changes indicate weak emotions and large changes indicate strong emotions. Examples such as depression and relief further illustrate this distinction. Depression is characterized by negative valence, low activity, and high intensity. Similarly, relief is characterized by positive valence, low to moderate activity (i.e., due to the release of tension), and fairly high intensity. The combination of high activity and low intensity is seen in emotions such as annoyance and dislike, with the relatively low level of intensity distinguishing them from related emotions such as anger, rage, hate, and contempt.

Despite the descriptive power of the intensity dimension, it has been largely overlooked in the emotion literature. Frijda, Ortony, Sonnemans, and Clore (1992) stated that this lack of attention "is all the more puzzling because intensity is such a salient feature of emotions. Our phenomenal experience acknowledges this fact, as do our behavior and our language; so how is it that our science essentially ignores it?" (p. 61). These authors go on to report data from an unpublished study by Clore, Ortony, Fujita, Kerr, and Pritchard, which demonstrated that emotions vary in terms of intensity range (i.e., the extent to which an emotion can be experienced as either "strong" or "weak") and average intensity (i.e., the intensity level with which the emotion is typically felt). Emotions such as dislike, like, happiness, and fear were found to have larger "intensity ranges" than emotions such as resentment, pride, and relief. Thus, as one would expect, more global emotion terms associate with the largest intensity ranges: We can feel mild or intense levels of happiness and fear, but resentment usually tends to be experienced as moderately intense.

The average intensity ratings also showed some interesting patterns. As can be

TABLE II   Emotions Sorted by Their Perceived Intensity[a]

	Anger group	Fear group	General emotions
Most intense	Rage	Terrified	Anger
↑	Irate	Dread	Pride
	Anger	Afraid	Resentment
↓	Aggravation	Nervous	Fear
Least intense	Annoyance	Concern	Sympathy

[a]This is a partial representation of the emotions listed in Frijda et al. (1992). Ordering is based on mean scores on an intensity measure.

seen in Table II, intensity helps differentiate related emotions in fairly common-sensical ways. Intensity also helps distinguish the broader spectrum of emotions. Anger and pride are emotions that tend to be experienced as intense, whereas fear and sympathy are generally experienced with less intensity.

Plutchik's Multidimensional Model

A convincing argument could be made to place Plutchik's (1962, 1980a,b, 1983, 1984) psychoevolutionary perspective on emotions into any one of the three categories we have identified here, as he addressed basic emotions, their dimensions, and how those can be arranged into hierarchies around prototypes. His perspective is best known for its structural model, however, which elaborates upon the discrete emotions approach by placing a set of basic emotions into a "three-dimensional emotion cone" (Plutchik, 1983, p. 226). Taking a functionalist perspective on the genesis and purpose of emotional expression, Plutchik (1962, 1980a) postulated eight primary emotions from which all other emotions are derived. His conceptualization of emotion is analogous to a color wheel of complementary pigments that blend into related but different colors (see Figure 2). As with primary colors, Plutchik noted that the eight basic emotions vary in *polarity, intensity,* and degree of *similarity* (Plutchik, 1962, 1980a). Polarity is illustrated by arranging the eight primary emotions in opposing pairs across from each other on the emotion wheel: joy versus sadness, acceptance versus disgust, fear versus anger, and surprise versus anticipation. Adjacent pairs on the wheel reflect emotional similarity; for instance, anger is placed between disgust and anticipation, joy is placed between anticipation and acceptance. Vertical levels of the cone extend the color wheel into three-dimensional space to represent emotional intensity; for example, fear varies from terror to apprehension, and joy varies from ecstasy to pleasure. Thus, Plutchik's model places the primary emotions and their respective extremes into systematic relationships with each other.

These relationships can provide a framework for understanding the approach and

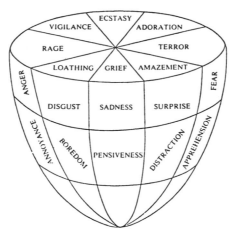

FIGURE 2   Plutchik's (1984) three-dimensional emotion cone. Reproduced with permission.

avoidance tendencies associated with more complex mixtures of emotions (Plutchik, 1980a). In the way that mixing red and yellow pigments results in orange paint, emotional blends that comprise adjacent pairs on the wheel are relatively pure and allow for a clear expression of emotion; for example, love is the blending of joy and acceptance (both positive emotions), whereas contempt blends disgust and anger (both negative emotions). On the other hand, combining complementary pigment colors in equal amounts produces the neutral color of gray. Similarly, the more removed the blended emotions are from each other on the wheel, the more likely they are to lead to conflicting motivations that will neutralize each other (i.e., concurrent feelings of acceptance and rejection can elicit a frozen state that precludes either approach or avoidance).

Plutchik's structural model is only one component of a set of interconnected ideas comprising the psychoevolutionary approach. In addition to structure, Plutchik (1983) described four other fundamental elements. First, Plutchik argued that emotions must be considered in an evolutionary context. Drawing upon Darwin's (1859) theory of natural selection, he noted that our primary physical features and basic behavioral responses exist because they had survival value for our ancestors. That is, emotions have been adaptive in handling survival threats and opportunities that present themselves in the environment. For example, it is adaptive to know when a creature in your environment is on the verge of attacking you so you can either avoid the confrontation by fleeing or take advantage by striking the first blow. Rage is commonly displayed by an enlarged body, whether exhibited in puffed feathers, erect body hair, or expanded air pouches. This display may be accompanied by a snarl, which also signals an intention to attack in both humans and animals (Darwin, 1872). Plutchik (1983) also relayed evidence that some emotional expression and reception, especially the emotional expressions of infants, may be linked to neurological mechanisms that have adaptive bonding qualities. For instance, visually impaired infants begin to smile to social stimuli at about the same time as sighted infants; and hearing-impaired infants coo at the same frequency as hearing infants until about 6 months of age, when more complex language begins to appear. From this perspective, emotions have evolved as a communicative device to let others gauge our internal feelings and predict potential actions that might result from such feelings, from recognition and welcome to attraction, submission, distress, dominance, and so forth (Plutchik, 1983). Emotions therefore help humans and other animals access the resources that are most necessary for survival: finding food, avoiding injury, and reproducing (Plutchik, 1980b).

A second important concept in Plutchik's model is that emotions are "complex chains of events that are triggered most often by environmental stimuli" (1983, p. 223). Emotions are neither disassociated from reality nor random, but a process of responding to an event in the environment that includes cognitive, visceral, behavioral, and outcome components. An enemy appearing nearby (stimulus event) and being evaluated as dangerous (cognition), can lead to fear (feeling) and running (behavior) in order to protect oneself (effect) (for other examples, see Table 1.1 in Plutchik, 1980b). In this way, emotions represent a complex feedback system that leads to actions that can reduce an environmental threat or embrace an environmental opportunity, thereby maintaining a state of homeostatic balance in the organism (Plutchik, 1983).

Third, Plutchik (1980a, 1983) noted that emotions are multifaceted constructs that we identify by piecing together a variety of evidence, including the stimulus conditions, our behavior over time, how our behavior affects others, how well the emotional inference may predict future behavior, and so forth. Although self-reports of emotions are popular methods of measurement, he noted that verbal accounts of emotions are not adequate evidence of emotional experience, as we are quite able to knowingly or inadvertently deceive others through emotional expression. Hence, the fleeting, telltale expression of shock that Aunt Molly would give you orange striped socks as a birthday gift can be quickly followed by compensatory verbal exclamations of delight that are intense and well-intentioned, yet insincere.

Finally, Plutchik (1962, 1980a, 1983) argued that the eight basic emotions are associated with a variety of derivative "domains of discourse," including interpersonal personality traits (e.g., the hostile personality is characterized by a mixture of anger and disgust); psychological diagnostic labels (e.g., depression is an extreme form of gloominess); and ego defense mechanisms (e.g., displacement is a method of dealing with anger that cannot be directly expressed to the provocateur). Linking emotions to behaviors that affect our interpersonal relationships supports the movement away from viewing emotion as an individual experience to viewing emotion as a communicative event.

In summary, Plutchik's psychoevolutionary model arranges eight basic emotions and their related emotions into a multidimensional space that is anchored by polarity, intensity, and similarity. Plutchik discusses his structural model of the emotions within an evolutionary framework that lends some theoretical coherence to the selection and placement of the model's dimensions, enhancing the model's heuristic value. His functionalist perspective on emotions examines not only why emotions exist, but also allows us to examine commonalities in emotions both within and across species. He also points out that some underlying neurological mechanisms may not only affect emotional expression, but emotional reception, as well (Plutchik, 1983). By connecting emotional states to interpersonal dynamics, Plutchik's model may provide a point of integration for communication scholars who are interested in how individual characteristics, such as genetic predispositions, chronic emotional states, and enduring personality characteristics, affect our relational communication. One serious criticism of the model is that the notion of true polar opposites is not perfectly realized by some of the basic emotions included in the model (for a critique of the model and an application to friendships, see Gaines et al., Chapter 19, this volume). His view that emotions can be arranged into hierarchies of intensity incorporates some considerations that are examined in the prototype approach to emotions.

The Prototype Approach

Like Plutchik's multidimensional approach, the prototype approach represents a compromise between the discrete emotions and dimensional approaches. Prototype families are distinguished from one another by a host of characteristics, including valence, common elicitors, functions, and expression. Within each prototype family, related clusters of emotion are separated by characteristics such as intensity. As Dillard and Wilson (1993) contended, the prototype approach can be considered a "middle ground" because emotions are "construed as *regions* in multidimensional space" (p. 638). Similarly, Shaver, Wu, and Schwartz (1992) argued that a strength of the prototype approach is that "it addresses both the contents of individual categories (e.g., the category of sadness episodes) and the hierarchical relations among categories (e.g., loneliness is a type of sadness, which itself is a type of negative emotion)" (p. 186).

The prototype approach (which is based on work by Rosch, 1977, 1978) rests on the idea that language, and knowledge structures related to language, shape how people conceptualize and categorize information. According to this perspective, people's experiences provide them with the information necessary to construct knowledge structures, including prototypes. For instance, by the time children are as young as 3 years old, they are likely to have witnessed and experienced anger and angry behavior. The common elicitors of this emotion (e.g., the child misbehaving), as well as the emotion's common features (e.g., hearing raised voices, being aroused, and feeling negative affect) are likely to be generalized and incorporated into one's prototypic view of anger.

The prototype itself is an abstract image that consists of a set of weighted features that represent the exemplar of a family of emotions (Fitness & Fletcher, 1993; Shaver et al., 1992). These features, which can include common emotion elicitors, physiological effects, cognitive appraisals, control strategies, and behavioral responses, define the core meaning of the category or emotion family (Fitness & Fletcher, 1993; Shaver et al., 1987). For example, the "joy family" (see Figure 3) contains emotions such as amusement, bliss, exhilaration, contentment, and pride. The features characterizing this prototype may include positive affective feelings and goal attainment. In contrast, research suggests that the anger prototype is associated with high levels of arousal and tension, feelings of helplessness, and the impulse to move against or strike out against someone (Davitz, 1969).

Two dimensions help organize the emotions within each category. The *vertical dimension* shows the hierarchical relationships among categories (see Figure 3). There are three levels. The most general level, the superordinate level, is defined by the positive or negative valence of the emotions within a given category. The middle or basic level represents the core emotion within the category. The core emotions are referenced more easily than the other members of the category and are likely to anchor the mental representations of all emotions within a given category. Shaver et al. (1987) classify love, joy, anger, sadness, fear, and perhaps surprise, as the basic-level emotions. Finally, the subordinate level consists of all other (nonbasic) emotions that are related to the prototype.

The *horizontial dimension,* in contrast, shows the relationships between members of the same category. For example, clusters containing adoration, love and liking,

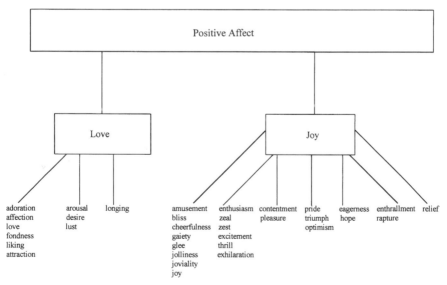

FIGURE 3   The prototype structure for joy and love. (Adapted from Shaver, Schwartz, Kirson, & O'Connor, 1987.)

arousal and desire, and longing all belong to the same family as the basic-level emotion of joy (see Figure 3). Emotions at the subordinate level can be compared to
the basic-level emotion that anchors the category. As Russell (1991) stated: "At the
heart of the prototype perspective is the idea that membership in a category is determined by resemblance to . . . protoypical exemplars" (p. 38). For example, the
subordinate emotions of contentment, bliss, and pleasure are probably better examples of joy than are pride or triumph (Russell, 1991), just as robins and bluejays
are more prototypical of birds than peacocks and ostriches. Subordinate-level emotions can also be compared to one another. Emotions that fall within the same hor-
izontial-level cluster are more strongly related to one another than they are to emotions from a different cluster. Thus, if someone is feeling desire, we would expect
them to be highly likely to also feel arousal and only somewhat likely to feel adoration (see Figure 3).

The prototype perspective is not without its critics (e.g., Clore & Ortony, 1991).
Some researchers have argued that people's accounts of emotional experiences may
be insufficient for describing the complex experience of emotions. Clore and
Ortony (1991) argued that although many people classify whales as fish rather than
mammals, this misconception does not lead zoologists to reclassify them. Thus, they
caution emotion researchers to remember that learning about people's conceptualizations tells us something about the everyday nature of emotional experience, but
does little to further objective scientific debate about the nature of emotion.

There is also disagreement over which emotions qualify as the basic-level exemplars. For example, Fitness and Fletcher (1993) provided evidence that jealousy
is a distinct prototype. Other research seems to confirm this, showing that jealousy
associates with a much wider array of emotions than just anger (see Guerrero &
Andersen, Chapter 6, this volume). Some studies also suggest that anger and hate
are separate prototypes (Davitz, 1969; Fitness & Fletcher, 1993).

Another concern is that some emotions may cross boundaries. Those supporting the prototype perspective readily accept that boundaries between categories are
sometimes "fuzzy" (e.g., Shaver et al., 1987). Surprise is a good example of a category that crosses boundaries at the superordinate level. As Shaver et al. (1992)
stated, it is unclear whether or not surprise is a basic emotion. Unlike the other
basic emotions, surprise can either be positive (e.g., feeling relieved when an expensive traffic ticket is unexpectedly dismissed) or negative (feeling disappointed
when Christmas bonuses are canceled).

Other emotions cross boundaries at the basic or subordinate levels. Shaver et al.
(1987) contended that emotions such as jealousy, hurt, and sympathy may constitute emotion blends. For example, they noted that although hurt fits within their
sadness category, it is likely to be a blend of both sadness and anger. Disappointment represents an even more complex case. Although disappointment was rated as
a fairly good example of an emotion, Shaver et al. (1987) were unable to classify it
within the prototype structure. This may be because disappointment associates with
sadness and surprise, and possibly anger. These examples demonstrate that consid-

erable work remains to be done if researchers hope to determine the structure of prototype hierarchies and make worthwhile distinctions between emotions at the subordinate level. *Emotion blends,* such as hurt and jealousy, appear to be distinct from other emotions at the subordinate level. For example, in the anger cluster, words such as "rage" and "annoyance" reflect changes in the intensity of the anger experience, whereas emotion blends such as jealousy appear to reflect the combined experience of anger and other emotions.

Perhaps prototype researchers should create a structure that better accommodates the distinction between emotions that are truly from the same family but vary in intensity (i.e., contentment, happiness, and bliss) and those that represent a blend of emotions associated with different prototype families (i.e., disappointment). Take jealousy as a case in point. Rather than classifying jealousy as an emotion falling solely under the anger category, prototype researchers should acknowledge that jealous individuals often experience emotions that fall within at least four different emotion families: anger, fear, sadness, and love. A revised hierarchical system could order emotions in terms of intensity level at the subordinate level and a new level could be created to represent the blend emotions.

IMPLICATIONS

Although the discrete emotions, dimensional, and prototype approaches to emotion represent distinct ways of characterizing emotion, we believe that the three approaches are complementary. Each provides unique information about the structure of emotions and each can be applied to communication research. For example, it is clear that dimensions such as valence, activity, and intensity have predictive and explanatory power. Measuring these dimensions in addition to identifying particular emotions gives researchers precise information on the nature of emotions. Similarly, dimensions help researchers obtain a clearer picture of the *overall* tone of an interaction. Rather than (or in addition to) listing the types of emotions that occur in a given interaction, such as conflictual or deceptive situations, researchers can determine the overall valence, activity, and intensity of the emotional experience. Prototypes are also important. For example, it may be useful to see if various emotions from within the same prototype family associate differentially with outcomes in conflict situations. Thus, all three approaches are valuable in the study of emotional communication.

Several very basic questions related to these approaches still need to be answered. For example, although we know that emotional experience and expression are influenced by both innate and cultural forces, we do not yet know how cultural differences influence the *patterns* of emotional expression that occur during cross-cultural interaction. In addition, it is possible that similarity in nonverbal emotional expression helps bridge the gap between two individuals from different cultures who have trouble communicating verbally. Such possibilities need further exploration. In terms of the dimensions underlying emotions, it is clear that valence is an important defining feature of emotional experience and expression. The role of other dimensions, including activity and intensity, is not as well understood. The associations between various emotion dimensions and different forms of emotional expression also remains a rich area for future research. Finally, as noted above, considerable work remains to be done on prototype structures. From a communication perspective, it would be interesting to see how people manage their emotional expression by substituting emotional displays from within the same or different prototype families. For instance, individuals may de-intensify anger by displaying annoyance rather than rage. They may mask sadness by acting happy, or they may intensify contentment by appearing overjoyed. In short, people's prototypic, commonsense models of emotion may guide their repertoire of emotional response patterns.

The dimensional and prototype approaches also have implications for patterns of reciprocity. As will be argued in Chapter 3 (Andersen & Guerrero, this volume), the reciprocal, synchronous expression of positive affect is one key to building satisfying relationships. When evaluating whether reciprocity has occurred, it may be particularly important to examine dimensions such as valence and intensity. Imagine, for example, an engaged couple discussing their future together. Both may be expressing emotion from the same prototype family (e.g., happiness), but if one partner's expression is more intensely positive than the other's, the more expressive partner might leave the interaction feeling disappointed and disconnected.

CONCLUSION

Our goal for this chapter was to acquaint readers with basic emotion concepts and popular approaches to studying emotion. We believe that this foundation, which is based on decades of work in social science disciplines such as anthropology and psychology, provides a starting point for understanding emotional communication. In this volume, various authors take different basic approaches to studying emotion. In Chapter 19, Gaines et al. examine the communication of emotion in friendship using Plutchik's (1984) multidimensional model. In Chapter 7, Canary et al. discuss a prototypic view of anger expression. Buller and Burgoon's chapter on deception (Chapter 14), as well as Metts, Sprecher, and Regan's chapter on sexual desire (Chapter 13), discuss issues related to arousal and affective valence.

The next two introductory chapters focus more squarely on how emotion functions within the context of social interaction. Chapter 2 discusses cues, channels, and processes that are related to emotional communication. Chapter 3 proposes six principles of emotional communication, which together show how biological, cultural, and relational factors shape emotional experience and expression, and how emotion and communication are inextricably linked to one another.

Dillard and Wilson (1993) predicted that the study of emotional communication would soon take flight. We hope that the introductory chapters, as well as the remaining chapters in this volume, will move us off the runway and toward the sky so that we are better equipped to understand and explain how emotions function in everyday interaction, and so that we can offer people such as "Caught in the Middle" sound answers to their questions about communication and emotion.

REFERENCES

Averill, J. R. (1980). A constructivist view of emotions. In R. Plutchik & H. Kellerman (Eds.), *Emotions: Theory, research, and experience* (Vol. 1, pp. 305–339). New York: Academic Press.

Batson, C. D., Coke, J. S., Chard, F., Smith, D., & Taliaferro, A. (1979). Generality of the "glow of goodwill": Effects of mood on helping and information acquisition. *Social Psychology Quarterly, 42,* 176–179.

Batson, C. D., Shaw, L. L., & Oleson, K. C. (1992). Differentiating affect, mood, and emotion: Toward functionally based conceptual distinctions. In M. S. Clark (Ed.), *Review of personality and social psychology: Emotion* (Vol. 13, pp. 294–326). Newbury Park, CA: Sage.

Blaney, P. H. (1986). Affect and memory: A review. *Psychological Bulletin, 99,* 229–246.

Bohner, G., & Schwarz, N. (1993). Mood states influence the production of persuasive arguments. *Communication Research, 20,* 696–722.

Bower, G. H. (1981). Mood and memory. *American Psychologist, 36,* 129–148.

Buck, R. (1984). *The communication of emotions.* New York: Guilford.

Burgoon, J. K. (1993). Interpersonal expectations, expectancy violations, and emotional communication. *Journal of Language and Social Psychology, 12,* 30–48.

Burgoon, J. K., Buller, D. B., & Woodall, W. G. (1996). *Nonverbal communication: The unspoken dialogue* (2nd ed.). New York: McGraw-Hill.

Campos, J. (1995). Foreword. In J. P. Tangney & K. W. Fischer (Eds.), *Self-conscious emotions: The psychology of shame, guilt, embarrassment, and pride* (pp. ix–xi). New York: Guilford.

Carnevale, P. J. D., & Isen, A. M. (1986). The influence of positive affect and visual access on the discovery of integrative solutions in bilateral negotiation. *Organizational Behavior and Human Decision Processes, 37,* 1–13.

Clark, M. S., & Isen, A. M. (1982). Toward understanding the relationship between feeling states and social behavior. In A. H. Hastorf & A. M. Isen (Eds.), *Cognitive social psychology* (pp. 73–108). New York: Elsevier.

Clore, G. L., & Ortony, A. (1988). The semantics of the affective lexicon. In V. Hamilton, G. H. Bower, & N. H. Frijda (Eds.), *Cognitive perspectives on emotion and motivations* (pp. 367–397). Norwell, MA: Kluwer Academic.

Clore, G. L., & Ortony, A. (1991). What more is there to emotion concepts than prototypes? *Journal of Personality and Social Psychology, 60,* 48–50.

Clore, G. L., Schwarz, N., & Conway, M. (1994). Affective causes and consequences of social information processing. In R. S. Wyer & T. K. Srull (Eds.), *Handbook of social cognition* (Vol. 1, pp. 323–417). Hillsdale, NJ: Erlbaum.

Daly, E. M., Lancee, W. J., & Polivy, J. (1983). A conical model for the taxonomy of emotional experience. *Journal of Personality and Social Psychology, 45,* 443–457.

Darwin, C. (1859). *The origin of the species.* New York: Philosophical Library.

Darwin, C. (1872). *The expression of the emotions in man and animals.* New York: Philosophical Library.

Davitz, J. R. (1969). *The language of emotion.* New York: Academic Press.

Dillard, J. P., & Wilson, B. J. (1993). Communication and affect: Thoughts, feelings, and issues for the future. *Communication Research, 20,* 637–646.

Ekman, P. (1972). Universal and cultural differences in facial expression of emotion. In J. R. Cole (Ed.), *Nebraska symposium on motivation* (pp. 207–283). Lincoln: University of Nebraska Press.

Ekman, P. (1984). Expression and the nature of emotion. In K. Scherer & P. Ekman (Eds.), *Approaches to emotion* (pp. 319–343). Hillsdale, NJ: Erlbaum.

Ekman, P. (1992). An argument for basic emotions. *Cognition and Emotion, 6,* 169–200.

Ekman, P., & Friesen, W. V. (1975). *Unmasking the face: A guide to recognizing emotions from facial clues.* Englewood Cliffs, NJ: Prentice-Hall.

Ekman, P., Friesen, W. V., & Ellsworth, P. (1972). *Emotion in the human face: Guidelines for research and an integration of findings.* New York: Pergamon Press.

Ekman, P., Levenson, R. W., & Friesen, W. V. (1983). Autonomic nervous system activity distinguishes among emotions. *Science, 221,* 1208–1210.

Ekman, P., Sorenson, E. R., & Friesen, W. V. (1969). Pan-cultural elements in facial displays of emotion. *Science, 164,* 86–88.

Ellis, H. C., & Ashbrook, P. W. (1988). Resource allocation model of the effects of depressed mood. In K. Fiedler & J. Forgas (Eds.), *Affect, cognition and social behavior* (pp. 25–43). Toronto, Canada: C. J. Hogrefe.

Fehr, B., & Russell, J. A. (1984). Concept of emotion viewed from a prototype perspective. *Journal of Experimental Psychology, 113,* 464–486.

Fiske, S. T., & Taylor, S. E. (1984). *Social cognition.* Reading, MA: Addison-Wesley.

Fitness, J., & Fletcher, G. J. O. (1993). Love, hate, anger, and jealousy in close relationships: A prototype and cognitive appraisal analysis. *Journal of Personality and Social Psychology, 65,* 942–958.

Forgas, J. P. (1995). Mood and judgment: The affect infusion model (AIM). *Psychological Bulletin, 117,* 39–66.

Frijda, N. H. (1986). *The emotions.* New York: Cambridge University Press.

Frijda, N. H. (1993). Moods, emotion episodes, and emotions. In M. Lewis & J. M. Haviland (Eds.), *Handbook of emotions* (pp. 381–404). New York: Guilford.

Frijda, N. H., Ortony, A., Sonnesmans, J., & Clore, G. L. (1992). The complexity of intensity: Issues concerning the structure of emotion intensity. In M. S. Clark (Ed.), *Review of personality and social psychology: Emotion* (vol. 13, pp. 60–89). Newbury Park, CA: Sage.

Galizio, M., & Hendrick, C. (1972). Effect of musical accompaniment on attitude: The guitar as a prop for persuasion. *Journal of Applied Social Psychology, 2,* 350–359.

Isen, A. M. (1984). Toward understanding the role of affect in cognition. In R. Wyer & T. Srull (Eds.), *Handbook of social cognition* (vol. 3, pp. 179–236). Hillsdale, NJ: Erlbaum.

Isen, A. M. (1987). Positive affect, cognitive processes, and social behavior. In M. Zanna (Ed.), *Advances in experimental social psychology* (vol. 20, pp. 203–253). New York: Academic Press.

Isen, A. M., Clark, M. S., & Schwartz, M. F. (1976). Duration of the effect of good mood on helping: "Footprints on the sands of time." *Journal of Personality and Social Psychology, 34,* 385–393.

Isen, A. M., Means, B., Patrick, R., & Nowicki, G. (1982). Some factors influencing decision-making strategy and risk-taking. In M. S. Clark & S. T. Fiske (Eds.), *Affect and cognition: The 17th Annual Carnegie Symposium on Cognition* (pp. 243–261). Hillsdale, NJ: Erlbaum.

Isen, A. M., Shalker, T., Clark, M., & Karp, L. (1978). Affect, accessibility of material in memory and behavior: A cognitive loop? *Journal of Personality and Social Psychology, 36,* 1–12.

Izard, C. E. (1971). *The face of emotion.* New York: Appleton-Century-Crofts.

Izard, C. E. (1977). *Human emotions.* New York: Plenum.

Izard, C. E. (1992). Basic emotions, relationship among emotions, and emotion-cognition relations. *Psychological Review, 99,* 561–565.

James, W. (1884). What is an emotion? *Mind, 9,* 188–205.

Janis, I. L., Kaye, D., & Kirschner, P. (1965). Facilitating effects of "eating while reading" on responsiveness to persuasive communications. *Journal of Personality and Social Psychology, 11,* 181–186.

Johnson-Laird, P. N., & Oatley, K. (1989). The language of emotions: An analysis of a semantic field. *Cognition and emotion, 3,* 81–123.

Kappas, A., Hess, U., & Scherer, K. R. (1991). Voice and emotion. In R. S. Feldman & B. Rimé (Eds.), *Fundamental of nonverbal vehavior* (pp. 200–237). Cambridge University Press.

Kenrick, D. T., Baumann, D. J., & Cialdini, R. B. (1979). A step in the socialization of altruism as hedonism: Effects of negative mood on children's generosity under public and private conditions. *Journal of Personality and Social Psychology, 37,* 747–755.

Lange, C. G. (1885). *The emotions* (trans., 1922). Baltimore, MD: Williams & Wilkins.

Larsen, R. J., & Diener, E. (1992). Promises and problems with the circumplex model of emotion. In M. S. Clark (Ed.), *Review of personality and social psychology: Emotion* (vol. 13, pp. 25–59). Newbury Park, CA: Sage.

Mackie, D. M., & Worth, L. T. (1989). Cognitive deficits and the mediation of positive affect in persuasion. *Journal of Personality and Social Psychology, 57,* 27–40.

Mackie, D. M., & Worth, L. T. (1991). Feel good, but not thinking straight: The impact of positive mood on persuasion. In J. Forgas (Ed.), *Emotion and social judgments* (pp. 201–219). Oxford, UK: Pergamon.

Metts, S., & Bowers, J. W. (1994). Emotion in interpersonal communication. In M. L. Knapp & G. R. Miller (Eds.), *Handbook of interpersonal communication* (2nd ed., pp. 508–541). Thousand Oaks, CA: Sage.

Natale, M. (1977). Effects of induced-elation depression on speech in the initial interview. *Journal of Consulting and Clinical Psychology, 45,* 45–52.

Orotny, A., Clore, G. L., & Foss, M. (1987). The referential structure of the affective lexicon. *Cognitive Science, 11,* 361–384.

Osgood, C. E., Suci, G. J., & Tannenbaum, P. (1957). *The measurement of meaning.* Urbana: University of Illinois Press.

Panksepp, J. (1992). A critical role for "affective neuroscience" in resolving what is basic about basic emotions. *Psychological Review, 97,* 554–560.

Planalp, S. (1993). Communication, cognition, and emotion. *Communication Monographs, 60,* 3–9.

Plutchik, R. (1962). *The emotions: Facts, theories, and a new model.* New York: Random House.

Plutchik, R. (1980a). *Emotion: A psychoevolutionary synthesis.* New York: Harper & Row.

Plutchik, R. (1980b). A general psychoevolutionary theory of emotion. In R. Plutchik & H. Kellerman (Eds.), *Emotion: theory, research, and experience* (Vol. 1, pp. 3–33). New York: Academic Press.

Plutchik, R. (1983). Emotions in early development: A psychoevolutionary approach. In R. Plutchik & H. Kellerman (Eds.), *Emotion: Theory, research, and experience* (Vol. 2, pp. 221–257). New York: Academic Press.

Plutchik, R. (1984). Emotions: A general psychoevolutionary theory. In K. R. Scherer & P. Ekman (Eds.), *Approaches to emotion* (pp. 197–219). Hillsdale, NJ: Erlbaum.

Rimé, B., Mesquita, B., Philippot, P., & Boca, S. (1991). Beyond the emotional event: Six studies of the social sharing of emotion. *Cognition and Emotion, 5,* 435–465.

Rosch, R. (1977). Human categorization. In N. Warren (Ed.), *Studies in cross-cultural psychology* (pp. 1–49). San Diego, CA: Academic Press.

Rosch, R. (1978). Principles of categorization. In E. Rosch & B. B. Lloyd (Eds.), *Cognition and categorization* (pp. 27–48). Hillsdale, NJ: Erlbaum.

Russell, J. A. (1978). Evidence of convergent validity of the dimensions of affect. *Journal of Personality and Social Psychology, 36,* 1152–1168.

Russell, J. A. (1980). A circumplex model of affect. *Journal of Personality and Social Psychology, 39,* 1161–1178.

Russell, J. A. (1983). Pancultural aspects of the human conceptual organization of emotions. *Journal of Personality and Social Psychology, 45,* 1281–1288.

Russell, J. A. (1989). Measures of emotion. In R. Plutchik & H. Kellerman (Eds.), *Emotion: Theory research, and experience* (pp. 83–111). New York: Academic Press.

Russell, J. A. (1991). In defense of a prototype approach to emotion concepts. *Journal of Personality and Social Psychology, 60,* 37–47.

Saarni, C. (1993). Socialization of emotion. In M. Lewis & J. M. Haviland (Eds.), *Handbook of emotions* (pp. 435–446). New York: Guilford.

Scherer, K. R. (1994). Affect bursts. In S. H. M. Van Goozen, N. E. Van de Poll, & J. A. Sergeant (Eds.), *Emotions: Essays on emotion theory* (pp. 161–193). Hillsdale, NJ: Erlbaum.

Scherer, K. R., Banse, R., Wallbott, H. G., & Goldbeck, T. (1991). Vocal cues in emotion encoding. *Motivation and Emotion, 15,* 123–148.

Scherer, K. R., & Wallbott, H. G. (1994). Evidence for universality and cultural variation of differential emotion response patterning. *Journal of Personality and Social Psychology, 66,* 310–328.

Schwarz, N. (1990). Feelings as information: Informational and motivational functions of affective states. In E. T. Higgins & R. Sorrentino (Eds.), *Handbook of motivation and cognition* (Vol. 2, pp. 527–561). New York: Guilford.

Schwarz, N., & Clore, G. (1988). How do I feel about it? Informative functions of affective states. In K. Fiedler & J. Forgas (Eds.), *Affect, cognition, and social behavior* (pp. 44–62). Toronto, Canada: C.J. Hogrefe.

Schwarz, N., & Clore, G. (1983). Mood, misattribution, and judgments of well-being: Informative and directive functions of affective states. *Journal of Personality and Social Psychology, 45,* 513–523.

Schwarz, N., Strack, F., Kommer, D., & Wagner, D. (1987). Soccer, rooms and the quality of your life: Mood effects on judgments of satisfaction with life in general and with specific life-domains. *European Journal of Social Psychology, 17,* 69–79.

Shaver, P. R., Morgan, J. J., & Wu, S. (1996). Is love a "basic" emotion? *Personal Relationships, 3,* 81–96.

Shaver, P. R., Schwartz, J., Kirson, D., & O'Connor, C. (1987). Emotion knowledge: Further explorations of a prototype approach. *Journal of Personality and Social Psychology, 52,* 1061–1086.

Shaver, P. R., Wu, S., & Schwartz, J. C. (1992). Cross-cultural similarities and differences in emotion and its representation: A prototype approach. In M. S. Clark (Ed.), *Review of personality and social psychology: Emotion* (vol. 13, pp. 175–212). Newbury Park, CA: Sage.

Singer, J. A., & Salovey, P. (1988). Mood and memory: Evaluating the network theory of affect. *Clinical Psychology Review, 8,* 211–251.

Strongman, K. T. (1987). *The psychology of emotion* (3rd ed.). New York: Wiley & Sons.

Tomkins, S. S. (1962). *Affect, imagery, consciousness: Vol. 1. The positive affects.* New York: Springer.

Tomkins, S. S. (1963). *Affect, imagery, consciousness: Vol. 2: The negative affects.* New York: Springer-Verlag.

Vangelisti, A. L. (1994). Messages that hurt. In W. R. Cupach & B. H. Spitzberg (Eds.), *The dark side of interpersonal communication* (pp. 53–82). Hillsdale, NJ: Erlbaum.

White, G. M. (1993). Emotions in side out: The anthropology of affect. In M. Lewis & J. M. Haviland (Eds.), *Handbook of Emotions* (pp. 29–39). New York: Guilford.

Wundt, W. (1897). *Outlines of psychology* (C. H. Judd, Trans.). Leipzig: Englemann.

CHAPTER 2

Communicating Emotion in Everyday Life: Cues, Channels, and Processes

Sally Planalp

University of Montana
Missoula, Montana

Research on how humans express emotions can be traced back at least to Darwin's seminal work, *The Expression of the Emotions in Man and Animals* (1872/1904). There Darwin set up assumptions that are still with us today, over a century later, and are apparent even from the title. Note the choices of terminology. He chose the word *emotions,* not *emotion,* implying that there are distinct emotions rather than ongoing emotional processes. The categories he used are surprisingly resilient, including what we now call the sadness, joy, anger, disgust, surprise, and shame families (but also including the "ill-temper" family, which is not recognized as a basic emotion today) (see debates in Ekman & Davidson, 1994; Stein & Oatley, 1992). Darwin also chose the word *expression,* not *communication,* thus making emotion the prime mover and expression only a by-product. Still today the phrases "emotional expression" or "facial expression" (Camras, Holland & Patterson, 1993; Fridlund, 1994; Heise & O'Brien, 1993) are seen more often than "emotional communication" or "facial communication" (for exceptions, see Buck, 1984; Metts & Bowers, 1994; Pittam & Scherer, 1993). Finally, Darwin focused on continuities between *man and animals,* not the unique emotional and communicative capacities of humans. This emphasis on biological continuities rather than on cultural variations may contribute to the emphasis today on facial expressions instead of on the verbal communication of emotion, the emphasis on unintentional displays of emotion rather than on messages intentionally adapted to other people, and on emotion removed from its social and everyday human context.

Recently, however, the paths of research on emotion have fanned out in a number of interesting directions, several of which challenge Darwin. In this chapter, I review existing research on the communication of emotion, focusing on emotion messages. I then describe a study that led my colleagues and me to question those assumptions and other research that points in similar directions. In the process, I argue for a view of emotional expression that I believe captures more fully what we now know about human communications as a complex, flexible, and creative process.

RESEARCH LITERATURE
ON EMOTION MESSAGES

Even a cursory glance at research on emotion messages reveals several patterns. First, the research is most often organized according to different types of cues—facial cues, vocal cues, body cues, verbal cues, physiological cues, and the like. Another related but much less common organizing scheme is the message channel divisions (e.g., visual, vocal, verbal, audio/visual) driven by the ability to record messages through audio- or videotaping or by transcribing verbal interaction. The third organizing principle is by category of emotion or emotion family—anger, fear, joy, shame, sadness, disgust, surprise, and so on. The pioneering work in this area was done primarily through naturalistic observation, overwhelmingly of infants and children (Tomkins, 1962, 1963; Izard, 1977). Often the assumption of separate cues and the assumption of distinct emotions are combined, as in research on the various cues and channels used to express basic emotions (e.g., Izard, 1991), or research on how the face differentially expresses anger, sadness, joy, and so forth (e.g., Ekman, 1982).

These are natural starting points, given the complexity of studying communication and emotion. It makes sense to divide messages into cues and emotions into distinct types. It provides a foothold from which we can learn a great deal—so much in fact, that the research is impossible to summarize in a few pages. For more complete reviews, consult articles by Bowers, Metts, and Duncanson (1985), Metts and Bowers (1994), chapters in Lewis and Haviland (1993) and the present volume, in addition to classic works by Buck (1984), Ekman (1982), Frijda (1986), Izard (1991), and Lazarus (1991). Although the complete range of cues is overwhelming, some important lines of research and trends can be identified. In this selective review, however, I focus on what the existing literature says about Darwin's assumptions and recent challenges.

Facial Cues

In many people's eyes emotional expression is nearly synonymous with facial cues, thanks to Darwin and to more latter-day pioneers such as Tomkins, Izard, and Ekman (for brief histories, see Camras et al., 1993 and Fridlund, 1994). Tomkins's (1962, 1963) and Izard's (1977) early work was founded on naturalistic observation of distinct emotions (such as joy, anger and shame), particularly facial expressions. Much of the work that has followed, however, has relied on controlled experiments that manipulate or measure facial expressions in order to determine if observers can accurately judge distinct emotions. Moreover, if you ask people how they express their own or recognize others' emotions, they mention facial expressions, smiles, frowns, eye gaze, gritting teeth, and other facial cues (Scherer, Wallbott, Matsumoto, & Kudoh, 1988; Shaver, Schwartz, Kirson, & O'Connor, 1987; Wallbott, Ricci-Bitti, & Bänninger-Huber, 1986). Taken together, there is no doubt that emotions are expressed through the face and that facial expressions are interpreted by others as indicative of emotions. Impressive bodies of research document substantial accuracy in recognizing emotions in the face even across cultures, although some emotions are more difficult to recognize than others (e.g., negative emotions are more easily confused with one another than with positive emotions, and blends are identified less accurately than simple emotions) (Ekman, 1993; Ekman & O'Sullivan, 1991; Ekman et al., 1987). Facial expressions have also been analyzed in such detail that researchers trying to code facial expression in ongoing interaction can turn to several generations of systems for coding facial expressions of affect, especially Ekman and Friesen's (1978) Facial Action Coding System.

Given the evidence available and basic common sense, one is tempted to conclude that Darwin was right—that all humans express emotions through the face. But there are complications. The first question is whether *distinct emotions* are expressed through the face, or whether a more continuous array of emotion might be operating. Russell (1994) argued that the assumption of distinct emotions is seldom challenged or tested, and when it is, the evidence is not strong. One major problem is that most studies of both encoding or expressing emotions and decoding or judging emotions simply assume distinct emotions (usually joy, surprise, sadness, fear, anger and disgust). On the encoding side, actors may be asked to pose those categories, making them much easier to identify than spontaneous expressions, perhaps unrealistically so (Motley & Camden, 1988). On the decoding side, many studies force observers to choose among those same categories of emotions without regard for whether the categories are suitable and whether there are methodological artifacts. Accuracy may be artificially enhanced if there are a small number of alternatives (Andersen & Buller, 1980). Accuracy scores may be inflated by easy distinctions between positive and negative emotions (such as between joy and sadness), which mask real difficulties in distinguishing among the negative emotions (sadness, anger, fear, disgust). Moreover, when left more to their own devices, observers may resist categorizing the facial expressions they observe, preferring instead to provide labels that are not emotions, but rather phrases, or stories (Russell, 1994).

The second issue is whether emotion is *expressed* or *communicated* through the face. In other words, is facial expression a simple by-product of emotion, or is the picture more complicated? Scholars have long recognized the importance of cultural display rules (Ekman & Friesen, 1975), which may amplify or attenuate facial displays that are assumed to be innate in order to follow culture-specific prescriptions (see Andersen & Guerrero, Chapter 3, this volume). For example, by our standards the Utku Eskimos (Briggs, 1970) consider expressions of anger nearly completely unacceptable and expect their children to learn to control this expression as a normal part of growing up. Children may struggle with emotional control, but by the time they are adults the rules seem natural to the point that violations call one's sanity or social acceptability into question (much as we disapprove of "temper tantrums").

In addition, research by Bavelas and colleagues (Bavelas, Black, Chovil, Lemery & Mullett, 1988; Bavelas, Black, Lemery, & Mullett, 1986), Chovil (1991), Fridlund (1994), and Kraut and Johnston (1979) on smiling, wincing, and other facial expressions indicates that the actual or imagined presence of others alters those expressions, usually making them more common or more pronounced (even controlling for felt emotion). For example, people are likely to wince when they see another person experience pain, especially if that person is facing them (Bavelas et al., 1988). Watching a funny film makes people laugh and smile, but such expressions increase in more social situations (Fridlund, 1991). This evidence supports a compelling case that emotion is not *expressed* (or at least not *just* expressed) but also *communicated* to others, whether consciously and intentionally or not, and whether as a part of deeply socialized cultural rules or in response to real or imagined strangers or friends.[1]

Darwin, of course, believed that emotions served the function of notifying other members of the species of important events such as danger, but he did not assume that emotional expressions were modified for communicative purposes. In seems, however, that adapting our messages to others may be as much a part of being human as is smiling with joy and staring in anger. Fridlund attributes the persistence of false dichotomy between "fake" and "felt" to a Rousseauean longing for

---

[1]By emotion being *expressed,* we mean that observable behaviors are determined by the emotion (e.g., smiles when happy, talking faster when afraid). By emotion being *communicated,* we mean that observable behaviors are guided by both the emotion and the presence of others who are available to observe them. In this sense, what distinguishes the two is adaptation to an audience. It is difficult to maintain the distinction, however, in light of Fridlund's (1994) demonstration that behaviors are adapted even to imagined audiences and evidence from comparison among cultures that by the time we reach adulthood, emotions themselves are inherently adapted to others through socialization and acculturation. This is not to suggest, however, that emotions that are expressed/communicated are necessarily noticed and interpreted (or misinterpreted) by anybody else, such that communication in its fullest sense has been realized (for a recent debate over whether "one cannot not communicate," see Andersen, 1991, Motley, 1991, and Clevenger, 1991).

authenticity unconstrained by society (1994, pp. 294–295).[2] It is becoming increasingly clear, however, that "felt" is as deeply socialized and adapted to social situations as is "fake." To give a concrete example, we all recognize that a "fake" emotion, such as appearing to be happy upon opening Aunt Gladys's fruitcake is socialized into us (often quite explicitly and overtly, probably through coaching), but we are less aware that the "felt" emotion of happiness at the luscious Godiva chocolates is also deeply socialized (though implicitly and covertly, probably through modeling). Unless one grows up in the clearly unnatural circumstance of social isolation, "there is no fundamental innocence to lose" (Fridlund, 1994, p. 295). Sociability and emotion may go together, even in our genes (Baumeister & Leary, 1995; see also Andersen & Guerrero, Chapter 3, this volume).

Vocal Cues

Vocal behaviors are not as widely recognized as cues to emotion as are facial expressions. Nonetheless, people will tell you that they express and observe others expressing emotion through screaming, yelling, speaking with a trembling voice, using a low, quiet, slow, monotonous voice, and talking very little or not at all (Shaver et al., 1987; Wallbott et al., 1986). Recent research has also established the indisputable importance of vocal cues to emotion (for reviews, see especially Frick, 1985; Scherer, 1986). In a recent review analyzing the vocal indicators of various emotions, Pittam and Scherer (1993) stated that most vocal cues are based on three perceptual dimensions: loudness, pitch, and time, with interactions among the three producing speech contours (Frick, 1985). Accuracy in detecting emotion based on vocal cues has been found well above chance levels and as good or better than what is found typically for facial expressions (Kappas, Hess, & Scherer, 1991).

Whether people can distinguish discrete categories of emotion through the voice or only underlying dimensions (especially arousal) is unclear. Vocal profiles of anger, fear, sadness, joy, disgust, boredom, and contempt can be found (Pittam & Scherer, 1993), but arousal underlies many of them. For example, vocal frequency, intensity, and rate of articulation goes up with anger, but the same is true for fear and elation, all intense emotions. Pittam and Scherer argued that due to a number of methodological limitations of existing research, we still may find distinctive vocal cues, so the jury is still out.

The expression/communication issue has also barely been explored. Kappas et al. (1991) argued that vocal cues are influenced by both "push" (trait and state) and "pull" (situation, social relationships, and cultural convention) factors, but their analysis is admittedly speculative. Still, after decades of research on facial expres-

---

[2]It should be noted, however, that the difference between "fake" and "felt" smiles has long been recognized. "Felt" smiles involve the orbicularis muscle, whereas "fake" ones do not. In nontechnical language, "felt" smiles crinkle the corners of the eyes (Ekman, Davidson, & Friesen, 1990).

sions, they admit that "we might have to give up the search for a handful of vocal parameters that serve as a 'window to our soul' " (p. 229) and explore how vocal cues are interpreted, presumably by real human beings in actual communicative encounters.

Body Cues

Surprisingly little research has been conducted on how emotion is manifest in body movement (as the term *e-motion* would suggest). People are aware of bodily emotional expressions, including a wide range of possibilities: being physically energetic, bouncy, jumping up and down, clenching hands or fists, making threatening movements, throwing things, walking heavily, holding the body rigidly, shuffling, or having a slumped, droopy posture, dancing around, and using hand emblems (Shaver et al., 1987; Wallbott et al., 1986). In fact, bodily expressions of emotion seem to be nearly as common as facial or vocal expressions for some emotions (see, for example, Scherer et al., 1988, Table 1.9, p. 23). Body movements, however, are seldom manipulated experimentally and tested for their ability to express emotion. Existing studies have shown that diagonal and angular movements convey threat and round patterns convey warmth (Aronoff, Woike, & Hyman, 1992), that gait characteristics such as arm swing, length of stride, walking with a heavy foot, and quick stride can be used to distinguish among anger, happiness, and sadness (Montepare, Goldstein, & Clausen, 1987; Walters & Walk, 1988), and that clusters of body cues can distinguish emotions across two cultures (Sogon & Masutani, 1989). Another common way of expressing emotion is through movement toward or away from others or movement directed at other people. In fact, Frijda, Kuipers, and ter Schure (1989) argued that tendencies to act, including the tendencies to move toward, away from, or against others, are central to the definition of emotion. Examples are kissing, touching, hitting, walking out, hugging, trying to spend time with another (or avoid spending time), cuddling, and having sex (Shaver et al., 1987). Nonverbal cues to *immediacy* such as proximity, body lean, and body orientation (Andersen, 1985; Wiener & Mehrabian, 1968) are well-known indicators of warmth in interpersonal interaction (see also Andersen & Guerrero, Chapter 11, this volume). A third type of body cue, largely uncontrollable physiological reactions, have at times been considered the sine qua non of emotional experience, but they may have overt manifestations as well that give them some status as cues. For example, changes in breathing, skin temperature, and heartbeat are detectable by others, especially others in close contact (Planalp, DeFrancisco, & Rutherford, 1996).

With body movements, as with vocal cues, there is too little evidence to draw conclusions about whether they fall into the clusters characteristic of discrete emotions or more continuous expressions of underlying dimensions such as valence and arousal. Because body movements are analogical, it is tempting to place them on continua of arousal, approach/avoidance, or intensity, but such connections have yet to be worked out (e.g., Sparks & Greene, 1992). Furthermore, there is evidence that such dimensions bear at least a moderate correspondence to distinct emotions anyway (Frijda et al., 1989).

The distinction between expressing and communicating emotion seems especially problematic for bodily movements. Clearly some body cues are largely controllable (e.g., hitting) and others largely uncontrollable (quivering) and so anchor the continuum of what can and cannot be used intentionally to communicate an emotional state. But there is one interesting case where intentionality and communication do not go together—blushing. Blushing is under very little conscious control, yet is triggered by certain social circumstances, such as concern for how one is regarded by others (Leary & Meadows, 1991). Embarrassment (and the shame family in general) seems to trigger an uncontrolled physiological response that communicates that the sender knows she has violated a norm. Leary and Meadows suggested that "the ultimate function of blushing and other embarrassment displays is to mitigate against negative evaluations and, ultimately, rejection or exclusion" (p. 261). The fact that people rarely, if ever, blush when they are alone indicates that blushing may never simply express an emotion, but serves a communicative function by its very nature.

Verbal Cues

Emotions are expressed, not just in the face, voice, and body, but in words as well. When we are sad we blame or criticize ourselves; when we are afraid we cry for help; when we are angry, we curse, verbally attack, complain, bitch, and talk about how lousy things are; when we are joyous we say positive things; when we are in love we say positive things about the loved one (Shaver et al., 1987). The possibilities are limitless. We can summarize a feeling in a word (love, jealousy, loneliness), or we can write sonnets, stories, or plays. We can blurt out exclamations or expletives, or we can analyze the emotion-provoking situations for hours. We manage our own and others' emotions through euphemisms, such as flight attendants referring to "incidents," not "accidents," (Hochschild, 1983), apologies (Tavuchis, 1991), or elaborate verbal interventions (Lutz, 1988). Verbal expressions of emotion reveal a great deal about how we think (Kövecses, 1990) and about our politics (Lutz & Abu-Lughod, 1990).

Do people speak of discrete emotions, or of more continual and more subtle emotional processes? Clearly, discrete emotion terms are part of our language, making it easy to talk about anger, sadness, joy, love, and fear. But in everyday life, these terms are not used very often (Shimanoff, 1985, 1987). Even the basic emotion terms of American English display huge variations. Clore, Ortony, and Foss (1987) found roughly 234 emotion terms, although there is no clear boundary between emotions and thoughts, bodily states, and external conditions (see Guerrero, Andersen, & Trost, Chapter 1, this volume, for more on these distinctions). Moreover, these 234 terms do not include phrases and more complex expressions.

Given free reign or some prompting, people describe what brought on the emotion, how long it lasted, their bodily reactions, their own expressions and actions, their attempts to control the emotion, the social implications of emotional expression, and other subtleties. People also differ in their ability or willingness to express emotions verbally, with older respondents showing more vividness of expression, more awareness of bodily reactions, and a greater degree of control (Labouvie-Vief, DeVoe, & Bulka, 1989). Nationality makes a difference (though it is confounded with language); for example, West Germans are more wordy than Spaniards (Cosnier, Dols, & Fernandez, 1986). Emotion matters, too; for example, anger is expressed verbally more than fear (Cosnier et al., 1986). In short, the variation in verbal expression of emotion is vast; it is not dominated by a few basic words used to express a few basic emotions.

One may question whether *expressed* is even the right word? Is it more accurate to say that we *communicate* emotion verbally? Again, the range is vast, and spontaneous expression and strategic communication are hard to disentangle in everyday life. Expletives, for example, have a way of popping out even when we are alone, though it seems that this is more likely for the well-practiced and in front of an appreciative audience.[3] Exclamations such as "help!" or "stop!", while brief and seeming almost involuntary, have both expressive and communicative value (Cosnier et al., 1986, p. 121). Whether people are expressing to privately vent feelings or communicating with others for some other purpose, we do not know, but an overwhelming majority of people report sharing their emotional experiences with others, usually quite soon after they occur, quite often, and with several people (Rimé, Mesquita, Philippot, & Boca, 1991).

The notion that it is therapeutic to express feelings can be traced, of course, back to Freud. More recent research, however, raises the question of whether the container metaphor ("letting your feelings out" or "spilling your guts," Kövecses, 1990) is really the most appropriate one. This metaphor suggests that the mere act of expressing emotion will release pressure and prevent strain. Several lines of recent research indicate that this is not true, that after trauma intrusive thoughts often persist despite talking or writing about feelings (Pennebaker, 1989; 1990; Rimé et al., 1991; Tait & Silver, 1989). The key is to find meaning in trauma (Silver, Boon, & Stones, 1983; see also Burleson & Goldsmith, Chapter 9, this volume) or to construct a coherent story analyzing causes and achieving insights (Pennebaker, 1993). For example, coming to understand losing a child as God's will or as a call to campaign against drunk driving incorporates the experience into a broader framework

---

[3]Phineas Gage, whose brain was damaged by a railroad spike driven through the frontal lobe, was emotionally impaired in many ways including "the grossest profanity which was not previously his custom" (Harlow, 1868, quoted in Damasio, 1994, p. 8).

of meaning and provides a renewed motivation for going on (Cochran & Claspell, 1987). This can be done alone or with others, but empathic responses and social support seem to provide additional therapeutic benefits beyond insight and understanding (Albrecht, Burleson, & Goldsmith, 1994). The warmth and caring that others can provide (if one is fortunate enough to get it) can be life-saving as well as life-enhancing (Atkins, Kaplan, & Toshima, 1991; Spiegel, Bloom, Kraemer, & Gottheil, 1989: Tait & Silver, 1989).

Cue and Channel Combinations

In the experimental work that dominates the research on cues to emotion, studies of single cues are typical; studies of cue combinations or channel combinations are more rare. Undoubtedly, this is because it is difficult enough to study one type of cue, and more difficult yet to study multiple cues in combination. The overall trends in multiple cue and channel studies are difficult to summarize except to say that the results depend strongly on specific operationalizations and experimental circumstances. They depend on the situation and attribute being judged (Ekman, Friesen, O'Sullivan, & Scherer, 1980). They depend on which actor is posing expressions, which emotion is posed, and what scenario is being acted out (Wallbott & Scherer, 1986). They depend on which cue is clearer and whether the cues are consistent or conflicting (Ekman, Friesen, & Ellsworth, 1982; Wallbott, 1988). They depend on sex and ethnicity (Gallois & Callan, 1986) and whether the emotion is expressed in public or private (Nakamura, Buck, & Kenny, 1990). They depend on whether expressions are posed or spontaneous and in or out of natural contexts (Motley, 1993). General conclusions about how different cues and channels go together seem unattainable at this point.

Even though researchers tend to study amputated heads, decapitated bodies, disembodied and content-free voices, and decontextualized words, we know that in some way they go together. What is singularly lacking is any plausible account of how cues are combined into complex, multichannel messages about emotion, much less accounts of how they are produced and interpreted. Perhaps it is because Darwin haunts us, saying communicative processes are hard-wired into our species, so this question is best left to neurophysiologists. Perhaps it is because the question is daunting and intractable through typical experimental design.

Clearly, people *can* communicate emotion through a variety of cues. But *do* they? And if they do, do observers notice? Which of the huge variety of cues, for instance, do observers rely on most? People *can* use subtle differences in the facial expressions of strangers to distinguish anger from joy from surprise.[4] But what if they

---

[4]Russell (1994) challenged the claim that people can consistently distinguish among negative emotions at levels better than chance. Instead he argued that discriminatory power comes between positive and negative emotions and is relatively weak among negative emotions.

are not told that an emotion is being expressed but have to figure out if any emotion occurred at all? What if they are not given a list of possibilities to choose from? What if they have to detect the emotions of other people while fixing dinner or driving to work? Is distinguishing anger from sadness what people even *do* when trying to understand the emotional lives of their friends and family? These are the questions that guided and arose from our own research.

VARIETIES OF CUES IN EVERYDAY LIFE

My colleagues and I asked the simple question—How can people tell when someone is feeling an emotion? To be consistent with earlier research, we focused on categories of cues (voice, face, body, etc.) that people use to detect standard emotions (like anger, joy, and sadness). But breaking from tradition in a way we did not consider particularly radical, we simply asked people, assuming that people could tell us something valid about how they interpret other people's emotions. Details of the study can be found in Planalp et al. (1996). We asked college students and working adults to monitor a person they knew well (preferably someone with whom they lived). They were asked to fill out a brief questionnaire the first time they noticed the other person experiencing an emotion. One format asked them to list the cues they detected; the other told them to describe in their own words "how they could tell" that the other was feeling an emotion." Their responses were coded for the types of cues and other relevant information.

Quantitative analyses showed some interesting patterns. First, almost everyone reported using multiple cues. Figure 1 shows a plot of the number of cues used (as bars) and the number of cues from different categories that were used (on the line). The modal number of cues reported was 4, although it was not uncommon for people to report using 6 or 7. A few people said they used just one, but an equal number said they used more than 10. The line above the bars indicates that cues came typically from 3 to 5 different categories (for details, see Planalp et al., 1996).

Figure 2 shows the percentage of all respondents who used at least one example of each category of cue (on the line), the percentage of all cues reported that were in each category (the open bars), and the percentage of cues identified as the "single most important cue" in each category (the shaded bars). There were no statistically significant differences when comparing the frequencies of all cues and of "most important" cues with one exception; context cues were identified less often as the most important cue than they were overall.

Vocal cues were reported most often, especially loudness, speed of talking, and amount of talking (talkative/quiet). *Indirect verbal* cues were diverse, ranging from name-calling and apologizing to long discourses describing the incident that provoked the emotion. *Facial* cues were common, including eye gaze, smiling, movements of lips or eyebrows, rolled eyes, puffy eyes, and a variety of others. *Activity* cues included solitary activities such as going for a walk, eating, drinking, smoking,

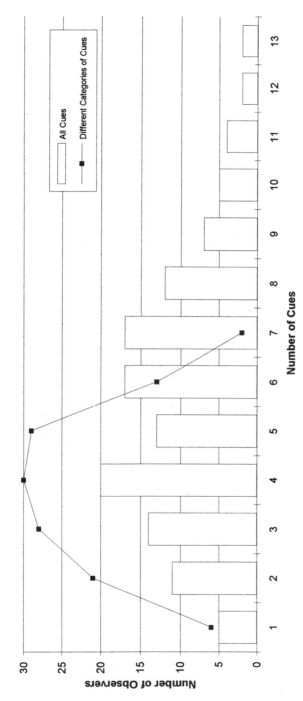

FIGURE 1   Number of observers using multiple cues.

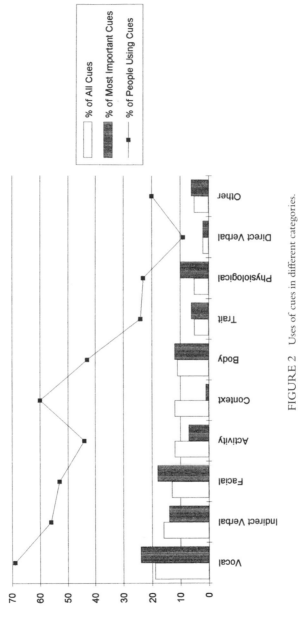

FIGURE 2 Uses of cues in different categories.

throwing things, and changing putters, but also interpersonal activities such as kissing, hugging, tickling, hitting, and touching. *Context* cues included facts that were relevant to understanding the emotion, such as knowing that the person had just received a letter or phone call, was getting married, had a school assignment due, was attending a hearing, and so forth. Because context cues were unlikely to be considered the "most important" cue and because they often came first in the sequence, we suspect that context alone is not sufficient to identify an emotion, but it provides background information and alerts the observer to a possible (even likely) emotion. *Body* cues were cited frequently and include clenched fists, walking heavily, stamping feet, throwing arms up, stomping around, and the like. *Trait* cues made reference to the other person's typical behaviors and took two forms. One was that the other person typically shows this expression when emotional (e.g., John's face always gets red when he's angry). The other was when the person behaves atypically (John didn't criticize my driving like he usually does). Neither type was used frequently. *Physiological* cues were rare and referred most often to crying, although other examples were blushing and changes in breathing. *Direct verbal* cues were very rare (e.g., saying directly "I'm happy" or "He pissed me off").[5] Finally, *other* cues fell outside all the categories above and referred most often either to qualities of behaviors rather than behaviors themselves (e.g., looked worried, acted irritable) or to timing (took a while to calm down). No two categories were more likely to occur together than any other, and there was no pattern to their order, except that context cues and, to a lesser extent trait cues, were more likely to be first in the reports. Thus, these cues appear to provide a backdrop for interpreting emotional messages.

To appreciate these findings, however, one must look at examples of our respondents' reports in their own words. The following are more or less typical:

Example A: I heard my friend arguing on the phone with her boyfriend. Her voice was raised above its usual pitch. She had a red face and her eyes were glazed. When she hung up she sat down on the couch not speaking. I asked her if she was all right. She did not answer me; however, tears started to run down her face. Her way is to contain her feelings until she is ready to talk. However, her face changed as if she was reviewing or reliving the conversation.

Example B: He was feeling remorse and sadness. We have broken up and he would like to make up and marry. He was talking nonstop—he's usually monosyllabic. His voice was quavering. He started crying. He talked about deep feelings he had for

---

[5]Although the infrequent use of emotion labels is surprising, it is a consistent finding (see also Shimanoff, 1985, 1987) for reasons we can only speculate about. Perhaps people believe that nonverbal cues are more informative, genuine, or subtle than verbal labels. Perhaps emotion labels are too brief to capture the full emotion process, such that more lengthy explanations are necessary. Or perhaps people do not want to be held accountable for some of the implications of labels. For example, saying someone is "jealous" opens them up for criticism more than pouting, being distant, and saying "you seem to be seeing a lot of Jane." One can imagine the rest of the conversation—"Oh, you're jealous!"—"No, I'm not, I just don't want you to neglect your work."

me—something he never did prior. He hugged me and was quivering. He apologized. He repeated himself over and over. He expressed fear of the future.

Example C: My mother's attitude became increasingly upset when she found out I was going down to Colorado Springs to see my boyfriend instead of studying. Her face began to get flustered and the tone of her voice became bitchy. She began to bring up irrelevant mistakes I'd made in my past as a way of eliciting response. She gave me that motherly disappointed face and finally . . . the silent treatment.

One gets the sense here, not of an array of cues that might be added up or averaged, or even of one important cue that might dominate others, but rather of a complex combination of cues that often unfold over a period of time. The observations are subtle and seem to be grounded in knowledge of the situation and the other's typical patterns of interacting. And the emotion messages do appear to be at least partially goal-oriented, at least in the eyes of the observers. In Example A, the observer interprets the roommate's behavior as trying to suppress emotional expressions until she is ready to talk. In Example B, the man's expressions of sadness and remorse suggest that they are at least partially an attempt to get his girlfriend to reconsider marrying him. In Example C, the mother seems to persuade or perhaps even coerce her daughter into staying home by expressing "upset" (what we would call some version of anger).

Another notable finding in this study was that when asked to identify the emotion that they observed, respondents usually used more than one word (*even though* they were prompted by the question, "What emotion did you observe (e.g., anger, happiness, fear, etc.)?" Some used one word (33%), but many used two (45%), and some used three or more words (22%). Many of the uses of multiple words were within basic emotion categories or prototypes (Shaver et al., 1987, e.g., anger and frustration or sadness and loneliness). But many combinations were across categories (24%), and the overwhelming majority of across-category emotions were negative (e.g., fear, sadness, and anger). This is consistent with Oatley and Duncan's (1992) finding that mixed emotions are common, especially anger and fear, or anger changing to sadness.

DARWIN REVISITED: PROCESS AND ADAPTATION

What do these findings and examples imply about how we view emotion messages? The first major implication is to question whether it is best to think of emotions primarily as distinct categories. Our review of research on different types of cues indicate no clear evidence that any one category of emotion can be distinguished from another. Facial cues may distinguish positive from negative emotions, and vocal cues or body cues may distinguish arousing from nonarousing emotions, but no single cue or set of cues seems clearly to distinguish among even the most widely recognized basic emotions—joy, fear, sadness, and anger. Verbal labels can be used, of course, but they rarely are, and people often resist applying a single label, preferring instead multiple labels for subtle or mixed emotions (for sadness, love, and fear, see Example B earlier). Given complete freedom, people may prefer to describe the situation imagined to produce the emotion (e.g., she looks like she's seeing a child about to be hit by a car; Frijda, 1953) or the social action to be accomplished by it (e.g., threat, greeting; Russell, 1994).

Perhaps it would be more fruitful to think of emotion as a process in which some emotion-eliciting event or events generate certain appraisals (novelty, valence, control, etc.), action tendencies, expressions, and processes by which all can be controlled. Only when certain prototypic configurations arise is the emotion clearly anger or joy or fear (Frijda, 1986). More often, the emotion falls into the crack between anger and fear, or is a combination of envy and hate, or is vague, ill-defined, and hard to label. If we thought of emotion this way, the questions we would ask about emotion messages would be different. We would not ask about accuracy, because accuracy assumes a right or wrong answer, a multiple choice test. From a process point of view, we would ask instead about understanding, which requires an essay test. Understanding can be achieved by gathering, unearthing, and reviewing evidence and fitting it into a framework that is coherent and consistent with what we know about the world, which is not always an easy task (Cochran & Claspell, 1987; Pennebaker, 1990). That is why we sometimes need friends, therapists, books, and insights to understand more deeply our own and other people's emotions.

This brings us back to the question of how and why such a variety of cues are used in emotion messages. Again, the answer is not entirely clear, but if we give up on the notion of discrete emotions, we largely give up on models such as adding cues, averaging cues, finding the single cue that dominates, or determining how cues fit the cue template of basic emotions. Instead, we would think about what information cues give us about the emotion process. Vocal cues, for example, might call strong emotions to our attention, or tell us how intense the emotion is. Verbal cues may speak to the situation that provoked the emotion and what the other person is thinking about it. Body cues may point to how much control is being exerted. Facial cues may portray subtle nuances of valence (see Example A earlier). More likely, though, the information carried by cues does not break out into categories of cues and channels quite as neatly.

An additional implication of the process perspective is that emotions are not snapshots that "click" on and off. They may come on gradually, evolve, dissipate, return, and just generally make interpretation more difficult because they change (Folkman & Lazarus, 1985; Frijda, Mesquita, Sonnemans, & Van Goozen, 1991). Even what appear to be static facial expressions can be microanalyzed into unfolding expressive patterns (Scherer, 1992). For example, the person in Example A (see above) noted that "her face changed as if she was reviewing or reliving the conversation." Emotions also change in response to changing circumstances, including changes in the provoking events and one's ability to control them (see Example C earlier).

The second major implication of the findings of this study and our previous analysis is that they make us take seriously the expressive *and* communicative functions of emotion (and make us question whether there is a functional difference). Certainly people express emotion because they feel it and have a hard time doing otherwise (Andersen & Guerrero, Chapter 3, this volume), no matter how hard they try (as in Example A). But equally certainly, people communicate their emotions to others for some purpose, whether intentionally or unintentionally. They may want to let the other know how much they care (Example B), perhaps asking in subtle ways for forgiveness and for another chance at connection. They may want to persuade (even coerce) the other into a different course of action (Example C), threatening social disruption in the bargain. They may communicate emotion in order to get support (e.g., sadness, loneliness), negotiate social roles (anger, jealousy), deflect criticism (shame, embarrassment), reinforce social bonds (love), or for any number of other reasons (Bailey, 1983; Frijda & Mesquita, 1991).

Indeed, the process of communicating emotion to serve some social purpose seems so basic that it is ingrained into automatic reactions like blushing, or solitary actions, like smiling and laughing at a funny film that you know your friends are watching too. So it seems that part of the process of interpreting other people's emotion involves determining their communicative motives or goals. Perhaps (as in Example A) you are simply an innocent bystander, but standing by to give support if needed. Perhaps (as in Example B), your boyfriend wants you to renew your relationship, or (as in Example C) your mother wants you to break it off. In any case, part of "getting the emotional message" must be to understand why the other is feeling as she or he does, what important concerns are at stake, and what you are able or expected to do about it.

If Darwin had not studied dogs, monkeys, and Victorian Britons, but some of the tribal peoples along the path of the Beagle instead, he might have been more aware of the social side of emotion. Australian aborigines, for example, see emotions as bound up in social activities (Heelas, 1986). The emotional lives of the Micronesian Ifaluk are inextricably bound up with social connection and disruption (Lutz, 1988). The Ilongots of the Philippines expect passion to be governed by knowledge of what is appropriate for one's social role and what is good for the group (Rosaldo, 1980). For the Malay, the pressures of demanding social rules and obligations result, under definable conditions, in the ostensible loss of emotional control called "running amok" (Winzeler, 1990). A closer investigation of animals (Masson & McCarthy, 1995) and, yes, even Victorian Britons might have revealed the social side of emotion that is coming into clearer focus today.

ACKNOWLEDGMENTS

The author thanks Victoria DeFrancisco for her ideas in formulating this chapter, for help in reviewing the literature, and for her ongoing emotional and intellectual support. She deserves more than a thanks, but she won't take it. Thanks also to both her and Diane Rutherford for co-authoring the research on which much of this chapter is based.

REFERENCES

Albrecht, T. L., Burleson, B. R., & Goldsmith, D. (1994). Supportive communication. In M. L. Knapp & G. R. Miller (Eds), *Handbook of interpersonal communication* (pp. 419–449). Thousand Oaks, CA: Sage.

Andersen, P. A. (1985). Nonverbal immediacy in interpersonal communication. In A. O. Siegman & S. Feldstein (Eds.), *Multichannel integrations of nonverbal behavior* (pp. 1–36). Hillsdale, NJ: Erlbaum.

Andersen, P. A. (1991). When one cannot not communicate: A challenge to Motley's traditional communication postulates. *Communication Studies, 42,* 309–325.

Andersen, P. A., & Buller, D. B. (1980). *Judging the accuracy of facial expressions: A methodological inquiry.* Paper presented to the Eastern Communication Association, Ocean City, MD.

Aronoff, J., Woike, B. A., & Hyman, L. M. (1992). Which are the stimuli in facial displays of anger and happiness? Configurational bases of emotion recognition. *Journal of Personality and Social Psychology, 62,* 1050–1066.

Atkins, C. J., Kaplan, R. M., & Toshima, M. T. (1991). Close relationships in the epidemiology of cardiovascular disease. In W. H. Jones & D. Perlman (Eds.), *Advances in personal relationships,* (vol. 3, pp. 207–231). London: Kingsley.

Bailey, F. G. (1983). *The tactical uses of passion.* Ithaca, NY: Cornell University Press.

Baumeister, R. F., & Leary, M. R. (1995). The need to belong: Desire for interpersonal attachments as a fundamental human motivation. *Psychological Bulletin, 117,* 497–529.

Bavelas, J. B., Black, A., Chovil, N., Lemery, C. R., & Mullett, J. (1988). Form and function in motor mimicry: Topographic evidence that the primary function is communicative. *Human Communication Research, 14,* 275–299.

Bavelas, J. B., Black, A., Lemery, C. R., & Mullett, J. (1986). "I *show* how you feel": Motor mimicry as a communicative act. *Journal of Personality and Social Psychology, 50,* 322–329.

Bowers, J. W., Metts, S. M., & Duncanson, W. T. (1985). Emotion and interpersonal communication. In M. L. Knapp & G. R. Miller (Eds.), *Handbook of interpersonal communication* (pp. 502–559). Beverly Hills, CA: Sage.

Briggs, J. L. (1970). *Never in anger.* Cambridge, MA: Harvard University Press.

Buck, R. (1984). *The communication of emotion.* New York: Guilford.

Camras, L. A., Holland, E. A., & Patterson, M. J. (1993). Facial expression. In M. Lewis & J. M. Haviland (Eds.), *Handbook of emotions* (pp. 199–208). New York: Guilford.

Chovil, N. (1991). Social determinants of facial displays. *Journal of Nonverbal Behavior, 15,* 141–153.

Clevenger, T., Jr. (1991). Can one not communicate? A conflict of models. *Communication Studies. 42,* 340–353.

Clore, G. L., Ortony, A., & Foss, M. A. (1987). The psychological foundations of the affective lexicon. *Journal of Personality and Social Psychology, 53,* 751–766.

Cochran, L., & Claspell, E. (1987). *The meaning of grief.* New York: Greenwood Press.

Cosnier, J., Dols, J. M. F., & Fernandez, A. J. (1986). The verbalisation of emotional experience. In K. R. Scherer, H. G. Wallbott, & A. B. Summerfield (Eds.), *Experiencing emotion: A cross-cultural study* (pp. 117–128). Cambridge, UK: Cambridge University Press.

Damasio, A. R. (1994). *Descartes' error.* New York: G. P. Putnam's Sons.

Darwin, C. (1872/1904). *The expression of the emotions in man and animals.* London: John Murray.

Ekman, P. (Ed.) (1982). *Emotion in the human face.* Cambridge, UK: Cambridge University Press.

Ekman, P. (1993). Facial expression and emotion. *American Psychologist, 48,* 384–392.

Ekman, P., & Davidson, R. J. (1994). *The nature of emotion: Fundamental questions.* Oxford, UK: Oxford University Press.

Ekman, P., Davidson, R. J., & Friesen, W. V. (1990). The Duchenne smile: Emotional expression and brain physiology II. *Journal of Personality and Social Psychology, 58,* 342–353.

Ekman, P., & Friesen, W. V. (1975). *Unmasking the face: A guide to recognizing emotions from facial cues.* Englewood Cliffs, NJ: Prentice-Hall.

Ekman, P., & Friesen, W. V. (1978). *Facial Action Coding System: A technique for the measurement of facial movement.* Palo Alto, CA: Consulting Psychologists Press.

Ekman, P., Friesen, W. V., & Ellsworth, P. (1982). What are the relative contributions of facial behavior and contextual information to the judgement of emotion? In P. Ekman (Ed.), *Emotion in the human face* (2nd ed., pp. 111–143). Cambridge, UK: Cambridge University Press.

Ekman, P., Friesen, W. V., O'Sullivan, M., Chan, A., Diacoyanni-Tarlatzis, I., Heider, K., Krause, R., LeCompte, W. A., Pitcairn, T., Ricci-Bitti, P. E., Scherer, K., Tomita, M., Tzavaras, A. (1987). Universals and cultural differences in the judgments of facial expressions of emotion. *Journal of Personality and Social Psychology, 53,* 712–717.

Ekman, P., Friesen, W. V., O'Sullivan, M., & Scherer, K. (1980). Relative importance of face, body, and speech in judgments of personality and affect. *Journal of Personality and Social Psychology, 38,* 270–277.

Ekman, P. & O'Sullivan, M. (1991). Facial expression: Methods, means, and moues. In R. S. Feldman & B. Rimé (Eds.), *Fundamentals of nonverbal behavior* (pp. 163–199). Cambridge, UK: Cambridge University Press.

Folkman, S., & Lazarus, R. S. (1985). If it changes it must be a process: Study of emotion and coping during three stages of a college examination. *Journal of Personality and Social Psychology, 48,* 150–170.

Frick, R. W. (1985). Communicating emotion: The role of prosodic features. *Psychological Bulletin, 97,* 412–429.

Fridlund, A. J. (1991). Sociality of solitary smiling: Potentiation by an implicit audience. *Journal of Personality and Social Psychology, 60,* 229–240.

Fridlund, A. J. (1994). *Human facial expression.* San Diego, CA: Academic Press.

Frijda, N. H. (1986). *The emotions.* Cambridge, UK: Cambridge University Press.

Frijda, N. H. (1953). The understanding of facial expression of emotion. *Acta Psychologica, 9,* 294–362.

Frijda, N. H., Kuipers, P., & ter Schure, E. (1989). Relations among emotion, appraisal, and emotional action readiness. *Journal of Personality and Social Psychology, 57,* 212–228.

Frijda, N. H., & Mesquita, B. (1991, July). *The various effects of emotion communication.* Paper presented at the 6th ISRE meeting, Saarbrücken, Germany.

Frijda, N. H., Mesquita, B., Sonneman, J., & Van Goozen, S. (1991). The duration of affective phenomena. In K. Strongman (Ed.), *International review of studies on emotion* (vol. 1, pp. 187–225). New York: Wiley.

Gallois, C., & Callan, V. J. (1986). Decoding emotional messages: Influence of ethnicity, sex, message type, and channel. *Journal of Personality and Social Psychology, 51,* 755–762.

Harlow, J. M. (1868). Recovery from the passage of an iron bar through the head. *Publications of the Massachusetts Medical Society, 2,* 327–347.

Heelas, P. (1986). Emotion talk across cultures. In R. Harré (Ed.), *The social construction of emotions* (pp. 234–266). Oxford, UK: Basil Blackwell.

Heise, D. R., & O'Brien, J. (1993). Emotion expression in groups. In M. Lewis & J. M. Haviland (Eds.), *Handbook of emotions* (pp. 489–497). New York: Guilford.

Hochschild, A. R. (1983). *The managed heart: Commercialization of human feeling.* Berkeley: University of California Press.

Izard, C. E. (1977). *Human emotions.* New York: Plenum.

Izard, C. E. (1991). *The psychology of emotions.* New York: Plenum Press.

Kappas, A., Hess, U., & Scherer, K. R. (1991). Voice and emotion. In R. S. Feldman & B. Rimé (Eds.), *Fundamentals of nonverbal behavior* (pp. 200–237). Cambridge, UK: Cambridge University Press.

Kövecses, Z. (1990). *Emotion concepts.* New York: Springer-Verlag.

Kraut, R. E., & Johnston, R. E. (1979). Social and emotional messages of smiling: An ethological approach. *Journal of Personality and Social Psychology, 37,* 1539–1553.

Labouvie-Vief, G., Devoe, M., Bulka, D. (1989). Speaking about feelings: Conceptions of emotion across the life-span. *Psychology and Aging, 4,* 425–437.

Lazarus, R. S. (1991). *Emotion and adaptation.* New York: Oxford University Press.

Leary, M. R., & Meadows, S. (1991). Predictors, elicitors, and concomitants of social blushing. *Journal of Personality and Social Psychology, 60,* 254–262.

Lewis, M., & Haviland, J. M. (Eds.) (1993). *Handbook of emotions.* New York: Guilford.

Lutz, C. A. (1988). *Unnatural emotions.* Chicago: University of Chicago Press.

Lutz, C. A., & Abu-Lughod, L. (1990). *Language and the politics of emotion.* Cambridge, UK: Cambridge University Press.

Masson, J. M., & McCarthy, S. (1995). *When elephants weep: The emotional lives of animals.* New York: Delacorte Press.

Metts, S., & Bowers, J. W. (1994). Emotion in interpersonal communication. In M. L. Knapp & G. R. Miller (Eds.), *Handbook of interpersonal communication* (2nd ed., pp. 508–541). Beverly Hills, CA: Sage.

Montepare, J. M., Goldstein, S. B., & Clausen, A. (1987). The identification of emotions from gait information. *Journal of Nonverbal Behavior, 11,* 33–42.

Motley, M. T. (1991). How one may not communicate: A reply to Andersen. *Communication Studies, 42,* 310–339.

Motley, M. T. (1993). Facial affect and verbal context in conversation. *Human Communication Research, 20,* 3–40.

Motley, M. T., & Camden, C. T. (1988). Facial expression of emotion: A comparison of posed expressions versus spontaneous expressions in an interpersonal communication setting. *Western Journal of Speech Communication, 52,* 1–22.

Nakamura, M., Buck, R., & Kenny, D. A. (1990). Relative contributions of expressive behavior and contextual information to the judgment of the emotional state of another. *Journal of Personality and Social Psychology, 59,* 1032–1039.

Oatley, K., & Duncan, E. (1992). Incidents of emotion in daily life. In K. T. Strongman (Ed.), *International review of studies on emotion* (vol. 2, pp. 249–293). Chichester, UK: Wiley.

Pennebaker, J. W. (1989). Confession, inhibition, and disease. In L. Berkowitz (Ed.), *Advances in experimental social psychology* (vol. 22, pp. 211–244). New York: Academic Press.

Pennebaker, J. W. (1990). *Opening up: The healing power of confiding in others.* New York: Avon.

Pennebaker, J. W. (1993). Putting stress into words: Health, linguistic, and therapeutic implications. *Behaviour Research and Therapy, 31,* 539–548.

Pittam, J., & Scherer, K. R. (1993). Vocal expression and communication of emotion. In M. Lewis and J. M. Haviland (Eds.), *Handbook of emotions* (pp. 185–198). New York: Guilford.

Planalp, S., DeFrancisco, V. L., & Rutherford, D. (1996). Varieties of cues to emotion in naturally occurring situations. *Cognition and Emotion, 10,* 137–153.

Rimé, B., Mesquita, B., Philippot, P., & Boca, S. (1991). Beyond the emotional event: Six studies of the social sharing of emotion. *Cognition and Emotion, 5,* 435–465.

Rosaldo, M. Z. (1980). *Knowledge and passion: Ilongot notions of self and social life.* New York: Cambridge University Press.

Russell, J. A. (1994). Is there universal recognition of emotion from facial expression? A review of the cross-cultural studies. *Psychological Bulletin, 115,* 102–141.

Scherer, K. R. (1986). Vocal affect expression: A review and a model for future research. *Psychological Bulletin, 99,* 143–165.

Scherer, K. R. (1992). What does facial expression express? In K. T. Strongman (Ed.), *International review of studies on emotion* (vol. 2, pp. 139–165). Chichester, UK: Wiley.

Scherer, K. R., Wallbott, H. G., Matsumoto, D., & Kudoh, T. (1988). Emotional experience in cultural context: A comparison between Europe, Japan, and the United States. In K. R. Scherer (Ed.), *Facets of emotion: Recent research* (pp. 5–30). Hillsdale, NJ: Erlbaum.

Shaver, P., Schwartz, J., Kirson, D., & O'Connor, C. (1987). Emotion knowledge: Further explorations of a prototype approach. *Journal of Personality and Social Psychology, 52,* 1061–1086.

Shimanoff, S. B. (1985). Expressing emotions in words: Verbal patterns of interactions. *Journal of Communication, 35*, 16–31.

Shimanoff, S. B. (1987). Types of emotional disclosures and request compliance between spouses. *Communication Monographs, 54*, 85–100.

Silver, R. L., Boon, C., & Stones, M. H. (1983). Searching for meaning in misfortune: Making sense of incest. *Journal of Social Issues, 39*, 81–102.

Sogon, S., & Masutani, M. (1989). Identification of emotion from body movements: A cross-cultural study of Americans and Japanese. *Psychological Reports, 65*, 35–46.

Sparks, G. G., & Greene, J. O. (1992). On the validity of nonverbal indicators as measures of physiological arousal. *Human Communication Research, 18*, 445–471.

Spiegel, D., Bloom, J. R., Kraemer, H. C., & Gottheil, E. (1989). Effects of psychosocial treatment of patients with metastatic breast cancer. *Lancet, 2*, 888–891.

Stein, N. L., & Oatley, K. (1992). Basic emotions (Special issue). *Cognition and Emotion, 6*, 161–319.

Tait, R., & Silver, R. C. (1989). Coming to terms with major negative life events. In J. S. Uleman & J. A. Bargh (Eds.), *Unintended thought* (pp. 351–382). New York: Guilford.

Tavuchis, N. (1991). *Mea culpa: A sociology of apology and reconciliation.* Stanford, CA: Stanford University Press.

Tomkins, S. S. (1962). *Affect, imagery, and consciousness Vol. 1: The positive affects.* New York: Springer.

Tomkins, S. S. (1963). *Affect, imagery, and consciousness Vol. 2: The negative affects.* New York: Springer-Verlag.

Wallbott, H. G. (1988). In and out of context: Influences of facial expression and context information on emotion attributions. *British Journal of Social Psychology, 27*, 357–369.

Wallbott, H. G., Ricci-Bitti, P. & Bänninger-Huber, E. (1986). Non-verbal reactions to emotional experiences. In K. R. Scherer, H. G. Wallbott, & A. B. Summerfield (Eds.), *Experiencing emotion: A cross-cultural study* (pp. 98–116). Cambridge, UK: Cambridge University Press.

Wallbott, H. G., & Scherer, K. R. (1986). Cues and channels in emotion recognition. *Journal of Personality and Social Psychology, 51*, 690–699.

Walters, K. L., & Walk, R. D. (1988). Perception of emotion from moving body cues in photographs. *Bulletin of the Psychonomic Society, 26*, 112–114.

Wiener, M. & Mehrabian, A. (1968). *Language within language: Immediacy, a channel in verbal communication.* New York: Appleton-Century-Crofts.

Winzeler, R. (1990). Amok: Historical, psychological, and cultural perspectives. In W. J. Karim (Ed.), *Emotions of culture: A Malay perspective* (pp. 97–122). Oxford, UK: Oxford University Press.

CHAPTER 3

Principles of Communication and Emotion in Social Interaction

Peter A. Andersen
San Diego State University
San Diego, California

Laura K. Guerrero
Arizona State University
Tempe, Arizona

> *The notion of communication presupposes both an ideational and an emotional state of speaker. Demonstration of an idea to others has its roots in feelings and attitudes which result from the speaker's having either directly or vicariously, experienced the thought.*
>
> (Thonssen & Baird, 1948, p. 357).

> *The centrality of other people is particularly evident in emotions. All the emotions are fundamentally social.*
>
> (Fischer & Tangney, 1995, p. 3)

Researchers of communication and emotion recognize the inherent inseparability of communication, emotion, and cognition. In this chapter we show that the origins, development, experience, and deployment of emotions are inherently communicative. Specifically, we outline six general principles and related theoretical concepts, including the ideas that social interaction is the primary elicitor of most emotions and that emotions are expressed through interpersonal communication. Taken together, these principles and concepts illustrate that social emotions can only be fully understood if they are examined along with the communication that surrounds them.

PRINCIPLES OF COMMUNICATION AND EMOTION

Our first two principles focus on two forces that influence how and when emotion is communicated: evolution and socialization. Though controversy has raged over which of these forces is predominant, most contemporary researchers now agree that evolution and socialization jointly affect the experience and expression of emotion. As Lewis and Saarni (1985) maintained, "Emotions are undisputedly multifaceted and derived from an interaction of biological and environmental socializing influences" (p. 1). Moreover, the forces of biological evolution and cultural socialization are not mutually exclusive; rather, they combine and interact to produce emotional communication. As Panksepp (1992) suggested, certain emotional tendencies have evolved to the point that they are related to basic brain functioning, yet considerable social learning still takes place. Scherer and Wallbott (1994) also debunked the controversy between evolutionary and cultural explanations for emotion expression. They argued that this debate is as futile as similar controversies that favor behavior or cognition, personality or situation, and biological determination or self-determination. In the next section, we discuss how evolution and socialization affect emotional communication. We begin by examining the evolution of emotional communication as a socially adaptive phenomenon.

THE EVOLUTION OF EMOTIONAL COMMUNICATION

Our position, as well as that of most emotion researchers, is that emotions evolved in human beings because they were adaptive and had survival benefits. As Berscheid (1983) stated, "Today, virtually all theorists of emotion agree that the experience and expression of emotion has served, and probably continues to serve, an important function in the survival of the species" (p. 120). Our first principle captures this idea.

Principle 1: Socially Adaptive Emotional Communication Is Positively Selected in the Evolutionary Process

Emotions evolved not just as internal control mechanisms, but as relatively universal communication systems that promoted the group survival of humans. Researchers have discovered a high degree of universality in the displays of basic emotions (Ekman, 1993; Izard, 1992; Plutchik, 1983), though this position is not without its critics (see Russell, 1994). These universal expressions had survival advantages or they would not have evolved. Panksepp (1992) provided considerable evidence for the position that "human affective experience ultimately emerges from neurosymbolic systems of the mammalian brain that unconditionally promote survival" (p. 558). Emerging evidence suggests that hard-wired neural links exist between emotions and their expression (Buck, 1995; Ekman, 1993; Panksepp, 1992; Plutchik, 1983), particularly their nonverbal expression (DePaulo, 1992). According to DePaulo (1992), "there may be automatic links between the elicitation of emotion and the expression of emotion for nonverbal, but not verbal, behavior" (p. 205).

The social functions of emotions have provided a particularly powerful evolutionary advantage. Emotions permit individuals to adapt successfully to a vast array of social demands and opportunities (Izard, 1992). Magai and McFadden (1995) maintained that, "emotions have evolved phylogenetically within the context of mammalian development needs and the properties of gregarious social organizations. Emotions are intrinsically social" (p. 279).

Perhaps the primary function of emotions and their expression is to minimize rejection by other humans. Humans and other primates gained a large survival advantage through cooperative group behavior. Being ostracized or abandoned by one's group had dire survival consequences for those individuals and their potential offspring. Emotions related to appeasement and harmony had obvious benefits related to group acceptance. Miller and Leary (1992) suggested that emotions confer reproductive advantage because they help individuals interact cooperatively with others, minimize rejection, and avoid attack from other group members. Specifically, Miller and Leary contended that emotions like embarrassment, shame, guilt, and social anxiety

> may have evolved because persons who experienced distress over concerns with others' impressions of them were more likely to survive as reproductive members of the group than persons who acted with disregard for other's opinion of them (who were likely to be ostracized or banished, if not killed). (p. 216)

Panksepp (1992) maintained that emotions such as embarrassment, guilt, jealousy, and shame "arise from higher evolutionary elaborations of separation-distress circuiting, perhaps within the frontal-circulate areas of the brain" (p. 557). Guerrero and Andersen (Chapter 6, this volume) summarize research suggesting that jealousy has sociobiological roots that enhance survival of one's genes through mate protection, paternal certainty, and resource conservation.

This sociobiological argument would hold for even the most basic emotions, such as anger, fear, and happiness. Hard-wired anger displays have functioned to warn and ward off dangerous predators and potential attacks by other humans. Fear expressions provided instantaneous warning messages to other group members. Happiness displays provided the pleasant affect necessary to bond mates and promote group solidarity.

Evidence suggests that emotional communication probably evolved through some variant of the process of group selection. As Noonan (1987) suggested, "throughout human history, . . . individuals could increase their reproductive success indirectly by helping to preserve the social group without which they could not reproduce at all" (p. 50). Because emotional communication facilitated group cohesiveness, emotional sending and receiving skills provided a survival advantage at the group level. Rejection or expulsion from a group usually was neither in the individual's or the group's best interest, thus both individual survival and group survival would be facilitated by members who were emotionally attuned to the social needs of the group.

THE SOCIALIZATION OF EMOTIONAL COMMUNICATION

Emotional communication, shaped by evolution through the millennia, is also molded by socialization. As Ekman (1993) contended, "it is not just our ontogenetic history but our phylogenetic history that makes an emotion more readily called forth in one circumstance than in another, and yet ontogeny has a great effect" (p. 389). The innate propensity to express emotions nonverbally and verbally is modified in each culture and each family by interpersonal forces that dictate norms and rules of emotional communication. Communication itself often provides the means by which a culture's young are socialized to express emotion. Of course, part of the socialization process involves learning when to inhibit, as well as express, emotion. Thus, we forward our second principle.

Principle 2: Socialization Processes Guide How Individuals Manage Their Communication of Emotion

Socialization Processes

Evidence suggests that emotions such as disgust, distress, and interest are present at birth and are largely a function of innate reactions to pleasant or unpleasant stimuli (see Izard, 1978). Emotions such as anger, surprise, and joy are expressed soon after birth, usually within the first seven months of life. Moreover, the social smile typically appears when a child is about two months old.

The process of learning how to interpret and manage emotions takes several forms. Ferguson and Stegge (1995) noted that the importance of caregivers as socializing agents is widely documented in clinical and experimental psychology. Moreover, they suggest that four processes, which we label parental modeling, parental directives, parent expectancy effects, and overt parental reinforcement, shape emotional communication. Of course, it should be noted that various individuals other than parents, including childcare workers, teachers, and peers, also shape and socialize emotional response. The focus on parental influence is a function of parents as the primary agents of socialization.

Parental Modeling

Few human behaviors fail to be influenced by modeling, and emotional communication is no exception (Saarni, 1993). Ferguson and Stegge (1995) demonstrated that direct parental modeling of affective styles is a function of the parent's own familial history and stressors in the parent–child environment. The modeling exists against a cultural background that prescribes appropriate expressions and proscribes inappropriate ones. Stearns's (1989) history of emotional suppression suggests that during American history, many emotional expressions such as anger or jealousy were discouraged and infrequently expressed. Hence, parental models showed few of these expressions for offspring to emulate. Conversely, romantic and familial love were socially approved emotions and conspicuously modeled for incorporation by offspring. Similarly, Lewis (1989), in her examination of mothers' manuals from the nineteenth century, shows that mothers were expected to teach their "children how to love; that is, to teach them what she knew best. She was to make her children like herself" (p. 215). Research on sex differences suggests that women may develop a greater repertoire of emotional expression because parents display a greater range of emotions to girls than to boys (Brody & Hall, 1993; Guerrero & Reiter, in press). Today, of course, an additional agent of socialization for emotional communication is the media. Television, in particular, provides numerous emotional displays for audience emulation and teaches children how to decode, as well as encode, emotions (see Wilson & Smith, Chapter 20, this volume).

Parental Directives

Parents do more than display certain behaviors for imitation by offspring. They provide active instruction and feedback to children on the appropriateness of various emotional expressions. Every parent has had the experience of saying "calm down," "cheer up," "don't cry," "say you're sorry," and a host of other affective communication directives. Ferguson and Stegge (1995) argued that emotional expression in children is influenced by "parental feedback to the child in emotion–eliciting situations that involve the child directly or indirectly" (p. 182). These parental directives often involve whether a particular emotion should be expressed at all and if it should be expressed in particular situations and in particular ways. In the American family, negative emotions like anger are often punished (especially for girls). Angry children are sent to their rooms to meditate on their evil ways, deprived of familial love, and made to feel guilty (Stearns, 1989).

Parental Expectancy Effects

Parents have strong expectations for how children should behave emotionally. Parents' subtle expectancies shape individuals' emotional expressions and even contribute to sex role differences in emotional expression (Guerrero & Reiter, in press). Subtle encouragement and discouragement of particular types of emotional communication shape these behaviors over time. It is not uncommon for a parent to ignore or smile at an angry boy, but to frown at an angry girl (Lemerise & Dodge, 1993). Similarly, Condry and Condry (1976) reported that supposed knowledge of a child's sex determines adult responses to negative affect displays. In this study, half the adult observers were told that they were watching an infant boy and the other half were told they were watching an infant girl, when in actuality the infants had been randomly labeled as boys or girls. The adults tended to interpret the supposed boys' negative affect as anger and the supposed girls' negative affect as fear. Jones's (1977) research shows parental expectations shape later emotional communication; when parents expected a child to be anxious or relaxed, the child's behavior conformed to these expectations over time (see also Rosenthal & DePaulo, 1979).

Overt Parental Reinforcement

Parents overtly reward children for good behavior both intrinsically through reinforcers such as love and attention, and extrinsically through raises in allowance, gifts, or various privileges. Saarni (1993), in her review of emotional socialization, suggested that contingency learning is a primary agent of emotional socialization. Parents will respond positively when a child behaves as they "ought" to behave (Ferguson & Stegge, 1995). Research by Fuchs and Thelen (1988), for example, suggests that parents react more positively to the expression of sadness in school-age girls than boys. In fact, boys expected their parents to react negatively if they displayed sadness, whereas girls expected their mothers to react negatively if they expressed anger, but positively if they expressed sadness. Not surprisingly, boys expressed less sadness to parents than did girls.

Display Rules

Display rules are products of socialization. Over the past several decades, researchers have discovered up to five display rules for various emotions (see J. F. Andersen, Andersen, & Landgraf, 1985; Ekman, 1978; Ekman & Friesen, 1975; Saarni, 1993; Shennum & Bugental, 1982, for reviews). In each case, these products of emotional socialization involve a learned response that modifies spontaneous emotional displays to be socially appropriate. Camras (1985), for example, discussed a process that we term *channeling*. This process involves the selective display of certain emotions in particular situations or contexts but not others. Examples of channeling are abundant. Anger may be displayed, and even exaggerated, on the ballfield, but inhibited in the classroom or at work. Private displays of affection and love are often inappropriate and unwanted in public but appropriate and desired in private. Emotional "maturity" of teens and young adults sometimes requires reduced involvement and "playing it cool." The successful channeling of emotions in situations such as these requires mastery of display rules, including simulation, inhibition, intensification, deintensification, and masking.

Simulation

Simulation involves displaying or feigning an emotion when no such emotion or feelings are present (J. F. Andersen et al., 1985; Shennum & Bugental, 1982).

Examples include smiling without experiencing happiness, expressing guilt when you have no remorse, or showing surprise when you fully expected an event to occur (i.e., a surprise party). Children learn to simulate emotions as early as infancy. As a case in point, young children sometimes pretend to cry to get attention. This skill is refined as children grow older and learn rules of social appropriateness. People typically simulate emotions to conform to politeness rituals and situational appropriateness (i.e., pretending to be happy when a co-worker you barely know tells you he is getting married). Simulations are common during acts of deception as well (Buller & Burgoon, Chapter 14, this volume; O'Hair & Cody, 1994). Simulation may be interpersonally competent behavior. For example, being pleasant or funny may be a relationally competent behavior that allows one to manage impressions and accomplish interpersonal facework (Cupach & Metts, 1994).

Inhibition

Whereas simulation involves expressing an emotion when no emotion is being experienced, inhibition (or neutralization) involves the reverse process—giving the impression of having no feelings when one truly experiences emotion (J. F Andersen et al., 1985; Ekman, 1978; Shennum & Bugental, 1982). Examples include keeping a straight face when something strikes one as funny, hiding attraction to a third party when one's spouse is present, or suppressing anger at one's boss. Children become increasingly skilled at inhibiting emotions as they move toward adolescence because impression management becomes more important. Branigan and Humphries (1969) reported that anger displays observed in nursery-school children disappear by school age. Similarly, P. A. Andersen, Andersen, and Mayton (1985) found that teachers observe dramatic reductions in emotional communication during the preteen years, particularly in sixth and seventh grade. Inhibition is also vital during deception because the concealment of guilt, anxiety, duping delight, arousal, and other emotions are necessary to avoid detection (Buller & Burgoon, Chapter 14, this volume; Ekman, 1978, 1993; O'Hair & Cody, 1994). When suspicious, receivers of potentially deceptive messages may also use inhibition so that they do not "tip off" the sender (see Buller & Burgoon, Chapter 14, this volume).

Intensification

Intensification, or maximization, involves giving the appearance of having stronger feelings than one actually has (J. F Andersen et al., 1985; Ekman, 1978; Saarni, 1985). In contrast to simulation, however, intensification necessarily involves experiencing a milder form of the emotion than is displayed. Examples include showing more grief at a funeral than one actually feels, laughing heartily at your boss's joke when you barely think it is funny, or communicating love to a distant relative for whom one only feels slight affection. Children learn to intensify their emotional expressions fairly early. For example, children who feel mild pain may cry loudly if a caregiver is available to soothe and comfort them. Yet these same children may merely whimper if alone or in the presence of peers. Intensification is also important in many deceptive situations (O'Hair & Cody, 1994). For instance, deceivers may convey a higher degree of liking and affection than they actually feel in order to appear trustworthy and credible (see Buller & Burgoon, Chapter 14, this volume). In other cases, intensification may simply be a confirming style of interpersonal interaction. For example, one might intensify expressions of empathy and concern when listening to another's problems.

Deintensification

Deintensification, which has also been termed minimization or miniaturization (J. F. Andersen et al., 1985; Ekman, 1978; Saarni, 1993), involves giving the appearance of experiencing an emotion with less intensity than one is actually feeling. According to Saarni (1993), minimization appears in children's communication as early as the second year of life. Examples include children raising their voices slightly rather than yelling when angry, or blasé teens smiling instead of laughing at a very humorous joke. Deintensification is often used to conform to rules of social appropriateness. Imagine, for example, a person who has just received a prestigious award. Although this individual may feel extremely proud, he or she may curb expressing pride in order to appear humble. Similarly, a person might be shocked to hear about a friend's personal or relational problems (e.g., the person has committed a crime or has abused a romantic partner), but may express only mild surprise and disappointment to avoid alienating the friend.

Masking

Masking, or substitution, involves communicating an emotion that is entirely different than the one a person is experiencing (J. F. Andersen et al., 1985; Ekman, 1978; Saarni, 1993; Shennum & Bugental, 1982). Masking appears later in the developmental cycle than intensification or deintensification, probably because it is easier to moderate an existing emotion than to express an emotion that is very different from what one is feeling. As Saarni (1993) stated: "Figuring out how to make a substitution or how to go poker-faced may require somewhat more complexity of thought and greater command of facial muscles, and it is sometimes assumed that children will demonstrate these expressive strategies somewhat later" (p. 437). Thus, inhibition, like masking, is a complex social skill that develops gradually. Masking is also a critical skill in deception (Buller & Burgoon, Chapter 14, this volume; O'Hair & Cody, 1994), such as when happiness is substituted for guilt or calm for excitement.

So far we have examined how evolutionary and socializing forces contribute to the expression, control, and modification of emotion in social contexts. We now turn to a discussion of the interrelationships between communication, emotion, and cognition within the context of social interaction. Four additional principles are advanced to illuminate these relationships. We argue that interpersonal communication constitutes a primary antecedent of emotion, that interpersonal schemata and cognitive processes affect how emotion is experienced and expressed, that interpersonal communication is a consequence of emotion, and that emotions generate other emotions and interaction chains. We begin with the idea that social interaction frequently elicits emotion.

INTERPERSONAL ELICITATION OF EMOTIONS

Certainly, emotions can exist apart from interpersonal interaction. Viewing a sunset may produce joy. Hitting one's thumb with a hammer may prompt anger. Fear can occur when being chased by a neighbor's dog. However, it is our position that these are exceptions to the rule. Most typically, emotions result from social interaction and interpersonal communication. Although emotions have been elicited in interaction for many millennia, this is more true than ever today because the number of messages we receive and the number of people we encounter is greater than ever. Thus, we advance a third principle.

Principle 3: Interpersonal Communication Is the Primary Elicitor of Most Emotions

During the past decade, research has revealed an emerging consensus that the primary antecedent of many, perhaps most, emotional experiences is interpersonal interaction. Many researchers argue that the vast majority of emotions that humans experience emerge from social interactions that occur in the context of interpersonal relationships (e.g., DeRivera, 1984; Metha & Clark, 1994; Miller & Leary, 1992; Schwartz & Shaver, 1987). Indeed, Bowlby (1979) argued that most intense emotions arise when people are forming, maintaining, disrupting, terminating, or renewing close relational ties with others. The formation and renewal of attachment associates with love and joy. Relationship disruption associates with emotions such as anxiety, anger, and jealousy. Relationship loss associates with sadness and grief. Ekman (1993) made a similar claim: "Typically, the events that call forth emotion are interpersonal actions, although the action of other animals, or natural events such as thunder can also call forth emotions" (p. 388). Oatley and Johnson-Laird (1987) argued that "with the exception of fear, which often occurs in modern life as the result of such events as near traffic accidents, the emotions of interest to humans occur in the course of our relations with others" (p. 41). Even fear sometimes results from real or imagined messages from others, including interpersonal fear appeals, television shows or movies, and mass media campaigns (see Wilson & Smith, Chapter 20, this volume; and Witte, Chapter 16, this volume). Thus, as Buck (1991) argued, "social emotions are basic to all social behavior and are activated in every social encounter" (p. 159).

Emotions can arise without social or communicative stimuli, but even in these instances emotions are usually the result of imagined or anticipated interaction. Greenwood's (1994) summary of literature suggests that when children first learn about emotion they "depend upon the actual presence of a social audience (e.g., parents and teachers), but eventually become independent of it, while retaining a conceptual link to the imagined response of a social audience" (p. 167). Ekman (1993) took a similar position by noting that emotions are typically elicited by "real, remembered, anticipated or imagined" (p. 385) social events. For example, happiness can be elicited by participating in, recalling, planning or imagining an interpersonal event such as a birthday party or a date. Although all emotions are primarily socially elicited, some emotions, such as the so-called self-conscious emotions, are especially socially dependent (Fischer & Tangney, 1995). These include jealousy, shame, guilt, embarrassment, and pride. In the following section, we discuss how communication and social interaction elicits emotions. We begin by looking at emotions typically characterized by positive affect and conclude with those emotions that often carry a negative valence.

Happiness/Joy

One of the most desirable emotions is happiness. Indeed, the U.S. Declaration of Independence casts the "pursuit of happiness" as an unalienable right. Babad and Walbott (1986) reported that happiness is particularly likely to occur in the context of social relationships. Diener, Sandvik, and Pavot (1991), for example, found that people who frequently feel positive affect through their interactions with others rate themselves as happy. McIntosh and Martin (1992) maintained that achieving goals leads to happiness. Research demonstrates that even positive achievements will most likely generate happiness if they are observed by, told to, shared with, or praised by others. Receiving love, liking, affection, and acceptance are the most prototypic triggers of joy (Shaver et al., 1987). Thus, people's most joyous moments probably involve sharing happy or euphoric states with others.

Even in infancy, social interaction produces joy. Magai and McFadden (1995) summarized the research on elicitors of joy in infants, going back more than a century to the work of Darwin, Preyer, and others. This summary shows that the primary elicitors of joy in babies are the sight of the mother, the father's face, a father's smile, playful shaking of the infant's limbs, tickling, animated faces, singing, and opening a curtain around the cradle. In contrast, few studies revealed nonsocial stimuli as antecedents of joy. Social interaction is a major elicitor of happiness across the life span. For most people it is probably difficult to think of many sources of happiness that are devoid of interpersonal interaction.

Love and Affection

Love constitutes an inherently interpersonal emotion because it is "evoked in relation to a particular other" (Shaver, Morgan, & Wu, 1996, p. 82) and is associated with "a desire to maintain a close relationship" with someone (Aron & Aron, 1991, p. 26). Similarly, affection involves feeling warmth and fondness *toward* someone. With the exception of total narcissism, love requires the presence of another person. Gaines et al. (Chapter 19, this volume) argue that love consists of the euphoric feelings and positive future expectations that arise from the addition of someone special in one's life. Dion and Dion (1996) contended that "love can only be understood by considering the societal structure defining personal relationships" (p. 1; see also Taraban, Hendrick, & Hendrick, Chapter 12, this volume). In their study of prototypic love, Shaver et al. (1987) discovered that the loved one provides something that the person wants, needs, or likes. Similarly, the feeling of being loved involves feeling needed and appreciated by another. Love and affection occur only in the context of shared time and experiences, when one finds the other psychologically or physically attractive, when "one enjoys exceptionally good communication with the other person, or because one feels open and trusting in the other person's presence" (Shaver et al., 1987, p. 1079). In this case, love is associated with positive affect. Interestingly, however, when love is unrequited and social interaction with the loved one is absent or limited, feelings of love can be associated with both intensely positive and negative feelings (Baumeister & Wotman, 1992; Baumeister, Wotman, & Stillwell, 1994; Taraban et al., Chapter 12, this volume).

Pride

Pride had been classified as one of the most "social" emotions (Barrett, 1995). Pride is frequently the result of another's approval that leads to positive self-evaluation and is associated with positive affect. However, pride is not always a positive emotion. Too much pride can make people feel guilt and cause others to see them as boastful. Indeed, pride is cast as one of the "seven deadly sins" and people are warned that "pride comes before a fall."

Typically, pride is generated by appraisals that one is responsible for socially valued outcomes or is a socially valued person (Mascolo & Fischer, 1995). Greenwood (1994) contended that pride is usually dependent on a social audience. Indeed, one's greatest accomplishments often fail to engender much pride until they are recognized by significant others. Shaver et al. (1987) reported an actual account of an individual's experience feeling pride and joy. As one can see, this account emphasizes how social interaction with others enhances prideful feelings, while the absence of others diminishes them:

> I was so proud. I never had so much fun or excitement as I did that closing night. Everyone was congratulating me, and it made me very naturally high . . . The feeling lasted for about 2 or 3 days. The thing that made it subside was when I realized it was over, and all the fun and excitement ended. (p. 1073)

Anger

Although anger can occur outside of social interaction, it is typically the result of a troubling interpersonal circumstance. Babad and Wallbott's (1986) research supports this contention by showing that anger more likely occurs in social versus nonsocial contexts. According to Shaver et al. (1987), the prototypical anger experience occurs when "something (usually another person, in these accounts) interferes with the person's execution of plans or attainment of goals (by reducing the person's power, violating expectations, frustrating or interrupting goal-directed activities)" (p. 1077). In 95% of the Shaver et al. accounts, angry individuals perceived that they had been harmed illegitimately. Similarly, Canary, Spitzberg, and Semic (Chapter 7, this volume) claim that anger is nearly always elicited by a personally relevant provocation.

Research also suggests that anger often originates as a reaction to the communication of others. Canary et al.'s (Chapter 7, this volume) synthesis of the literature on anger-inducing events indicates that there are nine primary causes of anger. Among these are events such as identity management, aggression, incompetence, and relationship threats. Specifically, people manage their identities by becoming angry when others insult, criticize, or reject them. People also become angry in response to another's physically or verbally aggressive attacks, incompetent behavior (i.e., thoughtless, inconsiderate, or rude behavior), and relationship-threatening behavior (i.e., unfaithful or disloyal behavior). These examples illustrate that anger is an overwhelmingly interpersonally induced emotion.

Fear and Anxiety

Fear represents an emotion that may or may not have roots in social interaction. Certainly, phobic responses to heights, enclosed spaces, dark water, and the like may have little or no genesis in communication, though they may surface as a response to a past negative experience (e.g., being locked in a closet for an extended time as a child). Fears of animals, of failure, of injury, and of death are also sometimes free from much social elicitation, though again, social events, such as criticism from others or the death of a loved one can promote these fears. Moreover, fear may be induced by parents, doctors, politicians, police officers, advertisers, and teachers to try to gain compliance and change the behavior of individuals (see Witte, Chapter 16, this volume). In the case of television and film, fear can also be induced for entertainment value (see Wilson & Smith, Chapter 20, this volume).

Fear has other interpersonal antecedents as well. Magai and McFadden's (1995) review of seminal fear studies in infants suggests that abrupt approaches to an infant's face, strange facial expressions, or the presence of a stranger are common fear elicitors. Similarly, attachment theory (Bowlby, 1969) suggests that young children experience "stranger anxiety" when they encounter unfamiliar adults. According to Shaver et al. (1987), the prototypical fear induction involves, among other factors, social rejection and failure. So interpersonal consequences appear to play a substantially central role in the induction of fear.

Interpersonal consequences also play a role in other types of anxiety. Numerous studies have examined emotional states related to social anxiety. Individuals experiencing social anxiety report feeling fear, worry, tenseness, and awkwardness when communicating with others. Moreover, social anxiety and communication apprehension can occur in several contexts, including speaking in public, meeting new people, and communicating in dyadic or small group interaction (e.g., Cheek & Buss, 1981; McCroskey, 1982). Socially anxious individuals worry that, when under the scrutiny of others, they will be embarrassed or rejected. Leary (1987) reported that social anxiety is a learned response to difficult or unpleasant interactions. The more an individual experiences negative social interaction, the more social anxiety is likely to develop.

Sadness, Grief, and Depression

This family of melancholic emotions have a primary basis in social interaction. In Magai and McFadden's (1995) review of historic studies of infant sadness and distress, social interaction was featured as the primary elicitor of sadness (Magai & McFadden, 1995). Fake weeping by a caregiver, harsh vocal tones, desired but unfulfilled contact, and physical harm by a sibling constitute the primary causes of infant sadness. Shaver et al. (1987) reported that sadness prototypes are largely socially induced: "The sad person has experienced an undesirable outcome; often he or she has experienced one of the events that the fearful person dreads—the death of a loved one, loss of a relationship, or social rejection" (p. 1077).

Grief, a special form of sadness, involves loss of a loved one through death or separation. Grief is characterized by high levels of preoccupation with the lost relationship and avoidance of objects, topics, or reminders of the loss in order to reduce emotional distress (Horowitz, 1991). Thus, grief is an inherently socially stimulated emotion.

Depression, defined as chronic, sad affect, is clearly intertwined with disturbed and negative communication patterns (see Segrin, Chapter 8, this volume). Research has shown that depressed individuals describe their families as rejecting, experience social isolation, have little intimacy or social support, and have poor social skills (see McCann & Lalonde, 1993; Segrin, Chapter 8, this volume). Research also indicates that sadness is somewhat more likely to occur in response to social rather than nonsocial events (Babad & Wallbott, 1986). In sum, empirical evidence suggests that the melancholic emotions, including sadness, grief, and depression, are often socially induced.

Jealousy

Jealousy is a social emotion. It occurs when an individual perceives that a rival poses a threat to the existence or quality of one's relationship (Guerrero & Andersen, Chapter 6, this volume). So jealous emotion is inextricably linked to real, anticipated, or imagined relational behavior and interpersonal interaction. Fitness and Fletcher (1993) reported that the prototypical jealousy experience occurs when a person's romantic partner is involved, even innocuously, with a third party. Even experimental operationalizations of jealousy employ interpersonal, social events to elicit jealousy. In a study that used hypothetical jealousy situations, Hupka and Eshett (1988) asked subjects to imagine a situation in which the subjects saw their mate interacting with, or alternatively kissing, another individual. On occasion, jealousy is also purposely induced by the relational partner (see Guerrero & Andersen, Chapter 6, this volume). Regardless of how jealousy is elicited, auxiliary emotions such as hurt, anger, sadness, and fear are central to the jealousy experience (Fischer & Tangney, 1995; Fitness & Fletcher, 1993). These emotions stem from the perceived betrayal of the partner and the potential loss of relational bonds. Thus, the auxiliary emotions associated with jealousy stem from the perception that the partner prefers interacting with the rival and has violated relational trust. In short, real or imagined interpersonal antecedents of jealousy are always present.

Guilt, Shame, and Embarrassment

Guilt, shame, and embarrassment are all members of a family of self-conscious emotions (Tangney, 1995). Guilt occurs when individuals perceive that they have injured, unjustly hurt, or failed to help someone (see Vangelisti & Sprague, Chapter 5, this volume). Thus, guilt is often focused on specific interpersonal events. "Shame is more of a dejection-based emotion encompassing feelings of helplessness, sadness, and depression but also anger. In shame, there is greater focus on other people's opinions of the self, accompanied by a sense of being exposed and observed" (Ferguson & Stegge, 1995, p. 176). As such, shame pertains to global feelings about oneself rather than feelings specific to a particular action (Baumeister, Stillwell, & Heatherton, 1994; Tangney, 1990, 1995). Embarrassment, in contrast, is defined as a form of social anxiety that occurs when unwanted attention is focused on a person. Like guilt, embarrassment is related to particular interpersonal events. Like shame, there is a strong focus on being observed by others. These three emotions can also be distinguished in terms of duration. Shame typically endures, whereas embarrassment is fleeting.

Each of these emotions result from social interaction. Recent conceptualizations suggest that guilt is more than a solely intrapersonal event. Indeed, guilt has recently been viewed as "an interpersonal phenomena based in close relationships, especially in certain interactions with relational partners" (Baumeister, Stillwell, & Heatherton, 1995, p. 255). For example, feeling overbenefited in comparison to one's partner (i.e., receiving more relational rewards than the partner) can lead to guilt, especially for women (Hatfield, Utne, & Traupmann, 1979). Engaging in relational transgressions such as sexual infidelity or deception often cause individuals to feel guilty (Metts, 1994). Individuals also intentionally induce guilt in their conversational partners (see Vangelisti, Daly, & Rudnick, 1991; Vangelisti & Sprague, Chapter 5, this volume), often as a way of gaining compliance or restoring emotional equity to the relationship. These findings illustrate that the self-judgment of guilt has its foundation in interpersonal dynamics. Thus, as Tangney (1992) demonstrated, the events that cause guilt are generally interpersonal.

Shame does not occur in solitude. It is a social emotion that originates in a person's moral or interpersonal transgressions, is forged in an interpersonal system, and is dependent on a real or imagined social audience (Averill, 1980; Greenwood, 1994; Magai & McFadden, 1995). Shame is a negatively valenced emotion that arises when individuals perceive themselves to be inferior, to have committed a significant transgression or omission, or have lost face (Ferguson & Stegge, 1995). In the case of transgressions, shame is an emotion that refocuses the hurt that was caused to a harmed other back to the negative characteristics of the self (Tangney, 1995). Instead of viewing the commission of the transgression as an isolated or infrequent event, shamed individuals see their transgressions as part of an enduring pattern of untoward behavior that reflects their negative personality characteristics and makes them unworthy of love and affection. Private shame is rare because feelings of inferiority usually arise out of a failure in interpersonal situations.

Embarrassment, by its very definition, involves social interaction. People become embarrassed when they are the recipients of unwanted attention. This attention can stem from presenting oneself unfavorably before peers (see Bradford & Petronio, Chapter 4, this volume) or from receiving excessive praise (Miller & Leary, 1992). Thus, embarrassment arises in real or imagined encounters when people believe that others have formed undesired impressions of them that threaten their public identities or have focused unwanted attention on them. Various models posit that embarrassment is a uniquely discomforting social phenomenon because it requires the presence of others as "interactive partners or as evaluative observers" (Miller, 1995, p. 323). Furthermore, Miller and Leary (1992) contended that because "embarrassment is a purely social event [it] can be understood only in terms of its interpersonal antecedents and consequences" (p. 204). Embarrassment may also be deliberately and strategically induced to highlight or alter another person's undesirable behavior through communication tactics or strategies (see Bradford & Petronio, Chapter 4, this volume).

Summary

In this section, we have demonstrated that the primary elicitor of emotions is interpersonal interaction. Emotions are more than private experiences, they are motivational states that originate in the interpersonal milieu and, as we will see later, also have significant impacts on interpersonal communication and long-term interpersonal relationships. Moreover, people often strategically induce emotional states in others as a way of achieving interpersonal goals.

INTERPERSONAL SCHEMATA AND COGNITIVE PROCESSING

Interpersonal communication does not occur in a vacuum. Rather, a multitude of relational and personal factors, including one's goals, desires, moods, and expectations are likely to affect how people interpret and respond to emotion-eliciting events. In the next section of this chapter, we discuss literature related to our fourth principle:

Principle 4: Interpersonal Schemata, Including Goals, Needs, Desires, and Expectations Affect How and When Emotion Is Experienced and Communicated

The links between cognition, emotion, and behavior have been a subject of great scholarly interest for several decades, although the focus on *communicative* behaviors has only surfaced relatively recently. Traditionally, research on emotion has been guided by the principle that emotional experience is "primarily data driven, caused by something that happens in the current situation" (Wilson & Klaaren, 1992, p. 2). According to this view, the emotion-eliciting stimulus is primarily, if not solely, responsible for the changes in arousal and behavior that accompany emotion. However, recent research suggests that "emotion results from the appraisal of events in relation to people's needs, wishes, and expectations" (Wilson & Klaaren, 1992, p. 2). Hence, the interpersonal and contextual factors that precede and surround the emotion-eliciting event shape how emotion is experienced and expressed.

Wilson and Klaaren (1992) illustrated the importance of these factors with an example of two people watching the Minnesota Twins win the World Series. They contended that the person who is a long-time Twins fan and has wagered a considerable sum on the game will have a very different emotional reaction than the person who is a less devoted (and nongambling) fan. As Wilson and Klaaren (1992) stated, though the two spectators "have access to the same 'data,' their needs and expectations cause quite different appraisals of the events, resulting in different emotions" (p. 3). These individuals are also likely to communicate their emotion differently. The devoted fan may show her elation by hugging those around her and jumping for joy. The less devoted fan is likely to have a much more subdued behavioral reaction.

Both data-driven (i.e., stimulus–response) and interpersonal approaches to studying emotion are valuable. However, we believe that when emotions occur in social interaction, they are *framed* by several interpersonal features, such as relational and personal schemata that encompass needs, goals, and expectations. We do not, however, ignore the fact that emotions are elicited by specific events or stimuli. Nor do we discount the importance of physiological arousal in emotional experience. Rather, we believe that these forces all work together to shape emotional experience and expression in interpersonal interaction. When emotions are experienced in nonsocial contexts (e.g., feeling fear because one is surrounded by a group of bumblebees), interpersonal features are less relevant, if relevant at all.

In the following pages, we review several theoretical perspectives that incorporate various interpersonal factors. These factors are theorized to affect the cognitive interpretation and evaluation of the emotion-eliciting event. We begin by reviewing research on goals and expectations. Next we turn to a discussion of Bradbury and Fincham's integrative model of affect and cognition, which includes both proximal context factors (i.e., expectations, temporary mood states) and distal context factors (i.e., information-processing biases, chronic mood states). Third, we review attachment theory literature, which suggests that mental models of self and others influence emotional communication.

Goals, Interruptions, and Expectations

Goals and action sequences are central in Berscheid's (1983) theory of emotion, which is based on interdependence theory (see Kelley et al., 1983). According to Berscheid (1983), highly interdependent relational partners have the ability to interrupt one another's organized action sequences. An action sequence is a series of well-learned actions that coincide with general goals and higher-order plans. Actions sequences have a hierarchical structure. For example, completing a work-related project may be part of an organized action sequence that centers on being successful in one's career; and being successful in one's career may be an integral part of an action sequence designed to preserve one's happiness and self-esteem. Developing and preserving intimate relationships is an important life goal (Hatfield, 1984), so action sequences often revolve around people's intimate relationships. As Berscheid (1983) put it:

> Given the prominent role close relationships play in most people's plans and purposes, and given the relationship between emotion and organized action sequences and plans, . . . it is not surprising that close relationships provide the setting for a range and intensity of emotion unmatched by any other context. (p. 131)

According to Berscheid, when action sequences are interrupted, arousal levels change and cognitive-labeling begins. When individuals perceive that the interruption hinders goal attainment, emotions are labeled negatively. However, if the interruption is appraised as facilitating goal attainment, or as being under the control of the individual experiencing the arousal change, emotions are labeled positively. This explains why the same event leads to various emotional responses in different relationships. Metha and Clark (1994) provided an applicable example. They described a situation where a person (we'll call her Jessica) receives two birthday gifts. The first is from an ardent admirer for whom she has no interest. The second is from her best friend. In the first case, the gift interrupts an action sequence. Jessica wishes to maintain a polite but distant relationship with the admirer. Receiving the gift makes her feel uncomfortable and perhaps even angry or fearful. In the second case, Jessica is pleased at her friend's thoughtfulness, presumably because the gift is a sign of their affection for one another and is consistent with an action sequence that focuses on maintaining the friendship. As a result, Jessica is likely to feel joy and appreciation when receiving the gift.

The situation in which one feels in complete control of the interruption is the least relevant to interpersonal interaction. In these situations, people voluntarily engage in behaviors that lead to psychological arousal. Riding a rollercoaster, bungy jumping, or viewing a snake close-up through a zoo window exemplify this type of interruption. In such cases, individuals appraise the situation positively because they can control the onset and offset of the event. Instead of labeling their arousal change as fear or anxiety, they report experiencing excitement and exhilaration.

Theories focusing on expectancy violations make similar predictions. Generally, positive violations of expectations lead to positive emotions, whereas negative violations of expectations lead to negative emotions. In many respects, expectancy violations are similar to interruptions. Both represent novel or unexpected stimuli that cause an individual to focus attention on the unexpected event. Cognitive processing, interpretation, and emotional-labeling then follow.

Expectancy violations theory (Burgoon, 1983, 1993; Burgoon & Hale, 1988) focuses on the role that expectancies play in predicting dyadic interaction patterns, including the communication of emotion. According to the theory, people develop expectancies about what is typical and appropriate communicative behavior in various types of social interaction. As Burgoon (1993) stated, "[t]hese proliferating expectancies thus form primary interaction schemata that should be activated in all human encounters" (p. 32). Expectancies frame social situations and "define and shape interpersonal interaction" (Burgoon, 1993, p. 32). When expectancies are violated, individuals focus attention on the violation and evaluate their partner as rewarding or nonrewarding, and the behavior as positive or negative. These judgments influence whether or not the expectancy violation is evaluated as positive or negative. Burgoon succinctly (1993) described the outcomes of this evaluation process.

> Positive violations, in which the enacted behavior is more positively valenced than the expected, are theorized to produce more positive interaction patterns and outcomes than conformity to expectancies; negative violations, in which the enacted behavior is more negatively valenced than the expected behavior, are theorized to be detrimental, relative to expectancy confirmation. (p. 40)

Thus, positive violations of expectations likely lead to the experience of positive emotions, such as joy, relief, and affection, as well as positive behaviors that reflect intimacy and involvement. In contrast, negative violations of expectations likely lead to the experience of negative emotions, such as anger, frustration, and sadness. In response to these negative emotions, people may either compensate by trying to return the interaction to a more positive state (e.g., trying to "cheer up" the partner) or reciprocate by engaging in negative behavior that reflects hostility, anxiety, and/or withdrawal (see Burgoon, Stern,& Dillman, 1995).

Other models have made similar predictions. Levitt (1991; Levitt, Coffman, Guacci-Franco, & Loveless, 1994) for example, proposed the social expectations model, which posits that when expectations are negatively violated, negative relational change and attendant negative emotion will occur. When expectations are exceeded (i.e., a positive violation in Burgoon's terminology), positive relational change, including positive emotional reactions, will occur. Finally, when expectations are confirmed, no emotional, behavioral, or relational change is predicted to occur. Levitt (1991) gave the following example to further illustrate the role that expectations play in predicting emotional and relational outcomes. Two middle-aged men had been friends since boyhood until one friend urgently requested financial help from the other and he refused. This refusal led to the termination of the friendship. Levitt (1991) suggested that the social expectations model can explain this incident because "the friend's failure to assist was a marked violation of the expectation that he would always 'come through if needed.' This violation was accompanied by strong feelings of disbelief, hurt, and anger" (p. 196).

Both Burgoon's and Levitt's models indicate that expectancy violations elicit emotion. Expectations also provide guidance for *how* emotions should be expressed within social contexts. As Burgoon (1993) argued, expectations help a person determine whether or not it is appropriate to display a particular emotion. For example, Aune, Buller, and Aune (1996) found that romantic partners (a) managed their expression of negative emotions, especially in early and late stages of relationship development; (b) viewed the management of negative emotion as an appropriate communication strategy; and (c) felt that expressing both positive and negative emotion was less appropriate in early (as compared to middle or late) stages of relationship development. Social expectations also help individuals decide when it is appropriate to use specific display rules such as masking, simulation, and deintensification.

The Integrative Model of Affect and Cognition

Like interdependence theory and expectancy theories, Bradbury and Fincham's (1987) integrative model focuses on factors that influence the cognitive processing of attention-eliciting stimuli. The model is based on six concepts: partner input, primary processing, secondary processing, proximal context factors, distal context factors, and behavioral output. *Partner input* includes all partner behaviors that one can observe. When a behavior is observed, a person may engage in *primary processing,* particularly if the behavior is negative or unexpected. As Bradbury and Fincham postulated; "negative relationship events are likely to attract attention and, when they do not pose an immediate threat to the safety of the individual, elicit cognitive processing which can influence the affective state of the individual" (p. 70). Both attention to and the processing of negative or unexpected relational events is automatic and operates largely "outside of immediate awareness" (Bradbury & Fincham, 1987, p. 75).

During *primary processing,* individuals judge behaviors along three dimensions: negativity/positivity, level of expectedness, and degree of self-relevance. This processing cumulates in an overall affective response, which can range from very positive, to neutral, to very negative. When the affective response is neutral, further processing is unnecessary. In addition, positively valenced affective states may require less cognitive processing than negatively valenced affective states. As Bradbury and Fincham (1987) suggested, affective responses characterized as highly negative, unexpected, and self-relevant are most likely to promote extended cognitive processing.

During *secondary processing,* individuals engage in a "causal search, resulting in the identification of a cause and, if relevant, the determination of responsibility" (Bradbury & Fincham, 1987, p. 77). The concept of a causal search is adopted from Weiner's (1985) work on attribution theory. According to Weiner, attributions are based on appraisals of locus (i.e., who is responsible?), stability, and controllability. Bradbury and Fincham note that several emotional responses are *attribution-dependent.* For example, pride and contempt are associated with the locus dimension, whereas despair, contentment, and hopelessness involve feeling that a cause is fairly stable. Bradbury and Fincham argue that emotions such as guilt, gratitude, and shame associate with the controllability dimension. These three emotions may also associate with the locus dimension, given that gratitude results from perceiving someone else as responsible for a positive action, while guilt and shame involve internalizing one's feelings and blaming oneself for a negative outcome. Fear may be a purer example of an emotion based on low controllability. These examples show that secondary processing leads to further refinement of emotional experiences. Secondary processing is also likely to affect emotional communication. For example, when individuals see their relational partners as the cause of their negative emotions, they are likely to feel justified in confronting and retaliating against them. In contrast, when individuals see themselves as the cause of the problem, they may apologize or withdraw from the situation. Canary et al. (Chapter 7, this volume) provide further evidence regarding how attributional processes affect the experience and expression of angry emotion.

According to Bradbury and Fincham's integrative model, two forces work together to affect both primary and secondary cognitive processing: proximal and distal context. *Proximal context factors* refer to the thoughts and feelings that occur immediately prior to interpreting the partner's behavior. These include expectations, temporary mood states, and physiological arousal. For example, when behaviors violate expectations, people are more likely to pay attention to them (see Burgoon & Hale, 1988; Le Poire, 1991). When people experience "bad moods" they are more likely to interpret neutral behaviors negatively. Forgas's (1994) found that individuals in happy moods attributed conflict to external, unstable, and specific causes, whereas those in sad moods attributed conflict to internal, stable, and global causes. Furthermore, in response to serious conflicts, "happy" individuals reported using cooperation (i.e., an active, positive communication style) and contention (i.e., an active, negative style) more than "sad" individuals. In contrast, individuals in sad moods reported more neglect (i.e., a passive, negative style) and patience (i.e., a passive, positive style) than did those who were in happy moods. Taken together, these results suggest that individuals who are feeling happy are likely to use outwardly directed communication strategies, presumably because they blame external forces for the conflict and see problems as specific and changeable. Individuals in sad moods, however, appear to use inwardly directed, passive strategies, presumably because they blame themselves and see problems as global and unchangeable.

Distal context factors include stable characteristics of individuals and relationships, including chronic mood states, level of relational satisfaction, and information-processing biases. Bradbury and Fincham postulated that people process information so that it is congruent with the predominant mood state of the relationship. When relationships are characterized by positive moods and behaviors, individuals are postulated to attend more to their partner's positive than negative behaviors. However, when relationships are characterized by negativity, partners attend more to one another's negative behaviors.

The final stage of this model is *behavioral output,* which refers to the individual's response to the partner's behavior. Bradbury and Fincham discuss two types of behavioral outputs: internal (e.g., physiological arousal) and external (e.g., verbal and nonverbal communication). This behavioral output is posited to be the result of the cognitive processing systems discussed above. Moreover, behavioral output often leads to partner responses, which produce new partner input and restarts the process.

Attachment Theory

Like the other theories reviewed in this section, attachment theory posits that expectations, interpersonal goals, and cognitive processing all exert influence on how emotions are experienced and expressed. According to attachment theory, past relationship experiences (especially social interaction with caregivers) lead people to develop mental models of oneself and others. These mental models can be conceptualized as falling along positive–negative continua. A positive mental *model of self* reflects "an internalized sense of self-worth that is not dependent on ongoing external validation" (Bartholomew, 1993, p. 40). A positive mental *model of others* reflects the view that people are accepting and supportive, and that relationships are rewarding. These mental models have been theorized to affect how people interpret information and how they regulate and express emotion.

Attachment theory originally focused on parent–child interactions, including children's emotional reactions to separation from and reunion with caregivers (see Ainsworth, Blehar, Waters, & Wall, 1978; Bowlby, 1969, 1973). Hazan and Shaver (1987) extended the theory's boundaries by demonstrating attachment style differences in adult love relationships. Bartholomew (1990) extended the theory further by proposing four distinct adult attachment styles.

According to Bartholomew's conceptualization, *Secures* have positive models of self and others. They trust others, have realistic relational expectations, acknowledge negative affect, and turn to others for support (Hazan & Shaver, 1987; Simpson & Rholes, 1994). *Preoccupieds,* in contrast, have positive models of others but negative models of themselves. These individuals depend on their relational partners for self-validation, worry about the well-being of their relationships (Bartholomew, 1993), dwell on negative affect, and seek support and comfort in a "hypervigilant manner" (Simpson & Rholes, 1994, p. 183). *Dismissives* have positive models of themselves, but negative models of others. They see relationships as nonessential, view themselves as highly self-sufficient, deny feeling negative affect, and insist on handling problems alone (Bartholomew, 1990, 1993). Finally, *Fearful Avoidants,* as a consequence of their negative models of self and others, fear rejection and worry about being hurt if they allow themselves to get too close to others. These individuals find it difficult to share emotions with others and report feeling anxiety in social situations (Bartholomew, 1993; Guerrero, 1996a).

The four attachment styles differ in terms of emotional regulation and expression. Collins and Read (1994) provided three reasons for the attachment-emotion link. First, they argued that working models, which are "heavily affect-laden," have *direct effects* on emotional response (p. 75). For example, fearful avoidants, who worry about being hurt in relationships, commonly experience emotions such as fear and anxiety. Second, attachment-style related *goals* influence emotional responses. As Collins and Read (1994) explained, events are evaluated based upon "the extent to which they fulfill one's currently active attachment goals and needs. And because adults with different attachment styles have different personal and interpersonal goals, they will respond to the same event with different emotions" (p. 75). Accordingly, an event such as a temporary separation is likely to produce sadness and jealousy in preoccupieds (who desire close contact with loved ones) and some degree of relief and happiness in dismissives (who value autonomy). Finally, different *interpretations* of a partner's behavior may lead to attachment style variations in emotional experience and expression (Collins & Read, 1994). As a case in point, consider the case of a woman receiving a brief hug from a co-worker after learning that she did not receive an expected promotion. A secure woman would likely interpret the co-worker's hug as appropriate and comforting. A preoccupied might interpret the hug as too brief. A dismissive, in contrast, may see the hug as unnecessary and perhaps condescending. Finally, a fearful avoidant would probably feel uncomfortable receiving public contact.

Research documents attachment-style differences in support seeking, support giving, and emotional sensitivity. An already seminal experimental study by Simpson, Rholes, and Nelligan (1992) demonstrated that in stressful situations, secure women actively seek support from their romantic partners. In contrast, avoidant women do not seek support. These tendencies to seek and avoid seeking support were strongest when anxiety levels were high. Simpson et al. found a similar pattern for support giving. Secure men gave their partners support, especially when their partners were highly anxious. But avoidant men failed to give support, particularly if their partner was highly anxious. A self-report study by Kunce and Shaver (1994) produced similar findings. Secures reported being the most emotionally sensitive and responsive to others. Dismissives and fearful avoidants, as compared to secures and preoccupieds, reported being less emotionally supportive and less accessible when their partners were distressed. Barbee, Lawrence, and Cunningham (Chapter 10, this volume) discuss other connections between attachment style and social support.

Other studies have examined differences in emotional control, expressiveness, and pleasantness. Feeney (1995) found that insecure couples report more emotional control of negative emotions (e.g., anxiety, sadness, anger) than do secure couples. In addition, insecure couples reported that they wanted their partners to inhibit their expression of negative affect. Guerrero (1996a), however, found preoccupieds to report being less successful at controlling their emotions than those with other attachment styles. Similarly, Bartholomew and Horowitz (1991) found preoccupieds to report having difficulty managing their emotional expression. Taken together, these results suggest that those with insecure attachment styles want to control their displays of negative emotion, but that preoccupieds may have a difficult time inhibiting their emotion as a consequence of their high expressiveness and overinvolvement in relationships. Research has also shown that secures and preoccupieds rate themselves as more expressive than dismissives and fearful avoidants (Guerrero, 1996a), and that observers see secures and preoccupieds as more vocally and facially pleasant than dismissives and fearful avoidants during short conversations with their romantic partners (Guerrero, 1996b).

Attachment-style differences have also surfaced for communicative responses to emotions such as jealousy, sadness, and anger (Guerrero, 1996a, in press). These findings are presented in Table 1. The findings for jealousy and sadness are generally consistent with other research (e.g., Sharpsteen & Kirkpatrick, 1995; Batgos &

TABLE I   Communicative Responses to Jealousy, Sadness, and Anger[a]

	S	P	D	F
Jealousy				
Integrative communication (i.e., talking about jealous feelings)	+	+	−	−
Compensatory restoration (i.e., efforts at improve the self or relationship)	+	+	−	−
Avoidance/denial (i.e., denying jealous feelings and avoiding the partner)	−	−	+	+
Expression of negative affect (i.e., nonverbally displaying negative emotion)	−	+	−	−
Surveillance behavior (i.e., spying on or "checking up" on the partner)	−	+	−	−
Sadness				
Social support seeking (i.e., talking about problems with others)	+	+	−	−
Social withdrawal (i.e., avoiding other people)	−	−	+	+
Dependent behavior (i.e., rely on others for help)	−	+	−	−
Activity (i.e., keeping busy with old and new activities)	+	−		
Acting impulsively (i.e., speaking without thinking about the consequences)		+	−	
Anger				
Nonassertive–Denial (i.e., denying angry feelings; keeping anger inside)	−	−	−	+
Passive–Aggression (i.e., ignoring the partner; pouting and moping)	−		−	+
Aggression (i.e., yelling at or arguing with the partner; slamming doors)			+	−

[a] S = Secure; P = Preoccupied; D = Dismissive; F = Fearful avoidant. Pluses and minuses indicate that one or more groups were significantly higher or lower, respectively, than one another on these communicative responses to emotion. Data are from Guerrero (1996a, in press).

Leadbeater, 1994). However, it should be noted that Feeney's (1995) research uncovered a different pattern for anger. She found secures to favor negotiation (e.g., talking things out); preoccupieds to favor indirect influence tactics (e.g., pouting); dismissives to favor avoidance; and fearful avoidants to favor aggression. Thus, the jury is still out on the precise nature of attachment-style differences in anger expression.

Summary

Taken together, the above theories and research findings suggest that a number of interpersonal variables frame how emotion is experienced and communicated within social contexts. In particular, people's goals, needs, desires, and expectations influence what relational events elicit attention and how these events are interpreted and evaluated.

EMOTIONS AS INTERPERSONAL COMMUNICATION

Emotion researchers, at long last, are reaching the conclusion that emotions reflect more than private, psychological experiences and reactions. Researchers are realizing that an essential part of emotional experience is the expression of emotion through various forms of interpersonal communication. Indeed, a primary purpose or function of emotion, perhaps *the* primary purpose, is to communicate feelings and needs to others. This contention leads to our fifth principle:

Principle 5: An Essential Feature of the Emotional Experience Is Expression via Interpersonal Communication

Various forms of general communicative responses to emotion have been documented. Both early and contemporary research has focused on the communication of emotion through facial or bodily movement and vocal behavior. Such nonverbal expressions were traditionally viewed as epiphenomenal or at least "merely expressive" and noncommunicative. During the past few decades, however, research has clearly shown that emotional displays are highly communicative and intended for reception by others (Bavelas et al., 1986, 1988; Buck, 1984; Chovil, 1991; Kraut & Johnson, 1979). In fact, emotional expressions that are present in public situations are often not present in private (see Planalp, Chapter 2, this volume), which demonstrates that these expressions function as forms of interpersonal communication rather than merely expressions of internal feelings. As Chovil's (1991) findings suggest, "facial displays are more likely to be exhibited in social interactions and illustrate the important role in conveying messages to others in face-to-face communication" (p. 153).

Even when the nonverbal expression of emotion is unintended, it can send a clear message to a receiver. Indeed, emotions so automatically generate communicative displays that they can be problematic for the maintenance of competent self-presentations during interaction, particularly when negative emotions are unwittingly revealed. As DePaulo (1992) maintained, "Emotions can undermine self-presentational efforts because of the automatic links . . . between the elicitation of the basic emotions and the nonverbal expression of these emotions" (p. 216). Emotional expression, whether intended or unintended, can have many positive consequences as well. Emotions exist so that one's affective states can be shared to ready others for parallel action, to forewarn others of an individual's feelings, and to create a particular affective atmosphere for communicating.

Some researchers now suggest that emotions are organizing structures that produce social scripts (Fischer & Tangney, 1995; Shaver et al., 1987). Considerable research shows that for a variety of emotions, particular social scripts are elicited that produce distinct patterns of communicative actions. Many of these scripts are discussed in more detail later in this section. Of course, as such social scripts are produced, receivers scan the sender's behavior for emotional communication. Successful reception of such information provides the very basis of social skill, empathy, and communication competence. Klinnert, Campos, Sorce, Emde, and Svejda (1983) demonstrated that "emotional expressions are causal events in the sense that they influence others and pervade almost all social interactions, whether they are between friends, strangers, or enemies" (p. 591). Monitoring another person's behavior for emotional cues and even asking questions regarding a partner's emotional state are keys to competent everyday interpersonal interaction.

As would be expected, people frequently express emotions verbally to other interactants. Rimé, Mesquita, Philippot, and Boca (1991) reported six studies showing that social sharing is an integral part of the emotional process. The overwhelming majority of their respondents reported speaking to at least one person about most of their emotional experiences. Moreover, these results seem to hold for virtually all types of emotion. White (1993) went as far as to suggest that "emotion is a widespread, probably universal topic of talk" (pp. 35–36) and Rimé et al. (1991) concluded that "social sharing [is] an integral facet of emotion that deserves scientific consideration of its own" (p. 452). Emotions are antecedent, or more specifically, a prerequisite to considerable interpersonal talk. The traditional position that the principle function of verbal communication is informational ignores the fact that the motivation, the content, and numerous relational aspects of most communicative exchanges are generated by emotion.

Research also supports the commonsense notion that people tend to communicate emotions on a variety of levels with a variety of nonverbal and verbal cues. Planalp (Chapter 2, this volume) demonstrates that people overwhelmingly use multiple cues to send emotional messages. Vocal cues, including volume and rate, were frequently reported, as were indirect verbal cues such as name calling and apologizing; facial cues such as gaze, smiling, and rolled eyes; activity cues such as going for a walk alone or hugging the partner; and body cues such as clenching one's fists or throwing one's arms in the air. Direct verbal cues, such as telling the partner, "I'm mad at you" or "I feel really happy" were also reported, but with less frequency (see Planalp, Chapter 2, this volume). These results suggest that communicators have a wide array of strategies at their disposal for communicating emotion.

In the following pages we will show that several selected emotions are inherently interactive and typically shared through interpersonal communication. In addition, this section illustrates the diversity of verbal and nonverbal responses to emotion.

Happiness/Joy

Because happiness is one of the most positive emotions its sharing is usually a reinforcing and pleasant experience for both parties. Unless another envies one's happiness, this emotion usually results in positive contagion, reciprocity, and affect sharing. Happiness is communicated via positive facial displays, particularly smiling (Ekman, Friesen, & Ellsworth, 1972). Research shows that people smile more commonly in the presence of friends and acquaintances than when alone (Kraut & Johnson, 1979). Shaver et al. (1987) showed that, prototypically, "the happy person is socially outgoing; he or she seeks contact with others (acts friendly, hugs people, etc.) and tends to communicate his or her good feelings" (p. 1078). According to this research, joy is portrayed as energetic, active, and bouncy, and is expressed by laughing, smiling, and talking enthusiastically (Shaver et al., 1987). Similarly, Rimé et al. (1991) found that all of the joyous emotions, including enthrallment, gaiety, and pleasure, were almost always expressed to friends, romantic partners, acquaintances, and/or colleagues. Indeed, in no case among the Rimé et al. subjects was happiness withheld! Typically, participants talked about their happy feelings and told their interactional partner the meaning of their happy emotion. These findings demonstrate that happiness is usually communicated to others. Since people are rarely violent or dangerous when experiencing happiness, the sharing of happy states may have functioned through the ages as positive relational overtures or appeasement displays (Van Hooef, 1972). Today, of course, people who exude happiness are viewed as more attractive and popular (Sommers, 1984), making the communication of happiness a rewarding experience for most people.

Love and Affection

It is hard to conceive of an emotion that is more interpersonal than love. With the exception of narcissism, love's manifestations are almost entirely communicative. Interestingly, however, Fischer and Tangney (1995) pointed out that despite hypotheses that lovers communicate through eye contact and other forms of spontaneous, nonverbal communication, no prototypical facial expression of love has been identified. However, research has uncovered a host of nonverbal behaviors that are likely to appear when people feel a "surge" of love (Shaver et al., 1996). These include blushing, pupil dilation, wet eyes, facial and bodily relaxation, slight smiles, slight head tilts, and mutual gaze (Bloch, Orthous, & Santibanez, 1987; Morris, 1971; Rubin, 1973). Verbal correlates of love have also been found. Some research has been conducted on the idioms close friends and lovers employ in interpersonal communication, as well as patterns of disclosure and nonverbal behavior characteristic of different types and stages of love relationships (Bell & Healy, 1992; Gaines et al., Chapter 19, this volume, Taraban et al., Chapter 12, this volume). This research shows that nicknames and special terminology reflect the close bond shared by dyadic partners. Moreover, love may be overtly expressed most often in escalating rather than beginning or established love relationships (see Taraban et al., Chapter 12, this volume).

Studies of lovers' prototypic expressions of love have begun to shed additional light on this topic. People expressing love move physically close to their partners, hug and kiss their partners, give their partners gifts, smile, and act excited and energetic (Fitness & Fletcher, 1993; Shaver et al., 1987). Although more research on love's expression certainly is needed, love is clearly an inherently interpersonal emotion that is manifested primarily in the nonverbal and verbal expression of affection and intimacy for the loved one.

Pride

Pride is an emotion associated with a person's success or creation of a socially valued outcome. While little research has been done on pride, some research suggests that it is associated with particular types of interpersonal communication. Proud individuals often stand taller or seek to become larger or stronger as signs of success, triumph, or esteem. They also display their worthy self to others, produce celebratory gestures like the high-five signal, and smile broadly (Mascolo & Fischer, 1995). Children are especially prone to seek eye contact with significant others when feeling proud of accomplishments, which indicates their desire to seek and share social approval (Leary & Meadows, 1991). Shaver et al. (1987) reported a man's account of verbally sharing pride after he successfully produced and directed a musical at his high school. The man recounts his communicative response this way: "I just kept saying, 'We did it, and we did it great!' I had the biggest smile on my face, and I was hugging all of the cast members" (p. 1073). This example illustrates that although pride certainly has internal components, people frequently engage in proud nonverbal displays and share their pride verbally with significant others (see also Mascolo & Fischer, 1995). Communicating pride probably has a central role in self-esteem development and is a way of interactively receiving recognition for one's accomplishments.

Anger

Anger is not only one of the most powerful emotions, it is also one of the most socially communicated and interpersonally dangerous. Anger's origins are in protection instincts, self-defense, and the display of interpersonal aggression. The emotion is inherently interactive. It functions to communicate one's motivated and perhaps irrational and/or dangerous state to other individuals. "Angry persons report becoming stronger (higher in potency) and more energized in order to fight or rail against the cause of anger. [Their] responses seem to rectify injustice—to reassert power, to frighten an offending person into compliance, to restore a desired state of affairs" (Shaver et al., 1987, p. 1078).

Anger has numerous nonverbal manifestations, starting with the angry facial expression (see Ekman et al., 1972) and including angry tones of voice, breaking things, slamming doors, making threatening gestures, staring at someone in a hostile fashion, decreasing distance and/or leaning forward to intimidate, giving someone the "silent treatment," holding a grudge, and walking out on another (Canary et al., Chapter 7, this volume; Guerrero, 1994; Scheff, 1995; Shaver et al., 1987).

Anger is often expressed verbally to others, particularly to the alleged cause of one's anger. It is also frequently disclosed to friends, acquaintances, colleagues, and lovers through interpersonal sharing of the emotion (Rimé et al., 1991). Anger results in expressive outbursts, such as, "I'm mad at you," disclosures, nasty or sarcastic comments, retaliatory remarks, interruptions, blaming, and challenges (Roseman, Wiest, & Swartz, 1994; Scheff, 1995; Shaver et al., 1987). Yet anger is not always communicated in an aggressive or threatening manner. Sometimes individuals disclose anger in a nonthreatening manner in order to talk about problems. Other times, individuals simply internalize their feelings and deny being angry (Buck, 1979; Guerrero, 1994). Even in these cases, some angry cues are likely to be leaked despite attempts to suppress them. The frequency of quarrels with friends, family, and strangers, and the high level of interpersonal violence in our society demonstrates that anger is often manifested inappropriately.

Fear and Anxiety

Fear emanates from humans' self-protection impulses and is quickly and involuntarily manifested in the fear facial expression (DePaulo, 1992; Ekman et al., 1972). Fearful communication is probably designed to appease potential aggressors or to prompt a rescue. Shaver et al. (1987) reported that prototypical fear expressions, including screaming, crying, and pleading, are presumably used to avert an impending disaster. Similar fear reactions such as running or hiding probably have the same function. Likewise, freezing, an effort to become invisible or inconspicuous, involves an attempt to curtail all behavior, including interaction. Another function of fear displays may be to warn friends and allies of impending danger. While little research has documented this function, Bavelas's research (Bavelas et al., 1986, 1988) suggests that motor-mimicry displays function to communicate danger quickly and effectively. Fear is communicated via verbal accounts and forms of feeling sharing more than any other emotion (Rimé et al., 1991), presumably in an attempt to have others alleviate fear and provide comfort. Fearful feelings often are shared with friends, partners, and acquaintances through discussions of feelings and full accounts of what happened (Rimé et al., 1991).

Fear is so commonly communicated and so automatically expressed that it may undermine one's interpersonal image. Appearing fearful may be viewed as weakness, cowardice, or incompetence. Thus, people often try to control their fear or anxiety or to avoid situations that elicit these emotions (Stearns, 1993). Acting unafraid is an important self-presentational goal, designed to reduce aggression, and to maintain face (Shaver et al., 1987). Unfortunately, like deception, fear may "leak," undermining an individual's self-presentational goals (DePaulo, 1992; Ekman,

1985). The very existence of leakage during the suppression of fear suggests its importance as an interpersonal phenomenon.

Interestingly, the fear of expressing nervousness or interacting in inappropriate ways that harm one's interpersonal image can lead to social anxiety or communication apprehension. Research indicates that people experiencing this form of anxiety may display their fear through nervous cues such as vocalized pauses, hesitancies, and long response latencies, or they may withdraw from social interaction, remain silent, or decrease eye contact (see Leary & Kowalski, 1995; McCroskey, 1982; Siegman, 1985). Manning and Ray (1993) found that socially anxious, shy individuals also exhibit distinct verbal communication patterns. Specifically, they tend to talk extensively about the setting (e.g., factual information such as the environment or weather); reject more topical areas of discussion; show unwillingness to initiate conversations at transitional periods between turns; and favor a particular topic. These findings suggest that socially anxious individuals may prefer talking about factual (rather than emotional) information and sticking to topics with which they are comfortable.

Sadness, Grief, and Depression

Sad or melancholic affect has a host of communicative manifestations. Whereas most sad reactions, especially extreme grief and chronic depression, are involuntary, communicative responses to sadness may function to gain sympathy or to seek help. Paradoxically, sadness and depression often involve withdrawal from social contact (Shaver et al., 1987). This may involve efforts at face saving, the inability to function interpersonally, or passive help-seeking behaviors. Guerrero and Reiter (in press) discuss several responses to sadness that involve social withdrawal. The first, *immobilization,* involves behaviors such as staying in bed, moping around the house, and skipping work or school. These strategies focus on ceasing normal activity. The second withdrawal strategy, *solitude,* comprises behaviors such as spending time alone and avoiding other people. Guerrero and Reiter (in press) also discuss a passive help-seeking strategy, which they termed *dependent behavior.* Waiting for others to help, trying to get the attention of others, and relying on friends for help are examples of dependent behaviors.

Numerous nonverbal behaviors display sadness, including frowning, sad or sober facial expressions, crying, whimpering, slouching, moping, a monotone voice, a sad voice, reduced smiling, less eye contact, longer response latencies, and indirect body positions (Ekman et al., 1972; Magai & McFadden, 1995; McCann & Lalonde, 1993; Segrin, Chapter 8, this volume; Segrin & Abramson, 1994). Overall, depressed or sad communication is manifested in negative tone and poor, inept communication. Moreover, the sad individual often has difficulty focusing on others during conversations (McCann & Lalonde, 1993; Segrin, Chapter 8, this volume).

Verbal sharing of sadness is quite common, including detailed accounts of what sadness personally means, full accounts of sad episodes, and disclosure of sad feelings (Rimé et al., 1991). Seeking social support by asking others for comfort and advice and spending time with one's close friends are also common responses to sadness (Guerrero & Reiter, in press). Friends and acquaintances are more common targets of sad verbal sharing than are romantic partners or family (Rimé et al., 1991). Research suggests that social support seeking, verbal sharing, engaging in activity (e.g., taking up new challenges) and trying to cheer oneself up (e.g., by acting cheerful or trying to keep one's mind off problems) are all fairly healthy responses to sadness, whereas social withdrawal and cognitive dwelling are likely to keep the depressed individual focused on problems (Guerrero, 1996a; Nolen-Hoeksema, 1987).

Coping with extreme sadness, such as grief, may involve distinct stages of communicative responses. Kubler-Ross (1969) suggested that individuals cope with dying by progressing through five stages: denial, anger, bargaining, depression, and acceptance. More recently, Horowitz (1991) suggested five stages of mourning and relational loss, including outcry, denial, intrusion, working though, and completion.

Jealousy

Recent research has revealed a variety of communicative responses to jealousy (Buss, 1988; Guerrero, Andersen, Jorgensen, Spitzberg, & Eloy, 1995; Guerrero & Andersen, Chapter 6, this volume; White & Mullen, 1989). These include negative affect expression, integrative or positive communication, distributive or aggressive communication, active distancing, avoidance/denial, violent communication/threats, signs of possession, derogation of competitors, relationship threats, surveillance/restriction, compensatory restoration, manipulation attempts, rival contacts, and violent behavior. Details of these communicative responses are reported in Chapter 6. The abundance of discrete tactics and strategies that individuals are able to report as responses to jealousy suggests that jealousy produces a great variety of communicative responses. It has been noted by Buss (1988, 1989) that jealousy may have evolved as an emotion to ensure mate retention. Similarly, many interpersonal behaviors probably function as attempts to regulate jealous feelings and to promote mate protection. Guerrero and Andersen (Chapter 6, this volume) also discuss several interpersonal functions of communicative responses to jealousy, including relationship maintenance and relational reassessment.

Guilt, Shame, and Embarrassment

These three self-conscious emotions have some similar manifestations, yet each is associated with a unique profile of interpersonal goals and communicative responses. Guilt typically involves active communication that is designed to repair the situation, redeem the guilty person, and/or reduce guilt. Shame, because of its focus on feelings of inferiority and low self-worth, tends to produce avoidance rather than active communication. Like guilt, embarrassment typically involves repairing a situation. However, the focus of the repair is different. Guilty people are concerned with making amends after somehow hurting another person. Embarrassed people try to save face after hurting their own self-images. The specific communicative responses related to these goals are delineated next.

So far, research has not uncovered nonverbal expressions *uniquely* associated with guilt (Izard, 1977). Research indicates that guilt and sadness, do, however, share similar nonverbal manifestations, such as a lump in the throat, long silences, and sad or worried facial expressions (e.g., Scherer & Wallbott, 1994). A number of scholars have found specific verbal reactions to guilt: repair through appeasements, apologies, confessions, corrective actions, explanations, and reparations (Barrett, 1995; Ferguson & Stegge, 1995; Keltner, 1995; Vangelisti & Sprague, Chapter 5, this volume). These verbal messages focus on reparation and are often designed to ameliorate others' indignation and one's own guilty feelings. As Barrett (1995) stated:

> Guilt-relevant behaviors act to repair the damage caused by a person's wrongdoing. Moreover, rather than removing the person from social contact, guilt often moves the individual to tell others about the wrongdoing, and thus to show them that he or she understands the standards and wishes to follow them. (p. 41)

In contrast to the active responses associated with guilt, the primary response to shame is avoidance of communication with other people. As Tangney (1995) stated: "The shamed individual seeks to hide the self from others, and to escape from the overwhelming pain of the situation. Thus, shame motivates behaviors that are likely to sever interpersonal contact" (p. 119). The negative affect experienced by a shamed individual is exacerbated by the presence of others, accounting for the predominance of avoidant responses in shame research. These avoidant behaviors include face hiding, gaze aversion, burying the face in one's hands, body slouching, head lowering, and fleeing from social contact (Barrett, 1995; Keltner, 1995; Mascolo & Fischer, 1995; Scheff, 1995). Some nonavoidant nonverbal responses have also been observed. Blushing is a typical response to shame, though less so than to embarrassment (Leary & Meadows, 1991; Roseman, Wiest, & Swartz, 1994). Control behaviors, such as biting or licking the lips, wrinkling the forehead, and false smiling are also common responses (Scheff, 1995) as are increased facial touches and an absence of smiling (Keltner, 1995).

When avoidant behavior, flight, or hiding is impossible or difficult, direct verbal behaviors represent a common shame response. Verbal admissions such as, "I'm so ashamed" have been reported (Fischer & Tangney, 1995). Retaliatory anger or humiliated fury can be directed by a shamed person toward a disapproving other (Tangney, 1995). Scheff (1995) reported a series of other verbal responses, including mitigation responses designed to reduce the pain of the shameful event, oblique references that depersonalize the shame event, as well as vague, denying, defensive, and indifferent responses. Rimé et al. (1991) have shown that despite the desire to avoid social contact in the shameful situation, a majority of respondents still share the shameful event with other people, particularly friends, acquaintances, and colleagues. Moreover, shame is typically shared with others during the very first interpersonal encounter following the shameful event.

It is interesting that even an emotion like shame, which prompts distinctly avoidant reactions, results in a number of communicative responses that range from nonverbal avoidance cues to overt discussions of one's feelings and accounts of the emotional episode. A significant response to shame, like its cousin embarrassment, is interpersonal facework to maintain one's image in the face of shameful emotions (see Cupach & Metts, 1994; Ferguson & Stegge, 1995).

Embarrassment is typically followed by nonverbal and verbal communication designed to redress or ameliorate the embarrassing situation. As Miller (1995) argued: "Embarrassment is thus much more than a private emotional response to an untoward social situation; it can also be a vivid social *communication* that has important, widespread, impact on what happens next" (p. 329).

Like shame, numerous nonverbal messages stem from embarrassment. Miller and Leary (1992) contend that the nonverbal cues that accompany embarrassment are highly recognizable and reliable. Some of these nonverbal behaviors are analogic apologies. Others may be designed to appease onlookers and/or release the tension associated with embarrassment. Such nonverbal displays include reductions in eye contact and interpersonal gaze; mirthless, fake, and silly smiles and laughter; blushing; less fluent speech; head turns and head-down positions; facial blocking or touching; and leave-taking behaviors (Cupach & Metts, 1990, 1994; Edelman, 1990; Keltner, 1995; Miller, 1995; Miller & Leary, 1992).

Recent research has also identified a number of verbal communicative strategies that result from embarrassment. According to Cupach and Metts (1990), over three-quarters of their respondents sought to repair their embarrassment through verbal behavior. These include accounts, excuses, comments about one's feelings, admissions, exclamations, apologies, justifications, topic shifts, and joking/humor (Bradford & Petronio, Chapter 4, this volume; Cupach & Metts, 1990, 1994; Edelman, 1990). This plethora of verbal tactics demonstrates the important role communication plays in helping individuals cope with embarrassment.

Summary

The above review of communicative responses to emotion suggests that people have a propensity to share emotions with others. Even when emotions are not intentionally communicated, they are often revealed through spontaneous, nonverbal manifestations that are difficult to manage. Moreover, contemporary society has created a new role for emotional communication. According to Stearns's (1993) excellent history of emotions in contemporary society, "the importance of managing emotions through talking out rather than active expression has become a dominant

theme" (p. 24). The recognition that disclosure, up to a point, has significant benefit has become a dogma of the social science literature. And these beliefs are not
without foundation. Pennebaker (1989) summarized a series of studies showing that
when people fail to articulate a traumatic event verbally, they fail to process it fully
or deal with it effectively. Clearly, then, communication plays a central role in coping with emotion.

PATTERNS OF MUTUAL INFLUENCE

Our last principle focuses on the interactive nature of emotional communication.
Understanding how one person in a dyad or group experiences and communicates
emotion is not enough. Communication researchers should also examine patterns
of mutual influence—what happens after the initial communication of emotion
and how the partner typically responds to various types of emotional communication. We believe that emotional communication involves a series of moves and
countermoves that can either intensify or deintensify the emotions being experienced. We also suspect that patterns of reciprocity generally govern the exchange
of emotional messages. In the next section of this chapter, we examine some of
these important issues by focusing on interchain events (i.e., events that occur *between* rather than within individuals) and mutual influence patterns related to emotional matching. This literature is consistent with our final principle:

Principle 6: Emotions Generate Other Emotions and Interaction Chains

Interdependence and Interchain Events

Berscheid's (1983) perspective is based on concepts from Kelley et al.'s (1983) interdependence theory and Mandler's (1975) theory of emotion. Berscheid argued
that emotions are a product of arousal change and cognitive-appraisal processes.
However, the events eliciting arousal change, as well as the intensity of felt emotions, are determined by factors such as relational interdependence and higher-
order goals. The degree of interdependence between two people determines the
degree of emotional investment (i.e., potential there to experience emotion within a particular relationship). Interdependent partners exert mutual influence upon
one another's thoughts, feelings, and actions. Thus, they have the power to elicit intense emotion in one another.

    The concept of interdependence has intriguing implications for how emotion-
al experience and expression differ across various types of relationships. For example, both close relational partners and enemies likely have the power to induce
strong emotional reactions in one another. This is because people generally care

what those close to them think, feel, and do. Ironically, people also appear to pay attention to their enemies' thoughts, feelings, and actions. In fact, enemies frequently induce intense negative emotions, such as frustration, anger, and contempt in one another. Thus, maintaining close, positive relationships may involve helping one another to attain goals. Maintaining intense, negative relations may involve continually interrupting another's goals.

The concepts of intra- and interchain events also have important implications for the study of emotional communication. According to the interdependence perspective, *events* comprise any change in a person's thoughts, feelings, or behaviors. Behaviors include both actions and reactions; and both verbal and nonverbal messages. An *interaction* occurs when two people's events occur in a sequence or pattern, as Kelley et al. (1983) explained:

> Events constitute the elements in the dynamics of interaction because they are changes that are causally connected with other changes. The changes in one person are caused by other changes, in that person, in the partner, in the environment, and so on. The changes in one person also cause further changes, in that person, in the partner, in the environment, and so on. (p. 26)

Intrachain events occur in the presence or absence of social interaction. It is the interchain events that are the substance of interpersonal interaction. Intrachain events occur *within* a person, whereas interchain events occur *between* people. Communication plays a central role in interchain events. As Kelley et al. (1983) stated: "Prominent instances of causal interconnections are communication and interpersonal perception . . . [including] both verbal and nonverbal communication" (p. 31).

The following example may help clarify the concepts of intrachain and interchain events, and how they work together. Imagine a young man who is nervous about asking a woman he likes out on a date. He may spot her at a party, ponder how to approach her, and then feel his hands begin to sweat and his mouth turn dry as he gets closer to her (intrachain events). Perhaps they say "hello," they engage in small talk, he asks her out, and she says "yes" (interchain events). This is a simplistic account of the thoughts, emotions, and behaviors that would accompany their interaction. In actuality, both individuals would experience intrachain events in between and during interchain events. Nonetheless, this example illustrates the dynamic nature of interpersonal interaction sequences that involve emotions.

Emotion researchers have spent considerable effort attempting to understand intrachain processes. For example, early research by James (1884) examined how people understand their feelings through the experience of internal (e.g., arousal) and external (e.g., facial expressions) bodily reactions. More research is needed to illuminate how interchain events operate, particularly when it comes to the links between one person's emotional communication and the partner's thoughts, feelings, and behavioral reactions. Most emotion research has focused on how the *individual* experiences and communicates emotion, rather than on how the *dyad* negotiates emotional experience and communication, yet research implicating interchain events is growing. For example, Metha and Clark (1994) reviewed some innovative research that begins to illustrate how interchain events function. They argued that other people's emotions influence our own emotions and behaviors. In particular, they reported research showing that people are unlikely to make requests of angry people (e.g., ask them for favors), more likely to offer help to those who look sad, and more likely to become hostile, anxious, and/or sad in the presence of depressed people (see also Segrin, Chapter 8, this volume). In this case, one person's emotional expression directly influences the behavior of a second person, which constitutes a clear interchain event.

Another type of interchain event, the *mood-similarity effect,* in which the emotional states of two individuals interact, is discussed by Metha and Clark (1994). They reported research by Locke and Horowitz (1990), which shows that dyadic partners who are in similar moods tend to be more satisfied than those in dissimilar moods. The study investigated interaction in dyads that included two people who were depressed, nondepressed, or mixed. People in the mixed dyads discussed increasingly negative topics and perceived one another as more hostile and cold as the interaction unfolded. In contrast, those in similar dyads, regardless of if they were depressed or nondepressed, experienced more satisfaction as the conversation developed. The authors suggest that people in similar dyads may validate one another's feelings, which leads to more liking and empathy. This type of interchain event demonstrates that the emotions of both dyadic partners interact to produce cognitive and behavioral sequences.

Communication and Emotional Matching

Emotional matching, which focuses on one partner matching the emotional state of another, has also been observed frequently. For example, happy individuals seem to promote happiness in their interactional partners, whereas sad individuals' partners seem to become sad (see Segrin, Chapter 8, this volume). Although the exact process or processes that produce emotional matching are not entirely understood, several theoretical perspectives shed light on the mechanisms by which partners communicate and match emotions. One thing is certain: The high degree of emotional matching observed by many scholars is not coincidence.

Several studies have shown that emotional matching not only occurs, but can create a positive emotional atmosphere. In the case of happiness, for example, Oatley and Johnson-Laird (1987) contend that "the social communication of emotions leads each actor to become aware of the other's euphoric feelings, and a euphoric mutual emotion is created. Such emotions act to cement social relations" (p. 46). Mutuality itself is a pleasant, happiness-inducing state. The smooth flow of positive, synchronous, and congruent behaviors has been shown to be a primary source of interpersonal intimacy (P. A. Andersen, 1985). Burgoon et al. (1995) discussed several forms of adaptation relevant to mutuality. *Matching* occurs when two individuals display similar behaviors. *Reciprocity* constitutes a special form of matching that occurs when one person responds to a partner's behavioral change by adopting a similar behavioral change. Giles (1980; Street & Giles, 1982), in his work on communication accommodation theory, discussed *convergence* as a form of behavioral matching that involves two individuals becoming increasingly similar to one another over time. Convergence is most likely to take place when individuals like and feel close to one another. We discuss another form of adaptation, motor mimicry, later in this section.

We contend that adaptation of positive or empathetic behavior, whether it be in the form of matching or reciprocity, is associated with feelings of happiness and comfort. As Oatley and Johnson-Laird (1987) stated: "Mutuality is important for the theory of emotions, partly because achieving social cooperation itself creates an emotion mode (happiness), and partly because failures to achieve it or sustain it have dysphoric emotional consequences" (p. 46).

Mutuality does not occur only in positive emotions, it also occurs in negative ones. Though the reciprocation or matching of some negative emotions are detrimental in many situations (e.g., spirals of hostility during conflict), when the sharing of negative affect leads to understanding and empathy it can be beneficial. According to Baumeister et al. (1995), when relational partners are able to redistribute negative affect so that they feel similar to one another, the sharing of negative affect facilitates communication and improves the relationship. The negative emotion of embarrassment is a case in point. A number of researchers have observed that both embarrassment and its communicative manifestations are frequently shared by interaction partners. Researchers have labeled this process "empathic embarrassment" (see Bradford & Petronio, Chapter 4, this volume; Miller, 1995). It occurs when one feels abashment for another's, as opposed to one's own, untoward behavior (Cupach & Metts, 1994). Observers may even articulate this emotion with statements such as "I feel so embarrassed for him." A similar process, embarrassment by association, occurs when individuals are associated with a person who enacts embarrassing behavior and then assumes that the negative attributions of the person's will be generalized to them (Cupach & Metts, 1990). Goffman (1967) suggested that empathic embarrassment actually may be more emotion-inducing than one's own embarrassment.

Across a number of emotions, including happiness, embarrassment, and sadness, mutuality or matching is a common process. But what explanations are there for emotional matching? The last section of this chapter addresses this question.

Contagion

One of the processes invoked as an explanation is emotional contagion, where people "catch" others' emotions (Hatfield, Cacioppo, & Rapson, 1994). Mob panic, mass euphoria, contagious laughter, group grief, and collective relief are prototypic examples of this phenomenon. Contagion occurs "in the more limited context of dyadic interaction" (Magai & McFadden, 1995, p. 282). Klinnert et al. (1983)

bemoan the lack of research on contagion but suggest that "it is well known, though frequently not emphasized, that the emotional expression of one person can elicit contagious emotional responses in another. This is particularly true for emotions such as sadness, joy, fear, and even anxiety" (p. 58). While contagion is invoked frequently as an explanation for emotional matching, the exact mechanisms underlying this communication process remain unexplained. Certainly communication of one's emotional state to another is a critical step in the process of contagion.

Social Referencing

Another process employed to explain emotional matching is social referencing and social proof. Klinnert et al. (1983) reviewed literature that describes social referencing as a process by which a person seeks information from others to make sense of an event that is beyond a person's own appraisal process. This may include observing various communicative responses to the situation. Kinnert et al. (1983) stated the importance of social referencing as follows: "Because the perceptual information that is sought out in social referencing is very often specifically emotional in nature, social referencing constitutes a prototypic example of how emotional expression can no longer be treated as epiphenomenal" (p. 64). Cialdini (1984) discussed a related phenomenon, social proof, which is a process whereby people determine what to do and how to feel based upon the actions of others. A key to social referencing is the communication of internal affective states by one person and the monitoring of the communication by another person.

Imitation

Individuals of all ages show expressions that match those of their interaction partner due to the process of imitation. "The literature on the proclivity of infants to match the facial and vocal expressions of social partners is now quite substantial" (Magai & McFadden, 1995, p. 282). Imitation is critical to the processes of learning, enculturation, and socialization. Adults also use imitation, especially when they encounter social situations that make them feel uncertainty or discomfort. For example, a newly promoted company executive may be uncertain about how to communicate during a business meeting. She may watch and imitate the company president's behaviors and emotional expressions. This example illustrates that processes of imitation and social referencing may work conjointly to promote matching emotional messages.

Motor Mimicry

One of the proposed mechanisms that produces matched emotional states and expressions is motor mimicry. Though the concept has been around since before the turn of the century, a series of fairly recent studies by Bavelas and her associates suggest that affect sharing is a common and important communication behavior (e.g., Bavelas et al., 1986, 1988). Motor mimicry occurs when observers display communicative behavior that is appropriate to the situation of the person (or persons) they are observing. Examples include wincing while another person is being injured, ducking as another person is about to be hit by a snowball, leaning across the finish line in support of an athlete's effort, or smiling at another person's happiness.

Bavelas and her associates suggest that motor mimicry is more than mere empathy. Rather, it is a powerful form of nonverbal communication by an observer that communicates appropriate affect to the observed person and shows concern or warning about the other's situation. In the vast majority of cases, the observer simultaneously and symmetrically mirrors (not simply imitates) the other's affect. Bavelas and her associates propose a parallel process whereby a stimulus simultaneously elicits a communicative display *and* an intrapersonal process. Since motor mimicry is an overt, symmetrical communicative behavior in response to another person, which only occurs in another's presence, it puts the interactants in similar emotional states. As Magai and McFadden (1995) maintained, "the mimicry of facial expressions of emotion is particularly germane to the issue of the contagion of emotional feelings" (p. 283). If, as Bavelas and her colleagues contend, behaviors instantly communicate parallel emotions between partners, parallel affective states should also occur. This is particularly true in light of the next explanation, the interpersonal facial feedback hypothesis (IFFH).

The Interpersonal Facial Feedback Hypothesis

Introduced by Cappella (1993), the IFFH is based on considerable research which demonstrates that people match or mimic other's facial expressions (e.g., Bavelas et al., 1988; Cappella & Palmer, 1990) and other nonverbal behaviors (see Burgoon et al., 1995). The IFFH is also based on research testing the original facial feedback hypothesis, which shows that there are consistent, albeit small, effects of a person's own facial expression on her/his emotional state (see Buck, 1984; Izard, 1991; Tomkins, 1980). For example, Cappella (1993) reported that when people smile they feel more attraction toward their partners. Similarly, Laird (1974) found that people who posed facial expressions of aggression and pain tended to experience negative affect. Burgoon, Buller, and Woodall (1996) summarized research in this area by concluding that "facial expressions may affect the intensity of the felt emotion or create general emotional feelings such as pleasantness or unpleasantness, but facial expressions may not produce specific emotional experiences such as disgust, anger, and contempt" (p. 275).

Based on the above research, Cappella proposed the IFFH, which states that people match one another's facial expressions, which in turn influences their moods and ultimately results in matched emotions. Thus, the IFFH extends the original facial feedback hypothesis by positing that the partner's facial expression (rather than a person's own facial expression), influences how one experiences emotion. "There is substantial research supporting the thesis that the unconscious mimicry of facial expression of emotion leads to congruent emotional experience" (Magai & McFadden, 1995, p. 283). McHugo, Lanzetta, Sullivan, Masters, and Englis (1985) provided an interesting example of this: They demonstrate that regardless of one's prior attitude toward a political candidate, viewers mimic a candidate's facial expressions, which in turn influences their general emotional states.

Congruent Interpretations

A final explanation that is somewhat different from the others focuses on interpretive processes. Metha and Clark (1994) reported studies showing that people often judge their partner's emotional states to be similar in intensity and/or valence to their own. Clark, Milberg, and Erber's (1984) study is an especially interesting example of this interpretation bias. In this study, one group of subjects exercised immediately before viewing a target person. Another group viewed the target person without exercising. The exercisers associated the target's positive verbal and nonverbal communication with more intense emotions than did the nonexercisers (e.g., joy versus contentment). Metha and Clark (1994) suggested that the implications of results such as these are that "if we are happy, we see others as happy and look forward to interacting with them. However, if we are sad or angry, we may judge the other's mood to be like ours and may decide to refrain from an interaction with the other" (p. 92).

Self-congruent interpretations of another's emotional state may set up self-fulfilling expectancies. For example, if Claire is angry and frustrated because she had a hard day at work, she may interpret her roommate's neutral emotional display as an expression of negative affect similar to her own. Claire is then likely to treat her roommate differently than if she had interpreted her expression positively. Claire may avoid interacting with the roommate or, perhaps, she may start complaining about her job with the expectation that the roommate will reciprocate with similarly negative disclosure. In either case, Claire's communicative behavior could generate negative emotion in the roommate, thus fulfilling Claire's expectancy regarding their congruent emotional states.

Summary

The above literature shows that emotions and emotional messages are often situated within dynamic sequences of interpersonal interaction. People bring their emotional states into interactions with others, and these emotions may affect how they behave toward others. Metha and Clark (1994) presented evidence showing that people in good moods are generally warm and affiliative toward others, whereas those in bad moods are generally hostile or withdrawn around others. People's emotions can also be modified or changed through social interaction with others. Someone can be "cheered up" or "made angry" during the course of an interaction. Most importantly, the emotions that two people bring with them at the outset of an interaction, along with the emotions that they feel during the interaction, produce dynamic patterns of emotional communication.

CONCLUSION

In this chapter, we have presented six principles relevant to emotional communication. Each of these principles suggests that communication is necessary to the process of emotional experience: Emotions evolved as communicative actions, emotional expression is shaped through socialization processes, the primary elicitor of most emotion is interpersonal communication, schemata affect how and when emotions are communicated, an inherent feature of emotional experience is emotional expression, and emotion generates other emotions and interaction chains. Over the past century emotion has been treated primarily as a physiological or subjective experience. However, contemporary social scientists have become increasingly interested in how people communicate their own emotions and respond to the emotional displays of others. Indeed, Hatfield et al. (1994) suggested that emotions are social viruses easily spread to others in one's social environment.

This new view of emotions as inherently communicative and processual is not trivial. Research and theory on marriages, families, organizations, and even countries can be radically transformed by understanding the process of emotional communication. Hatfield et al. (1994) suggested that understanding emotional contagion and communication is useful for psychotherapists and their clients, doctors and their patients, lawyers and their adversaries, teachers and their students, husbands and their wives, and parents and their children. The future well-being of our society, and indeed the human race, may depend, at least partially, on a better understanding of communication and emotion.

ACKNOWLEDGMENTS

We are grateful to Dan Canary and Brian Spitzberg for serving as reviewers for this chapter. Their suggestions greatly improved our work.

REFERENCES

Ainsworth, M. D. S., Blehar, M. C., Waters, E., & Wall, S. (1978). *Patterns of attachment: A psychological study of the strange situation.* Hillsdale, NJ: Erlbaum.

Andersen, J. F., Andersen, P. A., & Landgraf, J. (1985, May). *The development of nonverbal communication competence in childhood.* Paper presented at the annual convention of the International Communication Association, Honolulu, HI.

Andersen, P. A. (1985). Nonverbal immediacy in interpersonal communication. In A. W. Siegman & S. Feldstein (Eds.), *Multichannel integrations of nonverbal behavior* (pp. 1–36). Hillsdale, NJ: Erlbaum.

Andersen, P. A., Andersen, J. F., & Mayton, S. M. (1985). The development of nonverbal communication in the classroom: Teacher's perceptions of students in grades K–12. *Communication Education, 34,* 292–307.

Aron, A., & Aron, E. (1991). Love and sexuality. In K. McKinney & S. Sprecher (Eds.), *Sexuality in close relationships* (pp. 25–48). Hillsdale, NJ: Erlbaum.

Aune, K. S., Buller, D. B., & Aune, R. K. (1996). Display rule development in romantic relationships: Emotion management and perceived appropriateness of emotions across relationship stages. *Human Communication Research, 23,* 115–143.

Averill, J. R. (1980). A constructivist view of emotion. In R. Plutchik & H. Kellerman (Eds.), *Emotion: Theory, research, and experience, Vol. 1. Theories of emotion* (pp. 305–339). New York: Academic Press.

Babad, E. Y., & Wallbott, H. G. (1986). The effects of social factors on emotional relations. In K. R. Scherer, H. G. Wallbott, & A. B. Summerfield (Eds.), *Experiencing emotion: A cross-cultural study* (pp. 154–172). New York: Cambridge University Press.

Barrett, K. C. (1995). A functionalist approach to shame and guilt. In J. P. Tangney & K. W. Fischer (Eds.), *Self-conscious emotions: The psychology of shame, guilt, embarrassment, and pride* (pp. 25–63). New York: Guilford.

Bartholomew, K. (1990). Avoidance of intimacy: An attachment perspective. *Journal of Social and Personal Relationships, 7,* 147–178.

Bartholomew, K. (1993). From childhood to adult relationships: Attachment theory and research. In S. Duck (Ed.), *Learning about relationships* (pp. 30–62). Newbury Park, CA: Sage.

Bartholomew, K., & Horowitz, L. M. (1991). Attachment styles among young adults: A test of a four-category model. *Journal of Personality and social Psychology, 61,* 226–244.

Batgos, J., & Leadbeater, B. J. (1994). Parental attachment, peer relations, and dysphoria in adolescence. In M. B. Sperling and W. H. Berman (Eds.), *Attachment in adults: Clinical and developmental perspectives* (pp. 155–178). New York: Guilford.

Baumeister, R. F., Stillwell, A. M., & Heatherton, T. F. (1995). Interpersonal aspects of guilt: Evidence from narrative studies. In J. P., Tangney & K. W. Fischer (Eds.), *Self-conscious emotions: The psychology of shame, guilt, embarrassment, and pride* (pp. 255–273). New York: Guilford.

Baumeister, R. F., Stillwell, A. M., & Heatherton, T. F. (1994). Guilt: An interpersonal approach. *Psychological Bulletin, 115,* 243–267.

Baumeister, R. F., & Wotman, S. (1992). *Breaking hearts: The two sides of unrequited love.* New York: Guilford.

Baumeister, R. F., Wotman, S. R., & Stilwell, M. A. (1993). Unrequited love: On heartbreak, anger, guilt, scriptlessnesss, and humiliation. *Journal of Personality and Social Psychology, 64,* 377–394.

Bavelas, J. B., Black, A., Chovil, N., Lemery, C. R., & Mullett, J. (1988). Form and function in motor mimicry: Topographic evidence that the primary function is communicative. *Human Communication Research, 14,* 275–299.

Bavelas, J. B., Black, A., Lemery, C. R., & Mullett, J. (1986). "I *show* how you feel": Motor mimicry as a communicative act. *Journal of Personality and Social Psychology, 50,* 322–329.

Bell, R. A., & Healy, J. G. (1992). Idiomatic communication and interpersonal solidarity in friends' relational cultures. *Human Communication Research, 18,* 307–335.

Berscheid, E. (1983). Emotion. In H. H. Kelly, E. Berscheid, A. Christensen, J. H. Harvey, T. L. Huston, G. Levinger, E. McClintock, L. A. Peplau, & D. R. Peterson (Eds.), *Close relationships* (pp. 110–168). San Francisco, CA: Freeman.

Bloch, S., Orthous, P., & Santibanez, H. G. (1987). Effector patterns of basic emotions: A psychophysiological method for training actors. *Journal of Social and Biological Structures, 10,* 1–19.

Bowlby, J. (1969). *Attachment and loss: Vol. 1. Attachment.* New York: Basic Books.

Bowlby, J. (1973). *Attachment and loss: Vol. 2. Separation: Anxiety and anger.* New York: Basic Books.

Bowlby, J. (1979). *The making and breaking of affectional bonds.* London: Tavistock.

Bradbury, T. N., & Fincham, F. D. (1987). Affect and cognition in close relationships: Toward an integrative model. *Cognition and Emotion, 1,* 59–87.

Branigan, C., & Humphries, D. (1969, May 22). I see what you mean . . . *New Scientist, 42,* 406–408.

Brody, L. R., & Hall, J. A. (1993). Gender and emotion. In M. Lewis & J. M. Haviland (Eds.), *Handbook of emotions* (pp. 447–460). New York: Guilford.

Buck, R. (1979). Individual differences in nonverbal sending accuracy and electrodermal responding: The externalizing-internalizing dimension. In R. Rosenthal (Ed.), *Skill in nonverbal communication: Individual differences* (pp. 139–170). Cambridge, MA: Oelgechlager, Gunn, & Hain.

Buck, R. (1984). *The communication of emotion.* New York: Guilford.

Buck, R. (1985). Prime theory: An integrated view of motivation and emotion. *Psychological Review, 92,* 389–413.

Buck, R. (1991). Social factors in facial display and communication: A reply to Chovil and others. *Journal of Nonverbal Behavior, 15,* 155–162.

Buck, R. (1995). [Review of Human facial expression: An Evolutionary view]. *Communication Theory, 5,* 393–396.

Burgoon, J. K. (1983). Nonverbal violations of expectations. In J. M. Wiemann & R. P. Harrison (Eds.), *Nonverbal interaction* (pp. 77–111). Beverly Hills, CA: Sage.

Burgoon, J. K. (1993). Interpersonal expectations, expectancy violations, and emotional communication. *Journal of Language and Social Psychology, 12,* 30–48.

Burgoon, J. K., Buller, D. B., & Woodall, W. G. (1996). *Nonverbal communication: The unspoken dialogue.* New York: McGraw-Hill.

Burgoon, J. K., & Hale, J. L. (1988). Nonverbal expectancy violations: Model elaboration and application to immediacy behaviors. *Communication Monographs, 55,* 58–79.

Burgoon, J. K., Stern, L. A., & Dillman, L. (1995). *Interpersonal adaptation: Dyadic interaction patterns.* New York: Cambridge University Press.

Buss, D. M. (1988). The evolution of human intrasexual competition: Tactics of mate attraction. *Journal of Personality and Social Psychology, 54,* 616–628.

Buss, D. M. (1989). Conflict between the sexes: Strategic interference and the evocation of anger and upset. *Journal of Personality and Social Psychology, 56,* 735–747.

Camras, L. A. (1985). Socialization of affect communication. In M. Lewis & C. Saarni (Eds.), *The socialization of emotions* (pp. 141–160). New York: Plenum Press.

Cappella, J. N. (1993). The facial feedback hypothesis in human interaction: Review and speculation. *Journal of Language and Social Psychology, 12,* 13–29.

Cappella, J. N., & Palmer, M. T. (1990). Attitude similarity, relational history, and attraction: The mediating effects of kinesic and vocal behaviors. *Communication Monographs, 57,* 161–183.

Cheek, J. M., & Buss, C. M. (1981). The influence of shyness on loneliness in a new situation. *Personality and Social Psychology Bulletin, 7,* 572–577.

Chovil, N. (1991). Social determinants of facial displays. *Journal of Nonverbal Behavior, 15,* 141–153.

Cialdini, R. B. (1984). *Influence: How and why people agree to things.* New York: Quill.

Clark, M. S., Milberg, S., & Erber, R. (1984). Effects of arousal on judgments of others' emotions. *Journal of Personality and Social Psychology, 46,* 551–560.

Collins, N. L., & Read, S. J. (1994). Cognitive representations of attachment: the structure and function of working models. In K. Bartholomew & D. Perlman (Eds.), *Advances in personal relationships: Vol. 5. Attachment processes in adulthood* (pp. 53–90). Bristol, PA: Kingsley.

Condry, J., & Condry, S. (1976). Sex differences: A study of the beholder. *Child development, 47,* 812–819.

Cupach, W. R., & Metts, S. (1990). Remedial processes in embarrassing predicaments. In J. A. Anderson (Ed.), *Communication Yearbook,* (vol. 13, pp. 323–352). Beverly Hills, CA: Sage.

Cupach, W. R., & Metts, S. (1994). *Facework.* Thousand Oaks, CA: Sage.

DePaulo, B. M. (1992). Nonverbal behavior and self-presentation. *Psychological Bulletin, 111,* 203–243.

DeRivera, J. (1984). The structure of emotional relationships. In P. Shaver (Ed.), *Review of personality and social psychology: Vol. 5. Emotions, relationships, and health* (pp. 116–145). Beverly Hills, CA: Sage.

Diener, E., Sandvik, E., & Pavot, W. (1991). Happiness is the frequency, not the intensity, of positive versus negative affect. In F. Strack, M. Argyle, & N. Schwarz (Eds.), *Subjective well-being* (pp. 2–20). New York: Pergamon.

Dion, K. K., & Dion, K. L. (1996). Introduction: Toward understanding love. *Personal Relationships, 3,* 1–3.

Edelman, R. J. (1990). Chronic blushing, self-consciousness, and social anxiety. *Journal of Psychopathology and Behavioral Assessment, 12,* 119–127.

Ekman, P. (1978). Facial expression. In A. W. Siegman & S. Feldstein (Eds.), *Nonverbal behavior and communication* (pp. 96–116). Hillsdale, NJ: Erlbaum.

Ekman, P. (1985). *Telling lies.* New York: Norton.

Ekman, P. (1993). Facial expression and emotion. *American Psychologist, 48,* 384–392.

Ekman, P. & Friesen, W. V. (1975). *Unmasking the face: A guide to recognizing emotions from facial clues.* Englewood Cliffs, NJ: Prentice-Hall.

Ekman, P. Friesen, W. V., Ellsworth, P. (1972). *Emotion in the human face: Guidelines for research and an integration of findings.* New York: Pergamon Press.

Feeney, J. A. (1995). Adult attachment and emotional control. *Personal Relationships, 2,* 143–159.

Ferguson, T. J., & Stegge, H. (1995). Emotional states and traits in children: The case of guilt and shame. In J. P. Tangney & K. W. Fischer (Eds.), *Self-conscious emotions: The psychology of shame, guilt, embarrassment, and pride* (pp. 174–197). New York: Guilford.

Fischer, K. W., & Tangney, J. P. (1995). Self-conscious emotions and the affect revolution: Framework and overview. In J. P. Tangney & K. W. Fischer (Eds.), *Self-conscious emotions: The psychology of shame, guilt, embarrassment, and pride* (pp. 1–24). New York: Guilford.

Fitness, J., & Fletcher, G. J. O. (1993). Love, hate, anger, and jealousy in close relationships: A prototype and cognitive appraisal analysis. *Journal of Personality and social Psychology, 65,* 942–958.

Forgas, J. P. (1994). Sad and guilty? Affective influences on the explanation of conflict in close relationships. *Journal of Personality and Social Psychology, 66,* 56–68.

Fuchs, D., & Thelen, M. (1988). Children's expected interpersonal consequences of communicating their affective state and reported likelihood of expression. *Child Development, 59,* 1314–1322.

Giles, H. (1980). Accommodation theory: Some new directions. In S. De Silva (Ed.), *Aspects of linguistic behavior* (pp. 105–136). York: University of York Press.

Goffman, E. (1967). *Interaction ritual: Essays on face-to-face behavior.* Garden City, NY: Anchor Books Doubleday & Company.

Greenwood, J. D. (1994). *Realism, identity, and emotion: Reclaiming social psychology.* Thousand Oaks, CA: Sage.

Guerrero, L. K. (1994). "I'm so mad I could scream:" The effects of anger expression on relational satisfaction and communication competence. *The Southern Communiation Journal, 59,* 125–141.

Guerrero, L. K. (1996a, November). *Attachment-style differences in communication skills and the expression of anger and sadness.* Paper presented at the annual meeting of the speech Communication Association, San Diego, CA.

Guerrero, L. K. (1996b). Attachment-style differences in intimacy and involvement: A test of the four-category model. *Communication Monographs, 63,* 269–293.

Guerrero, L. K. (in press). Attachment-style differences in the experience and expression of jealousy. *Personal Relationships.*

Guerrero, L. K., Andersen, P. A., Jorgensen, P. F., Spitzberg, B. H., & Eloy, S. V. (1995). Coping with the green-eyed monster: Conceptualizing and measuring communicative responses to communicative responses to romantic jealousy. *Western Journal of Communication, 59,* 270–304.

Guerrero, L. K., & Reiter, R. L. (in press). Expressing emotion: Sex differences in social skills and communicative responses to anger, sadness, and jealousy. In D. J. Canary & K. Dindia (Eds.), *The handbook of sex, gender, and communication: Similarities and differences.* Hillsdale, NJ: Erlbaum.

Hatfield, E. (1984). The dangers of intimacy. In V. J. Derlega (Ed.), *Communication, intimacy, and close relationships* (pp. 207–220). New York: Academic Press.

Hatfield, E., Cacioppo, J. T., & Rapson, R. L. (1994). *Emotional contagion.* New York: Cambridge University Press.

Hatfield, E., Utne, M. K., & Traupmann, J. (1979). Equity theory and intimate relationships. In R. L. Burgess & T. L. Huston (Eds.), *Social exchange in developing relationships* (pp. 99–133). New York: Academic Press.

Hazan, C., & Shaver, P. (1987). Romantic love conceptualized as an attachment process. *Journal of Personality and Social Psychology, 52,* 511–524.

Horowitz, M. J. (1991). Person schemas. In M. J. Horowitz (Ed.), *Personal schemas and maladaptive interpersonal patterns* (pp. 13–31). Chicago: University of Chicago Press.

Hupka, R. B., & Eshett, C. (1988). Cognitive organization of emotion: Differences between labels and descriptors of emotion in jealousy situations. *Perceptual and Motor Skills, 66,* 935–949.

Izard, C. E. (1977). *Human emotions.* New York: Plenum.

Izard, C. E. (1978). Emotions as motivations: An evolutionary-developmental perspective. In R. A. Dienstvier (Ed.), *Nebraska symposium on motivation* (vol. 25, pp. 163–200). Lincoln: University of Nebraska Press.

Izard, C. E. (1991). *The psychology of emotions.* New York: Plenum Press.

Izard, C. E. (1992). Basic emotions, relationship among emotions, and emotion-cognition relations. *Psychological Review, 99,* 561–565.

James, W. (1884). What is an emotion? *Mind, 9,* 188–205.

Jones, R. A. (1977). *Self-fulfilling prophecies: Social, psychological, and physiological effects of expectancies.* Hillsdale, NJ: Erlbaum.

Kelley, H. H., Berscheid, E., Christensen, J. H., Harvey, T. I., Huston, G., Levinger, E., McClintock, L. A., Peplau, L. A., & Peterson, D. R. (1983). *Close relationships.* New York: W. H. Freeman.

Keltner, D. (1995). Signs of appeasement: Evidence for the distinct displays of embarrassment, amusement, and shame. *Journal of Personality and Social Psychology, 68,* 441–454.

Klinnert, M. D., Campos, J. J., Sorce, J. F., Emde, R. N., & Svejda, M. (1983). Emotions as behaviors regulators: Social referencing in infancy. In R. Plutchik & H. Kellerman (Eds.), *Emotion, Theory, Research, and experience: vol. 2. Emotions in early development* (pp. 57–86). New York: Academic Press.

Kraut, R. E., & Johnson, R. E. (1979). Social and emotional messages of smiling: An ethological approach. *Journal of Personality and Social Psychology, 37,* 1539–1553.

Kubler-Ross, E. (1969). *On death and dying.* Toronto: Macmillan.

Kunce, L. J., & Shaver, P. R. (1994). An attachment-theoretical approach to caregiving in romantic relationships. In K. Bartholomew & D. Perlman (Eds.), *Advances in personal relationships: Vol. 5. Attachment processes in adulthood* (pp. 205–237). Bristol, PA: Kingsley.

Laird, J. D. (1974). self-attribution of emotion: The effects of expressive behavior on the quality of emotional experience. *Journal of personality and Social Psychology, 29,* 475–486.

Leary, M. R. (1987). A self-presentation model for the treatment of social anxieties. In J. E. Maddux, C. D. Stoltenberg, & R. Resenvwig (Eds.), *Social processes in clinical and counseling psychology* (pp. 126–138). New York: Springer-Verlag.

Leary, M. R., & Kowalski, R. M. (1995). *Social anxiety.* New York: Gulford.

Leary, M. R., & Meadows, S. (1991). Predictors, elicitors, and concomitants of social blushing. *Journal of Personality and Social Psychology, 60,* 254–262.

Lemerise, E. A., & Dodge, K. A. (1993). The development of anger and hostile interactions. In M. Lewis & J. M. Haviland (Eds.), *Handbook of emotions* (pp. 537–546). New York: Guilford.

Le Poire, B. A. (1991). Orientation and defensive reactions as alternatives to arousal in theories of nonverbal reactions to changes in immediacy. *The Southern Communication Journal, 56,* 138–146.

Levitt, M. J. (1991). Attachment and close relationships: A life span perspective. In J. L. Gerwitz & W. F. Kurtines (Eds.), *Intersections with attachment* (pp. 183–206). Hillsdale, NJ: Erlbaum.

Levitt, M. J., Coffman, S., Guacci-Franco, N., & Loveless, S. C. (1994). Attachment relationships and life transitions: An expectancy model. In M. B. Sperling & W. H. Berman (Eds.), *Attachment in adults: Clinical and development perspectives* (pp. 232–255). New York: Guilford.

Lewis, J. (1989). Mother's love: The construction of an emotion in nineteenth-century America. In A. E. Barnes & P. N. Stearns (Eds.), *Social history and issues in human consciousness: Some interdisciplinary connections* (pp. 209–229). New York: New York University Press.

Lewis, M., & Saarni, C. (1985). Culture and emotions. In M. Lewis & C. Saarni (Eds.), *The socialization of emotions* (pp. 1–17). New York: Plenum Press.

Locke, K. D., & Horowitz, L. M. (1990). Satisfaction in interpersonal interactions as a function of similarity in level of dysphoria. *Journal of Personality and Social Psychology, 58,* 823–831.

Magai, C., & McFadden, S. H. (1995). *The role of emotions in social and personality development: History, theory, and research.* New York: Wiley.

Manning, P., & Ray, G. (1993). Shyness, elf-confidence, and social interaction. *Social Psychology Quarterly, 56,* 178–192.

Mascolo, M. F., & Fischer, K. W. (1995). Developmental transformations in appraisals for pride, shame, and guilt. In J. P. Tangney & K. W. Fischer (Eds.), *Self-conscious emotions: The psychology of shame, guilt, embarrassment, and pride* (pp. 64–113). New York: Guilford.

McCann, C. D., & Lalonde, R. N. (1993). Dysfunctional communication and depression: Social cognitive processes. *American Behavioral Scientist, 36,* 271–287.

McCroskey, J. C. (1982). Oral communication apprehension: a reconceptualization. In M. Burgoon (Ed.), *Communication yearbook 6* (pp. 136–170). Beverly Hills, CA: Sage.

McHugo, G. J., Lanzetta, J. T., Sullivan, D. G., Masters, R. D., & G. Englis (1985). Emotional reactions to a political leader's expressive displays. *Journal of Personality and social Psychology, 49,* 1513–1529.

McIntosh, W. D., & Martin, L. L. (1992). The cybernetics of happiness: The relation of goal attainment, runimation, and affect. In M. S. Clark (Ed.), *Review of personality and social psychology: Vol. 14, Emotion and social behavior* (pp. 222–246). Newbury Park, CA: Sage.

Metha, P., & Clark, M. S. (1994). Toward understanding emotions in intimate relationships. In A. I. Weber & J. H. Harvey (Eds.), *Perspectives on close relationships* (pp. 88–109). Boston, MA: Allyn & Bacon.

Metts, S. (1994). Relational transgressions. In W. R. Cupach & B. H. Spitzberg (Eds.), *The dark side of interpersonal communication* (pp. 217–239). Hillsdale, NJ: Erlbaum.

Miller, R. S. (1995). Embarrassment and social behavior. In J. P. Tangney & K. W. Fischer (Eds.), *Self-conscious emotions: The psychology of shame, guilt, embarrassment, and pride* (pp. 322–339). New York: Guilford.

Miller, R. S., & Leary, M. R. (1992). Social sources and interactive functions of emotion: The case of embarrassment. In M. S. Clark (Ed.), *Review of personality and social psychology* (vol. 14, pp. 202–221). Newbury Park, CA: Sage.

Morris, D. (1971). *Intimate behavior.* New York: Random House.

Nolen-Hoeksema, S. (1987). Sex differences in unipolar depression: Evidence and theory. *Psychological Bulletin, 101,* 259–282.

Noonan, K. M. (1987). Evolution: A primer for psychologists. In C. Crawford, M. Smith, & D. Krebs (Eds.), *Sociobiology and psychology: Ideas, issues, and applications* (pp. 31–60). Hillsdale, NJ: Erlbaum.

O'Hair, H. D., & Cody, M. J. (1994). Deception. In W. R. Cupach & B. H. Spitzberg (Eds.), *The dark side of interpersonal communication* (pp. 181–213). Hillsdale, NJ: Erlbaum.

Oatley, K., & Johnson-Laird, P. N. (1987). Towards a cognitive theory of emotions. *Cognition and Emotion, 1,* 29–50.

Panksepp, J. (1992). A critical role for "affective neuroscience" in resolving what is basic about basic emotions. *Psychological Review, 99,* 554–560.

Pennebaker, J. W. (1989). Confession, inhibition, and disease. In L. Berkowitz (Ed.), *Advances in experimental social psychology* (vol. 22, pp. 211–244). San Diego, CA: Academic Press.

Plutchik, R. (1983). Emotions in early development: a psychoevolutionary approach. In R. Plutchik & H. Kellerman (Eds.), *Emotion: Theory, research, and experience* (vol. 2, pp. 221–257). Orlando, FL: Academic Press.

Rimé, B., Mesquita, B., Philippot, P., & Boca, S. (1991). Beyond the emotional event: Six studies of the social sharing of emotion. *Cognition and Emotion, 5,* 435–465.

Roseman, I. J., Wiest, C., & Swartz, T. S. (1994). Phenomenology, behaviors, and goals differentiate discrete emotions. *Journal of Personality and Social Psychology, 67,* 206–221.

Rosenthal, R., & DePaulo, B. M. (1979). Sex differences in accommodation in nonverbal communication. In R. Rosenthal (Ed.), *Skill in nonverbal communication: Individual differences* (pp. 68–103). Cambridge, MA: Oelgeschlager, Gunn & Hain.

Rubin, Z. (1973). *Liking and loving: An invitation to social psychology.* New York: Holt, Rinehart, & Winston.

Russell, J. A. (1994). Is there universal recognition of emotion from facial expression? A review of the cross-cultural studies. *Psychological Bulletin, 115,* 102–141.

Saarni, C. (1985). Indirect processes in affect socialization. In M. Lewis & C. Saarni (Eds.), *The socialization of emotions* (pp. 187–209). New York: Plenum.

Saarni, C. (1993). Socialization of emotion. In M. Lewis & J. M. Haviland (Eds.), *Handbook of emotions* (pp. 435–446). New York: Guilford.

Scheff, T. J. (1995). Conflict in family systems: The role of shame. In J. P. Tangney & K. W. Fischer (Eds.), *Self-conscious emotions: The psychology of shame, guilt, embarrassment, and pride* (pp. 393–442). New York: Guilford.

Scherer, K. R. & Wallbott, H. G. (1994). Evidence for universality and cultural variation of differential emotion response patterning. *Journal of Personality and Social Psychology, 66,* 310–328.

Schwartz, J. C., & Shaver, P. (1987). Emotions and emotion knowledge in interpersonal relationships. In W. Jones & D. Perlman (Eds.), *Advances in personal relationships* (Vol. 1, pp. 197–241). Greenwich, CT: JAI.

Segrin, C., & Abramson, L. Y. (1994). Negative reactions to depressive behaviors: A communication theories analysis. *Journal of Abnormal Psychology, 103,* 655–668.

Sharpsteen, D. J., & Kirkpatrick, L. A. (1995, June). *Romantic jealousy as an attachment process: Individual differences in jealousy experiences.* Paper presented at the annual meeting of the International Network on Personal Relationships, Williamsburg, VA.

Shaver, P. R., Morgan, H. J., & Wu, S. (1996). Is love a "basic" emotion? *Personal Relationships, 3,* 81–96.

Shaver, P., Schwartz, J., Kirson, D., & O'Connor, C. (1987). Emotion knowledge: Further explorations of a prototype approach. *Journal of Personality and Social Psychology, 52,* 1061–1086.

Shennum, W. A., & Bugental, D. B. (1982). The development of control over affective expression in nonverbal behavior. In R. S. Feldman (Ed.), *Development of nonverbal behavior in children* (pp. 101–112). New York: Springer-Verlag.

Siegman, A. W. (1985). Expressive correlates of affective states and traits. In A. W. Siegman & S. Feldstein (Eds.), *Multichannel integrations of nonverbal behavior* (pp. 37–68). Hillsdale, NJ: Erlbaum.

Simpson, J. A., & Rholes, W. S. (1994). Stress and secure base relationships in adulthood. In K. Bartholomew & D. Perlman (Eds.), *Advances in personal relationships: Vol. 5, Attachment processes in adulthood* (pp. 181–204). Bristol, PA: Kingsley.

Simpson, J. A., Rholes, W. S., & Nelligan, J. S. (1992). Support-seeking and support-giving within couples in an anxiety-provoking situation: The role of attachment styles. *Journal of Personality and Social Psychology, 62,* 434–446.

Sommers, S. (1984). Reported emotions and conventions of emotionality among college students. *Journal of Personality and Social Psychology, 74,* 385–393.

Stearns, P. N. (1993). History of emotions: The issue of change. In M. Lewis & J. M. Haviland (Eds.), *Handbook of emotions* (pp. 17–28). New York: Guilford.

Stearns, P. N. (1989). *Jealousy: The evolution of an emotion in American history.* New York: New York University Press.

Street, R. L., Jr., & Giles, H. (1982). Speech accommodation theory: A social cognitive approach to language and speech behavior. In M. Roloff & C. Berger (Eds.), *Social cognition and communication* (pp. 193–226). Beverly Hills, CA: Sage.

Tangney, J. P. (1990). Assessing individual differences in proneness to shame and guilt: Development of the self-conscious affect and attribution inventory. *Journal of Personality and Social Psychology, 59,* 102–111.

Tangney, J. P. (1992). Situational determinants of shame and guilt in young adulthood. *Personality and Social Psychology Bulletin, 18,* 199–206.

Tangney, J. P. (1995). Shame and guilt in interpersonal relationships. In J. P. Tangney & K. W. Fischer (Eds.), *Self-conscious emotions: The psychology of shame, guilt, embarrassment, and pride* (pp. 114–139). New York: Guilford.

Thonssen, L., & Baird, A. C. (1948). *Speech criticism: The development of standards for rhetorical appraisal.* New York: Ronald Press Company.

Tomkins, S. S. (1980). Affect as amplification: Some modifications in theory. In R. Plutchik & H. Kellerman (Eds.), *Emotion: Theory, Research, and experience: Vol. 1.* (pp. 141–164). Orlando, FL: Academic Press.

Van Hoofe, J. A. R. A. M. (1972). A comparative approach to the phylogeny of laughter and smiling. In R. A. Hinde (Ed.), *Non-verbal communication* (pp. 209–238). Cambridge, UK: Cambridge University Press.

Vangelisti, A. L., Daly, J. A., & Rudnick, J. R. (1991). Making people feel guilty in conversations: Techniques and correlates. *Human Communication Research, 18,* 3–39.

Weiner, B. (1985). An attributional theory of achievement motivation and emotion. *Psychological Review, 92,* 548–573.

White, G. L., & Mullen, P. E. (1989). *Jealousy: Theory, research, and clinical strategies.* New York: Guilford.

White, G. M. (1993). Emotions inside out: The anthropology of affect. In M. Lewis & J. M. Haviland (Eds.), *Handbook of emotions* (pp. 29–39). New York: Guilford.

Wilson, T. D., & Klaaren, K. J. (1992). "Expectation whirls me round:" The role of affective expectations in affective experience. In M. S. Clark (Ed.), *Review of personality and social psychology: Vol. 14. Emotion and social behavior* (pp. 1–31). Newbury Park, CA: Sage.

PART II

The "Dark Side" of Emotions

Strategic Embarrassment: The Culprit of Emotion

Lisa Bradford
University of Wisconsin—Milwaukee
Milwaukee, Wisconsin

Sandra Petronio
Arizona State University
Tempe, Arizona

"In the wreckage left by embarrassment lie the broken foundations of social transactions. By examining such ruins, the investigator can reconstruct the architecture they represent" (Gross & Stone, 1964, p. 2). Among emotions, embarrassment may be considered one of the least desirable experiences. Spilling soup in a restaurant and inadvertently dragging toilet paper out of the rest room conjures up pictures of extreme emotional discomfort. Consequently, people make great efforts during social interaction to prevent themselves from becoming unintentionally embarrassed, sometimes entirely avoiding particular interactions altogether (Miller, 1995). Although embarrassment is an unpleasant emotional state, when it comes to someone else, people sometimes intentionally and strategically create embarrassing predicaments for others (Bradford, 1993; Petronio & Snider, 1990; Petronio, Snider, & Bradford, 1992; Petronio, 1992; Sharkey, 1990, 1991, 1993; Sharkey & Waldron, 1990; Snider, 1992). This paradoxical event takes a certain degree of planning to accomplish the desired level of emotional discomfort in others. Interestingly, strategic embarrassment is one circumstance where initiating an unpleasant emotional state is often viewed as acceptable or even expected in social interactions. Though people avoid embarrassment for themselves, they seem fully capable and actively engaged in creating embarrassment for others.

Handbook of Communication and Emotion: Research, Theory, Applications, and Contexts

The dynamics of strategic embarrassment seem to accentuate the emotional and social outcomes found in cases of unintentional embarrassment. Because there are some obvious linkages between unintentional and strategic embarrassment regarding emotions, this chapter briefly overviews the nature of unintentional embarrassment (for in-depth reviews see Cupach & Metts, 1990; Edelmann, 1987) then focuses principally on discussing strategic embarrassment as a culprit of emotion.

THE NATURE OF UNINTENTIONAL EMBARRASSMENT

Few people can escape the emotions of embarrassment. Embarrassment is experienced by people in all cultures[1] (Edelmann & Hampson, 1981; Lewis, 1995) and age groups,[2] with particular frequency during adolescence (Bradford, 1993; Gross & Stone, 1964; Harre, 1990). In the psychological literature, embarrassment is typically defined as "a form of social anxiety" (Edelmann, 1987, p. 1). The emotions of embarrassment, according to Sattler (1965) occur in interactions when three factors are present, these include: "(1) the presence of another person, or at least the thought of another person; (2) the person becoming aware that he[she] is the center of attention; and (3) the person feeling that he[she] is being judged" (p. 14). The emotional dimension of embarrassment is linked to social judgment. Even when embarrassment is elicited by more neutral stimuli (i.e., excessive attention) or positive stimuli (i.e., awards or compliments), the emotional component is evident if these situations lead to feelings of self-consciousness and a realization that others are making judgments (Miller & Leary, 1992). Sometimes emotional discomfort results because a "perceived discrepancy occurs between one's current self-presentation and one's standard for self-presentation" (Edelmann, 1987, p. 6). Other times "embarrassment reflects a failure in one's self presentation to others" (Modigliani, 1970, p. 16) or at least feelings of failure. Because embarrassment produces disquieting repercussions for individuals, many studies have focused on outcomes of or *reactions* to *unintentional* embarrassment.

Largely, studies in the fields of communication, sociology, and psychology have identified the manifestations of embarrassment (e.g., Cupach & Metts, 1990; Edelmann, 1987; Fink & Walker, 1975; Sharkey & Stafford, 1990; Singleis & Sharkey, 1995). In addition, strategies used to repair the recipients' self-presentation or *face* have been emphasized in a growing body of literature (e.g., Cupach, Metts, & Hazelton, 1986; Goffman, 1971; Miller, 1986; Petronio, 1984, 1990; Sharkey & Stafford, 1989).

---

[1]Although embarrassment has been accepted as a cultural universal, the cross-cultural research of Imahori and Cupach (1991) on embarrassment for Japanese and Americans suggests that cultures may differ in the types of events that trigger embarrassment.

[2]The potential for experiencing embarrassment may exist at least by age 5 when there is evidence of the social self (Buss, Iscoe, & Buss, 1979).

Recipient Reactions

When embarrassment occurs, recipients experience a variety of physical, emotional, communicative, and psychological reactions. Edelmann's (1987) research indicated that physiologically embarrassment is "characterized by blushing, rising in temperature, increased heart rate, muscle tension, grinning, smiling, or laughing, avoidance of eye contact and self-touching" (p. 68). These physiological outcomes are frequently referred to as objective symptoms. Gross and Stone (1964) suggested that they act as signals to the participants that something has gone awry in the interaction. Edelmann (1987) offered a model that incorporates Leventhal's (1979, 1980) perceptual-motor theory of emotion as a way to explain all of these physiological components of embarrassment. Briefly, Edelmann maintained that individuals are motivated to conduct self-appraisals when they experience an external event like a faux pas or an internal event like a personal shortcoming. These appraisals have an emotional outcome that is determined by elements of the environment and individual characteristics. The appraisal is affected by the salience of the event, individual differences in self-attention, and environmental factors affecting self-focus. If the appraisal results in feelings of embarrassment, Edelmann suggested that the emotional response may be behavioral, visceral, and subjective, or some combination. When embarrassment is the outcome, a coping response is launched.

Defining embarrassment as an emotional response infers a "complex sequence of reactions to a stimuli and includes cognitive evaluations, subjective changes, autonomic and neural arousal, impulses to action, and behaviour designed to have an effect upon the stimulus that initiated the complex sequence" (Plutchic, 1984, p. 217). Edelmann's model captured the complexity of the experience. Investigations of embarrassment reinforce the multidimensional nature of the phenomenon. For example, researchers have discovered that the intensity of embarrassment varies according to cultural norms, the situation, and the personality of the individual. Although the experience of embarrassment is universal, Edelmann et al. (1989) found that embarrassing encounters elicit different feelings of intensity and duration in people from the United Kingdom, Italy, Germany, Greece, and Spain.

The personality of recipients may also affect the likelihood and degree to which they become embarrassed. Modigliani (1968) offered the notion of embarrassibility as a way to understand individuals'

> susceptibility to embarrassment. Clearly there are substantial individual differences in embarrassibility. Some persons appear to be quite embarrassible, experiencing great discomfort in seemingly innocuous situations, while others appear to be relatively unembarrassible and capable of passing through the most awkward incidents with little discomfort. (p. 316)

Edelmann (1987) identified several personality characteristics influencing individual responses to embarrassment including, the need for social approval, fear of negative evaluation, self-consciousness, extroversion, empathy, and self-monitoring.

Contextual elements of the situation, including events eliciting embarrassment, may additionally affect the intensity of the recipient's experienced embarrassment. Some researchers suggest that the number of observers present when embarrassment occurs (Fink & Walker, 1975; Sharkey & Stafford, 1989) and their relative status determine how intensely people feel embarrassment (Edelmann, 1987). Thus, individuals embarrassed in front of many observers experience more intense embarrassment as do individuals embarrassed in front of higher status observers. Sharkey and Stafford (1989) also noted that there is a relationship between the type of event precipitating embarrassment and the degree of embarrassment experienced. They point out that most adults report violations of privacy as a source of intensely felt embarrassment. Moreover, researchers recognize that embarrassment outcomes are not limited solely to the recipient, but affect the nature of interaction, the interactants, as well as the observers.

Outcomes for Interaction and Observers

Although Edelmann's model emphasized the individual, a key factor in embarrassment is the audience, real or imagined. Thus, the context of communicative interaction and the publicness of the actions reflect the framework for this emotional response. Because embarrassment often impedes social interaction, it may be viewed as an obstacle or barrier temporarily affecting the exchange (Edelmann & Hampson, 1981; Martin, 1987). In fact, Apsler (1975) observed that etymologically, the French root from which embarrassment is derived, means obstacle. Embarrassment is disruptive, in part, because individuals wish to manage impressions or the social identity they project to others—the audience (Goffman, 1956). When this management is disturbed, the flow of communicative interaction is compromised.

Communicative interaction may be hindered further because embarrassment becomes infectious (Gross & Stone, 1964). People who observe embarrassment may be affected, and in some cases, experience embarrassment themselves. Miller (1986) called this "empathic embarrassment." He points out that,

> whenever a person suffers the flustered discomfort of embarrassment, observers may recognize and empathically share that embarrassment even though the person's actions do not reflect on the observer and the observer's social identity is not threatened. Moreover, observers may become empathically embarrassed if they are able to imagine themselves in another person's social predicament whether or not the person displays obvious embarrassment. (p. 1062)

The potential negative effects of embarrassment on the interaction and for those present lead Gross and Stone (1964) to label embarrassment as a "destructive dis-ease" (p. 2). The sense of "dis-ease" experienced by those involved in the embarrassment contributes to difficulties in their communicative interaction. The dis-ease of unintentional embarrassment may be somewhat different from that found with intentional acts aimed at embarrassing others. The dis-ease of strategic embarrassment is often compounded by the eventual knowledge that another person purposefully prompted the events leading to feelings of discomfort.

STRATEGIC EMBARRASSMENT

With a few exceptions (Gross & Stone, 1964; Martin, 1987; Petronio et al., 1989),[3] the examination of strategic embarrassment is relatively recent, yet promising (e.g., Bradford, 1993; Petronio, 1990, Petronio & Snider, 1990; Petronio et al., 1992; Sharkey, 1990, 1991, 1992, 1993; Sharkey & Waldron, 1990; Snider, 1992). This concept enjoys two labels in the literature, intentional embarrassment (Sharkey, 1990, 1991, 1992, 1993; Sharkey & Waldron, 1990) and strategic embarrassment (Bradford, 1993; Petronio, 1990; Petronio & Snider, 1990; Petronio et al., 1992; Snider, 1992) with little substantive difference in definition. In this chapter, we refer to the concept as strategic embarrassment. Strategic embarrassment may be defined as the deliberate (Gross & Stone, 1964) or intentional (Martin, 1987; Sharkey, 1990; Sharkey & Waldron, 1990) use of planned communication tactics (Petronio & Snider, 1990; Petronio et al., 1992) and strategies (Sharkey & Waldron, 1990) as a means of triggering embarrassment in another person.

Research on strategic embarrassment suggests that people instigate discomfort to achieve certain interactional goals (Sharkey & Waldron, 1990). As such, embarrassment may be used as a masterful vehicle for accomplishing communicative objectives (Petronio & Snider, 1990; Sharkey, 1990, 1991; Sharkey & Stafford, 1990; Sharkey & Waldron, 1990). For example, Petronio et al. (1988) reported that people may embarrass relational partners to highlight behaviors they dislike. Strategic embarrassment may also be employed to discredit an associate or rival. For example, if an employee feels an associate is taking undue credit for a report on which they both worked, strategic embarrassment might function to discredit the associate (Sharkey, 1990). During a presentation of the report, the employee may make the associate look unpoised by asking that person a question he or she could not answer.

Unlike the above example, sometimes strategic embarrassment is intended to achieve more positive goals. For instance, the following illustrates one of the most common uses of strategic embarrassment among adolescents (Bradford, 1993). James knows his friend Abe is very interested in Debra. He also knows that Abe is too shy to introduce himself to her. In order to help Abe meet Debra, James strategically embarrasses Abe by bumping him into Debra as they pass in the school hall-

---

[3]Petronio et al. (1988) discussed the effect of embarrassment on relationships of people who intentionally embarrassed their partners. Martin (1987) also reported cases in which students relate their concerns about being intentionally embarrassed by teachers. Gross and Stone (1964) are among the earliest researchers to mention the intentional use embarrassment, and suggest that embarrassment is used by parents and others in order to sanction negative behaviors as part of the socialization process.

way. In this situation, Abe experiences embarrassment, yet recognizes that James is motivated by a positive desire to help his friend. These examples illustrate that strategic embarrassment may be enacted to achieve both positive and negative goals (Sharkey, 1990, 1991, 1993; Sharkey & Waldron, 1990). They also speak to the way that people plan strategic embarrassment (Bradford, 1993; Petronio & Snider, 1990; Petronio et al., 1992; Snider, 1992), in addition to depicting the behavioral and emotional outcomes for both the target and initiator (Bradford, 1993; Petronio et al., 1992; Sharkey, 1990; Sharkey & Waldron, 1990; Snider, 1992).

Given the complexity of embarrassment in general, and strategic embarrassment in particular, a theoretical model is useful to capture the dynamic nature of this phenomenon. Petronio and Snider (1990) proposed applying Berger's Planning Theory (1995)[4] as a beneficial way to understand strategic embarrassment. This application answers criticisms of earlier embarrassment studies that lacked theoretical foundation (Petronio, 1990). Berger's (1995) Planning Theory serves as an effective model in a number of important ways. First, applying this model helps illustrate the emergent and processual nature of embarrassment, a prerequisite established by earlier researchers (Cupach & Metts, 1990; Edelmann, 1987). Second, it helps balance attention to include the initiator of strategic embarrassment rather than predominately focusing on the recipient. Third, Berger's theory extends previous perspectives by showing the importance of studying the process of embarrassment plans, the way they are constructed, and the selection criteria used in choosing strategies for the plan. Fourth, this application underscores the influence of participants' emotional and behavioral reactions to the outcome of embarrassment and subsequent effects on the planning process.

Berger's Planning Theory

Briefly, Berger (1995) maintained that strategic communicative behavior may be better understood when approached from a plan-based perspective (Berger & Bell, 1988; Berger & Jordan, 1989, 1992; Dillard, 1990). When communicators wish to achieve interactional goals, these goals play a role in the selection of behavioral strategies where "the content of communication is the result of choice" (Pavitt, 1991, p. 205). Berger (1995) noted that plans may be motivated by multiple interaction goals. These goals represent "desired end states toward which people strive" (p. 143). Three types of goals are discussed by Berger (1995) including meta-goals, explicit, and implicit goals. Berger theorizes that effective planning occurs when people choose the strategies that represent the best approach for obtaining their goals, as described in the following four-step process: "Planning is a process in which persons (a) devise action sequences, (b) anticipate the outcomes of action sequences,

---

[4]Berger's Planning Theory has been described in his research since 1987. Most recently, a full description of the model has been published (see Berger, 1995).

(c) adjust projected actions in terms of anticipated outcomes, and (d) finally realize their plans in actions" (p. 145).

Plans are depicted as "mental strategies that persons use to achieve goals" (Berger, Karol, & Jordan, 1989, p. 3). As such, "plans are not actions themselves but conceptual representations of actions" (Berger, 1995, p. 6). Plans vary in their levels of abstraction and contain both verbal and nonverbal communicative behaviors (Berger, 1988a). Plans also have an impact on the interaction and individuals involved in the plan. Thus, outcomes of planned actions are relevant for both the initiator of the plan and observers or others participating in the plan. This skeleton of Berger's Planning Theory helps set the stage for its application to strategic embarrassment and a more elaborate discussion.

MODEL OF PLANNED STRATEGIC EMBARRASSMENT

Obviously, not all interaction is planned. But when it is, as in the case of strategic embarrassment, the component parts of Berger's Planning Theory provide a scaffolding to build an explanatory tool. The elements of the Planned Strategic Embarrassment Model include attention to goals as they function within the context of strategic embarrassment, the planning stage, the plan of action, and outcomes that result. Figure 1 presents a model of planned strategic embarrassment.

Goals

Metagoals are the underlying objectives in every plan. Berger (1995) submitted that there are two meta-goals, *efficiency* and *social appropriateness*. The metagoal of efficiency, similar to Dillard's (1990) least effort principle, implies that plans are constructed to be cost effective in terms of the effort expended to pursue the goal(s). The metagoal of social appropriateness implies that planners are concerned with the extent to which the plan is compatible with the norms dictating acceptable behavior in a situational context. Plans may be considered socially appropriate to the extent that behaviors in the plan reduce conflict, minimize disruptions, and prevent loss of face for projected participants including the planner (Berger, 1995). Conversely, socially inappropriate plans may cause relational difficulties, a loss of face for the planner, and disrupt the communicative interaction.

At times, however, these two metagoals may come into conflict. For example, occasions exist where the most socially appropriate plan is not the most efficient (Berger, 1995). Petronio and Snider (1990) concluded that strategic embarrassment may represent a case of planned interaction in which the metagoal of social appropriateness is forfeited for efficiency. This means breaching social expectations for appropriate behavior by violating situational norms and rules in order to strategically embarrass the target efficiently.

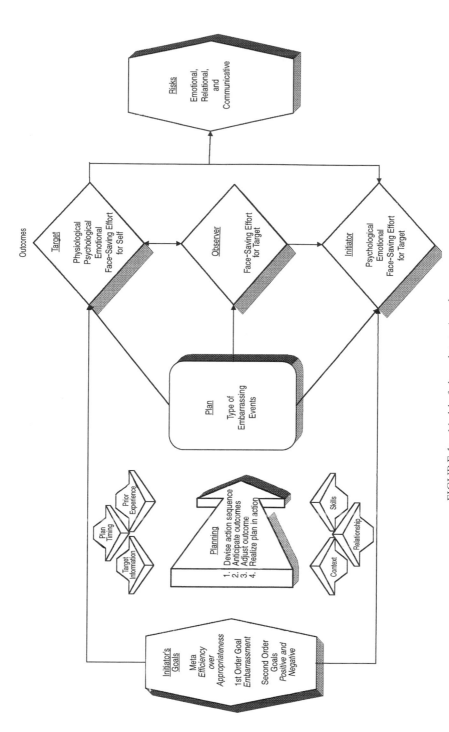

FIGURE 1: Model of planned strategic embarrassment.

Petronio and Snider (1990) expanded Berger's notion of explicit and implicit goals by suggesting that first-order and second-order goals guide the planning process in strategic embarrassment. However, their goal categories seem more conceptually equivalent to Dillard's goal classifications than Berger's. First-order goals represent the desired expectations for the outcome of the plan. Hence, in the case of strategic embarrassment, the first-order goal is the embarrassment of a target. A second-order goal "typically represents the intentions directing the plan" (Petronio et al., 1992, p. 4).

These second-order goals, like Dillard's (1990) secondary goals, are responsible for motivating and shaping the plan that is to produce the desired outcome of strategic embarrassment. Second-order goals provide the means for achieving the first-order goal of embarrassment and influencing the strategy choices. For example, if revenge is a second-order goal, it functions as a motivator for strategically embarrassing a target and determines the possible ways embarrassment might be accomplished. Petronio et al. (1992) further extended the conceptualization of goals proposing that second-order goals may have a positive or negative valence.

A second-order goal is positively valenced when the initiator of the plan desires a benevolent outcome and selects the least face-damaging strategy. Second-order goals are negatively valenced when the initiator of the plan desires humiliating, shameful, disreputable, or disgraceful outcomes. In this case, the most damaging strategies are chosen to embarrass a target. The valence, therefore, is hypothesized to influence the action plan for embarrassment. The metagoals, first-order, and second-order goals provide the fabric for the planning process.

Planning and Plans

A strategic embarrassment plan is defined as a conceptual representation of verbal and nonverbal behaviors perceived to have potential to attain positive or negative goals in embarrassment. Plans are distinguished from planning in terms of the process through which a plan is created (Berger, 1995). Planning, therefore, becomes the process of selecting strategies to accomplish interaction goals.

Berger (1995) observed that the process of planning may occur either prior to the action or "on-line" during the interaction. A plan may be well thought out before the initiator enters a situation. However, attributes of the situation, participants unknown to the initiator, or those that have changed since the conception of the plan, may force the initiator to modify or abandon a plan. At times, the initiators may construct plans that later are not enacted (Berger & Bell, 1988). All forms of plans (i.e., enacted and abandoned) may be stored in memory for future use (Berger, 1995; Berger & Jordan, 1989, 1992). As such, old plans often represent a major source of inspiration for new plans (Berger, 1988b; Miller, Galanter, & Pribram, 1960).

Old plans may be reemployed or redesigned (Berger, 1988a; Berger, 1995; Berger & Jordan, 1989). When initiators of strategic embarrassment construct a plan, they may also depend on plans that they have been constructed but not used before, direct instructions that they may have received for strategically embarrassing others, and observations based on watching others use strategic embarrassment as sources for constructing a plan that will meet their interaction goals (Berger, 1995; Berger & Jordan, 1989). Despite the number of potential plan sources, the success of a plan is largely dependent on information about the target and context. Berger (1995) suggested that to be successful, planners should possess a large knowledge base from which they can draw information necessary to construct and evaluate plans effectively.

However, as the model in Figure 1 suggests, devising a plan or action sequence for strategic embarrassment depends on anticipating outcomes and adjusting projected consequences. Together these ultimately lead to realizing a plan into action. At least six different contributors influence the planning, they include: (a) target information, (b) plan timing, (c) prior experiences, (d) context, (e) nature of relationships, and (f) skill.

Target Information

Petronio et al. (1992) indicated that plans for strategic embarrassment are more effective when the initiator possesses information about the target's personality, knows the target's fears (Watson & Friend, 1969), and understands the circumstances under which the target person feels self-conscious (Fenigstein, 1979). In addition, being aware of how shy a target is (Pilkonis, 1977), the extent to which the target self-monitors while interacting (Carver & Scheier, 1981), and how important the target person feels it is to control his or her public identity (Tedeschi & Riess, 1981) all contribute to forming effective plans for strategic embarrassment. Therefore, knowing someone on a personal or intimate level helps the initiator become more efficient and successful in addition to developing more elaborate plans. Berger and di Battista (1992) noted that the "greater diversity of person and situation information sought before the planning, the more elaborate plans are likely to be, when elaboration is indexed by the number of actions contained in plans" (p. 381). Plans in communicative interaction appear to be tailored to specific targets, thereby taking into account idiosyncratic information about a specific person (Berger & di Battista, 1992). Overall, target information may be a critical factor in plans for strategic embarrassment. Likewise, the timing of a plan is essential in determining how strategic embarrassment is planned.

Plan Timing

Plan timing is derived from Petronio and Snider's (1990) suggestion that where and when embarrassment takes place, and the amount of time spent constructing plans are elements that may affect the initiator's general ability to plan strategic embarrassment. For example, where and when strategic embarrassment takes place may be associated with the desired level of embarrassment (e.g., in front of high-status or low-status peers), and the use of embarrassment tactic. The more a person wishes to embarrass another, the greater the likelihood that he or she will pay attention to the timing of the event.

Petronio et al. (1992) found some support for an association between the amount of plan time and the planning process. Moreover, initiators who select positive embarrassment tactics tend to need more planning time. This implies that certain types of strategic embarrassment plans may require more complex planning and take more time to formulate. Although this research is exploratory, the efforts of Petronio et al. suggest future studies might focus on the planning process. In particular, the timing of plans and its influence on the selection of tactics or strategies seems important. Prior experience also contributes to an overall picture of strategic embarrassment.

Prior Experience

Berger (1995) argued that because individuals base their understanding, in part, on prior experiences, these "remindings" (Schank, 1982) allude to the process of applying similar meaning from past events to current situations. This process is relevant to strategic embarrassment planning (Bradford, 1993). The frequency with which someone uses strategic embarrassment, particularly with friends, seems to be related to the success of a plan (Petronio et al., 1992). Initiators who often employ strategic embarrassment probably have more plan options available and may become more adept because of their prior experiences. However, Waldron (1990) suggested that the link between preconversational planning knowledge and performance, such as strategic embarrassment, is not straightforward. Consequently, he proposed that one way to understand the connection is to examine conversational planning on three-tiers. The first tier is characterized by "prespecified plans" that may order individuals' interactions (Waldron, 1990, p. 185). These are automated behaviors where there is little attention to the selection and construction of new plans. Instead, individuals monitor conversations without an elaborate planning process. In this case, the dependence on prior knowledge is minimal. For example, using the least amount of prior information as a source for devising a plan may entail depending on gathering information during a dinner conversation. A quickly formulated plan to tease or strategically embarrass another at the table may be therefore based on limited experience and knowledge. These first tier decisions may be risky because the lack of knowledge might lead to poor choices for strategically embarrassing another. Sometimes, relying on minimal experiences, knowledge, and information may lead to the embarrassment misfiring, resulting in the initiator feeling disease instead of the target.

In the second tier, Waldron posited that a "knowledge-based" planning process occurs where a "conscious selection from long term memory of prefabricated plans that best match current conditions" (p. 185) is necessary for plans. Due to a "larger investment of cognitive resources than automatic planning" (Waldron, 1990, p. 185), there may be a greater reliance on prior knowledge. In this case, strategic embarrassment plans depend on using knowledge and experience of previous plans to construct a more elaborate plan to embarrass. These may be less risky than the first tiered plans because individuals take more information into account.

In the third tier, conversational planning involves the "replacement, modification, or supplementing of pre-specified plans when such plans match insufficiently with requirements of the situation" (Waldron, 1990, p. 185). This process is mostly used during plan construction for novel situations and represents more creative planning. For this last level of planning, the need for detailed prior knowledge appears necessary to accomplish this more complex kind of planning. This type of planning for strategic embarrassment means a substantial investment to gather pertinent information and draft a complicated set of tactics leading to dis-ease of one or more people. Waldron's typology illustrates the intricacy prior experience has in relationships to planning strategic embarrassment. Along with prior experience, plan timing, and target information, the context also is a critical factor in strategic embarrassment planning.

Context

Knowledge of the context, including cultural and social expectations, may help the initiator embarrass the target. Understanding the social rules for a given situation seems significant in devising a plan for strategic embarrassment. This is particularly true if the initiator has some indication that the target may not fully understand implicit rules. Not knowing social etiquette is a prime example. Understanding that guests may not be aware of uses for certain cutlery found in some formal dinner settings might prove fertile ground for strategic embarrassment.

Sometimes, social situations, such as a fraternity's "Hell Week," are purposefully embarrassing. The very point of the social experience is to feel embarrassed. Braithwaite (1995) provided a good example in her descriptions of coed weddings and baby showers. She pointed out that these social gatherings are intentionally created to embarrass the expecting parents and engaged couples. Particularly in the coed showers, men are not as familiar with the rules for this occasion and consequently are even more at risk. The guests play games that deliberately instigate discomfort. For example, coed wedding shower games often ask grooms to answer sexually laden questions, or expect brides to wear bows on their heads symbolizing the number children they will have with their spouse. In these cases, strategic embarrassment is embedded in the occasion, but the initiator often determines how the events will take place. As these points show, the context also plays a role in determining the planning process for strategic embarrassment. The nature of a relationship is also important to comprehending strategic embarrassment planning.

Nature of Relationships

Relationships between individuals contribute to the knowledge base of information used in strategic embarrassment. For example, there is a historical dimension to relationships that may serve to highlight pertinent experiences or vulnerabilities that might produce embarrassment. By comparison, strategically embarrassing strangers is more difficult because there is a level of uncertainty resulting in sketchy plans that have less potential for success. However, the ambiguity of the situation might be influenced by whether the stranger seems interesting and reciprocates interest in becoming acquainted.

Berger (1987, 1988b) suggested that college student dating requests tend to include multiple levels of plans. Because dating students do not wish to chance rejection, they assess how much interest the other person shows. When interest exists, they often construct multiple plans, perhaps to avoid embarrassment. Interest appears to be a factor in the number of contingencies developed for date request plans. Berger and Bell (1988) found that effective plans anticipate contingencies in a dating context, making the process more elaborate. Apparently, anticipated interest contributes to the kind of planning process developed, as does the nature of the relationship and gender.

Research on strategic embarrassment shows that the gender of both initiators and targets interact to influence the choice of embarrassment tactics used in strategic embarrassment (Sharkey, 1993). Women tend to embarrass intimate partners and their children more often, whereas men embarrass friends and subordinates. Women also tend to embarrass women targets more often and men embarrass other men. Consequently, women and men may plan differently given the kind of relational choice they make for strategic embarrassment.

Besides the trends found for gender, in some initiator-target relationships individuals may view embarrassment as a positive experience, even classifying it as a prosocial activity. For example, teasing about being asked out by a popular man may be strategic, yet, may be considered an opportunity to convey this news without seeming to brag. The person using strategic embarrassment may believe that this plan helps a friend rather than necessarily cause dis-ease. Strategic embarrassment may also be considered prosocial by the initiator. For instance, school-aged children may make a member of their group the center of attention because of a unique honor in school. In some relationships, embarrassment may also represent game playing between friends. Using a "whoopie" cushion on a friend, writing "just married" on a friend's car before he or she picks up a date, or playing "tricks" on each other is strategic embarrassment. Because of the relationship, the friend knows how to joke and game play effectively. Thus, the kind of relationships help to determine the plans they enact. Skill is also an important component of strategic embarrassment.

Skill

Berger (1995) argued that individuals have a wide array of information from which to draw planned action. Generalizations from previous plans that individuals adjust to fit the current situation, and information that they gather from the situation help in the planning process. Since there is some risk for initiators of becoming targets themselves, the plan to embarrass is often salient and deliberately crafted to accomplish embarrassing only the target. The ability to achieve the desired outcome may also depend on the person's capacity for detailed recall, generalizability to a new situation, as well as adequacy in synthesizing personal knowledge about the target, expectations of the situation, prior experiences, and history of the relationship. To be effective at embarrassment, individuals need to be motivated and capable. Berger and Bell (1988) maintained that "skilled planners may not always be motivated to enact their plans. . . . knowing what to do does not assure that one will perform well on the basis of knowledge" (p. 219). Yet, because a risk of self-embarrassment exists, this strategic phenomenon may uniquely require closer attention to the interface between skills and outcome.

Outcomes of Strategic Embarrassment

The emotional aftermath of any kind of embarrassment, including strategic embarrassment, calls for remediation of the situation. Saving face in this way is essential to reduce the recipient's embarrassment and feelings of abashment (Cupach & Metts, 1990). Once embarrassment produces an emotional outcome, the need to reduce these feelings is strong and face-saving is the course people usually take to remedy these feelings. Understanding the aftermath of strategic embarrassment necessitates an examination of three potential participants: (a) the target, (b) the observer, (c) the initiator (see Figure 1). The outcomes may vary depending on whose perspective is being examined. This is not to suggest that the embarrassment event does not touch all of these players, yet looking at each perspective in turn helps isolate the differences and commonalities.

Target

So far, research suggests little difference in the way that targets save face after intentional and unintentional embarrassment. Although more research is needed to look at differences, people often possess repertoires for responding to embarrassing events. Interestingly, being communicatively competent increases a person's "ability to successfully repair and recover from failure events" (Spitzberg & Cupach, 1989, pp. 23–24) such as strategic embarrassment. Apparently, the more competent a person is, the more likely she or he has a large repertoire of possible face-saving options and skills to correct the situation.

Face-saving "attempts to correct, minimize, explain away, or excuse the deficient demeanor that originally precipitated the embarrassment" (Modigliani, 1970, p. 17). The research on face-saving yields rich descriptions of strategies for remediating embarrassment (e.g., Cupach & Metts, 1990; Cupach et al., 1986; Goffman, 1971; Miller, 1986; Petronio, 1984), such as changing the topic, denying failure, scapegoating, accounts, explanations, justifications, and withdrawal (Cupach, et al., 1986; Modigliani, 1970; Petronio, 1984). Furthermore, Sharkey and Stafford (1989) noted that displays of objective symptoms (i.e., crying, blushing, laughing) may also be face-saving attempts.

As the evidence shows, numerous ways exist to alleviate embarrassment; however, the choices people make appear related to the *way* they are embarrassed (Cupach & Metts, 1990; Sharkey & Stafford, 1989). Cupach and Metts (1990) reported that for situations resulting in a loss of poise, recipients are more likely to report using strategies involving humor and escape. However, in situations involving improper identity, individuals most frequently report using description tactics. As these findings illustrate, face-saving is complex, and at times the strategies may fail to remediate embarrassment. Hence, Cupach and Metts (1990; Sharkey & Stafford, 1989) pointed out that individuals may need to use multiple face-saving strategies before they can successfully repair the damage caused by embarrassment. Sometimes, recipients may not be capable of successful repair by themselves. Often they turn for help to those present during the event.

In addition, both the gender of the recipient and cultural variables have been important in determining the choices of face-saving for the target. For example, Petronio (1984) reported that the gender of the recipient influences strategy choice; women are more likely to select excuses than justifications by blaming, and shifting the center of attention onto others. Men use more justifications than excuses by apologizing, denying the incident, and changing the topic. Subsequent research has not found support for gender differences (Cupach et al., 1986; Sharkey & Stafford, 1989). Therefore, this inconsistency calls for additional investigations.

Face-saving is presumed to be a universal phenomenon across cultures, yet Goffman (1967) theorized that each culture has its own unique "repertoire" of face-saving practices. Unfortunately, there is a paucity of research exploring embarrassment and subsequent face-saving strategy choices across cultures. However, Sueda and Wiseman (1992) offered some support for Goffman's suggestion, showing that culture influences the choice of remedial face-saving strategies for Japanese and American college students after embarrassment. More students from the United States report using justification and humor as remedial strategies when they are embarrassed than do Japanese students.

Observers

Researchers suggest that observers of embarrassing situations may help recipients face-save (Cupach & Metts, 1990; Goffman, 1967; Petronio, 1984, 1990) by ignoring the situation or attempting to rebuild the recipients' self-esteem (Sharkey & Stafford, 1989, 1990). Conversely, observers may also choose to intensify the embarrassment (Cupach & Metts, 1990) by teasing the recipients, laughing at them, or drawing more attention to their faux pas. However, Cupach and Metts (1990) noted that "it is much more common for others to assist the embarrassed actor in coping with the predicament" (p. 338) providing support, empathy, and variations of avoidance.

An observer's choice to save face for the target is related to the recipient's response to the embarrassment (Cupach & Metts, 1990). When recipients of embarrassment attempt to face-save by concealing their embarrassment, observers also respond by camouflaging their acknowledgment of the embarrassment. Considering this finding, Sharkey and Stafford (1989) examined how perceived intensity and type of embarrassment influences observers' decision to engage in face-saving for the recipient. Their findings suggest that although the perceived degree of embarrassment intensity does not influence the observers' decisions, the type of embarrassment may be associated with the observers' choice to save face for the recipient. The recipient's own face-saving efforts may also be related to the observer's face-saving decisions. Thus, when criticism precipitates embarrassment, the recipient is most likely to respond with some kind of hostility, while observers respond with some form of escape, such as changing the topic. Their perceptions of the event and the recipient's reaction influence the observers' choices to save face for the recipient. The responses of observers thereby interact with those of the recipient.

This relationship becomes obvious when looking at the observer's perceptions regarding who is responsible for the embarrassment. The judgment of responsibility may influence the observer's face-saving efforts (Cupach & Metts, 1990). The determination of who is responsible may also explain why an observer feels justified in disregarding the embarrassment of another or even intensifying the situation. Cupach and Metts (1990) argued that

> the greater the undesirability of an event and the greater the actor's ascribed responsibility for that event, the more threatening the predicament is for the actor's image. As predicaments become more severe, actors are more inclined to mitigate negative repercussions by employing appropriate remedial strategies. Paradoxically, as predicaments become more severe and more aggravating to observers, they are less willing to assist embarrassed actors to regain face, and are more likely to intensify face threat by calling for an account. (pp. 336–337)

Thus, both the undesirability of the event and the ascribed responsibility for the event are critical factors in determining whether observers alleviate embarrassment for the target through face-work. Although Cupach and Metts pointed out that the observer tends to be more helpful than detrimental, in at least one study, 43% of those reporting embarrassment (both intentional and unintentional) stated that observers intensified their discomfiture (Metts, Cupach, & Hazleton, 1987). For the issue of strategic embarrassment, more research is needed to identify the part this kind of predicament plays in the perceptions of both the observers and the targets of embarrassment.

Initiators

The extent to which the initiator intends to humiliate or help the target may be a factor in the initiator's willingness to save face for the target. Perhaps, one way we might identify the valence of second-order goals is through the initiator's efforts to engage in face-saving strategies for the target after the embarrassing incident (Petronio & Snider, 1990). If the initiator's second-order goal is positive, she or he might typically employ face-saving strategies to reduce the target's embarrassment (Petronio et al., 1992). For example, the initiator may plan to inform a friend about dressing inappropriately. However, to communicate his or her positive objective, the person may plan to use humor to help the friend overcome this intentional embarrassment.

Although initiators help save face for the target with positive second-order goals, when the goals are negative, people engage in face-threatening strategies. These strategies may increase embarrassment for targets, making them feel more conspicuous and incompetent in the communicative exchange. Hence, observing the degree of face-saving effort may identify the valence of the initiator's second-order goal. Berger (1987) offered some support for this proposal, noting that "goals related to relationship preservation or face-saving are frequently activated in parallel with other social goals" (p. 160). However, the target's perception of an initiator's second-order goal may influence the target's response to embarrassment. Berger (1988a) endorsed this idea, observing that "persons derive explanations for other's conduct by inferring what their goals are and the plans they are employing to reach those goals" (p. 94). Constructing strategies for face-saving, therefore, may be considered a part of the strategic embarrassment planning process.

In addition, Petronio et al. (1992) found that the degree of desired embarrassment for the target is negatively associated with the valence of the face-saving strategies used by the initiator. Initiators who want targets to become extremely embarrassed tend to use face-threatening behaviors or do nothing to help targets overcome their discomfort. However, initiators wishing targets to become only moderately embarrassed use face-saving strategies that temper the intensity of embarrassment.

The target's face-saving responses also seem to reflect a sequence of strategies used at different points in time during embarrassing interactions (Snider, 1992). Targets may use one face-saving strategy as they initially respond to strategic embarrassment and others later after embarrassment occurs. Research exploring the embarrassment process longitudinally is needed to more fully understand how recipients use face-saving with planned strategic embarrassment. Although there are some clear directions identified for outcomes of strategic embarrassment, more development is needed to isolate the differential ways this genre of embarrassment results in alternative face-saving routines. Particularly when the events are positive, examining how people overcome being the center of attention when the sentiment is supportive may be one avenue to explore.

Thus far, we have focused on ways that people aim for a successful plan to embarrass. As the model of planned strategic embarrassment indicates, potential risks exist that the plan will go bad. Failed plans do occur and studying them is helpful because these situations highlight plan adaptation (Berger, 1995; Berger & DiBattista, 1992). Examining situations where plans fail also illustrates the requirements of good plans.

Risks of Strategic Embarrassment

The use of strategic embarrassment poses a number of risks for initiators (Petronio & Snider, 1990; Petronio, 1992). Plans to embarrass targets may backfire by failing to embarrass the target or worse, embarrassing the initiators. Plans may fail because initiators make decisions that do not account for aspects of the context, their targets' reactions, or potential outcomes. These poor decisions may be due to insufficient knowledge or experiences with strategic embarrassment, lack of information about their targets, and little understanding about the context in which they attempt to use strategic embarrassment.

Individuals may also have constructed plans that go bad under stress. Berger (1995) contended that when there is an increase in stressful situations, people are less able to process complex levels of information. This limits the choices of planned actions and successful outcomes. Novel situations, such as trying strategically to embarrass someone from a different culture, may prove difficult. The implication is that strategic embarrassment presumes some competency linguistically and socially for both parties. When linguistic or social competencies do not exist, people may not see the incident as embarrassing.

Additionally, some may attempt strategic embarrassment with sketchy plans. As the interaction unfolds, the prospect of strategic embarrassment is turned back onto the initiator, rendering hopeless the expectation of discomfort for the target. Sketchy plans may result because a person has a low level of planning desire, but nevertheless elects to use strategic embarrassment. Low planning desires tend to activate the use of fewer complex plans that may be problematic for successful embarrassment (Berger, 1995). The risks of being ineffectual may be painful to the initiator, yet may also be troublesome for the target. For example, suppose the initiator means to instigate only a mildly embarrassing situation. Without a fully formed plan, the result turns to intense embarrassment for the target. The negative consequences may be difficult to overcome. Besides planning under stress and depending on sketchy plans, sustained use of embarrassment within relationships such as friendships and with intimate partners illustrates bad planning.

Although embarrassing events seem momentary (Sharkey, 1991), there appear to be cases where emotional consequences of strategic embarrassment on relationships are long-lasting. Continued embarrassment by relational partners is problematic for relational satisfaction (Petronio et al., 1989). In these relationships, strategic embarrassment represents a breach of trust for the partners because they often reveal information considered private by the target. In the most severe instances, taboo topics disclosed repeatedly appear to form the basis for resentment and humiliation. Due to potentially negative outcomes, partners in some relationships define strategic embarrassment as a relational taboo (Bradford, 1993).

As we have shown, the risks for using strategic embarrassment may be many. People wishing to use strategic embarrassment may be wise to calculate the hazards against the potential gains for themselves and their targets. Wanting to make someone the center of attention, constructing a plan to humiliate, or instigating mortification is not without potential liability for the initiator. To succeed, understanding the planning process seems imperative. The examination of risks underscores the importance of planning and illustrates the larger point of theoretical utility. By proposing a theoretical model for strategic embarrassment, we are able to capture an integrated system that frames this event giving import to how it is situated and the way it works.

CONCLUSION

Understanding the nature of strategic embarrassment affords researchers a way to broaden the scope of social predicaments. Applying Berger's Planning Theory lends a framework for amplifying the interrelationships in the process of strategic embarrassment and provides formulations for choicemaking. If embarrassment belongs to a class of self-conscious emotions that "require specific cognitions for their emergence" (Lewis, 1995, p. 205), causing embarrassment for someone else obliges us to discern how emotions and cognition interface so we can comprehend the way people plan this event. The proposed model sketches a promising route that leaves room for growth as we test these initial assumptions about strategic embarrassment.

Many avenues of growth for the model appear to have potential. One of the more important is considering developmental aspects of strategic embarrassment. Learning how and when children intentionally embarrass others may give clues to their social-emotional development. We already know that there may be age-related patterns and structure "relevant to children's experience and/or understanding of pride, shame, and embarrassment in middle childhood" (Griffin, 1995, p. 219). "Children construct a limited set of powerful organizing schemata . . . that shape the way physical and social reality are construed" (Griffin, 1995, p. 222). These organizing schemata may include not only emotional feelings as a result of pride, shame, and embarrassment, but also ways strategically to create these feelings in others of their own age. Their plans may be more effective with children the same age because their schemata match age-specific cognitive complexity levels. In other words, when they plan strategic embarrassment, they are most successful with their friends because they know what is salient and how to make the plan work. To enact a "strategic" plan, we propose the need for a baseline level of knowledge or experience, target information, consideration of the timing, understanding of the context, relationships, and some skill. Reaching beyond age-specific abilities and knowledge to cause others embarrassment might be more difficult and require more complexity than developmentally available. Exploring strategic embarrassment developmentally provides some basic information about the nature of embarrassment in general and intentional predicaments in particular. Doing so has the potential to enhance the existing model by identifying when certain elements in this theoretical proposal might become salient as individuals grow from children to adults. Currently, the model emphasizes adult embarrassment where self-judgment and audience judgment are central (Griffin, 1995). However, extending the model to include changes in judgment over the life cycle starting with children enhances the utility of this proposed model significantly.

Having a life-cycle perspective gives a broader understanding to this unique phenomenon. To some extent, strategic embarrassment is unusual because it frequently functions as an example of socially sanctioned discrediting. In very few circumstances do we allow, let alone expect that others will cause emotional discomfort in social settings. Yet when we attend our own birthday parties or wedding showers, we know that a social requirement of these events is our own embarrassment by others. Not all strategic embarrassment is socially sanctioned, but there are many instances where it is an acceptable part of an event. Strategic embarrassment is also paradoxical, in that we avoid feeling dis-ease, while joyously making someone else the target of our joking or teasing. Both of these characteristics prevail through out the life cycle because they typify the nature of this phenomenon. Exploring the nature of planned strategic embarrassment using Berger's theory has been a useful way to isolate critical issues; however, the model now challenges us to question the nature and function of intentionally causing dis-ease in others that we have not yet considered.

REFERENCES

Apsler, R. (1975). Effects of embarrassment on behavior toward others. *Journal of Personality and Social Psychology, 32,* 145–153.

Berger, C. R. (1987). Planning and scheming: Strategies for initiating relationships. In R. Burnett, P. McGhee, & D. D. Clarke (Eds.), *Accounting for relationships: Explanation, representation, and knowledge* (pp. 158–174). London: Methuen.

Berger, C. R. (1988a). Planning, affect, and social action generation. In R. L. Donohew, H. Sypher, & E. T. Higgens (Eds.), *Communication, social cognition, and affect* (pp. 93–116). Hillsdale, NJ: Erlbaum.

Berger, C. R. (1988b, May). *Communication plans and communicative performance.* Paper presented at the annual convention of the International Communication Association, New Orleans, LA.

Berger, C. R. (1995). A plan-based approach to strategic communication. In D. E. Hewes (Ed.), *The cognitive bases of interpersonal communication* (pp. 141–179). Hillsdale, NJ: Erlbaum.

Berger, C. R., & Bell, R. A. (1988). Plans and the initiation of social relationships. *Human Communication Research, 15,* 217–235.

Berger, C. R., & di Battista, P. (1992, May). *Communication failure and plan adaptation: If at first you don't succeed, say it louder and slower.* Paper presented at the annual convention of the International Communication Association, Miami, FL.

Berger, C. R., & Jordan, J. M. (1989, May). *Planning sources, planning difficulty, and social competence.* Paper presented at the annual convention of the International Communication Association, San Francisco, CA.

Berger, C. R., & Jordan, J. M. (1992). Planning sources, planning difficulty, and verbal fluency. *Communications Monographs, 59,* 130–149.

Berger, C. R., Karol, S. H., & Jordan, J. M. (1989). When a lot of knowledge is a dangerous thing: The debilitating effects of plan complexity on verbal fluency. *Human Communication Research, 16,* 91–119.

Bradford, L. (1993). *A cross-cultural study of strategic embarrassment in adolescent socialization.* Unpublished doctoral dissertation, Arizona State University, Tempe.

Braithwaite, D. O. (1995). Ritualized embarrassment at "coed" wedding and baby showers. *Communication Reports, 8,* 145–157.

Buss, A. H., Iscoe, I., & Buss, E. H. (1979). The development of embarrassment. *The Journal of Psychology, 103,* 227–230.

Carver, C. S., & Scheier, M. F. (1981). *Attention and self-regulation: A control-theory approach to human behavior.* New York: Springer-Verlag.

Cupach, W. R., & Metts, S. (1990). Remedial processes in embarrassing predicaments. In J. A. Anderson (Ed.), *Communication yearbook 13* (pp. 323–352). Newbury Park, CA: Sage.

Cupach, W. R., Metts, S., & Hazelton, V. Jr. (1986). Coping with embarrassing predicaments: Remedial strategies and their perceived utility. *Journal of Language and Social Psychology, 5,* 181–200.

Dillard, J. P. (1990). *Seeking compliance: The production of interpersonal messages.* Scottsdale, AZ: Gorsuch Scarisbrick.

Edelmann, R. J. (1987). *The psychology of embarrassment.* Chichester, UK: John Wiley & Sons.

Edelmann, R. J., Asendorf, J., Contarello, A., Zammuner, V., Georgas, J., & Villanueva, C. (1989). Self-reported expression of embarrassment in five European cultures. *Journal of Cross-cultural Psychology, 20,* 357–371.

Edelmann, R. J., & Hampson, S. (1981). Embarrassment in dyadic interaction. *Social Behavior and Personality, 9,* 171–177.

Fenigstein, A. (1979). Self-consciousness, self-attention, and social interaction. *Journal of Personality and Social Psychology, 37,* 75–86.

Fink, E. L., & Walker, B. A. (1975). Humorous responses to embarrassment. *Psychological Reports, 40,* 475–485.

Goffman, E. (1956). Embarrassment and the social organization. *The American Journal of Sociology, 70,* 1–15.

Goffman, E. (1967). *Interaction ritual: Essays on face-to-face behavior.* Garden City, NY: Anchor Books Doubleday & Company.

Goffman, E. (1971). *Relations in public: Microstudies of public order.* New York: Harper & Row.

Griffin, S. (1995). A cognitive-developmental analysis of pride, shame, and embarrassment in middle childhood. In J. P. Tangney and K. W. Fischer (Eds.), *Self-conscious emotions: The psychology of shame, guilt, embarrassment, and pride* (pp. 219–236). New York: The Guilford Press.

Gross, E., & Stone, G. P. (1964). Embarrassment and the analysis of role requirements. *The American Journal of Sociology.* LXX(1), 1–15.

Harré, R. (1990). Embarrassment: A conceptual analysis. In W. R. Crozer (Ed.), *Shyness and embarrassment: Perspectives from social psychology* (pp. 181–204). New York: Cambridge University Press.

Imahori, T. T., & Cupach, W. R. (1994). A cross-cultural comparison of the interpretation and management of face: U.S. American and Japanese responses to embarrassing predicaments. *International Journal of Intercultural Relations, 18*(2), 193–219.

Leventhal, H. (1979). A perceptual-motor processing model of emotion. In P. Pliner, K. R. Blankstein, & I. M. Spigel (Eds.), *Advances in the study of communication and effect* (pp. 1–46). New York: Plenum Press.

Leventhal, H. (1980). Toward a comprehensive theory of emotion. In L. Berkowitz (Ed.), *Advances in experimental social psychology* (vol. 13, pp. 139–207). New York: Academic Press.

Lewis, M. (1995). Embarrassment: The emotion of self-exposure and evaluation. In J. P. Tangney and K. W. Fischer (Eds.), *Self-conscious emotions: The psychology of shame, guilt, embarrassment, and pride* (pp. 198–218). New York: Guilford.

Martin, W. B. W. (1987). Student's perceptions of causes and consequences of embarrassment in the school. *Canadian Journal of Education, 12,* 277–293.

Metts, S., Cupach, W. R., & Hazleton, V. (1987, February) *Coping with social dis-ease: Remedial strategies and embarrassment.* Paper presented at the annual meeting of the Western Speech Communication Association, Salt Lake City, UT.

Miller, R. S. (1986). Embarrassment: Causes and consequences. In W. H. Jones, J. M. Cheek, & S. R. Briggs (Eds.), *Shyness: Perspectives on research and treatment* (pp. 295–311). New York: Plenum Press.

Miller, R. S. (1995). Embarrassment and social behavior. In J. P. Tangney & K. W. Fischer (Eds.), *Self-conscious emotions: The psychology of shame, guilt, embarrassment, and pride* (pp. 322–339). New York: Guilford.

Miller, G. A., Galanter, E., & Pribram, K. H. (1960). *Plans and the structure of behavior.* New York: Holt, Rinehart and Winston.

Miller, R. S., & Leary, M. R. (1992). Social sources and interactive functions of emotion: The case of embarrassment. In M. S. Clark (Ed.), *Review of personality and social psychology* (vol. 14, pp. 202–221). Newbury Park, CA: Sage.

Modigliani, A. (1968). Embarrassment and embarrassability. *Sociometry, 31,* 313–326.

Modigliani, A. (1970). Embarrassment, facework, and eye contact: Testing a theory of embarrassment. *Journal of Personality and Social Psychology, 17,* 15–24.

Pavitt, C. (1991). An analysis of artificial intelligence based models for describing communicative choice. *Communication Theory, 1,* 204–224.

Petronio, S. (1984). Communication strategies to reduce embarrassment differences between men and women. *The Western Journal of Speech Communication, 48,* 28–38.

Petronio, S. (1990). The use of a communication boundary perspective to contextualize embarrassment research. In J. Anderson (Ed.), *Communication yearbook 13* (pp. 365–373). Newbury Park, CA: Sage.

Petronio, S. (1992). *Planning strategic embarrassment: Testing a theory.* Paper presented at the annual convention of the Western States Communication Association, Boise, ID.

Petronio, S., Olson, C., & Dollar, N. (1989). Privacy issues in relational embarrassment: Impact on relational quality and communication satisfaction. *Communication Research Reports, 6,* 21–27.

Petronio, S., & Snider, E. (1990, November). *Planned strategic embarrassment.* Paper presented at the annual convention of the Speech Communication Association, Chicago, IL.

Petronio, S., Snider, E., & Bradford, L. (1992). *Planning strategic embarrassment of friends: An application and test of Berger's planning theory.* Unpublished manuscript.

Pilkonis, P. A. (1977). Shyness, public and private, and its relationships to other measures of social behavior. *Journal of Personality, 45,* 585–595.

Plutchik, R. (1984). Emotions: A general psychoevolutionary theory. In K. R. Scherer & P. Ekman (Eds.), *Approaches to emotion* (pp. 197–219). Hillsdale, NJ: Erlbaum.

Sattler, J. M. (1965). A theoretical, developmental, and clinical investigation of embarrassment. *Genetic Psychology Monographs, 71,* 19–59.

Schank, R. C. (1982). *Dynamic memory: A theory of reminding and learning in computers and people.* Cambridge: Cambridge University Press.

Sharkey, W. F. (1990). *Intentional embarrassment: Goals, tactics, responses, consequences.* Unpublished doctoral dissertation, Ohio State University, Columbus.

Sharkey, W. F. (1991). Intentional embarrassment: Goals, tactics, and consequences. In W. R. Cupach & S. Metts (Eds.), *Advances in interpersonal communication research—1991: Proceedings of the Western States Communication Association—Interpersonal communication interest group* (pp. 105–128). Normal, IL: Personal Relationships Research Group.

Sharkey, W. F. (1992). Uses and responses to intentional embarrassment. *Communication Studies, 43,* 257–275.

Sharkey, W. F. (1993). Who embarrasses whom? Relational and sex differences in the use of intentional embarrassment. In P. J. Kalbfleish (Eds.), *Interpersonal communication: Evolving interpersonal relationships* (pp. 147–168). Hillsdale, NJ: Lawrence Erlbaum.

Sharkey, W. F., & Stafford, L. (1989, May). *So, how embarrassing was it? . . . Whadja do?: The relationship between the situation, the degree of perceived embarrassment and responses to embarrassment.* Paper presented at the annual convention of the International Communication Association, San Francisco, CA.

Sharkey, W. F., & Stafford, L. (1990). Responses to embarrassment. *Human Communication Research, 17,* 315–342.

Sharkey, W. F., & Waldron, V. R. (1990, November). *The intentional embarrassment of subordinates in the work place.* Paper presented at the annual convention of the Speech Communication Association, Chicago, IL.

Singleis, T. M., & Sharkey, W. F. (1995). Culture, self-construal, and embarrassability. *Journal of Cross-Cultural Psychology, 26,* 622–644.

Snider, E. (1992). *Strategic embarrassment and face-saving strategies.* Unpublished master's thesis, Arizona State University, Tempe.

Spitzberg, B. H., & Cupach, W. B. (1989). *Handbook of interpersonal competence research.* New York: Springer-Verlag.

Sueda, K., & Wiseman, R. L. (1992). Embarrassment remediation in Japan and the United States. *International Journal of Intercultural Relations, 16*(2), 159–173.

Tedeschi, J. T., & Reiss, M. (1981). Identities, the phenomenal self, and laboratory research. In J. T. Tedeschi (Ed.), *Impression management theory and social psychological research* (pp. 3–22). New York: Academic Press.

Waldron, V. (1990). Constrained rationality: Situational influences on information acquisition plans and tactics. *Communication Monographs, 57,* 184–201.

Watson, D., & Friend, R. (1969). Measurement of social-evaluative anxiety. *Journal of Consulting and Clinical Psychology, 33,* 448–451.

CHAPTER 5

Guilt and Hurt: Similarities, Distinctions, and Conversational Strategies

Anita L. Vangelisti and Rhonda J. Sprague

University of Texas, Austin
Austin, Texas

> *My sister and I were teasing each other—you know, joking around,*
> *making fun of each other. At one point, I started to get a little irritated. We*
> *were still joking and laughing, but I hurled a pretty sharp insult at her. I*
> *don't even remember what it was. I just remember that her whole face*
> *changed. One second she was smiling and giggling, the next she looked like*
> *she was on the verge of tears. I felt awful. I might as well have slapped her.*
> *She just looked at me for a minute with those big sad eyes and then she*
> *turned around and slowly walked away.*

Guilt and hurt are two emotions that are often closely linked. When considering the circumstances that accompany guilt, scholars often note that guilt occurs when a person has injured, unjustly hurt, or failed to help someone (e.g., Friedman, 1985; Harwas-Napicrala, 1992). Those who are hurt may try to evoke guilt feelings in the other as a way to communicate their emotion, to retaliate against the perceived source of their pain, to prevent further harm, or to redistribute emotional distress in the relationship (Baumeister, Stillwell, & Heatherton, 1994). The purpose of this chapter is to examine guilt and hurt as they occur in the context of interpersonal relationships. To this end, the qualities of guilt and hurt will be discussed and aspects of communication associated with the two emotions will be explored.

Understanding the nature of guilt and hurt is important because the interplay between them and the way they are communicated serve as telling markers of *relational quality*. For instance, because those in close relationships usually feel some responsibility to care for and attend to their partner, the perception that they caused or failed to respond to the other's hurt is likely to make them feel guilty. From the perspective of those who are hurt, such guilt feelings may not only be justified, but may serve as a sort of salve for their wounds. If their partner communicates feelings

Handbook of Communication and Emotion: Research, Theory, Applications, and Contexts

of guilt, at least he or she is attending to the relationship. In contrast, if the partner knows that he or she has inflicted hurt, and does not communicate any guilt, the quality of the relational bond may be thrown into question.[1]

In addition, the ways partners communicate when they engender, experience, and respond to both guilt and hurt likely have important *relational consequences*. If a parent who is hurt evokes guilt in her child by denigrating the child's character, the relationship between the two may be damaged. If a spouse who feels guilty often communicates his feelings by verbally attacking his partner, any hurt the partner initially felt may turn to anger and dissatisfaction with the relationship. Of course, it is possible for one partner to feel hurt without the other detecting those feelings. And, one person may feel guilty about hurting another when no injury or damage was actually done. Having said this, even when hurt and guilt go undetected or are misinterpreted, the enactment of, and response to, these two emotions likely influence interpersonal relationships (Fitzpatrick & Ritchie, 1993; Sillars & Scott, 1983). People who feel hurt are liable to act upon their feelings even if their partner fails to detect or understand their injury. Likewise, those who feel guilty are apt to behave in ways that reflect their emotions even if no injury or damage was done. In short, guilt and hurt, the links between them, and more particularly, the nature of communication associated with them, play an important role in close relationships.

In this chapter, some of the similarities and differences between guilt and hurt are discussed. Then, a number of characteristics that define interactants' experience of these two emotions are examined. Conversational strategies for eliciting both emotions are described, as are concerns associated with the responses people have to guilt and hurt. Finally, several issues in the literature that would well be addressed by future research are considered.

COMPARING GUILT AND HURT

Similarities

Examining some of the core similarities between guilt and hurt illustrates how the two are connected as well as how they function in interpersonal relationships. Both emotions typically (a) are experienced as negative feelings; (b) arise as a result of a perceived transgression; (c) occur in, and are affected by, interpersonal contexts; and (d) have interpersonal functions.

Of these similarities, perhaps the most obvious is that both guilt and hurt are experienced as relatively unpleasant, *negative* feelings. Neither emotion is one that most people consciously enjoy. Guilt has been linked to shame (e.g., Kugler & Jones, 1992; Lewis, 1971; Tangney, 1990; Tangney, Wagner, Fletcher, & Gramzow, 1992),

---

[1] In a similar vein, one sign that a relationship is approaching demise may be the inability (or unwillingness) of one person, the other, or both to feel hurt because of a partner's actions.

anxiety, depression, loneliness, shyness, suspicion (Jones & Kugler, 1993), resentment, irritability (Vangelisti, Daly, & Rudnick, 1991), private self-consciousness (Buss, 1980), pain, agitation, negative self-evaluation, and expectations of punishment (Wicker, Payne, & Morgan, 1983). Although the correlates of hurt have not been systematically examined, prototype studies suggest that people associate hurt feelings with agony, suffering, and anguish (Shaver, Schwartz, Kirson, & O'Connor, 1987; see also, Metts & Bowers, 1994).

One of the reasons guilt and hurt involve such negative feelings is that both occur as a consequence of a perceived *transgression*. Whether conceptualized as an enduring condition or a temporary state, guilt is typically described as a response to having violated a moral imperative or social standard (e.g., Hoffman, 1982; Kugler & Jones, 1992; Lazarus, 1991; Mosher, 1979). Similarly, hurt is engendered because someone perceives a breach has occurred. People usually feel hurt when they believe they were injured or harmed (Vangelisti, 1994).

Importantly, transgressions associated with these two emotions often involve another individual. Both guilt and hurt occur in, and are influenced by, *interpersonal contexts*. In particular, relatively recent formulations of guilt suggest that it is "something that happens between people rather than just inside them" (Baumeister et al., 1994, p. 243). Horney (1937), one of the first to hint at this idea, noted that people feel guilty because they fear others' disapproval. Hoffman (1978) similarly argued that guilt feelings are a direct result of the damaging effects that wrongful acts have on others (see also Thompson & Hoffman, 1980). Friedman (1985) described guilt as a conscious or unconscious appraisal that one's own thoughts or actions are harmful to a significant other. Jones, Kugler, and Adams (1995) more broadly noted that people feel guilty about transgressions that threaten their relational bonds. Even when the transgression in question is not directly tied to other individuals, Brooke (1985) argued that "there is always an interpersonal dimension to guilt" (p. 37).

Hurt similarly occurs in interpersonal situations. Although not as widely discussed in the literature as guilt, hurt is typically conceptualized as a result of feeling emotionally injured or wounded by another (Folkes, 1982; L'Abate, 1977). People feel hurt because of something they perceive someone else said, did, or thought. As a consequence, communication—whether accurately or inaccurately interpreted—is required to evoke hurt feelings.

Empirical studies that focus on the interpersonal aspects of guilt and hurt indicate that both tend to be elicited in the context of relatively intimate relationships. For example, Baumeister, Stillwell, and Heatherton (1995a) reported that people tended to feel guilty about transgressions committed against valued partners in close relationships. Vangelisti et al. (1991) similarly found that when people were asked to describe a conversation in which guilt was elicited, the vast majority (80%) reported conversations that occurred in the context of very close relationships. In addition, when these researchers asked another group of respondents to describe a guilt-provoking conversation and to rate how typical it was for their conversational partner to make them feel guilty, typicality ratings were positively associated with intimacy. Similar results emerged from an investigation of intimacy and hurt (Vangelisti, 1994). When describing interactions in which someone hurt their feelings, people more frequently recalled situations centering on family members, friends, and romantic partners than interactions involving acquaintances or strangers. Furthermore, the topics of hurtful messages often emphasized relational events such as rejecting a partner, ridiculing the importance of a relationship, or disregarding another's desire for affiliation.

The associations between interpersonal relationships and both guilt and hurt raise the likelihood that the two emotions fulfill certain *interpersonal functions* (Baumeister et al., 1994). Studies suggest that guilt and hurt may constrain individuals' behavior, be used as a means of control over others, and redistribute emotional distress during interaction. In the literature on guilt, the first of these interpersonal functions—to constrain individuals' behavior—can be traced at least as far back as Freud's (1930/1961) writings. Broadly speaking, theorists argue that the negative feelings linked to guilt often prevent people from engaging in activities that deviate from social standards (Ausubel, 1955; Andersen & Guerrero, Chapter 3, this volume). From this perspective, "guilt may serve a warning function and lead to the inhibition of unacceptable behavior" (Mosher, 1979, p. 105). In addition, people's efforts to avoid guilt may lead them to engage in activities that are beneficial to their relationships. For instance, Baumeister, Stillwell, and Heatherton (1995b) suggested that individuals sometimes express affection or attend to their partner because failing to do so will make them feel guilty.

A second interpersonal function noted by scholars who study guilt is that this emotion can be used to exercise control or power in relationships (Miceli, 1992). Vangelisti et al. (1991) found that a substantial group of people acknowledged that either they, or their conversational partners, used guilt induction as a means of influence or persuasion. Baumeister et al. (1995b) also found that people often noted they learned a lesson and/or changed their behavior as a result of a guilt-inducing interaction. To deal with guilt, many of the respondents in this latter study reported that they restricted or changed their behavior in some way.

Baumeister and his colleagues (1995a, 1995b) also present data supporting a third interpersonal function of guilt: to redistribute emotional distress in relationships. Respondents who reported eliciting guilt in others felt better after the interaction. Because guilt is often evoked when one partner feels hurt, the elicitation of guilt may allow some of the negative feelings associated with the injury to be taken on by the guilty party. Redistribution, however, does not always carry such positive overtones. Vangelisti et al. (1991), for example, found that people elicited guilt to hurt others, to get revenge, and to express their own hurt, among other functions. Guilt evoked for purposes such as these may serve as a demonstration of remorse or an acknowledgement of the injured party's feelings.

Although the interpersonal functions of hurt are not articulated as clearly in the literature, it is not unreasonable to speculate that at least some of them overlap with the functions of guilt. For instance, hurt and the elicitation of hurt feelings likely restrict certain social behaviors and encourage others. Research suggests that to avoid hurting others' feelings, people offer external attributions for breaking social engagements (e.g., "because my car broke down") rather than internal ones (e.g., "because you're ugly") (Folkes, 1982; Weiner & Handel, 1985). Similarly, because dating partners are often concerned with the hurt that can accompany rejection, they tend to discuss some topics and retreat from others (Baxter & Wilmot, 1984). In short, people's desire to avoid hurt and to avoid causing hurt may encourage them to adhere to certain social and conversation norms (e.g., politeness rules, see Brown & Levinson, 1978).

Given that hurt, like guilt, is an unpleasant feeling, people may use hurt strategically to influence or persuade others. Ignoring social conventions that prevent hurt offers interactants the opportunity to wield a great deal of interpersonal power. For example, studies demonstrate that people sometimes engage in deception to avoid hurting others' feelings (Lippard, 1988; Metts, 1989). In such situations, when deception is typically employed to prevent hurt, truth-telling can be used to injure relational partners and possibly modify their behavior. As a conversational strategy, truth-telling can be quite powerful because if others draw attention to the conversational transgression (e.g., "How could you say such a thing?"), speakers can plead innocence by pointing to their honesty (e.g., "Well, did you want me to lie to you?"). As a consequence, people can inflict hurt to change others' behavior without portraying themselves as cruel or manipulative. Of course, those who are unconcerned with the image they portray have more latitude in how they use hurt to persuade others. Such individuals can directly induce hurt to punish behaviors they find disagreeable and can use it as a threat if the behaviors they desire are not performed.

Like guilt, hurt may also function as a means to rouse others' feelings and redistribute emotional distress. For example, when people are agitated or angry, they may say something to hurt their relational partner. This "venting" (Mace, 1976) may transfer part of the arousal associated with the initial anger to the injured party. The elicitation of hurt, in turn, may create guilt in the angry partner, again disseminating the distress. Although empirical evidence on the effect of this type of emotional distribution is sparse (but see related work by Christensen & Heavey, 1990; Gottman, 1993; Hatfield, Cacioppo, & Rapson, 1994), it is possible to imagine either positive or negative outcomes emerging from the process. If the redistribution results in an overall decrease in distress, it may have a positive effect on the interaction and the relationship. In contrast, if it encourages an escalation of emotionality, the consequences could be quite negative. The outcome may also be contingent upon other communication variables. For instance, scholars suggest that when interactants apologize for doing harm to another, the anger and aggression expressed by the injured party tend to decrease (Ohbuchi, Kameda, & Agarie, 1989; Tavuchis, 1991). This latter finding points out the need for empirical research to address both the functions of hurt and the roles various communication strategies play in the resolution of hurt and guilt in relationships.

Distinctions

Although guilt and hurt have a number of important similarities, they are obvious-ly quite different emotions. Distinctions between the two are apparent in: (a) the way they are conceptualized and categorized in the literature, (b) the source of the transgression that elicits each, and (c) the amount of attention to others' perspec-tives that each requires.

Guilt, more so than hurt, is portrayed in the literature as a *"primary"* affect (Izard, 1977; cf. Ekman, Friesen, & Ellsworth, 1982; Plutchik, 1962, 1980)[2] and is more closely associated with people's prototypical models of emotion (Fehr & Russell, 1984). Hurt, in contrast, is more likely to be termed an emotion *"blend"* (Weiner, personal communication). Although some have criticized the distinctions that have been drawn between primary and blended emotions (Ortony, Clore, & Collins, 1988), the differences implied by the two terms have important implications for the study of guilt and hurt. For instance, a number of scholars see primary emotions as the building blocks for emotion blends (Izard, 1977; Tomkins, 1981). From this per-spective, primary emotions are likened to the basic hues on a color wheel, and blended emotions emerge when the primaries are mixed together (Ekman, 1982; Plutchik, 1980). One conclusion that might be drawn from this analogy is that blended emotions are structurally more complex and likely harder to describe than primaries. Researchers taking this perspective may be interested in identifying the components parts of blended emotions such as hurt, because the amount or inten-sity of these basic components may influence the way the emotion is perceived and communicated. Because its composition is comparatively complex, it should be more difficult to make predictions about hurt than about a primary emotion such as guilt.

Some researchers, however, take issue with this "palette theory" (Scherer, 1984). They argue that blended emotions do not result from mixing primary emotions, but instead are unique states in and of themselves. Rather than emphasizing differ-ences between primary and blended states, Ortony, Clore, and Collins (1988) ar-gued that "the complexity of an emotion is determined by the degree to which it is a more differentiated form of a simple affective reaction" (p. 29). From this per-spective, hurt could be seen as a less complex emotion (than, e.g., guilt) because it is a fairly simple affective reaction to another's behavior. Scholars adopting this per-spective may be more interested in describing the elicitation or effects of hurt (for example) than in breaking it down into its component parts. Although theoretical issues such as these are not easily resolved, they clearly reflect some important con-siderations for researchers and theorists.

A second difference between guilt and hurt involves the locus or *source of the trans-*

---

[2]It is important to note that the emotions scholars deem as primary or basic vary a great deal. Thus, while some see guilt as a primary emotion, others do not. Hurt, however, was not characterized as a primary emotion in any of the literature we reviewed. The only arguable exceptions involve work by scholars such as Mowrer (1960), who conceptualize "pain" and "pleasure" as the two basic emotions.

gression that prompts each emotion. As previously noted, both guilt and hurt are instigated by a violation or breach of some sort. With guilt, the violation typically is committed by the individual feeling the emotion. In contrast, with hurt, the breach is made by someone other than the person who feels injured. Because the source of the transgression is distinct for the two emotions, people's efforts to deal with or resolve the two are also likely to differ. Those who feel guilty may perceive the onus for repairing any damage done lies within themselves; those who feel hurt may believe someone else should be held responsible for making amends.

Although assigning responsibility for a transgression to its source seems a simple, logical task, it can actually be quite complex. People who feel guilty must identify or label their unpleasant feelings as guilt (rather than, say, anger or hurt) in order to acknowledge their culpability. The literature on counseling is replete with examples of individuals who are unable or unwilling to recognize their guilty feelings (e.g., Lewis, 1971). Therapists cite a number of reasons why people may avoid accepting responsibility for a transgression, including the desire to escape punishment, to minimize negative evaluations from others, and to avoid making amends (Oatley, 1992).

In a similar vein, those who are hurt sometimes do not assign blame to the person who hurt them so that they can maintain a sense of positive regard for that individual. They may place responsibility for the other's behavior on external circumstances (e.g., "She has been under a lot of stress lately") or may even take on the blame themselves (e.g., "I started the argument"). Indeed, research on the elicitation of hurt demonstrates that recipients of hurtful messages often reported the other person did not intentionally hurt them (Vangelisti, 1994). Furthermore, intentionality was associated with the perceived impact of the hurtful message on the relationship—hurt viewed as unintentional had less of an impact. In extreme cases involving physical or emotional abuse, this pattern of thinking allows those who are abused to stay in relationships where their hurt can result in long-term damage (Herbert, Silver, & Ellard, 1991).

There are also situations when responsibility for the transgression is misplaced or misidentified. For instance, young children sometimes take responsibility for verbal aggression and hostility that occurs between their parents (Grych & Fincham, 1993). Anecdotal data further indicate that children who are sexually abused often feel guilty even though they are clearly victims, not transgressors (Cottle, 1980; Lamb, 1986; Pittman, 1989). Similarly, a substantial literature documents a phenomenon among those who lived through the Holocaust that has been termed "survivor guilt" (e.g., Lifton, 1967). Although individuals who report this experience usually do not exhibit exaggerated guilt feelings in their everyday interpersonal relationships (Lobel, Kav-Venaki, & Yahia, 1985), some suffer ongoing guilt for outliving loved ones or for feeling ambivalent toward those who died (Bettelheim, 1962; Krystal, 1968). In cases such as these, the people who were hurt—who were victims of others' actions—may take on feelings of guilt in an effort to create an illusion for themselves that they had (or have) some control over circumstances in their lives.

A third difference between guilt and hurt is that guilt requires more empathy or *attention to others' perspectives* than does hurt. Hoffman (1982) argued that guilt occurs when a person feels empathetic distress for another and simultaneously makes an attribution of responsibility to the self for the other's suffering. This conception of guilt suggests that those who feel the emotion must have enough awareness of others to recognize and, to some extent, comprehend others' distress. It also implies that those who are guilty must be able to understand causal links between their own behavior and others' feelings. Research by Zahn-Waxler and her colleagues (Zahn-Waxler & Radke-Yarrow, 1982; see Zahn-Waxler & Kochanska, 1990, for a review) supports this idea. Their longitudinal findings suggest that children must be old enough—approximately 2 years of age—to understand the effects of their own behavior on others before they begin to demonstrate signs of feeling guilt (for related work, see Kochanska, Casey, & Fukumoto, 1995).[3]

Although hurt also occurs as a result of an interpersonal event, it does not require that the injured person understand others' perspectives. Hurt is a response to another's behavior. The source of hurt lies outside the self, but the feelings are self-oriented and concern one's own distress. This is not to say that feeling hurt does not require some understanding of the associations between others' behavior and one's own emotions. It does. But it does not require the injured party to empathize with the other and/or understand the other's emotional state on the same level as does guilt.

DEFINING CHARACTERISTICS OF GUILT AND HURT

The assumptions that theorists, researchers, and therapists make about the characteristics that define guilt and hurt guide the questions they ask, the studies they conduct, and the treatments they implement involving the two emotions. Several potentially opposing characteristics are discussed in the literature. Guilt and hurt are often represented as (a) individual or interpersonal, (b) temporary or enduring, (c) intentional or unintentional, (d) prosocial or antisocial, and (e) rational or irrational. Disentangling some of the issues related to these characteristics helps to clarify existing research and concerns that face those interested in the communication processes associated with both guilt and hurt.

Individual versus Interpersonal

Perhaps the most cited theorist on guilt, Freud (1930/1961), portrayed guilt feelings as relatively individualistic phenomena. He identified guilt as a reaction to in-

---

[3]Children who were followed over time between the ages of 1 and 2-½ years were observed in situations where they caused another person's distress. The researchers found significant increases over time in the children's tendency to help or comfort the distressed individual.

appropriate impulses that can be traced to sexual or hostile feelings experienced during childhood toward parents. In part, guilt is a consequence of these impulses being repressed due to fear of punishment and/or of parental love. To say that psychoanalytic theory approaches guilt from an individualistic perspective is not to say that it completely ignores interpersonal or relational dynamics. Indeed, parent–child relationships play a substantial role in the theory. However, the focus is not on the relationship, what happens between relational partners, or even what is felt by the other (cf. Lewis, 1971). Instead, the emphasis is on what the child (the self) is trying to obtain from the parents (the other). Empathetic concern for the distress of others, as discussed by scholars such as Hoffman (1982), is not relevant. Because Freud assumed that all motivation is a result of people's efforts to rid themselves of accumulated stimulation, any attention to others' distress is necessarily self-motivated (Friedman, 1985).

It is certainly possible to take a similarly individualistic approach to the conceptualization of hurt. Researchers need only depict those who are hurt as motivated by self-preservation and a desire to avoid aversive (hurtful) stimuli. Relations with others would be relevant in so far as they contributed to the individual's goal of minimizing hurtful experiences. Duck and Sants (1983) argued that characterizing relational partners in this way—as relatively self-focused and oriented toward achieving their own goals—is not uncommon among those who study personal relationships.[4]

Examining guilt and hurt as interpersonal phenomena, by contrast, involves emphasizing what happens between interactants. Guilt and hurt feelings are contextualized in a social world—one where the thoughts and behaviors of others play an integral role in constructing individuals' emotions. Although this perspective does not preclude the possibility that emotions such as guilt and hurt may occur in the absence of others, it assumes that the emotions are based on social relationships (Friedman, 1985; Lazarus, 1991) rather than on individual drives, wants, or needs. People do have self-centered motivations, but those motivations are contextualized within relationships and tempered by a concern for relational partners.

The relevance of others to feelings of guilt is underlined by two studies examining the contexts in which guilt is typically elicited. Baumeister, Reis, and Delespaul (1995) asked respondents to describe their most recent experiences of guilt, anxiety, frustration, fear, sadness, anger, and irritation. The data revealed that of the seven emotions, guilt most often occurred when respondents were in the presence of others and that guilt episodes frequently emphasized neglecting a relational partner, failing to live up to an interpersonal obligation, or betraying a relational partner (also see Baumeister et al., 1995b). In a separate study, these researchers asked respondents to record their behaviors, thoughts, and feelings at random intervals when they were signaled by a beeper. The findings of the inves-

---

[4]In fact, Baumeister et al. (1994) argued that those who view guilt from such a perspective are adopting what has traditionally been termed an exchange orientation to relationships (Clark & Mills, 1979).

tigation indicated that although people were often alone when they felt guilty, the guilt usually centered on interpersonal issues or problems.

Although similar data concerning hurt are not available, hurt, almost by definition, should be considered as "interpersonal" an emotion as guilt. Human interaction of some sort is at the crux of both guilt and hurt. Scholars who define guilt from an interpersonal perspective suggest that it occurs when an individual feels distressed about harming another person (Baumeister et al., 1994, 1995b; Friedman, 1985; Hoffman, 1982; Jones et al., 1995). By contrast, hurt is engendered when a person feels distressed about being harmed *by* another (Vangelisti, 1994). When the two emotions are viewed in these ways, the interpersonal context of each becomes quite apparent. Given the centrality of social interaction to the elicitation of both emotions, it is not unreasonable to expect that people's experience of hurt, like their experience of guilt, accentuates interpersonal issues.

Temporary versus Enduring

Emotions, like many other human conditions, are typically represented in the literature either as attributes that persist over time or as more temporary qualities. Conceptualizing feelings of guilt and hurt as enduring tendencies or more temporary states affects the way researchers and therapists view the associations between the two emotions and interpersonal interaction.

Kugler and Jones (1992) noted that guilt has been operationalized in the literature in three different ways. They claimed first that guilt is often viewed as a temporary affective state, elicited when a person violates values or principles (e.g., Lazarus, 1991). Second, they noted that guilt is sometimes treated as an ongoing personality trait caused by past experiences or transgressions (e.g., Freud, 1930/ 1961). Third, they argued that guilt has been represented as a cognitive predisposition or state of readiness that is based on a person's moral standards (e.g., Mosher, 1968). Of these three approaches to measuring guilt, the latter two reflect relatively enduring characteristics, whereas the first is more transitory.

Thus far, the literature on hurt has treated the emotion as a temporary state. Hurt is typically connected to a particular event or interaction. It is interesting, however, to contemplate conceiving of hurt as a more sustained affective condition. If hurt, as a transitory state, is characterized as the negative feelings associated with being injured by another, then as a more enduring quality, the same negative feelings would be ongoing and would likely extend across a variety of situations. Enduring hurt would probably be associated with other generalized negative feelings such as anomie or depression (see Segrin, Chapter 8, this volume). It would differ, however, in that it would necessarily involve a perceived source and that source would reside outside the self. Presumably, ongoing feelings of hurt would vary in terms of whether the perceived injury was a single event with lasting consequences (e.g., an insult or accusation) or whether it involved a series of continuous events (e.g., verbal abuse).

Distinguishing temporary and enduring qualities of guilt and hurt has important ramifications not only for how the two emotions are defined, but also for the types of questions researchers ask concerning each and the ways therapists approach treatment of those who feel hurt or guilty. For instance, if guilt and hurt are seen as transitory, researchers and therapists are likely to examine variables associated with the elicitation of the emotions, factors that affect people's responses to them, and the typicality of various elicitation and response patterns in relational contexts. In contrast, those who view guilt and hurt as enduring may be more interested in identifying the patterns of thought and behavior that cause (and support) individuals' ongoing proclivities toward the emotions.

Furthermore, while temporary feelings of guilt and hurt are related to their more enduring counterparts (for studies on this issue relevant to guilt, see Jones & Kugler, 1993; Kugler & Jones, 1992), the passing affective conditions that make up the emotions, as temporary states, no doubt create different patterns of effects on interaction and relationships than do the more sustained conditions that comprise enduring feelings of guilt and hurt. When temporary, the two emotions are likely to reflect day-to-day fluctuations in relational partners' affections rather than ongoing attitudes toward partners. Indeed, in discussing the results of their research on distinctions between transitory and enduring guilt, Jones et al. (1995) suggested that temporary guilt feelings are "experienced following transgressions that harm relational partners and thereby threaten the emotional bond with significant others," whereas more lasting feelings of guilt "may reflect a continuing and habitual lack of mutual satisfaction and intimacy between the guilty person and his or her network of intimate and social relationships" (p. 318).

Intentional versus Unintentional

The influence of guilt and hurt on interaction and relationships in part depends on people's perceptions of whether the transgression in question was intentional or unintentional. Given that both guilt and hurt are unpleasant feelings, it is tempting to associate intentional transgressions with negative outcomes. The idea of intentionally causing violations linked to either emotion seems more damaging—both to individuals and to relationships—than unintentionally causing them. In making such predictions, however, it is important to consider that the source of the transgression differs for guilt and hurt. As a consequence, the locus of intentionality associated with the violation also differs. Because guilt involves distress over having committed a wrongful act, people who intentionally engage in such an act are actually less likely to feel guilty. In support of this, McGraw (1987) found that people felt more guilty when the harm they did was accidental than when it was purposeful.

By contrast, the source of transgressions associated with hurt resides with someone other than the person feeling the emotion. Intentionality, thus, may be judged by the individual who is harmed rather than the person who engages in the harmful act. Studies of romantic partners (Doherty, 1982; Fincham, Beach, & Nelson, 1987; Orvis, Kelley, & Butler, 1976) and roommates (Sillars, 1980) suggested that there is an association between recipients' judgments of intentionality or blame and relational outcomes. Those who felt their relational partner intentionally engaged in negative behaviors tended to report less satisfaction, more distress, and more negativity in their relationships than others. An investigation of the influence of intentionality on hurt similarly yielded a positive association between partners' perceptions of intentionality and their views about the impact of a particular transgression on their relationship (Vangelisti, 1994). Transgressions viewed as intentionally hurtful had a greater impact on the relationship than did those seen as unintentional. In concurrence with Stamp and Knapp (1990), the study suggested that recipients' judgments of intent seem to "change the nature of the stimulus" for them (p. 288).

Prosocial versus Antisocial

Although guilt and hurt are experienced by most as unpleasant feelings, both emotions can function in either positive or negative ways (Zahn-Waxler & Kochanska, 1990). The undesirable, aversive aspects of guilt and hurt can encourage people to avoid some behaviors and engage in others. For instance, scholars have long touted the value of guilt as a means of social control (Ausubel, 1955; Izard, 1977). Part of the reason people choose not to engage in certain activities is that they recognize a moral standard prohibiting the behavior and anticipate feeling guilty if they violate the standard. While many of the moral values associated with guilt are maintained by cultural or social groups, those values, when adopted by individuals, reduce the need for the larger group to concentrate its efforts on controlling or punishing wrongdoings (see, e.g., Mosher, 1965). Individuals who adopt the group's standards are likely to avoid or try to correct problematic behavior (e.g., Fehr, 1988).

With regard to hurt, the cognitive processes that discourage antisocial behavior may be more directly geared toward avoiding punishment (hurt) than adhering to a set of values. Given that the source or cause of hurt often is out of the recipient's direct control, relatively little can be gained by adopting a strong moral code of conduct. Instead, people may avoid performing certain behaviors as a way to avoid the negative affect associated with being hurt.

Another variable that may distinguish the ways that hurt and guilt discourage antisocial behavior is individuals' perception that their emotions are justified or warranted. People who feel guilty, on some level, probably believe they deserve to experience negative feelings because they committed a transgression. In contrast, those who are hurt may feel bad precisely because they believe they did not do anything to warrant feeling that way. And perhaps more importantly, because the transgression involved is committed by another person, part of their hurt may stem from a feeling of emotional betrayal. If this is the case, those who avoid certain behaviors because they foresee being hurt are probably somewhat cynical about their relationship with the person they anticipate may hurt them.

In addition to restricting behaviors that do not conform to social standards, guilt and hurt can encourage activities that contribute to the welfare of both individuals and relationships. Ferguson, Stegge, and Damhuis (1991) noted that "adaptive levels of guilt, at least in Western societies, flag a momentary break with our obligations to others and inform us to maintain our interpersonal relationships through approach and reparative action" (p. 837). In two different sets of studies, Baumeister and his colleagues (Baumeister et al., 1995b; Baumeister, Reis, & Delespaul, 1995) found that people's descriptions of guilt-inducing situations often highlighted neglecting a relational partner or failing to live up to an interpersonal responsibility. Vangelisti et al. (1991) also found that guilt-inducing messages frequently drew people's attention to unfulfilled relationship obligations. To prevent such feelings of guilt, people may engage in prosocial behaviors that maintain their relationships and their interpersonal obligations.

Preventing hurt may similarly be a basis for engaging in certain prosocial, relationship-enhancing behaviors. Once again, because the source of transgressions that elicit hurt resides outside the self, the processes that engender such behaviors probably differ from those associated with preventing guilt. Both processes likely involve sanctioning or punishment: If certain prosocial behaviors are not performed, people will feel hurt or guilty. What distinguishes the two is that the punishment associated with guilt is caused by a person's own behavior, whereas the punishment associated with hurt emanates from another. It is one thing to punish yourself for a transgression; it is another to have a relationship partner punish you. Over time, engaging in prosocial behaviors to avoid hurt is likely to create a very different relational environment than engaging in the same behaviors to avoid guilt.

It is important at this point to acknowledge that a transgression, by itself, does not increase prosocial behavior. When they see a breach of some sort, people are not necessarily willing to repair the damage or to volunteer to help others (Silverman, 1967). As Brock (1969) noted, transgressions are not invariably associated with guilt. Before feeling guilty, people must perceive that they have done something wrong. In the absence of this perception, they may not be motivated to make amends for their (wrongful) behavior. Similarly, people do not always feel hurt when someone commits a transgression against them. The transgression must be perceived and framed as hurtful (rather than, say, as an act that primarily evokes anger). In addition, guilt and hurt obviously are not the only emotions that motivate people to engage in prosocial behavior (see Konecni, 1972; Regan, 1971). Instead, there are likely a number of interpersonal variables that influence the association between guilt or hurt and the behaviors they evoke. For instance, the feelings of indebtedness often associated with guilt have been linked to increased altruistic behavior

(Darlington & Macker, 1966). Similarly, reminding people of their debts or obligations tends to increase their willingness to help others (Cunningham, Steinberg, & Grev, 1980).

Rational versus Irrational

When assessing the impact of guilt or hurt on social interaction, it is critical to consider variability in the way people detect and interpret transgressions. In some cases people's perceptions may be logical and sound, whereas in others their views may seem completely unreasonable. Importantly though, both rational and irrational perceptions of wrongdoings affect people's feelings and behaviors. Some people, for example, may react to very small, inconsequential acts as serious violations; others may go unaffected even when a wrongdoing has profound repercussions. Some may refuse to take responsibility for violations they clearly committed; others may feel culpable for events that did not even involve them. Some may ignore their partner's offenses; others may be affected by everything their partner does.

Taken to the extreme, any one of these positions can generate dysfunctional or problematic behavior. For instance, when people are unable (or unwilling) to feel guilt or hurt, they lack an important barometer for their own and others' activities. The inability to connect their feelings with transgressions leaves then unable to monitor the impact of behavior on relationships (Bulka, 1987). As a consequence, they may engage in activities that are harmful to their relationships and/or remain in relationships characterized by extremely negative behavior. In contrast, those who feel guilt or hurt with little or no provocation will tend to make inappropriate connections between feelings and transgressions (Friedman, 1985). In the case of guilt, this may involve taking responsibility for, and trying to repair, transgressions that are not theirs. This phenomenon is not at all uncommon among children who grow up with parents who are "absent" due to chemical dependency, marital problems, or mental illness (e.g., Minuchin, Roseman, & Baker, 1978). In the case of hurt, the same pattern may involve excessive sensitivity to others and the interpretation of even neutral or positive comments as hurtful. Individuals who interpret others' behavior in this way are unlikely to trust others and may withdraw from social interaction because they see people in their world as a constant source of pain (e.g., see the discussion of fearful avoidant attachment in Chapters 3, 10, and 18, this volume).

Zahn-Waxler and Kochanska (1990) discussed a neurophysiological model of "kindling" initially offered by Meyersberg and Post (1979) that explains the development of some irrational responses to guilt or hurt. Broadly interpreted, this model suggests that under certain conditions, people's responses to the two emotions may become "kindled" or exaggerated over time. In brief, Meyersberg and Post argued that when organisms are repeatedly exposed to a noxious stimulus (e.g., electric shock), they become sensitized so that, eventually, smaller doses of the stimulus are required to elicit a response (e.g., seizures). Ultimately, organisms may begin to display the response even in the absence of the stimulus.

Prior to applying this model to people's reactions to guilt and hurt, it is important to specify the conditions under which the process depicted in the model is thought to occur. First, "the organisms" in question (people) must be repeatedly exposed to the stimulus. The guilt or hurt feelings must be experienced again and again over a period of time. Second, the stimulus must be perceived as noxious or harmful. The guilt or hurt cannot, in other words, be seen as deserved, appropriate, or justified. Third, and finally, the stimulus must be externally imposed. In the case of hurt, this condition is easily fulfilled because hurt typically occurs as a result of an external transgression (one committed by someone other than the self.) The external imposition of guilt, however, is a bit more complex. Usually, guilt-related transgressions are internal; they are committed by the person who feels the guilt. Externally imposed feelings of guilt are those where the transgression was committed by someone else. These guilt feelings likely occur when people inappropriately take responsibility for a transgression they did not commit.

Whether people's reaction to guilt or hurt is to ignore the transgression or to become extremely distressed, Meyersberg and Post's (1979) model of kindling suggests that those reactions may become more extreme over time. Unfortunately, there is an abundance of anecdotal data to support this proposition. When children are repeatedly hurt (e.g., physically or sexually abused), they often become withdrawn and seemingly unresponsive to social interaction or the develop what appears to be an exaggerated sensitivity or defensiveness toward others (Arias & Pape, 1994). Similarly, when placed in a position of responsibility for transgressions that are not theirs (e.g., their parents' marital problems), children can become either overly willing to experience guilt or completely unwilling to accept responsibility for even their own behavior (Ruesch, 1957). Given the possible consequences of these patterns of behavior for individuals and relationships, research on the applicability of the Meyersberg and Post model to situations such as these would be useful.[5]

THE ELICITATION OF GUILT AND HURT

Recent theoretical and empirical work suggests not only that guilt and hurt frequently concern interpersonal issues (Baumeister et al., 1994; Jones et al., 1995; Vangelisti, 1994), but also that the two emotions are often elicited through social interaction (Andersen & Guerrero, Chapter 3, this volume). The strategies people use to evoke guilt and hurt in others very likely influence the extent to which the emotions are elicited and the effect of the elicitation on individuals and relationships.

---

[5]An alternative to the Meyersberg and Post model is a model in which recipients habituate or "get used to" ongoing transgressions. If a habituation model applies to recurrent guilt and hurt, we would expect recipients' responses to decrease (rather than become more exaggerated) over time.

Making Others Feel Guilty

Miceli (1992) argued conversational strategies that evoke guilt can be categorized along two broad dimensions: *aggressive/adoptive* and *communicative/noncommunicative*. She defined aggressive strategies as those that induce guilt by obstructing the transgressor's goals. Accusations, for example, may be used to thwart goals such as keeping a transgression hidden from others or avoiding sanctions. Similarly, reproaches that focus on the moral or relational consequences of transgressions can block goals associated with evading responsibility for a wrongdoing. Adoptive strategies, in contrast, create guilt by taking on (adopting) the goals of the transgressor. Miceli claimed that offering forgiveness or providing excuses for a wrongful act implies acceptance of the guilty party's goals. She also noted, however, that these strategies often provide the speaker with substantial power (e.g., to guide the course of the conversation) as they place the guilty party in a position of indebtedness.

In claiming that any of these, and other, guilt-inducing techniques can be communicative or noncommunicative, Miceli (1992) suggested that guilt can be elicited via direct or indirect means. She argued that strategies are noncommunicative if, for example, the transgressor hears of guilt-eliciting information indirectly, from a third party (e.g., "your mother is sick"). This technique is akin to what Berger and Bradac (1982) referred to as a passive strategy. By comparison, she defined as communicative those techniques that directly acknowledge the elicitor's desire to provide the transgressor with information (e.g., "I'm sick").

An empirical investigation conducted to explore the underlying dimensions of strategies that create guilt confirms many of Miceli's (1992) arguments. Vangelisti et al. (1991) reported that guilt-eliciting techniques may be arranged along three continua. The first, an *active–passive* dimension, reflects part of what Miceli referred to when she distinguished aggressive and adoptive strategies. Active techniques are those that demand more overt involvement from the elicitor (e.g., strategies that point out debt or inequity), whereas passive strategies allow the elicitor to appear more compliant and submissive (e.g., strategies that acquiesce to the transgressor's goals). The second dimension, a *direct–indirect* one, captures Miceli's distinction between communicative and noncommunicative techniques. Direct strategies are those that explicitly point to a transgression (e.g., those that enunciate an unfulfilled obligation). Indirect techniques, in contrast, involve more subtle, elusive conversational moves (e.g., hinting that a deception has occurred). The third, and final dimension is a *self–other* continuum. Techniques that are self-oriented emphasize the role of the guilt elicitor (e.g., they use the self as a basis for comparison), whereas those that are other-oriented focus primarily on the transgressor (e.g., they emphasize the transgressor's goals or desires).

The events that underlie these dimensions are remarkably similar across studies conducted by two different groups of researchers (Baumeister et al., 1995b; Vangelisti et al., 1991). Both groups found that one of the central issues in the elicitation of guilt was the transgressor's violation of relationship obligations or norms.

Baumeister et al. reported that the most common incidents causing guilt involved neglecting a relationship partner, failing to live up to an interpersonal obligation, and betraying a romantic relationship. Vangelisti et al. (1991) similarly noted that conversational techniques most frequently used to engender guilt feelings were stating relationship obligations, enunciating a sacrifice that was made, stating role obligations, and making comparisons. (Table I contains descriptions and examples of the categories used in the latter study, listed in order of the frequency with which they were cited by participants.)

Both groups of researchers also provide evidence that people may regard guilt elicitation as an undesirable conversational strategy. Vangelisti et al. (1991) noted a negative association between social approval seeking (Crowne & Marlowe, 1964) and people's self-reported guilt use. These researchers also reported that individuals claimed they were less likely than others to use guilt as a technique. Baumeister et al. (1995b) further found that a number of their respondents felt "metaguilt"—guilt about engendering guilt in their conversational partner. Thus, while guilt elicitation clearly is used and has important functions in interpersonal relationships, there seem to be occasions when it is accompanied by a negative evaluation (Rubin & Shaffer, 1987). Eliciting guilt may break unspoken rules associated with holding relational partners in high regard or respecting their actions.

Using Words That Hurt

Like those that elicit guilt, strategies that create hurt have a strong relational component. Data from two different studies suggest that when asked to describe messages that hurt their feelings, over one-third of people focused on topics concerning romantic or nonromantic relationships (Vangelisti, 1994). In addition, a smaller but substantial portion of respondents recalled hurtful messages emphasizing their personality traits—characteristics that were relatively stable and unchangeable. Although statements focusing on an individual's personality do not provide direct information about relational issues, they do comprise an indirect commentary on the relationship at the time they are spoken.[6] Table II includes the topics that were the focus of people's accounts of hurtful messages in order of their frequency.

The form of hurtful messages also yields interesting information about the interpersonal dynamics that contribute to hurtful episodes—particularly when the messages are examined in terms of the extent to which they elicit hurt. In two different studies, the most commonly noted forms of hurtful messages were accusations, evaluations, and informative statements (see Table II). These message forms,

---

[6]Furthermore, when considering the substantial number of hurtful messages about personality traits, it is important to keep in mind that the transgression that engenders hurt feelings is embedded in the message. The elicitation of hurt, itself, is a transgression. By comparison, the elicitation of guilt merely points to a previous transgression. And that prior transgression, like some of those that evoke hurt, may involve an attack on someone's personality.

TABLE I   Categories of Guilt Elicitation[a]

Definitions	Examples
State relationship obligation: A tells B that B is not meeting an obligation that is part of B's relationships with either A or a third party.	A: Are you going to watch the baby tomorrow while I'm in school? B: No, I want to go fishing. A: Fine. When he grows up and asks who daddy is I'll say he never had time for you.
Nature of things: A points out that B should "know" how to think or behave appropriately with regard to a particular issue or situation, and that his or her behavior does not reflect that knowledge.	A: Are you going to eat that ice cream cone? B: Yes. A: I thought you wanted to lose weight.
State role obligation: A tells B that B has a role obligation that B is not fulfilling.	A: There's a meeting after school today. B: Do I have to go? A: Depends on how professional you are. B: That means I have to go.
Sacrifice: B says that B is engaging in an undesirable or atypical behavior because of A's actions.	A: I won't be able to come into work today. B: Well, I guess that's O.K., I'll try to find someone to watch the desk while you're not here and I'm at lunch. A: Well, I'm not putting you out, am I? B: No, no. I'll just skip lunch if I don't find anyone. It's O.K.
Comparison: A contrasts an act performed by B either with A's own performance or with a third party's performance of the same act with the implication that B's performance is wanting.	A: What time did you get up today? B: About noon. A: By that time I was having my lunch.
Deception recognition: A points out that B is either deceiving or making obviously false excuses for a behavior.	A: Have you been taking my messages? B: I think so. A: Well, Peter said that he called today, but I never got the message.
Debt: A points out that B "owes" A because of past actions.	A: Sue, can I borrow your car? B: No, I really don't like to loan out my car. A: Well, I'm glad you appreciate all the times you've driven my car to work!
Describe disproportionality: A notes that B did not (or does not intend to) fulfill B's part of a task or obligation that is typically a shared one, and that A did (or does) a greater share of the task.	A: When I get home you can help me bathe the kids and we'll put them to bed. B: Now wait a minute, I have to study for a test, pack, and get ready for a job interview. I think you can bathe the kids.
Consistency demand: A reminds B that B agreed in the past to some behavior and is now acting in a way inconsistent with the agreed upon behavior.	A: Mom, can I have Brandy over this evening? B: No, we've had company all day. I start class tomorrow. We just finished your dance recital and Girl Scout project. A: You said I could have Brandy over sometime.

TABLE I (*continued*)

Definitions	Examples
Acquiescence: A grudgingly permits B to engage in a behavior of which A does not approve.	A: Are you playing golf again? B: Yes, starting time is 11:30. A: Well, have fun, but you could have started earlier. B: I know, maybe I'll call and cancel. A: No, go ahead, you love to golf and you haven't very much lately.
State rule violation: A points out that B is ignoring or violating a general "rule" that both A and B consider to be a moral or ethical issue.	A: I did not get to put any money in church today. I forgot and paid a bill and did not leave enough money for church. B: Well, church should be the most important thing and you probably should have allowed for it.
Self-focus: A says that A's condition is worse than B's.	A: How are you? B: O.K., I have been going to school for 2 weeks and I'm getting behind in my housework. It's very tiring. A: At least you have had it easier than I have. I have been spending the nights at the hospital. We found out Saturday that my mother is dying of cancer.

[a]Adapted from Vangelisti, A. L., Daly, J. A., & Rudnick, J. R. (1991). Making people feel guilty in conversations: Techniques and correlates. *Human Communication Research, 18,* 10–11.

however, impacted receivers differently. Accusations, for example, were more frequently rated low in hurtfulness, while informative statements were more often seen as extremely hurtful.

This difference in the tendency of accusatory and informative statements to elicit hurt can be explained, in part, by the ability of recipients to "repair" or offer alternatives to each. When accused (e.g., "You are a such a selfish person!"), people are usually afforded the opportunity to defend themselves; they can respond by denying the accusation, offering an explanation, or attacking their accuser. However, when presented with an informative statement ("I'm in love with someone else"), there is little recipients can do to counter what was said. As a consequence, they have less control over the conversation. Furthermore, given that over one-third of the hurtful messages described in these two studies emphasized relational issues, many of the respondents may have felt the ramifications of this lack of conversational control in their personal relationships.

The ability of recipients to exert such control may be particularly salient in hurtful episodes because the transgressions that elicit hurt are externally imposed. In contrast, the transgressions that create guilt feelings are more often internally im-

TABLE II   Forms and Topics of Hurtful Messages[a]

Forms		Topics	
Category	Examples	Category	Examples
Inform: A disclosure of information.	"You aren't a priority in my life."	Romantic relations	"He never liked you anyway. He just used you to get back at me."
Evaluation: A description of value, worth, or quality.	"Going out with you was the biggest mistake of my life."		
Accusation: A charge of fault or offense.	"You're such a hypocrite."	Personality traits	"Well, I think you're selfish and spoiled!"
Directive: An order, set of directions, or a command	"Just leave me alone, why don't you?"	Nonromantic relations	"You're trying too hard to be popular . . . you're ignoring your 'real' friends."
Express desire: A statement of preference.	"I don't ever want to have anything to do with you."	Physical appearance	"God almighty you're fat!"
Advise: A suggestion for a course of action.	"Break up with her so you can have some fun."	Abilities/intelligence	"I guess it's hard for you teenage illiterates to write that stuff."
Joke: A witticism or prank.	"The statement was really an ethnic joke against my ethnicity."	Time	"We don't do things together like we used to."
Threat: An expression of intention to inflict some sort of punishment under certain conditions.	"If I find out you are ever with that person, *never* come home again."	Self-worth	"I don't need you anymore."
		Sexual behavior	"Why? Do you still want to sleep around?"
Lie: An untrue, deceptive statement or question.	"The worst part was when he lied about something."	Ethnicity/religion	"You're a stupid Jew!"

[a] Adapted from Vangelisti, A. L. (1994). Messages that hurt. In W. R. Cupach & B. H. Spitzberg (Eds.), *The dark side of interpersonal communication* (pp. 53–82). Hillsdale, NJ: Erlbaum.

posed. They are committed by the person who feels guilty. Thus, while guilt may be very distressing, the nature of the transgressions associated with the emotion may provide guilty parties with a larger repertoire of responses.

RESPONSES TO GUILT AND HURT

Although responses to guilt and hurt clearly play a role in shaping interaction associated with the two emotions, there has been little research directly investigating this issue. Studies conducted to date, however, do underline the importance of these reactions to the well-being of both individuals and relationships. They also raise a number of interesting questions about the conversational and relational constraints people face when confronted with the two emotions.

As noted in the previous section of this chapter, the nature of the transgression committed may limit people's reactions to guilt or hurt. In most cases, the transgressions associated with guilt are committed by an internal source (the self) and those associated with hurt are imposed by an external source (another person). When people feel guilty, they can try to repair what they have done by apologizing, explaining themselves, or otherwise making amends. Guilt often engenders a desire for people to confess or offer reparations for their behavior (Tangney, Wager, Fletcher, & Gramzow, 1992). Even "bystanders" (Cunningham et al., 1980), who feel guilty about observing a transgression may attempt reparations for the offense because they are not hampered by having been injured themselves. By contrast, when people feel hurt, they can make moves to cope with their feelings (e.g., by excusing the wrongdoing, inviting repair, or ignoring the situation), but it is relatively difficult for them to repair a transgression they did not commit.

Because people may perceive their ability to resolve or recover from hurt as somewhat limited, their reaction to the emotion may involve defensive or even offensive posturing, rather than repair. Furthermore, in cases where hurt is extreme, people may be unable or unwilling to exert the effort required for either a defensive or an offensive stance and may instead withdraw from interaction. Results of an exploratory study support these notions (Vangelisti & Crumley, in press). The findings revealed that people who were hurt by others sometimes reacted by lashing out at the person they saw as the source of their pain. However, recipients of extremely hurtful messages more frequently said that they reacted by withdrawing—often by crying or acquiescing to their conversational partner.

Although, in general, the transgressions associated with hurt may place more restrictions on recipients' reparative behavior than those associated with guilt, it is very important to acknowledge that there are some types of guilt that are also extremely difficult to resolve. As previously noted, people can experience guilt without committing a transgression. In such cases, individuals take on responsibility for violations that are not of their doing. The violation may be instigated by another person, or it may lack a specific cause. Either way, it is relatively difficult for the person who feels guilty to repair or make amends for the wrongdoing.

One particularly poignant example of this phenomena can be found in the guilt experienced by bereaved parents. Oftentimes, parents who experience the death of a child not only are devastated by the loss, but also feel culpable for the events surrounding the death. Miles and Demi (1983–1984) noted that these parents may suffer a range of guilt feelings including those associated with beliefs that they contributed to the death (death causation guilt), that they should not outlive their child (survivor guilt), that they are being punished for a prior act (moral guilt), or that they are not grieving properly (grief guilt). Furthermore, parents of children who committed suicide or died in an accident reported more guilt than did parents of children who died of chronic illness (Miles & Demi, 1991–1992). As argued by these researchers, deaths linked to suicide or accidents may be perceived as preventable, and thus may be more likely to elicit guilt. By contrast, the extended time often associated with chronic illness may allow parents to resolve many issues that later create guilt feelings.

The tendency to take responsibility for the welfare of others is certainly not limited to bereaved parents. Indeed, people in a variety of close relationships may experience guilt when they are unable to "fix" or repair a problem faced by a loved one. The guilt these individuals experience may be particularly difficult to deal with when they perceive the person they feel responsible for is physically, psychologically, or emotionally dependent on them. For instance, grown children caring for an elderly parent (Blieszner & Shifflett, 1990), family members dealing with the serious illness of a loved one (Rolland, 1993), and parents raising a child with disabilities (Nixon & Singer, 1993) all may have trouble recognizing that they cannot repair or erase the challenges that face those they love.

In part because the circumstances most of these people deal with are impossible for them to repair (sadly, a person cannot prevent an existing disability, be a "better parent" to a child who has died, or eliminate the symptoms of chemical dependency), the guilty party's reactions may be quite different than they would be to other types of guilt. Indeed, Miles and Demi (1983–1984) found that rationalizing, sharing, and believing in religion were responses common to parents who were dealing with the death of a child. Also, people faced with these seemingly "impossible" situations might dedicate time and effort to a cause associated with the issue in an effort to "do something" and/or gain a sense of control in a very uncontrollable situation.

DIRECTIONS FOR FUTURE STUDY

The goal of this chapter was to begin to disentangle some of the complex associations between guilt and hurt and to examine some aspects of communication associated with the two emotions. In reviewing the literature relevant to guilt and hurt, one thing that becomes apparent is that the two emotions, almost by their nature, are interpersonal events. They affect and are affected by the relational context in which they occur. Feeling guilt is linked with taking responsibility for a transgression and, according to research (Baumeister et al., 1995b; Baumeister, Reis, & Delespaul, 1995; Jones et al., 1995; Vangelisti et al., 1991), many of the transgressions that evoke guilt are associated with interpersonal relationships. Similarly, when individuals feel hurt by another, they demonstrate the ability of that person to affect them. Even in cases where people feel inappropriate guilt (i.e., they take responsibility for a transgression that is not theirs) or hurt (i.e., they feel injured by a transgression that did not occur), the emotions they feel shape, and are shaped by, their interactions with others.

Although the transgressions linked to guilt and hurt frequently emphasize relational issues, the processes involved in identifying and evaluating relational transgressions are not altogether clear. Researchers and theorists have long claimed that the tendency of people to hold and adhere to a set of moral standards inhibits certain behaviors, in part because engaging in those behaviors creates feelings of guilt (Ausubel, 1955; Mosher, 1979). The implication is that moral standards provide individuals with a yardstick to measure behavior and identify transgressions. Accordingly, research by Jones et al. (1995) demonstrates that there are negative associations between people's tendencies to subscribe to a moral code (e.g., "I believe in a strict interpretation of right and wrong") and to engage in both relational and nonrelational transgressions. Importantly, though, moral standards are "generally more extensively and strongly related to nonrelational than to relational transgression categories" (p. 316). These findings suggest that people's general moral standards provide only a weak hint as to whether they uphold certain relational behaviors.

If scholars are to understand the elicitation of guilt and hurt in personal relationships, they must continue to explore the ways people identify and evaluate transgressions. The relatively weak link between general moral standards and relational wrongdoings found by Jones et al. (1995) implies that people may use a more specific set of relational standards to evaluate relational behavior. Researchers suggest that moral standards provide an indicator of people's ethics—their moral conscience. Given this, it is not unreasonable to suggest that people's relational standards reflect what might be termed a *relational conscience*. And, although moral and relational consciences are likely related, it is not difficult to imagine people who have a strong moral conscience (e.g., a very strict sense of "right" and "wrong"), but a weak relational one (e.g., a general belief that they should have "free reign" in personal relationships). Exploring and measuring individuals' relational standards may provide a more clear idea of how people identify and evaluate transgressions that occur in their relationships (Baucom, Epstein, Sayers, & Sher, 1989). This, in turn, should yield important information about the cognitive processes associated with the elicitation of guilt and hurt.

Of course, as soon as the possibility of studying relational standards is raised, difficulties associated with identifying a single group of standards become relevant. Individuals, relationships, societies, and cultures all construct and endorse different standards for interpersonal communication and relationships (Knapp, 1984; Montgomery, 1988). People may even have different rules or guidelines for applying those standards to their daily lives. At the same time, there is evidence of some commonality—at least within larger cultural groups. Bringing a loved one to tears in public would make many feel at least a twinge of guilt. Being told they aren't important by a relational partner is bound to cause most people pain. Even hardened criminals, who commit acts deemed as irreparable by many societies, tend to band together against those who prey upon small children.

Perhaps the most compelling evidence that there is commonality among people's standards is a phenomenon called *collective guilt*. Collective guilt occurs when a whole group of people feels culpable for the same event. Individuals in the group identify a transgression and take responsibility either for committing it or for failing to prevent it. Family members or circles of friends can experience this type of guilt when they realize that one of their group has been unjustly harmed by the activities of the whole or when, on a daily basis, they must confront ongoing transgressions (e.g., abuse) that they contribute to by acting (or failing to act) in ways they believe they should. One of the most powerful examples of collective guilt discussed by scholars is the Holocaust (Bulka, 1987; Frankl, 1984). Whether accepted in recognition of their crimes, imposed upon them by those who suffered, or taken on due to their associations with others who committed transgressions (Sichrovsky, 1988), a strong sense of guilt for the suffering that occurred at the hands of the Nazi Party permeates the lives of many who lived in Germany during World War II.

Although there is no literature documenting a parallel phenomenon under the rubric of *collective hurt,* the issue certainly seems worthy of study. Anecdotal data suggest that groups of people, at times, feel hurt by the same event. Members of a family may be hurt when they are stigmatized by others in their community (Imber-Black, 1993), and siblings may experience a unified sense of pain due to transgressions committed by their parents (Kahn & Lewis, 1988). Many African Americans feel a deep hurt when they contemplate the bigotry that they, and their children, still have to tolerate (Boyd-Franklin, 1993). Similarly, people who are HIV-positive experience emotional pain when they confront the hostility of those who blame them for their illness (Weiner, Perry, & Magnusson, 1988).

Closely related to collective hurt and guilt is another emotional experience termed *survivor guilt* (Lifton, 1967). As noted earlier, this phenomenon, like collective guilt, has been extensively discussed in the context of the Holocaust. Different from collective guilt, however, survivor guilt is not associated with having actually violated a set of moral standards. Instead, it is felt by individuals who survived or endured a transgression. Thus, those who lived through the heinous crimes committed in Nazi Germany often feel guilty because they outlived friends and family members (Bettelheim, 1962; Krystal, 1968). Although these individuals probably also feel a collective hurt, their experience of survivor guilt is different in that it involves taking some responsibility for the transgressions committed against them and their loved ones (Friedman, 1985).

The concept of survivor guilt has also been used to study the feelings of those who keep their jobs when others in their company are fired or terminated. In two different studies, Brockner and his colleagues (Brockner, Davy, & Carter, 1985; Brockner, Greenberg, Brockner, Bortz, & Carter, 1986) set up an experimentally induced "layoff" where a confederate departed after being told he or she was not allowed to complete the investigation. Results indicated that participants felt guilty about being allowed to continue the study when the confederate was dismissed.

Survivor guilt, such as this, may occur in the context of personal relationships. Following relational disengagement, for example, those who "move on" and develop another satisfying, long-term relationship may feel guilty if their former partner is unable (or unwilling) to do so. Similarly, siblings who move through the experience of growing up in a problematic family environment and begin to flourish may feel a sense of guilt about brothers or sisters who are less able to deal with the transgressions that occurred in their family.

Although examining various forms of guilt and hurt should yield important data about the standards people use to judge transgressions and the situations that elicit guilt and hurt, it may or may not provide information about the conversational patterns that create and support the two emotions. Given that guilt and hurt are often inextricably linked to interpersonal associations, the communication that evokes, maintains, and resolves these two emotions is a key to understanding how they operate. As noted in this chapter, strategies that elicit both guilt and hurt have been examined (Baumeister et al., 1995b; Miceli, 1992; Vangelisti et al., 1991). For the most part, however, the techniques that have emerged in the literature are those used by someone other than the individual feeling the emotion. Are there instances when people engage in communication that evokes guilt or hurt in themselves? Do people sometimes use communication to seek guilt or hurt? While the notion that individuals would try to make themselves feel unpleasant seems counterintuitive, some of the forms of guilt and hurt reviewed in this chapter lend themselves to this possibility. For instance, people who experience survivor guilt may seek confirmation for their feelings through communication with others because they lack the more overt evidence of having committed a transgression. Similarly, those who feel collective guilt or hurt may engage in communication strategies that help them relate to others in their group who feel the emotion and, in doing so, may reinforce their own feelings.

Seeking guilt or hurt may also occur in an effort to restore or cope with interpersonal inequities (Baumeister et al., 1994). Although studies suggest that overbenefited people tend to feel guilty (Walster, Walster, & Traupmann, 1978), researchers have not examined the extent to which overbenefited people seek out this guilt. Instead, the assumption has been that the guilt is almost an automatic consequence of this inequity. It is very possible that being overbenefited first creates an image of the self (e.g., inconsiderate, egocentric) that is inconsistent with a desired image (e.g., considerate, other-oriented), and that the need to resolve this inconsistency in turn encourages people to interact in ways that make them feel guilty. People may reason that someone who feels guilty about being overbenefited at least is not altogether selfish, inconsiderate, or egocentric.

Feeling guilty, of course, is not the only way to respond to interpersonal inequity. Among other things, people may choose to change their overbenefited status by seeking out hurt in their relationships. If they position themselves to be hurt, or construe their partner's behavior as hurtful, they will increase their perceived costs and thus restore equity. Individuals who choose this course of action, for example, may communicate intense feelings of hurt when their partner questions or denies their access to some benefit. Whether feigned, or actually felt, these hurt feelings may be interpreted as relational costs and, as a consequence, may decrease the overbenefited person's liability.

Missing from this, and many other scenarios discussed in the literature, is the interactive nature of guilt and hurt. Whether considering communication strategies associated with the elicitation, maintenance, or response to the two emotions, researchers and theorists need to begin to look at the utterances and relationships that surround guilt and hurt. For example, some data suggest that people respond to guilt they feel about harming outgroup members by derogating those they have hurt (Katz, Glass, & Cohen, 1973). What communication contexts encourage and discourage derogation as a response to guilt? If people are placed in situations where they must interact with outgroup members prior to committing the harmful act, are they less likely to cope with their guilt by derogating the others? Also, what are the outgroup members' responses to this type of derogation and what variables differentiate situations where the interaction escalates into conflict from those where it does not?

Clearly, research can be conducted to address these, and similar issues, on an individual level. Studies, for instance, suggest that people who are prone to guilt and tend to feel more guilty after derogating others than those who are not prone to the emotion (Okel & Mosher, 1968). Given this, it is possible that individuals' tendency toward guilt feelings will predict the extent to which they derogate outgroup members. Individual-level data such as these are both interesting and theoretically important. However, because guilt and hurt frequently occur in interpersonal contexts, this information should be supplemented with data that focus on interactions between people. Communication between those who are hurt and those who hurt them should affect the guilt feelings experienced by transgressors as well as the ways both parties cope with their feelings. Similarly, feelings of hurt should be influenced by the ways the transgressors respond to their guilt—whether it be with derogation or with some other communication strategy.

If, as theorists argue, people engage in behaviors that reinforce their views of themselves and their relationships (Swann, Hixon, & De La Ronde, 1992), it is also possible that individuals seek out emotions that are familiar to them and that provide them with a familiar role. For instance, therapists argue that people who are used to being abused by others tend to find themselves in relationships where they regularly feel hurt (Evans, 1992). If this is the case, these individuals likely participate in the construction of a relational environment where they engage in, and encounter, communication patterns associated with the elicitation of hurt. Similarly, those who are accustomed to taking responsibility for transgressions that are not theirs may gravitate toward relationships with people who are willing to give them that responsibility. Zahn-Waxler and Kochanska (1990) argued that "Guilt may be learned through parental modeling of negative attributional styles ('it's my fault')" (p. 211). Given this, researchers should be able to identify and describe ongoing patterns of communication associated with the elicitation of guilt that are passed from parent to child and subsequently enacted in the child's adult relationships.

Of course, the ethics of discussing and studying some of these issues can be quite complex. For many in middle-class, Western culture, both guilt and hurt carry with them an ethic of disclosure—a standard that suggests it is important to reveal one's feelings to others. In the case of guilt, this ethic translates into disclosing one's transgressions and, at times, confronting others who may have helped to engender guilt feelings. In the case of hurt, the ethic may involve discussing felt pain and facing those who initially caused the hurt. From this perspective, failure to engage in these types of disclosure can result in stress, problematic interpersonal relationships, physical ailments, and pathological behavior. Although researchers and therapists provide substantial evidence to support these claims (e.g., Lazarus & Lazarus, 1994; Mowrer & Veszelovszky, 1980; Pennebaker, 1990), the influence of such disclosures on personal relationships has yet to be thoroughly examined. It is one thing to disclose the source of one's guilt or hurt to a therapist or a therapeutic group. It is entirely another to disclose it to a friend, spouse, or child. Researchers have cautioned against unrestricted self-disclosure (Bochner, 1984; Parks, 1982), but we have yet to define the circumstances and parameters under which we should reveal, and avoid revealing, guilt and hurt in our personal relationships.

REFERENCES

Arias, I., & Pape, K. T. (1994). Physical abuse. In L. L'Abate (Ed.), *Handbook of developmental family psychology and psychopathology* (pp. 284–308). New York: John Wiley & Sons.

Ausubel, D. P. (1955). Relationships between shame and guilt in the socializing process. *Psychological Review, 62,* 378–390.

Baucom, D. H., Epstein, N., Sayers, S., & Sher, T. G. (1989). The role of cognitions in marital relationships: Definitional, methodological, and conceptual issues. *Journal of Consulting and Clinical Psychology, 57,* 31–38.

Baumeister, R. F., Reis, H. T., & Delespaul, P. (1995). Subjective and experiential correlates of guilt in daily life. *Personality and Social Psychology Bulletin, 21,* 1256–1268.

Baumeister, R. F., Stillwell, A. M., & Heatherton, T. F. (1994). Guilt: An interpersonal approach. *Psychological Bulletin, 115,* 243–267.

Baumeister, R. F., Stillwell, A. M., & Heatherton, T. F., (1995a). Interpersonal aspects of guilt: Evidence from narrative studies. In J. P. Tangney & K. W. Fischer (Eds.), *Self-conscious emotions: The psychology of shame, guilt, embarrassment, and pride* (pp. 255–273). New York: Guilford.

Baumeister, R. F., Stillwell, A. M., & Heatherton, T. F. (1995b). Personal narratives about guilt: Role in action control and interpersonal relationships. *Basic and Applied Social Psychology, 17,* 173–198.

Baxter, L. A., & Wilmot, W. W. (1984). Taboo topics in close relationships. *Journal of Social and Personal Relationships, 2,* 253–270.

Berger, C. R., & Bradac, J. J. (1982). *Language and social knowledge: Uncertainty in interpersonal relations.* London: Edward Arnold.

Bettelheim, B. (1962). *The informed heart.* Glencoe, IL: The Free Press.

Blieszner, R., & Shifflett, P. A. (1990). The effects of Alzheimer's disease on close relationships between patients and caregivers. *Family Relations, 39,* 57–62.

Bochner, A. P. (1984). The functions of human communication in interpersonal bonding. In C. C. Arnold & J. W. Bowers (Eds.), *Handbook of rhetorical and communication theory* (pp. 544–621). Boston: Allyn & Bacon.

Boyd-Franklin, N. (1993). Racism, secret-keeping, and African-American families. In E. Imber-Black (Ed.), *Secrets in families and family therapy* (pp. 331–354). New York: W. W. Norton.

Brock, T. C. (1969). On interpreting the effects of transgression upon compliance. *Psychological Bulletin, 72,* 138–145.

Brockner, J., Davy, J., & Carter, C. (1985). Layoffs, self-esteem, and survivor guilt: Motivational, affective, and attitudinal consequences. *Organizational Behavior and Human Decision Processes, 36,* 229–244.

Brockner, J., Greenberg, J., Brockner, A., Bortz, J., Davy, J., & Carter, C. (1986). Layoffs, equity theory, and work performance: Further evidence of the impact of survivor guilt. *Academy of Management Journal, 29,* 373–384.

Brooke, R. (1985). What is guilt? *Journal of Phenomenological Psychology, 16,* 31–46.

Brown, P., & Levinson, S. (1978). *Politeness: Some universals in language usage.* Cambridge, UK: Cambridge University Press.

Bulka, R. P. (1987). Guilt from, guilt towards. *Journal of Psychology and Judaism, 11,* 72–90.

Buss, A. (1980). *Self-consciousness and social anxiety.* San Francisco: Freeman.

Christensen, A., & Heavey, C. L. (1990). Gender and social structure in the demand/withdrawal patterns of marital conflict. *Journal of Personality and Social Psychology, 59,* 73–81.

Clark, M. S., & Mills, J. (1979). Interpersonal attraction in exchange and communal relationships. *Journal of Personality and Social Psychology, 37,* 12–24.

Cottle, T. J. (1980). *Children's secrets.* Reading, MA: Addison-Wesley.

Crowne, D. P., & Marlowe, D. (1964). *The approval motive: Studies in evaluative dependence.* New York: Wiley.

Cunningham, M. R., Steinberg, J., & Grev, R. (1980). Wanting to and having to help: Separate motivations for positive mood and guilt-induced helping. *Journal of Personality and Social Psychology, 38,* 181–192.

Darlington, R. B., & Macker, C. E. (1966). Displacement of guilt-produced altruistic behavior. *Journal of Personality and Social Psychology, 4,* 442–443.

Doherty, W. J. (1982). Attribution style and negative problem solving in marriage. *Family Relations, 317,* 23–27.

Duck, S. W., & Sants, H. K. A. (1983). On the origins of the specious: Are interpersonal relationships really interpersonal states? *Journal of Social and Clinical Psychology, 1,* 27–41.

Ekman, P. (1982). (Ed.), *Emotion in the human face.* New York: Cambridge University Press.

Ekman, P., Friesen, W. V., & Ellsworth, P. (1982). Research foundations. In P. Ekman (Ed), *Emotion in the human face* (2nd ed., pp. 1–143). New York: Cambridge University Press.

Evans, P. (1992). *The verbally abusive relationship: How to recognize it and how to respond.* Holbrook, MA: Bob Adams

Fehr, B., & Russell, J. A. (1984). Concept of emotion viewed from a prototype perspective. *Journal of Experimental Psychology, 113,* 464–486.

Fehr, L. A. (1988). Guilt in alcoholics: An evaluation of the Mosher guilt scales. *Psychological Reports, 62,* 92–94.

Ferguson, T. J., Stegge, H., & Damhuis, I. (1991). Children's understanding of guilt and shame. *Child Development, 62,* 827–839.

Fincham, F. D., Beach, S., & Nelson, G. (1987). Attribution processes in distressed and non-distressed couples: III. Causal and responsibility attributions for spouse behavior. *Cognitive Therapy and Research, 11,* 71–86.

Fitzpatrick, M. A., & Ritchie, L. D. (1993). Communication theory and the family. In P. Boss, W. Doherty, R. La Rossa, W. Schumm, & S. Steinmetz (Eds.), *Sourcebook of family theories and methods: A contextual approach* (pp. 565–585). New York: Plenum.

Folkes, V. S. (1982). Communicating the causes of social rejection. *Journal of Experimental Social Psychology, 18,* 235–252.

Frankl, V. (1984). *Man's search for meaning: An introduction to logotherapy.* New York: Simon and Schuster.

Freud, S. (1961). *Civilization and its discontents* (J. Strachey, Trans.). New York: Norton. (Original work published 1930).

Friedman, M. (1985). Toward a reconceptualization of guilt. *Contemporary Psychoanalysis, 21,* 501–547.

Gottman, J. M. (1993). A theory of marital dissolution and stability. *Journal of Family Psychology, 7,* 57–75.

Grych, J. H., & Fincham, F. D. (1993). Children's appraisals of marital conflict: Initial investigations of the cognitive-contextual framework. *Child Development, 64,* 215–230.

Harwas-Napierala, B. (1992). Some psychological aspects of shame and guilt in school children. *Acta Paedopsychiatrica, 55,* 251–254.

Hatfield, E., Cacioppo, J. T., & Rapson, R. L. (1994). *Emotional contagion.* Cambridge: Cambridge University Press.

Herbert, T. B., Silver, R. C., & Ellard, J. H. (1991). Coping with an abusive relationship: 1. How and why do women stay? *Journal of Marriage and the Family, 53,* 311–325.

Hoffman, M. L. (1978). Empathy, its development and prosocial implications. In C. B. Keasey (Ed.), *Nebraska Symposium on Motivation* (Vol. 26). Lincoln: University of Nebraska Press.

Hoffman, M. L. (1982). Development of prosocial motivation: Empathy and guilt. In N. Eisenberg (Ed.), *The development of prosocial behavior* (pp. 281–313). New York: Academic.

Horney, K. (1937). *The neurotic personality of our time.* New York: Norton.

Imber-Black, E. (Ed.). (1993). *Secrets in families and family therapy.* New York: W. W. Norton.

Izard, C. E. (1977). *Human emotions.* New York: Plenum.

Jones, W. H., & Kugler, K. (1993). Interpersonal correlates of the guilt inventory. *Journal of Personality Assessment, 61,* 246–258.

Jones, W. H., Kugler, K., & Adams, P. (1995). You always hurt the one you love: Guilt and transgressions against relationship partners. In J. P. Tangney & K. W. Fischer (Eds.), *Self-conscious emotions: The psychology of shame, guilt, embarrassment, and pride* (pp. 301–321). New York: Guilford.

Kahn, M. D., & Lewis, K. G. (1988). *Siblings in therapy: Lifespan and clinical issues.* New York: W. W. Norton.

Katz, I., Glass, D. C., & Cohen, S. (1973). Ambivalence, guilt, and the scapegoating of minority group victims. *Journal of Experimental Social Psychology, 9,* 423–436.

Knapp, M. L. (1984). *Interpersonal communication and human relationships.* Boston: Allyn & Bacon.

Kochanska, G., Casey, R. J., & Fukumoto, A. (1995). Toddlers' sensitivity to standard violations. *Child Development, 66,* 643–656.

Konecni, V. J. (1972). Some effects of guilt on compliance: A field replication. *Journal of Personality and Social Psychology, 23,* 30–32.

Krystal, H. (Ed.). (1968). *Massive psychic trauma.* New York: International Universities Press.

Kugler, K., & Jones, W. H. (1992). On conceptualizing and assessing guilt. *Journal of Personality and Social Psychology, 62,* 318–327.

L'Abate, L. (1977). Intimacy is sharing hurt feelings: A reply to David Mace. *Journal of Marriage and Family Counseling, 3,* 13–16.

Lamb, S. (1986). Treating sexually abused children: Issues of blame and responsibility. *American Journal of Orthopsychiatry, 56,* 303–307.

Lazarus, R. S. (1991). *Emotion and adaptation.* New York: Oxford University Press.

Lazarus, R. S., & Lazarus, B. N. (1994). *Passion and reason: Making senses of our emotions.* New York: Oxford University Press.

Lewis, H. B. (1971). *Shame and guilt in neurosis.* New York: International Universities Press.

Lifton, R. J. (1967). *Death in life.* New York: Simon & Schuster.

Lippard, P. V. (1988). "Ask me no questions, I'll tell you no lies": Situational exigencies for interpersonal deception. *Western Journal of Speech Communication, 52,* 91–103.

Lobel, T. E., Kav-Venaki, S., & Yahia, M. (1985). Guilt feelings and locus of control of concentration camp survivors. *International Journal of Social Psychology, 31,* 170–175.

Mace, D. R. (1976). Marital intimacy and the deadly love–anger cycle. *Journal of Marriage and Family Counseling, 2,* 131–137.

McGraw, K. M. (1987). Guilt following transgression: An attribution of responsibility approach. *Journal of Personality and Social Psychology, 53,* 247–256.

Metts, S. (1989). An exploratory investigation of deception in close relationships. *Journal of Social and Personal Relationships, 6,* 159–179.

Metts, S., & Bowers, J. W. (1994). Emotion in interpersonal communication. In M. L. Knapp & G. R. Miller (Eds.), *Handbook of interpersonal communication* (2nd ed., pp. 508–541). Thousand Oaks, CA: Sage.

Meyersberg, H. A., & Post, R. M. (1979). An holistic development view of neural and psychological processes: A neurobiologic-psychoanalytic integration. *British Journal of Psychiatry, 135,* 139–155.

Miceli, M. (1992). How to make someone feel guilty: Strategies of guilt inducement and their goals. *Journal for the Theory of Social Behaviour, 22,* 81–104.

Miles, M. S., & Demi, A. S. (1983–1984). Toward the development of a theory of bereavement guilt: sources of guilt in bereaved parents. *Omega, 14,* 299–314.

Miles, M. S., & Demi, S. A. (1991–1992). A comparison of guilt in bereaved parents whose children died by suicide, accident, or chronic disease. *Omega, 24,* 201–215.

Minuchin, S., Roseman, B. L., & Baker, L. (1978). *Psychosomatic families: Anorexia nervosa in context.* Cambridge, MA: Harvard University Press.

Montgomery, B. M. (1988). Quality communication in personal relationships. In S. W. Duck (Ed.), *Handbook of personal relationships* (pp. 343–359). New York: John Wiley & Sons.

Mosher, D. L. (1965). Interaction of fear and guilt in inhibiting unacceptable behavior. *Journal of Consulting Psychology, 29,* 161–167.

Mosher, D. L. (1968). Measurement of guilt in females by self-report inventories. *Journal of Consulting and Clinical Psychology, 32,* 690–695.

Mosher, D. L. (1979). The meaning and measurement of guilt. In C. E. Izard (Ed.), *Emotions in personality and psychopathology* (pp. 105–129). New York: Plenum.

Mosher, D. L., O'Grady, K. E., & Katz, H. A. (1980). Hostility-guilt, guilt over aggression, and self-punishment. *Journal of Personality Assessment, 44,* 34–40.

Mowrer, O. H. (1960). *Learning theory and behavior.* New York: John Wiley & Sons.

Mowrer, O. H., & Veszelovszky, A. V. (1980). There may indeed by a "right way": Response to James D. Smrtic. *Psychotherapy: Theory, Research, and Practice, 17,* 440–447.

Nixon, C. D., & Singer, G. H. S. (1993). Group cognitive-behavioral treatment for excessive parental self-blame and guilt. *American Journal on Mental Retardation, 97,* 665–672.

Oatley, K. (1992). *Best-laid schemes: The psychology of emotions.* Cambridge: Cambridge University Press.

Ohbuchi, K., Kameda, M., & Agarie, N. (1989). Apology as aggression control: Its role in mediating appraisal of and response to harm. *Journal of Personality and Social Psychology, 56,* 219–227.

Okel, E., & Mosher, D. L. (1968). Changes in affective states as a function of guilt over aggressive behavior. *Journal of Consulting and Clinical Psychology, 32,* 265–270.

Ortony, A., Clore, G. L., & Collins, A. (1988). *The cognitive structure of emotions.* Cambridge: Cambridge University Press.

Orvis, B. R., Kelly, H. H., & Butler, D. (1976). Attributional conflict in young couples. In J. H. Harvey, W. J. Ickes, & R. Kidd (Eds.), *New directions in attribution research* (Vol. 1, pp. 353–386). Hillsdale, NJ: Lawrence Erlbaum Associates.

Parks, M. R. (1982). Ideology and interpersonal communication: Off the couch and into the world. In M. Burgoon (Ed.), *Communication yearbook 5* (pp. 79–107). New Brunswick, NJ: Transaction Books.

Pennebaker, J. W. (1990). *Opening up: The healing power of confiding in others.* New York: Avon Books.

Pittman, F. (1989). *Private lies: Infidelity and the betrayal of intimacy.* New York: W. W. Norton.

Plutchik, R. (1962). *The emotions: Facts, theories, and a new model.* New York: Random House.

Plutchik, R. (1980). *Emotion: A psychoevolutionary synthesis.* New York: Harper & Row.

Regan, J. W. (1971). Guilt, perceived injustice, and altruistic behavior. *Journal of Personality and Social Psychology, 18,* 124–132.

Rolland, J. S. (1993). Mastering family challenges in serious illness and disability. In F. Walsh (Ed.), *Normal family processes* (2nd ed., pp. 444–473). New York: Guilford.

Rubin, J., & Shaffer, W. F. (1987). Some interpersonal effects of imposing guilt versus eliciting altruism. *Counseling and Values, 31,* 190–193.

Ruesch, J. (1957). *Disturbed communication: The clinical assessment of normal and pathological communicative behavior.* New York: W. W. Norton.

Scherer, K. R. (1984). Emotion as a multicomponent process: A model and some cross-cultural data. In P. Shaver (Ed.), *Review of personality and social psychology, Vol. 5, Emotions, relationships, and health* (pp. 37–63). Beverly Hills, CA: Sage.

Shaver, P., Schwartz, J., Kirson, D., & O'Connor, C. (1987). Emotion knowledge: Further exploration of a prototype approach. *Journal of Personality and Social Psychology, 52,* 1061–1086.

Sichrovsky, P. (1988). *Born guilty: Children of Nazi families.* New York: Basic Books.

Sillars, A. L. (1980). Attributions and communication in roommate conflicts. *Communication Monographs, 47,* 180–200.

Sillars, A. L., & Scott, M. D. (1983). Interpersonal perception between intimates: An integrative review. *Human Communication Research, 10,* 153–176.

Silverman, I. W. (1967). Incidence of guilt reactions in children. *Journal of Personality and Social Psychology, 7,* 338–340.

Stamp, G. H., & Knapp, M. L. (1990). The construct of intent in interpersonal communication. *Quarterly Journal of Speech, 76,* 282–299.

Swann, W. B., Hixon, J. G., & De La Ronde, C. (1992). Embracing the bitter truth: Negative self-concepts and marital commitment. *Psychological Science, 3,* 118–121.

Tangney, J. P. (1990). Assessing individual differences in proneness to shame and guilt: Development of the self-conscious affect and attribution inventory. *Journal of Personality and Social Psychology, 59,* 102–111.

Tangney, J. P., Wagner, P., Fletcher, C., & Gramzow, R. (1992). Shames into anger?: The relation of shame and guilt to anger and self-reported aggression. *Journal of Personality and Social Psychology, 62,* 669–675.

Tavuchis, N. (1991). *Mea culpa: A sociology of apology and reconciliation.* Stanford, CA: Stanford University Press.

Thompson, R. A., & Hoffman, M. L. (1980). Empathy and the development of guilt in children. *Developmental Psychology, 16,* 155–156.

Tomkins, S. S. (1981). The quest for primary motives: Biography and autobiography of an idea. *Journal of Personality and Social Psychology, 41,* 306–329.

Vangelisti, A. L. (1994). Messages that hurt. In W. R. Cupach & B. H. Spitzberg (Eds.), *The dark side of interpersonal communication* (pp. 53–82). Hillsdale, NJ: Lawrence Erlbaum.

Vangelisti, A. L., & Crumley, L. P. (in press). Reactions to messages that hurt: The influence of relational contexts. *Communication Monographs.*

Vangelisti, A. L., Daly, J. A., & Rudnick, J. R. (1991). Making people feel guilty in conversations: Techniques and correlates. *Human Communication Research, 18,* 3–39.

Walster, E., Walster, G. W., & Traupmann, J. (1978). Equity and premarital sex. *Journal of Personality, 36,* 82–92.

Weiner, B., & Handel, S. J. (1985). A cognition-emotion-action sequence: Anticipated emotional consequences of causal attributions and reported communication strategy. *Developmental Psychology, 21,* 102–107.

Weiner, B., Perry, R. P., & Magnusson, J. (1988). An attributional analysis of reactions to stigmas. *Journal of Personality and Social Psychology, 55,* 738–748.

Wicker, F. W., Payne, G. C., & Morgan, R. D. (1983). Participant descriptions of guilt and shame. *Motivation and Emotion, 7,* 25–39.

Zahn-Waxler, C., & Kochanska, G. (1990). The origins of guilt. In R. A. Thompson (Ed.), *Nebraska Symposium on Motivation* (pp. 183–258). Lincoln, NE: University of Nebraska Press.

Zahn-Waxler, C., Radke-Yarrow, M., & King, R. (1983). Early altruism and guilt. *Academic Psychology Bulletin, 5,* 247–259.

Zahn-Waxler, C., & Radke-Yarrow, M. (1982). The development of altruism: Alternative research strategies. In N. Eisenberg (Ed.), *The development of prosocial behavior.* New York: Academic Press.

CHAPTER 6

Jealousy Experience and Expression in Romantic Relationships

Laura K. Guerrero

Arizona State University
Tempe, Arizona

Peter A. Andersen

San Diego State University
San Diego, California

Biblical writers, Renaissance playwrights, contemporary historians and social scientists have all portrayed jealousy as a powerful emotion that has consequences for personal relationships and society at large. In the *Song of Solomon* (8:6), jealousy was pronounced to be "as cruel as the grave," and in *Proverbs* (27:4) jealousy was described as more overwhelming and debilitating than angry rage. In *Othello*, Shakespeare depicted jealousy as "the green-eyed monster." Stekel (1921) asked, "Has anyone counted the victims of jealousy? . . . What are all the hideous battles, narrated by history, when compared to this frightful passion jealousy?" (p. 65). Brehm (1992) stated: "Jealousy is like a San Andreas fault running beneath the smooth surface of an intimate relationship. Most of the time, its potential lies hidden. But when its rumblings begin, the destruction can be enormous" (p. 263). These vivid comparisons to death, rage, monsters, battles, and earthquakes illustrate that jealousy has captured the imagination of poets and playwrights, and the scholarly attention of social scientists.

A more scientific definition of jealousy was provided by White and Mullen (1989), who conceptualized romantic jealousy as

> a complex of thoughts, emotions, and actions that follows loss of or threat to self-esteem and/or the existence of quality of the romantic relationship. The perceived loss or threat

is generated by the perception of a real or potential romantic attraction between one's partner and a (perhaps imaginary) rival" (p. 9).

This definition has important implications for the study of communication about jealousy. First, it implies that jealous cognition and affect are inextricably linked to jealous actions and communication. Second, jealousy is situated within interpersonal relationships, making it likely that communication (or lack of communication) between members of the "love triangle" can clarify, repair, or exacerbate jealous feelings. Third, although it is the *perception* of a rival relationship that leads to jealousy, such perceptions are rooted in real or imaginary social interaction. For example, individuals who notice that their partners are paying extra attention to someone else are likely to feel neglected and jealous. Thus, jealousy is an interpersonal phenomenon.

In this chapter, we highlight the interpersonal nature of jealousy. After overviewing a componential model, we examine several antecedents of jealousy, including biological and relational factors. Next, we discuss the emotion and cognition that accompany the jealousy experience. The final section of the chapter focuses on a variety of communicative responses to jealousy, and the functions and relational consequences associated with these responses.

OVERVIEW

To illustrate how these factors of jealousy experience and expression may work together, we present a componential model (see Figure 1). This model, which is based on a synthesis of literature on the causes and consequences of jealousy, reflects the concepts we discuss in this chapter. The model is presented as a descriptive device, rather than as a causal process model. As more research is conducted, the exact causal connections between these factors will become clearer.

Our model stresses components of the jealous person's emotional experience and expression. This focus emphasizes separate chains of jealous cognition, emotion, and communication, rather than examining patterns of mutual influence between all three members of the romantic triangle. This emphasis reflects the research conducted on jealousy to date. Moreover, we hold that researchers must understand the jealous person's experience and expression before examining more complex patterns reflecting interaction dynamics (e.g., patterns of reciprocity).

The model is framed by six antecedent factors. According to current research, these factors, which probably interact with one another, can influence all aspects of jealousy experience and expression, including a person's initial perception of jealousy threat. We include perceptions of threat as a generative mechanism in our model because threat is central to most definitions of jealousy (e.g., Bryson, 1991; Sharpsteen, 1993; White & Mullen, 1989). Such threats can be the result of paranoid suspicions, witnessing communication between the partner and the rival (e.g.,

Antecedent Factors:
1. Biology
2. Culture
3. Personality
4. Relational Factors
5. Situational Factors
6. Strategic Moves

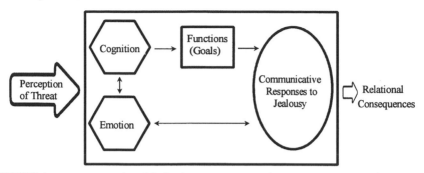

FIGURE 1   A componential model of jealousy experience and expression in romantic relationships.

seeing the partner and rival sitting close together and laughing), hearing "rumors" about the partner, discovering evidence that the partner is interested in someone else, and so forth. Regardless of the event that triggers perceptions of threat, research suggests that individuals encountering such threat will experience a number of jealousy-related emotions and cognitions. These internal factors comprise jealousy experience.

It is likely that jealous emotion and cognition, along with the antecedent factors that frame jealousy experience, contribute to the goals that guide individuals' communicative responses to jealousy. For example, people who feel intense fear at the possibility of losing their partners are likely to strive to maintain their relationships. Such individuals should engage in specific communication strategies (e.g., being especially nice to the partner) designed to facilitate this goal. However, emotion can also have a direct effect on communicative responses to jealousy. This contention is based on theory showing that high levels of arousal or emotional intensity can circumvent cognitive processing and goal formation, which leads to automatic or habitual behavioral responses (Andersen, in press; Zillman, 1990). For instance, jealous individuals who find their partners in a compromising position may be so angry that they begin yelling and cursing at their partners without thinking about the relational consequences. Similarly, someone who is overwhelmed with fear over losing their partner may desperately "cling" to the relationship without realizing that such action drives the partner further away. Thus, communicative responses to jealousy, in addition to jealousy experience factors, are likely to influence relational consequences.

ANTECEDENTS OF JEALOUSY EXPERIENCE AND EXPRESSION

We begin our discussion of the elements in our componential model by examining how antecedent conditions influence jealousy experience and expression. White and Mullen (1989) included culture, personality, and relationship factors as three such antecedents. However, evidence also shows that jealousy is biologically based and has distinct phylogenetic origins, and that situational and strategic forces shape jealousy. In the following pages, we outline how these six antecedents influence the experience and expression of jealousy. We begin with the broadest of the antecedents—biology.

Sociobiological Factors

Scholars have argued that although the conditions that lead to jealousy as an appraisal of threat vary interculturally, the experience of jealousy is a ubiquitous, cross-cultural phenomena (Clanton & Smith, 1977; Hupka, 1981; White & Mullen, 1989). Moreover, sociobiologists argue that biological issues of paternal uncertainty and mate retention make jealousy and possessiveness biologically based and culturally universal (Buss, 1988; Daly & Wilson, 1987). The central premise of this perspective is that humans are motivated to reproduce and to ensure the survival of offspring through instinctive processes via natural selection, sexual selection, and mate protection.

According to the sociobiological perspective, males could enhance maximal reproductive potential through multiple inseminations leading to more potential offspring (Buss, 1988, 1989; Daly & Wilson, 1983, 1987). But there's a catch. If females engaged in a similarly promiscuous reproductive strategy, paternity would be uncertain and males would waste resources in raising children who are not genetically theirs (see Buss, 1988). Thus, a male can only ensure paternity by restricting the access of other males to his mate. Uncertain paternity may lead males to a number of different reproductive and interpersonal strategies, with jealous anger and possessive behaviors as principal ones. Moreover, paternal uncertainty may be the reason why men in all societies tend to experience more sexual than emotional jealousy.

Female reproductive strategies are somewhat different, but may still explain jealousy. Because females have a limited number of reproductive opportunities due to long gestation and lactation periods, they should be choosier than males (Walters & Crawford, 1994) and be more attracted to a mate's resources and loyalty rather than the health, youth, and physical attractiveness typically preferred by males (Buss, 1988; Kenrick & Trost, 1989). Although women may be less concerned about a mate's occasional promiscuous behavior, sociobiologists would predict that any threat to their long-term *relationship* would result in female jealousy. Thus, female jealousy should be less focused on infidelity per se, and more focused on losses of relational, emotional, and economic resources (Buss, 1988; Greenlees & McGrew, 1994; Kenrick & Keefe, 1992; Kenrick & Trost, 1989).

Buss (1988) provided some support for the contention that sociobiological forces shape the ways in which jealous men and women attempt to retain their mates. He found that males used the following tactics more than women: (a) *resource display,* which includes spending money on gifts or flowers for the partner; (b) *mate concealment,* which focuses on restricting the partner's access to rivals; (c) *submission and debasement,* which included promising to "change to please the partner" and giving in to the partner's wishes; (d) *intrasexual threats,* which focus on sending threatening messages to potential rivals, such as giving the rival a hostile stare or threatening to hit the rival; and (e) *violence,* which involves actually engaging in violent acts toward the rival's person or property. In contrast, Buss (1988) found that women use the tactics of *enhancing appearance* and *fidelity threats* (e.g., flirting with others to make the partner jealous) more than men. Similarly, in a study by Guerrero and Reiter (in press), jealous men reported contacting rivals, restricting their partners' access to rivals, and buying gifts or spending money on their partners more than did jealous women. Jealous women, in contrast, reported trying to enhance their physical appearance more often than did jealous men. These findings are generally consistent with the sociobiological principles that (a) men focus on mate protection and sexual aspects of jealousy; and (b) women know that men value physical attractiveness and sexual faithfulness in their mates.

Of course, the sociobiological basis of jealousy is not without criticism. Why would jealousy be a primary mate protection strategy? Jealousy often occurs after the mate has already become involved with others. Other strategies, such as isolation and the use of moral prohibitions, would seem to have greater efficacy. Although some data support a sociobiological explanation, the evidence is, at best, indirect (White & Mullen, 1989). Moreover, jealous instincts are likely to operate at an unconscious level. Finally, cultural and individual factors may prevent certain instinctual behaviors from being predominant.

Cultural and Historical Factors

The prevalence of jealousy in literature from the Siege of Troy throughout centuries of writing, including Shakespeare's *Othello* and Hawthorne's *The Scarlet Letter,* attests to its long history. Indeed, both historical and cultural factors seem to have created the necessary conditions for jealousy and probably fostered it as well. In patriarchal societies, jealousy seems to have been an emotional state designed for the protection of male property. For women, jealousy was part of the emotional fabric that held the family together. Despite a man's affairs, the longing for security and emotional bonds that jealousy inspired reaffirmed a woman's desire to maintain and nurture her marriage and the family.

In the West, Christian and Jewish admonitions against adultery, along with patriarchal marriage rights, provided a cultural, religious, and legal basis for jealousy. Russell (1957) maintained that jealousy helps a patriarchal society function properly, noting that without paternal certainty the patriarchal family would not work. The Judeo-Christian bible depicts and encourages jealousy as an emotion based on love, ownership, hurt, and anger. Watts (1958) maintained that Christian and Jewish societies encouraged jealousy when marriage was viewed as a property right and adultery was an infringement of that right. Morality, including the control of sexuality, became a foundation of "civilized" Western society.

Jealousy, however, is not only limited to Western society. Anthropologists have found evidence of jealousy in all cultures, though it varies in intensity and consequences as well as in the situations which elicit it. In highly masculine cultures, sexual freedom for women is virtually nonexistent and jealousy is more prevalent (Hofstede, 1980; Rathas, Nevid, & Fichner-Rathus, 1993). Similarly, Whitehurst (1977) argued that jealousy is most prevalent in cultures with rigid sex roles, and Hupka and Ryan (1981) found that male jealousy was most likely in cultures where marriage and property ownership were important for social status, and sex outside marriage was socially condemned. In such cultures, jealous behavior has been used as a tool to inhibit sexual promiscuity, particularly for women. This moral code also affected communication about jealousy. Women in such cultures were advised to "look the other way" when their spouses had affairs, yet men had a right to be morally outraged and to vent anger at their wives. Of course, cultures low in jealousy also exist. Hupka (1981) stated that cultures that place little emphasis on marriage, discourage individual property rights, view sexual experiences and intimate relationships as readily available, and do *not* foster a need to have genetic offspring, tend to exhibit lower levels of jealousy.

The experience and communication of jealousy has also been shown to vary across cultures throughout history. In an ambitious study of cross-cultural jealousy, Hupka et al. (1985) investigated how individuals in Hungary, Ireland, Mexico, the Netherlands, the (former) Soviet Union, the United States, and (the former) Yugoslavia experienced jealousy. They found that jealous individuals from all seven cultures were concerned about relationship exclusivity and experienced self-deprecation and envy. Individuals from six of the seven cultures also identified relationship dependency (or feeling unable to cope without the partner) as part of the jealousy experience. Despite these similarities, some cultural variation emerged. For example, Mexicans were most likely to identify distrust as a major factor in the jealousy experience, and those from the Netherlands appeared to worry most about sexual exclusivity.

Ethnographic research has also shown that cultures vary in terms of jealous communication. In some tribes, such as the Maori of New Zealand, a husband has the right to demand goods, property, or labor from his wife's lover (Mishkin, 1937). Interestingly, however, if a Maori wife leaves her husband for another man, the husband may be "plundered [because] he should have been more discerning than to be unaware of such an affair" (Mishkin, 1937, p. 450). Thus, Maori men are rewarded for detecting affairs early and punished for detecting them too late. Hupka (1981) reported that in many cultures, women commonly divorce or desert unfaithful husbands, yet in other cultures, women cannot leave the husband without reaping severe consequences. For example, Hupka (1981) reported that Murngin wives are hunted by the family of the deserted husband, returned to the husband, and usually beaten.

In contemporary Western culture, and particularly starting in the 1960s, jealousy has often been equated with an obsolete sexual morality, patriarchal values, and a lack of individual freedom. Clanton and Smith (1977) contended that, within modern society, jealousy is widely regarded as the new sin of the liberated generation. Such sentiments may be having some effect: The murder rate from romantic triangles has steadily declined in the United States (Delgado & Bond, 1993). A competing historical factor that may increase jealousy at a societal level is the AIDS epidemic. Since the mid-1980s when AIDS education began to take root, the media and educators have touted the virtues of monogamy. Clearly, the health risks that infidelity poses could affect both the reasons for and the emotions connected to romantic jealousy.

Personality Factors

Scholars have argued that insecurity and low self-esteem are key personality characteristics predicting jealousy because they make people more vulnerable to third-party threats (e.g., Berscheid & Fei, 1977; Francis, 1977). Salovey and Rodin (1986) had individuals list synonyms of the word "jealousy" and found that "insecurity, low self-esteem, and self-blame" represented one of five clusters of jealousy-related concepts. Research has shown jealousy to associate positively with insecurity and uncertainty (Afifi & Reichert, 1996; McIntosh, 1989; Parker, 1996). In addition, Guerrero (in press) found that individuals who lack confidence experience more cognitive suspicion, cognitive worry, fear, sadness, and envy when they are jealous. Bringle and Buunk (1986) argued that "low self-esteem has been regarded both as a predisposing characteristic to jealous reactions and as a consequence of having been jealous" (p. 228).

The relationship between jealousy and self-esteem, however, is not clear-cut. Some scholars have found small to moderate negative associations between self-esteem and jealousy experience (e.g., Bringle, 1981; Bringle & Evenbeck, 1979; De Moja, 1986; McIntosh, 1989; Salovey & Rodin, 1985; Stewart & Beatty, 1985). Others have found no relationship (e.g., Amstutz, 1982; Buunk, 1981; Mathes & Severa, 1981; Shettel-Neuber, Bryson, & Young, 1978). Still others have found this relationship to hold for females only (e.g., Buunk, 1982), or males only (e.g., White, 1981d). More consistent findings may be obtained if researchers focus on relationship-specific rather than global self-esteem (Brehm, 1992), and anticipated instead of actual jealousy.

Research also indicates that individual differences in self-esteem and security levels lead to different ways of coping with jealousy. McIntosh and Tangri (1989) found that jealous individuals who reported low self-esteem indicated using more indirect coping behaviors (e.g., giving their partners the silent treatment) as opposed to direct behaviors (e.g., confronting their partners). Similarly, Guerrero (in press) found that those who lack confidence tended to use active distancing (e.g., ignoring the partner), surveillance behavior, and negative affect expression when coping with jealous threat. All three of these strategies, and particularly the first two, are indirect ways of communicating jealousy. Another study by McIntosh (McIntosh & Tate, 1990) found that, in jealous situations, insecurity associates more highly with indirect coping strategies ($r = .35$) than direct coping strategies ($r = .16$).

Individuals low in self-esteem and security may also feel little control over the events leading to jealousy. Research demonstrates that chronically jealous individuals tend to be more externally controlled than nonjealous individuals (e.g., Bringle & Buunk, 1986). Bringle and Williams (1979) suggested that jealousy is related to one's locus of control. Externally controlled individuals believe that rewards come from uncontrollable sources, such as fate, luck, or the influence of others. They also feel that they cannot control third-party threats. Individuals with internal loci of control, on the other hand, feel that they are responsible for creating their own rewards. Interestingly, McIntosh and Tangri (1989) found that individuals who were internally controlled reported using more direct and confrontational strategies to deal with jealousy, suggesting that externally controlled individuals feel less able to change the situation through communication.

Research has also shown that jealousy experience and expression vary based upon one's love type or attachment style. White (1977) found that individuals endorsing the eros (passionate), storge (friendship), and mania (obsessive) love styles tended to experience the most romantic jealousy. Erotic lovers reported experiencing jealous anxiety, storgic lovers reported feeling jealous anxiety and depression, and manic lovers reported feeling jealous anxiety, depression, and anger. In contrast, jealousy associated negatively with ludus (game-playing) love, presumably because ludic lovers tend to desire low levels of relationship commitment (see Taraban, Hendrick, & Hendrick, Chapter 12, this volume, for more on these love styles). Individuals with *preoccupied* attachment styles (sometimes referred to as "anxious ambivalence") experience high levels of jealousy, whereas individuals with *dismissive* styles experience low levels of jealousy (e.g., Collins & Read, 1990; Guerrero, in press; Hazan & Shaver, 1987). *Preoccupieds* have negative models of themselves and positive models of others. Thus, they tend to rely on their relational partners for rewards. *Dismissives* hold positive models of themselves, negative models of others, and are so independent that they may be unconcerned about relational commitment and less prone to jealousy (Bartholomew, 1990; also see Andersen & Guerrero, Chapter 3, this volume; Feeney, Noller, & Roberts, Chapter 18, this volume). Preoccupieds appear to dwell on jealousy, to focus on feelings of sadness, fear, inferiority, self-blame, and envy, and to engage in behaviors such as spying on the partner, expressing negative affect to the partner, and clinging to the relationship. In contrast dismissives are *less* likely to dwell on jealousy and to experience jealousy-related fear or sadness, but are *more* likely to direct blame and anger toward the rival, engage in avoidant coping strategies such as denying jealous feelings, and handle jealousy alone rather than seeking social support (Guerrero, in press; Radecki-Bush, Farrell, & Bush, 1993; Sharpsteen & Kilpatrick, 1995).

The above findings show that personality variables can affect jealousy experience and expression. It should be noted, however, that the quality of the relationship can moderate these personality-based reactions. For example, a preoccupied individual who generally has low self-esteem may feel secure within the confines of a long-term romantic relationship. Thus, we explore relational antecedents of jealousy next.

Relational Factors

Research on social exchange and relational investment (e.g., Rusbult, 1983; Thibaut & Kelley, 1959) provides scholars with a theoretical foundation for studying how relational factors affect jealousy. In particular, emotional dependency, and the related concepts of comparison level of alternatives, investment, and commitment, have been found to affect jealousy experience and expression.

Emotional dependency is the relative extent to which people rely on their relationships to provide them with rewards and happiness, as compared to their reliance on other aspects of their lives (Berscheid, 1983; Berscheid & Fei, 1977; Buunk, 1982). Emotional dependency is strongest when individuals have put significant investment (i.e., time and effort) into the relationship, have a low comparison level of alternatives (i.e., potential alternative relationships are unappealing), and are highly committed to the relationship (Rusbult, Drigotas, & Verette, 1994). Research shows that emotional dependency associates with jealousy. Buunk found that, across three different samples, emotional dependency was positively related to anticipated jealousy for males. In two of the three samples, emotional dependency associated positively with anticipated jealousy for females as well (see Bringle & Buunk, 1986).

Other research suggests that a combination of high investment and undesirable alternatives leads to considerable jealousy in the face of relational threat. For men, Trost, Brown, and Morrison (1994) found that jealousy increases as they invest more in their relationships. Metts and Bowers (1994) maintained that "to the extent that a person feels his or her romantic partner is the only possible source of happiness, any perceived threat to the relationship may lead to rumination and eventually to excessive or dispositional jealousy" (p. 533). White (1981b) found that jealousy is more likely when one person believes that s/he is putting more effort into the relationship than the partner. A jealous individual who has poor alternatives and has made sizable, unrecoverable relational investments is likely to cling to the relationship and engage in maintenance behaviors (e.g., being especially attentive and affectionate) to try to "win back" the partner. In contrast, a jealous individual who has good alternatives might engage in fidelity testing, display relational anger, and/or terminate the relationship.

Researchers have also investigated how commitment levels and relational stages affect jealousy. It appears that couples who feel romantic love for one another, but are not in a committed marital relationship, are most prone to jealousy. Several studies have found that couples who are seriously dating or cohabiting are more likely to experience and express jealousy than are those in other types of relationships, such as opposite-sex friend, casually dating, married, divorced, or separated relationships (Aune & Comstock, 1991, 1995; Bringle & Boebinger, 1990; Guerrero, Eloy, Jorgensen, & Andersen, 1993; Salovey & Rodin, 1985; White, 1985). Guerrero et al. (1993) argued that these results suggest that "romantic love and attraction are positively related to jealousy, but that security is negatively related. Thus, the commitment afforded by marriage may aid in combating jealousy" (p. 118). Communicative responses to jealousy have also been found to vary based upon relationship type. In Guerrero et al.'s (1993) study, daters reported using more negative and avoidant types of behavior (e.g., arguing, ignoring the partner, and denying jealousy) than did marrieds. Married couples may refrain from using negative or avoidant strategies if they have negotiated relational rules. Daters, who have been found to experience more intense jealousy-induced emotion, may find it difficult to conceal negative affect. Alternatively, daters who fear losing their relationships or wish to reduce their emotional load may deny jealous feelings and avoid discussing jealousy with their partner.

Sexual exclusivity also affects jealousy. People who value and expect sexual exclusivity are likely to feel intense jealousy *if* their partners violate (or are perceived to violate) this expectation (White, 1981b,c,d). In contrast, those who have (or plan to have) affairs of their own are less likely to experience jealousy (Buunk, 1982). Interestingly, Pines and Aronson (1983) found that individuals who valued monogamy tended *not* to experience much actual jealousy, presumably because they are in long-term monogamous relationships and feel that their partners are unlikely to have affairs. Similarly, Trost et al. (1994) found sexual openness to correlate positively with jealousy, possibly because those in sexually open relationships feel that their partners are more likely to have affairs. Combined, this research leads to two conclusions. First, individuals who value sexual exclusivity are not likely to feel jealousy unless they perceive that their partners have violated their trust. In other words, those in monogamous relationships *expect* their partners to be faithful and, thus, do not anticipate jealousy. However, if they do come to suspect that their partner is having an extradyadic relationship, their jealous feelings will be especially intense. Second, it is important that there is a *match* in attitudes toward sexual exclusivity. If both partners value exclusivity, infidelity is less likely to occur. If both partners value sexual freedom, jealousy is likely to be less intense because infidelity is expected. However, if one partner values sexual exclusivity and the other does not, sexual jealousy is likely.

Situational Factors

The situation is a critical factor in events that may promote jealousy. Indeed, Sharpsteen (1993) argued that for better or worse, in academe "a consensus is emerging that romantic jealousy is best defined in terms of a situation" (p. 69). As a case in point, extradyadic sexual activities are often the result of relatively unplanned situational factors. This is evidenced by surveys of attitudes toward extramarital affairs from a number of countries that show respondents disapprove of extramarital affairs under virtually all circumstances (Bringle & Buunk, 1991). Nonetheless, surveys of involvement in extramarital relationships indicate that at least 50% of the global population has extramarital sexual relationships (Bringle & Buunk, 1991). Evidently, contextual or situational factors such as the attractiveness of the partner, the distance from home, the invitation to have sex, and the presence of drugs or alcohol have an impact on one's decision to have such relations.

Situational factors also influence jealousy-related attributions. Several studies summarized by White and Mullen (1989) showed that a person sees her or his own jealousy as situational (e.g., I was jealous because she was dancing with him all night), but regards the partner's jealousy as dispositional (e.g., he's always been such a jealous person). Such attributions may lead people to feel that they are justified in confronting their partners when they are jealous, but that their partners are unjustified in confronting them.

Situational justifications for jealousy-evoking events are also common (Bringle & Buunk, 1991). Justifications may include the degree of involvement (e.g., we were just having lunch), situational rationalizations (e.g., that small affair I had could never threaten our relationship), or situational improvement (e.g., my affair led me to realize how much I value our relationship). Situational excuses are commonly used, including blaming life events or explaining that one was intoxicated in a particular situation. When individuals are confronted by jealous partners, they are likely to offer situational excuses for their behavior (e.g., I was depressed over losing my job).

Other research shows that the type of jealous threat (e.g., emotional or sexual) is an important situational factor that predicts jealous reactions. Hansen (1985) showed that situations involving sexual involvement by one's partner are the most jealousy-invoking, followed by situations in which emotional support is exchanged between one's partner and a perceived rival. Similarly, scholars have argued that situations that threaten sexual exclusivity produce the most intense and destructive reactions to jealousy (Bringle & Buunk, 1986; Buunk & Hupka, 1987; Parker, 1996; Reiss, 1986). Although some individuals experiencing sexual jealousy may focus on restoring passion to their relationships, most are likely to react with anger, threats, or even violence. Parker (1994) found that individuals responding to hypothetical situations involving sexual infidelity reported that they would be *un*likely to engage in relationship-maintaining communication, "such as being supportive of the beloved, spending more time with the beloved, and giving the beloved compliments" (p. 26). In contrast, individuals experiencing emotional (rather than sexual) jealousy may react with more sadness than anger. They could also focus on increasing intimacy through communication.

Whether jealousy is emotional, sexual, or both, research indicates that the characteristics of the rival play a role in determining jealous reactions. Shettel-Neuber et al. (1978) showed that people were the most jealous in situations where they perceived the rival to be *less* attractive than themselves. Similarly, research conducted in the Netherlands showed that people report experiencing more negative feelings when a rival is physically unattractive, has little to offer others, and is disliked by others (see Buunk, 1981). Apparently, it is a greater blow to the jealous person's self-esteem to learn that the partner is interested in someone they perceive as less desirable than themselves. Shettel-Neuber et al. found that in this situation, jealous individuals often felt anger and embarrassment in conjunction with jealousy. Jealousy may also be especially intense when the rival is a friend of the jealous person, presumably because feelings of strong betrayal emerge (Parker, 1994). Parker also found that when the rival was a friend, jealous individuals engaged in more derogation and less social-support seeking. Together, these findings indicate that situations where the partner has a (real or perceived) sexual relationship with a less attractive rival or a close friend are highly threatening and engender considerable anger.

The situation is also likely to affect what forms of communication are socially appropriate. Most, though not all, displays of violence occur in private. Displays of negative affect, such as crying or anger, may be inhibited by public situations. Also, different behavioral strategies are available in different situations. For example, one common jealousy-response strategy is to make the offending partner jealous as well. This strategy, which is especially like to occur in social situations such as parties or at nightclubs where it is easy to find potential targets of flirtation, is discussed next as one of several "strategic" or "partner-initiated" factors that can precipitate jealousy.

Strategic Factors

Individuals are rarely aware of the sociobiological or cultural factors that precipitate certain behaviors. They may not even fully appreciate the dispositional, relational, or situational factors that promote a particular communication behavior. However, people do behave strategically and are often conscious of their strategies. They recognize that certain actions, such as jealousy inductions through third-party involvements, or feigned jealousy, may affect their partner's thoughts, feelings, and behaviors.

Several researchers (Baxter & Wilmot, 1984; Guerrero, Andersen, Jorgensen, Spitzberg, & Eloy, 1995; White, 1980) have investigated these processes, which typically involve "secret tests" of the relationship. White (1980) reported that couples employ such actions to test the status of the relationship or to attain specific rewards, such as more involvement, commitment, or attention from one's partner. White found that jealousy was often induced by exaggerating or discussing one's attraction to another person, flirting with others, or actually dating others for the sole purpose of producing jealousy. Individuals may also make their partners jealous if they feel they are being taken for granted. Baxter and Wilmot (1984) reported several types of jealousy tests, including *describing alternatives* and *beginning alternatives.* One respondent, who used the describing alternatives strategy, talked about her "old boyfriend back home" when with her current college boyfriend. She reported doing this to assess his reaction. Another respondent, who engaged in the beginning alternatives strategy, went out with other women to see what kind of commitment his girlfriend really wanted. Baxter and Wilmot (1984) described another secret test, called *fidelity checks,* which appear to test whether jealousy is warranted. This type of test included tactics such as leaving one's partner alone with one's attractive roommate, unobtrusively observing one's partner at parties, and pressing the redial button on the partner's phone to ascertain with whom s/he was last speaking. Of course, jealousy inductions, while effective tests of relational status, can be dangerous. They can hurt the partner's feelings, precipitate a relational crisis or breakup, and even induce jealous violence. Obviously, jealousy tests should be used cautiously. Similarly, fidelity checks should be employed only if one really wants to know the loyalty level of one's partner.

In a study of communicative responses to jealousy, Guerrero et al. (1995) reported a category called *manipulation attempts,* which is similar to Baxter and Wilmot's notion of secret tests. Manipulation attempts included the counterjealousy induction, attempts to secure the partner's attention (e.g., by pouting), guilt inductions, and fidelity tests, among others. Of these, the counterjealousy induction was the most frequently mentioned by respondents. Guerrero et al. (1995) found that individuals reported using counterjealousy inductions as a way to get back at partners who had made them jealous. Presumably, this strategy would show the offending partner "how it feels to be jealous" while affirming that the partner still cares enough to be jealous.

These examples show that jealousy is often created deliberately as a strategic attempt to glean relational information, improve a relationship, or get revenge on a partner. Communication can be a means to induce jealousy as well as to respond to it. The next sections of this chapter focus on what happens after jealousy is induced. We start by examining how jealousy is experienced affectively and cognitively, and how the quality of the jealousy experience may influence communication. We then focus on communicative responses to jealousy and their relational consequences.

COGNITIVE AND EMOTIONAL COMPONENTS OF JEALOUSY EXPERIENCE

Cognitive Appraisal Processes

White and Mullen (1989) delineated several types of cognitive appraisals that occur as jealous feelings develop. *Primary appraisals* are assessments regarding the existence and nature of the rival relationship. White and Mullen (1989) identified three cognitively based types of primary appraisal that are characteristic of jealousy experience. First, individuals ponder the possibility that a rival relationship could exist. Second, individuals judge whether or not a rival relationship actually exists. Finally, jealous individuals determine the degree of threat the rival constitutes. According to White and Mullen (1989), these appraisals shape the type and intensity of felt emotions, and influence how individuals cope with and communicate about jealousy. Of course, emotion can also influence primary appraisals.

Secondary appraisal processes are particularly important to the planning of coping strategies and may affect communication. White and Mullen (1989) described four types of secondary appraisal that are used to gather information and interpret the situation: (a) motives assessment, (b) social comparison to rival, (c) alternatives assessment, and (d) loss assessment. An example best illustrates how these forms of appraisal work. Imagine a husband, Barney, noticing that his wife, Betty, is spending a considerable amount of time with a neighbor, Fred. Barney decides that the rival relationship is a definite threat to his relationship with Betty (primary appraisal) and he starts to question why his wife would prefer to spend time with Fred rather than with him. He decides that Betty likely finds a new relationship more stimulating and exciting that her marriage (motives assessment) and that Fred is more attractive and successful than he is (social comparison to rival). Barney realizes that he would rather be married to Betty than to anyone else he knows (alternatives assessment) and that if he loses her he will be lonely and depressed (loss assessment). Given these assessments, Barney is likely to feel depressed and to fear losing Betty.

Two final forms of secondary appraisal are related to coping and communication. White and Mullen (1989) theorized that after jealous individuals gather information and interpret the situation, they will *plan coping strategies* and *assess coping outcomes*. Thus, Barney (in the example above) is likely to plan ways that he can improve his relationship with Betty. He may decide to workout at Boulder Gym to make himself more attractive, buy Betty flowers for her rock garden, and take Betty out for brontosaurus steaks more often. Barney will assess the likelihood of success of his efforts before and during his enactment of them.

Emotional Responses to Jealousy

Researchers have investigated the many emotions that comprise the jealousy experience (e.g., Bryson, 1976, 1991; Mathes, Phillips, Skowran, & Dick, 1982; Pines & Aronson, 1983; Salovey & Rodin, 1986; Tipton, Benedictson, Mahoney, & Harnett, 1978). Some of this research suggests that jealousy is first experienced as a heightened state of arousal (e.g., Pines & Aronson, 1983) or a "jealousy flash" (Ellis & Weinstein, 1986). According to this view, the jealous individual's sudden perception of threat triggers a strong physiological response. Perceived loss of control over the partner's feelings may exacerbate distress and arousal (Duck, 1986). In a similar vein,

Bringle and Buunk (1985) and McIntosh and Tangri (1989) defined jealousy as any aversive emotional reaction to the real or potential threat of a partner engaging in a relationship with a rival.

Research has also demonstrated that jealousy is a unique emotion, or prototype, because it is connected to a distinctive cluster of emotions (Fitness & Fletcher, 1993; Sharpsteen, 1993). A considerable amount of research indicates that fear (or anxiety), anger, and sadness are the three emotions most central to the jealousy experience (Bers & Rodin, 1984; Clanton & Smith, 1977; Fisher & Tangney, 1995; Plutchik, 1980; Salovey & Rodin, 1988; Teismann & Mosher, 1978; White, 1981b). Bryson's (1976, 1977) and Sharpsteen's (1993; Sharpsteen & Kirkpatrick, 1995) research indicated that in addition to feelings of anger and sadness, jealous individuals report feeling hurt, upset, threatened, betrayed, invaded, pressured, confused, insecure, helpless, aroused, embarrassed, rejected, and frustrated when experiencing jealousy. Further, Bryson (1976) found that jealous individuals often felt the desire to get revenge and/or seek social support. Other research indicates that anticipation or expectancy (Panskepp, 1982), envy (Clanton & Smith, 1977; Hupka & Rusch, 1977; Parrott & Smith, 1993; Tipton et al., 1978), love and happiness (Arnold, 1960; Pines & Aronson, 1983), mistrust (Spielman, 1971), and sexual arousal or passion (Pines & Aronson, 1983) accompany feelings of jealousy. Pride and appreciation may also be related to jealousy in some situations. For instance, it may make jealous individuals feel proud when others are attracted to their partners. Similarly, jealousy may lead individuals to re-evaluate their relationships (especially if they had been taking them for granted), and, possibly, to appreciate their partners more.

White and Mullen (1989) consolidated the above findings and proposed that there are six basic composites of jealousy-related emotion: Anger, fear, sadness, envy, sexual arousal, and guilt. These composites represent clusters of emotions. *Anger,* for example, includes hate, disgust, contempt, and annoyance. *Fear* is comprised of anxiety, tension, worry, and distress. *Sadness* includes depression, hopeless, and melancholy. Resentment and covetousness relate to *envy,* whereas lust, desire, and passion associate with *sexual arousal.* Finally, *guilt* comprises emotions such as regret, shame, and embarrassment. Based on the research reviewed above, there may be at least one other important cluster of jealousy-related emotion—a *positive affect* cluster that revolves around feelings of appreciation, love, loyalty, pride, and warmth.

To our knowledge, little research has been aimed at investigating the links between affective and communicative responses to jealousy. It stands to reason that certain clusters of emotion, such as the anger cluster, would be related to verbally aggressive and violent responses to jealousy. Similarly, the fear and sadness clusters may associate with information-gathering strategies, whereas the sexual arousal and positive affect clusters may associate with relationship-maintaining behaviors, such as restating one's love for the partner or engaging in romantic acts (e.g., fixing a candlelight dinner for one's partner).

Such connections between affect and communication are likely, given White and Mullen's (1989) research on jealousy complexes. A jealousy complex refers to the pattern of thoughts, feelings, and behaviors that are experienced and expressed by a jealous individual. White and Mullen (1989) give the following example of a potential jealousy complex: An individual experiences "*thoughts* of revenge and comparison to the rival, *feelings* of anger and rage," and repeatedly engages in "*behaviors* intended to damage the rival relationship" (p. 13; emphasis added). Clearly, this example shows that cognition, emotion, and behavior are intertwined.

TYPES, FUNCTIONS, AND CONSEQUENCES OF COMMUNICATIVE RESPONSES TO JEALOUSY

Several researchers have lamented that interpersonal communication is often overlooked in scholarship on romantic jealousy (e.g., Afifi, Einwich, & Johnson, 1992; Aune & Comstock, 1991; Le Poire & Strzyzewski, 1991) and that emotions such as jealousy are often studied without examining them within their relational context (e.g., Fitness & Fletcher, 1993). Duck (1992) argued that most jealousy research concentrates on the intrapersonal processes of cognition and affect, or on behaviors performed when one is alone (e.g., reading a book on relationships or looking through the partner's belongings for evidence of an affair). Although a focus on intrapersonal processes is important, Duck maintained that a more complete account of how jealousy functions in relationships must also include interpersonal communication. In response to these calls for more work on communication about jealousy, we developed a program of research that focuses on the jealous individual's communicative responses to jealousy, and the functions and consequences associated with those responses. In this work, we have defined a communicative response to jealousy as "a behavioral reaction to jealousy that carries communicative value and has the potential to fulfill individual and/or relational goals" (Guerrero et al., 1995, p. 272).

Types of Communicative Responses to Jealousy

To determine the types of communicative responses that accompany jealousy, we (Guerrero et al., 1995) conducted three studies that focused on uncovering qualitative categories of communicative responses to jealousy, developing reliable scales to measure these responses, and providing preliminary evidence for the factorial structure and validity of the scales. We found eleven communicative responses to jealousy (see Table I). Six of these were labeled "interactive responses" because of their focus on engaging in or avoiding face-to-face communication. Five additional responses were labeled "general responses" because they often involved engaging in actions or behavioral responses that have communicative value but do not necessarily involve face-to-face communication. For example, fixing a special dinner for the partner involves action that is often conducted out of the presence of the

TABLE I   Communicative Responses to Jealousy[a]

---

1. Negative affect expression: Nonverbal expressions of jealousy-related affect that the partner can see

    Examples: acting anxious when with the partner and rival, appearing hurt, wearing "displeasure" on face, crying in front of the partner

2. Integrative communication: Direct, nonaggressive communication about jealousy with the partner

    Examples: disclosing jealous feelings to the partner, asking the partner probing questions, trying to reach an understanding with the partner; reassuring the partner that we can "work it out"

3. Distributive communication: Direct, aggressive communication about jealousy with the partner

    Examples: accusing the partner of being unfaithful, being sarcastic or rude toward the partner, arguing with the partner, bringing up the issue over and over again to "bombard" the partner

4. Active distancing: Indirect, aggressive means of communicating jealousy to the partner

    Examples: giving the partner the "silent treatment," storming out of the room, giving the partner cold or dirty looks, withdrawing affection and sexual favors

5. Avoidance/denial: Indirect, nonaggressive communication that focuses on avoiding the jealousy-invoking issue, situation, or partner

    Examples: denying jealous feelings when confronted by the partner, pretending to be unaffected by the situation, decreasing contact with the partner, avoiding jealousy-invoking situations

6. Violent communication/threats: Threatening or actually engaging in physical violence against the partner

    Examples: threatening to harm the partner if she continues to see the rival, scaring the partner by acting as if he was about to hit her, roughly pulling him away from the rival, pushing or slapping him

7. Signs of possession: Publicly displaying the relationship to others so they know the partner is "taken"

    Examples: putting an arm around the partner and saying "she's taken," constantly introducing the partner as "my girlfriend," telling potential rivals that we plan to be married, kissing the partner in front of potential or actual rivals

8. Derogating competitors: Making negative comments about potential rivals to the partner and to others

    Examples: "bad-mouthing" the rival in front of the partner and his/her friends, telling the partner that the rival was a "ladies' man" who would hurt her, expressing disbelief that anyone would be attracted to the rival

9. Relationship threats: Threatening to terminate or de-escalate the primary relationship or to be unfaithful

    Examples: threatening to end the relationship if the partner continued to see the rival, threatening infidelity, telling the partner that they should both start dating other people if he continued to see others

10. Surveillance/restriction: Behavioral strategies designed to find out about or interfere with the rival relationship

    Examples: spying or checking up on the partner, looking through the partner's belonging for evidence of a rival relationship, pressing the redial button to see who the partner phoned last, restricting the partner's access to rivals at parties

---

(continues)

TABLE I (*continued*)

11. Compensatory restoration: Behavior aimed at improving the primary relationship and/or making oneself more desirable
    Examples: Sending the partner flowers or gifts, keeping the house especially clean and nice, trying to present oneself as "better" than the rival, trying to appear more physically attractive, reading a self-help book on jealousy and love relationships

12. Manipulation attempts: Moves to induce negative feelings in the partner and/or shift responsibility for communicating about the problem to the partner
    Examples: flirting with others to make the partner jealous, inducing guilt, calling the partner's "bluff" by daring him to break-up and go off with the rival, bringing the rival's name up in conversation to check for a reaction, asking a friend to talk to the partner about the situation

13. Rival contacts: Direct communication with the rival about the jealousy situation, rival relationship, or partner
    Examples: telling the rival to stop seeing the partner, informing the rival that the partner is "already in a relationship," saying something "mean" to the rival, asking the rival about the relationship without revealing her "identity" as the girlfriend, making negative comments about the partner in order to discourage the rival from pursuing her/him

14. Violent behavior toward objects: Directing violence toward objects, either in private or in the presence of others
    Examples: slamming doors, breaking dishes, throwing the partner's possessions out of the house, throwing the partner's makeup across the room

*a*All examples are taken from Guerrero et al.'s (1995) qualitative data.

romantic partner, yet the action has communicative value (e.g., the partner may feel "special" because the jealous individual prepared a nice meal).

Interactive Responses

The six interactive responses included: (a) negative affect expression, (b) integrative communication, (c) distributive communication, (d) active distancing, (e) avoidance/denial, and (f) violent communication/threats. These responses resemble jealous behaviors found by other researchers. For example, scholars have found jealous individuals to negotiate relational rules (Francis, 1977), share jealous feelings, and ask for explanations (Bryson, 1991), all of which fall under integrative communication. Other scholars have also proposed active distancing responses, such as giving the partner the cold shoulder (Byers & Overdorf, 1991; Pines, 1992; Rich, 1991); and distributive responses, such as nagging, complaining, blaming (Buunk & Bringle, 1987; Rich, 1991), and sarcasm (Byers & Overdorf, 1991). Jealous responses of threat (Francis, 1977; Rich, 1991) and avoidance or denial (White & Mullen, 1989) have also surfaced in other literature.

At least three other distinct interactive responses to jealousy have appeared in research on jealousy: Signs of possession, derogating competitors, and relationship threats. These three responses were found in Guerrero et al.'s (1995) qualitative data (though they did not emerge in their factor analysis), and in Buss's (1988) study on mate retention strategies. In addition, in Le Poire and Strzyzewski's (1991) experimental study of jealousy, participants often increased nonverbal immediacy (e.g., put an arm around the partner) when someone showed interest in their partner. Thus, nonverbal communication can function as a display of possession. Other examples of signs of possession, derogating competitors, and relationship threats are found in Table I.

General Responses

The five general responses to jealousy uncovered by Guerrero et al. (1995) are (a) surveillance/restriction, (b) compensatory restoration, (c) manipulation attempts, (d) rival contacts, and (e) violent behavior (see Table I). Other social scientists have investigated similar responses. In fact, surveillance behaviors have been a staple in the psychology literature on jealousy. Researchers focusing on "behavioral jealousy" tend to emphasize actions such as spying, checking up on the partner, and looking through a partner's purse or pockets for evidence of an affair (Pfeiffer & Wong, 1987). Buss (1988) found a strategy labeled "concealment of mate," which focused on restricting the partner's access to the rival. Past research has also tapped into behaviors reflecting compensatory restoration, such as telling the partner how much you value the relationship, making positive comments about the partner to others (Rich, 1991), trying to improve the relationship, and increasing affection and/or sexual activities (Bryson, 1991). Strategies of emotional manipulation and infidelity threats, such as making the partner feel guilty (Buss, 1988), and inducing counterjealousy in the partner (Byers & Overdorf, 1991) are examples of manipulation attempts found in past literature. Violent actions such as throwing objects (Byers & Overdorf, 1991) have also been found by other researchers. Finally, demanding that the partner stop seeing the rival, threatening the rival (Bryson, 1991), and derogating the partner in front of the rival (Buss, 1988) fall under the category labeled rival contacts.

Functions of Communicative Responses to Jealousy

Although some of the above communicative responses to jealousy are likely based on automatic reactions to physiological arousal and emotion, or are the result of purely habitual behavior, it is likely that jealous individuals often use communication to accomplish relational or individual goals (see Figure 1 above). Guerrero and Afifi (1993, 1997) contended that six communicative functions help predict the type of communication in which a jealous person will engage. These functions, which were derived from theory in the areas of social comparison, relationship maintenance, uncertainty reduction, equity, and relationship dissolution, include desires to (a) preserve or bolster self-esteem; (b) maintain the primary relationship; (c) reduce uncertainty about the primary relationship; (d) reduce uncertainty about the rival relationship; (e) restore relational equity; and (f) reassess the relationship.

Preserving or Bolstering Self-Esteem

Researchers studying jealousy and envy have sometimes adopted a social comparison perspective (Bers & Rodin, 1984; Buunk, Bringle, & Arends, 1984; Salovey & Rodin, 1984, 1986; Schmidt, 1988; White, 1981a). Social comparison theory posits that individuals compare themselves with less desirable others as a way of bolstering their self-esteem. However, when jealousy occurs, individuals must concede that their romantic partners have compared them unfavorably to a rival. Some level of forced social comparison is virtually inevitable. Jealous individuals are often left wondering, "What does the rival have that I don't have?" Such comparisons can pose a serious threat to one's self-esteem (Buunk et al., 1984; Ellis & Weinstein, 1986). Therefore, an important function of communication about jealousy is to preserve or restore self-esteem. Indeed, White and Mullen (1989) argued that the cognitive process of making social comparisons to the rival influences how individuals cope with the jealousy situation. These coping mechanisms include communication with members of the romantic triangle as well as one's social support system. Guerrero and Afifi (1993, 1997) found that one way jealous individuals try to preserve self-esteem is by denying jealous feelings or avoiding communication with the partner. Such avoidance strategies may help a jealous individual "save face" in front of the partner. Such strategies may also dampen jealous affect by keeping individuals away from the jealousy-provoking person or situation. This reasoning is consistent with other research (reported earlier in this chapter), which has shown that insecurity and low self-esteem associate positively with indirect communication strategies.

Maintaining the Primary Relationship

Events leading to jealousy, such as extradyadic affairs and perceiving that one's partner is romantically interested in others, have been defined as major relational transgressions (Metts, 1994). Such transgressions must be explained and contained if relationships are to continue. Communication about jealousy plays a central role in either repairing or further harming the relationship. Research on relational maintenance indicates that constructive and prosocial behaviors, such as acting cheerful, being especially affectionate, and sharing tasks or activities function to maintain relationships (Canary & Stafford, 1994). Guerrero and Afifi (1993) found that one prosocial strategy, integrative communication, was used frequently by jealous individuals who wished to maintain their relationships. In addition, Guerrero and Afifi (1993) found that those who wanted to maintain their relationships but did not care about maintaining self-esteem tended to use compensatory restoration behaviors. This last finding comports with Bryson's (1977) prediction that those who have high needs for relationship maintenance and low needs for self-esteem are likely to "cling" to their relationships.

Some antisocial behaviors may also help maintain relationships after a bout with jealousy. For instance, some researchers have argued that antisocial behaviors, such as avoiding the discussion of conflict-inducing subject matter, are associated with relational satisfaction (Baxter & Dindia, 1990). Certainly, romantic partners may avoid talking about past romantic partners and sexual experiences to promote relational closeness and prevent conflict and distress.

Reducing Uncertainty about the Primary Relationship

Besides goals based on concerns for self-esteem preservation and relationship maintenance, goals related to reducing uncertainty are likely to be operative when individuals are jealous. Uncertainty reduction theory (Berger, 1988; Berger & Calabrese, 1975) presents a theoretical foundation from which to explain the impact of uncertainty on behavior (see Afifi & Reichert, 1996). Although originally a theory of initial interactions, it has been employed to study long-term relationships. The theory claims that individuals faced with uncertainty are highly motivated to reduce this undesirable state through active, passive, or interactive means. The experience of romantic jealousy is prototypic of a situation high in uncertainty (Guerrero & Afifi, 1993). When jealousy occurs, the primary relationship, which is usually a source of love and security, becomes plagued with uncertainty, particularly about the future of the relationship and appropriate interpersonal behavior (see Livingston, 1980). Afifi and Reichert (1996) found a positive relationship between uncertainty and jealousy across two studies. Similarly, Parker (1996) found that uncertainty was much higher in situations characterized by threats to sexual exclusivity or verbal intimacy than in situations characterized by no threat.

The effects that increased uncertainty has on information seeking and jealous communication are still unclear. Afifi and Reichert (1996) found that jealousy increased motivation to reduce uncertainty, but that uncertainty associated with a tendency to avoid expressing jealousy. They argued that uncertainty about the partner's reaction to jealousy expression could discourage communication. Two other studies suggest the opposite—that uncertainty may promote communication. First, Guerrero and Afifi (1997) found that jealous individuals who were concerned about relational uncertainty tended to engage in integrative communication with their partners. Second, Parker's (1996) jealousy study showed that uncertainty associated with information seeking, and that individuals in a jealous threat condition thought they would engage in more interactive behavior than did those in a no-threat condition.

Reducing Uncertainty about the Rival Relationship

Communication and information-gathering techniques are likely used to reduce uncertainty about the rival relationship. White and Mullen's (1989) discussion of primary and secondary appraisal processes highlight the importance of this form of uncertainty reduction. Primary appraisal processes involve determining the existence and quality of the rival relationship, as well as assessing the degree of threat that the rival relationship poses. Before making these primary appraisals, the jealous person is likely to feel suspicion and uncertainty, and to be unsure of the extent of attraction and permanence that characterizes the rival relationship. Secondary appraisal processes also involve information gathering, such as determining the partner's motives for participating in a rival relationship. Prior to this appraisal process, the jealous individual is uncertain as to why the partner would be attracted to someone else.

Clearly, communication aimed at *discovering* the nature of the rival relationship is a primary information-gathering strategy used to help individuals reduce uncertainty. Guerrero and Afifi (1993, 1997) confirmed that the desire to reduce uncertainty about the rival relationship was associated with surveillance behavior, manipulation attempts, and rival contact. Parker (1996) reported a similar finding, although she did not differentiate between uncertainty about the rival versus the primary relationship. Parker found that individuals in jealous threat conditions reported being more likely to engage in passive, surveillance behaviors than those in a no-threat condition. Thus, a jealous individual might attempt to find out about the rival relationship by engaging in tactics such as spying, checking the partner's whereabouts, testing fidelity (e.g., bringing up the rival's name to check for a response), and talking with the rival.

Restoring Relational Equity

A fifth function of communicative responses to jealousy centers on equity restoration (Guerrero & Afifi, 1993). According to equity theory, there is a general tendency for partners who perceive their relationships as inequitable to attempt to restore equity (Hatfield, Utne, & Traupmann, 1979). An inequitable relationship is one in which romantic partners have dissimilar ratios of rewards to costs. For example, a wife may put twice as much effort into her marriage as her husband, yet each receives the same amount of relational benefits. In such a case, the wife is said to be "underbenefited," while the husband is said to be "overbenefited." When jealousy occurs, the jealous individual is likely to feel that the relational balance has been tipped, leading to a feeling of underbenefitedness. According to equity theory, there is an especially strong tendency for underbenefited relational members to attempt equity restoration by either increasing their own rewards or decreasing the rewards of their partners (Austin & Walster, 1974; Walster, Walster, & Berscheid, 1978). This may lead the jealous individual to engage in "rewarding" behaviors such as finding better relational alternatives. On the other hand, the jealous individual may try to make the partner feel guilty or attempt to induce counterjealousy. Thus, hurting or getting revenge at the partner may serve the purpose of restoring equity by increasing the partner's costs in the relationship (see also Vangelisti & Sprague, Chapter 5, this volume). Engaging in angry, conflictual, or violent behavior may serve a similar purpose for some individuals.

Research by Guerrero and Afifi (1993) indicated that jealous individuals do indeed use a variety of "negative" strategies to restore relational equity. They found that jealous individuals who felt a need to "get back at the partner" or "even the score" tended to use distributive communication, manipulation attempts, and active distancing. Thus, a jealous individual may attempt to restore relational balance by venting anger, communicating contempt, inducing partner guilt, inducing counterjealousy, or giving the partner the silent treatment. Other strategies, such as withholding sex or threatening infidelity may function similarly.

Reassessing the Primary Relationship

Research on relational stages and relationship dissatisfaction support the existence of psychological assessment of the self and/or the relationship as a motivation underlying jealous reactions. Duck (1982) argued that such assessment is the principle component of the intrapsychic phase of relational dissolution and may lead to further relational dissolution or relational compromise. Specifically, Duck argues that when individuals feel dissatisfied with their relationships, they are likely to go through a period of introspection where they weigh costs and rewards and determine if they are justified in feeling dissatisfaction. At this time, an individual may construct evidence to bring to a dyadic discussion of relational problems. Since researchers have found a strong relationship between the experience of jealousy and relationship dissatisfaction (Bringle, Evenbeck, & Schemdel, 1977; Guerrero & Eloy, 1992), such introspection is likely in jealousy situations.

Research on relational events and turning points also shows that individuals take time to determine their relational feelings when experiencing jealousy. Planalp and Surra (1992) suggested that unexpected relational events often result in a change in the individual's relational schema and an increased motivation to explain the event. In fact, these authors cite jealousy-inducing behaviors as "precipitating events" leading to subjective evaluation of the relationship and increased motivation to change the relationship. Similarly, research on relational turning points has consistently shown that the threat of a new rival may produce relational change and adaptation (Baxter & Bullis, 1986; Bullis, Clark, & Sline, 1992). Andersen, Eloy, Guerrero, and Spitzberg (1995) found relationship dissatisfaction to associate with jealous cognition, distributive communication, and avoidance. Guerrero and Afifi (1993) found that jealous individuals who were reassessing their relationships used avoidance, integrative communication, and distributive communication. These findings suggest that dissatisfied individuals engage in avoidance and extended jealous cognition or mulling. If jealous individuals remain dissatisfied after such deliberation, they may resort to verbal aggression to vent their negative emotion.

Consequences of Communicative Responses to Jealousy

In its "darkest" form, jealousy co-occurs with possessiveness, control, and violence (see Guerrero & Andersen, in press). In fact, in most respects jealousy is a detriment to close relationships. Jealousy is both a symptom and a cause of relational distress. Recent research has shown that cognitive, affective, and behavioral jealousy are all inversely associated with relational and marital satisfaction (Andersen et al., 1995; Buunk & Bringle, 1987; Guerrero & Eloy, 1992; Salovey & Rodin, 1989; Trost et al., 1994) and positively associated with discussions regarding potential relational termination (Guerrero & Jorgensen, 1991).

Even more problematic is the connection between jealousy and violence. In the midst of a blizzard of media coverage of interpersonal violence in sensational cases such as the O. J. Simpson trial, researchers have shown jealousy to be a major contributor to relational violence. Researchers have concluded that male sexual jealousy is probably the leading cause of spousal homicides (Hansen, 1991) and dating violence (Sugarman & Hotaling, 1989) in North America. Moreover, Daly and Wilson (1987) maintained that jealousy is a major source of spousal homicides worldwide and concluded: "The restriction of female sexual freedom by the use and threat of male violence appears to be cross-culturally universal" (p. 304). White and Mullen (1989) estimated that up to 20% of all murders involve a jealous lover. Moreover, men are not the only perpetrators of violence. Stets and Pirog-Good (1987) found that jealousy more than tripled females' use of violence in dating relationships.

In its "brightest" form, jealousy shows how much relational partners care about one another and, if feelings of love or passion are rekindled, jealousy can strengthen relational and sexual bonds. In insecure relationships, such as in new romances and affairs, jealousy may be a particularly telling sign of love and affection. In fact, feeling jealous in a new relationship may lead a person to conclude that s/he really cares about the partner. Research has also shown that individuals who feel a great deal of love for their partners tend to anticipate feeling jealous (White & Mullen, 1989). As we have discussed, jealousy may also provide a means for repairing or maintaining a relationship, opening channels of communication, and reaching new levels of understanding.

Despite the knowledge that jealousy can either enhance or diminish relational satisfaction, it was not until recently that scholars began to investigate how various communicative responses to jealousy influence relationship quality. Since it is plausible to expect both positive and negative relational effects of communication about jealousy, we (Andersen et al., 1995) sought to determine the effects of jealous feelings, jealousy thoughts, and jealousy-induced communication on relational satisfaction. Three important findings emerged from this study and from related studies (e.g., Guerrero & Eloy, 1992). First, various negative and positive types of jealous communication co-occur, and these combinations show complex associations with indices of relational satisfaction. Second, jealous cognition is a more potent predictor of relational dissatisfaction than is jealous emotion. Third, communicative responses to jealousy account for larger portions of variance in relational satisfaction than do jealous cognition or jealous emotion. Thus, jealousy itself is not always the culprit. Rather, it is how jealousy is communicated that appears to have the most significant effects on relationships. In the following pages, we discuss communicative responses to jealousy that appear to have a negative impact on relationships. We then turn to a discussion of communicative responses that often have positive relational consequences.

Negative Moves

Distributive Communication

Aside from violence, the most negative set of communicative behaviors involves distributive communication. Prior research has shown that distributive strategies result in negative affect and perpetuate interpersonal conflict (Gottman, 1994; Guerrero, 1994; Sillars, 1980; Spitzberg, Canary, & Cupach, 1994). Research on jealousy also illustrates the detrimental effects of distributive communication. Buss (1988) found the least effective mate retention strategies to include mate derogation (e.g., making negative comments to others about the partner), which is a distributive strategy. Recently, Andersen et al. (1995) reported an inverse correlation ($r = -.44$) between distributive communicative responses to jealousy and relational satisfaction. Little research basis exists for the folk wisdom that severe arguments or accusations bring people closer together. Indeed, our data suggest that it is one of the most deleterious communication strategies.

Avoidant Strategies

Both active distancing and avoidance/denial have also been found to be counterproductive. As with distributive strategies, our data have shown that active distancing is moderately and inversely associated with relational satisfaction ($r = -.36$; Andersen et al., 1995). Active distancing strategies, such as ignoring the partner, may both confuse the partner and reduce the opportunity for meaningful relational communication. Avoidance/denial strategies, such as pretending that nothing is wrong, may also shut down channels of communication and increase uncertainty (Afifi & Burgoon, 1996). Recent research by Guerrero (in press) found that individuals with negative models or expectations of relational partners tend to use avoidance and denial as ways to cope with jealousy. In other words, jealous individuals who generally perceive relationships to be unrewarding engaged in avoidance/denial, perhaps reinforcing their negative attitudes toward relationships. Similarly, Andersen et al. (1995) found a significant negative relationship ($r = -.24$) between avoidance/denial and relational satisfaction. This finding is consistent with other research (see Sillars, 1980), which has shown that avoidance is an ineffective means of managing conflict.

Violent Communication / Threats

As discussed above, some individuals engage in extreme strategies, such as threatening or actually using physical violence. Buss (1988) reported that violence is an extremely ineffective mate retention strategy. Several scholars have reported that vi-

olence is actually more likely and more severe against an allegedly unfaithful partner than against the alleged rival (Mathes & Verstraete, 1993; White & Mullen,
1989). This suggests that violence may be an immediate reaction that stems from
anger, and that angry feelings may be exacerbated when an angry individual confronts the partner. Our recent research (Andersen et al., 1995) showed a significant
negative correlation ($r = -.21$) between violent communication/threats and relational satisfaction, which indicates that such displays tend to make matters worse in
one's relationship. The magnitude of this correlation may appear surprisingly small.
However, it should be remembered that violence is often underreported (Marshall,
1994) and, thus, a restricted range may attenuate the relationship.

Manipulation Attempts

Manipulation attempts, which include counterjealousy and guilt inductions, are also
likely to affect relationship quality. However, little research has investigated the relational consequences of deploying these tactics. Buss's (1988) research on infidelity threats (e.g., flirting with others to make the partner jealous) showed that tactics
based on manipulation are more effective mate retention strategies for women than
men. Buss (1988) concluded: "Male jealousy . . . may be *elicited intentionally by females* through the implied threat to fidelity as a tactic for retaining mates" (p. 314).
More research is needed to determine if this sex difference extends to relationship
quality indicators. Perhaps certain manipulation attempts can lead to more relational
commitment, especially if they are performed by women.

Positive Moves

Fortunately, recent research has discovered some strategies that, alone or in combination, have the effect of ameliorating jealousy and improving interpersonal relationships. These strategies include integrative communication, negative affect expression, and compensatory restoration behaviors.

Integrative Communication

A solid body of literature shows that integrative communication is beneficial in several types of problematic relationships (Sillars, 1980; Spitzberg et al., 1994). Similarly, to prevent the disruptive effects of extradyadic relationships, Rusbult and
Buunk (1993) suggested that successful couples actively negotiate relational rules
such as (a) *restricted intensity,* which refers to toning down relational involvements
with extradyadic partners, (b) *marriage primacy,* which involves making sure the marriage comes first, and (c) *invisibility,* which focuses on making sure that extradyadic
contacts are discrete and secret. Other couples may agree not to flirt with others or

that all extramarital relationships are wrong. These tactics may prevent jealousy from occurring or at least lessen its intensity and frequency.

Even after jealousy has occurred, integrative communication is relationally beneficial. Andersen et al. (1995) failed initially to find a significant bivariate correlation between integrative communication and satisfaction. However, a hierarchical regression model in which cognitive jealousy and relational type were entered first produced more promising results. In this model, integrative communication showed a small but significant positive relationship with relational satisfaction. Distributive communication, on the other hand, showed a negative association. Interestingly, our research (Andersen et al., 1995; Guerrero et al., 1995) has shown that integrative and distributive forms of communication about jealousy are positively correlated, perhaps because they are both direct means of communicating jealousy to the partner. It may be that initially neutral or positive talk can turn negative when discussion revolves around a volatile issue such as jealousy. Thus, a positive association between integrative communication and relational satisfaction is more likely to emerge when distributive communication is covaried out of the equation.

Negative Affect Expression

What effect does expression of jealousy-related emotions have on relational satisfaction? Such expression includes nonverbally communicating anger, fear, frustration, sadness, and a host of other negative emotions. Our research (Andersen et al., 1995) has shown that under some circumstances, negative affect expression is relationally beneficial. When jealousy occurs, negative affect expression can be used in conjunction with integrative communication to promote relational satisfaction. But when negative affect is expressed alongside either distributive communication and/or active distancing, it appears to be detrimental to relationships. These findings have intuitive appeal. If an individual is hurt and angry, then positive, solution-oriented, expressive communication promotes catharsis, disclosure, and mutual problem solving. In contrast, when expressions of negative affect are accompanied by distributive strategies (e.g., verbal attacks, blaming, or screaming), revealing negative emotions can intensify an already negative interaction. Similarly, when negative emotions are combined with active distancing behaviors, like giving the cold shoulder or decreasing affection, the resulting message is hardly an elixir for a wounded relationship. Thus, the case of negative affect expression highlights the importance of studying various combinations of communicative responses to jealousy.

Compensatory Restoration

Because restoration behaviors focus on repairing the relationship, it makes intuitive sense that such strategies should work to increase closeness and promote partner responsiveness. Of course, paradoxically, too much compensatory restoration could reflect an overdependence on a relationship, and could push the partner away. Guerrero (in press) found that insecure individuals who were preoccupied with their relationships were most likely to use compensatory restoration. She concluded that if used too dramatically, the partner may interpret compensatory restoration as a desperate move and s/he may respond by feeling engulfed and retreating. This is consistent with both expectancy violations theory (Burgoon, 1983; Burgoon & Hale, 1988) and cognitive valence theory (Andersen, in press), which predict that excessive intimacy from an unrewarding or low valence communicator will produce compensatory reactions and reduced relational closeness. Still, moderate or moderately high levels of compensatory restoration appear to have positive effects on relationships. Buss (1988) reported that demonstrating love and caring for one's partner, both of which are arguably compensatory restoration behaviors, were the most effective mate retention strategies, suggesting that these tactics may work in promoting relational satisfaction.

SUMMARY AND CONCLUSION

Numerous factors affect the experience and expression of romantic jealousy. We have suggested that six antecedent factors—biology, culture, personality, relationships, situations, and strategic (partner-initiated) maneuvers—provide a backdrop for the study of romantic jealousy. These six factors work together to influence the type and intensity of affective responses, the extent of jealous cognition, and ultimately, the ways that members of the romantic triangle communicate about jealousy. We also suggest that jealous affect and cognition influence one another, and often determine how one communicates about jealousy. Sometimes, communicative responses to jealousy are automatic responses to arousal or to intense emotions. At other times, the six antecedents, jealous cognition, and jealous affect may singly or in combination influence the goals that a jealous person attempts to fulfill. We outlined six goals, or communicative functions, related to jealousy: (a) preserving self-esteem, (b) maintaining the primary relationship, (c) reducing uncertainty about the primary relationship, (d) reducing uncertainty about the rival relationship, (e) restoring relational equity, and (f) reassessing the primary relationship. All of these functions have been shown to correspond with particular types of communicative responses to jealousy, such as negative affect expression, integrative communication, distributive communication, active distancing, surveillance behavior, and compensatory restoration.

The research summarized in this chapter describes how jealous individuals affectively, cognitively, and communicatively respond to jealousy. More research is needed to address the experiences of the other members of the romantic triangle. How the partner and rival respond to the jealous individual's communication, and how their communication affects the jealous person's goals, decisions, and behaviors are interesting and important questions that have yet to be addressed. We expect that communication about jealousy is a highly dynamic process, with members of the romantic triangle exerting considerable mutual influence on one another. Investigating these dynamics is a challenging new enterprise in communication research.

ACKNOWLEDGMENTS

We thank Walid Afifi and Dan Canary for serving as reviewers for this chapter. Their insights greatly improved our work.

REFERENCES

Afifi, W. A., Einwich, V., & Johnson, M. (1992, November). 'We're only friends': A comparison of friends and daters on jealousy. Paper presented at the annual meeting of the Speech Communication Association, Chicago, IL.

Afifi, W. A., & Burgoon, J. K. (1996, November). Behavioral violations in interactions: The combined consequences of valence and change in uncertainty on interaction outcomes. Paper presented at the annual meeting of the Speech Communication Association, San Diego, CA.

Afifi, W. A., & Reichart (1996). Understanding the role of uncertainty in jealousy experience and expression. Communication Reports, 9, 93–103.

Amstutz, D. (1982). Androgyny and jealousy. Unpublished doctoral dissertation, Northern Illinois University, DeKalb.

Andersen, P. A. (in press). The cognitive-valence theory of intimate communication. In M. Palmer (Ed.), Mutual influence in interpersonal communication. Hillsdale, NJ: Erlbaum.

Andersen, P. A., Eloy, S. V., Guerrero, L. K., & Spitzberg, B. H. (1995). Romantic jealousy and relational satisfaction: A look at the impact of jealousy experience and expression. Communication Reports, 8, 77–85.

Arnold, M. B. (1960). Emotion and personality. New York: Columbia University Press.

Aune, K. S., & Comstock, J. (1991). The experience and expression of jealousy: A comparison between friends and romantics. Psychological Reports, 69, 315–319.

Aune, K. S., & Comstock, J. (1995). The effects of relational development on the experience, expression, and perceived appropriateness of jealousy. Manuscript under review at Social Psychology.

Austin, W., & Walster, E. (1974). Reactions to confirmations and disconfirmations of expectancies of equity and inequity. Journal of Personality and Social Psychology, 30, 208–213.

Bartholomew, K. (1990). Avoidance of intimacy: An attachment perspective. Journal of Social and Personal Relationships, 7, 147–178.

Baxter, L. A., & Bullis, C. (1986). Turning points in developing romantic relationships. Human Communication Research, 12, 469–493.

Baxter, L. A., & Dindia, K. (1990). Marital partners' perceptions of marital maintenance strategies. Journal of Social and Personal Relationships, 7, 187–208.

Baxter, L. A., & Wilmot, W. (1984). Secret tests: Social strategies for acquiring information about the state of the relationship. Human Communication Research, 11, 171–201.

Berger, C. R. (1988). Uncertainty and information exchange in developing relationships. In S. Duck (Ed.), Handbook of personal relationships: Theory, research, and interventions (pp. 239–256). Chichester: Wiley and Sons.

Berger, C. H., & Calabrese, R. J. (1975). Some explorations in initial interaction and beyond: Toward a developmental theory of interpersonal communication. Human Communication Research, 2, 33–50.

Bers, S. A., & Rodin, J. (1984). Social comparison jealousy: A developmental and motivational study. Journal of Personality and Social Psychology, 47, 766–769.

Berscheid, E. (1983). Emotion. In H. H. Kelly, E. Berscheid, A. Christensen, J. H. Harvey, T. L. Huston, G. Levinger, E. McClintock, L. A. Peplau, & D. R. Peterson (Eds.), *Close relationships* (pp. 110–168). San Francisco, CA: Freeman.

Berscheid, E., & Fei, J. (1977). Romantic love and sexual jealousy. In G. Clanton & L. G. Smith (Eds.), *Jealousy* (pp. 101–109). Englewood Cliffs, NJ: Prentice-Hall.

Brehm, S. S. (1992). *Intimate relationships* (2nd ed.). New York: McGraw-Hill.

Bringle, R. G. (1981). Conceptualizing jealousy as a disposition. *Alternative Lifestyles, 4,* 274–290.

Bringle, R. G., & Boebinger, K. L. G. (1990). Jealousy and the "third" person in the love triangle. *Journal of Social and Personal Relationships, 7,* 119–133.

Bringle, R. G., & Buunk, B. (1985). Jealousy and social behavior. *Review of Personality and Social Psychology, 6,* 241–264.

Bringle, R. G., & Buunk, B. (1986). Examining the causes and consequences of jealousy: Some recent findings and issues. In R. Gilmour & S. Duck (Eds.), *The emerging field of personal relationships* (pp. 225–240). Hillsdale, NJ: Erlbaum.

Bringle, R. G., & Buunk, B. (1991). Extradyadic relationships and sexual jealousy. In K. McKinney & S. Sprecher (Eds.), *Sexuality in close relationships* (pp. 135–153). Hillsdale, NJ: Erlbaum.

Bringle, R. G., & Evenbeck, S. (1979). The state of jealousy as a dispositional characteristic. In M. Cook & G. Wilson (Eds.), *Love and attraction* (pp. 201–204). Oxford: Pergamon Press.

Bringle, R. G., Evenbeck, S. E., & Schmedel, K. (1977, September). *The role of jealousy in marriage.* Paper presented at the annual meeting of the American Psychological Association, San Francisco, CA.

Bringle, R. G., & Williams, L. J. (1979). Parental–offspring similarity on jealousy and related personality dimensions. *Motivation and Motion, 3,* 265–286.

Bryson, J. B. (1976, September). *The nature of sexual jealousy: An exploratory paper.* Paper presented at the annual meeting of the American Psychological Association, Washington, D.C.

Bryson, J. B. (1977, September). *Situational determinants of the expression of jealousy.* Paper presented at the annual meeting of the American Psychological Association, San Francisco, CA.

Bryson, J. B. (1991). Modes of responses to jealousy-evoking situations. In P. Salovey (Ed.), *The psychology of envy and jealousy* (pp. 1–45). New York: Guilford.

Bullis, C., Clark, C., & Sline, R. (1992). From passion to commitment: Turning points in romantic relationships. In P. Kalbfleish (Ed.), *Interpersonal communication: Evolving interpersonal relationships* (pp. 213–236). Hillsdale, NJ: Erlbaum.

Burgoon, J. K. (1983). Nonverbal violations of expectations. In J. M. Wiemann & R. P. Harrison (Eds.), *Nonverbal interaction* (pp. 77–111). Beverly Hills, CA: Sage.

Burgoon, J. K., & Hale, J. L. (1988). Nonverbal expectancy violations: Model elaboration and application to immediacy behaviors. *Communication Monographs, 55,* 58–79.

Bush, C. R., Bush, J. P., & Jennings, J. (1988). Effects of jealousy threat on relationship perception and emotions. *Journal of Social and Personal Relationships, 5,* 285–303.

Buss, D. M. (1988). From vigilance to violence: Tactics of mate retention in American undergraduates. *Ethology and Sociobiology, 9,* 291–317.

Buss, D. M. (1989). Conflict between the sexes: Strategic interference in the evocation of anger and upset. *Journal of Personality and Social Psychology, 56,* 735–747.

Buunk, B. (1981). Jealousy in sexually open marriages. *Alternative Lifestyles, 4,* 357–372.

Buunk, B. (1982). Anticipated sexual jealousy: Its relationship to self-esteem dependency, and reciprocity. *Personality and Social Psychology Bulletin, 8,* 310–316.

Buunk, B., & Bringle, R. G. (1987). Jealousy in love relationships. In D. Perlman & S. Duck (Eds.), *Intimate relationships development, dynamics, and deterioration* (pp. 123–147). Newbury Park, CA: Sage.

Buunk, B., Bringle, R. G., & Arends, H. (1984). *Jealousy: A response to threatened self-concept?* Paper presented at the International Conference on Self and Identity, Cardiff, Wales, UK.

Buunk, B., & Hupka, R. B. (1987). Cross-cultural differences in the elicitation of sexual jealousy. *Journal of Sex Research, 23,* 12–22.

Byers, P. Y., & Overdorf, S. A. (1991, November). *A descriptive analysis of female perceptions of romantic marital jealousy.* Paper presented at the annual meeting of the Speech Communication Association, Atlanta, GA.

Canary, D. J., & Stafford, L. (1994). Maintaining relationships through strategic and routine interaction. In D. J. Canary & L. Stafford (Eds.), *Communication and relational maintenance* (pp. 3–22). San Diego, CA: Academic Press.

Clanton, G., & Smith, L. G. (Eds.). (1977). *Jealousy.* Englewood Cliffs, NJ: Prentice-Hall.

Collins, N. L., & Read, S. J. (1990). Adult attachment, working models, and relationship quality in dating couples. *Journal of Personality and Social Psychology, 58,* 644–663.

Daly, M., & Wilson, M. (1983). *Sex, evolution, and behavior.* Boston, MA: Willard Grant Press.

Daly, M., & Wilson, M. (1987). Evolutionary psychology and family violence. In C. Crawford, M. Smith, & D. Krebs (Eds.), *Sociobiology and psychology: Ideas, issues, and applications* (pp. 293–309). Hillsdale, NJ: Erlbaum.

De Moja, C. A. (1986). Anxiety, self-confidence, jealousy, and romantic attitudes toward love in Italian undergraduates. *Psychological Reports, 58,* 138.

Delgado, A. R., & Bond, R. A. (1993). Attenuating the attribution of responsibility: The lay perception of jealousy as a motive for wife battery. *Journal of Applied Social Psychology, 23,* 1337–1356.

Duck, S. W. (1982). A topography of relationship disengagement and dissolution. In S. Duck (Ed.), *Personal relationships 4: Dissolving personal relationships* (pp. 1–30). London: Academic Press.

Duck, S. W. (1986). *Human relationships: An introduction to social psychology.* Beverly Hills, CA: Sage.

Duck, S. W. (1992). *Human relationships* (2nd edition). Newbury Park, CA: Sage.

Ellis, C., & Weinstein, E. (1986). Jealousy and the social psychology of emotional experirence. *Journal of Social and Personal Relationships, 3,* 337–357.

Fisher, K. W., & Tangney, J. P. (1995). Self-conscious emotions and the affect revolution: Framework and overview. In J. P. Tangney & K. W. Fisher (Eds.), *Self-conscious emotions: The psychology of shame, guilt, embarrassment, and pride.* New York: Guilford.

Fitness, J., & Fletcher, G. J. O. (1993). Love, hate, anger, and jealousy in close relationships: A prototype and cognitive appraisal analysis. *Journal of Personality and Social Psychology, 65,* 942–958.

Francis, J. (1977). Toward the management of sexual jealousy. *Journal of Marriage and the Family, 39,* 61–69.

Gottman, J. (1994). *What predicts divorce?* Hillsdale, NJ: Erlbaum.

Greenless, I. A., & McGrew, W. C. (1994). Sex and age differences in preferences and tactics of mate attraction: An analysis of published work. *Ethology and Sociobiology, 15,* 59–72.

Guerrero, L. K. (1994). "I'm so mad I could scream:" The effects of anger expression on relational satisfaction and communication competence. *Southern Communication Journal, 59,* 125–141.

Guerrero, L. K. (in press). Attachment-style differences in the experience and expression of jealousy. *Personal Relationships.*

Guerrero, L. K., & Afifi, W. A. (1993, June). *Coping with romantic jealousy: Accomplishing goals via communication.* Paper presented at the biennial meeting of the International Network on Personal Relationships, Milwaukee, WI.

Guerrero, L. K., & Afifi, W. A. (1997, June). *Toward a functional approach for understanding strategic communicative responses to jealousy.* Paper presented at the annual meeting of the International Network on Personal Relationships, Oxford, OH.

Guerrero, L. K. & Andersen, P. A. (in press). The dark side of jealousy and envy: Desire, delusion, desperation, and destructive communication. In B. H. Spitzberg & W. R. Cupach (Eds.), *The dark side of relationships.* Hillsdale, NJ: Erlbaum.

Guerrero, L. K., Andersen, P. A., Jorgensen, P. F., Spitzberg, B. H., & Eloy, S. V. (1995). Coping with the green-eyed monster: Conceptualizing and measuring communicative responses to romantic jealousy. *Western Journal of Communication, 59,* 270–304.

Guerrero, L. K., & Eloy, S. V. (1992). Relational satisfaction and jealousy across marital types. *Communication Reports, 5,* 23–31.

Guerrero, L. K., Eloy, S. V., Jorgensen, P. F., & Andersen, P. A. (1993). Hers or his? Sex differences in the communication of jealousy in close relationships. In P. Kalbfleisch (Ed.), *Interpersonal Communication in Evolving Interpersonal Relationships* (pp. 109–131). Hillsdale, NJ: Erlbaum.

Guerrero, L. K., & Jorgensen, P. F. (1991, November). *The nature of marital jealousy: Effects of threats to permanence and interdependence.* Paper presented at the annual meeting of the Speech Communication Association, Atlanta, GA.

Guerrero, L. K., & Reiter, R. L. (in press). Expressing emotion: Sex differences in communication skills and the expression of anger, sadness, and jealousy. In D. J. Canary & K. Dindia (Eds.), *Handbook of sex, gender, and communication: Similarities and differences.* Hillsdale, NJ: Erlbaum.

Hansen, G. L. (1985). Dating jealousy among college students. *Sex Roles, 12,* 713–721.

Hansen, G. L. (1991). Jealousy: Its conceptualization, measurement, and integration with family stress theory. In P. Salovey (Ed.), *The psychology and jealousy of envy* (pp. 211–230). New York: Guilford.

Hatfield, E., Utne, M. K., & Traupmann, J. (1979). Equity theory and intimate relationships. In R. L. Burgess & T. L. Huston (Eds.), *Social exchange in developing relationships* (pp. 99–133). New York: Academic Press.

Hazan, C., & Shaver, P. (1987). Romantic love conceptualized as an attachment process. *Journal of Personality and Social Psychology, 52,* 511–524.

Hofstede, G. (1980). *Culture's consequences: International differences in work-related values.* Beverly Hills, CA: Sage.

Hupka, R. B. (1981). Cultural determinants of jealousy. *Alternative Lifestyles, 4,* 310–356.

Hupka, R. B., Buunk, B., Falus, G., Fulgosi, A., Ortega, E., Swain, R., & Tarabrina, N. V. (1985). Romantic jealousy and romantic envy: A seven nation study. *Journal of Cross-Cultural Psychology, 16,* 423–446.

Hupka, R. B., & Rusch, P. A. (1977, April). *The interpersonal relationships scale.* Paper presented at the annual meeting of the Western Psychological Association, Seattle, WA.

Hupka, R. B., & Ryan, J. M. (1981, April). *The cultural contribution to emotions: Cross-cultural aggression in sexual jealousy situations.* Paper presented at the annual meeting of the Western Psychological Association, Los Angeles.

Kenrick, D. T., & Keefe, R. C. (1992). Age preferences in mates reflect sex differences in human reproductive strategies. *Behavioral and Brain Sciences, 15,* 75–137.

Kenrick, D. T., & Trost, M. R. (1989). A reproductive exchange model of heterosexual relationships: Putting proximate economics in ultimate perspective. In C. Hendrick (Ed.), *Close relationships* (pp. 92–118). Newbury Park, CA: Sage.

Le Poire, B. A., & Strzyzewski, K. (1991, May). *Gender differences in the nonverbal expression of jealousy.* Paper presented at the annual meeting of the International Communication Association, Chicago, IL.

Livingston, K. R. (1980). Love as a process of reducing uncertainty—cognitive theory. In K. S. Pope (Ed.), *On love and loving* (pp. 133–151). San Francisco, CA: Jossey-Bass.

Marshall, L. L. (1994). Physical and psychological abuse. In W. R. Cupach & B. H. Spitzberg (Eds.), *The dark side of interpersonal communication* (pp. 281–311). Hillsdale, NJ: Erlbaum.

Mathes, E. W., Phillips, J. T., Skowran, J., & Dick, W. E. (1982). Behavioral correlates of the Interpersonal Jealousy Scale. *Educational and Psychological Measurement, 42,* 1227–1230.

Mathes, E. W., & Severa, N. (1981). Jealousy, romantic love, and liking: Theoretical considerations and preliminary scale development. *Psychological Reports, 49,* 23–31.

Mathes, E. W., & Verstraete, C. (1993). Jealous aggression: Who is the target, the beloved or the rival? *Psychological Reports, 72,* 1071–1074.

McIntosh, E. G. (1989). An investigation of romantic jealousy among black undergraduates. *Social Behavior and Personality, 17,* 135–141.

McIntosh, E. G., & Tangri, S. S. (1989). Relationship between jealous feelings and behaviors. *Perceptual and Motor Skills, 69,* 765–766.

McIntosh, E. G., & Tate, D. T. (1990). Correlates of jealous behaviors. *Psychological Reports, 66,* 601–602.

Metts, S. (1994). Relational transgressions. In W. R. Cupach & B. H. Spitzberg (Eds.), *The dark side of interpersonal communication* (pp. 217–239). Hillsdale, NJ: Erlbaum.

Metts, S., & Bowers, J. W. (1994). Emotion in interpersonal communication. In M. L. Knapp & G. R.

Miller (Eds.), *Handbook of interpersonal communication* (2nd ed., pp. 508–541). Thousand Oaks, CA: Sage.

Mishkin, B. (1937). The Maori of New Zealand. In M. Mead (Ed.), *Cooperation and competition among primate peoples* (pp. 428–457). New York: McGraw-Hill.

Panskepp, J. (1982). Towards a general psychobiological theory of emotions. *Behavioral and Brain Sciences, 5,* 407–467.

Parker, R. G. (1994, November). *An examination of the influence of situational determinants upon strategies for coping with romantic jealousy.* Paper presented at the annual meeting of the Speech Communication Association, New Orleans, LA.

Parker, R. G. (1996, February). *The influence of sexual infidelity, verbal intimacy, and gender upon secondary appraisal processes in romantic jealousy.* Paper presented at the annual meeting of the Western States Communication Association, Pasadena, CA.

Parrott, W. G., & Smith, R. H. (1993). Distinguishing the experiences of envy and jealousy. *Journal of Personality and Social Psychology, 64,* 906–920.

Pfeiffer, S. M., & Wong, P. T. (1989). Multidimensional jealousy. *Journal of Social and Personal Relationships, 6,* 181–196.

Pines, A. M. (1992). *Romantic jealousy: Understanding and conquering the shadow of love.* New York: St. Martin's Press.

Pines, A., & Aronson, E. (1983). Antecedents, correlates, and consequences of sexual jealousy. *Journal of Personality, 51,* 108–136.

Planalp, S., & Surra, C. A. (1992). The role of account-making in the growth and deterioration of close relationships. In J. H. Harvey, T. L. Orbuch, & A. L. Webber (Eds.), *Attributions, accounts, and close relationships* (pp. 71–92). New York: Springer-Verlag.

Plutchik, R. (1980). *Emotion.* New York: Harper & Row.

Radecki-Bush, C., Farrell, A. D., & Bush, J. P. (1993). Predicting jealous responses: The influence of adult attachment and depression on threat appraisal. *Journal of Social and Personal Relationships, 10,* 569–588.

Rathus, S. A. Nevid, J. S., & Fichner-Rathus, L. (1993). *Human sexuality in a world of diversity.* Boston, MA: Allyn & Bacon.

Reiss, I. L. (1986). A sociological journey into sexuality. *Journal of Marriage and the Family, 48,* 233–242.

Rich, J. (1991). A two-factor measure of jealous response. *Psychological Reports, 68,* 999–1007.

Rusbult, C. E. (1983). A longitudinal test of the investment model: The development (and deterioration) of satisfaction and commitment in heterosexual involvement. *Journal of Personality and Social Psychology, 45,* 101–117.

Rusbult, C. W., & Buunk, B. P. (1993). Commitment processes in close relationships: An interdependence analysis. *Journal of Social and Personal Relationships, 10,* 175–204.

Rusbult, C. E., Drigotas, S. M., & Verette, J. (1994). The investment model: An interdependence analysis of commitment processes and relationship maintenance phenomena. In D. J. Canary & L. Stafford (Eds.), *Communication and relational maintenance* (pp. 115–140). San Diego, CA: Academic Press.

Russell, B. (1957). *Why I am not a Christian.* New York: Simon and Shuster.

Salovey, P., & Rodin, J. (1984). Some antecedents and consequences of social-comparison jealousy. *Journal of Personality and Social Psychology, 47,* 780–792.

Salovey, P., & Rodin, J. (1985). The heart of jealousy. *Psychology Today, 19*(9), 22–25, 28–29.

Salovey, P., & Rodin, J. (1986). Differentiation of social-comparison jealousy and romantic jealousy. *Journal of Personality and Social Psychology, 50,* 1100–1112.

Salovey, P., & Rodin, J. (1988). Coping with envy and jealousy. *Journal of Social and Clinical Psychology, 7,* 15–33.

Salovey, P., & Rodin, J. (1989). Envy and jealousy in close relationships. In C. Hendrick (Ed.), *Close relationships* (pp. 221–246). Newbury Park: Sage.

Schmidtt, B. H. (1988). Social comparison in romantic jealousy. *Personality and Social Psychology Bulletin, 14,* 374–387.

Sharpsteen, D. J. (1993). Romantic jealousy as an emotion concept: A prototype analysis. *Journal of Social and Personal Relationships, 10,* 69–82.

Sharpsteen, D. J., & Kirkpatrick, L. A. (1995, June). *Romantic jealousy as an attachment process: Individual differences in jealousy experiences.* Paper presented at the annual meeting of the International Network on Personal Relationships, Williamsburg, VA.

Shettel-Neuber, J., Bryson, J. B., & Young, C. E. (1978). Physical attractiveness of the "other person" and jealousy. *Personality and Social Psychology Bulletin, 4,* 612–615.

Sillars, A. (1980). The sequential and distributional structure of conflict interactions as a function of attributions concerning the locus of responsibility and stability of conflicts. In D. Nimmo (Ed.), *Communication yearbook 4* (pp. 217–235). New Brunswick, NJ: Transaction Books.

Spielman, P. M. (1971). Envy and jealousy: An attempt at clarification. *Psychoanalytic Quarterly, 40,* 59–82.

Spitzberg, B. H., Canary, D. J., & Cupach, W. R. (1994). A competence-based approach to the study of interpersonal conflict. In D. D. Cahn (Ed.), *Conflict in personal relationships* (pp. 183–202). Hillsdale, NJ: Erlbaum.

Solomon, R. C. (1976). *The passions.* Garden City, NY: Doubleday.

Stekel, W. (1921). *The depths of the soul* (S. A. Tannenbaum, Trans.). London: Kegan Paul.

Stets, J. E., & Pirog-Good, M. A. (1987). Violence in dating relationships. *Social Psychology Quarterly, 50,* 237–246.

Stewart, R. B., & Beatty, M. J. (1985). Jealousy and self-esteem. *Perceptual and Motor Skills, 60,* 153–154.

Sugarman, D. B., & Hotaling, G. T. (1989). Dating violence: Prevalence, context, and risk markers. In M. A. Pirog-Good & J. E. Stets (Eds.), *Violence in dating relationships: Emerging social issues* (pp. 3–32). New York: Praeger.

Teismann, M. W., & Mosher, D. L. (1978). Jealous conflict in dating couples. *Psychological Reports, 42,* 1211–1216.

Thibault, J. W., & Kelley, H. H. (1959). *The social psychology of groups.* New York: Wiley.

Tipton, R. M., Benedictson, C. S., Mahoney, J., & Harnett, J. (1978). Development of a scale for assessment of jealousy. *Psychological Reports, 42,* 1217–1218.

Tolman, R. M. (1989). The development of a measure of psychological maltreatment of women by their male partners. *Violence and Victims, 4,* 159–177.

Trost, M. R., Brown, S., & Morrison, M. (1994, November). *Jealousy as an adaptive communication strategy.* Poster presented at the annual meeting of the Speech Communication Association, New Orleans, LA.

Walster, E., Walster, G. W., & Berscheid, E. (1978). *Equity: Theory and research.* Boston, MA: Allyn & Bacon.

Walters, S., & Crawford, C. B. (1994). The importance of mate attraction for intersexual competition in men and women. *Ethology and Sociobiology, 15,* 5–30.

Watts, A. W. (1958). *Nature, man, and women.* New York: Vintage Books.

White, G. L. (1977). *Jealousy and attitudes toward love.* Unpublished manuscript.

White, G. L. (1980). Inducing jealousy: A power perspective. *Personality and Social Psychology Bulletin, 6,* 660–668.

White, G. L. (1981a). Jealousy and partner's perceived motives for attraction to a rival. *Social Psychology Quarterly, 44,* 24–30.

White, G. L. (1981b). A model of romantic jealousy. *Motivation and Emotion, 5,* 295–310.

White, G. L. (1981c). Relative involvement, inadequacy, and jealousy: A test of a causal model. *Alternative Lifestyles, 4,* 291–309.

White, G. L. (1981d). Some correlates of romantic jealousy. *Journal of Personality, 49,* 129–147.

White, G. L. (1984). Comparison of four jealousy scales. *Journal of Research in Personality, 18,* 115–130.

White, G. L. (1985). *Gender, power, and romantic jealousy.* Unpublished manuscript.

White, G. L., & Mullen, P. E. (1989). *Jealousy: Theory, research, and clinical strategies.* New York: Guilford.

Whitehurst, R. N. (1977). Jealousy and American values. In G. Clanton & L. G. Smith (Eds.), *Jealousy* (pp. 136–239). Englewood Cliffs, NJ: Prentice-Hall.

Zillman, D. (1990). The interplay of cognition and excitation in aggravated conflict. In D. D. Cahn (Ed.), *Intimates in conflict: A communication perspective* (pp. 187–208). Hillsdale, NJ: Erlbaum.

CHAPTER 7

The Experience and Expression of Anger in Interpersonal Settings

Daniel J. Canary

Pennsylvania State University
University Park, Pennsylvania

Brian H. Spitzberg

San Diego State University
San Diego, California

Beth A. Semic

Pennsylvania State University
University Park, Pennsylvania

Historical analyses suggest that the prevailing *zeitgeist* regarding anger has varied considerably over time, from ancient and medieval conceptions (Kemp & Strongman, 1995) to Victorian prohibitions against its destructive nature, to more contemporary conceptions of its proper channeling and use in interaction (Stearns & Stearns, 1986). Not only do meanings of anger change, but apparently social and scholarly paradigms of anger vary over time (Stearns & Stearns, 1986) and culture (Tavris, 1982). It follows from these analyses that *anger* constitutes a difficult concept to locate and generalize theoretically. In this chapter, we attempt to synthesize the scholarship on anger. We focus on both the experience and expression of anger, especially in reference to one of its most common and potentially destructive manifestations—aggression.

As a social phenomenon, anger involves expression as well as its experience. As Fehr and Baldwin (1996) noted, "anger, especially intense anger, is an interpersonal event" (p. 221). In our view, people must somehow *communicate* their anger to others in order for it to have social significance (e.g., effects on partner, relational outcomes, productivity outcomes). Accordingly, we explore both the experience and expression of anger in interpersonal contexts. Besides our personal perspective, other reasons warrant such an effort.

First, people who find it difficult to communicate anger in an appropriate manner risk physical problems. An important case concerns how suppressing *or* overexpressing anger leads to heart disease (e.g., Helmers, Posluszny, & Krantz, 1994). In an extensive review, Siegman (1994) concluded that

> this much is clear then: The two traits, that is, the expression of anger and the experience of anger, relate differentially to CVR [cardiovascular reactivity], with only the expression of anger, not its mere experience, correlating with CVR. . . . It is the expression of anger, not the mere experience of these feelings, that seems to be the toxic factor in CAD [coronary artery disease]. (pp. 181–182)

Holt (1970) noted a variety of other physical ailments that accompany the *in*expression of anger, including hives, acne, arthritis, and ulcers.

Second, failure to communicate anger can render people dysfunctional for a time (Helmers et al., 1994). The inexpression of anger can perpetuate cognitive inefficiency, and one may find it near impossible to work with someone who has recently provoked anger (Holt, 1970). In a similar manner, angered people may need to vent their feelings against the perpetrator in order to feel normal again. "Whatever the explanation, we evidently feel better when we see that the person who angered us has been hurt" (Berkowitz, 1970, p. 6).

Finally, the appropriate communication of anger appears critical for relational reasons as well. Buss (1989) found that sources of anger and upset negatively correlated with marital satisfaction (rs $= -.31$ to $-.52$). Likewise, Krokoff (1991) found that for couples who approach or engage in conflict (but not for those who avoid conflict), both the wife's and the husband's expression of anger strongly predicted wife's concurrent marital satisfaction, and lack of anger expression negatively affected wife satisfaction measured 3 years later. Kubany, Bauer, Muraola, Richard, and Read (1995) found that the "explicit" communication of anger (i.e., blaming messages of anger) is attributed with provoking more anger, antagonism, and retaliation, and less empathy and conciliation, relative to self-attributions of anger or expressions of general distress. Tavris (1984) observed that

> many studies indicate a host of negative aspects of expressing anger, including miscommunication with the target of one's anger; emotional distance as a person angry with you; rehearsal of grievances; acquiring a hostile disposition; angry habits; making a bad situation worse; losing self-esteem, respect of others; 'anti-catharsis'; raising blood pressure, signs of tension; feeling angrier. (pp. 171–172)

Consequences of anger are not uniformly negative, however (Stearns & Stearns, 1986). Tavris (1984) observed that the appropriate expression of anger can lead to many *positive* outcomes, including the following: "communicating with another person (one's target or a third party); emotional closeness; shared experience and understanding; changing a bad situation; achieving justice, redress of grievances; catharsis; reduction of tension and anxiety; lowering of blood pressure; getting one's way (gaining power, authority, status)" (p. 171). In addition, although honest expression of anger may lead to concurrent relational dissatisfaction, Gottman and

Krokoff (1989) found that expressions of anger were positively associated with increases in satisfaction 3 years following the anger episode. The communication of ideas energized by anger can help underscore one's beliefs, attitudes, and values, making them hard to miss.

In the following pages, we discuss how people experience and express anger in interpersonal interactions. Scientific and social constructionist understandings of anger and the implications of these views for communicative responses to anger are examined. We first review research on the nature of anger, emphasizing its types and causes. Next, we offer a set of propositions regarding links between anger and aggression that have been examined empirically. Finally, we examine various communicative responses to anger.

ANGER IN INTERPERSONAL SETTINGS

Scientific Parameters of Anger

As a scientific construct, *anger* remains a tough nut to crack. "Anger is one of the most frequently experienced emotions; moreover, we seldom have difficulty deciding when we are angry or understanding when others are angry at us. Yet, when asked to state what we mean by anger, we are often at a loss of words" (Averill, 1993, p. 171). The propensity for humans to express anger is illustrated by infants, who communicate anger as early as 4 months of age (Lemerise & Dodge, 1993). Rubin (1986) concluded, "To further the understanding of the anger expression controversy, the definition of anger needs to be clarified. Currently, no generally agreed upon definition exists" (p. 116). Some researchers have attempted to define anger in fairly narrow terms, for example, by considering as necessary the perceptions of the target's blameworthiness and negative consequences arising from the target's behavior (Clore, Ortony, Dienes, & Fujita, 1993). Other researchers have expanded the potential meaning of the construct, for example, by defining it situationally. As an illustration of this later approach, Russell and Fehr (1994) concluded that "the word *anger* takes on a specific meaning in a specific context" (p. 203).

Researchers also disagree about the fundamental features of anger. Russell and Fehr (1994) outlined several issues under current scholarly dispute, including the following: (a) the status of anger as a primary or a secondary emotion (e.g., whether or not anger follows fear); (b) its causes (e.g., goal impediment vs. reproach); (c) the correspondence of anger to related emotional constructs, such as frustration and resentment; (d) subcategories of anger (e.g., envy, frustration, hatred); (e) the association of anger to physiological arousal; and importantly (f) how anger associates with aggression.

Much of the research on the layperson's experience of anger has emerged under the auspices of emotional prototypes. This view holds that people rely on exemplar models to understand their affective experiences—how emotions arise, how people respond to them physically, and how people express emotions (see Guerrero, Andersen, & Trost, Chapter 1, for a more detailed description of prototypes). Accordingly, Shaver, Schwartz, Kirkson, and O'Connor (1987; see also Russell & Fehr, 1994) conceived of emotions as fuzzy-set categories. Shaver and colleagues asked social actors to provide information about emotions in general and used a cluster analysis to identify "basic" level emotions. These researchers found five basic emotional categories of love, joy, fear, sadness, and anger. At a lower, more specific level, the following six clusters represented anger:

1. *Rage* represents the most generic form of anger (it also included the term "anger"). Terms linked with rage included outrage, anger, fury, wrath, hostility, bitterness, hate, and the like.
2. *Irritation* associated with the terms aggravation, agitation, annoyance, grumpiness, and grouchiness.
3. *Exasperation,* which was hierarchically similar to irritation and associated with the term frustration.
4. *Disgust* linked to revulsion and contempt. As Shaver et al. noted, "Thus, although disgust may be a separate, identifiable physical reaction across the life span, in the adult emotion lexicon it becomes metaphorically transformed into a type of anger akin to contempt" (p. 1069).
5. *Envy* comprised another form of anger, and it was linked with the emotion of jealousy.
6. *Torment* was the final basic level cluster, and as a term it stood alone.

In like manner, Storm and Storm (1987) asked children and adults to list emotional terms that correspond to abstract emotional clusters. The cluster involving anger also included the terms jealously, irritation, rage, disgust, hatred, contempt, loathing, and revulsion. Judges then classified the participants' 525 terms into seven emotional categories, one of which involved the emotions of anger, hatred, and disgust. Storm and Storm's results were quite similar to those of Shaver et al., with one exception: Storm and Storm found many more emotional references that indicated personal vendetta, including revenge, rebelliousness, malice, dislike, distrust, suspicion, contempt, and the like.

Sites of Anger Provocation

Locating where anger arises, or "sites" of anger, provides a useful demarcation point for understanding people's reactions to anger. Researchers have presented many alternative categories of anger provocations in interpersonal interaction (e.g., Buss, 1989; Campbell & Muncer, 1987; Harris, 1993; Törestad, 1990). In Table I, we present several of the common causes of anger indicated by the research literature.

The first site of anger provocation, *identity,* refers to the perception that one's self-concept or public image is under attack. People appear to be quite sensitive to

TABLE I   Sites of Anger[a]

I. Identity management
   Integrity threat (C & M)
   Insult (B; F; S et al.; T)
   Self-esteem threat (F)
   Condescension (B; H)
   Blame/reproach (S; T)
   Personal criticism (F&B)
   Rebuff/rejection (F&B)
   Teasing (T)
   Loyalty—defending another's dignity (C&M)
   Neglecting/rejecting/unreliable (Bu)

II. Aggression
   Physical threat or harm (B; C&M; S et al.; T)
   Physical harassment (T)
   Verbal abuse (B; H)
   Sexually aggressive (Bu)

III. Frustration
   Goal interference (Ba; S et al.)
   Violation of expectations (S et al.)
   Impotence—inability to influence others (C&M)
   Powerlessness (F&B)
   Thwarted plans (T)
   Environmental frustrations (T)
   Negative consequences linked to blameworthy action (C et al.)

IV. Fairness
   Inequity/lack of fairness (F&B; F&F; S et al.)
   Situation is illegitimate, wrong (S et al.)
   Hurts another's feelings (H)
   People's belongings (T)

V. Incompetence
   A. Due to ignorance
      Incompetence of another (C&M)
      Thoughtless behaviors (T)
      Moody (Bu)
      Emotionally constricted (Bu)
      Disheveled (Bu)
   B. Due to egocentric motives
      Self-centered (Bu)
      Self-opinionated (T)
      Inconsiderate/insensitive to others (B; C&M; F&B)
      Rudeness (F&B)
      Physically self-absorbed (Bu)
      Nagging (T)
      Sexualizes others (Bu)
      Harassment/being bugged (F&B)

(continues)

TABLE I (*continued*)

VI. Relationship threat
Jealousy (B, C&M; S et al.)
Unfaithfulness (Bu)
Betrayal (F&B)
VII. Predispositions
Predisposition to anger due to experiences (S et al.)
Predisposition to anger due to stress, fatigue, etc. (S et al.)
Alcoholism (Bu)
Possessiveness/dependent behaviors (Bu)
Scripts (R&F)
VIII. General reaction
Aggression-related tendencies following negative affect (Be)
Threat appraisal and coping processes (R)
Response to aversion (Ba)
Excitation (Z)

[a]Ba = Bandura, 1973; Be = Berkowitz, 1993; Bu = Buss, 1989; C&M = Campbell & Muncer, 1987; C et al.= Clore, Ortony, Dienes, & Fujita, 1993; F = Feschback, 1986; F&B = Fehr & Baldwin, 1996; F&F = Fitness & Fletcher, 1993; H = Harris, 1993; R = Rubin, 1986; R&F = Russell & Fehr, 1987; S = Schönback, 1990; S et al. = Shaver, Schwartz, Kirson, & O'Connor, 1987; T = Törestad, 1990; Z = Zillmann, 1990.

both direct and indirect attacks on their private and public identities (e.g., Dobash & Dobash, 1984; Feschback, 1986; Retzinger, 1991, 1995; Schönbach, 1990; Ting-Toomey, 1988). Both men and women report that attacks on one's identity represent a primary reason for becoming angry (Cupach & Canary, 1995). Direct attacks include integrity threats to self or to a friend, blame/reproaches, and insults, whereas less direct but nonetheless anger-producing behaviors include teasing and condescension. Identity challenges vary in intensity from simple requests for information (e.g., Tracy, Craig, Smith, & Spisak, 1984) to public ridicule (including intentional embarrassment; see Bradford and Petronio, Chapter 4, this volume).

An intriguing variation on the identity view of anger can be found in the work of Clark, Pataki, and Carrer (1996). From their perspective, anger occurs more frequently in episodes wherein the social actor wants to appear dominant. The desire to appear dominant thus operates as a personal self-presentation (identity) objective. Wanting to appear dominant can be unrelated and perhaps negatively associated with desires to appear likable or competent. The desire for a dominant public image appears to cue people into behaviors of others who oppose such dominance, leading to anger episodes. Regardless of one's preferred public image, research indicates that people vigilantly protect their identity and face management needs (Cupach & Metts, 1994).

Aggression represents the second site of anger provocation. Viewing aggression as an antecedent of anger represents the opposite of the popular anger–aggression causal link (that anger leads to aggression). Researchers have found that physical and verbal aggression are viewed as common causes of anger. Men in particular appear to view perpetrators of aggression with more revulsion than do women, regardless of the sex of the perpetrator (Harris, 1993), although research fails to find many sex differences in the expression of anger (Cupach & Canary, 1995). One study of nurses and nurse managers found that women primarily responded to verbal abuse with anger (Cox, 1987). Regardless of the sex difference issue, it appears that other people's aggression prompts anger in oneself.

Goal impediment focuses on the frustrations people experience when their plans are interrupted. This site of anger most often references another person's behavior. However, "environmental frustration" concerns how impersonal forces (e.g., ice on the highways; smothering heat during the Olympics) can impede someone from achieving a valued objective (Törestad, 1990). Similarly, some conflict scholars have identified goal obstruction or incompatibility as the primary basis of interpersonal conflict (e.g., Deutsch, 1973).

Fairness comprises the fourth site of anger. Fitness and Fletcher (1993) found that people often connect the cause of their anger to perceptions that they are being inequitably treated, whereas causes of hatred more closely tie to perceptions of being personally harmed. Directly investigating the experience of emotions due to inequity, Sprecher (1986) found that men in particular feel anger in response to being underbenefited in their romantic involvements, whereas women tend to feel more passive emotions, such as sadness and depression (emotions related to anger and aggression; Berkowitz, 1993).

Two sites of anger concern people's incompetence. Anger appears to vary according to the reasons for a person's incompetence. *Incompetence due to ignorance* reflects anger arising from the partner's relatively benign "cluelessness." Here the person is seen as a social dolt, unconsciously incompetent, unaware of self and/or other, and disheveled. *Incompetence due to egocentric motives* relies on assessments of selfishness. Here the egocentric incompetent thinks that he or she knows best, nags others, cannot see the value of other people's opinions, and remains inconsiderate of others. An extreme form of egocentric-based incompetence may involve the sexual objectification of the other person (limiting one's view of the partner to a sexual dimension; Buss, 1989). The attribution of egocentric motives suggests a stable, global, internal, and selfish explanation for one's actions. Later we elaborate on how attributions in general operate during anger episodes.

Relationship threat constitutes an anger site that typically refers to jealousy-evoking situations. Jealousy is by far the most common cause attributed to dating violence (Sugarman & Hotaling, 1989). Interestingly, people often become angry at the partner instead of the third party who is ostensibly threatening the relationship (Fitness & Fletcher, 1993). Of course, at times people act aggressively toward a rival (see Guerrero & Andersen, Chapter 6, this volume). In addition to jealousy, the tendencies of one's partner to be unfaithful and/or possessive appear to generate anger.

The next site, *predispositions* to anger, refers to individual tendencies that influence expressions of anger. Anger stemming from predispositions include shame-proneness (Tangney, Wagner, Fletcher, & Gramzow, 1992), how one's upbringing affects current behavior, and how alcohol dependence negatively affects one's judgment and ability to control one's emotions (Shaver et al., 1987). Social science researchers also explore personality predispositions that moderate one's response to anger-provoking events, such as competitiveness, locus of control, self-efficacy, and aggressiveness (Canary, Cupach, & Messman, 1995). As one might expect, lay concepts of predispositions typically refer to background characteristics, acute tendencies, and alcohol.

Examinations of alcohol as a trigger to anger and subsequent aggression are warranted. For instance, Rosenbaum and O'Leary (1981) found that alcohol use was associated with spousal aggression, and that 40% of abusive husbands in the study were alcoholic. Zillmann (1990) noted that intoxicated people suffer from cognitive deficits to the extent that during interpersonal conflicts they offer irrational responses, cannot accurately read partner cues, and distort expectations for appropriate social behavior.

Finally, *generalized learned responses* refer to the view that anger is a broad syndrome or set of response tendencies, such that expressions of anger can be elicited through a number of aversive stimuli (e.g., Bandura, 1973; Berkowitz, 1993). In other words, negative stimuli can lead to anger-like responses, given that anger is connected to related emotions. And given that emotions blend in experience as well as expression, anger may be inferred from similar emotional states like pain or frustration. Berkowitz (1993) explicated how people respond aggressively when they experience discomfort, depression, and even pollution. Berkowitz reported two studies wherein women either experienced discomfort (keeping in hand in very cold water) or no discomfort (by keeping a hand in room temperature water). Participants evaluated other people's ideas, and they rewarded or punished the other person. The women experiencing discomfort offered fewer rewards and more punishments than the women who did not experience the same discomfort. There was no apparent anger-provoking event, as we might typically conceive. The only ostensible cause of variation in anger-like responses was due to variation in the women's pain. Likewise, in a second study, Berkowitz reported that women exposed to pain (vs. those who were not exposed to pain) recalled more conflict interactions with their boyfriends.

Summary

Research reveals little scholarly consensus on the nature of anger. In addition, laypersons' prototypes of the emotion suggest a construct with several associated components—all of which carry a negative valence (Johnson & Arneson, 1991; Fitness & Fletcher, 1993). Moreover, various causes of anger arise from many types of events that entail a complex array of emotional responses (instead of only one response). Nevertheless, almost all causes of anger indicate it as a primary emotional response to a personally relevant provocation. One of the most common responses to provocation and its consequent anger is thought to be aggression.

ANGER AND AGGRESSION

At this juncture, we review scholarly conceptions and correlates of aggression. By focusing on theoretic analyses of aggression, we should be able to discover the role of anger in aggressive behaviors.

The Presumed Link between Anger and Aggression

Some researchers suggest a strong causal connection between the experience of anger and the use of aggressive behaviors. For instance, people typically infer that "anger" and the associated experience of "frustration" are the two most common causes of courtship violence (Sugarman & Hotaling, 1989). Anger has been found to combine with other emotions—for example, with empathy—in predicting premarital sexual aggression (Christopher, Owens, & Stecker, 1993) and courtship violence (Betancourt & Blair, 1992). Makepeace (1986) noted that "uncontrollable anger" represents the most common motive for men—and the second most common motive for women (after self-defense)—regarding the use of violence (see also Sugarman & Hotaling, 1989). Likewise, Margolin, John, and Gleberman (1988) found that physically abusive husbands appeared angrier in discussions than did verbally abusive, withdrawing, or nondistressed husbands.

Other researchers present a weaker version of the anger-aggressiveness link. For example, Törestad (1990) argued that anger and aggression often act independently: One can experience anger without behaving aggressively (e.g., "pure" anger), and one can act aggressively in an instrumental fashion without being angry (e.g., executioner using lethal poison). In providing a broad interpretation of the criminology research, Törestad wrote that "nonaggressive behaviors follow anger arousal in more than half the cases, and that overt aggression following anger is seldom physical" (p. 11). Consistent with this reasoning, Lloyd (1990) found that nondistressed and nonviolent couples reported *more anger* than distressed and nonviolent couples, although she also found that significantly fewer nondistressed and nonviolent couples experience anger than did nondistressed and violent or distressed and violent couples. According to Averill (1993), "anger no more causes aggression than a blueprint causes the construction of a building" (p. 189). Clearly, anger can instigate aggression, though anger is not a necessary condition for people to behave aggressively.

Definition of Aggression

Alternative research perspectives highlight different verbal, physical, and psychological characteristics or components of aggression. Some scholars refer to aggression as an overarching concept that includes covert and overt harm to another (e.g., Rubin, 1986). Some divide aggression into psychological and physical components (e.g., Murphy & O'Leary, 1989). Others discuss aggression in terms of its verbal and nonverbal components (e.g., Infante & Wigley, 1986; Kinney, 1994). Still others shy away from the term aggression in favor of *abuse* or *violence* (Marshall, 1994). Despite this divergence, a widely accepted definition focuses on aggression as a behavior sequence that seeks to bring about physical or psychological pain for another person (Bandura, 1973; for similar definitions, see Berkowitz, 1962; Buss, 1961; Infante, 1987). We now examine some empirical generalizations concerning behavior intentionally performed to hurt another person.

Empirical Generalizations Regarding Aggression

Research has uncovered several predictors of aggressive behavior. We selected four, which we cast as theoretically guided propositions, highlighting particular research programs examining each.

Proposition 1: Aggression Arises from Initial Situation Appraisal

Several researchers have documented that people's appraisals of an anger episode affect how they respond with aggression (e.g., Frijda, Kuipers, & ter Shure, 1989). The line of work by Zillmann and associates illustrates one way this proposition has been studied.

Cognition–excitation explains how physiological arousal affects thought processes that lead to aggression. Zillmann (1994) explained that the "recognition of endangerment" causes "agonistic experiences and agonistic behaviors" (p. 52). Confronted with threatening conditions, an individual will tend to respond in a fight or flight fashion. Zillmann argued that forceful action can resolve the crisis whatever option is taken. If excitation occurs within an optimal range, cognition modifies one's reactions through appraisal of the situation. Zillmann demonstrated that thought processes allow continual assessment, allowing excitation from a threatening condition to diminish. On this view, cognition warns people of danger and allows excitation to continue, or cognition lowers awareness of danger and reduces excitation. But if excitation is too high, cognition fails (Zillmann, 1988, 1990).

Research illustrates that aggression depends on excitation of cognition. For example, Zillmann and Cantor (1976) had a "rude" confederate provoke men who were later given an opportunity to retaliate. Participants were placed in one of three experimental conditions in which cognitive appraisal of the situation was varied (allowed or not). In two of the conditions, participants were told before (or after) being provoked that the confederate was "uptight" because of an impending midterm exam. In the third condition, no excuse was presented. Results indicated that those who had prior knowledge of the experimenter's circumstances were relatively unaffected by the mistreatment. However, those who were able to appraise the situation reacted less severely when allowed to retaliate. In another study (Zillmann, Johnson, & Day, 1974), men aggressively induced were asked to engage in strenuous exercise or were asked not to exercise, and then, when excitation from exercising was still apparent, the participants were allowed to retaliate. Those men experiencing excitation from exercise displayed pronounced aggressive reactions. Similar research in which men and women were provoked, exposed to pleasant or unpleasant films, and then given a chance to retaliate showed that participants with greater excitation exhibited more intense aggression (Bryant & Zillmann, 1977; Zillmann, 1971).

Anger plays a central role in this body of literature. Zillmann (1994) explained that unjust, unfair, or rude provocations "tend to produce intense feelings of anger toward antagonists and tormentors" (p. 47). Such anger increases excitation that can exceed the optimum range, which would cause a breakdown in cognitive appraisal and lead to aggressive behavior (Zillmann, 1988).

Proposition 2: Aggression Arises from Learned Responses

This proposition reflects the notion that people engage in behaviors they believe are rewarding (and, by implication, less punishing). To elaborate this proposition adequately, we turn to Bandura's social learning theory.

Bandura (1973) argued that people learn to behave aggressively through direct experience and modeling. One's family of origin, subculture, and media—particularly TV—provide sources of modeling. Modeling works by *inhibiting* aggression if the model's behavior is punished, and by *disinhibiting* aggression if the model's behavior leads to failure or is met with social condemnation. According to Bandura, aggression continues to be reinforced by obtaining positive consequences, self-rewards, and through the neutralization of self-condemnation (e.g., through gradual desensitization to hurting others). Moreover, aggression continues as long as the social actor finds it rewarding. Aggression does not cease when one's emotions are vented; it ceases when rewards no longer accrue to aggressive acts. *Anticipated,* rather than immediate, consequences sustain aggression (see also Rubin, 1986). Bandura (1973) specified three ways to alter aggression: (1) *modeling,* including use of appropriate assertiveness, law enforcement officers' reduction of aggression, and controlling violence on TV; *differential reinforcement,* including parental rewards for positive (not negative) behavior; and *punishment,* including reward withdrawal for aggressive behavior and aversive punishment. Interestingly, Bandura (1973) maintained that "at the highest level of psychological functioning, individuals regulate their own behavior by self-evaluative and other self-produced consequences" (p. 48).

Later, Bandura (e.g., 1983; 1991) elaborated how one's self-regulation according to assessments of desired goals and self-efficacy affects one's behavior.

This theory has promoted extensive research. O'Leary (1988) linked aggression to social learning in five areas: violence in family of origin, aggressive personality style, stress, alcohol, and marital discord. For example, children learn through direct experience and by modeling parental behavior. O'Leary (1988) found that violence in the family of origin (observation of parental aggression, and being beaten as a child) predicted aggression. Likewise, Straus, Gelles, and Steinmetz (1980) discovered that a disproportionate number of individuals who engage in physical aggression against their partners come from homes in which their parents hit one another. Several studies of abusive husbands indicate that the majority have witnessed similar behavior from their fathers. One study showed that abusive parents engage in more aversive behaviors with each other than do nondistressed or nonabusive families (Straus, 1980). In another study, wives were less likely to seek refuge from their abusive husbands if the wives witnessed their mothers being abused (Gelles & Straus, 1979).

Social learning theory does not presume anger as necessary to aggression. As Bandura (1973) stated, "Considerable evidence that hurtful aggression can be enhanced, sustained, and eliminated simply by altering its consequences calls into question theories that postulate anger arousal as an essential and primary determinant of aggression" (p. 136). On this view, anger might trigger the use of learned responses (including aggression), though one might turn to aggressive actions whenever such actions appear to offer a viable means to obtain rewards.

Proposition 3: Aggression Is Moderated by Higher Order Cognitions

Beyond the initial appraisal of anger provocation and learned response associations, people can invoke higher-ordered beliefs, such as expectations, assessment of outcomes, and attributions (Berkowitz, 1993). People more mindful of their own behavioral consequences appear less likely to respond aggressively (Bandura, 1973). Such higher-ordered processes act as means of self-control that moderate how one's initial anger affects aggression (e.g., Berkowitz, 1993; Feschback, 1986). We reference attribution theory, which refers to people's explanations for events, as an example.

People's attributions predictably suffer from biases. Two of the more widely recognized biases concern the "actor–observer" bias (or the fundamental attribution error) and the "activity" bias (Canary & Spitzberg, 1990). The *actor-observer bias* refers to the general inferential tendency of people to explain the partner's behavior as due to some internal feature of the partner, whereas people tend to attribute their own behavior in terms of external causes. Storms (1973), using experimental procedures, found that people attend more to behaviors of others rather than to themselves in social situations. Accordingly, people "respond" to the partner's particular communication behavior and remain less mindful of their own communicative behaviors when constructing attributions for the anger episode. The *activity bias* concerns the general inferential tendency of people to attend to active and extraordinary stimuli and to ignore passive and ordinary stimuli. An important variation of this bias concerns how negative messages violate one's expectations for normative behavior and therefore appear more salient than do expected positive behaviors. Research in conflict and competence shows that people rely more on partner (vs. self) behavior to assess the competence of the communicator, and that people rely more on negative (vs. positive) messages to evaluate their partner's competence (Canary & Spitzberg, 1990).

Researchers utilize a finite set of dimensions to depict people's attributions. The dimensions most critical to conflict appear to be globality, stability, locus, intent, selfishness, and blameworthiness (Fincham, Bradbury, & Scott, 1992). *Globality* refers to the extent to which people view the cause of the event as specific to the event or general across situations. *Stability* refers to how consistently the cause can be applied over time; unstable causes only apply for short periods. *Locus* concerns whether the problem resides internal to the person and/or relationship or external to the person and/or relationship. *Intent* involves the assessment of the extent to which the cause presumes a conscious decision for the event. *Selfishness,* of course, regards the extent to which the cause suggests a person's motive as exclusively self-serving. Finally, *blameworthiness* refers to whether the cause indicts someone as responsible for the failure event, whereas *praiseworthiness* focuses on being responsible for a success. Using the attribution "inconsiderate," for example, one can generalize to a variety of events and behaviors over a long period of time that are also internal to the partner and reflect a selfish, blameworthy motive. In contrast, using the attribution "young," one might still generalize to other behaviors but convey a sense of transition without intentional or selfish or blameworthy motivation.

The research appears clearest regarding the use of globality, followed by stability, locus, and selfish versus unselfish motivation (Fincham et al., 1992). More precisely, people who see the cause of relational problems as reflecting global, stable, internal, and selfish dimensions more likely engage in negative communicative behavior and less likely to experience positive relational outcomes. Sillars (1980) found that those who viewed the cause as stable and internal to the partner were more likely to engage in distributive conflict behavior (e.g., threats, sarcasm, etc.). Gottman (1994) reported that dissatisfied married couples infer from the other's negative behavior more global causes, and that these inferences of global causes in term cause people to question the marriage itself.

In brief, attributions largely moderate the communication of anger as people consider the underlying causes for an anger-provoking event. People who take more personal responsibility for the event (vs. those who attribute the cause of their anger to others) are less likely to respond in an aggressive manner. Moreover, those who refrain from generalizing from the negative event to broader issues and who attribute partner behavior to unstable, external, and unselfish causes appear less likely to engage in aggressive behaviors.

Proposition 4: Aggression Arises from Deficient Communication Skills

Research on skill deficiency casts aggressiveness as an inability to manage interpersonal problems in a constructive manner. For example, Infante, Chandler, and Rudd (1989) argued that violence occurs "if undissipated anger creates a latent hostile disposition in at least one partner and the individuals have an argumentative skill deficiency which increases the probability of verbal aggression" (p. 169). Similarly, Gelles (1974) emphasized that verbal deficiencies constitute a primary predictor of violence: "When the husband and wife are engaged in a verbal fight . . . one partner simply runs out of ammunition . . . and begins to flail away at the other" (p. 163).

Findings support a skill-deficiency model in examinations of abusive relationships (Marshall, 1994). Clearhout, Elder, and Janes (1982) compared the problem-solving skills of women in abusive and nonabusive relationships. Nonabused women (vs. abused women) were able to generate more alternatives for problem solving and more effective alternatives. In a similar vein, Margolin, Burman, and John (1989) found that couples who reported using physical aggression were more hostile to each other during a role playing of a recent conflict. Additionally, physically aggressive husbands enacted a lack of involvement, defensiveness, and coldness in comparison to verbally abusive and withdrawn husbands. Nondistressed couples (vs. abusive types) relied more on problem solving and warmth to manage their conflicts (see also Jansen & Meyers-Able, 1981). In other research, Purdy and Nickle (1981) concluded that males in abusive relationships are "victimized by their own lack of communication skills" (p. 111). Balswick and Peek (1971) noted that males in violent relationships suffer from an extreme inability to express their emotions verbally. This body of literature suggests that the inability to express emotion increases the likelihood of using aggression as a "default" option to communicate one's anger.

Whereas most people do not use aggression as the result of a communicative skill deficiency, everyone does appear vulnerable to house-variety expressions of anger that can plague any relationship. Siegman (1994) reported that people who are angered "raise their voice, accelerate their speech rate, and interrupt their partner. However, the heightened levels of BP [blood pressure] HR [heart rate] and catecholamines will further intensify the speaker's angry voice and feelings of anger" (p. 189). In brief, some of the microscopic behavioral correlates of anger can convey a general sense of negativity.

One's physiological reactions to the other person's negative behavior do not diminish entirely before subsequent sets of reactions follow, and the dovetailing of physiological arousal may lead to "over-reactions" to the cause of one's anger, including aggression (Zillmann, 1990) or withdrawal (Gottman, 1994). In addition, several studies have shown that the ongoing reciprocation of negative affect works against couples, and that the tendency to mirror the partner's behavior appears to be quite strong (for a review, see Sillars & Wilmot, 1994). For instance, Kubany et al. (1992) found that one's angry statements (whether assertive or aggressive) were likely to evoke behavioral reciprocation of partner, justification of the partner's be-havior, and raising of the partner's voice. However, aggressive (vs. assertive) angry statements were more likely to evoke anger and defiance, less likely to evoke sym-pathy, and more likely to evoke negative reactions from women (vs. men).

Research on communication skill deficits has found that anger plays various roles. For example, Infante et al. (1989) considered an act of verbal aggression as producing a negative emotional reaction that can be construed as anger. In this light, anger represents an emotion that follows an aggressive act. Gottman (1994) and col-leagues (Levenson & Gottman, 1985) have observed that couples—and men in par-ticular—experience diffuse and negative physiological arousal when confronted by the partner, and this negative arousal presents a noxious state that leads to fight or flight tendencies. This research implies that confrontative *behavior* serves as a pri-mary cause for aggressive behavior, with anger playing various roles in the onset of aggressive responses.

ANGER-RELEVANT RESPONSES

In this section, we emphasize different modes for expressing anger, including ag-gression and its alternatives. In our view, the research literature implies several modes of response. First, however, we begin with people's prototypical understanding of responses to anger.

Prototypical Responses

Anger prototypes involve negative, and often aggressive, responses. Based on proto-type and analyses, Russell and Fehr (1994) claimed that "to know the concept of anger is to know a script (to be able to simulate a scenario) in which prototypical antecedents, feelings, expressions, behaviors, physiological changes, and conse-quences are laid out in a causal and temporal sequence" (p. 202). Fehr and Baldwin (1996) developed the script notion in claiming that "the most critical elements of an emotion script may well be its interpersonal features" (p. 228), which almost al-ways involve another person as the target of anger.

Shaver et al. (1987) found that social actors typically equate *anger* with interper-sonal aggression. These researchers cluster-analyzed accounts of recalled and hypo-thetical emotion episodes, including anger (i.e., causes, thoughts, feelings, actions, and duration of emotion). Table II reports Shaver et al.'s results regarding anger re-sponses. (Causes of anger are omitted, since these were all clustered apart from re-sponses and are presented in Table I.) The clusters of angry behaviors follow: Clus-ter 1—verbal attacks of all kinds, yelling, and complaining; Cluster 2—physical attack threats involving clenched fists and threatening gestures, and emotional and physical attacks on objects; Cluster 3—nonverbal displays of protest and anger, in-

TABLE II   Prototypes of Angry Responses[a]

Cluster 1 (4.44): Verbal attacks
Obscenities, cursing
Verbally attacking the cause of the anger
Yelling, loud voice, screaming, shouting
Complaining, bitching, etc.

Cluster 2 (4.04): Physical attacks
Hands and fists clenched
Aggressive, threatening gestures
Attacking something other than the cause of anger (e.g., throwing things)
Attacking the cause of anger
Incoherent, out of control, emotional behavior
Imagined attacks or hurting cause of anger

Cluster 3 (3.87): Nonverbal disapproval
Heavy walk, stomping
Tightness in body
Nonverbally communicating disapproval (e.g., slamming doors)
Frowning, mean or unpleasant expression
Gritting and showing teeth
Flushed face

Cluster 4 (3.50): Uneasiness
Crying
Feelings of nervousness, anxiety, and discomfort

Cluster 5 (4.00): Internal withdrawal
Brooding, withdrawing from episode
Narrowing of attention to all but anger situation
Thinking, "I'm all right—others are wrong."

Cluster 6 (4.00): Avoidance
Suppressing the anger, trying not to show or express anger
Redefining the situation so anger is no longer appropriate

---

[a]Adapted from Shaver, Schwartz, Kirson, and O'Connor (1987) p. 1078. Cluster coefficients in parentheses reflect a similarity score, where 1 = dissimilar and 5 = similar. Clusters 1, 2, and 3 had a 3.75 similarity score, and Clusters 4 and 5 had a 3.87 similarity score.

cluding stomping, slamming doors, frowning, gritting teeth, and being flushed; Cluster 4—crying and feelings of anxiety and discomfort; Cluster 5—internal escape mechanisms, including brooding or focusing on the anger; and Cluster 6—avoidance by suppressing or redefining one's anger as inappropriate.

We should note, however, that Shaver et al. (1987) were more interested in the basic content of emotion prototypes than they were in the communicative management of any single emotion. Nevertheless, anger prototypes can reveal implicit understandings of anger-relevant responses. In this light, Berkowitz (1993) reported a study predicting that behaviors consistent with prototypical responses elicit angry responses, but not other emotional responses. Specifically, Berkowitz predicted that participants who clenched their fists at a precalibrated level for four minutes would become angry at recalling an angry incident, because clenching one's fist comprises a prototypical, angry response. But people who clinched their fist and recalled a sad incident would report less sadness than those who did not clinch their fists, since the sadness prototype does not involve clenched fists. As Berkowitz and colleagues predicted, those with clenched fists felt angrier but less sad than their counterparts without clenched fists. This finding implies that prototypes have a self-fulfilling nature in producing scripted responses to anger.

Although people might think of a "model" anger episode in terms of destructive and aggressive behaviors, research indicates that people also respond to anger in constructive and less threatening ways. Fitness and Fletcher (1993) found that participants reported they were *less* in control of their anger in hypothetical, prototypical situations versus actual accounts of anger episodes. It appears that people generating prototypical accounts of anger underestimate the degree to which people control their own volatile reactions to anger. In addition, Clore and Ortony (1991) faulted prototypical analyses of anger on the basis that only intense forms of anger come to mind and milder forms of anger (e.g., irritation) are excluded. As Clore and Ortony (1991) pointed out, "large-scale empirical research conducted on anger shows that aggressive actions are actually quite uncommon. . . . Conclusion: There is no widespread agreement about the anger script" (p. 50).

Alternatives to Prototypical Anger Responses

Holt (1970) distinguished between *constructive* and *destructive* modes of anger expression. In constructive anger, parties express their anger "in such a way as to give direct and genuine expression to [their] own feelings, while maintaining enough control so that their intensity is no greater than what is necessary to convey their true quality" (pp. 8–9). Holt noted that more kinds of destructive expressions of anger appear to exist, including physical attack, verbal denunciation, and indirect manipulation. Likewise, Törestad (1990) argued that anger expressions can function positively as "preservers and protectors of private and social norms" (p. 15). Similarly, Deutsch (1973) claimed that, more generally, people can manage social conflict using constructive or destructive orientations.

Besides noting that anger expressions can reveal constructive or destructive orientations, research also suggests an activity dimension (e.g., Sillars & Wilmot, 1994; Van de Vliert & Euwema, 1994). In other words, responses to anger entail interactional decisions about the approach one takes with the partner. Accordingly, one's strategic orientation varies along the dimensions of affect (i.e., cooperative/constructive vs. competitive/destructive) and directness/activity (Sillars & Wilmot, 1994).

As the previous sections indicate, strategic orientations toward expressing anger occur as the result of many factors, including initial appraisals, learned response tendencies, higher-ordered cognitions, and one's ability to enact the strategy in a competent fashion. However, Frijda et al. (1989) conceived of strategic orientations as similar to action control states, which reference more general types of action programs that spontaneously function in response to emotional states. Given that people appear to choose their strategic orientations based on their conversational objectives, attributions for the event, and other concerns, we believe that choices to respond to anger are largely under the conscious control of interactants. More precisely, higher-ordered cognitions mediate the effect of initial response tendencies on one's strategy selection and use (Zillmann, 1988).

Research suggests that people do employ alternative communicative orientations to anger that partners appreciate more than prototypical aggressive responses. Kubany and colleagues (Kubany, Richard, Bauer, & Muraoka, 1992a,b; Kubany et al., 1995) conceptualized anger expression in terms of assertive (e.g., "I'm getting angry") or aggressive (e.g., "You're making me angry") modes. As expected, assertive modes of expression were seen as less antagonizing and aversive. Sereno, Welch, and Braaten (1987) differentiated among assertive, aggressive, and nonassertive modes of anger expression, finding that aggressive anger expression was significantly less satisfying than either alternative, and less competent and appropriate than the nonassertive mode of expression. Tangney et al. (1996) presented four behavioral alternatives to managing anger: *maladaptive responses,* such as physical aggression, malediction; *adaptive behaviors,* such as discussing the issue with the target; *escapist-diffusing responses,* including distracting activities, leaving the situation; and *cognitive reappraisals,* such as reinterpreting the intentions of the other person. As expected, maladaptive responses correlated positively with hostility and assessments of maladjustment, whereas adaptive responses and cognitive appraisals correlated negatively with hostility and maladjustment (Tangney et al., 1996).

Alternative modes of communicating anger relate differentially to relational satisfaction as well. For example, Guerrero (1994) demarcated types of anger expressions along similar dimensions of directness and threat. *Distributive-aggression* refers to direct and threatening messages, such as screaming, criticizing, and using threats. *Integrative-assertion* includes those behaviors that reflect a direct but nonthreatening orientation, such as listening, attempts to be fair, and sharing of feelings. *Passive-aggression* concerns indirect and threatening actions, such as giving the partner the "silent treatment," leaving the scene, and giving dirty looks. *Nonassertive-denial* tactics reference those that are both indirect and nonthreatening (e.g., hiding from partner, denying feelings). Guerrero found that perceptions of integrative-assertiveness were positively linked to assessments that the partner managed the episode in a competent manner. However, contrary to expectations, Guerrero (1994) did not find that relational satisfaction was linked to the strategy of distributive-aggressiveness. Guerrero offered two alternative explanations: (a) Anger is atypical, such that evaluations of satisfaction resist isolated episodes of anger; and/or (b) the expression of anger involves sending two messages—a positive one that indicates a degree of investment and caring and a negative one that indicates some kind of disdain. A third interpretation, implied from prototypical analyses, holds that "anger" episodes *typically* entail negative responses, which can be forgivable (given the episode prototype), and therefore may operate in a more complex manner with assessments of relational quality (Spitzberg, 1997).

We do not believe that people can easily trade their prototypically defined scripts for more circumspect models of anger and aggression, simply because anger is anything but risible[1] and can be extremely absorbing. People must often make strategic decisions about managing their anger in the context of emotional turbulence and competing preoccupations. For example, people might experience rage (Retzinger, 1991) or emotional flooding (Gottman, 1994), or otherwise become too excited and thus suffer from cognitive deficits (Zillmann 1988, 1990). In such instances, people cannot efficiently process higher-ordered information.

Other factors work against cooperative communicative responses to anger. Given that conflict often "surprises" people when they perform other activities, like balancing a checkbook (Sillars & Weisberg, 1987), the experience of anger may become exacerbated by environmental or activity "noise" (e.g., arguing while the teakettle screams for attention; dealing with a complaint while watching television). Moreover, competing goals—especially maintaining one's own identity while arguing for one's instrumental or relational goal—can compound one's ongoing, "online" decisions to enact cooperation. As Feschback (1986) observed, "In general, deliberate blows to self-esteem are far more powerful elicitors of anger than impediments that frustrate one's pursuit of some material goals" (p. 127). In addition, controlling anger can be quite difficult when interacting with hostile company. As Siegman (1994) noted, "emotions have another characteristic: they are contagious. With the best intentions to remain calm, it is very difficult to interact with an angry person without becoming angry oneself" (p. 189). People suffering from communicative deficits would appear to be most handicapped in providing alternative responses to a partner's aggressive messages.

Some of the research explores the communicative progression of anger. Gergen and Gergen (1988) provided an analysis of anger narratives and found that anger generally provokes a partner's inquiry into the cause, which evokes an explanation, which in turn tends to elicit a response of remorse, a reframing account, or further anger. Schönbach (1990) argued that when a person's identity is challenged, he or she responds in an egocentric manner to show the partner evidence of competence and control of the situation. Such displays likely reproach the partner, who in turn feels slighted and engages in egocentric identity management her- or himself. Of course, both partners probably resent the other as they each present a "desired" public image. Kovecses (1990) proposed a prototype stage scenario with considerable similarities to Schönbach's concepts, as well as models of confrontation episodes.

---

[1]In our initial draft, we used the term *risorial,* a synonym for "risible." The senior (and eldest) author preferred this term because he learned it playing *Balderdash* with Laura Guerrero, her husband Vico, and other friends. But "risorial" appears to be arcane, so we sadly relinquish the term risorial—however recondite it might have sounded to the senior (and older) editor.

Kovecses' prototype involves five stages: an offensive event (in which blame and intent are attributed), the experience of anger, attempt at control, loss of control, and act(s) of retribution.

Observational analyses of naturally occurring anger episodes and responses to anger are needed to verify such portrayals of the evolution of anger. Certainly, it appears likely that people enact alternatives to the above sequences. For instance, an alternative to providing social proof of one's competence involves the use of silence. Regarding the use of silence, Feschback (1986) claimed that delaying one's response to an identity challenge allows one time to become less absorbed in the event. And Tavris (1984) likewise considered the wisdom of "counting to 10."

CONCLUSION

Despite the widely accepted proposition that anger represents a fundamental emotional response, scholars do not agree on its nature or its causes. Reflection on the lack of definitional consensus about *anger* could lead one to adopt such terms as "anger-like" when discussing anger-relevant experiences (e.g., responses to aversive emotions; Berkowitz, 1993), or the lack of consensus could prompt one to specify types of anger (e.g., Clore et al., 1993). In addition, the presumption that anger necessarily causes aggression has been critically questioned by researchers (e.g., Bandura, 1973). Aggression can stem from several causes (e.g., being too hot or too cold), as well as from a specific anger-provoking event involving a perpetrator and victim.

Research clearly suggests that people may enact communicative responses to their anger that vary from the anger prototype. However, doing so can be quite difficult. People apparently understand the experience of anger enough to excuse their own behaviors (and sometimes) their partners. Eventually, however, chronic and aversive responses to anger would probably be interpreted with attributions that call into question the partner's qualities and one's satisfaction with the entire relationship, in addition to desires to protect one's identity from unfair attack.

Finally, we believe that educating people about cooperative ways that people can communicate anger in interpersonal contexts would help override the monolithic, negative anger script to which most people appear to subscribe. Both popular literature (e.g., McKay, Rogers, & McKay, 1989; Williams & Williams, 1993) and scholarly writings (e.g., Spitzberg, 1997; Tavris, 1984) provide guidelines for social actors' management of anger and aggression. Averill (1993), for instance, provided succinct and coherent advice regarding the expression of anger (pp. 182–184). We conclude our chapter with his rules:

1. People have the right to become angry in the face of intentional wrongdoing or unintended misdeeds if those misdeeds can be corrected (e.g., negligence);

2. People should direct anger at people or objects responsible for the action(s);
3. People should not displace anger onto innocent third parties, "nor should it be directed at the target for reasons other than the instigation;"
4. The goal should be to correct the situation and restore fairness—not intimidation;
5. The response to anger should be in proportion to the instigation—it should not "exceed what is necessary to correct the situation, restore equity, or prevent the instigation from happening again;"
6. The response to anger should closely follow the provoking event—it should not last longer than the time needed to remediate the situation;
7. The expression of anger should entail resolve and follow through when necessary.

REFERENCES

Averill, J. R. (1982). *Anger and aggression: An essay on emotion.* New York: Springer-Verlag.

Averill, J. R. (1993). Illusions of anger. In R. B. Felson & J. T. Tedeschi (Eds.), *Aggression and violence: Social interactionist perspectives* (pp. 171–193). Washington, DC: American Psychological Association.

Balswick, J., & Peek, C. (1971). The inexpressive male: A tragedy of American society. *Family Coordinator, 20,* 363–368.

Bandura, A. (1991). Social cognitive theory of self-regulation. *Organizational Behavior and Human Decision Processes, 50,* 248–287.

Bandura, A. (1983). Psychological mechanisms of aggression. *Journal of Communication, 28,* 12–29.

Bandura, A. (1973). *Aggression: A social learning analysis.* Englewood Cliffs, NJ: Prentice-Hall.

Berkowitz, L. (1962). *Aggression: A social psychological analysis.* New York: McGraw-Hill.

Berkowitz, L. (1970). Experimental investigations of hostility catharsis. *Journal of Consulting and Clinical Psychology, 35,* 1–7.

Berkowitz, L. (1993). Towards a general theory of anger and emotional aggression: Implications of the cognitive-neoassociationistic perspective for the analysis of anger and other emotions. In R. S. Wyer, Jr., & T. K. Srull (Eds.), *Perspectives on anger and emotion: Vol. VI. Advances in social cognition* (pp. 1–46). Hillsdale, NJ: Erlbaum.

Betancourt, H., & Blair, I. (1992). A cognition (attribution)-emotion model of violence in conflict situations. *Personality and Social Psychology Bulletin, 18,* 343–350.

Bryant, J., & Zillmann D. (1977). The mediating effect of the intervention potential of communications on displaced aggressiveness and retaliatory behavior. In B. D. Ruben (Ed.), *Communication Yearbook 1* (pp. 291–306). New Brunswick, NJ: Transaction Press.

Buss, A. H. (1961). *The Psychology of Aggression.* New York: John Wiley.

Buss, D. M. (1989). Conflict between the sexes: Strategic interference and the evocation of anger and upset. *Journal of Personality and Social Psychology, 56,* 735–747.

Campbell, A., & Muncer, S. (1987). Models of anger and aggression in the social talk of women and men. *Journal for the Theory of Social Behavior, 17,* 489–511.

Canary, D. J., Cupach, W. R., & Messman, S. J. (1995). *Relationship conflict: Conflict in parent–child, friendship and romantic relationships.* Thousand Oaks, CA: Sage.

Canary, D. J., & Spitzberg, B. H. (1990). Attribution biases and associations between conflict strategies and competence outcomes. *Communication Monographs, 57,* 139–151.

Christopher, F. S., Owens, L. A., & Stecker, H. L. (1993). Exploring the darkside of courtship: A test of a model of male premarital sexual aggressiveness. *Journal of Marriage and the Family, 55,* 469–479.

Clark, M. S., Pataki, S. P., & Carrer, V. H. (1996). Some thoughts and findings on self-presentation of emotions in relationships. In J. O. Fletcher & J. Fitness (Eds.), *Knowledge structures in close relationships: A social psychological approach* (pp. 247–274). Mahwah, NJ: Erlbaum.

Clearhout, S., Elder, J., & Janes, C. (1982). Problem-solving skills of rural battered women. *American Journal of Community Psychology, 10,* 605–613.

Clore, G. L., & Ortony, A. (1991). What more is there to emotion concepts than prototypes? *Journal of Personality and Social Psychology, 60,* 48–50.

Clore, G. L., Ortony, A., Dienes, B., & Fujita, F. (1993). Where does anger dwell? In R. S. Wyer, Jr., & T. K. Srull (Eds.), *Perspectives on anger and emotion: Vol. VI. Advances in social cognitionI* (pp. 57–87). Hillsdale, NJ: Erlbaum.

Cupach, W. R., & Canary, D. J. (1995). Managing conflict and anger: Investigating the sex stereotype hypothesis. In P. Kalbfleisch & M. J. Cody (Eds.), *Gender, power, and communication in human relationships* (pp. 233–252). Hillsdale, NJ: Erlbaum.

Cupach, W. R., & Metts, S. (1994). *Facework.* Thousand Oaks, CA: Sage.

Deutsch, M. (1973). *The resolution of conflict: Constructive and destructive processes.* New Haven, CT: Yale University Press.

Dobash, R. W., & Dobash, R. P. (1984). The nature and antecedents of violent events. *British Journal of Criminology, 24,* 269–288.

Fehr, B., & Baldwin, M. (1996). Prototype and script analyses of lay people's knowledge of anger. In G. J. O. Fletcher & J. Fitness (Eds.), *Knowledge structures in close relationships: A social psychological analysis* (pp. 219–246). Hillsdale, NJ: Erlbaum.

Feschback, S. (1986). Reconceptualizations of anger: Some research perspectives. *Journal of Social and Clinical Psychology, 4,* 123–132.

Fincham, F. D., Bradbury, T. N., & Scott, C. K. (1992). Cognition in marriage. In F. D. Fincham & T. N. Bradbury (Eds), *The psychology of marriage: Basic issues and applications* (pp. 118–149). New York: Guilford.

Fitness, J., & Fletcher, G. J. O. (1993). Love, hate, anger, and jealousy in close relationships: A prototype and cognitive appraisal analysis. *Journal of Personality and Social Psychology, 65,* 942–958.

Frijda, N. H., Kuipers, P., & ter Shure, E. (1989). The relationships between emotion, appraisal, and emotional action readiness. *Journal of Personality and Social Psychology, 57,* 212–228.

Gelles, R. J. (1974). *The violent home.* Beverly Hills, CA: Sage.

Gelles, R. J., & Straus, M. A. (1979). Determinants of violence in the family: Toward a theoretical integration. In W. R. Burn, R. Hill, F. I. Nye, & J. L. Reiss (Eds.), *Contemporary theories about the family* (pp. 549–581). New York: Free Press.

Gergen, K. J., & Gergen, M. M. (1988). Narrative and the self as relationship. In L. Berkowitz (Ed.), *Advances in experimental social psychology* (Vol. 21, pp. 17–56). San Diego, CA: Academic Press.

Gottman, J. M. (1994). *What predicts divorce? The relationship between marital processes and marital outcomes.* Hillsdale, NJ: Erlbaum.

Gottman, J. M., & Krokoff, L. J. (1989). Marital interaction and marital satisfaction: A longitudinal view. *Journal of Consulting and Clinical Psychology, 57,* 47–52.

Guerrero, L. K. (1994). "I'm so mad I could scream:" The effects of anger expression on relational satisfaction and communication competence. *The Southern Communication Journal, 59,* 125–141.

Harris, M. B. (1993). How provoking! What makes men and women angry? *Aggressive Behavior, 19,* 199–211.

Helmers, K. F., Posluszny, D. M., & Krantz, D. S. (1994). Associations of hostility and coronary artery disease: A review of studies. In A. W. Siegman & T. W. Smith (Eds.), *Anger, hostility, and the heart* (pp. 67–96). Hillsdale, NJ: Erlbaum.

Holt, R. R. (1970). On the interpersonal and intrapersonal consequences of expressing or not expressing anger. *Journal of Consulting and Clinical Psychology, 35,* 8–12.

Infante, D. A. (1987). Aggressiveness. In J. C. McCroskey and J. A. Daly (Eds.), *Personality and Interpersonal Communication* (pp. 157–192). Beverly Hills, CA: Sage.

Infante, D. A., Chandler, T. A., & Rudd, J. E. (1989). Test of an argumentative skill deficiency model of interspousal violence. *Communication Monographs, 56*, 163–177.

Infante, D. A., & Wigley, C. J. (1986). Verbal aggressiveness: An interpersonal model and measure. *Communication Monographs, 53*, 61–69.

Jensen, M. A., & Meyers-Abel, J. (1981). Assertive training for battered women: A pilot program. *Social Work, 26*, 164–165.

Johnson, J., & Arneson, P. (1991). Women expressing anger to women in the workplace: Perceptions of conflict resolution styles. *Women's Studies in Communication, 14*, 24–41.

Kemp, S., & Strongman, K. T. (1995). Anger theory and management: A historical analysis. *American Journal of Psychology, 108*, 397–417.

Kinney, T. A. (1994). An inductively derived typology of verbal aggression and its association to distress. *Human Communication Research, 21*, 183–222.

Kovecses, Z. (1990). *Emotion concepts.* New York: Springer-Verlag.

Krokoff, L. J. (1991). Communication orientation as a moderator between strong negative affect and marital satisfaction. *Behavioral Assessment, 13*, 51–65.

Kubany, E. S., Richard, D. C., Bauer, G. B., & Muraoka, M. Y. (1992a). Impact of assertive and accusatory communication of distress and anger: A verbal components analysis. *Aggressive Behavior, 18*, 337–347.

Kubany, E. S., Richard, D. C., Bauer, G. B., & Muraka, M. Y. (1992b). Verbalized anger and accusatory "you" messages as cues for anger and antagonism among adolescents. *Adolescence, 27*, 505–516.

Kubany, E. S., Bauer, G. B., Muraoka, M. Y., Richard, D. C., & Read, P. (1995). Impact of labeled anger and blame in intimate relationships. *Journal of Social and Clinical Psychology, 14*, 53–60.

Lemerise, E. A., & Dodge, K. A. (1993). The development of anger and hostile interactions. In M. Lewis & J. M. Haviland (Ed.), *Handbook of emotions* (pp. 537–546). New York: Guilford.

Levenson, R. W., & Gottman, J. M. (1985). Physiological and affective predictors of change in relationship satisfaction. *Journal of Personality and Social Psychology, 49*, 85–94.

Lloyd, S. A. (1990). Conflict types and strategies in violent marriages. *Journal of Family Violence, 5*, 269–284.

Makepeace, J. M. (1983). Life events, stress, and courtship violence. *Family Relations, 30*, 97–102.

Makepeace, J. M. (1986). Gender differences in courtship violence victimization. *Family Relations, 35*, 383–388.

Margolin, G., Burman, B., & John, R. S. (1989). Home observations of married couples reenacting naturalistic conflicts. *Behavioral assessment, 11*, 101–118.

Margolin, G., John, R. S., & Gleberman, L. (1988). Affective responses to conflictual discussions in violent and nonviolent couples. *Journal of Consulting and Clinical Psychology, 56*, 24–33.

Marshall, L. L. (1994). Physical and psychological abuse. In W. R. Cupach & B. H. Spitzberg (Eds.), *The dark side of interpersonal communication* (pp. 281–311). Hillsdale, NJ: Erlbaum.

McKay, M., Rogers, P., & McKay, J. (1989). *When anger hurts.* New York: MJF.

Murphy, C. M., & O'Leary, K. D. (1989). Psychological aggression predicts physical aggression in early marriage. *Journal of Consulting and Clinical Psychology, 57*, 579–582.

O'Leary, K. D. (1988). Physical aggression between spouses: a social learning theory perspective. In V. B. Van Hassett, R. C. Morrison, A. S. Bellack, & M. Hersen (Eds.), *Handbook of family violence* (pp. 31–55). New York: Plenum.

Purdy, R. & Nickle, N. (1981). Practice principles for working with groups of men who batter. *Social Work with Groups, 4*, 111–122.

Retzinger, S. M. (1991). *Violent emotions: Shame and rage in marital quarrels.* Newbury Park, CA: Sage.

Retzinger, S. M. (1995). Shame and anger in personal relationships. In S. Duck & J. T. Wood (Eds.), *Understanding relationship processes: Vol. 5: Confronting relationship challenges* (pp. 22–42). Thousand Oaks, CA: Sage.

Rosenbaum, A., & O'Leary, K. D. (1981). Marital violence: Characteristics of abusive couples. *Journal of Consulting and Clinical Psychology, 49*, 63–71.

Rubin, J. (1986). The emotion of anger: Some conceptual and theoretical issues. *Professional psychology research and practice, 17,* 115–124.

Russell, J. A., & Fehr, B. (1994). Fuzzy concepts in a fuzzy hierarchy: Varieties of anger. *Journal of Personality and Social Psychology, 67,* 186–205.

Schönbach, P. (1990). *Account episodes: The management of escalation of conflict.* New York: Cambridge University Press.

Sereno, K. K., Welch, M., & Braaten, D. (1987). Interpersonal conflict: Effects of variations in manner of expressing anger and justification for anger upon perceptions of appropriateness, competence, and satisfaction. *Journal of Applied Communication Research, 15,* 128–143.

Siegman, A. W. (1994). Cardiovascular consequences of expressing and repressing anger. In A. W. Siegman & T. W. Smith (Eds.), *Anger, hostility, and the heart* (pp. 173–197). Hillsdale, NJ: Erlbaum.

Sillars, A. L. (1980). The sequential and distributional structure of conflict interactions as a function of attributions concerning the locus of responsibility and stability of conflicts. In D. Nimmo (Ed.), *Communication Yearbook 4* (pp. 217–235). New Brunswick, NJ: Transaction.

Sillars, A. L., & Weisberg, J. (1987). Conflict as a social skill. In M. E. Roloff & G. R. Miller (Eds.), *Interpersonal processes: New directions in communication research* (pp. 140–171). Newbury Park, CA: Sage.

Sillars, A. L., & Wilmot, W. W. (1994). Communication strategies in conflict and mediation. In J. A. Daly & J. M. Wiemann (Eds.), *Strategic interpersonal communication* (pp. 163–190). Hillsdale, NJ: Erlbaum.

Shaver, P., Schwartz, D., Kirkson, D., & O'Connor, C. (1987). Emotion knowledge: Further exploration of a prototype approach. *Journal of Personality and Social Psychology, 52,* 1061–1086.

Spitzberg, B. H. (1997). Violence in intimate relationships. In W. R. Cupach & D. J. Canary (Eds.), *Competence in interpersonal conflict* (pp. 175–201). New York: McGraw-Hill.

Sprecher, S. (1986). The relation between emotion and equity in close relationships. *Social Psychological Bulletin, 49,* 309–321.

Stearns, C. Z., & Stearns, P. N. (1986). *Anger: The struggle for emotional control in America's history.* Chicago: University of Chicago Press.

Storm, C., & Storm, T. (1987). A taxonomic study of the vocabulary of emotions. *Journal of Personality and Social Psychology, 53,* 805–816.

Storms, M. D. (1973). Videotape and the attribution process: Reversing actors' and observers' points of view. *Journal of Personality and Social Psychology, 27,* 165–175.

Straus, M. A. (1980). Victims and aggressors in marital violence. *American Behavioral Scientist, 23,* 681–704.

Straus, M. A., Gelles, R. J., & Steinmetz, S. K. (1980). *Behind closed doors: Violence in the American family.* Garden City, NY: Anchor.

Sugarman, D. B., & Hotaling, G. T. (1989). Dating violence: Prevalence, context, and risk markers. In M. A. Priog-Good & J. E. Stets (Eds.), *Violence in dating relationships: Emerging social issues* (pp. 3–32). New York: Praeger.

Tangney, J. P., Barlow, D. H., Wagner, P. E., Marschall, D. E., Borenstein, J. K., Sanftner, J., Mohr, T., & Gramzow, R. (1996). Assessing individual differences in constructive versus destructive responses to anger across the lifespan. *Journal of Personality and Social Psychology, 70,* 780–796.

Tangney, J. P., Wagner, P., Fletcher, C., & Gramzow, R. (1992). Shamed into anger? The relation of shame and guilt to anger and self-reported aggression. *Journal of Personality and Social Psychology, 62,* 669–675.

Tavris, C. (1982). *Anger: The misunderstood emotion.* New York: Simon and Schuster.

Tavris, C. (1984). On the wisdom of counting to ten: Personal and social dangers of anger expression. In P. Shaver (Ed.), *Review of personality and social psychology: Vol. 5* (pp. 170–192). Newbury Park, CA: Sage.

Ting-Toomey, S. (1988). Intercultural conflict styles: A face-negotiation theory. In Y. Kim & W. Gundykunst (Eds.), *Theories in intercultural communication* (pp. 213–235). Newbury Park: Sage.

Törestad, B. (1990). What is anger-provoking? A psychophysical study of perceived causes of anger. *Aggressive Behavior, 16,* 9–26.

Tracy, K., Craig, R. T., Smith, M., & Spisak, F. (1984). The discourse of requests: An assessment of compliance-gaining requests. *Human Communication Research, 10,* 513–538.

van de Vliert, E., & Euwema, M. C. (1994). Agreeableness and activeness as components of conflict behaviors. *Journal of Personality and Social Psychology, 66,* 674–687.

Williams, R., & Williams, V. (1993). *Anger kills.* New York: Harper Collins.

Zillmann, D. (1994). Cognition-excitation interdependencies in the escalation of anger and angry aggression. In M. Potegal & J. F. Knutson (Eds.), *The dynamics of aggression: Biological and social processes in dyads and groups* (pp. 45–71). Hillsdale, NJ: Erlbaum.

Zillmann, D. (1990). The interplay of cognition and excitation in aggrevated conflict. In D. D. Cahn (Ed.), *Intimates in conflict: A communication perspective* (pp. 187–208). Hillsdale, NJ: Erlbaum.

Zillmann, D. (1988). Cognition-excitation interdependence in aggressive behavior. *Aggressive Behavior, 14,* 51–64.

Zillmann, D. (1971). Excitation transfer in communication-mediated aggressive behavior. *Journal of Experimental Social Psychology, 7,* 519–434.

Zillmann, D., & Cantor, J. R. (1976). Effect of timing of information about mitigating circumstances on emotional responses to provocation and retaliatory behavior. *Journal of Experimental Social Psychology, 12,* 38–55.

Zillmann, D., Johnson, R. C., & Day, D. K. (1974). Provoked and unprovoked aggressiveness in athletes. *Journal of Research in Personality, 8,* 139–152.

CHAPTER 8

Interpersonal Communication Problems Associated with Depression and Loneliness

Chris Segrin
University of Kansas
Lawrence, Kansas

At any given point in time, approximately 3 to 9% of the population suffer from Major Depressive Disorder. Lifetime prevalence estimates for the disorder in the general population are approximately 17%, but climb to as high as 25% among women (Blazer, Kessler, McGonagle, & Swartz, 1994). One recent prospective epidemiological investigation found that 9% of the male population, and 25% of the female population had been treated for depression *by age 30* (Angst, 1992). Apart from being particularly common, depression is also associated with a high mortality rate. Up to 15% of all people afflicted with severe depression die from suicide (American Psychiatric Association, 1994). Keep in mind that the prevalence rates referenced above are for those with clinically diagnosable cases of depression. Less severe episodes and cases of depression, sometimes referred to as dysphoria, are something that the majority of the population have suffered (or will suffer) from at some point(s) in time.

Because loneliness is not a disorder with recognized and agreed upon diagnostic criteria, its prevalence is more difficult to estimate. In Roscoe and Skomski's (1989) survey of over 1600 adolescents, approximately 20% were classified as "lonely." Other authors have noted similar rates of loneliness among the general population (e.g., Peplau, Russell, & Heim, 1979). These findings suggest that like depression, loneliness is a common and substantial problem for many people.

The term *depression* has a dual meaning. Members of the lay public often use the term to describe a rather temporary affective state, as in "He's feeling depressed about X." Social scientists frequently use the word to describe an identifiable syndrome that has as its main feature sad affect, along with a host of other symptoms such as sleep disturbance, an inability to experience pleasure, feelings of fatigue, significant weight loss or gain, to name but a few (American Psychiatric Association, 1994). Accordingly, a person is considered to be "depressed" if s/he exhibits a number of these symptoms for at least 2 weeks time. Both of these uses of the term depression recognize the fact that it is a state of profound unhappiness, despair, hopelessness, sadness, and negative self-worth. The majority of research on depression employs the social scientific conceptualization, yet not all participants in depression research are clinically diagnosed as such. Nevertheless, it is safe to assume that all were afflicted with some degree of sad, negative affect.

The concept of *loneliness* also has suffered from conceptual confusion. Loneliness is a discrepancy between one's *desired* and *achieved* levels of social contact and interaction (Peplau & Perlman, 1982; Peplau et al., 1979). This definition has two important implications. First and contrary to popular belief, not all people who have small or nonexistent social networks are lonely. Social network size is notoriously unrelated to feelings of loneliness (e.g., Hamid, 1989; Medora & Woodward, 1986). Second, some lonely people have large social networks and a lot of social contact. I describe such a state as the "Marilyn Monroe Syndrome," as she was reputed to have an unusually large social network but at the same time suffered from chronic loneliness and depression. It is widely agreed that loneliness has a distinct emotional component (e.g., Vaux, 1988; Vincenzi & Grabosky, 1990) that is characterized by feelings of not having a close friend, not wanting to burden others, and being undesirable to others.

DEPRESSION AND INTERPERSONAL INTERACTION

The extensive research on depression and social interaction can usefully be segmented into that which focuses on the nature of the relationships and interpersonal reactions of others to depression and that which focuses on depressed persons' social behaviors. The former line of research, often connected with Coyne's (1976a,b) interactional model of depression, focuses on the way that other people respond to depression in a friend, roommate, romantic partner, family member, or parent. Much of this work examines the quality of depressed people's relationships with others. The later area of research examines what depressed people actually do in social situations, and is often associated with the "social skills deficit hypothesis" from Lewinsohn's (1974, 1975) behavioral theory of depression. The amalgamation of these two lines of research, that focuses on what depressed people do in communicative situations and how others react to them, provides a true interpersonal analysis of depression (Segrin & Abramson, 1994).

INTERPERSONAL RELATIONSHIPS AND REACTIONS TO DEPRESSION

Interpersonal Responses to Depression

A substantial body of evidence indicates that an important interpersonal problem for people afflicted with depression is rejection from others (e.g., Amstutz & Kaplan, 1987; Gotlib & Beatty, 1985; Gurtman, 1987; Siegel & Alloy, 1990). Much of the research on this phenomenon is guided by Coyne's interactional model of depression (Coyne, 1976a,b). According to this model, depressed people are hypothesized to induce a negative mood in their interactional partners through a process of emotional contagion. This hypothesis is predicated on the assumption that it is an irritating, negative experience to interact with depressed people. As a consequence of this negative mood induction, others are expected to move from initially offering nongenuine reassurance and support to outright rejection and avoidance of the depressed individual.

Numerous attempts to experimentally test Coyne's interactional model often have failed to demonstrate the hypothesized negative mood–induction effect (e.g., Gotlib & Robinson, 1982; McNiel, Arkowitz, & Pritchard, 1987; but see Coyne, 1976b), although this effect may become more evident over repeated interactions with the depressed target (Hokanson & Butler, 1992). However, the rejection of depressed persons by their interactional partners appears to be a reliable and robust phenomenon (e.g., Amstutz & Kaplan, 1987; Elliott, MacNair, Herrick, Yoder, & Byrne, 1991; Gurtman, 1987), and holds up across different cultures (Vanger, Summerfield, Rosen, & Watson, 1991) and age groups (Connolly, Geller, Marton, & Kutcher, 1992; Peterson, Mullins, & Ridley-Johnson, 1985; Rudolph, Hammen, & Burge, 1994).

This interpersonal rejection effect associated with depression appears to be moderated by a number of different variables. For example, depressed males elicit more rejection from others, especially other females, than do depressed females (Hammen & Peters, 1977, 1978; Joiner, Alfano, & Metalsky, 1992). Some evidence also indicates that friends are less rejecting of depressed persons than strangers (Segrin, 1993b; but see Sacco, Milana, & Dunn, 1985), that other people who assume a "helper" role are less rejecting (Marks & Hammen, 1982), and that those who rely on advice giving and joking with the depressed person are more rejecting (Notarius & Herrick, 1988). Other potential moderators of the depression-rejection effect include physical attractiveness of the depressed target (less rejection of attractive targets; Amstutz & Kaplan, 1987) and self-esteem of the target; depressed people who are low in self-esteem and seek reassurance from their partners are especially prone to eliciting rejection (Joiner et al., 1992).

A meta-analysis of the literature on interpersonal responses to depression indicates that the phenomenon of interpersonal rejection of depressed persons is very reliable and moderate in magnitude across studies (Segrin & Dillard, 1992). However, the extent to which depressed people create a negative affective state in others through social interaction is weaker and more sporadic. Research conducted since this meta-analysis has continued to produce results that generally are consistent with this conclusion (e.g., Connolly et al., 1992; Joiner et al., 1992; Marcus & Davis, 1993; Rudolph et al., 1994; Segrin, 1993b). Interested readers may wish to consult Coyne (1990), Coyne, Burchill, and Stiles (1990), Coyne, Kahn, and Gotlib (1987), McCann (1990), and Segrin and Dillard (1992) for more in-depth reviews of this literature.

Personal Relationships of Depressed Persons

The personal relationships of depressed people are characterized by dissatisfaction (Burns, Sayers, & Moras, 1994), diminished influence and intimacy (Nezlek, Imbrie, & Shean, 1994; Patterson & Bettini, 1993), and diminished activity and involvement (Gotlib & Lee, 1989). Some evidence indicates that the *quality* of social interaction with others is more strongly associated with depression than the sheer *quantity* (e.g., Rotenberg & Hamel, 1988). As might be expected, the availability of a confidant with whom one can self-disclose and engage in rewarding conversation is negatively associated with depression. It is the case, however, that many depressed people lack a close intimate relationship all together (Brown & Harris, 1978; Costello, 1982). This finding is particularly important in that lack of a close confiding relationship appears to create a heightened vulnerability to experiencing depression (Brown & Harris, 1978; Henderson, 1991).

Research on the personal relationships of depressives leads one to question the worth of their relational partners. For example, in Fiske and Peterson's (1991) investigation, depressed participants complained of dissatisfaction and anger with their romantic partners, as well as increased quarreling relative to nondepressed participants. These same respondents reported being hurt or upset by their romantic partners more frequently than did nondepressed controls, despite (or perhaps as a cause of) their greater desire for more love in the relationship. Depressed people also perceive their intimate partners as more hostile than nondepressed persons do (Thompson, Whiffen, & Blain, 1995). One recently studied group of depressed women reported that they received less social support from their confidants than did a group of nondepressed controls (Belsher & Costello, 1991). Indeed, the confidants of these depressed women exhibited more depressogenic speech (e.g., "I can't do anything right anymore," "I'm never going to find a job") than confidants of either nondepressed or psychiatric controls. Although serious consideration must be given to the possibility that this merely reflects an echoing phenomenon (i.e., the confidants are simply repeating the content uttered by the depressed women), an equally tantalizing possibility is that these confidants somehow have a hand in maintaining, if not creating the depressed state in which these women find themselves.

Evidence reviewed earlier in this chapter established that depressed people have a negative interpersonal impact on others. However, that evidence should not displace the fact that being in dysfunctional, hostile, and unsupportive relationships that are wanting in intimacy may itself precipitate depression and other undesirable affective states (Coyne & DeLongis, 1986; Coyne et al., 1987). Furthermore, depressed people may harbor certain vulnerabilities such as dependent or self-critical personalities that predispose them to both the experience of depression as well as disrupted interpersonal relationships (Coyne & Whiffen, 1995).

If this is the case that depressed persons typically find themselves in low-quality interpersonal relationships, it is necessary to at least contemplate the extent to which (a) the depressed person is causing or contributing to the disruption of the interpersonal interactions and relationships, and (b) the relationships may actually be better than the depressed person makes them out to be. Research findings reviewed below on social-skills deficits suggest that many depressed persons may not be equipped with the interpersonal tools that are adequate for ensuring satisfying and rewarding interpersonal interactions. Additionally, depressed people have a tendency to be overly negative in evaluating their interpersonal relationships (Hokanson, Hummer, & Butler, 1991) and estimating the frequency with which negative interpersonal events occur (Kuiper & MacDonald, 1983). In fact, for depressed males at least, there appears to be a bias to hold negative beliefs about people in general (Shapiro, 1988). Undoubtedly, many depressed people are in dysfunctional or dissatisfying interpersonal relationships. However, there is reason to suspect that at least some of the variance in these reports of aversive and dissatisfying interpersonal relationships is due to the depressed person's general tendency toward negatively biased assessments of such relationships.

Depression and Family Interaction

In addition to the experience of disrupted personal relationships, depression is also associated with problems in marital interactions and relationships (see Beach, Sandeen, & O'Leary, 1990, and Coyne et al., 1987 for reviews). Repeatedly, this research has shown that depression and marital distress go hand in hand (Beach & O'Leary, 1993; Beach et al., 1990; Hinchliffe, Hooper, & Roberts, 1978). Estimates indicate that 50% of all women in distressed marriages are depressed (Beach, Jouriles, & O'Leary, 1985), and 50% of all depressed women are in distressed marriages (Rounsaville, Weissman, Prusoff, & Herceg-Baron, 1979).

The communication between depressed people and their spouses is often negative in tone and tends to generate more negative affect in each spouse than that of nondepressed couples (Gotlib & Whiffen, 1989; Kahn, Coyne, & Margolin, 1985; Ruscher & Gotlib, 1988). Biglan and his co-workers suggested that depressed persons and their spouses often find themselves in dysfunctional vicious cycles of interaction (Biglan et al., 1985; Hops et al., 1987). Their findings indicate that depressed persons are often "rewarded" by their spouses for emitting depressive behaviors in that the depressive behaviors tend to inhibit the hostile and irritable behaviors of the spouse (see also Nelson & Beach, 1990). A recent investigation by McCabe and Gotlib (1993) showed that over the course of a 10–15-minute marital interaction, the verbal behavior of depressed wives becomes increasingly negative. It is therefore not surprising that this study demonstrated that couples with a depressed spouse viewed their marital interactions as more hostile and less friendly than did the nondepressed couples.

In an impressive program of research, Hinchliffe and her colleagues investigated a number of specific marital communication problems experienced by depressed people (e.g., Hinchliffe, Hooper, & Roberts, 1978, Hinchliffe, Hooper, Roberts, & Vaughan, 1978; Hinchliffe, Vaughan, Hooper, & Roberts, 1978, Hooper, Vaughan, Hinchliffe, & Roberts, 1978). These investigations reveal that when interacting with their spouses, depressed persons exhibit distorted patterns of responsiveness such that there is a lack of synchrony between the husband and wife. In addition, depressed people tend to be most expressive with their spouses when they are discussing issues that are negative in nature. It is interesting to note that in one study, acute depression was associated with a tendency to control and influence the other spouse (Hooper et al., 1978). These and other investigations indicate that the marital interactions of depressed persons are not always withdrawn and avoidant; they can take on a hostile and manipulative tone as well.

Expressed emotion (EE) is a type of communication behavior that entails excessive criticism, hostility, and an attitude of emotional overinvolvement, typically toward a family member. Research on EE shows that it is a problem for both depressed persons and their spouses (Florin, Nostadt, Reck, Franzen, & Jenkins, 1992; Hooley & Teasdale, 1989). Typically, high EE in the family has been a good predictor of a patient's relapse (e.g., Hooley & Teasdale, 1989). In this case the depressed person would be the recipient of the EE. However, there is now evidence to suggest that depressed people themselves exhibit high EE along with their spouses (Florin et al., 1992). These findings indicate that in depressive marital interactions active, not just passive, negativity is evident.

A variety of other investigations into marital interaction find depression to be associated with poor communication during problem-solving interactions (Basco, Prager, Pite, Tamir, & Stephens, 1992), negative self-evaluations and statements of negative well-being (Hautzinger, Linden, & Hoffman, 1982; Linden, Hautzinger, & Hoffman, 1983), verbal aggressiveness (Segrin & Fitzpatrick, 1992), and problems in establishing intimacy (Bullock, Siegel, Weissman, & Paykel, 1972; Basco et al., 1992). Given all of these negative communication behaviors and marital problems, it is easy to understand why depression and marital distress are so powerfully relat-ed. Some evidence indicates that these communication problems may be the result of marital distress more than depression per se (Schmaling & Jacobson, 1990). How-ever, the similarity of these findings with those of depressed persons' other person-al relationships point to obvious and pervasive interpersonal problems across a va-riety of different relationships.

Depressed persons experience as many problems in their role as a parent as they do in their role as a spouse. In numerous investigations depression has been linked to disrupted and dysfunctional parenting behavior (e.g., Hamilton, Jones, & Ham-men, 1993; Hammen et al., 1987). In general, the parenting behavior of depressives is characterized by similar negativity, hostility, complaining, and poor interperson-al problem solving that is associated with their other relationships. Apparently as a consequence of this disrupted parenting behavior, the children of depressed parents are at a much higher risk for behavioral, cognitive, and emotional dysfunction than are those of nondepressed parents (e.g., Lee & Gotlib, 1991; Whiffen & Gotlib, 1989; see Downey & Coyne, 1990; Gelfand & Teti, 1990; and Morrison, 1983, for re-views). Among the problems experienced by children of depressed mothers is de-pression itself (Hammen et al., 1987; Warner, Weissman, Fendrich, Wickramaratne, & Moreau, 1992). Although the effects of maternal depression have received much attention in the literature, evidence suggests that paternal depression also has ill effects on children (Forehand & Smith, 1986; Thomas & Forehand, 1991).

Children of depressed mothers typically exhibit a behavioral pattern indicative of rejection. During interaction with their parents, children of depressives express negative affect, are generally tense and irritable, spend less time looking at their par-ent, and appear less content than children who interact with their nondepressed par-ents (e.g., Cohn, Campbell, Matias, & Hopkins, 1990; Field, 1984).

Instead of using parents' depression to predict children's psychosocial problems as an outcome, some authors have examined the issue by using parental depression to explain retrospective or concurrent reports of parental and family functioning from adult children. Consistent results indicate that people who are depressed typ-ically describe their family of origin as rejecting (Lewinsohn & Rosenbaum, 1987) and uncaring (Gotlib, Mount, Cordy, & Whiffen, 1988). One study with college students found that siblings of depressed students were themselves more depressed than those of nondepressed students (Oliver, Handal, Finn, & Herdy, 1987).

SOCIAL SKILLS DEFICITS ASSOCIATED WITH DEPRESSION

Social skills are those skills and abilities that allow people to communicate appro-priately and effectively with others. Communication researchers sometimes study these skills under the heading of "communication competence" or "interpersonal competence." Lewinsohn (1974, 1975) hypothesized that people who lack adequate social skills would be at heightened risk for developing depression because these deficient skills make it difficult to obtain positive reinforcement and to avoid negative outcomes from the social environment. Indeed, a large body of research indicates that depressed people exhibit disruption in their communicative and social skills.

Self-Reports and Observer Ratings of Social Skill

Depressed subjects exhibit a tendency to evaluate themselves as less socially skilled than nondepressed subjects on a variety of self-report inventories (e.g., Cole, Lazarick, & Howard, 1987; Lewinsohn, Mischel, Chaplin, & Barton, 1980; Meyer & Hokanson, 1985; Segrin & Dillard, 1993; Vanger, 1987; Youngren & Lewinsohn, 1980). It is often the case, however, that depressed–nondepressed differences in social skills are most evident when social skills are measured with self-report instruments, and less evident on observers' ratings of social skill (Lewinsohn et al., 1980; Segrin & Dillard, 1993). However, observers do tend to evaluate the social skills of depressed research participants as lower than those of their nondepressed peers (Dalley, Bolocofsky, & Karlin, 1994; Dykman, Horowitz, Abramson, & Usher, 1991; Segrin, 1990, 1992). Additionally, depressed people's general tendency to evaluate themselves negatively does not fully account for the often-noted self-reported social-skills deficits associated with the disorder (Dow & Craighead, 1987; Gotlib & Meltzer, 1987; Kuiper, Olinger, & Swallow, 1987).

Communication Behaviors Related to Social Skills

In contrast to the rather global self-report and observer-rated assessment techniques, a number of researchers employed a behavioral approach to the study of depression. The focus in this orientation is on the specific communication behaviors that appear to be disrupted by the experience of depression. Analyses of the relationship between social skills and many of these communication behaviors are available elsewhere (e.g., Bellack, 1979; Dillard & Spitzberg, 1984; Millbrook, Farrell, & Curran, 1986; Spitzberg & Cupach, 1985). These analyses currently provide the best explanation as to exactly what depressed actors do, or fail to do, in social situations that might lead to negative reactions from others. Although not all of the studies reviewed below were explicitly designed to gather data on social skill and depression, all share the view that social behavioral deficits play an important role in the disorder.

Paralinguistic Behaviors

Some evidence indicates that depressed subjects differ from nondepressed subjects in the noncontent portion of their speech. Studies have shown that people who are depressed speak slower (Pope, Blass, Siegman, & Raher, 1970; Siegman, 1987; Weintraub & Aronson, 1967; Youngren & Lewinsohn, 1980), speak less (Breznitz & Sherman, 1987; Edison & Adams, 1992; Ellgring, Wagner, & Clarke, 1980; Fossi, Faravelli, & Paoli, 1984; Hinchliffe, Lancashire, & Roberts, 1971a; Williams, Barlow, & Agras, 1972), with less volume (Darby, Simmons, & Berger, 1984; Gotlib, 1982), and more silences (Greden, Albala, Smokler, Gardner, & Carroll, 1981; Natale, 1977a; Nilsonne, 1988; Pope et al., 1970; Rutter & Stephenson, 1972; Vanger, Summerfield, Rosen, & Watson, 1992), and hesitancies (as established by the Ah ratio: Pope, Blass, et al., 1970) than nondepressed persons. Depressed subjects also take longer than nondepressed persons to respond to the speech behaviors of others (Breznitz & Sherman, 1987; Talavera, Saiz-Ruiz, & Garcia-Toro, 1994).

Investigators who measured voice pitch and fundamental frequency typically found that depressed persons spoke in a monotonous tone (i.e., diminished f_o variability) and with a lower pitch than nondepressed persons (Darby et al., 1984; Kuny & Stassen, 1993; Nilsonne, 1988; Talavera et al., 1994; see Scherer, 1987, for review). The voices of depressed people are often sad and/or tense (Tolkmitt, Helfrich, Standke, & Scherer, 1982). Flint and his colleagues recently recorded greater spirantization in voice samples of depressed elderly patients versus nondepressed elderly controls (Flint, Black, Campbell-Taylor, Gailey, & Levinton, 1993). Spirantization is the presence of voice-related noise during what would normally be total closure of the vocal tract.

It is not surprising that nondepressed subjects have been rated as clearer in their communication (Lewinsohn et al., 1980) and easier to hear and understand than depressed subjects (Dow and Craighead, 1987). In one particular investigation, depressed subjects were asked to speak about a happy, sad, and angry experience they had (Levin, Hall, Knight, & Alpert, 1985). The vocal qualities of the depressed persons did not differentiate between happy and angry experiences. Levin et al. concluded that it was only sad affect that depressed people communicate effectively and appropriately through their voices. It may be that depressed persons are very "skilled" or capable of communicating sadness and despair paralinguistically. However, they may be less attuned to or concerned about cultural display rules that often proscribe the outward display of such emotional states. Alternatively, depressed people may be unable to mask their negative affect paralinguistically since vocal cues such as pitch, speech rate, intonation, and so on are difficult to consciously control.

Speech Content

In a unique investigation of depressive verbal interaction, Hautzinger et al. (1982) had distressed married couples come into a research laboratory and talk to each other about eight different topics. In half of the couples there was a partner suffering from a clinically significant depressive episode. The couples with a depressed partner were more likely than the nondepressed couples to verbally express dysphoric feelings, negative well-being, talk more about well-being, ask questions about well-being, and in the case of the depressed partner, engage in negative self-evaluation. Depressed spouses have also reported being more verbally aggressive and less constructive in problem-solving, a view corroborated by their spouses, when engaged in marital interaction (Kahn et al., 1985).

When depressed students were asked to get acquainted with another student for 15 minutes, they emitted fewer statements that reflected a positive appraisal of their partner, and made more directly negative statements than their nondepressed peers (Gotlib & Robinson, 1982). Similar findings of negative verbal content among depressives were obtained in studies of stranger interactions (Coyne, 1976b), unstructured interviews (Hinchliffe, Lancashire, & Roberts, 1971b), 10-min monologues (Weintraub & Aronson, 1967), telephone conversations with confidants (Belsher & Costello, 1991), and psychotherapy sessions (Weissman & Klerman, 1973). Likewise, Blumberg and Hokanson (1983) demonstrated that depressed individuals communicate self-devaluataion, sadness, and general negativity to their interpersonal partners.

It appears that another trouble area for depressive speech behaviors is with self-disclosure (Gibbons, 1987; Gurtman, 1987; Jacobson & Anderson, 1982). Jacobson and Anderson (1982) demonstrated that depressed students delivered negative statements about the self at a higher rate than nondepressed students. Of greater significance is that depressed subjects were more inclined to emit unsolicited self-disclosures, and were more likely to self-disclose following a partner self-disclosure, than were the nondepressed subjects. This indicates that depressed subjects not only self-disclose more than their nondepressed counterparts, but that their timing of these disclosures is often inappropriate and the content is often negative. Self-disclosures have been shown to be a key ingredient in the rejection of depressed persons by others (Gurtman, 1987).

In a rare examination into evaluations of topics for self-disclosure by depressed people, Kuiper and McCabe (1985) gave depressed and nondepressed respondents 30 different items from Jourard and Lasakow's (1958) scale of self-disclosure. Items ranged from topics such as work, money, personality, body, and opinions. A panel of judges labeled items as positive if they thought that they would feel comfortable or good discussing it with another person, and that a positive social interaction would follow in the pursuit of the topic. Items labeled negative were those that judges thought would make them unhappy, uncomfortable, and lead to negative social interaction. As might be expected, the depressed subjects rated the negative topics as more appropriate for discussion than the nondepressed subjects. There were no group differences for the positive topics.

Gaze

Gaze is an important indicator of interest and attention in conversation and is an important component of social skill (Cherulnik, Neely, Flanagan, & Zachau, 1978). Depressed persons engage in less eye contact with their interpersonal partners than nondepressed interactants (Dow & Craighead, 1987; Ellgring et al., 1980; Fossi et al., 1984; Hinchliffe et al., 1971a; I. H. Jones & Pansa, 1979; Kazdin, Sherick, Esveldt-Dawson, & Rancurello, 1985; Natale, 1977b; Waxer, 1974; Youngren & Lewinsohn, 1980). Rutter and Stephenson (1972) discovered a significant interaction between depression and the presence or absence of speech, such that depressed subjects were less likely than controls to be looking while speaking. It is possible that the decrease in looking while speaking (relative to controls) is a phenomenon associated with low self-esteem. People with low self-esteem may be less confident, less comfortable, and thus less likely to engage in visual contact with the partner as they speak. Similarly, people who hold high status will engage in more looking while speaking than low-status, submissive individuals (Andersen & Bowman, 1990; Exline, Ellyson, & Long, 1975). Taken together, these results suggest that the diminished eye contact evident in depressive social interactions may be driven by feelings of inferiority, low status, and low self-esteem on the part of the depressed person.

Facial Expression

Differences in facial affective displays of depressed subjects versus nondepressed controls have been investigated extensively. In two laboratory studies by Schwartz and his colleagues (Schwartz, Fair, Salt, Mandel, & Klerman, 1976a,b), participants were connected to electromyographic (EMG) electrodes that measure subtle facial activity in the form of muscle movements. In the first investigation depressed subjects evidenced an attenuated EMG response while trying to imagine happy situations and images, and an exaggerated reaction (relative to controls) while trying to imagine sad situations and feelings. In a second and similar investigation, both depressed subjects and nondepressed controls evidenced similar abilities to self-regulate a happy facial state when requested to do so; however, when no instructions were offered, the controls spontaneously assumed a happy expression while the depressed subjects showed no evidence of a happy expression (cf. Schwartz et al., 1978).

In a related investigation, no depressed–nondepressed differences were noted under conditions of physical pain, yet at rest the depressed group had a higher incidence of corrugated brow, squinting or closed eyes, turned down mouth, and were more frequently judged as looking "depressed" (Ganchrow, Steiner, Kleiner, & Edelstein, 1978). Significant correlations between depressed mood and corrugator (brow region) EMG activity were also observed by other investigators (Greden, Genero, Price, Feinberg, & Levine, 1986; Teasdale & Bancroft, 1977) including I. H. Jones and Pansa (1979), who found depressed patients less likely to have their brows raised than controls. Other inquiries revealed differences as a function of depression in mouth position (Waxer, 1974), facial expression of pleasantness and arousal (Youngren & Lewinsohn, 1980), smiles (Ellgring, 1989; Williams et al., 1972), expressions of anger (Berenbaum, 1992), and facial expressions of happiness, sadness, fear, surprise, and interest (less in the depressed group; Fossi et al., 1984). Generally, depressed people exhibit diminished animation of involuntary facial expression of emotion (Gaebel & Wolwer, 1992).

Although results clearly converge to suggest a deficit in the encoding of facial expressions, depression shows no such association with performance on decoding tasks. When asked to decode emotional facial expressions, depressed individuals perform similarly to the nondepressed (Gaebel & Wolwer, 1992; Rubinow & Post, 1992).

Posture and Gesture

A small body of data indicates that depression may be associated with certain patterns or tendencies in gesture and posture (Dittmann, 1987; Ekman & Friesen, 1974; Miller, Ranelli, & Levine, 1977). For example, depressed patients have been observed to engage in significantly less gesturing and head nodding than controls (Fossi et al., 1984). Similarly, depressed children appear to have a diminished tendency to use illustrators, which are gestures that accompany speech (Kazdin et al., 1985). Ekman and Friesen (1972) found that the tendency to use illustrators increased dramatically in depressed individuals as symptoms lifted (see also Ekman & Friesen, 1974).

Depressed subjects have been noted to engage in more body contact (self-touching, including rubbing and scratching) while at rest, and when presented with a number of different stimuli, than nondepressed subjects (I. Jones & Pansa, 1979; Ranelli & Miller, 1981). Also, there is some evidence that depressed individuals are more likely to hold their head in a downward position than nondepressed persons (Waxer, 1974).

Summary

In review, a vast body of data indicates that interpersonal rejection is a common phenomenon associated with depression (Segrin & Dillard, 1992). Perhaps it follows logically that depressed people would experience disrupted and often dissatisfying personal relationships with their friends, roommates, romantic partners, and even with strangers with whom they briefly interact. The pervasiveness of relational problems associated with depression clearly extends into the domain of family interaction and relationships. The marital interactions and relationships of depressives are characterized by negativity, hostility, and often coercive manipulation. Depressed persons typically raise children who exhibit various behavioral and adjustment problems.

The studies on depressed people's social and communicative skills provide a compelling explanation of *why* depressed people so often experience interpersonal rejection (Segrin & Abramson, 1994). Many of the communication behaviors that are disrupted by depression are correlated with rejection from others (Segrin, 1992, study 2). Overall, depressed persons show a behavioral pattern of low interpersonal involvement, unresponsiveness, withdrawal, and negativity. Behavioral studies of social skill and depression indicate that depressed persons speak slowly, with little volume, take a long time to respond, gaze very little at their partner, gesture infrequently, exhibit sad facial expressions, and talk about negative issues related to the self and environment. It is very likely that many of the behavioral deficits associated with depression can be explained by social withdrawal and unwillingness to communicate, which are common in those afflicted with this disorder.

A meta-analysis of the depression–social skill literature indicated that the largest depressed–nondepressed difference in social skill was evident when social skill was measured with a self-report instrument (Segrin, 1990). This may reflect partial contamination from a negative self-evaluation bias associated with depression. However, when asked to make evaluations, conversational partners and third-party observers always rated depressed subjects lower in social skill than nondepressed subjects. Finally, of the various behaviors indicative of social skill, vocal pitch variation, gestures, and silences proved to be the most powerful discriminators between depressed and nondepressed communicators.

It appears that it is not particularly rewarding to interact with depressed people. They may often violate people's expectations and desires for appropriate and cheerful behavior, attentiveness, and responsiveness (Segrin & Abramson, 1994). As a consequence of these problems with social skills, other people react with rejection and outright avoidance, and the depressed person finds him- or herself in dissatisfying and often corrosive interpersonal relationships.

LONELINESS AND INTERPERSONAL INTERACTION

Like the literature on depression, research on loneliness illustrates numerous social and interpersonal problems associated with the condition. Given that loneliness is a discrepancy between a person's desired and achieved level of social interaction (Peplau et al., 1979), it is perhaps a foregone conclusion that lonely people have problems with interpersonal communication and relationships. Like depression, loneliness appears to be a phenomenon that is prevalent in many different cultures (Brewin, Furnham, & Howes, 1989; Jones, Carpenter, & Quintana, 1985; Pearl, Klopf, & Ishii, 1990).

Loneliness and Personal Relationships

Perhaps the most substantial affliction experienced by lonely persons is a lack of intimacy in their social and personal relationships (e.g., Hamid, 1989; Revenson & Johnson, 1984; Vaux, 1988). This may be explained by the fact that lonely people have a difficult time making friends (Medora & Woodward, 1986), and experience poor communication with family members (Brage, Meredith, & Woodward, 1993) and low social integration (Vaux, 1988).

What appears to be particularly lacking for the lonely person are meaningful and intimate friendships. Even relationships with co-workers can serve to suppress loneliness (Bell, Roloff, Van Camp, & Karol, 1990). Quality relationships with family members, on the other hand, do little to prevent or ameliorate the experience of loneliness (e.g., Jones & Moore, 1990). In fact, Jones and Moore found that the more social support students had from their family, the *more* lonely they were. Although the increased family social support may be a result of the students' loneliness, it is clear that these types of relationships do little to help the lonely person's situation. In a study with truly mind-bending results, Andersson further explored the role of family relationships in the experience of loneliness (Andersson, Mullins, & Johnson, 1990). He obtained retrospective reports of parent–child relationships from a large sample of elderly women in their 70s and 80s. Children who had an excessively close, warm, and nurturing relationship with at least one parent, were significantly *more* lonely as elderly adults than a group of controls. Andersson et al. (1990) concluded that the effects of overinvolvement from parents can be as noxious as underinvolvement or neglect when it comes to producing lonely children. This is due in part to the fact that parental overinvolvement can create a sense of narcissism in the child. One reason that family relationships and involvement might be so ineffective at buffering against loneliness is because they are relationships of obligation. Consequently, lonely people may find little solace in social support from persons who they feel are obligated to offer it.

One might additionally hypothesize that extremely close parent–child relationships build great expectations that other relationships chronically fail to meet. Such a phenomenon could easily create a sense of dissatisfaction and longing for greater intimacy in one's interpersonal relationships. Finally, excessive closeness and interaction with parents may displace the interactions that children would have with peers. This could lead to a corruption of the processes that lead to peer-referent social skills. An individual lacking in such social skills would again experience difficulty in establishing and maintaining satisfying social relations.

Additional suspicion about the ill effects of relationships with the family of origin have been raised by results of a recent investigation from Henwood and Solano (1994). These authors surveyed a sample of first-grade children and their parents and found that children's loneliness was significantly correlated with that of their mothers (see also Lobdell & Perlman, 1986). Whether parental loneliness is transmitted via genetics, environment, socialization, or a combination of these factors, the family does not appear to be a source of buffers against the loneliness experience.

One possible cause of the lonely person's problems in establishing intimate relationships may involve social anxiety. There is a powerful link between loneliness and the experience of social anxiety (e.g., Moore & Schultz, 1983; Segrin, 1993c;

Segrin & Kinney, 1995; Solano & Koester, 1989). The socially anxious tend to approach social interactions with discomfort and nervousness, and in more severe cases, avoid them altogether. As a consequence, other people typically respond rather unfavorably to these awkward and reserved interactions. It is easy to see how the experience of social anxiety could create barriers to establishing meaningful relationships with others.

Loneliness and Social Skills

As in the depression literature, much of the research on interpersonal communication and loneliness has involved investigations of social skills. In a now classic paper, W. Jones, Hobbs, and Hockenbury (1982) developed the hypothesis that lonely people exhibit deficits in social skills. Poor social skills could obviously make it difficult to establish quality relationships with others, and thus cause and perpetuate the experience of loneliness. Indeed, W. Jones (1982) found that during dyadic interactions lonely people made fewer partner references, asked fewer questions, and emitted fewer statements indicative of partner attention. These authors concluded that one area of social skill in which lonely people experience particular difficulty is with partner attention. In their social interactions, lonely people fail to send messages of involvement or concern with their partners. This lack of partner attention may be a manifestation of the general inhibited sociability that is common to loneliness (Horowitz & French, 1979).

Since the appearance of the Jones et al. (1982) investigation, numerous other studies indicate that lonely people consistently describe their social skills as lesser in nature than nonlonely controls (e.g., Roscoe & Skomski, 1989; Segrin 1993c; Solano & Koester, 1989; Wittenberg & Reis, 1986). Furthermore, observers appear to concur with these negative assessments (Segrin, 1994; Spitzberg & Canary, 1985), as do conversational partners (Spitzberg & Hurt, 1990), and teachers of lonely adolescents (Inderbitzen-Pisaruk & Solano, 1992). A number of cross-sectional studies indicate that correlations between loneliness and various aspects of social skills are in the $-.30$ to $-.50$ range (e.g., Buhrmester, Furman, Wittenberg, & Reis, 1988; Riggio, Throckmorton, & DePaola, 1990; Riggio, Watring, & Throckmorton, 1993). In Spitzberg and Hurt's (1989) longitudinal investigation, between 34 and 42% of the variance in loneliness was explained by various measures of social skills, including some that referenced appropriate use of communication behaviors from a 5–7-min "get acquainted" interaction.

Behaviorally, lonely people talk less in conversations with strangers and roommates (Sloan & Solano, 1984), engage in less self-disclosure with opposite-sex partners (Solano, Batten, & Parish, 1982), and emit fewer back-channels and interruptions (Bell, 1985). Lonely subjects in the latter investigation rated themselves and were rated by others as less involved in a laboratory conversation than were nonlonely subjects. The general lack of behavioral (and cognitive, see Bell, 1985) involvement in conversations illustrates an interesting paradox associated with loneliness: The lonely are people who, by definition, desire more intimate and meaningful contact with others, while at the same time sending messages of disinterest and noninvolvement to others. After a 10-min interaction, lonely participants in Bell's (1985) investigation were rated as less desirable for future interaction, and seen as less interested in friendship by their conversational partners. This message is presumably the exact opposite of what the lonely person wants to send! It is difficult to understand why a group of people who desire greater quality social contact would come across as, and indeed be (Joubert, 1986), disinterested in social interaction.

Lonely People's Views of Social Interaction

An explanation for lonely people's diminished sociability and social interest, despite the longing for more intimate contact, may come from research on lonely persons' interpersonal perceptions. Although some studies suggest that the social perceptions of lonely people are no different than those of nonlonely people (e.g., Gerson & Perlman, 1979; Segrin, 1993a), a growing number of studies reveal that lonely people often hold negative views toward other people (e.g., Hanley-Dunn, Maxwell, & Santos, 1985; W. Jones, Freemon, & Goswick, 1981). Lonely persons will make negative ratings of strangers whom they have just interacted with (W. Jones et al., 1981; W. Jones, Sansone, & Helm, 1983), as well as their well-known friends (Wittenberg & Reis, 1986). Lonely subjects have also been demonstrated to make more negative attributions about the motives of others in interpersonal situations (Hanley-Dunn et al., 1985, see also Jones et al., 1981), and to exhibit very little trust in other people, even their close peers (Rotenberg, 1994). Some have hypothesized that the lack of trust in others serves to rationalize the lonely person's failure to develop rewarding relationships with other people (W. Jones et al., 1981).

In one recent investigation, lonely subjects characterized a relationship with one of their friends and rated the quality of their communication with that friend more negatively than nonlonely participants (Duck, Pond, & Leatham, 1994). What is particularly intriguing about Duck et al.'s findings is that lonely students made negative global inferences about their relationships in the absence of any complaints about particular aspects of their conversations with a friend. It appears as if lonely people feel that "I don't like my friends, but I can't explain why."

Commensurate with their negative evaluations of others, lonely people also expect others to hold negative views toward them (Jones et al., 1981). This feeling, along with their generally negative view of others, may partially explain why lonely people send a message of detachment and noninvolvement during social interactions with others. If one holds a negative view toward others, and expects others to hold a negative toward the self, it stands to reason that such a person would be avoidant, detached, and somewhat withdrawn in social interactions.

It is unfortunately the case that lonely people are trapped in an emotional and cognitive conundrum: They want more intimacy and meaningful relationships, while simultaneously holding negative views of others, and expecting others to do the same. In conversation, they behave in such a way, perhaps as a result of deficient social skills, to virtually ensure a negative outcome.

As Spitzberg and Canary (1985) aptly noted, loneliness and social skills deficits evidently have a reciprocal relationship. The prolonged avoidance of social interaction that could be expected as a result of the lonely person's social anxiety and negative view toward others could lead to an atrophy of social skills. The consequent deficits in social skills will make it all the more difficult to initiate and maintain satisfying interpersonal relationships, therefore exacerbating the feelings of loneliness.

Summary

It is perhaps tautological to assess the personal relationships of lonely people as lacking in intimacy, dissatisfying, and at times, few in number. What may be less obvious, however, is the generally ineffective and occasionally negative impact of family relationships on loneliness. People who are too close with family members, particularly parents, appear to be at heightened risk for loneliness.

As with depression, one must regard poor social skills as a strong contributor to the unfortunate state of the lonely person's interpersonal relationships. Lonely people often exhibit poor communicative skills that are most likely reciprocally related to the experience of loneliness. Problems associated with these disrupted social skills are no doubt exacerbated by the lonely person's general distrust and dim view of others.

THE RELATIONSHIP BETWEEN DEPRESSION AND LONELINESS

It is difficult to overlook similarities in the interpersonal communication and relational problems of depressed and lonely people. Both show strong evidence of social-skills deficits. Both have difficulties establishing and maintaining rewarding and intimate relationships with other people. It should therefore come as to no surprise that there is an exceptionally high rate of comorbidity between these two problems (e.g., Brage et al., 1993; Rich & Scovel, 1987; Weeks, Michela, Peplau, & Bragg, 1980). Correlations between depression and loneliness typically fall in the $r = .40–.60$ range (Brage et al., 1993; Moore & Schultz, 1983; Rich & Bonner, 1987) with some studies indicating a relationship closer to $r = .70$ (e.g., Moore & Schultz, 1983).

Why is it that these two pervasive problems should coexist with such regularity? Some observers might conclude that depression and loneliness are manifestations of the same phenomenon, somewhat akin to generalized emotional distress. In an effort to explore this possibility, Jackson and Cochran (1991) examined the correlation between depression and loneliness while partialing out the effect for general psychological distress. Although this correlation ($r = .23$) was considerably lower than the zero-order correlation between depression and loneliness ($r = .54$), it was still statistically significant. Thus these two problems are not simply manifestations of the same generalized phenomenon.

Without doubt, depression and loneliness reside in the same nomological network, yet they remain theoretically and conceptually distinct phenomena. One compelling attempt to explain their empirical relationship involved an appeal to a social role theory that states that "an interpersonal deficit . . . will impact on a wider variety of personal, social, and adjustment states to the extent that there is a heightened dependency on the social environment" (Schultz & Moore, 1988, p. 277). According to these authors, among persons who are dependent on their social environment, an interpersonal problem such as a social-skills deficit would have an impact on a number of different adjustment states such as loneliness, depression, anxiety, self-esteem, and so on. Like the ripples generated by a rock thrown into a pond, an interpersonal deficit will impact a number of different variables in the nomological network of "adjustment/distress." It should be pointed out that these authors hypothesized that adolescents would be very dependent on their social environments, and accordingly found a stronger correlation between loneliness and depression among adolescents versus either college students or elderly individuals (Schultz & Moore, 1988).

A number of methodologically and statistically sophisticated studies have been undertaken to explore the precise nature of the relationship between depression and loneliness. At least two studies, one a path analysis, and one a cross-lagged panel correlation analysis, indicate that loneliness is a causal factor in depression (Brage & Meredith, 1994; Rich & Scovel, 1987). However, in their structural equation analysis Weeks et al. (1980) found no such causal relation between the two variables. In this study cross factor paths for depression and loneliness were ruled out indicating that neither caused the other. Although the results of this investigation are difficult to reconcile with those of the studies previously mentioned, this investigation established that depression and loneliness could be empirically distinguished. Ultimately, Weeks et al. (1980) concluded that depression and loneliness may share a common causal origin.

As a clinical phenomenon, depression is a heterogeneous family of disorders. One could argue plausibly that it is patently inadvisable to search for *the* single cause of the condition. Similarly, loneliness is a complex state that involves both emotional and social components (Vaux, 1988), and is similarly ill suited to a monolithic hypothesis of etiology. Having said that, both depression and loneliness have clear links to problems with interpersonal communication and relationships. Such problems when sufficiently severe and chronic, surely have the potential to precipitate episodes of either state. However, interpersonal communication problems are clearly not the cause of *all* cases of depression or loneliness.

A number of longitudinal studies are currently underway at our lab to explore the hypothesis that social-skills deficits are a distal, rather than proximal, contributory cause of various psychosocial problems such as depression and loneliness (e.g., Segrin, 1996, 1997). In these studies, social skills are conceptualized as a vulnerability factor that interacts with other variables such as negative life events to predict the development of depression and loneliness. This approach assumes that those who exhibit problematic social skills will experience difficulty in establishing and maintaining rewarding interpersonal interactions and relationships. Unfortunately, it is these interactions and relationships that allow people to marshall the social support that can buffer against the ill effects of stress. The person with inadequate communication competencies who is often consequently lacking in such protective social relationships is therefore predicted to be particularly vulnerable to the experience of depression, loneliness, and social anxiety when faced with stressors, particularly those that are social in nature. This "social skills deficit as vulnerability" approach is consistent with Weeks et al.'s (1980) suggestion that depression and loneliness covary due to a common causal origin. It should be stressed that problematic interpersonal communication is therefore hypothesized to be a key ingredient in the empirical relationship between depression and loneliness.

CONCLUSION

Depression and loneliness are two emotional problems on which we are remarkably well informed by studies on interpersonal communication and relationships. Each are interpersonal problems as much as they are psychological problems. The allure of these emotions to future communication researchers may lie in the possibility of discovering specific causal antecedents through basic communication research, that will not only enhance our understanding of these problems, but contribute to their effective treatment and/or prevention.

REFERENCES

American Psychiatric Association. (1994). *Diagnostic and statistical manual of mental disorders* (4th ed.). Washington, D.C.: American Psychiatric Association.

Amstutz, D. K., & Kaplan, M. F. (1987). Depression, physical attractiveness, and interpersonal acceptance. *Journal of Social and Clinical Psychology, 5,* 365–377.

Andersen, P. A., & Bowman, L. L. (1990). Positions of power: Nonverbal behavior in organizational communication. In J. A. DeVito & M. L. Hecht (Eds.), *The nonverbal communication reader* (pp. 391–411). Prospect Heights, IL: Waveland Press.

Andersson, L., Mullins, L. C., & Johnson, D. P. (1990). Parental intrusion versus social isolation: A dichotomous view of the sources of loneliness. In M. Hojat & R. Crandall (Eds.), *Loneliness: Theory, research, and applications* (pp. 125–134). Newbury Park, CA: Sage.

Angst, J. (1992). Epidemiology of depression. *Psychopharmacology, 106,* S71–S74.

Basco, M. R., Prager, K. J., Pite, J. M., Tamir, L. M., & Stephens, J. J. (1992). Communication and intimacy in the marriages of depressed patients. *Journal of Family Psychology, 6,* 184–194.

Beach, S. R. H., Jouriles, E. N., & O'Leary, K. D. (1985). Extramarital sex: Impact on depression and commitment in couples seeking marital therapy. *Journal of Sex and Marital Therapy, 11,* 99–108.

Beach, S. R. H., & O'Leary, K. D. (1993). Marital discord and dysphoria: For whom does the marital relationship predict depressive symptomatology? *Journal of Social and Personal Relationships, 10,* 405–420.

Beach, S. R. H., Sandeen, E. E., & O'Leary, K. D. (1990). *Depression and marriage.* New York: Guilford.

Bell, R. A. (1985). Conversational involvement and loneliness. *Communication Monographs, 52,* 218–235.

Bell, R. A., Roloff, M. E., Van Camp, K., & Karol, S. H. (1990). Is it lonely at the top? Career success and personal relationships. *Journal of Communication, 40,* 9–23.

Bellack, A. S. (1979). Behavioral assessment of social skills. In A. S. Bellack & M. Hersen (Eds.), *Research and practice in social skills training* (pp. 75–104). New York: Plenum.

Belsher, G., & Costello, C. G. (1991). Do confidants of depressed woman provide less social support than confidants of nondepressed women? *Journal of Abnormal Psychology, 100,* 516–525.

Berenbaum, H. (1992). Posed facial expressions of emotion in schizophrenia and depression. *Psychological Medicine, 22,* 927–937.

Biglan, A., Hops, H., Sherman, L., Friedman, L. S., Arthur, J., & Osteen, V. (1985). Problem-solving interactions of depressed women and their husbands. *Behavior Therapy, 16,* 431–451.

Blazer, D. G., Kessler, R. C., McGonagle, K. A., & Swartz, M. S. (1994). The prevalence and distribution of major depression in a national communication sample: The National Comorbidity Survey. *American Journal of Psychiatry, 151,* 979–986.

Blumberg, S. R., & Hokanson, J. E. (1983). The effects of another person's response style on interpersonal behavior in depression. *Journal of Abnormal Psychology, 92,* 196–209.

Brage, D., & Meredith, W. (1994). A causal model of adolescent depression. *The Journal of Psychology 128,* 455–468.

Brage, D., Meredith, W., & Woodward, J. (1993). Correlates of loneliness among Midwestern adolescents. *Adolescence, 28,* 685–693.

Brewin, C. R., Burnham, A., & Howes, M. (1989). Demographic and psychological determinants of homesickness and confiding among students. *British Journal of Psychology, 80,* 467–477.

Breznitz, Z., & Sherman, T. (1987). Speech patterning of natural discourse of well and depressed mothers and their young children. *Child Development, 58,* 395–400.

Brown, G. W., & Harris, T. (1978). *Social origins of depression.* New York: Free Press.

Buhrmester, D., Furman, W., Wittenberg, M. T., & Reis, H. T. (1988). Five domains of interpersonal competence in peer relationships. *Journal of Personality and Social Psychology, 55,* 991–1008.

Bullock, R. C., Siegel, R., Weissman, M., & Paykel, E. S. (1972). The weeping wife: Marital relations of depressed women. *Journal of Marriage and the Family, 34,* 488–495.

Burns, D. D., Sayers, S. L., & Moras, K. (1994). Intimate relationships and depression: Is there a causal connection? *Journal of Consulting and Clinical Psychology, 62,* 1033–1043.

Cherulnik, P. D. Neely, W. T., Flanagan, M., & Zachau, M. (1978). Social skill and visual interaction. *The Journal of Social Psychology, 104,* 263–270.

Cohn, J. R., Campbell, S. B., Matias, R., & Hopkins, J. (1990). Face-to-face interactions of postpartum depressed and nondepressed mother–infant pairs at 2 months. *Development Psychology, 26,* 15–23.

Cole, D. A., Lazarick, D. L., & Howard, G. S. (1987). Construct validity and the relation between depression and social skill. *Journal of Counseling Psychology, 34,* 315–321.

Connolly, J., Geller, S., Marton, P., & Kutcher, S. (1992). Peer responses to social interaction with depressed adolescents. *Journal of Clinical Child Psychiatry, 21,* 365–370.

Costello, C. G. (1982). Social factors associated with depression: A retrospective community study. *Psychological Medicine, 12,* 329–339.

Coyne, J. C. (1976a). Toward an interactional description of depression. *Psychiatry, 39,* 28–40.

Coyne, J. C. (1976b). Depression and the response of others. *Journal of Abnormal Psychology, 85,* 186–193.

Coyne, J. C. (1990). Interpersonal processes in depression. In G. I. Keitner (Ed.), *Depression and families* (pp. 31–54). Washington, D.C.: American Psychiatric Press.

Coyne, J. C., Burchill, S. A. L., & Stiles, W. B. (1990). An interactional perspective on depression. In C. R. Snyder & D. R. Forsyth (Eds.), *Handbook of social and clinical psychology* (pp. 327–349). New York: Pergamon Press.

Coyne, J. C., & DeLongis, A. (1986). Going beyond social support: The role of social relationships in adaptation. *Journal of Consulting and Clinical Psychology, 54,* 454–460.

Coyne, J. C., Kahn, J., & Gotlib, I. H. (1987). Depression. In T. Jacob (Ed.), *Family interaction and psychopathology* (pp. 509–533). New York: Plenum.

Coyne, J. C., Kessler, R. C., Tal, M., Turnbull, J., Wortman, C. B., & Greden, J. F. (1987). Living with a depressed person. *Journal of Consulting and Clinical Psychology, 55,* 347–352.

Coyne, J. C., & Whiffen, V. E. (1995). Issues in personality as diathesis for depression: The case of sociotropy/dependency and autonomy/self-criticism. *Psychological Bulletin, 118,* 358–378.

Dalley, M. B., Bolocofsky, D. N., & Karlin, N. J. (1994). Teacher-ratings and self-ratings of social competency in adolescents with low- and high-depressive symptoms. *Journal of Abnormal Child Psychology, 22,* 477–485.

Darby, J. K., Simmons, N., & Berger, P. A. (1984). Speech and voice parameters of depression: A pilot study. *Journal of Communication Disorders, 17,* 75–85.

Dillard, J. P., & Spitzberg, B. H. (1984). Global impressions of social skills: Behavioral predictors. In R. N. Bostrom (Ed.), *Communication yearbook* (Vol. 8, pp. 446–463). Beverly Hills: Sage.

Dittmann, A. T. (1987). Body movements as diagnostic cues in affective disorders. In J. D. Maser (Ed.), *Depression and expressive behavior* (pp. 17–36). Hillsdale, NJ: Lawrence Erlbaum.

Dow, M. G., & Craighead, W. E. (1987). Social inadequacy and depression: Overt behavior and self-evaluation processes. *Journal of Social and Clinical Psychology, 5,* 99–113.

Downey, G., & Coyne, J. C. (1990). Children of depressed parents: An integrative review. *Psychological Bulletin, 108,* 50–76.

Duck, S., Pond, K., & Leatham. G. (1994). Loneliness and the evaluation of relational events. *Journal of Social and Personal Relationships, 11,* 253–276.

Dykman, B. M., Horowitz, L. M., Abramson, L. Y., & Usher, M. (1991). Schematic and situational determinants of depressed and nondepressed students' interpretation of feedback. *Journal of Abnormal Psychology, 100,* 45–55.

Edison, J. D., & Adams, H. E. (1992). Depression, self-focus, and social interaction. *Journal of Psychopathology and Behavioral Assessment, 14,* 1–19.

Ekman, P., & Friesen, W. V. (1972). Hand movements. *Journal of Communication, 22,* 353–374.

Ekman, P., & Friesen, W. V. (1974). Nonverbal behavior and psychopathology. In R. J. Friedman & M. M. Mintz (Eds.), *The psychology of depression* (pp. 203–224). Washington, D.C.: V. H. Winston.

Ellgring, H. (1989). *Nonverbal communication in depression.* Cambridge: Cambridge University Press.

Ellgring, H., Wagner, H., & Clarke, A. H. (1980). Psychopathological states and their effects on speech and gaze behavior. In H. Giles, W. P. Robinson, & P. M. Smith (Eds.), *Language: Social psychological perspectives* (pp. 267–273). Oxford, U.K.: Pergamon.

Elliot, T. R., MacNair, R. R., Herrick, S. M., Yoder, B., & Byrne, C. A. (1991). Interpersonal reactions to depression and physical disability in dyadic interactions. *Journal of Applied Social Psychology, 21,* 1293–1302.

Exline, R. V., Ellyson, S. L., & Long, B. (1975). Visual behavior as an aspect of power role relationships. In P. Pliner, L. Krames, & T. Alloway (Eds.), *Nonverbal communication of aggression* (Vol. 2, pp. 21–52). New York: Plenum.

Field, T. (1984). Early interactions between infants and their post-partum depressed mothers. *Infant Behavior and Development, 7,* 517–522.

Fiske, V., & Peterson, C. (1991). Love and depression: The nature of depressive romantic relationships. *Journal of Social and Clinical Psychology, 10,* 75–90.

Flint, A. J., Black, S. E., Campbell-Taylor, I., Gailey, G. F., & Levinton, C. (1993). Abnormal speech articulation, psychomotor retardation, and subcortical dysfunction in major depression. *Journal of Psychiatric Research, 27,* 309–319.

Florin, I., Nostadt, A., Reck, C., Franzen, U., & Jenkins, M. (1992). Expressed emotion in depressed patients and their partners. *Family Process, 31*, 163–172.

Forehand, R., & Smith, K. A. (1986). Who depressed whom? A look at the relationship of adolescent mood to maternal and paternal depression. *Child Study Journal, 16*, 19–23.

Fossi, L., Faravelli, C., & Paoli, M. (1984). The ethological approach to the assessment of depressive disorders. *Journal of Nervous and Mental Disease, 172*, 332–341.

Gaebel, W., & Wolwer, W. (1992). Facial expression and emotional face recognition in schizophrenia and depression. *European Archives of Psychiatry and Clinical Neuroscience, 242*, 46–52.

Ganchrow, J. R., Steiner, J. E., Kleiner, M., & Edelstein, E. L. (1978). A multidisciplinary approach to the expression of pain in psychotic depression. *Perceptual and Motor Skills, 47*, 379–390.

Gelfand, D. M., & Teti, D. M. (1990). The effects of maternal depression on children. *Clinical Psychology Review, 10*, 329–353.

Gerson, A. C., & Perlman, D. (1979). Loneliness and expressive communication. *Journal of Abnormal Psychology, 88*, 258–261.

Gibbons, F. X. (1987). Mild depression and self-disclosure intimacy: Self and others' perceptions. *Cognitive Therapy and Research, 11*, 361–380.

Gotlib, I. H. (1982). Self-reinforcement and depression in interpersonal interacation: The role of performance level. *Journal of Abnormal Psychology 91*, 3–13.

Gotlib, I. H., & Beatty, M. E. (1985). Negative responses to depression: The role of attributional style. *Cognitive Therapy and Research, 9*, 91–103.

Gotlib, I. H., & Lee, C. M. (1989). The social functioning of depressed patients: A longitudinal assessment. *Journal of Social and Clinical Psychology, 8*, 223–237.

Gotlib, I. H., & Meltzer, S. J. (1987). Depression and the perception of social skills in dyadic interaction. *Cognitive Therapy and Research, 11*, 41–54.

Gotlib, I. H., Mount, J. H., Cordy, N. I., & Whiffen, V. E. (1988). Depression and perceptions of early parenting: A longitudinal investigation. *British Journal of Psychiatry, 152*, 24–27.

Gotlib, I. H., & Robinson, L. A. (1982). Responses to depressed individuals: discrepancies between self-report and observer-rated behavior. *Journal of Abnormal Psychology 91*, 231–240.

Gotlib, I. H., & Whiffen, V. E. (1989). Depression and marital functioning: An examination of specificity and gender differences. *Journal of Abnormal Psychology, 98*, 23–30.

Greden, J. R., Albala, A. A., Smokler, I. A., Gardner, R., & Caroll, B. J. (1981). Speech pause time: A marker of psychomotor retardation in endogenous depression. *Biological Psychiatry, 16*, 851–859.

Greden, J. F., Genero, N., Price, L., Feinberg, S., & Levine, S. (1986). Facial electromyography in depression. *Archives of General Psychiatry, 43*, 269–274.

Gurtman, M. B. (1987). Depressive affect and disclosures as factors in interpersonal rejection. *Cognitive Therapy and Research, 11*, 87–100.

Hamid, P. N. (1989). Contact and intimacy patterns of lonely students. *New Zealand Journal of Psychology, 18*, 84–86.

Hamilton, E. B., Jones, M., & Hammen, C. (1993). Maternal interaction style in affective disordered, physically ill, and normal women. *Family Process, 32*, 329–340.

Hammen, C. L., Gordon, D., Burge, D., Adrian, C., Janicke, C., & Hiroto, D. (1987). Communication patterns of mothers with affective disorders and their relationship to children's status and social functioning. In K. Hahlweg & M. J. Goldstein (Eds.), *Understanding major mental disorder* (pp. 103–119). New York: Family Process Press.

Hammen, C. L., & Peters, S. D. (1977). Differential responses to male and female depressive reactions. *Journal of Consulting and Clinical Psychology, 45*, 994–1001.

Hammen, C. L., & Peters, S. D. (1978). Interpersonal consequences of depression: Responses to men and women enacting a depressed role. *Journal of Abnormal Psychology, 87*, 322–332.

Hanley-Dunn, P., Maxwell, S. E., & Santos, J. R. (1985). Interpretation of interpersonal interactions: The influence of loneliness. *Personality and Social Psychology Bulletin, 11*, 445–456.

Hautzinger, M., Linden, M., & Hoffman, N. (1982). Distressed couples with and without a depressed partner: An analysis of their verbal interaction. *Journal of Behavior Therapy and Experimental Psychiatry, 13,* 307–314.

Henderson, A. S. (1991). Social support and depression. In H. O. F. Veiel & U. Baumann (Eds.), *The meaning and measurement of social supoprt* (pp. 85–92). New York: Hemisphere Publishing.

Henwood, P. G., & Solano, C. H. (1994). Loneliness in young children and their parents. *Journal of Genetic Psychology, 155,* 35–45.

Hinchliffe, M. K., Hooper, D., & Roberts, F. J. (1978). *The melancholy marriage.* New York: John Wiley & Sons.

Hinchliffe, M. K., Hooper, D., Roberts, F. J., & Vaughan, P. W. (1978). The melancholy marriage: An inquiry into the interaction of depressoin. IV. Disruptions. *British Journal of Medical Psychology, 51,* 15–24.

Hinchliffe, M. K., Lancashire, M., & Roberts, F. J. (1971a). Depression: Defense mechanisms in speech. *British Journal of Psychiatry, 118,* 471–472.

Hinchliffe, M. K., Lancashire, M., & Roberts, F. J. (1971b). A study of eye-contact changes in depressed and recovered psychiatric patients. *British Journal of Psychiatry, 119,* 213–215.

Hinchliffe, M. K., Vaughan, P. W., Hooper, D., & Roberts, F. J. (1978). The melancholy marriage: An inquiry into the interaction of depression. III. Responsiveness. *British Journal of Medical Psychology, 51,* 1–13.

Hokanson, J. E., & Butler, A. C. (1992). Cluster analysis of depressed college students' social behaviors. *Journal of Personality and Social Psychology, 62,* 273–280.

Hokanson, J. E., Hummer, J. T., & Butler, A. C. (1991). Interpersonal perceptions by depressed college students. *Cognitive Therapy and Research, 15,* 443–457.

Hooley, J. M., & Teasdale, J. D. (1989). Predictors of relapse in unipolar depressives: Expressed emotion, marital distress, and perceived criticism. *Journal of Abnormal Psychology, 98,* 229–235.

Hooper, D., Vaughan, P. W., Hinchliffe, M. K., & Roberts, J. (1978). The melancholy marriage: An inquiry into the interaction of depression. V. Power. *British Journal of Medical Psychology, 51,* 387–398.

Hops, H., Biglan, A., Sherman, L., Arthur, J., Friedman, L., & Osteen, V. (1987). Home observations of family interactions of depressed women. *Journal of Consulting and Clinical Psychology, 55,* 341–346.

Horowitz, L. M., & French, R. D. S. (1979). Interpersonal problems of people who describe themselves as lonely. *Journal of Consulting and Clinical Psychology, 47,* 762–764.

Inderitzen-Pisaruk, H., Clark, M. L., & Solano, C. H. (1992). Correlates of loneliness in midadolescence. *Journal of Youth and Adolescence, 21,* 151–167.

Jackson, J., & Cochran, S. D. (1991). Loneliness and psychological distress. *The Journal of Psychology, 125,* 257–262.

Jacobson, N. S., & Anderson, E. A. (1982). Interpersonal skill and depression in college students: An analysis of the timing of self-disclosures. *Behavior Therapy, 13,* 271–282.

Joiner, T. E., Alfano, M. S., & Metalsky, G. I. (1992). When depression breeds contempt: Reassurance-seeking, self-esteem, and rejection of depressed college students by their roommates. *Journal of Abnormal Psychology, 101,* 165–173.

Jones, I. H., & Pansa, M. (1979). Some nonverbal aspects of depression and schizophrenia occurring during the interview. *The Journal of Nervous and Mental Disease, 167,* 402–409.

Jones, W. H., Carpenter, B. N., & Quintana, D. (1985). Personality and interpersonal predictors of loneliness in two cultures. *Journal of Personality and Social Psychology, 48,* 1503–1511.

Jones, W. H., Freemon, J. E., & Goswick, R. A. (1981). The persistence of loneliness: Self and other determinants. *Journal of Personality, 49,* 27–48.

Jones, W. H., Hobbs, S. A., & Hockenbury, D. (1982). Loneliness and social skill deficits. *Journal of Personality and Social Psychology, 42,* 682–689.

Jones, W. H., & Moore, T. L. (1990). Loneliness and social support. In M. Hojat & R. Crandall (Eds.), *Loneliness: Theory, research, and applications* (pp. 145–156). Newbury Park, CA: Sage.

Jones, W. H., Sansone, C., & Heim, B. (1983). Loneliness and interpersonal judgements. *Personality and Social Psychology Bulletin, 9,* 437–441.

Joubert, C. E. (1986). Social interest, loneliness, and narcissism. *Psychological Reports, 58,* 870.

Jourard, S. M., & Lasakow, P. (1958). Some factors in self-disclosure. *Journal of Abnormal and Social Psychology, 56,* 91–97.

Kahn, J., Coyne, J. C., & Margolin, G. (1985). Depression and marital disagreement: The social construction of despair. *Journal of Social and Personal Relationships, 2,* 447–461.

Kazdin, A. E., Sherick, R. B., Esveldt-Dawson, K., & Rancurello, M. D. (1985). Nonverbal behavior and childhood depression. *Journal of the American Academy of Child Psychiatry, 24,* 303–309.

Kleinke, C. L. (1986). Gaze and eye contact: A research review. *Psychological Bulletin, 100,* 78–100.

Kuiper, N. A., & MacDonald, M. R. (1983). Schematic processing in depression: The self-based consensus bias. *Cognitive Therapy and Research, 7,* 469–484.

Kuiper, N. A., & McCabe, S. B. (1985). The appropriateness of social topics: Effects of depression and cognitive vulnerability on self and other judgments. *Cognitive Therapy and Research, 9,* 371–379.

Kuiper, N. A., Olinger, L. J., & Swallow, S. R. (1987). Dysfunctional attitudes, mild depression, views of self, self-consciousness, and social perceptions. *Motivation and Emotion, 11,* 379–401.

Kuny, S., & Stassen, H. H. (1993). Speaking behavior and voice sound characteristics in depressive patients during recovery. *Journal of Psychiatric Research, 27,* 289–307.

Lee, C. M., & Gotlib, I. H. (1991). Adjustment of children of depressed mothers: A 10-month follow-up. *Journal of Abnormal Psychology, 100,* 473–477.

Levin, S., Hall, J. A., Knight, R. A., & Alpert, M. (1985). Verbal and nonverbal expression of affect in speech of schizophrenic and depressed patients. *Journal of Abnormal Psychology, 94,* 487–497.

Lewinsohn, P. M. (1974). A behavioral approach to depression. In R. J. Friedman & M. M. Katz (Eds.), *The psychology of depression: Contemporary theory and research* (pp. 157–185). Washington DC: Winston-Wiley.

Lewinsohn, P. M. (1975). The behavioral study and treatment of depression. In M. Hersen, R. M. Eisler, & P. M. Miller (Eds.), *Progress in behavior modification: Vol 1* (pp. 19–64). New York: Academic Press.

Lewinsohn, P. M., Mischel, W., Chaplin, W., & Barton, R. (1980). Social competence and depression: The role of illlusory self-perceptions. *Journal of Abnormal Psychology, 89,* 203–212.

Lewinsohn, P. M., & Rosenbaum, M. (1987). Recall of parental behavior by acute depressives, remitted depressives, and nondepressives. *Journal of Personality and Social Psychology, 52,* 611–619.

Linden, M., Hautzinger, M., & Hoffman, N. (1983). Discriminant analysis of depressive interactions. *Behavior Modification, 7,* 403–422.

Lobdell, J., & Perlman, D. (1986). The intergenerational transmission of loneliness: A study of college freshmen and their parents. *Journal of Marriage and the Family, 48,* 589–595.

Marcus, D. K., & Davis, K. K. (1993). Depression and interpersonal rejection: The role of anticipated interaction. *The Journal of Social Psychology, 134,* 251–252.

Marks, T., & Hammen, C. L. (1982). Interpersonal mood induction: Situational and individual determinants. *Motivation and Emotion, 6,* 387–399.

McCabe, S. B., & Gotlib, I. H. (1993). Interactions of couples with and without a depressed spouse: Self-report and observations of problem-solving interactions. *Journal of Social and Personal Relationships, 10,* 589–599.

McCann, C. D. (1990). Social factors in depression: The role of interpersonal expectancies. In C. D. McCann & N. S. Endler, (Eds.), *Depression: New directions in theory, research, and practice* (pp. 27–47). Toronto: Wall & Emerson.

McNiel, D. E., Arkowitz, H. S., & Pritchard, B. E. (1987). The response of others to face-to-face interaction with depressed patients. *Journal of Abnormal Psychology, 96,* 341–344.

Medora, N., & Woodward, J. C. (1986). Loneliness among adolescent college students at a Midwestern university. *Adolescence, 82,* 391–402.

Meyer, E. B., & Hokanson, J. E. (1985). Situational influences on social behaviors of depression-prone individuals. *Journal of Clinical Psychology, 41,* 29–35.

Millbrook, J. M., Farrell, A. D. & Curran, J. P. (1986). Behavioral components of social skills: A look at subject and confederate behaviors. *Behavioral Assessment, 8,* 203–220.

Miller, R. E., Ranelli, C. J., & Levine, J. M. (1977). Nonverbal communication as an index of depression. In I. Hanin & E. Usdin (Eds.), *Animal models in psychiatry and neurology* (pp. 171–180). New York: Pergamon.

Moore, D. & Schultz, N. R. (1983). Loneliness at adolescence: Correlates, attributions, and coping. *Journal of Youth and Adolescence, 12,* 95–100.

Morrison, H. L. (Eds.). (1983). *Children of depressed parents: Risk, identification, and intervention.* New York: Grune & Gratton.

Natale, M. (1977a). Effects of induced elation-depression on speech in the initial interview. *Journal of Consulting and Clinical Psychology, 45,* 45–52.

Natale, M. (1977b). Induction of mood states and their effect on gaze behaviors. *Journal of Consulting and Clinical Psychology, 45,* 960.

Nelson, G. M., & Beach, S. R. H. (1990). Sequential interaction in depression: Effects of depressive behavior on spousal aggression. *Behavior Therapy, 21,* 167–182.

Nezlek, J. B., Imbrie, M., & Shean, G. D. (1994). Depression and everyday social interaction. *Journal of Personality and Social Psychology, 67,* 1101–1111.

Nilsonne, A. (1988). Speech characteristics as indicators of depressive illness. *Acta Psychiatrica Scandinavia, 77,* 253–263.

Notarius, C. I., & Herrick, L. R. (1988). Listener response strategies to a distressed other. *Journal of Social and Personal Relationships, 5,* 97–108.

Oliver, J. M., Handal, P. J., Finn, T., & Herdy, S. (1987). Depressed and nondepressed students and their siblings in frequent contact with their families: Depression and perceptions of the family. *Cognitive Therapy and Research, 11,* 501–515.

Patterson, B. R., & Bettini, L. A. (1993). Age, depression, and friendship: Development of a general friendship inventory. *Communication Research Reports, 10,* 161–170.

Pearl, T. Klopf, D. W., & Ishii, S. (1990). Loneliness among Japanese and American college students. *Psychological Reports, 67,* 49–50.

Peplau, L. A., & Perlman, D. (Eds.) (1982). *Loneliness: A sourcebook of current theory, research, and therapy.* New York: Wiley Interscience.

Peplau, L. A. Russell, D., & Heim, M. (1979). The experience of loneliness. In I. H. Frieze, D. Bar-Tal, & J. S. Caroll (Eds.), *New approaches to social problems* (pp. 53–78). San Francisco: Josey-Bass.

Peterson, L., Mullins, L. L., & Ridley-Johnson, R. (1985). Childhood depression: Peer reactions to depression and life stress. *Journal of Abnormal Child Psychology, 13,* 597–609.

Pope, B., Blass, T., Siegman, A. W., & Raher, J. (1970). Anxiety and depression in speech. *Journal of Consulting and Clinical Psychology, 35,* 128–133.

Ranelli, C. J., & Miller, R. E. (1981). Behavioral predictors of amitriptyline response in depression. *American Journal of Psychiatry, 138,* 30–34.

Revenson, T. A., & Johnson, J. L. (1984). Social and demographic correlates of loneliness in late life. *American Journal of Community Psychology, 12,* 71–85.

Rich, A. R., & Bonner, R. L. (1987). Interpersonal moderators of depression among college students. *Journal of College Student Personnel, 28,* 337–342.

Rich, A. R., & Scovel, M. (1987). Causes of depression in college students: A cross-lagged panel correlation analysis. *Psychological Reports, 60,* 27–30.

Riggio, R. E., Throckmorton, B., & DePaola, S. (1990). Social skills and self-esteem. *Personality and Individual Differences, 11,* 799–804.

Riggio, R. E., Watring, K. P., & Throckmorton, B. (1993). Social skills, social support, and psychosocial adjustment. *Personality and Individual Differences, 15,* 275–280.

Roscoe, B., & Skomski, G. G., (1989). Loneliness among late adolescents. *Adolescence, 96,* 947–955.

Rotenberg, K. J. (1994). Loneliness and interpersonal trust. *Journal of Social and Clinical Psychology, 13,* 152–173.

Rotenberg, K. J., & Hamel, J. (1988). Social interaction and depression in elderly individuals. *International Journal of Aging and Human Development, 27,* 305–318.

Rounsavile, B. J., Weissman, M. M., Prusoff, B. A., & Herceg-Baron, R. L. (1979). Marital disputes and treatment outcome in depressed women. *Comprehensive Psychiatry, 20,* 483–490.

Rubinow, D. R., & Post, R. M. (1992). Impaired recognition of affect in facial expression in depressed patients. *Biological Psychiatry, 31,* 947–953.

Rudolph, K. D., Hammen, C., & Burge, D. (1994). Interpersonal functioning and depressive symptoms in childhood: Addressing the issues of specificity and comorbidity. *Journal of Abnormal Child Psychology, 22,* 355–371.

Ruscher, S. M., & Gotlib, I. H. (1988). Marital interaction patterns of couples with and without a depressed partner. *Behavior Therapy, 19,* 455–470.

Rutter, D. R., & Stephenson, G. M. (1972). Visual interaction in a group of schizophrenic and depressive patients. *British Journal of Social and Clinical Psychology, 11,* 57–65.

Sacco, W. P., Milana, S. & Dunn, V. K. (1985). Effect of depression level and length of acquaintance on reactions of others to a request for help. *Journal of Personality and Social Psychology, 49,* 1728–1737.

Sacco, W. P., Milana, S., & Dunn, V. K. (1988). The effect of duration of depressive episode on the response of others. *Journal of Social and Clinical Psychology, 7,* 297–311.

Scherer, K. R. (1987). Vocal assessment of affective disorders. In J. D. Maser (Ed.), *Depression and expressive behavior* (pp. 57–82). Hillsdale, NJ: Lawrence Erlbaum.

Schmaling, K. B., & Jacobson, N. S. (1990). Marital interaction and depression. *Journal of Abnormal Psychology, 99,* 229–236.

Schultz, N. R., & Moore, D. (1988). Loneliness: Differences across three age levels. *Journal of Social and Personal Relationships, 5,* 275–284.

Schwartz, G. E., Fair, P. L., Mandel, M. R., Salt, P., Meiske, M., & Klerman, G. L. (1978). Facial electromyography in the assessment of improvement in depression. *Psychosomatic Medicine, 40,* 355–360.

Schwartz, G. E., Fair, P. L., Salt, P., Mandel, M. R., & Klerman, G. L. (1976a). Facial expression and imagery in depression: An electromyographic study. *Psychosomatic Medicine, 38,* 337–347.

Schwartz, G. E., Fair, P. L., Salt, P., Mandel, M. R., & Klerman, G. L. (1976b). Facial muscle patterning to affective imagery in depressed and nondepressed subjects. *Science, 192,* 489–491.

Segrin, C. (1990). A meta-analytic review of social skill deficits in depression. *Communication Monographs, 57,* 292–308.

Segrin, C. (1992). Specifying the nature of social skill deficits associated with depression. *Human Communication Research, 19,* 89–123.

Segrin, C. (1993a). Effects of dysphoria and loneliness on social perceptual skills. *Perceptual and Motor Skills, 77,* 1315–1329.

Segrin, C. (1993b). Interpersonal reactions to depression: The role of relationship with partner and perceptions of rejection. *Journal of Social and Personal Relationships, 10,* 83–97.

Segrin, C. (1993c). Social skills deficits and psychosocial problems: Antecedent, concomitant, or consequent? *Journal of Social and Clinical Psychology, 12,* 336–353.

Segrin, C. (1994). Social skills and psychosocial problems among the elderly. *Research on Aging, 16,* 301–321.

Segrin, C. (1996). The relationship between social skills deficits and psychosocial problems: A test of a vulnerability model. *Communication Research, 23,* 425–450.

Segrin, C. (1997). *Social skills, stressful life events, and the development of psychosocial problems.* Manuscript submitted for publication.

Segrin, C., & Abramson, L. Y. (1994). Negative reactions to depressive behaviors: A communication theories analysis. *Journal of Abnormal Psychology, 103,* 655–668.

Segrin, C., & Dillard, J. P. (1992). The interactional theory of depression: A meta-analysis of the research literature. *Journal of Social and Clinical Psychology, 11,* 43–70.

Segrin, C., & Dillard, J. P. (1993). The complex link between social skills and dysphoria: Conceptualization, perspective, and outcome. *Communication Research, 20,* 76–104.

Segrin, C., & Fitzpatrick M. A. (1992). Depression and verbal aggressiveness in different marital couple types. *Communication Studies, 43,* 79–91.

Segrin, C., & Kinney, T. (1995). Social skills deficits among the socially anxious: Loneliness and rejection from others. *Motivation and Emotion, 19,* 1–24.

Shapiro, J. P. (1988). Relationships between dimensions of depressive experience and evaluative beliefs about people in general. *Personality and Social Psychology Bulletin, 14,* 388–400.

Siegel, S. J., & Alloy, L. B. (1990). Interpersonal perceptions and consequences of depressive significant-other relationships: A naturalistic study of college roommates. *Journal of Abnormal Psychology, 99,* 361–373.

Siegman, A. W. (1987). The pacing of speech in depression. In J. D. Maser (Ed.), *Depression and expressive behavior* (pp. 83–102). Hillsdale, NJ: Erlbaum.

Sloan, W. W., & Solano, C. H. (1984). The conversational styles of lonely males with strangers and roommates. *Personality and Social Psychology Bulletin, 10,* 292–301.

Solano, C. H., Batten, P. G., & Parish, E. A. (1982). Loneliness and patterns of self-disclosure. *Journal of Personality and Social Psychology, 43,* 524–531.

Solano, C. H., & Koester, N. H. (1989). Loneliness and communication problems: Subjective anxiety or objective skills. *Personality and Social Psychology Bulletin, 15,* 126–133.

Spitzberg, B. H., & Canary, D. J. (1985). Loneliness and relationally competent communication. *Journal of Social and Personal Relationships, 2,* 387–402.

Spitzberg, B. H., & Cupach, W. R. (1985). Conversational skill and locus of perception. *Journal of Psychopathology and Behavioral Assessment, 7,* 207–220.

Spitzberg, B. H., & Hurt, T. (1989). The relationship of interpersonal competence and skills to reported loneliness across time. In M. Hojat & R. Crandall (Eds.), *Loneliness: Theory, research, and applications* (pp. 157–172). Newbury Park: CA: Sage.

Talavera, J. A. Saiz-Ruiz, J., & Garcia-Toro, M. (1994). Quantitative measurement of depression through speech analysis. *European Psychiatry, 9,* 185–193.

Teasdale, J. D., & Bancroft, J. (1977). Manipulation of thought content as a determinant of mood and corrugator electromyographic activity in depressed patients. *Journal of Abnormal Psychology, 86,* 235–241.

Thomas, A. M., & Forehand, R. (1991). The relationship between parental depressive mood and early adolescent parenting. *Journal of Family Psychology, 4,* 260–271.

Thompson, J. M., Whiffen, V. E., & Blain, M. D. (1995). Depressive symptoms, sex, and perceptions of intimate relationships. *Journal of Social and Personal Relationships, 12,* 49–66.

Tolkmitt, F., Helfrich, H., Standke, R., & Scherer, K. R. (1982). Vocal indicators of psychiatric treatment effects in depressives and schizophrenics. *Journal of Communicative Disorders, 15,* 209–222.

Vanger, P. (1987). An assessment of social skill deficiencies in depression. *Comprehensive Psychiatry, 28,* 508–512.

Vanger, P., Summerfield, A. B., Rosen, B. K., & Watson, J. P. (1991). Cultural differences in interpersonal responses to depressives' nonverbal behavior. *The International Journal of Social Psychiatry, 37,* 151–158.

Vanger, P., Summerfield, A. B., Rosen, B. K., & Watson, J. P. (1992). Effects of communication content on speech behavior of depressives. *Comprehensive Psychiatry, 33,* 39–41.

Vaux, A. (1988). Social and emotional loneliness: The role of social and personal characteristics. *Personality and Social Psychology Bulletin, 14,* 722–734.

Vincenzi, H., & Grabosky, F. (1990). Measuring the emotional/social aspects of loneliness and isolation. In M. Hojat & R. Crandall (Eds.), *Loneliness: Theory, research, and applications* (pp. 257–270). Newbury Park, CA: Sage.

Warner, V., Weissman, M. M., Fendrich, M., Wickramaratne, P., & Moreau, D. (1992). The course of major depression in the offspring of depressed parents: Incidence, recurrence, and recovery. *Archives of General Psychiatry, 49,* 795–801.

Waxer, P. (1974). Nonverbal cues for depression. *Journal of Abnormal Psychology, 83,* 319–322.

Weeks, D. G., Michela, J. L., Peplau, L. A., & Bragg, M. E. (1980). Relation between loneliness and depression: A structural equation analysis. *Journal of Personality and Social Psychology, 39,* 1238–1244.

Weintraub, W., & Aronson, H. (1967). The application of verbal behavior analysis to the study of psychopathological defense mechanisms. IV: Speech pattern associated with depressive behavior. *The Journal of Nervous and Mental Disease, 144,* 22–28.

Weissman, M. M. & Klerman, G. L. (1973). Psychotherapy with depressed women: An empirical study of content themes and reflection. *British Journal of Psychiatry, 123,* 55–61.

Whiffen, V. E., & Gotlib, I. H. (1989). Infants of postpartum depressed mothers: Temperament and cognitive status. *Journal of Abnormal Psychology, 98,* 274–279.

Williams, J. G., Barlow, D. H., & Agras, W. S. (1972). Behavioral measurement of severe depression. *Archives of General Psychiatry, 27,* 330–333.

Wittenberg, M. T., & Reis, H. T. (1986). Loneliness, social skills, and social perception. *Personality and Social Psychology Bulletin, 12,* 121–130.

Youngren, M. A., & Lewinsohn, P. M. (1980). The functional relation between depression and problematic interpersonal behavior. *Journal of Abnormal Psychology, 89,* 333–341.

PART III

The "Bright Side" of Emotions

How the Comforting Process Works: Alleviating Emotional Distress through Conversationally Induced Reappraisals

Brant R. Burleson

Purdue University
West Lafayette, Indiana

Daena J. Goldsmith

University of Illinois
Urbana, Illinois

What becomes of the brokenhearted,
Who had love that's now departed?
I know I've got to find
Some kind of peace of mind.
Help me, please.

—James Dean, Paul Riser, and William Weatherspoon

In the course of our daily lives, we all experience fear, disappointment, anger, sadness, and other negative emotional states, and many of us turn to friends and loved ones for comfort. There is growing evidence that for everyday hurts and hassles, the informal communicative assistance we receive from our network of personal relationships can be effective at helping us overcome various forms of distress (for reviews see Albrecht & Adelman, 1987; Albrecht, Burleson, & Goldsmith, 1994; Burleson, Albrecht, & Sarason, 1994). However, our networks do not always come through: Sometimes people with good intentions say harmful things, sometimes those close to us are unwilling or unable to provide comfort, and sometimes people just don't know what to say to make us feel better (for reviews see Albrecht et al., 1994; Dunkel-Schetter, Blasband, Feinstein, & Herbert, 1992). Consequently, considerable effort has been devoted to identifying features of effective comforting strategies—messages that generally do a good job of helping people overcome emotional distress and feel better about themselves, their lives, and their circumstances (for reviews see Burleson, 1994a,b; Goldsmith, 1994).

There is now a substantial body of research on what features of messages are effective and ineffective at comforting; however, these findings do not do much to help us understand *why* some messages are more effective than others. Until recently, we have had little understanding of how comforting messages work; we lacked knowledge of the underlying mechanisms through which messages bring about (or fail to bring about) changes in the emotions of their targets. Developing a better grasp of these mechanisms would have obvious theoretical and practical value. Understanding why some messages are effective at altering negative emotional states should contribute to our knowledge of both how messages have effects and how the emotions work. And understanding how certain message forms reduce distress would have obvious practical value for all those who provide emotional support, both professionally and informally—and that is all of us.

Although existing literature provides little theoretical understanding of the mechanisms through which comforting messages bring about emotional change, a great deal has been learned about human emotion in the last 30 years, particularly about the circumstances resulting in specific emotions and some general conditions of emotional change. A review of emotion theory, coupled with a consideration of messages that comfort effectively, has the potential to shed considerable light on mechanisms through which comforting messages bring about affective change.

This chapter provides an overview and integration of what we know about human emotion and features of effective comforting messages in order to suggest how the two are linked. The first section of the chapter summarizes the results of several streams of research examining the features of more and less effective comforting messages. Next, we provide an extended discussion of *appraisal theories* of emotion, focusing particularly on how affective distress is conceptualized by appraisal theories. We then present a reformulation of the comforting process from the perspective of appraisal theory, specifying how supportive conversations can assist distressed persons in coping with their emotions. Finally, we describe how a variety of conversational behaviors and message strategies can help accomplish critical functions in constituting and conducting effective supportive interactions, detailing some of the mechanisms through which these behaviors and strategies may work. We conclude the chapter by elaborating some implications of our analysis for future empirical work examining the comforting process.

EFFECTIVE FORMS OF COMFORTING

Definitions and Distinctions

We view "comforting" as encompassing communicative attempts to alleviate the emotional distress of another. "Communicative attempts" include both verbal and nonverbal forms of behavior that are conventionally recognized as intended to bring about a lessening of emotional distress. Our view of comforting encompasses both successful and unsuccessful attempts at alleviating distress, where "alleviation" includes both attempting to help another work through emotions and attempting to change another's emotional state. This notion of comforting is broader than the commonsense or everyday notion of comfort as sympathizing and agreeing with a distressed other's emotional reaction: We also include in our conception those behaviors that attempt to alleviate negative feelings by denying emotions, challenging inappropriate emotional reactions, or encouraging the other to elaborate and express negative emotions.

For us, comforting behaviors are a subset of "social support" behaviors (see also Barbee, Lawrence, & Cunningham, Chapter 10, this volume). Comforting focuses specifically on dealing with emotional distress, whereas "social support" may encompass a range of ways in which (and mechanisms through which) individuals benefit from involvement in caring relationships. Comforting also differs from psychotherapy, not only because we are concerned primarily with the behaviors of laypersons interacting with each other (rather than therapists interacting with their clients), but also because we focus on responses to relatively short-term, transient emotional upsets rather than enduring and deep-seated emotional pathologies (e.g., paranoia, phobias, depression).

Research on Effective Comforting Behaviors: Findings and Problems

Many research programs have addressed the question of what features of messages are more effective at providing comfort and emotional support. Yet each of these programs exhibits significant limitations, and none provides a full account of how and why specific message forms bring about affective change. Burleson (1994a), Dunkel-Schetter et al. (1992), and Goldsmith (1994) have recently reviewed several bodies of research that inform our understanding of effective comforting messages. In what follows, we draw from these reviews, focusing on the conclusions about effective comforting that can be deduced from the research and identifying some significant lacunae in our current knowledge.

Comparisons of Support Types

One large body of research has aimed to determine which behaviors distressed recipients perceive as most "helpful" by comparing the reported effects of different types of social support (e.g., emotional support, informational support, tangible support, companionship). Some of these studies have proceeded inductively, asking people who have experienced stressful life events (e.g., cancer, heart disease, incest) to respond to open-ended questions about the behaviors of others in these circumstances. Taxonomies of both helpful and unhelpful behaviors have then been developed from these retrospective self-reports (for reviews, see Dunkel-Schetter et al., 1992; Goldsmith, 1992). Other studies have utilized a preexisting taxonomy of support types (e.g., emotional support, problem-solving support) and have tested predictions about the types of support perceived as most helpful by different respondents under different conditions. This approach is utilized in several ongoing research programs, including research on the optimal matching model (e.g., Cutrona & Suhr, 1992, 1994), sensitive interaction systems theory (e.g., Barbee & Cunningham, 1995), and a series of experimental studies by Winstead and colleagues (e.g., Winstead, Derlega, Lewis, Sanchez-Hucles, & Clarke, 1992).

Studies comparing the effects of different forms of support are most useful for what they tell us about the *topical focus* of effective comforting messages: Should a provider talk about the distressed other's immediate emotional reaction, the nature of the problem that is the source of the other's distress, or possible solutions to the problem? Is it helpful to discuss one's own similar experiences? Should the distressed other be distracted from negative feelings, encouraged to cheer up, or assisted in ventilating negative feelings?

Not surprisingly, the helpfulness of different topical foci varies with the type of problem (Cutrona & Russell, 1990), the relationship between support provider and recipient (Dakof & Taylor, 1990; Metts, Geist, & Gray, 1994), and the timing of the response, both within a conversation (Pearlin & McCall, 1990) and over the course of a person's coping with a problem (Jacobsen, 1986). However, there is evidence that, across a wide variety of situations, focusing on the feelings of the distressed other is consistently evaluated as helpful. Some studies do find that information or advice about solutions to a problem can be beneficial under some circumstances, but responses characterized as "emotional support" or "empathic response" appear to have the greatest likelihood of helping (Cramer, 1990; Cutrona, Cohen, & Igram, 1990; Cutrona & Suhr, 1992; Dunkel-Schetter et al., 1992). Similarly, allowing talk about feelings is typically more comforting than denying or minimizing the other's experience, or than providing information about one's own experiences (Barbee & Cunningham, 1995; Barbee, Lawrence, & Cunningham, Chapter 10, this volume; Dunkel-Schetter et al., 1992), although some studies suggest distraction may be perceived as helpful when one is anticipating a short, stressful experience such as giving a public speech (e.g., Costanza, Derlega, & Winstead, 1988; Winstead & Derlega, 1991; Winstead et al., 1992). The utility of distraction, problem-solving attempts, or social comparison information is highly dependent on the quality of the message, its placement in a conversation, and the appropriateness of the information in a particular situation; in contrast, talk about feelings is more generally and consistently perceived as helpful.

There are, however, several constraints on using these findings to infer what features of messages are most effective at comforting. First, the outcomes these studies measure typically are not specific to the alleviation of emotional distress. The most frequently used outcome measure is a rating of "helpfulness." Messages might be helpful in a number of ways other than or in addition to their particular effect on emotional distress. Studies that have employed multiple specific outcome measures find different aspects of support associated with different outcomes. For example, Winstead and colleagues (1992) found talk about feelings was related to less fear of public speaking but was not related to recipients' self-reports of "supportiveness."

Second, these studies employ broad categories of social support (e.g., tangible, emotional, informational) that do not capture particular behaviors and message features. Even the inductively derived taxonomies of helpful and unhelpful behaviors include such global categories as "being there" or "shows concern." It is unclear what messages and behaviors produced these interpretations or how helpful messages that "show concern" are different from unhelpful messages that are "overly concerned" or "show too little concern" (Burleson, 1994b; Goldsmith, 1994, 1995). Unfortunately, many of the studies obtaining actual support messages have reduced this rich source of data to simple, global categories such as "problem-solving" versus "emotion-focused," and have then correlated frequencies in these categories with perceived helpfulness or interaction satisfaction. This research approach suggests that the topic of a message translates unproblematically into coping behavior by the other—if I express empathy with your emotion, this presumably induces you to engage in more effective emotion-focused coping. The possibility that information about the problem might also have implications for emotion, or that some statements about feelings might hinder emotional coping, is not considered. This approach fails to examine how it is that a message influences a recipient, and further fails to recognize variability in quality among messages having a similar topical focus.

Therapist Response Modes

Another body of research has focused on the outcomes for distressed individuals of different therapist behaviors (for reviews see Elliott et al., 1982; Hill et al., 1988; Truax & Carkhuff, 1967). Research on therapist response modes provides detailed codings of specific acts and intentions of therapists and often measures the immediate impacts of acts in a counseling session as well as the overall effect of an entire session on client progress. Although we see the job of comforting as different in important respects from the job of therapy, this literature offers several insights into how a provider's orientation to a topic may be related to the helpfulness of a message.

Whether a provider focuses on emotions, or even on some other topic (e.g., the problem itself), there are more and less effective ways of doing so. Elliott and colleagues (1982) cautioned that several response modes are associated with different impacts in different samples of therapy sessions; in general, however, there is good evidence that *providing and encouraging description or explanation* of a problematic situation and the feelings associated with it appears to be more helpful than evaluation of the other's actions and feelings (also see the review by Hoyt, Xenakis, Marmer, & Horowitz, 1983). For example, Elliott (1985) found that posing open questions to clients was positively related to one helpful outcome, generating a "new perspective" on the situation. "Reflections" that represented what a client said or meant were significantly related to the helpful outcome of "understanding." Hill and colleagues (1988) noted that the response mode "interpretation" (that is, offering an explanation or labeling the client's thoughts or behaviors) was effective across the greatest number of conditions and studies.

The greatest difficulty in generalizing about effective comforting messages from research examining therapist response modes is that there is no clear theoretical account linking the distinctions drawn among response mode types to the outcomes experienced by clients. This body of literature yields insights into what works, but does not articulate the process that accounts for *why*. A related concern is the lack of parsimony in the often complex patterns of findings in these studies. This body of work shows that there are links between therapist intentions, therapist behaviors, client interpretations, and client outcomes; however, without a theory to unify these categories and linkages, we are left without an explanation for the patterns.

Facework and Person-Centered Comforting Messages

A third body of research has examined how variability in the quality or sophistication of comforting messages is functionally associated with outcomes. For example, Goldsmith (1992) suggested supportive acts vary in appropriateness to the situation, competence in execution, and sensitivity to face. *Sensitivity to face* is particularly important because disclosing a problem and expressing negative emotion threatens an individual's public identity as a competent and composed person. To further complicate matters, many actions that are intended to be supportive may further threaten face by implying criticism of the other's feelings or actions, or by imposing the support provider's interpretations or recommendations on the recipient. A preliminary study by Goldsmith (1994) suggested the same supportive message is perceived as more helpful when it includes clauses and phrases that accomplish face work than when it does not display sensitivity to face. These findings need to be replicated in a wider variety of situations and with a more comprehensive set of supportive messages and face work strategies. Nonetheless, the findings suggest that threats to face may be a significant risk of supportive interactions—a risk that could prevent support seeking or undermine the utility of support that is offered. However, it is unclear how face work facilitates or hinders the process of emotional change. It is also necessary to consider situations in which challenging the face of a distressed other might be necessary to convey a sense of urgency or to question inappropriate interpretations of the problem or expressions of emotion.

How variability in the quality of messages is functionally related to differences in outcomes has been most directly addressed in a series of studies by Burleson and his colleagues on the "person-centeredness" or "sophistication" of comforting strategies (Burleson & Samter, 1985a,b; Kunkel, 1995; Samter, Burleson, & Basden-Murphy, 1987). In this research, comforting messages have been scaled for the extent to which the feelings and perspective of a distressed other are explicitly acknowledged, elaborated, and granted legitimacy. The least sophisticated messages are those that deny or challenge the legitimacy of the other's feelings. Moderately sophisticated messages implicitly recognize the other's feelings while highly sophisticated messages do so explicitly. Messages that deny, ignore, or challenge the feelings of the distressed other are consistently rated as less sensitive and effective than messages that implicitly or explicitly recognize the other's emotional state. When raters observe taped interactions containing all types of messages or read transcripts containing a full range of messages varying in sophistication, significant differences also emerge between implicit and explicit recognition of feelings.

The categorization of messages in this program of research was originally motivated by an interest in message production and in how features of messages covaried with social perception skills (e.g., Applegate, 1980; Burleson, 1983, 1984). Sophisticated messages are formally "better" in that they reflect greater capacity at taking the perspective of the distressed other. Production of these sophisticated messages has been shown to vary with the abstractness and differentiation of the provider's interpersonal construct system (see the review by Burleson, 1987). However, messages that are formally better turn out also to be functionally more effective at comforting a distressed other. This suggests a need for a theoretical explanation of what it is about sophisticated messages that make them functionally better at comforting (some possibilities are proposed by Burleson, 1990, 1994a; and Burleson & Samter, 1985a).

Although promising, Burleson's research program has, to date, focused on a very narrow range of situations in which distressed others are sad or disappointed about events for which they are blameless and lack control (e.g., the break-up of a relationship, failure to win a scholarship). It is unclear whether findings based on this class of situations will generalize to other kinds of emotional distress or whether further distinctions in features of comforting messages may be necessary (see Jones, 1996). For example, the hierarchy of comforting messages used in this research does not differentiate among (a) legitimating the particular feeling of a distressed other, (b) legitimating having an emotional experience, but not necessarily the particular emotion the other is experiencing, and (c) simply explaining or elaborating the feeling the other is experiencing. When a distressed other has experienced an irrevocable loss of something valuable, legitimating feelings of sadness may be just as effective as explaining and elaborating those feelings. However, for other forms of emotional distress, a more fine-grained analysis of potential comforting messages may be necessary to distinguish the optimally effective response. For example, unwarranted anger could require elaboration (and perhaps even a challenge) of emotion rather than legitimation of the anger. A person who feels guilt when anger is more appropriate might require legitimation of some negative emotion coupled with reassessment of the appropriate type of emotion.

Limitations in Existing Research on Effective Comforting

In sum, it is possible to propose several features of messages that are effective at comforting. It appears that a topical focus on emotional states may be more generally and consistently effective at alleviating distress than focusing on solutions to the problem or attempting to deny, minimize, or avoid talking about the emotions. Similarly, a descriptive and explanatory orientation to whatever topic is discussed appears to be effective. Finally, sensitivity to the face concerns of the distressed other may facilitate the provision of comfort.

Drawing these conclusions, however, requires glossing over several serious limitations in and differences among these studies. Many studies do not provide a detailed look at the particular message features contributing to a global assessment that "emotional support" was provided. Nor do they examine the message features that differentiate among better and worse offerings of emotional support. Furthermore, there is no consistent set of coding schemes for or experimental manipulations of comforting messages; consequently, there is the possibility that widely varying behaviors are subsumed in categories with similar labels. A similar problem can be seen in the outcome measures that have been frequently used. Although most studies are comparable in using "helpfulness" as a criterion, none have provided an explicit conceptualization of this measure. Moreover, the few studies that have used multiple measures (e.g., Jones, 1996) suggest that "helpfulness," "sensitivity," "appropriateness," and changes in specific emotional states are not necessarily comparable outcomes. Finally, little of the extant research offers explicit theoretical accounts about *how* and *why* a topical focus on emotion, a descriptive and explanatory orientation, and sensitivity to face should be effective in alleviating emotional distress.

The variability in measurement of comforting, the paucity of conceptualizations regarding outcomes, and the absence of theoretical explanation are interrelated problems. If we had a better notion of how and why messages have an effect on the emotional states of others this would provide a coherent basis for identifying those features of messages and conversations that are likely to be effective. Such understandings would further be useful for identifying criteria that researchers should use in measuring "effectiveness" at alleviating emotional distress.

If comforting is about alleviating negative emotional states, then a theory of comforting effects requires an understanding of the nature and source of emotional distress. Perhaps the most surprising limitation in the extant comforting literature is the absence of clear, well-articulated theories of emotional distress. Many of the conceptual and methodological problems we have identified cannot be solved without elaborated theories of emotion and distress. Fortunately, the extensive literature on human emotion constitutes a rich resource from which to draw theories of emotional distress and its modification. It is to this literature that we now turn.

EMOTION AND APPRAISAL

Theories of Emotion

What causes emotion? Why do people feel the emotions they do? Although theories of emotion have proliferated in recent years (see Lewis & Haviland, 1993; Metts & Bowers, 1994), most treatments of the emotional experience can be classed in one of three groups: feedback theories, labeling theories, or appraisal theories.

Feedback or *self-perception* theories (e.g., Izard, 1977; Laird & Bresler, 1992) "assume that emotion arises as a consequence of bodily reactions and not as a function of cognitive appraisals of the prevailing situation" (Parkinson & Manstead, 1992, p. 139). Bodily responses—including facial expressions, postural changes, neurological activity, and other visceral reactions—follow directly from perception of some object, and the sensing of these bodily responses *is* the emotion. As Laird and Bresler (1992, p. 213) put it, "We do not smile because we are happy. Instead, we are happy because we smile, and also angry because we frown, sad because we sit slumped and listless, and so forth, for all emotions." On this view, then, people become aware of what they are feeling by sensing or recognizing distinct patterns of physiological response.

Although feedback theories maintain that distinct patterns of physiological arousal are associated with each emotion, a second group of theories holds that the physiological arousal associated with most emotions is undifferentiated and must be interpreted or labeled to acquire significance. Such *labeling theories* of emotion (e.g., Mandler, 1984; Schachter, 1964) maintain that undifferentiated arousal gives rise to a search by the individual for the cause of the arousal. In the effort to explain an aroused state, persons examine features of the setting, their degree of success or failure with respect to goal-directed behavior, and a variety of other contextual cues. Evaluation of such factors presumably leads to the internal articulation of a plausible explanation for the arousal and a concomitant labeling of that arousal as a particular type of emotion. Hence, for labeling theories, "emotion arises as a function of the interpretation of physiological arousal within its situational context" (Parkinson & Manstead, 1992, p. 140).

Appraisal theories constitute a third approach to explaining the emotional experience (e.g., Frijda, 1986; Lazarus, 1991; Ortony, Clore, & Collins, 1988; Roseman, 1984). In contrast to both feedback and labeling theories, which see physiological arousal preceding the emotional experience, appraisal theories maintain that bodily reactions of various sorts are typically generated as *consequences* of the individual's cognitive interpretation or appraisal of the situation (see Smith, 1989). Specifically, appraisal theories see emotions as arising from an individual's cognitive evaluation of a situation and its implications for personal well-being. Appraisal theories are intrinsically transactional in that they view emotion as being generated by cognitive evaluations of specific person–environment relationships. Hence, different judgments about how the environment impacts on well-being lead to the experience of distinct emotions.

We believe that analyses of emotional distress, the comforting process, and, especially, psychological effects of comforting efforts can be developed most productively in the context of appraisal theories of emotion. For example, in the great majority of cases in which helpers seek to alleviate another's sadness, we do not think that the sad feelings were caused by someone sitting in a "slumped and listless" manner. Rather, we see people becoming distressed because unpleasant things happen to them, situations do not work out as they hoped, or features of the environment become unpromising or threatening. In other words, consistent with the tenets of appraisal theory, we see people's emotional reactions as *responses* to their interpretations and evaluations of events.

Appraisal and the Emotional Experience

There are at least a dozen distinct appraisal theories of emotion, each of which provides a somewhat novel analysis of the character of various emotions, the circumstances provoking different emotions, the behavioral tendencies associated with each emotion, and so forth (see the review by Omdahl, 1995). Our aim here is not to provide a thorough review of different appraisal theories, but to present an overview of the core elements shared by most appraisal theories. Our understanding of appraisal and emotion has been particularly influenced by the work of Lazarus (1968, 1984, 1991, 1995; Lazarus & Folkman, 1984; Lazarus & Lazarus, 1994; Smith & Lazarus, 1990), who has articulated an increasingly comprehensive and elegant theoretical framework over the last 30 years.

Lazarus (1991) maintained that associated with each particular emotion is a *core relational theme,* a specific *appraisal pattern,* and a distinct *action tendency.* A core relational theme expresses, in summary form, the adaptational significance of a particular person–environment relationship. Lazarus described a core relational theme as "simply the central (hence core) relational harm or benefit in adaptational encounters that underlies each specific kind of emotion" (Lazarus, 1991, p. 121). Each individual emotion or (family of emotions) is defined by a specific core relational theme. For example, the core relational theme for *anger* is "a demeaning offense against me and mine"; the theme for *anxiety* is "facing an uncertain, existential threat"; the theme for *guilt* is "having transgressed a moral imperative"; the theme for *shame* is "having failed to live up to an ego-ideal"; and the theme for *sadness* is "having experienced an irrevocable loss" (Lazarus, 1991, p. 122).

Core relational themes crystalize the multiple judgments that constitute an appraisal pattern. That is, an *appraisal pattern* is the set of cognitive evaluations an individual makes about a person–environment relationship. Several different dimensions of the person–environment relationship are evaluated in the appraisal process. For example, Lazarus (1991) maintained that the adaptational significance of an event is determined by both primary and secondary appraisals of that event. "*Primary appraisals* refer to whether what is happening is personally relevant; *secondary appraisals* refer to coping options and prospects" (Lazarus, 1991, p. 87, italics added). Primary appraisals include evaluations of *goal relevance* (the extent to which the event impacts personal goals or concerns), *goal congruence* (the extent to which an event facilitates or frustrates the achievement of a personally relevant goal), and *ego involvement* (the aspects of identity involved in an event). All negative emotions share a common primary appraisal pattern (Lazarus, 1991). That is, all negative emotions arise from appraisals that the current situation is goal relevant and goal incongruent.

What distinguishes particular negative emotions, then, are the specific goals viewed as relevant in the situation and the secondary appraisal patterns for the event. Secondary appraisals include judgments regarding *accountability* (who or what should receive blame or credit for the event), *coping potential* (the capacities of the individual to solve the problem and manage emergent feelings), and *future expectancy* (the likelihood that things will change for better or worse). Other researchers have suggested somewhat different sets of dimensions for the appraisal process (e.g., see Frijda, 1986, Roseman, 1984; Scherer, 1988; Smith & Ellsworth, 1985). Indeed, different appraisal theories are distinguishable primarily in terms of the general dimensions they see people using in appraising situations, as well as in the specific appraisal patterns associated with emotion.

Considerable work has been directed at elaborating appraisal patterns for diverse emotions (see the review by Omdahl, 1995). For example, the appraisal pattern for *sadness* includes the loss of an object more or less closely connected to one's identity; the closer the connection, the more intense the sadness. In pure sadness, there is no blame for the loss; other emotions are likely to result if blame is assigned externally (anger) or internally (guilt or shame). Because the loss is irrevocable, the person can do nothing about the loss, so coping potential will be low. Furthermore, due to the irrevocability of the loss, there is nothing to do but accept this loss and, perhaps, locate it in the larger context of ongoing life events. *Anger* arises from interference with or blockage of a desired goal, especially when such blockages are viewed as undeserved or unfair (Canary, Spitzberg, & Semic, Chapter 7, this volume; Smith & Ellsworth, 1985; Roseman, 1984). The angry person has suffered damage or threat to his or her ego–identity through actions of another that are viewed as arbitrary, inconsiderate, or malevolent (see also Canary et al., Chapter 7, this volume). Blame is a key secondary appraisal element for anger; someone is held to have committed a demeaning offense. *Shame* and *embarrassment* both involve a loss of face associated with an inadequate, inept, or inappropriate role performance (see Bradford & Petronio, Chapter 4, this volume; Scheff, 1990). In shame, an individual is disgraced or humiliated in her or his own eyes by the failure to live up to an ego ideal (Lazarus, 1991). In embarrassment, the individual suffers public humiliation and loss of face by failing to comport himself or herself in a manner consistent with a publicly claimed social identity (Gross & Stone, 1964). In both shame and embarrassment, the individual blames himself or herself for the problematic role performance.

Action tendencies are biologically based behavioral responses that have the function of helping the person cope adaptively with the emotion-arousing event. As such, action tendencies "provide the link between an emotion and its physiological response pattern" (Lazarus, 1991, p. 87). Associated with each action tendency are characteristic subjective feeling states (affects) and patterns of physiological arousal or activity. For example, the action tendency for anger is attack on the offending party; for fear, the action tendency is avoidance or escape; for sadness, the action tendency is disengagement from a lost object or commitment and seeking help to cope with this loss; and for guilt, the action tendency is to expiate, atone, or make reparations for the harm done another (see Lazarus, 1991; Smith & Lazarus, 1990; Smith & Pope, 1992). Obviously, action tendencies are not hard-wired reflexes or programs automatically run off by the person. These tendencies may be (and often are) inhibited, ignored, suppressed, denied, or transformed. Regardless of whether they are exhibited or suppressed, action tendencies provide a behavioral orientation toward the emotion-arousing event.

Appraisal theory views emotions as complex syndromes that combine particular patterns of thought (cognitive appraisals), feeling (affects or arousal), and behavior (latent or manifest actions). Greenberg, Rice, and Elliott (1993) nicely summarized the multifold character of emotions from the vantage point of appraisal theory:

> Emotion[s] . . . are thus complex synthesizing structures that integrate *cognition* (in the form of appraisals, expectations, and beliefs) and *motivation* (in the form of needs, concerns, intentions, and goals) with *affect* (in the form of physiological arousal and sensory, bodily feeling) and *action* (in the form of expressive-motor responses and action tendencies). (p. 5, italics added)

Furthermore, emotions serve both an informative function (communicating to the self and other how an event is being appraised) and an adaptive function (providing a framework for coping with the event).

The Coping Process

A core feature of the appraisal analysis of emotion is its focus on the coping process. Coping "is what we do and think in an effort to manage stress and the emotions associated with it" (Lazarus & Lazarus, 1994, p. 152). More formally, coping "consists of cognitive and behavioral efforts to manage specific external or internal demands (and conflicts between them) that are appraised as taxing or exceeding the resources of the person" (Lazarus, 1991, p. 112). Coping may be viewed as an effect or outcome of a particular emotion in that emotions stimulate efforts directed at changing the conditions that aroused the emotion, the emotion itself, or both. But coping efforts are also causally antecedent to emotions in that coping efforts influence subsequent appraisals (i.e., reappraisals) of events and, thus, emotional reactions to them.

Lazarus and his colleagues have distinguished two forms of coping, problem-focused and emotion-focused. *Problem-focused coping* efforts are directed at changing features of a specific person–environment relationship. Most problem-focused coping efforts can be viewed as action-centered attempts to modify some aspect of the environment that is viewed as problematic (e.g., the attitudes and behaviors of others). However, the individual's goals are a key feature of the person–environment relationship, so changes in these can also be viewed as a form of problem-focused coping (e.g., changes in what the distressed person wants or seeks to accomplish). *Emotion-focused coping* efforts "change only the way in which the relationship is *attended to* (e.g., a threat that one avoids perceiving or thinking about) or *interpreted* (e.g., a threat that is dealt with by denial or psychological distancing)" (Lazarus, 1991, p. 112, italics in the original). Thus, emotion-focused coping strategies are directed at controlling what is felt about a particular person–environment relationship. Forms of emotion-focused coping include distraction (focusing attention on some other feature of life and thereby changing the emotions felt), denial or suppression (telling oneself that problematic circumstances and/or the accompanying negative emotional responses do not exist), and reappraisal (modifying how a particular person–environment relationship is represented and evaluated).

Distraction and denial are likely to be effective forms of coping when the problematic circumstance is comparatively trivial or is likely to change of its own accord. But when the situation is a serious one and neither features of the person (i.e., goals) or environment are likely to change, then distraction and denial are unlikely to be effective, especially when the frustrated goal is an important one. Indeed, attempts to cope with troubled person–environment relationships through distraction and denial may well exacerbate the problem, contributing to intrusive or ruminative thoughts about the situation (see Harber & Pennebaker, 1992; Tait & Silver, 1989). If neither personal goals nor environmental conditions are likely to change, and distressful feelings cannot be ignored, then the person needs to change how the situation is represented and evaluated (i.e., how the situation is appraised).

There is substantial evidence that changing appraisals results in changed emotions (e.g., Ross, Rodin, & Zimbardo, 1969; Valins & Nisbett, 1972; Wilson & Linvell, 1982; see the reviews by Lazarus, 1991; Smith & Pope, 1992). Moreover, the affective changes brought about through reappraisal are more stable and functional than those achieved through distancing, avoidance, or denial, especially when dealing with consequential matters (see Lazarus & Lazarus, 1994, pp. 156–173). Thus reappraisal emerges as a key—and, perhaps, the central—coping mechanism through which emotional change occurs.

Many discussions of coping treat it as a singular, intrapersonal process; indeed,

Lazarus and Lazarus presented coping as "the self-management of emotion" (1994, p. 152). Obviously, people do cope with a great many problems on their own. But they also frequently turn to others for help when confronting distressful circumstances. Indeed, there is a great deal of evidence indicating that people *want* to talk to others about their troubles (see Clark, 1993, pp. 25–26; Stiles, 1987). Moreover, people with whom we interact, especially intimates, frequently offer help upon noticing that we have encountered a troubling circumstance or are exhibiting distress cues. In all such cases, coping becomes an *interpersonal* process. In fact, some researchers explicitly advocate conceptualizing social support as "coping assistance" (e.g., Thoits, 1984). We see value in viewing emotional support as those efforts aimed at helping people cope with emotional distress.

In sum, appraisal theory offers a rich set of analyses about the circumstances and reactions that lead to a variety of negative emotions addressed in support efforts. Appraisal theory underscores that emotions such as sadness, shame, anger, fear, embarrassment, and guilt stem from cognitive evaluations of certain events, and not from the events themselves. Appraisal theory also provides useful information about the individual's natural coping inclinations with respect to these emotions (i.e., the action tendencies for each emotion) and the modes of coping people may rely upon. However, people rarely rely exclusively on their own resources when dealing with emotional distress; they frequently are afforded assistance, comfort, and support by caring others in their social network. The next section considers more fully the implications of appraisal theory for the emotional support process.

APPRAISAL THEORY, COMFORTING, AND CONVERSATION

Viewing Comforting as a Process of Facilitating Reappraisal

Perhaps the most important implication of appraisal theory for the comforting process stems from its analysis of the nature and source of emotional distress. According to appraisal theory, the source of emotional distress does not lie in some external state of affairs, but rather in how external states of affairs are appraised and evaluated in the context of personal goals. Consequently, the only way a distressed emotional state can be altered is through an individual changing the appraisals that underlie and constitute the emotional distress. Furthermore, although the words and deeds of others may facilitate a reappraisal of a stressful circumstance, no one can directly alter or modify the appraisals of another. Rather, the only way to change a feeling state is to change what produced that feeling state in the first place: the appraisals of the distressed person.

This account of emotional distress suggests a distinctive perspective on the processes of "providing" comfort: Comfort is not a substance given by one individual to another or a salve applied by a helper to an emotional wound suffered by a victim. All any helper can do is assist the distressed other in developing new appraisals about the stressful situation. Consequently, the study of how comfort is communicated should focus on how specific features of conversations contribute to or inhibit the constructive reappraisal of stressful circumstances (e.g., characteristics of the conversational exchange, the issues discussed, and the manner in which topics are addressed).

This view of comforting carries several subtle, but important, implications. Some of these implications may be counterintuitive and are inconsistent with lay views of the comforting process, as well as with some scientific models of social support. For example, this view challenges the usefulness of "matching" models of support that suggest effective emotional support is that which is appropriately matched to externally defined characteristics of a stressor (e.g., Cohen & McKay, 1984; Cutrona & Russell, 1990). Emotional distress is a result of an individual's appraisal of his or her environment, goals, and resources. Although the external environment imposes real constraints on individuals, a given situation may be amenable to more than one appraisal. Comforting works by *discursively constructing* useful appraisals of particular person–environment configurations, not by simply *matching* the right type of support to a predefined and static environmental circumstance.

Our appraisal-based view is also at odds with the vernaculars of both everyday life and formal theories that represent different types of social support as commodities that are "exchanged," "provided," or "given." People can (and do) express affection, care, and concern for another and sometimes speak of "providing care" or "exchanging affection." But if receiving expressions of such sentiments assists in ameliorating emotional distress, it is not because they provide some commodity the distressed other previously lacked in sufficient quantity. Rather, it is because they prompt or motivate a reappraisal of a troubled person–environment relationship.

Similarly, our conception of the comforting process challenges the notion that there are "magic bullet" words and phrases that will reliably bring relief to victims of emotional distress. Such a view is captured in everyday phrases such as "I wish I knew what to say," and "If I could only find the right words." It may also be an implicit assumption underlying several lines of research (e.g., Barbee & Cunningham, 1995; Burleson & Samter, 1985a; Dunkel-Schetter et al., 1992) that have sought to differentiate "effective" from "ineffective" support messages by examining features of individual messages and their relationship to desirable outcomes such as perceived helpfulness or lessened distress. Our appraisal analysis of comforting suggests that the search for verbal magic bullets is misguided: Any effect an act or message has on another's distress does not come about directly, but only through the effect it has on the other's reappraisal of his or her situation. There may be instances when a single message dramatically affects another person's appraisal and brings about rapid reduction of distress. However, it seems likely that messages will more often have their effects over a sequence of acts in which the distressed other continues to think through and talk through her or his appraisal. The effects that comforting messages have on the conversation (e.g., length and number of turns granted to the distressed other, degree to which distressed other explores topics relevant to a reappraisal) are likely to be important mediators of any effects comforting messages have on the other's appraisals and distress.

Although our analysis challenges some implicit ways of thinking about comforting, it does fit with and render explicable the feelings of *powerlessness* people may experience when confronted with a distressed other. People often report feeling inadequate because they can only express sympathy and concern; they see nothing they can *do* to *make* the other feel better (e.g., Coyne, Wortman, & Lehman, 1988; DePaulo, 1982; Gottlieb & Beatty, 1985). People want to help, but become frustrated with themselves, the distressed other, and the situation because they correctly sense that there is no tangible or instrumental action that they can perform to affect meaningful emotional change in the other. This frustration may lead to futile or even counterproductive reactions, such as undertaking well-intended but pointless actions, exiting from the situation, issuing simple imperatives about how the other should think or feel, or even condemning the other's feelings and plight (see Dunkel-Schetter & Bennett, 1990; Herbert & Dunkel-Schetter, 1992).

In fact, our appraisal theory analysis of distress suggests that there *is* something functional that a helper can *do:* talk to the distressed other and help the other work through his or her emotions, thereby facilitating relief-generating reappraisals. Indeed, all that can be done in many situations of emotional distress is to "be there" and help the other work through her or his feelings by being a good conversational partner.

How Conversation Facilitates Reappraisals

How is it that conversing helps reduce another's emotional distress and facilitates reappraisal of the stressful circumstances? By way of overview, we see conversation as a medium in which a distressed person can express, elaborate, and clarify relevant thoughts and feelings. As a result of concretizing and exploring these thoughts and feelings, the distressed person may be led to modify his or her goals, views of the situation, and/or coping efforts. Modifications in motives, perceptions, or actions constitute a new appraisal of the situation and, if these changes are functional, an improved affect state should result.

Several different bodies of literature emphasize the stress-relieving potential of supportive conversations, including work in communication (e.g., Burleson & Samter, 1985a; Goldsmith, 1992; Metts, Backhaus, & Kazoleas, 1995), sociology (e.g., Hochschild, 1979, 1990; Jefferson, 1988), counseling psychology (e.g., Carkhuff & Berenson, 1977: Greenberg & Safran, 1987) health psychology (e.g. Harber & Pennebaker, 1992; Pennebaker, 1989), and social psychology (e.g., Clark, 1993; Thoits, 1986). Our appraisal analysis of distress and support provides a useful framework for integrating these literatures and developing a detailed understanding of how conversational processes can contribute to functional reappraisals of stressful circumstances.

One of the oldest traditions extolling the stress-relieving potential of conversational interactions is associated with the "experiential" or "client-centered" counseling approach of Rogers (e.g., 1957, 1975) and his followers (Carkhuff & Berenson, 1977; Greenberg et al., 1993; Truax & Carkhuff, 1967). Rogers (1957) maintained that for a counselor to bring about improvement in a client, it was necessary and sufficient that the counselor express *empathy* (awareness and understanding of the client's feelings), nonpossessive *warmth* (prizing or unconditional positive regard), and *genuineness* (authenticity or congruence). These "therapeutic conditions" supposedly bring about improvement by creating a climate that maximizes the client's self-exploration, self-understanding, and development of appropriate plans of action (see Carkhuff & Berenson, 1977). Emotional hurt often stems from the invalidation of the self, either directly (e.g., rejection by a valued other) or indirectly (e.g., failing at something connected to one's self-concept). The therapeutic conditions convey to distressed others that their feelings are recognized and appreciated, that they are valued as persons, and that they are accepted by another (the helper) in the context of an honest relationship.

A key insight of this perspective is the idea that the therapeutic conditions by themselves do not remove the source of distressed others' hurts (e.g., personal rejections, task failures); rather they provide the context in which people can explore and seek understanding of their feelings (i.e., reappraise the stressful situation). Indeed, "facilitating clients to access and explore feelings is a central focus of client-centered therapy" (Greenberg et al., 1993, p. 36). The reappraisals attained through guided exploration of feelings provide a basis for the development of coping strategies that assist in moving distressed persons "from where they are to where they want to be" (see Carkhuff & Berenson, 1977, p. 18).

We view the work of Rogers and his associates as useful in helping articulate conditions that facilitate the conversational expression and exploration of thoughts and feelings by a distressed other. Although it has been very influential, we view the Rogerian doctrine as limited in that it provides little detail about specific behaviors that assist others in exploring their feelings or the mechanisms through which these behaviors work. Recent work in health psychology, as well as social psychology, details some of the mechanisms through which the expression of feelings in conversation can assist the process of elaborating stress-reducing reappraisals of events.

For example, Pennebaker and his associates (e.g., Harber & Pennebaker, 1992; Pennebaker, 1989, 1993); have provided compelling documentation that the discursive expression (in conversation or writing) of feelings engendered by a traumatic event aids persons in developing less stress-inducing understandings of those events. Harber and Pennebaker (1992) suggested that traumatic events can deeply challenge the fundamental assumptions we all make about our self-worth and the benevolence and meaningfulness of the world. The disruption of these beliefs is distressful and destabilizing. Successful coping requires assimilating (i.e., reappraising) the particulars of the stressful circumstance in such a way that they are reconciled with the fundamental assumptions giving meaning to life. However, achieving such an assimilation is often difficult since

> all the emotions, images, and thoughts attending to a trauma are held together solely by the traumatic incident itself. This integrated structure may complicate the winnowing of assumptive morals from traumatic dramas. At the same time, the distress that traumas evoke when encountered *in toto* discourages efforts at making this translation. (Harber & Pennebaker, 1992, p. 378)

Talking or writing about a traumatic event "may help dismantle the phenomenal whole that traumas constitute" (Harber & Pennebaker, 1992, p. 378). The constraints of language require that distinct features of the event be presented in separate sentences, with these sentences then organized in some overall narrative structure. Hence, describing a traumatic event necessarily requires the assumption of an analytic attitude toward it which, in turn, helps the distressed individual get some cognitive distance on the event and his or her feelings about it. Furthermore, the processes of putting one's thoughts into words, and those words into a coherent narrative, help make the event more understandable to the person constructing the narrative. In sum, discoursing about a traumatic event helps the distressed person get some distance on the event, reappraise it, and integrate new perspectives on it within a broader view of life.

Clark (1993) also emphasized how talking about a stressful event can help distraught persons make sense out of their experiences and cope more effectively with the reappraised situation. She maintained that several distinct features of conversational behavior promote reappraisal of the problematic situation and serve to combat the negative consequences of stress. The syntactic and pragmatic demands to produce cohesive, coherent utterances in the course of conversation can enhance a distressed other's clarity about a situation and increase his or her understanding of relevant perceptions and reactions to the stressful event. Furthermore, conversation inherently requires consideration of multiple perspectives (i.e., the listener's as well as the speaker's viewpoint). Focusing on another's perspective can lead to new insights about and appraisals of the troubled person–environment relationship. Clark thus argued that participation in conversation fosters the kind of reflection and reappraisal that facilitates both improved affect and more functional coping.

The research reviewed here underscores the importance of conversation in the emotional support process and points to some mechanisms through which conversational interaction may facilitate more functional appraisals of events, as well as the development of more appropriate coping strategies. However, this research also makes it quite clear that not just *any* conversational interaction will have helpful outcomes. Rather, if conversations are to promote functional reappraisals of events, those conversations must focus on appropriate topics, and those topics must be explored and elaborated in useful ways.

FEATURES OF CONVERSATIONS THAT FACILITATE REAPPRAISAL

Appraisal theory suggests an alternative way of viewing comforting and generates a novel account of how conversations may assist with the reduction of distress. Our appraisal analysis of the comforting process provides a basis for revisiting and expanding our understanding of the features of effective comforting: Our analysis suggests three requirements for effective conversations. First and foremost, participants—especially the distressed other—must be willing to enter into conversations during which painful and upsetting matters will be discussed. Second, there is growing evidence that conversations about stressful incidents have constructive outcomes only if the right issues are discussed. For example, Pennebaker (e.g., Pennebaker & Beall, 1986) finds that discussions of stressful events are only helpful when focused on the individual's emotional reactions to those events. Third, these issues need to be discussed in ways that facilitate reappraisals. Recent research (Pennebaker, 1993; Pennebaker, Kiecolt-Glaser, & Glaser, 1988) shows that the revelation of feelings is maximally useful when those feelings are expressed in an elaborated, narrative form.

Constituting a Supportive Conversational Environment

The willingness and ability to express and explore negative feelings will be enhanced if participants feel safe and secure about doing so. People may be hesitant to discuss negative feelings for a great many reasons. The expression or exhibition of strong feelings, especially negative ones, violates emotional display rules in many cultures (e.g., Hochschild, 1979; Liu, Karasawa, & Weiner, 1992; Scheff, 1984). Expression of emotional distress creates numerous self-presentation dilemmas (Coates & Winston, 1987; Goldsmith & Parks, 1990; Silver, Wortman, & Crofton, 1990), including making the self appear weak or incompetent, revealing undesirable information about the self, and risking stigmatization (see the summary by Albrecht et al., 1994, p. 433). The expression of negative feelings also leaves the discloser open to the risks of ridicule and violated confidences (Stiles, 1987). Furthermore, friends and family members have been found to discourage the open expression of negative feelings (Dunkel-Schetter & Wortman, 1982; Herbert & Dunkel-Schetter, 1992; Wortman & Lehman, 1985). People are sometimes ostracized, and even punished, by others for their honest expressions of emotional distress (e.g., Coates, Wortman, & Abbey, 1979; Silver, Boon, & Stones, 1983; Silver et al., 1990).

For all these reasons, most people are hesitant to talk about their distressed feelings and the circumstances producing those feelings. Yet, conversations are likely to be maximally beneficial only if the distressed other can give free voice to her or his feelings and explore those feelings fully. This conclusion is supported by extensive research in both everyday contexts (e.g., Pennebaker, 1993; Pennebaker & Beall, 1986; Stiles, 1987; see Clark, 1993, pp. 47–48) and clinical contexts (e.g., Elliott,

1985; Greenberg et al., 1993; Hoyt et al., 1983). Under what conditions can conversational partners overcome the general reluctance to openly discuss negative feelings? And what features of conversations enact or promote these conditions?

We suspect there are a number of conditions that contribute to people's willingness and ability to discuss negative emotion. Four are particularly important: trust in one another, a sense that talk about feelings is appropriate, sufficient emotional control to discuss the situation coherently, and ease with the setting in which the conversation occurs. An understanding of these prerequisites to comforting conversations provides one explanation for why previous research has found that a topical focus on emotion, a descriptive and explanatory orientation, and sensitivity to face are associated with helpfulness.

The "emotional support" messages that have been found to be so helpful include expressions of care, concern, and affection (see the reviews by Dunkel-Schetter et al., 1992; and Goldsmith, 1994). In fact, some social support researchers see the category of "emotional support" exhausted by such expressions of acceptance and concern. One pathway through which these messages bring about comfort is through their enactment of a trusting relationship and of a conversation in which expression of feelings is safe. Research conducted in clinical contexts indicates that trust and acceptance are developed both paraverbally (through vocal tone; see Rice & Kerr, 1986) and through expressions of warmth, respect, and positive regard (Andersen & Guerrero, Chapter 11, this volume; Barrett-Lennard, 1962, 1986; Elliott, 1985; Greenberg et al., 1993). Similarly, a descriptive and explanatory orientation to topics may evoke less defensiveness and vulnerability than an evaluative orientation (Carkhuff & Berensen, 1977; Greenberg et al., 1993). Finally, to the extent that disclosing negative feelings detracts from a composed public "face," facework that conveys acceptance of the other (both verbally and nonverbally) can provide reassurance that the distressed other will not be stigmatized or rejected (see Goldsmith, 1992, 1994).

Expressions of affection, care, and concern may help to foster feelings of trust and acceptance, but a different approach may be needed to encourage and legitimize the expression of feeling states by the distressed other. If supportive conversations are to help, the distressed person must not only feel accepted, but must also feel that it is acceptable to *have* negative feelings and to *express* those feelings during the interaction. A variety of verbal and nonverbal strategies are available for legitimizing the expression of feelings, and research on helping in both clinical contexts (e.g., Elliott, 1985; Greenberg et al., 1993; Truax & Carkhuff, 1967) and everyday settings (Burleson & Samter, 1985a; Goldsmith, 1994; Notarius & Herrick, 1988; Stiles, 1987) suggests the efficacy of many of these strategies. For example, the helper can directly legitimize the expression of feelings (e.g., "Say whatever you are feeling. It's OK to be emotional; it's OK to cry."), and can reinforce this by asserting that having the experienced feelings is understandable (e.g., "Gee, if that happened to me, I'd be very upset, too"). "Giving voice" to emotions and expressing empathy for the other also help legitimize the expression of feelings (e.g.,

"That had to be really tough; no wonder you're upset."). However, the research also suggests that efforts to legitimize the expression of emotion should not focus extensively on the helper's own emotional experiences (i.e., should avoid statements like: "Gosh, I know exactly how you feel. Something like that happened to me and I felt . . .") since this may draw attention away from the experiences and feelings of the distressed other. Acknowledgements, "minimal encouragers," and following responses (e.g., head nods and vocalizations such as "Uh-huh," "Mm-hmm," "Yes," "I see; I understand") both legitimize the expression of feelings and encourage the elaboration of those feelings (see Burleson & Samter, 1985a; Carkhuff & Berensen, 1977; Greenberg et al., 1993).

There are, then, a variety of conversational actions that helpers can employ to build trust, convey acceptance, and legitimize the expression of feelings. Other conditions must also be met if supportive conversations are to occur. For example, sometimes the other may be too aroused or distraught to discuss her or his feelings in a coherent fashion. In such cases, the helper may need to facilitate the reduction of arousal through encouraging the other to engage in emotional venting (see Albrecht & Adelman, 1987), though there are also dangers associated with venting certain emotions, especially anger (see Tavris, 1984). The helper may also assist in reducing the other's arousal level by suggesting some physical activity that will help consume excess arousal, or by distracting the other from the distressful circumstance until the level of emotional intensity declines to a point where coherent conversation becomes possible.

Finally, supportive conversations need to occur in settings where both participants feel secure and comfortable with discussing troubling events and the feelings aroused by those events. Obviously, settings subject to distractions, intrusions, interruptions, and other disturbances do not lend themselves to the open disclosure and searching exploration of distressed feeling states. Thus, the helper may need to create a setting conducive to supportive conversations (e.g., closing doors to shut out potential distractions), relocate the participants to a private and secure setting, or postpone the conversation until such a setting has been found.

Identifying and Pursuing Topics of Talk in Supportive Conversations

Creating and sustaining a supportive conversational environment is no small feat. The recognition by distressed others that such an environment is present—that trustworthy, caring others are available, that the expression and exploration of feelings is possible and legitimate—may itself be curative. Indeed, research has found that the perception of support availability, especially in stressful contexts, has facilitative effects on coping, health, and psychological well-being (see the reviews by Cohen & Wills, 1985; Cutrona & Russell, 1990; Pierce, Sarason, & Sarason, 1990). Rogers (1957) even argued that the conditions we have described as constitutive of supportive conversational environments are the necessary and sufficient conditions of therapeutic change.

Contemporary practitioners of experiential therapy continue to emphasize the importance of the Rogerian therapeutic relationship. However, many contemporary clinicians also believe that the therapist can do more than offer the client a therapeutic relationship. As Greenberg et al. (1993, p. 102) put the matter, "the therapeutic relationship is always *necessary* (for providing the basis for therapeutic work), generally *sufficient* in the long run (i.e., curative in itself), but not always *efficient* (i.e., can be enhanced by task-focused interventions)." That is, functional change in clients can be more reliably and rapidly facilitated by identifying specific therapeutic tasks and directing the therapeutic process so as to address these tasks in a coherent, focused way.

The concept of "conversational topic" in everyday emotional support may be a useful analogue for the concept of "therapeutic task" in experiential therapy. That is, once the conditions of supportive conversations have been more or less met, the participants must talk about *something*. Much of the research previously reviewed in this chapter makes it clear that conversations are most likely to be helpful when distressed others talk about their "thoughts and feelings" regarding the upsetting situation (e.g., Clark, 1993; Pennebaker, 1993). But such global characterizations of talk topics provide little assistance to helpers in guiding conversations so that they are most productive: What *specific* aspects of another's thoughts and feelings should be amplified and explored? Nor are global characterizations of conversational foci particularly useful to researchers in their efforts to (a) make sense of the topics pursued in supportive interactions and (b) learn why discussion of some topics rather than others is associated with functional outcomes. What is needed is an understanding of the various topics having the potential to be addressed in the course of supportive conversations, as well as an appreciation of the factors that make some of these topics more relevant than others in particular circumstances. But is there a general set of topics for supportive conversations? If so, how are they to be identified and arrayed?

We believe that a general set of issues or topics for emotional support situations can be derived from Lazarus's (1991) appraisal theory of emotion. This is a second major contribution of appraisal theory to our analysis of emotional support: Suggesting a general set of potential issues for emotional support situations, some of which are likely to be relevant in any particular supportive conversation. A set of these issues, and the circumstances making them conversationally relevant, are summarized in Figure 1.

Recall that appraisal theory distinguishes between primary and secondary appraisals, as well as between problem-focused and emotion-focused coping. Primary appraisals concern whether an event is relevant to a person's goals and, if so, whether the event is congruent or incongruent with the achievement of those goals. Secondary appraisals pertain to coping options and prospects. Problem-focused coping efforts are directed at changing a troubled person–environment relationship whereas emotion-focused coping efforts are directed at how the person–environ-

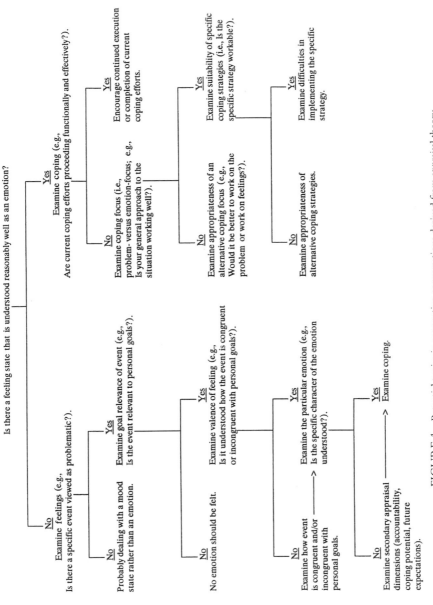

FIGURE 1 Potential topics in supportive conversations derived from appraisal theory.

ment relationship is attended to or interpreted. Detailing the circumstances when discussions of particular appraisal patterns and coping modes are relevant can help generate a set of potential topics that may be usefully pursued in the course of supportive conversations.

Specifically, once a supportive conversational environment has been established, the other can be encouraged to articulate her or his emotional state and understanding of the circumstances leading to that state ("What happened? And how are you feeling about things?"). This discussion should lead to a fuller appreciation of the emotional state, the reasons for it occurrence, and an assessment of its appropriateness. However, it is possible that either during initial discussion or sometime later in the conversation, a sense may emerge that the felt emotion is not well understood or is not fully appropriate to the circumstances. There may be confusion about what is felt, or even whether anything is felt. In such cases, appraisal theory suggests several topics that may be conversationally relevant.

At the most general level, talk might focus on whether something is actually felt or whether the situation warrants a significant emotional response ("Are you feeling something? Can you describe the feeling? Do you know why you are feeling this way?"). Not all feeling states are emotions (see Batson, Shaw, & Oleson, 1992), and one of the most important ways of discriminating between an emotion and some other affective state (e.g., a mood) is to explore whether current feelings are tied to a specific, provoking incident ("Did something happen that made you feel this way? What happened?"). If some provoking event is identified, appraisal theory suggests the appropriateness of examining the relevance of that event to the other's personal goals ("How did that event affect you and what you want or care about?"). It is conceivable that such a discussion could reveal (or lead to the appraisal) that an event had no real impact on the other's goals. In that instance, appraisal theory suggests that the problematic emotion should disappear.

More likely, an event will be seen as impacting the other's goals, thus making some emotional response appropriate, although it may remain unclear as to which specific emotion is (or should be) felt. If there is some uncertainty about the basic character (i.e., valence) of the emotion experienced by the other, it becomes relevant to explore how an event is congruent or incongruent with personal goals ("Did the event help you or hurt you? How?"). Or, the conversation may consider whether the event, while incongruent with one goal, is congruent with a more important, superordinate goal ("How did the event both help you and hurt you and which do you think was the most important?"). Such discussions should clarify (or lead to a reappraisal of) the valence of the emotion felt in the situation.

If the valence of the emotion (positive *versus* negative) is understood and viewed as appropriate to the circumstance, but there is confusion about the specific character of the emotion, it becomes relevant to discuss topics suggested by the secondary appraisal dimensions (i.e., accountability, coping potential, and future expectancy). Here, conversations may focus on the character of specific secondary appraisals and their implications for the other's emotional state (e.g., "Do you think you're feeling mostly angry or mostly anxious about failing the exam?"). Discussions of secondary appraisal dimensions should lead to a clear understanding of the specific emotion (or set of emotions) experienced by the other.

If the experienced emotion is understood reasonably well and is viewed as appropriate to the circumstances, it becomes relevant in subsequent conversation to consider the adequacy of coping activities. The most immediately relevant topics in such discussions concern the character of current coping activities ("So what are you doing about the situation?") and the outcome of those activities ("How is that working? Is that solving the problem? And how are you feeling as a result of trying that?"). If the discussion suggests that the enacted (or planned) coping efforts are functional, then it becomes relevant to focus the conversation on facilitating the execution or completion of these efforts ("Are you motivated to keep doing this? Do you feel like you'll be able to see this through? How are you going to keep yourself on course?"). If it appears that the experienced emotion is appropriate to the situation and coping efforts are proceeding functionally, it is relevant to let the other structure the conversation, talking about the troubling situation if he or she chooses, but also allowing the other to pursue other topics as well.

If coping activities are not proceeding functionally, it is possible that an inappropriate coping focus (problem *versus* emotion) has been selected, or that no coping focus has been selected. Under such circumstances, topics regarding the appropriateness of coping focus become relevant ("You said you were just trying to forget about the situation and put that behind you. How's that working out?" or "You indicated that you were trying to change some feature of the situation. How successful has that been?"). If discussion suggests that an inappropriate coping focus has been chosen then consideration of an alternative focus becomes relevant ("What do you think would happen if you tried changing some feature of the problematic environment?").

On the other hand, if the conversation suggests that coping activities are not going well even though an appropriate coping focus has been chosen, then it becomes relevant to examine the suitability of the specific strategies enacted to realize the coping focus ("How are you trying to rethink the situation and how's that going?" or "How are you trying to change the situation and how's that coming along?"). If the strategy doesn't seem to be working, it becomes relevant to consider alternative strategies that are consistent with the chosen coping focus ("What other kinds of thing might you try in this situation? What are the advantages and limitations of the various alternatives?"). If the strategy seems to be working (or appears to be workable) but is still not achieving the desired results, this suggests that something else (e.g., a motivational problem) is inhibiting the effective implementation of the strategy. Hence, a relevant topical focus for the conversation would become diagnosing and resolving the obstacle inhibiting enactment of the coping strategy ("Are you finding it difficult to do that? Do you understand why?").

The analysis developed here provides a much more detailed and differentiated view of what it means to "talk about thoughts and feelings" in supportive interactions. Of course, we are not claiming that all these topics are explicitly talked about in supportive interactions, or should be if a conversation is to facilitate functional changes. Nor are we trying to describe or prescribe the sequencing of topics in a helper's thoughts or during the course of a supportive conversation. Rather, our effort is directed at supplying some detail about the topics potentially pursuable in supportive conversations, deriving these topics from a logical analysis of factors implicated in emotion and coping. This list of topics may assist researchers in making sense of the matters discussed in supportive conversations. It is possible that this list may provide for helpers some useful ideas about issues to consider, topics to pursue, and the circumstances that make a specific topic particularly relevant.

Encouraging Functional Conversational Contributions

Although appraisal theory helps in identifying topics that may be discussed during the course of supportive conversations, it provides no insight into *how* these topics should be discussed to facilitate functional change. That is, in addition to understanding what issues may be addressed in supportive interactions, both helpers and researchers need a detailed understanding of the various ways these topics may be discussed, which of these ways are helpful, and which are not. Extant research suggests that a descriptive and explanatory orientation to topics and an approach that is face-sensitive are helpful. Our appraisal analysis of comforting suggests why these conversational strategies are helpful and identifies some additional ways of discussing topics that may promote reappraisals.

Participants in comforting conversations must work to overcome two natural inclinations that may inhibit the process of reappraisal. Helpers may experience pressure to *fix* the other's distress by telling her or him what to think, do, or feel. At the same time, distressed others may experience pressure to keep their conversational turns brief rather than extended. Each of these natural inclinations is at odds with what we suspect are the optimal conversational features for facilitating reappraisals: the elicitation by helpers and the performance by distressed others of extended talk about feelings and coping options.

When confronted with another person's disclosure of a problem and experience of distress, it is common for hearers to respond by telling the distressed other what to do, think, or feel (Cowen, 1982; Cutrona & Suhr, 1994; Cutrona, Suhr, & Mac-Farlane, 1990; D'Augelli & Levy, 1978; Pearlin & McCall, 1990; Reisman & Shorr, 1980). This may spring from a sincere desire to help the other person and to express caring and concern (Goldsmith & Fitch, 1994). Helpers may see solutions to the other's situation—perhaps even simple solutions—and believe that simply stating the solution will bring about relief. The desire to tell the distressed other what to do may also be motivated by discomfort with the expression of negative emotion— we want to make distressed others feel better fast so we don't have to endure their distress (Gottlieb & Wagner, 1991; Pearlin & McCall, 1990). Finally, helpers may interject recommendations about what to do, think, or feel because they feel the norms of conversation require that they contribute substantial turns at talk rather than continuously providing "ritualized signs of appreciation" for the other's distress, such as "that's too bad" (Metts et al., 1995).

The appraisal perspective developed in this chapter suggests that no matter how well-intended or well-informed a helper may be, he or she can only assist in alleviating another's distress by facilitating reappraisals. As a general rule, "telling" the other person how to reappraise the situation is likely to be less consistently effective at comforting than promoting a discussion in which the other has the opportunity to make sense of the situation and feelings about it. For example, Elliott and colleagues (1982) reported that on the occasions when "advisements" by therapists are effective, they are embedded in a more complex string of behaviors that includes interpretations, disagreements, reassurances, and self-disclosures.

Our appraisal analysis suggests several reasons why simply telling another how to reappraise a situation should be less consistently comforting than assisting the other in talking through reappraisal-relevant topics. First, the distressed other's responses will provide information that allows a comforter to assess what topics are relevant. As Figure 1 makes clear, there are many directions comforting conversations can go. The likelihood of reaching a functional reappraisal will be greater when the comforter has a better understanding of how the distressed other is appraising and coping with the situation (Metts et al., 1995; Pearlin & McCall, 1990). Even when a comforter feels confident that he or she knows how a distressed other ought to appraise or cope (e.g., through past experience with the individual or the situation), it is still preferable to allow the other to articulate and elaborate the recommended way of thinking, feeling, or doing rather than to simply tell her or him. If distress is to be alleviated, a change in appraisal must take place, and this is more likely to occur if the other articulates and elaborates a new way of viewing things or new way of coping for herself or himself. In addition, some distressed others may be resistant to a comforter's recommendations; letting others reach their own conclusions about how to reappraise situations should evoke less resistance and may minimize threats to face.

If encouraging the other to talk through a reappraisal is preferable to telling the other how to reappraise, how does a helper do so? Metts and colleagues (1995) suggested asking questions may enable a helper to contribute substantive conversational turns and gather information on which to base sophisticated comforting messages. However, findings on the utility of questions as a therapist response mode are mixed. In one study, open questions were associated with client perceptions that they achieved a "new perspective" but were not related to client ratings of helpfulness and were negatively related to the positive outcome "understanding" (Elliott, 1985; see also Elliott, James, Reimschuessel, Cislo, & Sack, 1985). In another study, questions were unrelated to perceptions of helpfulness for one sample and negatively related to perceived helpfulness in another sample (Elliott et al., 1982). A comparison of therapist and client perceptions found therapists perceived open questions as more helpful than clients did, but that open questions and paraphrases were positively related to measures of actual change in anxiety (Hill et al., 1988). Understanding of the potential role of asking questions in comforting will probably require considering the questioning mode in conjunction with topic. For example, Metts et al. (1995) coded "troubles talk" between strangers for questions about the event, the degree of the event's severity, the distressed other's feelings, and options for the future. The therapist response mode findings also underscore the importance of selecting appropriate outcome measures: Questions may achieve reappraisal (i.e., "a new perspective") and reduce anxiety even when recipients do not immediately recognize that these outcomes are "helpful."

Several bodies of research point to other conversational moves that can serve the function of seeking information and encouraging talk; these might be examined for their utility in the comforting context. For example, research on strangers interacting for the first time (Berger & Kellermann, 1983; Kellermann & Berger, 1984) found that when people had a goal of seeking information, they not only asked more questions but asked different kinds of questions aimed at generating explanations for acts and beliefs. They also made fewer statements and yielded the floor right after asking questions. Back-channel cues and shorter pauses were also employed by information seekers as a way of putting the other at ease. In conversations about problems between known others, these same conversational moves may be useful not only in eliciting information but also in generating extended talk. Research on how participants in conversations naturally acknowledge and encourage extended talk by others suggests a variety of verbal tokens (e.g., "oh," "mm-hm," or "yeah") and nonverbal behaviors (e.g., head nods, eye movements, body lean) that can function to acknowledge the newsworthiness of a topic and encourage further talk about it (see review by Nofsinger, 1991, pp. 115–121).

In research on talk between young and elderly strangers, as well as talk among the elderly, Coupland, Coupland, and Giles (1991) identified a range of responses to a "painful self-disclosure" that varied in the degree to which they encouraged further talk. For example, these researchers found that in addition to minimal "oh dear" responses, the recipient of a self-disclosure may encourage further talk through fuller conversational moves such as asking for specific clarification of some detail, asking nonspecific questions (e.g., "Were you?" in response to a statement by the other about an experience or feeling), or providing sympathetic evaluative responses (e.g., "Oh, that couldn't have been easy"). Sometimes helpers may wish not just to encourage talk, but to direct talk to particular topics; research on how participants recognize topic changes and rules for appropriate topic change suggest some ways this might be accomplished (see the review by McLaughlin, 1984, pp. 56–62).

Distressed others may find it difficult to engage in extended elaboration of their negative emotions, even when encouraged to do so by helpers. In ordinary conversation, the telling of an extended narrative requires the teller to gain hearers' cooperation in granting the teller extended turns at talk (see reviews by McLaughlin,

1984, pp. 186–189; Nofsinger, 1991, pp. 155–162). Metts et al. (1995) note that the normal means of gaining cooperation for extended turns may be complicated when the "story" a distressed other wishes to tell involves the expression of negative emotion. In addition to the normal tasks of getting hearers to acknowledge the significance or topical relevance of the impending talk about a problem, the distressed other must gain cooperation in suspending the societal preference for the expression of positive emotions. Jefferson (1984) noted how "troubles tellers" sometimes laugh during the course of telling their troubles or take time out to discuss "buffer topics" unrelated to the troubles. She speculates that this may occur because troubles tellers feel compelled to show that they are managing well. Thus, research on the structure of ordinary conversations and troubles tellings suggest that tellers may encounter challenges in licensing extended talk about problems and negative emotions. Jefferson (1988) also proposed a set of descriptive categories for understanding the types of conversational moves that occur in troubles talk and their sequencing. This may provide a starting point for testing hypotheses about more and less effective strategies available to both helpers and troubles tellers who wish to create conversational spaces in which talk about problems and negative emotions can occur.

CONCLUSION

Our aim in this chapter has been to sketch a theoretical framework capable of making sense of findings regarding the features of effective comforting behaviors. Although limitations in this literature make it difficult to extract reliable generalizations, it appears that comforting efforts that display a topical focus on emotion, reflect a descriptive and explanatory orientation, and exhibit sensitivity to face concerns are most likely to be associated with positive affective change in emotionally distressed others. We argued that these three message features serve several important functions over the course of comforting interactions. In particular, messages exhibiting these properties help constitute a supportive conversational environment, aid in focusing the discussion on emotions and coping efforts, and encourage the distressed other to elaborate on these topics through detailed narratives. We also reviewed evidence indicating that these conversational processes assist in reducing emotional distress and its noxious correlates.

What has received little attention is *why* these particular message features and conversational processes are associated with improved affect and *how* these interactional elements facilitate functional emotional change. We argued that this question can be best answered by understanding how distressed emotional states arise in the first place. In appraisal theory, we found a compelling account of the circumstances leading to emotional states and their modification. Within this perspective, emotions are the product of appraisals of events; hence, emotional states change when events are reappraised.

The cognitive reappraisal of events thus emerges as a key mechanism of emotional change. The features of comforting messages and supportive conversations identified in our review are critical precisely because they appear to assist distressed others with the process of reappraisal. That is, messages encouraging distressed others to elaborate detailed narratives focusing on feelings and coping efforts help people with the reappraisal process. These messages appear to assist people in making sense out of troubling situations, developing coherent interpretations of events, considering alternative perspectives, grasping the nature and source of experienced feelings, and assimilating problematic events within the frame of larger understandings about life.

This chapter has sketched only the outline of a new theoretical perspective on the comforting process. A great deal more conceptual work remains to be done in fleshing out the theory. In particular, the precise character of the reappraisal process needs further specification, as do the mechanisms through which reappraisals are facilitated (or inhibited) by various communicative efforts. And, although our emergent theory gives us improved ways of viewing the comforting process and the communicative activities that play roles in this process, much work remains to be done in identifying specific features of messages and conversations that facilitate or inhibit reappraisals. In particular, a more elaborated model of the comforting process needs to provide an integrated treatment of (a) the conversational goals to be addressed by helpers when attempting to facilitate reappraisals by distressed others, (b) the obstacles or issues helpers may face in attempting to achieve these goals, and (c) the conversational strategies that can assist with overcoming such obstacles and in addressing such issues.

Despite its nascent state, our theory of the comforting process does have several important implications for future research examining emotional support efforts and their outcomes. For example, most research examining the effects of different comforting messages on varied outcomes (e.g., improved affect, subjective well-being, health) has employed, however implicitly, a direct effects model. That is, most studies have examined the direct link or association between message behavior of helpers and outcomes experienced by message targets. Our theoretical analysis of the comforting process suggests that future research should examine and test a mediational model of comforting effects. Specifically, our analysis implies that the communicative efforts of a helper are more or less effective in virtue of facilitating reappraisals by the distressed other. These reappraisals are generated, and conversationally marked, by narratives focused on feelings and coping efforts. Hence, the communicative activities of the distressed other (i.e., the extent to which narratives about feelings are elaborated) should mediate the effect of the helper's communicative efforts on outcomes experienced by the other.

Second, our theoretical framework suggests that the common practice of coding support-intended messages for "type of support" (e.g., informational support, emotional support, esteem support) is not particularly useful. Such approaches deflect attention from both the form and function of utterances during the course of conversations. They also frequently assume a one-to-one correspondence between particular message forms and particular message functions (e.g., emotional support affects emotions, problem-solving support affects problems). In contrast, we recommend focusing on the varied features of messages that facilitate or inhibit the reappraisal process. Surface content of a message is only one relevant feature, and it may not be the most reliable indicator of whether a message promotes reappraisals. After all, information about a problem can impact on the emotions, whereas some statements about feelings can hinder emotional coping.

Finally, our analysis makes it imperative to examine the conversational interactions in which comforting activities occur. Obviously, a great deal has been learned about comforting through methods that do not involve the observation of interactions (e.g., self-reports, structured exercises, message evaluation tasks, etc.). Although such techniques will remain important research tools, our appraisal approach to comforting underscores that emotional support is a *conversational process,* not a behavioral act or a message strategy. Understanding how supportive conversational environments get constituted and maintained, how topics are managed, and how extended conversational turns are negotiated and allocated will, quite naturally, require studying these processes as they are realized in conversation. Clearly, there are formidable challenges to be overcome in obtaining the kinds of conversations needed to study these processes. Nonetheless, these challenges must be addressed if we are to further our understanding of how conversation facilitates reappraisals, and how these reappraisals lead to feeling better.

REFERENCES

Albrecht, T. L., & Adelman, M. B. (Eds.). (1987). *Communicating social support.* Newbury Park, CA: Sage.

Albrecht, T. L., Burleson, B. R., & Goldsmith, D. (1994). Supportive communication. In M. L. Knapp & G. R. Miller (Eds.), *Handbook of interpersonal communication* (2nd ed., pp. 419–449). Thousand Oaks, CA: Sage.

Applegate, J. L. (1980). Adaptive communication in educational contexts: A study of teachers' communicative strategies. *Communication Education, 29,* 158–170.

Barbee, A. P., & Cunningham, M. R. (1995). An experimental approach to social support communications: Interactive coping in close relationships. In B. R. Burleson (Ed.), *Communication yearbook 18* (pp. 381–413). Thousand Oaks, CA: Sage.

Barrett-Lennard, G. T. (1962). Dimensions of therapist response as causal factors in therapeutic change. *Psychological Monographs, 76* (43), Whole No. 562.

Barrett-Lennard, G. T. (1986). The Relationship Inventory now: Issues and advances in theory, method, and use. In L. S. Greenberg & W. M. Pinsof (Eds.), *The psychotherapeutic process: A research handbook* (pp. 439–476). New York: Guilford.

Batson, C. D., Shaw, L. L., & Oleson, K. C. (1992). Differentiating affect, mood, and emotion: Toward functionally based conceptual distinctions. In M. S. Clark (Ed.), *Emotion* (pp. 294–326). Newbury Park, CA: Sage.

Berger, C. R., & Kellermann, K. A. (1983). To ask or not to ask: Is that the question? In R. N. Bostrom (Ed.), *Communication yearbook 7* (pp. 342–368). Beverly Hills, CA: Sage.

Burleson, B. R. (1983). Social cognition, empathic motivation, and adults' comforting strategies. *Human Communication Research, 10,* 295–304.

Burleson, B. R. (1984). Age, social-cognitive development, and the use of comforting strategies. *Communication Monographs, 51,* 140–153.

Burleson, B. R. (1987). Cognitive complexity. In J. C. McCroskey & J. A. Daly (Eds.), *Personality and interpersonal communication* (pp. 305–349). Newbury Park, CA: Sage.

Burleson, B. R. (1990). Comforting as everyday social support: Relational consequences of supportive behaviors. In S. Duck (Ed.) with R. Silver, *Personal relationships and social support* (pp. 66–82). London: Sage.

Burleson, B. R. (1994a). Comforting communication: Significance, approaches, and effects. In B. R. Burleson, T. L. Albrecht, & I. G. Sarason (Eds.), *Communication of social support: Messages, interactions, relationships, and community* (pp. 3–28). Thousand Oaks, CA: Sage.

Burleson, B. R. (1994b). Comforting messages: Features, functions, and outcomes. In J. A. Daly & J. M. Wiemann (Eds.), *Strategic interpersonal communication* (135–161). Hillsdale, NJ: Erlbaum.

Burleson, B. R., Albrecht, T. L., & Sarason, I. G. (Eds.) (1994). *Communication of social support: Messages, interactions, relationships, and community.* Thousand Oaks, CA: Sage.

Burleson, B. R., & Samter, W. (1985a). Consistencies in theoretical and naive evaluations of comforting messages. *Communication Monographs, 52,* 103–123.

Burleson, B. R., & Samter, W. (1985b). Individual differences in the perception of comforting messages: An exploratory investigation. *Central States Speech Journal, 36,* 39–50.

Carkhuff, R. R., & Berenson, B. G. (1977). *Beyond counseling and therapy* (2nd ed.). New York: Holt, Rinehart, & Winston.

Clark, L. F. (1993). Stress and the cognitive-conversational benefits of social interaction. *Journal of Social and Clinical Psychology, 12,* 25–55.

Coates, D., & Winston, T. (1987). The dilemma of distress disclosure. In V. J. Derlega & J. H. Berg (Eds.), *Self-disclosure: Theory, research, and therapy* (pp. 229–255). New York: Plenum.

Coates, D., Wortman, C. B., & Abbey, A. (1979). Reactions to victims. In I. H. Frieze, D. Bar-Tal, & J. S. Carroll (Eds.), *New approaches to social problems* (pp. 21–52). San Francisco: Jossey-Bass.

Cohen, S., & McKay, G. (1984). Social support, stress, and the buffering hypothesis: A theoretical analysis. In A. Baum, J. E. Singer, & S. E. Taylor (Eds.), *Handbook of psychology and health* (pp. 253–267). Hillsdale, NJ: Erlbaum.

Cohen, S., & Willis, T. A. (1985). Stress, social support, and the buffering hypothesis. *Psychological Bulletin, 98,* 310–357.

Coupland, N., Coupland, J., & Giles, H. (1991). *Language, society and the elderly.* Oxford: Blackwell.

Costanza, R., Derlega, V. J. & Winstead, B. A. (1988). Positive and negative forms of social support: Effects of conversational topics on coping with stress among same-sex friends. *Journal of Experimental Social Psychology, 24,* 182–193.

Cowen, E. L. (1982). Help is where you find it. *American Psychologist, 37,* 385–395.

Coyne, J. C., Wortman, C. B., & Lehman, D. R. (1988). The other side of social support: Emotional overinvolvement and miscarried helping. In B. Gottlieb (Ed.), *Marshalling social support: Formats, processes, and effects* (pp. 305–330). Newbury Park, CA: Sage.

Cramer, D. (1990). Helpful actions of close friends to personal problems and distress. *British Journal of Guidance and Counseling, 18,* 280–292.

Cutrona, C. E., Cohen, B. B., & Igram, S. (1990). Contextual determinants of the perceived helpfulness of helping behaviors. *Journal of Social and Personal Relationships, 7,* 553–562.

Cutrona, C. E., & Russell, D. W. (1990). Types of social support and specific stress: Toward a theory of optimal matching. In B. R. Sarason, I. G. Sarason, & G. R. Pierce (Eds.), *Social support: An interactional view* (pp. 319–366). New York: Wiley.

Cutrona, C. E., & Suhr, J. A. (1992). Controllability of stressful events and satisfaction with spouse support behaviors. *Communication Research, 19,* 154–174.

Cutrona, C. E., & Suhr, J. A. (1994). Social support communication in the context of marriage: An analysis of couples' supportive interactions. In B. R. Burleson, T. L. Albrecht, & I. G. Sarason (Eds.), *Communication of social support: Messages, interactions, relationships, and community* (pp. 113–135). Thousand Oaks, CA: Sage.

Cutrona, C. E., Suhr, J. A., & MacFarlane, R. (1990). Interpersonal transactions and the psychological sense of support. In S. Duck with R. Silver (Eds.), *Personal relationships and social support* (pp. 30–45). London: Sage.

D'Augelli, A. R., & Levy, M. (1978). The verbal helping skills of trained and untrained human service paraprofessionals. *American Journal of Community Psychology, 6,* 23–31.

Dakof, G. A., & Taylor, S. E. (1990). Victims' perceptions of support attempts: What is helpful from whom? *Journal of Personality and Social Psychology, 58,* 80–89.

DePaulo, B. M. (1982). Social-psychological processes in informal help seeking. In T. A. Wills (Ed.), *Basic processes in helping relationships* (pp. 255–279). New York: Academic Press.

Dunkel-Schetter, C., & Bennett, T. L. (1990). Differentiating the cognitive and behavioral aspects of social support. In B. R. Sarason, I. G. Sarason, & G. R. Pierce (Eds.), *Social support: An interactional view* (pp. 267–296). New York: Wiley.

Dunkel-Schetter, C., Blasband, D., Feinstein, L., & Herbert, T. (1992). Elements of supportive interactions: When are attempts to help effective? In S. Spacapan & S. Oskamp (Eds.), *Helping and being helped: Naturalistic studies* (pp. 83–114). Newbury Park, CA: Sage.

Dunkel-Schetter, C., & Wortman, C. B. (1982). The interpersonal dynamics of cancer: Problems in social relationships and their impact on the patient. In H. S. Friedman & M. R. DiMatteo (Eds.), *Interpersonal issues in health care* (pp. 349–380). New York: Academic Press.

Elliott, R. (1985). Helpful and nonhelpful events in brief counseling interviews: An empirical taxonomy. *Journal of Counseling Psychology, 32,* 307–322.

Elliott, R., James, E., Reimschuessel, C., Cislo, D., & Sack, N. (1985). Significant events and the analysis of immediate therapeutic impacts. *Psychotherapy, 22,* 620–630.

Elliott, R., Stiles, W. B., Shiffman, S., Barker, C. B., Burstine, B., & Goodman, G. (1982). The empirical analysis of help-intended communications: Conceptual framework and recent research. In T. A. Wills (Ed.), *Basic processes in helping relationships* (pp. 333–356). New York: Academic Press.

Frijda, N. H. (1986). *The emotions.* New York: Cambridge University Press.

Goldsmith, D. (1992). Managing conflicting goals in supportive interaction: An integrative theoretical framework. *Communication Research, 19,* 264–286.

Goldsmith, D. J. (1994). The role of facework in supportive communication. In B. R. Burleson, T. L. Albrecht, & I. G. Sarason (Eds.), *Communication of social support: Messages, interactions, relationships, and community* (pp. 29–49). Thousand Oaks, CA: Sage.

Goldsmith, D. J. (1995). The communicative microdynamics of support. In B. R. Burleson (Ed.), *Communication yearbook 18* (pp. 414–433). Thousand Oaks, CA: Sage.

Goldsmith, D. J., & Fitch, K. (1994, July). *Giving and receiving advice in some American speech.* Paper presented at the International Communication Association convention, Sydney, Australia.

Goldsmith, D., & Parks, M. (1990). Communicative strategies for managing the risks of seeking social support. In S. Duck with R. Silver (Eds.), *Personal relationships and social support* (pp. 104–121). London: Sage.

Gottlieb, B. H., Beatty, E. (1985). Negative responses to depression: The role of attributional style. *Cognitive Therapy Research, 9,* 91–103.

Gottlieb, B. H., & Wagner, F. (1991). Stress and support processes in close relationships. In J. Eckenrode (Ed.), *The social context of coping* (pp. 165–188). New York: Plenum.

Greenberg, L. S., Rice, L. N., & Elliott, R. (1993). *Facilitating emotional change: The moment-by-moment process.* New York: Guilford Press.

Greenberg, L. S., & Safran, J. D. (1987). *Emotion in psychotherapy: Affect, cognition, and the process of change.* New York: Guilford Press.

Gross, E., & Stone, G. P. (1964). Embarrassment and the analysis of role-requirements. *American Journal of Sociology, 70,* 1–15.

Harber, K. D., & Pennebaker, J. W. (1992). Overcoming traumatic memories. In S. A. Christianson (Ed.), *The handbook of emotion and memory: Research and theory* (pp. 359–387). Hillsdale, NJ: Erlbaum.

Herbert, T., & Dunkel-Schetter, C. (1992). Negative social reactions to victims: An overview of responses and their determinants. In L. Montada, S. Filipp, & M. Lerner (Eds.), *Life crises and experiences of loss in adulthood* (pp. 497–518). Hillsdale, NJ: Erlbaum.

Hill, C. E., Helms, J. E., Tichenor, V., Spiegel, S. B., O'Grady, K. E., & Perry, S. E. (1988). Effects of therapist response mode in brief psychotherapy. *Journal of Counseling Psychology, 35,* 222–233.

Hochschild, A. (1979). Emotion work, feeling rules, and social structure. *American Journal of Sociology, 85,* 551–575.

Hochschild, A. (1990). Ideology and emotion management: A perspective and path for future research. In T. D. Kemper (Ed.), *Research agendas in the sociology of emotions* (pp. 117–142). Albany, NY: SUNY Press.

Hoyt, M. F., Xenakis, S. N., Marmer, C. R., & Horowitz, M. H. (1983). Therapists' actions that influence their perceptions of "good" psychotherapy sessions. *Journal of Nervous and Mental Disease, 171,* 400–404.

Izard, C. E. (1977). *Human emotions.* New York: Plenum.

Jacobson, D. E. (1986). Types and timing of social support. *Journal of Health and Social Behavior, 27,* 250–264.

Jefferson, G. (1984). On the organization of laughter in talk about troubles. In J. M. Atkinson & J. C. Heritage (Eds.), *Structures of social action: Studies in conversational analysis* (pp. 346–369). Cambridge: Cambridge University Press.

Jefferson, G. (1988). On the sequential organization of troubles-talk in ordinary conversation. *Social Problems, 35,* 418–441.

Jones, S. M. (1996). *The impact of situational variables on the perception of comforting messages.* Unpublished master's thesis, Indiana University, Bloomington.

Kellermann, K., & Berger, C. R. (1984). Affect and social information acquisition: Sit back, relax, and tell me about yourself. In R. N. Bostrom (Ed.), *Communication yearbook 8* (pp. 412–445). Beverly Hills, CA: Sage.

Kunkel, A. W. (1995, November). *Assessing the adequacy of explanations for gender differences in emotional support: An experimental test of the different cultures and skill deficit accounts.* Paper presented at the Speech Communication Association convention, San Antonio, TX.

Laird, J. D., & Bresler, C. (1992). The process of emotional experience: A self-perception theory. In M. S. Clark (Ed.), *Emotion* (pp. 213–234). Newbury Park, CA: Sage.

Lazarus, R. S. (1968). Emotions and adaptation: Conceptual and empirical relations. In W. J. Arnold (Ed.), *Nebraska Symposium on Motivation* (Vol. 16, pp. 175–266). Lincoln: University of Nebraska Press.

Lazarus, R. S. (1984). On the primacy of cognition. *American Psychologist, 39,* 124–129.

Lazarus, R. S. (1991). *Emotion and adaptation.* New York: Oxford University Press.

Lazarus, R. S. (1995). Vexing research problems inherent in cognitive-mediational theories of emotion—and some solutions. *Psychological Inquiry, 6,* 183–196.

Lazarus, R. S., & Folkman, S. (1984). *Stress, appraisal, and coping.* New York: Springer.

Lazarus, R. S., & Lazarus, B. N. (1994). *Passion and reason: Making sense of our emotions.* New York: Oxford University Press.

Lewis, M., & Haviland, J. M. (Eds.) (1993). *Handbook of emotions.* New York: Guilford.

Liu, J. H., Karasawa, K., & Weiner, B. (1992). Inferences about the causes of positive and negative emotions. *Personality and Social Psychology Bulletin, 18,* 603–615.

Mandler, G. (1984). *Mind and body: Psychology of emotions and stress.* New York: Norton.

McLaughlin, M. L. (1984). *Conversation: How talk is organized.* Beverly Hills, CA: Sage.

Metts, S., Backhaus, S., & Kazoleas, D. (1995, February). *Social support as problematic communication.* Paper presented at the Western States Communication Association convention, Portland, OR.

Metts, S., & Bowers, J. W. (1994). Emotion in interpersonal communication. In M. L. Knapp & G. R. Miller (Eds.), *Handbook of interpersonal communication* (pp. 508–541). Thousand Oaks, CA: Sage.

Metts, S., Geist, P., & Gray, J. L. (1994). The role of relationship characteristics in the provision and effectiveness of supportive messages among nursing professionals. In B. R. Burleson, T. L. Albrecht, & I. G. Sarason (Eds.), *Communication of social support: Messages, interactions, relationships, and community* (pp. 229–246). Thousand Oaks, CA: Sage.

Nofsinger, R. E. (1991). *Everyday conversation.* Newbury Park, CA: Sage.

Notarius, C. I., & Herrick, L. R. (1988). Listener response strategies to a distressed other. *Journal of Social and Personal Relationships, 5,* 97–108.

Omdahl, B. L. (1995). *Cognitive appraisal, emotion, and empathy.* Mahwah, NJ: Erlbaum.

Ortony, A., Clore, G. L., & Collins, A. (1988). *The cognitive structure of emotions.* New York: Cambridge University Press.

Parkinson, B., & Manstead, A. S. R. (1992). Appraisal as a cause of emotion. In M. S. Clark (Ed.), *Emotion* (pp. 122–149). Newbury Park, CA: Sage.

Pearlin, L. I., & McCall, M. E. (1990). Occupational stress and marital support: A description of microprocesses. In J. Eckenrode & S. Gore (Eds.), *Stress between work and family* (pp. 39–60). New York: Plenum.

Pennebaker, J. W. (1989). Confession, inhibition, and disease. In L. Berkowitz (Ed.), *Advances in experimental social psychology* (Vol. 22, pp. 211–244). New York: Academic Press.

Pennebaker, J. W. (1993). Putting stress into words: Health, linguistic, and therapeutic implications. *Behavioral Research and Theory, 31,* 539–548.

Pennebaker, J. W., & Beall, S. K. (1986). Confronting a traumatic event: Toward an understanding of inhibition and disease. *Journal of Abnormal Psychology, 95,* 274–281.

Pennebaker, J. W., Kiecolt-Glaser, J., & Glaser, R. (1988). Disclosure of traumas and immune function: Health implications for psychotherapy. *Journal of Consulting and Clinical Psychology, 56,* 239–245.

Pierce, G., Sarason, I., & Sarason, B. (1990). Integrating social support perspectives: Working models, personal relationships, and situational factors. In S. Duck with R. Silver (Eds.), *Personal relationships and social support* (pp. 173–189). London: Sage.

Reisman, J. M., & Shorr, S. (1980). Developmental changes in friendship-related communication skills. *Journal of Clinical Child Psychology, 9,* 67–69.

Rice, L. N., & Kerr, G. P. (1986). Measures of client and therapist vocal quality. In L. S. Greenberg & W. M. Pinsof (Eds.), *The psychotherapeutic process: A research handbook* (pp. 73–105). New York: Guilford.

Rogers, C. R. (1957). The necessary and sufficient conditions of therapeutic personality change. *Journal of Consulting Psychology, 21,* 95–103.

Rogers, C. R. (1975). Empathic: An unappreciated way of being. *Counseling Psychologist, 5(2),* 2–10.

Roseman, I. J. (1984). Cognitive determinants of emotion: A structural theory. In P. Shaver (Ed.), *Emotions, relationships, and health* (pp. 11–36). Beverly Hills, CA: Sage.

Ross, L., Rodin, J., & Zimbardo, P. G. (1969). The reduction of fear through induced cognitive-emotional misattribution. *Journal of Personality and Social Psychology, 12,* 279–288.

Samter, W., Burleson, B. R., & Basden-Murphy, L. B. (1987). Comforting conversations: Effects of strategy type on evaluations of messages and message producers. *Southern Speech Communication Journal, 52,* 263–284.

Schachter, S. (1964). The interaction of cognitive and physiological determinants of emotional state. In L. Berkowitz (Ed.), *Advances in experimental social psychology* (Vol. 1, pp. 49–80). New York: Academic Press.

Scheff, T. J. (1984). The taboo on coarse emotions. In P. Shaver (Ed.), *Review of personality and social psychology: Emotions, relationships, and health* (Vol. 5, pp. 146–169). Beverly Hills, CA: Sage.

Scheff, T. J. (1990). *Microsociology: Discourse, emotion, and social structure.* Chicago: University of Chicago Press.

Scherer, K. R. (1988). Criteria for emotion-antecedent appraisal: A review. In V. Hamilton, G. Bower, & N. H. Frijda (Eds.), *Cognitive perspectives on emotion and motivation* (pp. 89–126). Dordrecht, The Netherlands: Kluwer.

Silver, R., Boon, C., & Stones, M. H. (1983). Searching for meaning in misfortune: Making sense of incest. *Journal of Social Issues, 39,* 81–102.

Silver, R. C., Wortman, C. B., & Crofton, C. (1990). The role of coping in support provision: The self-presentational dilemmas of victims of life crises. In B. R. Sarason, I. G. Sarason, & G. R. Pierce (Eds.), *Social support: An interactional view* (pp. 397–426). New York: Wiley.

Smith, C. A. (1989). Dimensions of appraisal and physiological response in emotion. *Journal of Personality and Social Psychology, 56,* 339–353.

Smith, C. A., & Ellsworth, P. C. (1985). Patterns of cognitive appraisal in emotion. *Journal of Personality and Social Psychology, 48,* 813–838.

Smith, C. A., & Lazarus, R. S. (1990). Emotion and adaptation. In L. A. Pervin (Ed.), *Handbook of personality: Theory and research* (pp. 609–637). New York: Guilford.

Smith, C. A., & Pope, L. K. (1992). Appraisal and emotion: The interactional contribution of dispositional and situational factors. In M. S. Clark (Ed.), *Emotion and social behavior* (pp. 32–62). Newbury Park, CA: Sage.

Stiles, W. B. (1987). "I have to talk to somebody": A fever model of disclosure. In V. J. Derlega & J. H. Berg (Eds.), *Self-disclosure: Theory, research, and therapy* (pp. 257–282). New York: Plenum.

Tait, R., & Silver, R. C. (1989). Coming to terms with major negative life events. In J. S. Uleman & J. A. Bargh (Eds.), *Unintended thought* (pp. 351–382). New York: Guilford.

Tavris, C. (1984). On the wisdom of counting to ten: Personal and social dangers of anger expression. In P. Shaver (Ed.), *Review of personality and social psychology: Emotions, relationships, and health* (Vol. 5, pp. 170–191). Beverly Hills, CA: Sage.

Thoits, P. A. (1984). Coping, social support, and psychological outcomes. In P. Shaver (Ed.), *Review of personality and social psychology: Emotions, relationships, and health* (Vol. 5, pp. 219–238). Beverly Hills, CA: Sage.

Thoits, P. A. (1986). Social support as coping assistance. *Journal of Counseling and Clinical Psychology, 54,* 416–423.

Truax, C. B., & Carkhuff, R. R. (1967). *Toward effective counseling and psychotherapy.* Chicago: Aldine.

Valins, S., & Nisbett, R. E. (1972). Attribution processes in the development and treatment of emotional disorders. In E. E. Jones, D. E. Kanouse, H. H. Kelley, R. E. Nisbet, S. Valins, & B. Weiner (Eds.), *Attribution: Perceiving the causes of behavior* (pp. 137–150). Morristown, NJ: General Learning Press.

Wilson, T. D., & Linville, P. W. (1982). Improving the academic performance of college freshman: Attribution therapy revisited. *Journal of Personality and Social Psychology, 42,* 367–376.

Winstead, B. J., & Derlega, V. J. (1991). An experimental approach to studying social interaction and coping with stress among friends. In W. H. Jones & D. Perlman (Eds.), *Advances in personal relationships* (Vol. 2, pp. 107–131). London: Jessica Kingsley.

Winstead, B. A., Derlega, V. J., Lewis, R. J., Sanchez-Hucles, J., & Clarke, E. (1992). Friendship, social interaction, and coping with stress. *Communication Research, 19,* 193–211.

Wortman, C. B., & Lehman, D. R. (1985). Reactions to victims of life crises: Support attempts that fail. In I. G. Sarason & B. R. Sarason (Eds.), *Social support: Theory, research, and application* (pp. 463–489). Dordrecht: Martinus Nijhoff.

CHAPTER 10

When a Friend Is in Need: Feelings about Seeking, Giving, and Receiving Social Support

Anita P. Barbee, Tammy L. Rowatt, and Michael R. Cunningham

University of Louisville
Louisville, Kentucky

It has been well documented that receiving social support from friends and loved ones leads to mental and physical well-being (e.g., Cutrona, 1986; Matthews, Davis, Stoney, Owens, & Caggiula, 1991). Although it is important to understand general outcomes of the receipt of social support, it is equally important to understand the variables that affect when and how support is given and received in close relationships (Dunkel-Schetter & Skokan, 1990; Barbee & Cunningham, 1995). One of the most important variables to examine in this context is emotion.

This chapter will examine the role of emotion before, during, and after a supportive interaction takes place. Both the perspective of the support seeker and the support giver will be considered. Previous work focused on reasons for *not* seeking social support, most of which stemmed from negative emotional outcomes (Fisher, Goff, Nadler, & Chinsky, 1988). We will build on this previous work in four major ways. First, we draw upon our theory of interactive coping, *Sensitive Interaction Systems Theory* (SIST). With this theoretical base, we explore other ways in which emotion can affect support seekers, including their choice of support activation behaviors, as well as their response to their partner's attempt to comfort them. Next, we examine the role that emotion plays in a potential supporter's willingness and ability to give effective support, and in their response to their partner's reaction to

Handbook of Communication and Emotion: Research, Theory, Applications, and Contexts

their supportive attempts. Finally, we examine how all of these expressions of emotion function within a supportive context to affect both short-term and long-term outcomes.

SENSITIVE INTERACTION SYSTEMS THEORY

Relationships are often robust and resilient, but specific interactions can be delicate and easily thrown off track by forces that are either internal or external to the system. SIST reflects the dialectics of flexibility and brittleness that occur in communication between members of close relationships (Barbee & Cunningham, 1995). SIST is predicated on the notion that internal emotional conflicts and ambivalencies may be reflected in the communication of both the support seeker and the support giver in particular supportive interactions.

We developed a model to reflect many of the variables that could play a part in the unfolding of supportive interactions (Barbee & Cunningham, 1995). The model includes the impact of seekers' emotional state on their choice of support activation behavior, the impact of the supporters' emotional state on their willingness and ability to give support, as well as the impact of the expression of emotional reactions to particular support activation and helping behaviors. For the purpose of this chapter, we will focus primarily on the role that emotion plays at each juncture of the interactive coping process (see Figure 1).

Support Activation

Emotions influence the types of strategies that both the seekers and the supporters use when in a supportive episode. To understand the impact of emotion, however, it is first necessary to describe some of the basic dimensions that people use to elicit social support. A distressed person's tactics for activating social support may be either direct and unambiguous about the desire for help, or indirect and ambiguous about whether help is being sought (Cutrona, Suhr, & MacFarlane, 1990). Direct support seeking behaviors may be verbal, by *asking* for help, which includes talking about the problem in a factual manner, telling the supporter about the problem, giving details of the problem, and disclosing what has been done so far about the problem.

Direct support seeking also may involve nonverbal communication such as showing distress about the problem through *crying*, or using other direct behaviors such as eye contact with furrowed brow, or putting one's head on the partner's shoulder. Seekers using these behaviors wordlessly communicate their emotional state, and convey that they want some form of help to solve the problem or make them feel better. Indirect support-seeking behaviors, by contrast, are more subtle and less informative.

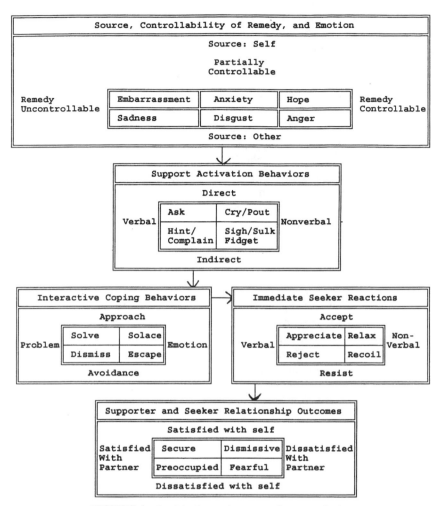

FIGURE 1   Sensitive interaction system theory typologies.

Indirect verbal strategies for activating social support are exemplified by global-ly *complaining* about a situation without requesting aid, or by *hinting* that a problem exists. Hints may let the supporter know there is a problem, or reveal how the seek-er feels without the seeker having to directly state her or his problems or feelings. Hints and complaints may protect the support-seeker's self-esteem, but may not convey the nature of the problem in such a way that the support giver can provide effective solutions and consequently may cause the support giver to dismiss the problem. Indirect support activation behaviors also may employ nonverbal com-munication by subtly showing negative affect in the form of *sighing, sulking,* or *fid-*

geting. Indirect nonverbal behaviors may induce a caring support giver to ask what is wrong, but they run the risk of causing the potential support giver to ignore the gestures or escape from the situation.

Interactive Coping Responses

Support activation behaviors are generally intended to elicit helpful responses from the partner. The range of socially supportive behaviors provided by a supporter are incorporated into what we call the Interactive Coping Typology. It is useful to briefly describe this typology of support-giver reactions prior to discussing the role of emotions in support activation and support giving. The Interactive Coping Typology of support-giving strategies subsumes two major theoretical dimensions of the coping process. This typology incorporates the Roth and Cohen (1986) dimension of either *approaching* or *avoiding* the problem or emotion, which is crossed with the Folkman and Lazarus (1985) dimension of *focusing on the problem* versus *focusing on the emotion*. The resulting Interactive Coping typology includes: *solve* behaviors, which are problem-focused/approach behaviors designed to find an answer to the problem, such as giving informational and tangible support, asking questions, and making suggestions; *solace* behaviors, which are emotion-focused/approach behaviors designed to elicit positive emotions and express closeness, such as saying the friend is a good person. *Dismiss* behaviors are problem-focused/avoidance behaviors that minimize the significance of the problem, such as saying the problem is not serious; and *escape* behaviors, which are emotion-focused/avoidance behaviors that discourage the display of negative emotion in the seeker of support, often for the benefit of the support, such as making fun of the problem, or showing irritability (Barbee, 1990; Barbee & Cunningham, 1995). As the following section will clarify, each interactive coping behavior may be sought, and given, under different emotional circumstances.

SEEKER'S PERSPECTIVE

An interactive coping episode generally begins with a problem, and with a support seeker who communicates the need for assistance. The nature of the problem, the temperament of the support seeker, and past supportive interactions with the partner can affect the intensity of the anxiety, anger, sadness, or embarrassment that is to be dealt with in the interaction. These emotions stem from either the nature of the problem or the anticipation of the potential supporter's reaction.

A seeker may feel anxious because of an upcoming test, for example, and may need solace, such as reassurance that he or she will probably do as superbly on the test as he or she has in the past. Or, he or she may need the support giver to provide a solve behavior, such as taking over household responsibilities so that the support seeker has more time to study in order to master the material for the test. But a support seeker may feel embarrassed about sharing her or his test anxiety with her or his partner, especially if the partner has dismissed the concerns in the past. As a result, the support seeker may be reluctant to make a direct request for help.

The considerable literature on why people are reluctant to seek help was reviewed by Fisher and Nadler (1982). They found that people are generally uncomfortable seeking help because (a) it has the potential to lower self-esteem (Chesler & Barbarin, 1984; Wortman & Dunkel-Schetter, 1979); (b) it has the potential to change the balance of equity in a relationship (Fisher, Nadler, & Whitcher-Alagna, 1983; Hatfield & Sprecher, 1983); and (c) it calls into question the competence of the person asking for help (DePaulo, 1982). Although we found no studies that have directly assessed the underlying emotional states that prevent the seeking of support, we speculate that anxiety and depression may be linked to the motivation to preserve self-esteem. Concern about the partner's negative arousal and angry irritation may be linked to the motivation to preserve equity in the relationship (Hatfield & Sprecher, 1983). Finally, fear of embarrassment and a sense of pride may be linked to the motivation to appear competent and independent (Shapiro, 1983).

If emotions about the partner and the self keep people from seeking help with a problem, then they may not communicate their need for support. If they do seek help, their communication may be in the form of indirect seeking attempts, such as hinting or complaining, rather than direct communication. The arousal that accompanies the negative emotions may leak out in the form of sighing or fidgeting, which may lead the supporter to detect the distress without clearly knowing what is wrong or exactly how to help.

Research on the sequencing of supportive exchanges (Gulley, 1993) found that the use of indirect forms of help seeking, such as hinting and sighing, often lead to avoidance strategies by supporters in the form of dismiss and escape behaviors. Gulley (1993) examined the communication behavior of 120 pairs of close associates who were discussing several different types of problems. Sequential analyses were conducted to determine whether the direct support activation behaviors of ask and cry, versus the indirect categories of hint and sulk, lead to the interactive coping approach categories of solve and solace versus the avoidance categories of dismiss and escape.

Direct requests for support were more likely to produce approach rather than avoidance behaviors (Gulley, 1993). Indirect support activation behaviors also could stimulate approach behaviors, but direct activation behaviors more reliably led to approach behaviors than did indirect behaviors. Further analysis also showed that support seekers more often employed a direct support activation behavior following a supporter's use of an approach behavior and employed an indirect support activation behavior most often in response to an avoidant behavior. These findings were true for both males and females.

These results demonstrate that partners were communicating in synchrony, such that each individual's behavior tended to elicit a reciprocal behavior from their interaction partner. Other variables, such as the subject's gender, whether the relationship was romantic or a friendship, and the category of problem discussed did *not* effectively predict the patterns of behaviors employed during the conversations. This finding bolsters the notion that support seekers share some of the responsibility for the type of support that is given to them. Supporters may not be solely responsible if poor support is given, because it is the support seeker who must convey the form of support that is needed. Support seekers may differ in the competency with which they communicate their needs (Burleson, 1982).

We located no research that examined how the type of emotion experienced by seekers of support affected either their desire for a particular form of social support, or their use of a particular verbal or nonverbal request for assistance. However, Emmons and Colby (1995) found that ambivalence in expressing emotion was associated with low perceived social support, use of avoidant coping strategies, and fewer efforts to seek social support in distressing situations.

There is no reason to believe that any emotion is inevitably linked to a specific type of interactive coping response, or a specific support activation behavior. Cutrona and Russell (1990), however, have suggested that the more a situation is seen as uncontrollable, the more the individual may focus on their emotions; whereas the more a situation is seen as potentially controllable, the more the individual focuses on the problem. The SIST model incorporates this insight, and adds the additional dimension of whether the cause of the problem is the self or another source, to predict desired interactive coping behaviors and likely support-activation behaviors.

Emotion and the Seeker's Support Expectations

Each emotion may be based on a specific pattern of attributions and both the attributions and the emotions may be linked to the help-seeker's expectations about what form of social support would be most helpful, and to the use of different support activation behaviors (See Figure 2). *Sadness* often occurs following a negative event, such as the loss of a loved one, in which the individual feels no control over the resolution of the situation (Ellsworth & Smith, 1988). Under those circumstances the individual may desire *Solace*, such as compassionate expressions of care and reassurances of worth. In a situation in which the individual feels no guilt for the cause of the emotion, he or she may be more likely to use direct nonverbal support activation behaviors. *Crying* or *pouting* may be the most likely to elicit such *Solace*.

If an individual feels *embarrassed* because of a situation that reflects negatively on the self and which cannot be altered, the person may desire an *Escape* behavior to avoid those feelings (Hull, Young, & Jouriles, 1986). The support seeker might wish to avoid calling additional attention to the self by using an indirect, nonverbal support activation behavior, such as a *sigh* or a *fidget,* which attracts attention but side-

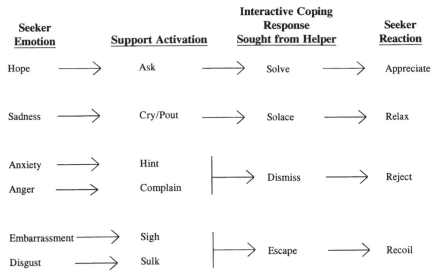

FIGURE 2   Hypothetical emotion, activation, interaction, and reaction links.

steps direct personal responsibility. If a potentially embarrassing situation is controllable because it is not clear that other people saw the faux pas, or saw the faux pas as a detraction to ones' reputation, then the emotion might be better described as anxiety rather than embarrassment, and involves an alternate pattern.

If an individual is feeling *anxious* about an event's future negative consequences, then the determination of what behaviors occur next may depend on precisely how controllable the person sees the situation as being. If the person feels little control over the solution to the problem, the person may desire *Dismiss* behavior from the partner in order to minimize the problem's apparent threat. Discussing or even just mentioning the problem may cause the distressed person to experience more arousal, so an anxious support seeker may use indirect nonverbal support activation behaviors, such as *hinting* and *complaining* to elicit the desired *Dismiss* behaviors from the partner (Kowalski, 1996). Some anxiety-inducing events, such as anticipating getting fired or going to prison after being convicted of a crime, are controllable only by cognitive coping. Other anxiety-inducing events, such as facing a challenging test, may be handled through direct action.

Anger is one of the most difficult emotions to cope with (Tice, personal communication, September 1995), perhaps in part because the solution to the problem is perceived to be controllable, but the control is in the hands of another person (Weiner, 1980). If angry support seekers focus on their own emotions, which are yoked to the uncontrollable problem, they may feel disgusted, and desire an *Escape*. A *sulk* or *fidget* may elicit *Escape* suggestions from the partner, such as recommendations to watch television, go jogging, or get drunk. If angry support seekers focus on the fact that the solution to the problem is in the hands of another person, they may feel increasingly irritated. One way to minimize the irritation is to reduce the significance of the problem, by *Dismissing* the importance of the issue. *Hints* or *complaints* may serve to elicit problem minimization from the partner.

If a situation that provokes anger or anxiety entails some personal control over the outcome, the feeling of hope may be mixed with the other emotions. Hope is likely to be linked to the desire for a *Solve* from the partner, and the use of a direct verbal *Ask* behavior. *Ask* behaviors, however, may be most likely when either the uncontrollable nature of the problem or the closeness of the relationship conveys that there is minimal risk of embarrassment for not coming up with a solution on one's own. Although the foregoing predictions are speculative, it is certainly plausible that different supporting actions might be more effective with different causes of unhappiness. Future research should examine the link between reasons for direct avoidance of help, particularly the emotions driving such reasons. Future research also needs to explore the relationship between the seeker emotion and the type of support-seeking strategy, as well as the link between type of seeker's emotion and preference for type of support given.

SUPPORTER PERSPECTIVE

According to the SIST perspective, contextual variables that produce negative thoughts, and the internal dynamics of the supporter that produce ambivalent feelings, may upset the delicate balance of the supporter's interactive coping communications. Only a few studies have examined the variables that affect a *supporter's* willingness and ability to support a close associate (e.g., Barbee, 1990, 1991; Barker, & Lemle, 1987; Otten, Penner, & Waugh, 1988; Simpson, Rholes, & Nelligan, 1992) or specifically *how* individual provide social support to help regulate the mood and solve the problems of their associates (Barbee & Cunningham, 1995; Cutrona & Suhr, 1992; Dakof & Taylor, 1990; Winstead & Derlega, 1991). A few of these studies have focused on the effect of a supporter's mood or emotional state on the giving of support.

In contrast to the social support literature, there is a long tradition in social psychology of examining the effect of various types of mood on *helpers* (Darley & Latane, 1968). Much of that research focused on manipulating the mood of a helper in either a laboratory or field setting. These positive or negative events were then followed by an opportunity for the participant to help in order to examine how transient moods affected people's willingness to help.

One theory suggests that positive and negative moods operate through separate motivational processes (Cunningham, Steinberg, & Grev, 1980; Cunningham, Shaffer, Barbee, Wolff, & Kelly, 1990; Forgas, 1995). Positive mood tends to make people more helpful (Carlson, Charlin, & Miller, 1988; Salovey, Mayer, & Rosenhan, 1991; Shaffer, 1986). Cunningham noted that in positive moods, people are more helpful because they are more outwardly and socially focused (Cunningham et al., 1980, 1990; Shaffer & Smith, 1985), and because they are cued to concomitants of positive affect (Manucia, Baumann, & Cialdini, 1984), such as liking for others (Forgas & Bower, 1987; Mayer & Gaschke, 1988), optimism (Cunningham, 1988a; Forgas, Bower, & Krantz, 1984), and recollections of positive experiences (Isen, 1984). In addition, people in positive moods may be helpful in order to enhance their own good feelings (Mayer, DiPaolo, & Salovey, 1990), or to maintain the positive mood (Isen, Shalker, Clark, & Karp, 1978).

Negative mood may decrease or increase helping behavior, depending on the helper's focus of attention and feelings of personal responsibility to help (Carlson & Miller, 1987; Miller & Carlson, 1990; Salovey et al., 1991; Shaffer, 1986). People in negative moods tend to be self-focused (Cunningham, 1988b; Pyszcynski & Greenberg, 1987; Wood, Saltzberg, Neale, Stone, & Rachmiel, 1990), in part because focusing inward enables distressed people to focus their resources on understanding why they are distressed and retain the energy to alleviate the negative state (Pratto & Johns, 1991; Taylor, 1991). Negative affect includes other concomitants, including pessimism (Cunningham, 1988a), risk avoidance (Isen, 1984), and low energy levels (Cunningham, 1988b). All of these factors can deter those in negative moods from being helpful.

Much of the mood research has concentrated on simple forms of helping such as picking up dropped packages (Isen, 1970), giving to charity (Cunningham et al., 1980), or volunteering for an experiment (Shaffer & Graziano, 1983). The mood research has largely neglected more effortful and complex forms of helping, such as help given in a support interaction between close associates. Previous research has found that if the helping task is aversive, those in a negative mood are less inclined to help (Shaffer & Graziano, 1983).

Because much of the helping research has involved strangers, it does not account for an alternate possibility, that people may be motivated to overcome their own bad moods to help a distressed person with whom they have a close relationship. This may occur when the benefits for helping, and the costs for *not* helping a close friend, are high (Piliavin, Rodin, & Piliavin, 1969).

People's capacity to overcome their own emotions in order to help others may be limited. Studies have found that interacting with a depressed friend or family member over an extended period of time affects a person's mood state and willingness to help the depressed companion. More specifically, the depression of one member of a dyad causes the helper to be nurturant, concerned, and helpful (Sacco, Milana, & Dunn, 1985), but also to feel depressed and annoyed toward the originally depressed person (See Segrin, Chapter 8, this volume). The changed emotion of the helper leads to some negative behaviors, such as avoidance and conflict (Coyne, 1976a,b; Howes, Hokanson, & Lowenstein, 1985; Hokanson, Lowenstein, Hedeen, & Howes, 1986; Kahn, Coyne, & Margolin, 1985; Sacco & Dunn, 1990). Although occasionally people may be helpful when they themselves are feeling down (especially early in a relationship when impression management is high), over time they may wear down and be unable or unwilling to put forth much effort. In support of this notion, other research has found that the support process becomes strained when spouses of chronically ill patients become depressed themselves (Dunkel-Schetter & Bennett, 1990; Coyne et al., 1990).

Inducing Affect in Support Givers

All of these findings suggest that negative mood exerts a detrimental impact on helping between friends. We confirmed this in our studies of the effects of helper mood on social support (Barbee, 1990, 1991). In a series of four investigations, We combined the methodological strengths from the helping literature with the more naturalistic orientation of the social support literature. Our basic paradigm for examining the effect of emotion and cognition on the behaviors that people chose to engage in when interacting with a distressed friend involved asking people in close relationships (i.e. friends, romantic partners) to volunteer for a study of "communication." Once in a laboratory, each partner filled out questionnaires, including demographic, personality, and mood measures. Then each person was randomly, but covertly, assigned to be either a recipient in need of comfort, or to be a supporter. The recipients then were exposed to an event that produced depressed sadness, such as a tragic movie, or a failure experience on a cognitive or physiological test. In several of these studies (Barbee, 1990, 1991; Yankeelov, Barbee, Cunningham, & Druen, 1991; Yankeelov, Barbee, Cunningham, Druen, & Berry, 1993), the supporters were simultaneously induced to be in either a happy, saddened, or neutral mood. Once the pair was reunited, their conversation about the first person's experience with the movie or test was covertly videotaped for 5 min. After the interaction, each participant gave a self-report account of their feelings (e.g., empathy and annoyance), thoughts (e.g., attributions concerning the importance, cause, and controllability of the problem), and the behaviors that they engaged in during the interaction. Participants also indicated how they believed their partner felt and acted during the interaction. The videotapes were later coded by trained assistants using both the Interactive Coping Behavioral Coding System and the Support Activation Behavioral Coding System (Barbee & Cunningham, 1995).

We found that people in experimentally induced positive moods were much more likely to notice a friend's distress, and address it with effective supportive and problem-solving strategies, as compared to people who were either in neutral or negative moods (Barbee, 1991; Yankeelov et al., 1991). In fact, people who were sad and depressed often were so self-focused and passive that they rarely realized that their friend was in need of support. Even when they did notice, saddened supporters lacked the energy to act effectively (See Figure 3).

Contrary to what might be expected from the Negative State Relief model (see Cialdini & Kenrick, 1976) or the notion that people are motivated to help loved ones, depressed supporters did not take the interaction as an opportunity to cheer

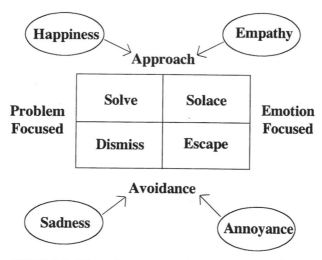

FIGURE 3   Effects of supporter emotions on interactive coping.

themselves up by helping their friends or to simply expend the extra effort to help their friend. We found that supporters in negative moods were less likely to make a support attempt, were less active in cheering the partner up, were less successful when an attempt was made, and were less willing to endorse the use of Solace and Solve behaviors, compared to positive mood supporters.

Overall, our data suggest that if people are in need of social support, they are more likely to receive it from friends who are themselves feeling good. A negative mood tends to reduce the perceived importance of the friend's problems. Even though some empathy occurs, negative mood tends to inhibit the kinds of support that recipients will view as most effective.

Attributions, Emotions, and Social Support

The supporter's attributions about the legitimacy of the depressed person's mood also has an impact on the supporter's feelings and on the interactive coping strategy that they employ (Barden, Garber, Lieman, Ford, & Masters, 1985). Weiner (1980) reported that subjects expected to feel sympathy and pity for strangers in need and would offer assistance if they attributed the problem to circumstances beyond the control of the stranger. When subjects believed the problem was controllable by the stranger, they anticipated feeling anger and a lower inclination to help.

In order to examine the impact of these attributions on the support process, we replicated and extended our laboratory work in three studies using role-playing scenario, experimental designs (Barbee, 1991), and structural equation modeling.

These models show that induced positive affect, as well as feelings of subjective closeness, caused support givers to regard the problem as more important, which increased empathy. Feelings of empathy, in turn, increased the likelihood that *solve* and *solace* behaviors would be used. One other study also found a positive relationship between empathy and the intention to give social support to a friend (Trobst, Collins, & Embree, 1994). The next step would be to manipulate empathy and see if it exerts direct effects on the interactive coping process between close friends.

Our research also found that the more supporters attributed the support-seeker's problems to internal, controllable causes, the more that they blamed the support seeker, and the more blame, the more they displayed the avoidance behaviors of dismiss and escape (Barbee, 1991). Given their annoyance, such supporters may have wished to provide a token effort and then distance themselves from the person who had caused the problems (Pleban & Tesser, 1981). The use of avoidant behaviors may have been rationalized as potentially helpful. The problem-minimization strategies of *Dismiss,* and the sarcastic humor and emotion-suppression strategies of *Escape* could have been seen as potentially effective coping reactions (Morrow & Nolen-Hoksema, 1990).

We can conclude from these studies that if the relationship is close, if the problem is viewed as a crisis that is important, if the cause of the problem is attributable to external causes, if the problem does not make the supporter feel personally threatened, and if the problem seems to have a controllable solution, then the support giver will feel positive and strongly motivated to provide all the assistance that is required. The flip side of these circumstances may make the supporter feel angry, frustrated, distressed, or sad. Thus, the initial emotions that supporters bring to the situation, and those that are aroused by the seeker's problem, all can affect a support giver's willingness and ability to be supportive.

Emotional Deterrents to Providing Support

Just as the support seeker's self-esteem is at risk when presenting a problem, the support giver's self-esteem is challenged when attempting to provide an effective solution or to relieve distress. If the support seeker's problem seems insoluble, support givers may feel threatened by the fact that they are capable of providing only limited assistance. Thus, their choice of an interactive coping behavior may be avoidant rather than approach-oriented.

A second emotional deterrent to providing support may be due to what we call an "attributional conflict." The support seeker's use of a specific support-activation behavior provides the support giver with clues regarding both the support seeker's attributions about the cause of the problem and the controllability of the solution. The support giver may not always agree with the support seeker's perceptions. As Figure 1 suggests, a *pout* may convey that the seeker believes the problem is caused by a source outside the self, and that the solution is uncontrollable. If the support giver believes that the support seeker caused the problem and that the solution is controllable, however, the difference of opinion may cause the support giver to feel a bit of anger, and the support giver may offer a *dismiss* or a *solve* rather than the *solace* that the support seeker desired. The frustrated support seeker may redouble efforts to obtain *solace* by further pouting or by *crying,* or may respond with retaliatory anger and *sulking.* But pouting or crying are not likely to change the support giver's attributions, whereas sulking is likely to lead the support giver to offer *escape* behaviors.

The failure to obtain desired support may itself become a problem for the relationship. A perceptive and gracious support giver, of course, will provide *solace* regardless of the support activation behavior, or whether the solution to the partner's problem is personally believed to be uncontrollable. With an irritated or stubborn support partner, unfortunately, the only way out of a covert attributional conflict may be for the support seeker to explicitly *ask* the partner for a *solution* first to the communication problem, and second to the presenting problem (i.e., "I feel upset about tomorrow's test. How can I get a hug from you?"). Because the support seeker is already feeling uncomfortable about the presenting problem, however, he or she may be prone to feel even more embarrassed or defensive about the communication problem, and be reluctant to address it directly.

Our studies (Barbee, 1990, 1991; Yankeelov et al., 1991, 1993) focused on the impact of happiness or depressed sadness on a support giver's behavior. Future research might explore how other emotions affect supporters' willingness to listen attentively to partners' concerns and their effectiveness in addressing them. It could be that those who are already angry may be primed to have the negative attributions found in the Barbee (1991) and Yankeelov et al. (1993) studies. Such preexisting supporter anger could lead not only to ineffective forms of support, but to increased conflict between the partners as the interaction unfolds. Another interesting scenario could involve a potential supporter who is feeling envious of a friend's good fortune in life, and who then is confronted with that friend when he or she is in need of support. The supporter may be likely to minimize the problem and appear dismissive, because the support-giver is judging the magnitude of the seeker's problem in light of the bounty of the rest of the seeker's life. These examples illustrate the wide range of emotions experienced in the fabric of relationships that could affect the interactive coping process.

IMMEDIATE EMOTIONAL OUTCOMES

How a support seeker responds to the interactive coping efforts of a supporter may be influenced by several factors. First, as noted earlier, the extent to which the support giver's interactive coping responses meet the seeker's expectations will affect the extent to which the seeker is comforted. Second, the seeker's response to support may be tied to why he or she was reluctant to seek support in the first place. If the individual was already feeling embarrassed or inadequate, then strong (or condescending) advice by the supporter could make the support seeker feel even worse (See Burleson & Goldsmith, Chapter 9, this volume). If the person feared rejection, then dismiss or escape behaviors from the partner may confirm that fear, and exacerbate the negative emotions. Finally, the seeker's own verbal and nonverbal reaction to the supporter's initial support efforts may determine the subsequent course of the interaction.

We are currently investigating a typology of the support-seeker's immediate response to the support giver's interactive coping efforts, and how those responses affect subsequent communication. This interest was stimulated by Cheuck and Rosen's (1992) intriguing findings concerning the spurned helper in close relationships. Rosen and his colleagues found that those whose help is rejected experience greater expectancy violation, see the potential recipient of help as unduly defensive, and cope more by ventilating negative affect, compared to those whose help is accepted (Rosen, Mickler, & Collins, 1987; Rosen, Mickler, & Spiers, 1986), but this research did not examine how the seeker rejected the helper.

The SIST's response-to-support typology expands on this insight by suggesting that seeker's reactions to social support may be expressed in four basic patterns (Barbee & Cunningham, 1995). Responses to support may be verbal or nonverbal, and they may entail acceptance or resistance. A support seeker may convey acceptance through verbal *appreciation* of the support giver's efforts, or may convey the same positivity nonverbally by *relaxing* or smiling. By contrast, a support seeker may convey resistance by verbally *rejecting* an interactive coping effort, or may convey the same resistance with a *recoil* or a sneer.

If the seeker gives accepting responses to support, the support giver may persist with the current effort, perhaps restating what seemed to be most helpful, and revising what did not seem to contribute to cheering up the partner. If, by contrast, the support seeker rejects the advice or recoils from the supporter's interactive coping efforts in other ways, then the supporter may be inclined to confront the support seeker ("So, you haven't liked anything I've done, exactly what do you want me to do to help you?") or subvert the process by abruptly switching to dismissive comments ("It's not a big deal, you should just forget about it") or escape statements ("What you need is a stiff drink. Here's ten dollars; why don't you go to the liquor store and buy yourself something?")

We know that depressed roommates exhaust the willingness of their partners to be supportive (Coyne, 1976a,b), but it is not yet clear how many *rejects* and *recoils* it takes to reach that point. The seeker's acceptance or resistance to help will, in turn, affect how the supporter feels about the supportive interaction, about the seeker, and about themselves.

LONG-TERM RELATIONSHIP OUTCOMES

Individual differences in the support seeker's use of verbal and nonverbal support activation behaviors, the supporter's willingness to provide nurturant solace and insightful solutions or to suggest dismissive and escape interactive coping behaviors, and the seeker's responses of acceptance or resistance to support may all have reciprocal links with attachment experiences. Bowlby (1988) described attachment as an affective bond. He focused on the mother–child bond, but noted that the quality of an individual's affectional bond to another is determined by both the individual's perception of themselves as worthy of affection and the individual's perception of the other as being responsive to their needs. Bowlby explained that these internal representations of self and other, initially established during childhood through interactions with one's primary caregiver, could shape one's relationships throughout the life span. Thus, the early working models of self and others could act as filters for all future relational feedback, thereby perpetrating itself.

In her work with mothers and infants, Ainsworth (1979) discovered three styles of attachment: secure, insecure-ambivalent, and insecure-avoidant. Hazan and Shaver (1987) extended Ainsworth's work by studying these three styles in the context of adult romantic attachments. Collins and Read (1990) and Bartholomew (1990) returned to the Bowlby notion of working models. But, the work of Bartholomew and her colleagues (Bartholomew, 1990; Bartholomew & Horowitz, 1991) is particularly important in the way it expanded Bowlby's conception of an internal working model into four distinct attachment styles. She crossed the dimension of positive–negative view of self with the dimension of positive–negative views of others. The four resulting types included: a *secure type* who has a positive view of self and others, a *preoccupied type* who has a positive view of others, but a negative view of self, a *dismissing type* who has a negative view of others, but a positive view of oneself, and a *fearful type* who has a negative view of both oneself and others (see Andersen & Guerrero, Chapter 3, this volume; and Feeney, Noller, & Roberts, Chapter 18, this volume, for more information on attachment styles). Griffin and Bartholomew (1994) noted that very few adults are likely to correspond perfectly to one pattern. They suggested providing a continuous scale for each type to assess an individual's tendency toward each of the four patterns.

Although internal attachment styles may shape relationships, the partner's behavior also may have an impact. Indeed, attachment styles may not be completely fixed, but instead may be altered by ongoing experiences (Berman & Sperling, 1994; Cohn, Silver, Cowan, Cowan, & Pearson, 1992; Fox, 1995; Koback & Hazan, 1991). The SIST model suggests that attachment styles may be viewed as dependent variables rather than just independent variables, and that experience with a repeated pattern of interactive coping outcomes may either reinforce a particular attachment schema, or cause a subtle shift towards an alternate style.

Outcomes for Seeker's Emotions and Attachment

The SIST model focuses on whether the supporter meets versus disappoints the support seeker's expectations for a specific type of interactive coping behavior, and whether the felt need for support has been satisfied or not (see Figure 1).

If support seekers' partners meet their expectations, and the issue seems under control, seekers may feel more positive about both their partners and themselves. The outcome of these positive views of self and other could lead the seeker to feel increased levels of love in the relationship if it was already secure, or could shift a person with a more insecure pattern toward greater feelings of security in the relationship. But if the support seekers' partners disappoint their expectations, and the presenting issue has not been effectively addressed, then support seeker's are likely to feel sad and negative about both their partners and themselves, which could either reinforce a *fearful* attachment style or move the relationship in a more *fearful* direction.

Mixed outcomes in social support interactions also may affect the relationship. If the partner provides the interactive coping behavior that they expect, yet the issue still does not seem under control (perhaps because they sought the wrong type of support), the person may feel positive about the partner but negative about the self. The belief that one can just barely get by even when given high levels of social input can be guilt and dependency inducing, increasing a *preoccupied* attachment style. A *preoccupied* attachment style might also be induced by social support that is provided intermittently, reinforcing the seeker's habit of trying to attain it, rather than becoming self-reliant.

The converse may also occur. If a support seeker's partner disappoints her or his expectations for a comforting interaction (due either to the seeker's poor support activation behaviors, or the partner's ineffective interactive coping efforts), but the seeker goes on to handle the problem or improve the emotions independently, the seeker may feel angry about the partner but smugly positive about the self. Perceived betrayal that is followed by self-assertion may reinforce or shift the seeker toward a *dismissive* attachment style. It should be noted that none of the foregoing relations between received social support and attachment style have been established, and all should be regarded as hypotheses in need of verification.

Outcome for the Support-Giver's Emotions and Attachment

The outcome of a support interaction may influence the attachment feelings of the supporter as well. The SIST model suggests that the dimensions of acting congruently versus incongruently with the partner's seeking behavior, and receiving a positive versus negative seeker response, may affect both the supporter and the relationship. If the supporter acts congruently with the seeker's support activation behavior (ask is met by solve, cry is met by solace, and so on), and the seeker responds positively with appreciation or relaxation, then the supporter is likely to feel lovingly positive about both the self and the other person, which could increase a *secure* attachment. By contrast, if the supporter acts congruently with the seeker's support activation behavior but the seeker responds with resistance behavior, such as a rejection or recoil, the individual may feel positive about the self and angry and negative about the partner. Such a spurned helper may be tilted to a more *dismissive* attachment style, and may develop a "social allergy" (Cunningham et al., in press) to her or his unappreciative partner.

An unskilled supporter may have a hard time responding congruently to a seeker's support activation behavior, but sometimes the seeker expresses appreciation and relaxation just for the supporter's attention and care. Although grateful for their partners' appreciation, such supporters may feel self-critical and guilty about their maladroitness. The feelings of negativity about the self and positivity about the partner may lead to a more *preoccupied* attachment style. Finally, a support giver may respond incongruently to the seeker's support activation behavior (a sigh is given a solve; a cry is given a dismiss) and receive resistant feedback, such as rejection or recoil. The clear failure of the cheering-up interaction may cause the supporter to feel sadly negative about both the self and the partner, leaning toward a more *fearful* attachment style.

CONCLUSIONS AND IMPLICATIONS

Successful and unsuccessful interactive coping patterns may have substantial long-term consequences for the maintenance of relationships in which they take place. We examined the extent to which one member of 120 couples provided effective or ineffective interactive coping behaviors to the other in a laboratory situation (Barbee & Yankeelov, 1992). Both partners of each couple were called 10 months after their participation in the study to see which couples were still together and which couples had separated. We found that the lack of an attempt to cheer up a partner, and the use of dismiss behaviors during the experimental session, were significant predictors of later romantic relationship dissolutions. It is likely that the inattentiveness and poor interactive coping displayed in the experimental context was a representative sample of the communication problems that led to the deterioration of the relationship.

In conclusion, this chapter has suggested four ways in which emotions can play a role in relational communication. Emotions that are produced by the perception of the initial problem may influence a needy person's support activation behaviors. The potential supporter's emotional state may influence her or his willingness to provide approach or avoidance interactive coping to the seeker. The clarity of the seeker's support activation behavior, and the effectiveness of the supporter's interactive coping, may influence the extent to which the seeker cheers up. Finally, the outcome of the support interaction may influence the short-term emotions and long-term relationship attachment of both the seeker and the supporter. Clearly, supportive attention to the emotions of one's partner can be helpful not only to the partner, but to one's own emotions and to the relationship itself.

REFERENCES

Ainsworth, M. D. S. (1979). Infant–mother attachment. *American Psychologist, 34,* 932–937.

Barbee, A. P. (1990). Interactive coping: The cheering up process in close relationships. In S. W. Duck (Ed.), *Personal relationships and social support* (pp. 46–65). London: Sage.

Barbee, A. P. (1991, October). *The role of emotions and cognitions in the interactive coping process.* Symposium chaired by Roy Baumiester on "Interpersonal Causes of Emotions." Society of Experimental Social Psychologists, Columbus, Ohio.

Barbee, A. P., & Cunningham, M. R. (1995). An experimental approach to social support communications: Interactive coping in close relationships. *Communication Yearbook, 18,* 381–413.

Barbee, A. P., & Yankeelov, P. A. (1992, July). *Social support as a mechanism for relationship maintenance.* Conference of the International Society of the Study of Personal Relationships, Orono, Maine.

Barden, R. C., Garber, J., Leiman, B., Ford, M. E., & Masters, J. C. (1985). Factors governing the effective remediation of negative affect and its cognitive and behavioral consequences. *Journal of Personality and Social Psychology, 49,* 1040–1053.

Barker, C., & Lemle, R. (1987). Informal helping in partner and stranger dyads. *Journal of Marriage and the Family, 49,* 541–547.

Bartholomew, K. (1990). Avoidance of intimacy: An attachment perspective. *Journal of Social and Personal Relationships, 7,* 147–178.

Bartholomew, K., & Horowitz, L. (1991). Attachment styles among young adults: A test of a four-category model. *Journal of Personality and Social Psychology, 61,* 226–244.

Berman, W. H., & Sperling, M. B. (1994). The structure and function of adult attachment. In M. B. Sperling & W. H. Berman (Eds.), *Attachment in adults* (pp. 2–28). New York: Guilford.

Bowlby, J. (1988). *A secure base.* New York: Basic Books.

Burleson, B. R. (1982). Social cognition, empathic motivation, and adults' comforting strategies. *Human Communication Research, 10,* 295–304.

Carlson, M., Charlin, V., & Miller, N. (1988). Positive mood and helping behavior: A test of six hypotheses. *Journal of Personality and Social Psychology, 55,* 211–229.

Carlson, M., & Miller, N. (1987). Explanation of the relation between negative mood and helping. *Psychological Bulletin, 102,* 91–108.

Chesler, M. A., & Barbarin, O. A. (1984). Difficulties of providing help in a crisis: Relationships between parents of children with cancer and their friends. *Journal of Social Issues, 40,* 113–134.

Cheuck, W. H., & Rosen, S. (1992). Helper reactions: When help is rejected by friends or strangers. *Journal of Social Behavior and Personality, 7,* 445–458.

Cialdini, R. B., & Kenrick, D. T. (1976). Altruism as hedonism: A social development perspective on the relationship of negative mood state and helping. *Journal of Personality and Social Psychology, 34,* 907–914.

Cohn, D. A., Silver, D. H., Cowan, C. P., Cowan, P. A., & Pearson, J. (1992). Working models of childhood attachment and couple relationships. *Journal of Family Issues, 13,* 432–449.

Collins, N. L., & Read, S. J. (1990). Adult attachment, working models, and relationship quality in dating couples. *Journal of Personality and Social Psychology, 58,* 644–663.

Coyne, J. C. (1976a). Depression and the response of others. *Journal of Abnormal Psychology, 85,* 186–193.

Coyne, J. C. (1976b). Toward an interactional description of depression. *Psychiatry, 39,* 28–40.

Coyne, J. C., Ellard, J. H., & Smith, D. A. F. (1990). Social support, interdependence, and the dilemmas of helping. In B. R. Sarason, I. G. Sarason, & G. R. Pierce (Eds.), *Social Support: An interactional view.* New York: John Wiley & Sons.

Cunningham, M. R. (1988a). What do you do when you're happy or blue?: Mood, expectancies and behavioral interest. *Motivation and Emotion, 12,* 309–331.

Cunningham, M. R. (1988b). Does happiness mean friendliness? The effects of mood and self-esteem on social interaction and self-disclosure. *Personality and Social Psychology Bulletin, 14,* 283–297.

Cunningham, M. R., Barbee, A. P., Druen, P. B., & Pospisil, J. (in press). Social antigens and the allergies that they produce: Escalation of annoyance and disgust in long-term relationships. In R. Kowalski (Ed.), *Aversive interpersonal behaviors.* New York: Plenum.

Cunningham, M. R., Shaffer, D. R., Barbee, A. P., Wolff, P. L., & Kelly, D. J. (1990). Separate processes in the relation of elation and depression to helping: Social versus personal concerns. *Journal of Experimental Social Psychology, 26,* 13–33.

Cunningham, M. R., Steinberg, J., & Grev, R. (1980). Wanting to and having to help: Separate motivations for positive mood and guilt-induced helping. *Journal of Personality and Social Psychology, 38,* 181–192.

Cutrona, C. E. (1986). Behavioral manifestations of social support: A microanalytic investigation. *Journal of Personality and Social Psychology, 51,* 201–208.

Cutrona, C. E., & Russell, D. W. (1990). Type of social support and specific stress: Toward a theory of optimal matching. In B. R. Sarason, I. G. Sarason, & G. R. Pierce (Eds.), *Social support: An interactional view.* New York: Wiley.

Cutrona, C. E., & Suhr, J. A. (1992). Controllability of stressful events and satisfaction with spouse support behaviors. *Communication Research, 19,* 154–174.

Cutrona, C. E., Suhr, J. A., & MacFarlane, R. (1990). Interpersonal transactions and the psychological sense of support. In S. W. Duck (Ed.), *Personal relationships and social support* (pp. 30–45). London: Sage.

Dakof, G. A., & Taylor, S. E. (1990). Victims' perception of social support: What is helpful from whom? *Journal of Personality and Social Psychology, 58,* 80–89.

Darley, J. M., & Latane, B. (1968). Bystander intervention in emergencies: Diffusion of responsibility. *Journal of Personality and Social Psychology, 10,* 202–214.

DePaulo, B. M. (1982). Social psychology processes in asking for help. In T. A. Wills (Ed.), *Basic processes in helping relationships* (pp. 255–279). New York: Academic press.

Dunkel-Schetter, C., & Bennett, T. L. (1990). Differentiating the cognitive and behavioral aspects of social support. In B. R. Sarason, I. G. Sarason, & G. R. Pierce (Eds.), *Social support: An interactional view* (pp. 267–296). New York: Wiley.

Dunkel-Schetter, C., & Skokan, L. A. (1990). Determinants of social support provision in personal relationships. *Journal of Social and Personal Relationships, 7,* 437–450.

Ellsworth, P. C., & Smith, C. A. (1988). From appraisal to emotion: Differences among unpleasant feelings. *Motivation and Emotion, 12,* 271–302.

Emmons, R. A., & Colby, P. M. (1995). Emotional conflict and well-being: Relation to perceived, availability, daily utilization, and observer reports of social support. *Journal of Personality and Social Psychology, 68,* 947–959.

Fisher, J. D., Goff, B. A., Nadler, A., & Chinsky, J. M. (1988). Social psychological influences on help seeking and support from peers. In B. H. Gottlieb (Ed.), *Marshaling social support* (pp. 267–304). London: Sage.

Fisher, J. D., & Nadler, A. (1982). Determinants of recipient reactions to aid: Donor-recipient similarity and perceived dimension of problems. In T. A. Wills (Ed.), *Basic processes in helping relationships* (pp. 131–152). New York: Academic Press.

Fisher, J. D., Nadler, A., & Whitcher-Alagna, S. (1983). Four theoretical approaches for conceptualizing reactions to aid. In J. D. Fisher, A. Nadler, & B. M. DePaulo (Eds.), *New directions in helping: Vol 1. Recipient reactions to aid* (pp. 147–163). New York: Academic Press.

Folkman, S., & Lazarus, R. S. (1985). If it changes it must be a process: A study of emotion and coping during three stages of a college examination. *Journal of Personality and Social Psychology, 48,* 150–170.

Forgas, J. P. (1995). Mood and judgement: The affect infusion model (AIM). *Psychological Bulletin, 117,* 39–66.

Forgas, J. P., & Bower, G. H. (1987). Mood effects on person–perception judgments. *Journal of Personality and Social Psychology, 53,* 53–60.

Forgas, J. P., Bower, G. H., & Krantz, S. E. (1984). The influence of mood on perceptions of social interactions. *Journal of Experimental Social Psychology, 20,* 497–513.

Fox, N. A. (1995). Of the way we were: Adult memories about attachment experiences and their role in determining infant–parent relationships: A commentary on van Ijzendoorn (1995). *Psychological Bulletin, 117,* 404–410.

Griffin, D., & Bartholomew, K. (1994). The metaphysics of measurement: The case of adult attachment. *Advances in personal relationships, Vol. 5: Attachment processes in adulthood* (pp. 17–52). London: Kingsley.

Gulley, M. R. (1993). *Sequential analyses of social support elicitation and provision behaviors.* Unpublished doctoral dissertation, University of Louisville, Kentucky.

Hatfield, E., & Sprecher, S. (1983). Equity theories and recipient reactions to aid. In J. D. Fisher, A. Nadler, & B. M. DePaulo (Eds.), *New directions in helping: Vol 1. Recipient reactions to aid.* New York: Academic Press.

Hazan, C., & Shaver, P. (1987). Romantic love conceptualized as an attachment process. *Journal of Personality and Social Psychology, 52,* 511–524.

Hokanson, J. E., Loewenstein, D. A., Hedeen, C., & Howes, M. J. (1986). Dysphoric college students and roommates: A study of social behaviors over a three-month period. *Personality and Social Psychological Bulletin, 12,* 311–324.

Howes, J. S., Hokanson, J. E., & Loewenstein, D. A. (1985). Induction of depressive affect after prolonged exposure to a mildly depressed individual. *Journal of Personality and Social Psychology, 49,* 1110–1113.

Hull, J. G., Young, R. D., & Jouriles, E. (1986). Applications of self-awareness model of alcohol consumption: Predicting patterns of use and abuse. *Journal of Personality and Social Psychology, 51,* 79–96.

Isen, A. M. (1970). Success, failure, attention and reaction to others: The warm glow of success. *Journal of Personality and Social Psychology, 15,* 294–301.

Isen, A. M. (1984). Towards understanding the role of affect in cognition. In R. S. Wyer & T. K. Srull (Eds.), *Handbook of social cognition* (Vol. 3, pp. 179–236). Hillsdale: Erlbaum.

Isen, A. M., Shalker, T. E., Clark, M., & Karp, L. (1978). Affect, accessibility of material in memory, and behavior: A cognitive loop? *Journal of Personality and Social Psychology, 36,* 1–12.

Kahn, J., Coyne, J. C., & Margolin, G. (1985). Depression and marital disagreement: The social construction of despair. *Journal of Social and Personal Relationships, 2,* 447–461.

Kobak, R., & Hazan, C. (1991). Attachment in marriage: Effects of security and accuracy of working models. *Journal of Personality and Social Psychology, 60,* 861–869.

Kowalski, R. (1996). Complaints and complaining: Functions, antecedents and consequences. *Psychological Bulletin, 119,* 179–196.

Manucia, G. K., Baumann, D. J., & Cialdini, R. B. (1984). Mood influences on helping: Direct effects or side effects? *Journal of Personality and Social Psychology, 46,* 357–364.

Matthews, K. A., Davis, M. C., Stoney, C. M., Owens, J. F., & Caggiula, A. R. (1991). Does the gender relevance of the stressor influence sex differences in psychophysiological responses? *Health Psychology, 10,* 112–120.

Mayer, J. D., & Gaschke, Y. N. (1988). The experience and meta-experience of mood. *Journal of Personality and Social Psychology, 55,* 102–111.

Mayer, J. D., DiPaolo, M., & Salovey, P. (1990). Perceiving affective content in ambiguous visual stimuli: A component of emotional intelligence. *Journal of Personality Assessment, 54,* 772–781.

Miller, N., & Carlson, M. (1990). Valid theory-testing meta-analyses further question the negative state relief model of helping. *Psychological Bulletin, 107,* 215–225.

Morrow, J., & Nolen-Hoeksema, S. (1990). Effects of responses to depression on the remediation of depressive affect. *Journal of Personality and Social Psychology, 58,* 519–527.

Otten, C. A., Penner, L. A., & Waugh, G. (1988). That's what friends are for: The determinants of psychological helping. *Journal of Social and Clinical Psychology, 7,* 34–41.

Pleban, R., & Tesser, A. (1981). The effect of relevance and quality of another's performance on interpersonal closeness. *Social Psychology Quarterly, 44,* 178–285.

Piliavin, I. M., Rodin, J., & Piliavin, J. A. (1969). Good Samaritanism: An underground phenomenon? *Journal of Personality and Social Psychology, 13,* 289–299.

Pratto, F., & Johns, O. P. (1991). Automatic vigilance: The attention-grabbing power of negative information. *Journal of Personality and Social Psychology, 61,* 380–391.

Pyszczynski, T., & Greenberg, J. (1987). Self-regulatory perseveration and the depressive self-focusing style: A self-awareness theory of depression. *Psychological Bulletin, 102,* 122–138.

Rosen, S., Mickler, S., & Collins, J. E. (1987). Reactions of would-be helpers whose offer of help is spurned. *Journal of Personality and Social Psychology, 53,* 288–297.

Rosen, S., Mickler, S., & Spiers, C. (1986). The spurned philanthropist. *Humboldt Journal of Social Relations, 13,* 145–158.

Roth, S., & Cohen, L. J. (1986). Approach, avoidance, and coping with stress. *American Psychologist, 41,* 813–819.

Sacco, W., & Dunn, V. K. (1990). Effect of Actor Depression on observer attributions: Existence and impact of negative attributions toward the depressed. *Journal of Personality and Social Psychology, 59,* 517–524.

Sacco, W. P., Milana, S., & Dunn, V. K. (1985). Effects of depression level and length of acquaintanceship on reactions of others to a request for help. *Journal of Personality and Social Psychology, 49,* 1728–1737.

Salovey, P., Mayer, J., Rosenhan, D. L. (1991). Mood and helping: Mood as a motivator of helping and helping as a regulator of mood. In M. Clark (Ed.), *Review of personality and social psychology* (pp. 215–264). London: Sage.

Shaffer, D. R. (1986). Is mood-induced altruism a form of hedonism? *Humboldt Journal of Social Relations, 13,* 195–216.

Shaffer, D. R., & Smith, J. (1985). Effects of preexisting moods on observers' reactions to helpful and nonhelpful models. *Motivation and Emotion, 9,* 101–122.

Shaffer, D. R.,& Graziano, W. G. (1983). Effects of positive and negative moods on helping tasks having pleasant or unpleasant consequences. *Motivation and Emotion, 7,* 269–278.

Shapiro, E. G. (1983). Embarrassment and help-seeking. In A. Nadler (Ed.), *New directions in helping* (pp. 143–165). New York: Academic Press.

Simpson, J. A., Rholes, J. A., & Nelligan, J. S. (1992). Support seeking and support giving within couples in an anxiety-provoking situation: The role of attachment styles. *Journal of Personality and Social Psychology, 62,* 434–446.

Taylor, S. (1991). Asymmetrical effects of positive and negative events: The mobilization-minimization hypothesis. *Psychological Bulletin, 110,* 67–85.

Trobst, K. K., Collins, R. L., & Embree, J. J. (1994). The role of emotion in social support provision: Gender, empathy and expressions of distress. *Journal of Social and Personal Relationships, 11,* 45–62.

Weiner, B. (1980). A cognitive (attribution)-emotion-action model of motivated behavior: An analysis of judgments of help giving. *Journal of Personality and Social Psychology, 39,* 186–200.

Winstead, B. A., & Derlega, V. J. (1991). An experimental approach to studying social interaction and coping with stress among friends. In W. H. Jones & D. Perlman (Eds.), *Advances in personal relationships* (Vol. 2, pp. 107–131). London: Kingsley.

Wood, J. V., Saltzberg, J. A., Neale, J. M., Stone, A. A., & Rachmiel, T. B. (1990). Self-focused attention, coping responses, and distressed mood in everyday life. *Journal of Personality and Social Psychology, 58,* 1027–1036.

Wortman, C., & Dunkel-Schetter, C. (1979). Interpersonal relationships and cancer. *Journal of Social Issues, 35,* 120–155.

Yankeelov, P. A., Barbee, A. P., Cunningham, M. R., & Druen, P. (1991, May). *Interactive coping in romantic relationships.* Paper presented at the meeting of the International Network on Personal Relationships, Normal, IL.

Yankeelov, P., Barbee, A. P., Cunningham, M. R., Druen, P., & Berry, M. (1993, June). *Cognitive and emotional influences on the interactive coping process in romantic couples.* Paper presented at the meeting of the International Network on Personal Relationships Milwaukee, WI.

CHAPTER 11

The Bright Side of Relational Communication: Interpersonal Warmth as a Social Emotion

Peter A. Andersen

San Diego State University
San Diego, California

Laura K. Guerrero

Arizona State University
Tempe, Arizona

From quiet homes and first beginning, out to undiscovered ends,
there's nothing worth the wear of winning, but laughter and the love of friends.

—Hilaire Belloc

Of all the gifts that wise Providence grants us to make life full and happy,
friendship is the most beautiful.

—Epicurus

I want a warm and faithful friend, to cheer the adverse hour;
Who ne'er to flatter will descend, nor bend the knee to power,—
A friend to chide me when I'm wrong, my inmost soul to see;
And that my friendship prove as strong for him as his for me.

—John Quincy Adams

Almost without exception, our relationships with friends and loved ones are the cornerstone of our happiness and emotional well-being. The warm feelings of an intimate conversation, a reassuring hug, seeing a close friend after a long absence, or sharing joy with one's family are uniquely satisfying experiences. Indeed, the brightest side of life's experiences often occurs in close, intimate relationships during the exchange of warm, involving, immediate messages.

Handbook of Communication and Emotion: Research, Theory, Applications, and Contexts

In recent years, the focus in communication research on "good" people speaking well, on self-actualization, and on interpersonal growth has been balanced by the publication of Cupach and Spitzberg's (1994) *The Dark Side of Interpersonal Communication,* Spitzberg and Cupach's (in press) *The Dark Side of Relationships,* and Goldberg's (1993) *The Dark Side of Love.* Indeed, Parks (1982) argued that such research is necessary if scholars are to get "off the couch and into the [real] world" (p. 79). In other words, rather than idealizing communication as a cure-all solution to interpersonal problems, scholars and practitioners need to realize that communication can have both adverse and beneficial consequences in relationships. Thus, researchers have become increasingly interested in communication patterns related to the dark side of interpersonal communication.

Conversely, research on emotions appears to have evolved in the opposite direction, with more research focusing on negative than positive emotions. With the exception of books on love (e.g., Walster & Walster, 1978; Hendrick & Hendrick, 1992), books on emotion have tended to focus on "dark side" emotions such as anger and aggression (e.g., Averill, 1982; Tarvis, 1982); depression (e.g., Seligman, 1975), shame, guilt, embarrassment (e.g., Tangney & Fischer, 1995), and jealousy (e.g., Stearns, 1989; White & Mullen, 1989). Even the theoretical literature on basic emotions rarely includes positive or bright emotions. Among Plutchick's (1984) eight basic emotions of sadness, disgust, acceptance, fear, anger, surprise, anticipation, and joy, only joy is an unequivocally "bright" emotion. Although Izard (1971) claimed that the ten emotions he classifies as fundamental—interest, joy, surprise, sadness, anger, disgust, contempt, fear, shame, and guilt—cannot be categorized as inherently positive or negative, only joy and perhaps interest belong on the "bright side" list. Similarly, Ekman and Friesen's (1975) six basic facial expressions contain only happiness—among sadness, fear, surprise, disgust, and anger—as a positive, bright emotion. Perhaps emotions are primarily negative and evolved to provide the motivation for survival in a dangerous and hostile world (see Andersen & Guerrero, Chapter 3, this volume). Or perhaps some positive emotions are too mundane and commonplace to have attracted much attention.

This chapter focuses on one of the most common, most important, and perhaps least understood emotions—interpersonal warmth. Interpersonal warmth is the pleasant, contented, intimate feeling that occurs during positive interactions with friends, family, colleagues, and romantic partners. Warmth can also be conceptualized as the pleasant emotional connection or attachment that we feel when communicating with loved ones. Similar feelings arise when we feel connected to nature. For example, viewing a spectacular sunset or watching ocean waves crash against craggy rocks may cause us to feel "connected to nature." Interpersonal warmth leads us to feel connected to others.

Although interpersonal warmth has not attracted much attention in the literature on emotion, we will argue for its centrality as an emotional experience. In support of this position, we contend that warmth is related to a plethora of interpersonal constructs, such as intimacy and attachment, which we discuss below. We believe warmth can be conceptualized as a basic emotion, as well as a context for the experience of pleasant emotions, a label for a type of relational experience, and a dimension that underlies many positive experiences. Research on warmth as an emotion by Clarke, Allen, and Dickson (1985) revealed that warmth was not only a very positive emotion, but also highly characteristic of wives' feelings for their husbands and parents' feelings for their children. While warmth per se has attracted little research, an abundance of studies employing interrelated terms suggests that warm feelings are at the "heart" of emotional experience and emotional communication in close, intimate relationships.

INTERPERSONAL WARMTH

Admittedly, the selection of warmth as the central conceptual metaphor for this chapter is rather arbitrary. A number of concepts including feelings of intimacy, attachment, bondedness, and emotional connectedness might have sufficed. Interestingly, none of these terms are commonly discussed as emotions in and of themselves in the English language. Rather, warm feelings are viewed as part of a cluster of thoughts, feelings, and behaviors that comprise concepts such as intimacy and attachment. Within Shaver, Schwartz, Kirson, and O'Connor's (1987) list of 213 potential emotion terms, love, affection, delight, pleasure, tenderness, enjoyment, fondness, and caring come the closest to describing interpersonal warmth. Yet warmth is distinctly different from these emotions.

It may be that the English language does not have a single emotion word that properly describes feelings of interpersonal warmth and emotional bondedness. In Danish, *hygge* best captures feelings of cozy, positive warmth. In fact, *hygge* is as central to the Danish culture as the concept of "things" or "possessions" is to American culture. Just as it would be difficult for Americans to imagine talking without referencing things, it would be difficult for Danes to imagine talking without describing experiences as "*hygge*" or "*nonhygge.*" The Germans have a somewhat similar word, *gemütlichkeit,* which refers to a feeling of emotional connectedness. The English translation for *gemütlichkeit* includes adjectives such as cozy, pleasant, comfortable, amiable, and sanguine, but no one word adequately captures the concept. It is likely that other languages also have similar terms for the emotion we are labeling "interpersonal warmth."

Unlike words such as *hygge* and *gemütlichkeit,* English words such as warmth and intimacy must be qualified in order to fit the criteria of an emotion. This may be because our language uses the same word to refer to various components (e.g., affective versus cognitive) of experiences such as intimacy and attachment. These multiple loci defy simple operationalization. For example, in Chapter 1 we discussed Clore and Ortony's (1988; Ortony, Clore, & Foss, 1987) conceptualization of emotions as focusing on internal, affective states rather than on external, bodily, cognitive, or behavioral states. The difficulty with terms such as warmth, intimacy, and attachment is that they refer to multiple states. For example, warmth can be a bio-logical state (e.g., feeling hot). Intimacy can refer to cognitive processes (e.g., making a commitment) and behavioral processes (e.g., engaging in intimate behaviors such as kissing or hugging). Similarly, the processes of *being* attached and *feeling* attached to someone are related, but not isomorphic. Thus, when referring to these constructs as emotions, scholars qualify them with labels such as "interpersonal warmth" and "intimate feelings."

Nonetheless, a cluster of constructs demonstrates that interpersonal warmth is both ubiquitous and important in our emotional and relational lives. All of these constructs—intimacy, relational closeness, bondedness, attachment, and involvement—can be conceptualized as multicomponential constructs that include or are relevant to interpersonal warmth.

MULTICOMPONENTIAL CONSTRUCTS RELATED TO INTERPERSONAL WARMTH

Intimacy

Intimacy researchers have struggled with capturing the conceptual essence of our first multicomponential construct, intimacy. In her recent, *tour de force* of intimacy research and theory, Praeger (1995) suggested that intimacy is a conjunctive concept that includes warmth as an affective component. She stated:

> Capturing the essence of intimate experience, according to most conceptions, seems to require an acknowledgment of both cognitive and *affective* aspects of that experience. Theorists have done this by combining two aspects of experience into one concept, like validation. Validation seems to combine within it experiences of understanding, acceptance and *warmth*. (p. 47, italics added)

In Acitelli and Duck's (1987) already classic article, "Intimacy as the Proverbial Elephant," intimacy researchers are depicted as a group of blind people who, while feeling the same elephant, reach very different conclusions about the shape of the beast. Nonetheless, while Acitelli and Duck illustrated the academic struggle with distinctions between love, intimacy, and satisfaction, they located intimacy in *both* thoughts and feelings. Similarly, Bochner (1984) acknowledged that intimacy is used to describe both a "type of relationship" and "an emotional state of arousal" (p. 559), and Hatfield (1984) discussed cognitive, behavioral, and emotional forms of intimacy as crucial components within close relationships. These examples further illustrate that the elusiveness of interpersonal emotions such as intimacy and warmth may stem from their multiple loci.

Certainly, interpersonal warmth is centrally featured in most definitions of intimacy. In his triangular theory of love, Sternberg (1986, 1988) employs thermal metaphors for love's three components: passion (hot); commitment (cool); and intimacy (warm). According to Sternberg (1988), intimacy refers to relational *feelings* that "promote closeness, bondedness, and connectedness" (p. 38). Praeger (1995) summarized the centrality of intimacy as an emotion:

> Intimate interactions are best defined not only by the kind of behavior that characterizes them, but by the intimate experiences of the partners during or as a result of the interaction. The affective component consists of involvement in, interest in, or feelings about oneself, the interaction, and the partner. (p. 22)

Intimacy, thus conceptualized, includes warm emotions generated in the relationship (Hatfield, 1988), which Praeger calls the affectively intimate experience.

Relational Closeness

Interpersonal or relational closeness are terms that are frequently employed as virtual synonyms for intimacy. In a recent study of laypeople's conceptualizations of the terms closeness and intimacy, half the respondents viewed them as equivalent terms (Parks & Floyd, 1996). Similarly, terms such as closeness, intimacy, and satisfaction are often used interchangeably in the relational communication literature (e.g., Berscheid, Snyder, & Omato, 1989; Parks & Floyd, 1996).

Close relationships are affectively intense with positive emotions typically dominating. For example, in Perlman and Fehr's (1987) summary of how casual and close relationships differ, one key difference was that close relationships were characterized by greater positive affect (e.g., liking or loving) and greater caring, commitment, and trust. Similarly, Baumeister and Leary (1995) contended that

> happiness in life is strongly correlated with having some close personal relationships. Research suggests that it does not seem to make a great deal of difference what sort of relationship one has, but the absence of close social bonds is strongly linked to unhappiness, depression, and other woes. (p. 56)

Berscheid et al. (1989) concurred that for most laypeople, as well as many social scientists, the concepts of close relational bonds and positive affective ties are inextricably linked to one another.

Of course, not all close relationships are unilaterally positive in emotional tone. The majority of violent acts, including rapes and murders, occur in close relationships (see Marshall, 1994). Research has shown that in most close relationships, both negative and positive emotions are present (see Parks & Floyd, 1996; Wood & Duck, 1995). Berscheid et al. (1989) reported that long-lasting relationships may be characterized by less closeness than some shorter relationships. Moreover, although Berscheid et al. reported that close relationships contain significantly more positive emotions such as delight, joy, elation, and so forth, they are also marked by a significant number of negative emotions. In sum, close relationships are typically warm and intimate, and although they are frequently characterized by mixed patterns of affect, they are generally described as having a primarily positive emotional tone.

Indeed, close relationships may be maintained by feelings of interpersonal warmth, comfort, and emotional connection that are similar to the Danish concept of *hygge*.

Bonding

Another term associated with the aforementioned social emotions is *bonding*. Natural groups, tribes, villages, and organizations characterize all human interaction (Brown, 1991). Deep bonds between members have probably had distinct survival advantages for human beings throughout history. Bochner (1984) discussed four historic reasons why humans bond: (a) to neutralize aggressive instincts; (b) to provide one another with security; (c) to give and receive caring and love; and (d) to expand themselves and transcend individual experience. Similarly, Baumeister and Leary (1995) concluded that people are strongly inclined to bond spontaneously and naturally, and to experience universal distress at the breaking of interpersonal bonds. The key element in bonding is belonging, which, according to Baumeister and Leary (1995), is more than mere affiliation. Only frequent contact *and* emotional attachment can satisfy the need for belonging. They state:

> The need to belong is something other than a need for affiliation. Frequent contacts with nonsupportive, indifferent others can go only so far in promoting one's general well-being and would do little to satisfy the need to belong. Conversely, relationships characterized by strong feelings of attachment, intimacy or commitment but lacking in regular contact will also fail to satisfy the need. (p. 500)

The feelings of interpersonal warmth, intimacy, security, and attachment are the emotional experiences that produce strongly bonded interpersonal relationships.

Attachment

Attachments have been defined as enduring affectional bonds (Ainsworth, 1989) that focus on intimacy and security. The attachment system is composed of cognitions, behaviors, and emotions that help an individual maintain a particular type of relationship with a loved one. In the cognitive domain, attachment theory posits that mental models of self and other guide people's emotions and behaviors (see Andersen & Guerrero, Chapter 3, this volume). Attachment is also characterized by the perception that a particular partner is irreplaceable (Ainsworth, 1989).

The emotional component of attachment has received considerable attention. In fact, as Hazan and Shaver (1987) argued, Bowlby developed attachment theory to "describe and explain how infants become emotionally attached to their primary caregivers and emotionally distressed when separated from them" (p. 511). Bowlby (1969) also contended that similar emotional bonds characterize adult relationships. Hazan and Shaver (1987) argued that attachment theory provides a framework for investigating love, fear of intimacy, jealousy, emotional ups and downs, caring, intimacy, happiness, and trust. Other researchers have used attachment theory to study anger, anxiety, comfort, depression, emotional expressiveness, interpersonal warmth, sadness, and security (e.g., Bartholomew & Horowitz, 1991; Feeney, 1995; Guerrero, 1996a; Kobak & Hazan, 1991; Simpson, Rholes, & Nelligan, 1992).

The interrelationships between attachment and various emotions are illustrated by Shaver and Hazan (1988), who posit emotional profiles for both infants and adults. For infants, "feelings of joy and distress depend on the [caregiver's] perceived availability and responsiveness" (p. 481). Shaver and Hazan also noted that when infants are separated from their caregivers they feel distress. If the separation is prolonged or permanent, this distress may turn into despair. For adults, feeling a close attachment to someone is associated with relaxation, decreased worry, less defensiveness, and more creativity and spontaneity. Moreover, Shaver and Hazan (1988) contended that "adult lover's moods depend on his or her current perceptions of the partner's reciprocation or rejection" (p. 481) and that separation from those with whom we have formed attachments leads to intense distress and potential grief.

Research has also demonstrated that various attachment styles are characterized by differences in emotional experience and expression (see Andersen & Guerrero, Chapter 3, this volume; Feeney, Noller, & Roberts, Chapter 18, this volume) and that emotional experiences help shape and modify attachment styles (see Barbee, Lawrence, & Cunningham, this volume). For example, Bartholomew and Horowitz (1991) found compelling evidence that emotional expressiveness and interpersonal warmth are key features underlying different attachment styles. Secures, who have positive models of themselves and others, are characterized by moderate levels of warmth and expressiveness. Dismissives, who have positive models of themselves but negative models of others, are characterized as relatively cold and inexpressive. Fearful avoidants, who have negative models of themselves and others, are characterized by a neutral emotional tone (i.e., neither cold nor warm) and very low levels of expressiveness. Last, preoccupieds, who have positive models of others but negative models of themselves, are characterized by the highest levels of interpersonal warmth and emotional expressiveness (Bartholomew & Horowitz, 1991).

Finally, the behavioral component of attachment focuses on the actions and communicative messages people use to keep them close to their partners or, conversely, to facilitate autonomy by placing physical distance between themselves and others. Shaver and Hazan (1988) focused on the former. They reported that infants engage in attachment behaviors that focus on proximity seeking, such as caressing, cuddling, rocking, and following the caregiver. Infants also display positive affect through smiling, eye contact, and cooing. Adult lovers engage in similar behaviors. They caress, kiss, hold each other, smile, and use "affectionate baby-like names" for one another (Shaver & Hazan, 1988, p. 481). Both infants and adults also feel an intense desire to share discoveries, reactions, and feelings with one another, which presumably leads to intimate self-disclosure. Adults also express attachment by giving gifts to one another (Shaver & Hazan, 1988). Clearly, these behaviors not only display attachment; they communicate interpersonal warmth and affection.

Attachment-style differences in intimacy behavior have also been found. Guerrero (1996b) found that during conversations with romantic partners, secures and preoccupieds generally exhibit more nonverbal intimacy and positive affect than their dismissive and fearful avoidant counterparts. Another study by Guerrero (1996a) investigated how those with different attachment styles perceive their social skills. The four styles could be distinguished from one another based on two skills: (a) *social sensitivity/vulnerability,* which ranged from being "overly sensitive" to what others think, to being "unconcerned" about what others think; and (b) *sociability/expressiveness,* which ranged from being highly engaged and expressive, to being detached and inhibiting emotional displays. Secures reported moderately high scores on sociability/expressiveness, and moderately low scores on social sensitivity/vulnerability. Dismissives reported moderately low sociability/expressiveness and low social sensitivity/vulnerability. Fearful avoidants reported low sociability/expressiveness and moderately high social sensitivity/vulnerability. Finally, preoccupieds reported high sociability/expressiveness and high social sensitivity/vulnerability. These findings suggest that preoccupieds and secures engage in more active, involved communication, and that fearful avoidants and preoccupieds may be overly concerned about what others think of them.

Involvement

Involvement behavior signals that an individual is available for communication and is interested in the conversation at hand. Several studies (e.g., Burgoon & Newton, 1991; Coker & Burgoon, 1987; Spitzberg & Hecht, 1984; Spitzberg & Hurt, 1987) have uncovered at least five dimensions of involvement: immediacy (e.g., touch, close proxemic distancing); expressiveness (e.g., vocal and kinesic animation); smooth interaction management (e.g., fluent speech, smooth turn taking); moderately low social anxiety (e.g., moderate relaxation), and altercentrism (e.g., attentiveness to the partner). When individuals convey messages related to these five dimensions, they show that they are actively engaged and interested in an interaction. Burgoon (1994) also discussed a sixth dimension, positive affect, which is relevant to the interpretation of involvement cues.

When involvement cues convey both interest and positive affect, they are likely to promote feelings of interpersonal warmth and emotional connectedness. Cappella (1983) argued that messages can be characterized by involvement (i.e., approach vs. avoidance) and affect (i.e., positive vs. negative). However, Cappella does not regard involvement and affect as completely separate dimensions. He argued that the same type of behavior can convey either positive or negative affect, depending upon factors such as context, relational history, and expectations. Cappella (1983) gave the following example:

> Imagine two impassioned lovers greeting one another in public after a long separation. They are likely to touch, to spend time in physical proximity, to gaze at one another, to

orient their bodies toward one another, to have a great deal to say, and to be animated in saying it. Now imagine a divorcing husband and wife in an impassioned custody battle over children, home, and resources. They too will touch, gaze, be near physically, be oriented toward one another, and be vocally animated. They will of course, be more likely to gaze with sneers rather than smiles and to touch with malice rather than nurturance. (p. 115)

This example illustrates that involvement behaviors themselves are meaningless unless other information, such as context and relational history, are considered. The reunited lovers and the divorcing couple, in the example above, are both highly aroused, involved, and interested in the interaction at hand. Yet, quite obviously, the valence of the affect being communicated is very different. Gaze and touch are particularly good examples of involvement behaviors that can communicate either hostility or warmth: Unfriendly stares and violent touches signal involvement and negative affect. Looking into someone's eyes lovingly and giving someone a comforting hug signal involvement and positive affect. Thus, messages that convey both interest and positive affect are most likely to promote interpersonal warmth.

Other Constructs

Several other multicomponential concepts appear to be associated with interpersonal warmth. For example, confirmation, which involves the acceptance and validation of a person's definition of self, is likely to engender feelings of interpersonal warmth. Watzlawick, Beavin, and Jackson (1967) believed that a major function of communication is the emotional confirmation of self and others. Confirming messages acknowledge, recognize, endorse, and validate the feelings of others (Cissna & Sieburg, 1981). Such communication leads to relational growth and feelings of closeness.

Confirmation is also similar to what Gottman and his colleagues call validation (Gottman, 1994; Gottman, Notarius, Gonso, & Markman, 1976). Validation messages occur when interactional partners know that you understand what they are thinking and feeling, and that you think it is reasonable for them to feel the way they do. Thus, validation may be related to empathy, feelings of interpersonal warmth, and emotional connectedness.

Another similar concept is that of qualification/disqualification. Disqualifying messages are characterized by incongruity, rejection, and invalidation of other people and their messages (see Bavelas, Black, Chovil, & Mullet, 1990; Watzlawick et al., 1967). Qualifying messages align interactants and promote supportive, congruent feelings.

The concepts of confirmation, validation, and qualification are associated with social support and comfort (see Barbee et al., Chapter 10, this volume; Burleson & Goldsmith, Chapter 9, this volume). Supportive, prosocial behavior has remarkable effects, both direct and indirect, on physiology, cognition, and emotion (Burleson,

Albrecht, Goldsmith, & Sarason, 1994). Supportive behaviors are "emotion-focused approach behaviors designed to produce positive feelings in the help seeker and to convey a sense of being cared for and supported (e.g., giving affection or a hug: telling the support seeker of his or her positive qualities)" (Derlega, Barbee, & Winstead, 1994, pp. 137–138). Support has been shown to result from and produce warm, intimate relationships characterized by a positive emotional tone.

COMMUNICATIVE BEHAVIORS RELATED TO INTERPERSONAL WARMTH

Thus far, we have demonstrated that the emotional experience of interpersonal warmth is related to a number of broader interpersonal constructs, including relational closeness, attachment, and involvement. In each of these cases, the degree of interpersonal warmth that characterizes a relationship or an interaction provides tell-tale clues about the nature of that relationship. For example, individuals whose relationships are characterized by low levels of interpersonal warmth may become dissatisfied. Indeed, maintaining feelings of interpersonal warmth may be one key to maintaining healthy, satisfying relationships. Attachment-style differences in relational communication may also be partially governed by differences in interpersonal warmth, with some individuals providing their partners with warm, expressive, nurturing behaviors, and others acting cold and distant. Involvement provides yet another example of the importance of interpersonal warmth. When relational partners exhibit behavior that reflects both involvement and positive affect, they are likely to feel emotionally connected to one another.

Interpersonal warmth both defines our relational experiences and constitutes an important type of emotional communication. Thus, the next section of this chapter focuses on *how* relational partners communicate interpersonal warmth to one another.

Nonverbal Intimacy and Warmth

A substantial body of literature now exists on nonverbal intimacy behaviors. This research has been conducted under several labels, including nonverbal immediacy (P. Andersen, 1985; Mehrabian, 1971), nonverbal involvement and positive affect (Burgoon, 1994; Cappella, 1983), physical affection (e.g., Dainton, 1991); and affiliation behaviors (Mehrabian & Ksionzky, 1970), as well as interpersonal warmth (Bayes, 1972). In this chapter, we refer to nonverbal and verbal intimacy behaviors as those messages that signal involvement, interest, and interpersonal warmth. These behaviors can be further conceptualized as (a) approach behaviors that signal availability for interaction (J. Andersen, Andersen, & Jensen, 1979; Burgoon & Hale, 1988; Mehrabian, 1971); (b) arousing behaviors that increase sensory stimulation

(Andersen, 1985; Patterson, 1976); and (c) interpersonal behaviors that communicate warmth and closeness (Andersen et al., 1979; Andersen, 1985, in press, b).

Nonverbal intimacy almost always occurs as a multichanneled behavioral combination (see Andersen, 1985, in press, b; Burgoon, Buller, & Woodall, 1996) that is sent and received as a gestalt. Intimacy involves numerous discrete behaviors, but interactants are rarely aware of the specific behavior they employ to send or interpret intimacy.

Although many factors determine how intimacy behaviors are received and what they mean for respondents, research has demonstrated that in general, these behaviors have direct, positive effects on other people. This *direct-effects* model holds that in most circumstances immediate interactants are perceived as warmer, friendlier, and more attractive. Furthermore, these direct, positive effects emerge whether the interaction occurs among romantic partners, friends, or strangers (Andersen, 1985; Coutts, Schneider, & Montgomery, 1980). Research supports a similar model of nonverbal involvement, the *social meaning* model (Burgoon, Coker, & Coker, 1986; Burgoon & Newton, 1991). According to this model, many nonverbal behaviors have such a clear, consensual social meaning that most interactants react to them in the same way across most relationships. Support for the direct-effects and social meaning models has been accumulating, suggesting that many nonverbal intimacy behaviors have strong positive meanings in social interaction. Of course, intimacy behaviors interact with personal or situational variables in some circumstances, which are discussed later in this chapter.

A host of nonverbal intimacy cues have been identified and are discussed in detail elsewhere (for summaries see P. Andersen, 1985, in press, a; Bayes, 1972; Burgoon et al., 1996; Taraban, Hendrick, & Hendrick, Chapter 12, this volume). The nonverbal behaviors that communicate warmth, intimacy, and closeness encompass the following:

1. *Proxemic behaviors,* including close conversational distances, direct body orientations, forward leans, and communicating at the same level or in the same physical plane.
2. *Haptic or tactile behaviors,* including pats, squeezes, hugs, kisses, soothing contact, massages, sexual contact, handshakes, and even some instrumental and incidental touches.
3. *Oculesic behaviors,* including increased gaze, mutual eye contact, pupil dilation, and decreased eye movements.
4. *Kinesic behaviors,* including smiling, general facial pleasantness, affirmative head nods, gestural animation (especially illustrators), head tilts, bodily relaxation, lack of random movement, open body positions, and postural congruence.
5. *Vocalic behaviors,* including more variation in pitch, amplitude, duration, and tempo; reinforcing interjections such as "uh-huh" and "mm-hmm;" greater fluency, warmth, pleasantness, expressiveness, and clarity; and smooth turn-taking.

6. *Chronemic behaviors,* including time spent with people, punctuality, patience, and a focus on the conversation alone (rather than on multiple tasks) at a given time.

As noted in Chapter 3, these behaviors promote the most positive relational outcomes, and are likely to be associated with the strongest feelings of interpersonal warmth when they are matched or reciprocated by dyadic partners.

Verbal Intimacy and Warmth

Though research has generally shown that nonverbal communication is the primary vehicle of warm, intimate communication, several types of verbal messages are also essential to this process. Moreover, verbal and nonverbal intimacy expressions co-occur and provide a complete intimacy message system. If congruent, verbal and nonverbal messages can converge to reflect a gestalt of warm, intimate behavior. If incongruent (i.e., saying "I love you" while frowning and crossing your arms across your chest), the nonverbal behavior is likely to carry more weight and undercut the verbal message (see Burgoon et al., 1996). Nonetheless, verbal expressions of intimacy have been found to relate to love (see Taraban et al., this volume) and relational maintenance (Canary & Stafford, 1994).

Self-Disclosure

Perhaps the primary mode for the verbal expression of intimacy in close relationships is self-disclosure (see Derlega, Metts, Petronio, & Margulis, 1993). Certainly, the literature on this topic is abundant. Recent research shows that the most common definitions of intimacy and closeness revolve around disclosure, and that this holds true for both males and females in same- and cross-sex friendships (Chelune, Robinson, & Kommor, 1984; Monsour, 1992; Parks & Floyd, 1996; Perlman & Fehr, 1987). As a case in point, Afifi and Guerrero (1997) found that for male same-sex friends, frequency of self-disclosure was the strongest predictor of relational closeness. For female same-sex friends, similarity of disclosure between partners was the strongest predictor of closeness. Other scholars consider self-disclosure to be so central to warmth, intimacy, and closeness that they consider these terms to be virtually isomorphic (Hatfield, 1984). Of course, more disclosure is not always better (Bochner, 1984; Mikulincer & Nachshon, 1991; Parks, 1982). Several studies have reported a curvilinear relationship between self-disclosure and variables such as liking and intimacy (Cozby, 1973; Duck & Miell, 1986; Hays, 1985). Appropriate, well-timed, generally positive disclosure is highly associated with intimacy. Indiscriminant and frequent self-disclosure, especially when it is often negative in tone, can cause relational partners to pull away and seek interpersonal distance. Infrequent self-disclosure with friends and loved ones is associated with coldness and detachment.

Emotional Expressiveness

This sister construct of self-disclosure is also a necessary ingredient in warm, intimate relationships (Altman, Vinsel, & Brown, 1981; Dosser, Balswick, & Halverson, 1986; Montgomery, 1988; Norton, 1983). Recent studies have shown that dyadic partners widely believe that feelings of closeness and intimacy are associated with honest, open communication about emotions (Monsour, 1992; Parks & Floyd, 1996; Reeder, 1995). Of course, these emotional expressions may often be unstated, nonverbal emotional expressions as well as verbal communication. In general, the expression of positive emotions tends to characterize close relationships (Berscheid et al., 1989).

Verbal Immediacy

Like nonverbal immediacy, verbal immediacy increases intimacy while reducing the psychological distance between communicators. This is typically accomplished through the use of plural first-person pronouns such as "we" rather than "I" or even "you and I" (Wiener & Mehrabian, 1968). Communication characterized by negative emotions rather than positive emotions is highly correlated with nonimmediacy (Conville, 1974), perhaps because people internalize negative emotions and readily share positive emotions. Another explanation was provided by Bradac, Bowers, and Courtright (1979), who argued that a major generalization of communication research is that "verbal immediacy is directly related to receiver attributions of positiveness of source affect" (p. 262). Bradac et al. reported that this is a reciprocal relationship because positive affect generates verbal immediacy and verbal immediacy increases positive relational affect. Praeger (1995) suggested that more immediate pronoun use (i.e., "this" and "these" versus "that" and "those"), adverb use (i.e., "here" vs. "there"), and verb tense (i.e., present versus past), as well as the use of active versus passive voice, all contribute to verbal immediacy.

Forms of Address

Intimate feelings can be reflected in the way that we address another person. King and Sereno (1984) have shown that forms of address (e.g., President Knight vs. Mr. Knight vs. Tom) have considerable relational implications. Likewise, nicknames are major forms of expressing relational intimacy and have been associated with partner perceptions of love and closeness (Bell, Buerkel-Rothfuss, & Gore, 1987; Hopper, Knapp, & Scott, 1981), though one ought to be careful to use nicknames that are acceptable and appropriate to the partner. For example, a subordinate who addresses senior executives by their first names or students who address their professors by nicknames often violate interpersonal expectations and are viewed as disrespectful and too familiar. Moreover, some people take umbrage at "cute" nicknames conceived by other people.

Personal Idioms

Personal idioms are a major verbal vehicle for expressing warmth and intimacy in close relationships. Some of these idioms include teasing insults, sexual references and euphemisms, unique labels for others outside the relationship, and special greetings (Bell et al., 1987; Hopper et al., 1981). Bell et al. (1987) found that many idioms associated with loving, liking, commitment, and closeness. As with nicknames, however, it is important to remember that personal idioms which are appropriate for one person to use may be inappropriate for another. As a case in point, imagine a brother and sister who grew up teasing each other with names such as "bubble-butt" and "bubblehead." In adulthood, when the brother teasingly calls his sister a "bubblebutt," the idiom is likely to reflect affection and nostalgia. However, if the brother's wife calls the sister "bubblebutt," she is likely to take offense.

Assurances

Verbal messages that emphasize positive feelings about the relationship are an important type of affective communication. Verbalizations such as "I love you," "You're important to me," and "I hope we are friends for a long time" exemplify this type of message. These statements feature simultaneously both the content and relational aspects of communication (King & Sereno, 1984) and are vital to relational intimacy (P. Andersen, 1989, in press, b). Research has also demonstrated that verbal assurances associate with relational satisfaction, caring, commitment, and the stability of relationships (Bayes, 1972; Guerrero, Eloy, & Wabnik, 1993; Stafford & Canary, 1991). In a study on the importance of various maintenance behaviors, Canary and Stafford (1993) noted that: "The maintenance strategy of assurances was *the* primary predictor of liking and was a significant predictor of trust" (p. 254, italics added).

Mundane Talk

The importance of sharing time through everyday conservation has been underestimated as a generator of warm, intimate, affectional bonds. Canary and Stafford (1994) proposed that both routine and strategic behaviors help maintain relationships. Similarly, Duck and his colleagues have repeatedly shown that "routine mundane everyday life behaviors influence a range of psychological and communicative dimensions of interpersonal interaction, such as the maintenance of relationships, coping with stressors, and many aspects of social participation" (Duck, Rutt, Hurst, & Strejc, 1991, p. 228). Leading among these routine behaviors is talk. As Duck and Pond (1989) maintained: "Talk is the crucible wherein relationships are conducted: Almost every day we need to communicate effectively, to influence or inform others, to ask advice, to deliver comfort, to offer help, to chat informally" (p. 25). It is mundane, daily discourse that refurbishes and constructs close, intimate relationships (Duck et al., 1991; Montgomery, 1994). Baxter (1992) conceptualized routine talk as "intimate play," a low-risk way of reducing negative affect and creating close, intimate relationships. In her study, intimate play was highly correlated with relational closeness for both friendships and romances.

THE ACCEPTANCE OF INTERPERSONALLY WARM MESSAGES

Of course, warm, intimate behaviors must be perceived and reciprocated by the relational partner if high levels of relational closeness are to be achieved. Clearly, there are times when attempts to increase intimacy are rebuffed. For example, inappropriate touch, excessive disclosure, and unwanted intimacy are relationally detrimental and emotionally negative (P. Andersen, 1992). The question then becomes, what factors predict whether messages of intimacy and warmth are accepted or rejected by others?

Cognitive-valence theory (formally arousal-valence theory; see P. Andersen, 1985, in press, b) helps explain how people respond to the intimacy messages of others. According to this theory (see Figure 1), an increase in intimacy behavior is inherently arousing when perceived by others. When the resultant arousal change is low, no behavioral reaction is likely. When arousal change is very high, the partner is likely to view the intimacy display negatively and to react with compensation (e.g., pulling away when encountering inappropriate touch). When arousal change is moderate, which is the most likely scenario (see P. Andersen 1985, in press, b), the theory predicts that the intimacy behavior will be judged based on six factors, which Andersen calls "cognitive valencers." If the intimacy increase is regarded favorably in light of these valencers, a person is likely to feel positive affect and to reciprocate. In contrast, if the intimacy increase is regarded unfavorably, a person should feel negative affect and compensate. The six cognitive valencers that mediate this process are discussed next.

Culture

Culture is a learned repository of beliefs and values that influence our attitudes toward most communicative behavior. Culture is such a basic and pervasive force that it is often confused with human nature itself (Andersen, in press, a). Cultural schemata are knowledge structures that permeate all relational behaviors. As P. Andersen (1993) stated: "Cultural schemata are so habitual, overlearned, and automatic that cross-cultural intimacy behaviors are likely to violate one's cultural schemata in a variety of ways" (p. 17). Hecht, Andersen, and Ribeau (1989) have shown that cultures vary in the degree to which they desire high levels of nonverbal intimacy. In general, cultures that are outwardly warm and immediate are located in South America, southern and eastern Europe, and the Middle East (Hecht et al., 1989). Low

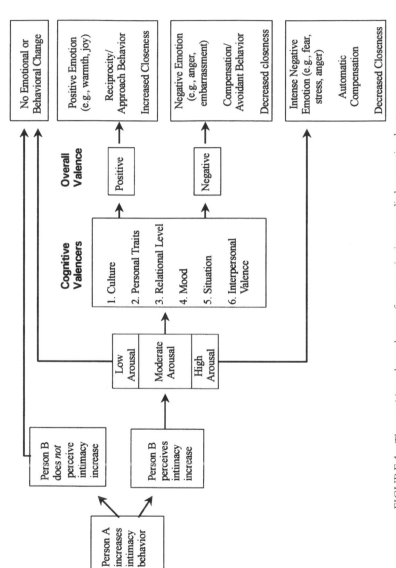

FIGURE 1   The cognitive–valence theory of communication as applied to emotional outcomes.

contact cultures are most likely to be found in Asia (McDaniel & Andersen, in press). North American and Northern European cultures are also fairly low in terms of contact (Burgoon et al., 1996). Cultural differences are particularly proscriptive when it comes to public displays of intimacy. According to Burgoon (1993), "public displays of affection through tie signs, proximity, kissing, and the like are acceptable in some places, but considered tacky and embarrassing in others" (p. 42).

Personal Traits

Individuals vary greatly in a number of ways. These individual differences are variously called traits, personality variables, or predispositional variables. Indeed, it is estimated that there are 20,000 trait terms in the English lexicon (P. Andersen, 1987). Many of these trait terms are relevant to interpersonal relationships (Park & Waters, 1988). Although perhaps dozens of personality traits are relevant to the process of the experience and reception of warm, intimate interpersonal emotion, several are most important. Among these are extroversion, communication apprehension, touch avoidance, and attachment styles.

Extroverts, communication apprehensives, and touch avoiders fear certain types of social contact. Extroverts, according to Eysenck (1967), have chronically low levels of cortical arousal and favor stimulating and intimate interactions with others. Introverts, in contrast, have higher levels of arousal and prefer more distant interactions. Similarly, communicative apprehensives (McCroskey, 1982) are inhibited, asocial, and unfriendly (Cheek & Buss, 1981), less communicatively skilled (Allen & Bourhis, 1996), less vocally relaxed (Guerrero, 1997), manifest and elicit less disclosure from others (Miller, Berg & Archer, 1983), and are less open and socially confirming (Lustig & Andersen, 1991). Touch avoiders (P. Andersen & Leibowitz, 1978) have been shown to have negative emotional reactions to touch (Sorensen, 1979) and to be less tactically interactive than others (Guerrero & Andersen, 1991). Touch avoidance also associates negatively with verbal openness (Andersen, Andersen, & Lustig, 1987).

Research has also uncovered attachment-style differences in interactional patterns. Guerrero and Burgoon (1996) found that although most individuals tend to compensate intimacy decreases and reciprocate intimacy increases by their romantic partners, those who are preoccupied with their relationships exhibit this pattern most strongly. A study by Kobak and Hazan (1991) found that insecurely attached wives are more likely to display negative affect and to criticize their husbands during problem-solving tasks than are securely attached wives. In addition, Kobak and Hazan found that the husbands of secure wives are more likely to accept and be supportive of their wives' emotional distress than are the husbands of insecure wives.

Taken together, this research suggests that social anxiety, security, and preoccupation with relationships are key traits contributing to the acceptance or refusal of expressed intimacy. McAdams (1988) also contended that "intimacy motivation" (which is probably a cousin construct to preoccupation) predicts one's own intimacy level, readiness for close relationships, thoughts about positive relationships, levels of eye contact and smiling, and interpersonal affect. Certainly, many individual differences impact the capacity to experience, express, and exchange warm, intimate emotions.

Relational Level

Obviously, since warmth and intimacy are inherently interpersonal emotions, the nature of a relationship will determine a persons's readiness to experience warmth and intimacy. Baxter (1987) reported that individuals have two types of relational schemata: relational type (e.g., friend, lover, spouse, etc.) and relational trajectory (e.g., growth or decline). Studies using a variety of different methodologies have shown that intimate communication differs as a function of both relational type and relational trajectory.

Not surprisingly, friends exhibit more intimate behavior than strangers (e.g., Hale & Burgoon, 1984). Romantics and friends also differ from one another. In the verbal realm, Pilkington and Bilbro (1993) found that romantics engage in longer and more frequent interactions with one another. In the nonverbal realm, Guerrero (1997) found that romantics engage in more touch, closer conversational distances, more gaze, less fluency, longer response latencies, and more silence than friends; whereas friends engage in more head nodding and exhibit more vocal interest than romantics. Research has also shown that relational stage makes a difference. In Chapter 12, this volume, Taraban et al. review literature showing that romantic partners tend to engage in the most verbal and nonverbal intimacy when they are in the process of escalating their relationships. Similarly, Guerrero et al. (1993) found that individuals who reported that their romantic relationships had "become more serious" after a 6-week period also reported increasing their use of maintenance behavior (e.g., more verbal assurances and positivity) over the 6 weeks. In contrast, those who reported that their relationships had "become less serious" reported using less maintenance behavior.

Studies also show that when intimacy displays are inappropriate within the context of a particular relational type and/or relational trajectory, they are usually negatively valenced and perceived as unwanted intimacy (P. Andersen, 1992) or even sexual harassment (Wertin & Andersen, 1996). Planalp (1985) suggested that "people enter interactions with some sense of what communication behaviors are appropriate for the type of relationship" (p. 3). Therefore, although communication definitely affects the relationship, the relationship also affects the type of communication in which interactants engage. Baldwin (1992) argued that when a particular relational schema is activated, related feelings are activated as well. These feelings of intimacy, sexual arousal, dislike, or whatever, create behavior that is consistent with the emotion being experienced. Such behavior can positively or negatively influence a relationship.

Mood

Moods are a mezzo or midlevel construct when compared to traits or dispositions that are stable and enduring (macrolevel) and to emotions that are connected to particular stimuli and are of relatively short duration (microlevel). Unlike emotions, moods are affective states without necessarily being connected to current causes or objects (Frijda, 1993; see also Guerrero et al., Chapter 1, this volume). Undoubtedly, moods have an impact on people's ability to experience warmth and intimacy, but the nature of this association is poorly understood.

Some studies suggest a direct relationship between mood and feelings of warmth and intimacy, such that positive moods associate with greater warmth and intimacy, whereas negative moods associate with greater coldness and detachment. When people are in a depressed mood, typically pleasurable events are perceived as less intimate and positive (Frijda, 1993; Segrin, Chapter 8, this volume). Similarly, Ruch (1993) reported that a cheerful mood increases feelings of humor-induced exhilaration when other people are present, but not during solitary situations. Recently, Smyth and Aaron (1995) found that cheerful moods correlated positively and sad moods correlated negatively with being in love. Conversely, a study of mood-induced social decisions revealed that sad subjects preferred interpersonally rewarding rather than task-competent partners (Forgas, 1991). However, happy subjects seem to be better processors of social information than sad subjects. Barbee, Lawrence, and Cunningham (Chapter 10, this volume) argue that individuals in positive moods are more helpful because they are outwardly focused and cued to liking and positive affect. Negative moods tend to make an individual self-focused and to decrease helping behavior. Clearly, the moods that people are in influence the way they interpret, evaluate, and respond to the partner's intimacy behaviors.

Situation

Certainly, the situation frames how intimacy behavior is interpreted and affects whether or not intimacy is reciprocated. As Andersen (1989) put it: "It has become axiomatic that any human action cannot be interpreted and understood outside of its context. The term 'out of context' has become synonymous with meaningless or misleading" (p. 27). Spitzberg and Bruner (1991) demonstrated the importance of integrating contextual features, such as how typical a situation is, into a comprehensive theory of interpersonal communication competence. The situational context is vital to whether a given behavior will produce warmth or intimacy. A hug at the office may be substantially less intimacy-inducing than a hug in a social or private setting. Acitelli and Duck (1987) suggested that cognitive appraisals of the situation are critical to appropriate emotional and relational outcomes. Specifically, they contend that "elements of intimacy are both dynamic and static, both personal and situational: The mediating factor is the perspective on it that is taken by the participants, particularly their judgment about the level of intimacy appropriate for a given situation or occasion" (p. 301). In a similar vein, Chelune et al. (1984) showed that certain physical settings are more conducive to intimacy than others. Task-oriented environments such as courtrooms, offices, or lecture halls, as well as public environments such as streets, malls, parking lots, and elevators, tend not to foster intimacy. Personal, private environments such as bedrooms, family rooms, cars, and jacuzzis tend to foster greater intimacy. In short, the feelings of warmth and intimacy have everything to do with the environmental and situational contexts in which intimate interactions take place.

Interpersonal Valence

So far, we have touched upon factors related to culture, the situation, moods, the relationship, and the individual characteristics of the person *receiving* intimacy. A sixth factor, interpersonal valence, deals with the characteristics of the person who has *initiated* an increase in intimacy. According to cognitive valence theory, when people respond to increases in intimacy, they evaluate the personal characteristics of their partners. This concept is nearly identical to Burgoon's (1978, 1983) concept of *communicator reward valence,* which is a central construct in her expectancy violations theory. Burgoon, Stern, and Dillman (1995) described communicator reward valence as "a net assessment of how favorably regarded the other is" at a particular point in time (p. 95). Several preinteractional and interactional factors can influence this net assessment. Examples of preinteractional characteristics include physical attractiveness, initial credibility, similarity, status, gender, and age. Interactional characteristics include conversational style, derived credibility, sense of humor, relevant task knowledge, and responsiveness.

Of the many preinteractional and interactional features that influence interpersonal valence, attractiveness has probably received the most scholarly attention. Dion, Berscheid, and Walster's (1972) seminal work on the "what is beautiful is good hypothesis" shows that people generally perceive good-looking people to possess a number of positive qualities, including being warmer and more responsive, sensitive, kind, outgoing, nurturant, poised, and interesting. Similarly, research on the "what sounds beautiful is good" hypothesis has shown that attractive voices, which are pleasant and expressive, associate with a host of positive personal attributes (Zuckerman & Driver, 1989). It is likely that people view physically and vocally attractive people in a positive light because it is easier to make consistent judgments (i.e., someone who looks and sounds good is good) than inconsistent judgments (i.e., someone who looks and sounds good is bad). Right or wrong, it appears that attractive people have an edge in terms of interpersonal valence.

Of course, there are other types of attractiveness. In addition to physical attraction, McCroskey and McCain (1974) identified social and task attraction. Social attraction refers to the perception that someone would make a good companion and would fit easily into one's social circle. Individuals who are perceived as warm, competent, and responsive are likely to be socially attractive. In addition, a sense of humor appears to be central to judgments of social attractiveness. Buss (1988) found that both men and women rated humor as *the* most potent predictor of interpersonal attraction. Task attractiveness refers to a person's ability to help someone complete instrumental tasks and solve problems. Research suggests that in certain circumstances, task attraction may be an important predictor of reciprocity and compensation. For example, Burke, Weir, and Harrison (1976) showed that spouses avoid disclosure when they perceive that their partner lacks knowledge that is relevant to their problems.

Similarity and credibility have also received considerable attention as interpersonal valences. Generally, research suggests that similarity which is positive and reinforcing breeds liking (see Brehm, 1992, for a review; but also see Sunnafrank, 1992). Bryne, Clore, and Smeaton (1986) argued that similarity and dissimilarity associate with approach and avoidance behavior, respectively. Specifically, they theorize that dissimilarity leads to negative affect and avoidance, low levels of similarity lead to indifference, and high levels of similarity lead to attraction, positive affect, and approach behavior. People who are perceived to be high in credibility and/or status may also receive more positive responses from others. As a case in point, Burgoon and Aho (1982) investigated how status affects a salesperson's decision to let a customer use the store telephone. The confederates in this experiment were either: (a) dressed professionally and indicated that they wished to purchase an expensive item; or (b) dressed casually and indicated that they wished to purchase an inexpensive item. Not surprisingly, the salespeople showed greater interest, more positive affect, and more willingness to comply when the confederates were perceived as high in status. This experiment, and others like it, illustrate the importance of interpersonal valence as a factor influencing emotional and behavioral responses.

CONCLUSION

In this chapter we have argued that emotion researchers have neglected a potentially important emotion—that of interpersonal warmth. In the past, emotions have been conceptualized primarily as private intrapersonal experiences. A more social view of emotions suggests that some emotions, like warmth, occur exclusively in interpersonal communication settings. We demonstrated that interpersonal warmth is a key component within several multicomponential constructs, including intimacy, relational closeness, and attachment. The exact nature and function of interpersonal warmth has yet to be fully understood. Yet clearly, several nonverbal and verbal behaviors elicit feelings of warmth, especially when they are reciprocated. Continuing research in this area should help scholars better understand the emotional underpinnings of close relationships. Interpersonal warmth is undoubtedly a "fuzzy" concept, yet we expect that it provides a solid foundation for the development and maintenance of close relationships.

ACKNOWLEDGMENTS

We thank Janis Andersen and Brian Spitzberg who served as reviewers for this piece. Their valuable insights improved this chapter substantially.

REFERENCES

Acitelli, L. K., & Duck, S. (1987). Postscript: Intimacy as the proverbial elephant. In D. Perlman & S. Duck (Eds.)., *Intimate relationships: Development, dynamics, and deterioration* (pp. 297–308). Newbury Park, CA: Sage.

Afifi, W. A., & Guerrero, L. K. (1997). *Maintenance behaviors in same-sex friendships: Sex differences, equity, and associations with relational closeness.* Unpublished manuscript, University of Delaware.

Ainsworth, M. D. (1989). Attachments beyond infancy. *American Psychologist, 44,* 709–716.

Allen, M., & Bourhis (1996). The relationship of communication apprehension and communication behavior: A meta-analysis. *Communication Quarterly, 44,* 214–226.

Altman, I., Vinsel, A., & Brown, B. B. (1981). Dialectic conceptions in social psychology: An application to social penetration and privacy regulation. In L. Berkowitz (Ed.), *Advances in experimental social psychology* (vol. 14, pp. 107–160). New York: Academic Press.

Andersen, J. F., Andersen, P. A., & Jensen, A. D. (1979). The measurement of nonverbal immediacy. *Journal of Applied Communication Research, 7,* 153–180.

Andersen, J. F., Andersen, P. A., & Lustig, M., W. (1987). Opposite-sex touch avoidance: A national replication and extension. *Journal of Nonverbal Behavior, 11,* 89–109.

Andersen, P. A. (1985). Nonverbal immediacy in interpersonal communication. In A. O. Siegman & S. Feldstein (Eds.), *Multichannel integrations of nonverbal behavior* (pp. 1–36). Hillsdale, NJ: Erlbaum.

Andersen, P. A. (1987). The trait debate. A critical examination of the individual differences paradigm in interpersonal communication. In B. Dervin & M. J. Voigt (Eds.), *Progress in communication Sciences* (Vol. 8, pp. 47–82). Norwood, NJ: Ablex.

Andersen, P. A. (1989, May). *A cognitive-valence theory of intimate communication.* Paper presented at the biennial meeting of the International Network on Personal Relationships, Iowa City, IA.

Andersen, P. A. (1992, July). *Excessive intimacy: An account analysis of behaviors, cognitive schemata, affect, and relational outcomes.* Paper presented at the biennial meeting of the International Society of the Study of Personal Relationships, Orono, ME.

Andersen, P. A. (1993). Cognitive schemata in personal relationships. In S. Duck (Ed.), *Individuals in relationships* (pp. 1–29). Newbury Park, CA: Sage.

Andersen, P. A. (in press, a). *Beside language: Nonverbal communication in interpersonal relationships.* Mountain View, CA: Mayfield.

Andersen, P. A. (in press, b). The cognitive valence theory of intimate communication. In M. Palmer (Ed.), *Mutual influence in interpersonal communication: Theory and research in cognition, affect, and behavior.* Norwood, NJ: Ablex.

Andersen, P. A., & Leibowitz, K. (1978). The development and nature of the construct, touch avoidance. *Environmental Psychology and Nonverbal Behavior, 3,* 89–106.

Averill, J. R. (1982). *Anger and aggression: An essay on emotion.* New York: Springer-Verlag.

Baldwin, M. W. (1992). Relational schemas and the processing of social information. *Psychological Bulletin, 112,* 461–484.

Bartholomew, K., & Horowitz L. M. (1991). Attachment styles among young adults: A test of a four-category model. *Journal of Personality and Social Psychology, 61,* 226–244.

Baumeister, R. F., & Leary, M. R. (1995). The need to belong: Desire for interpersonal attachments as a fundamental human motivation. *Psychological Bulletin, 117,* 497–529.

Bavelas, J. B., Black, A., Chovil, N., & Mullet, J. (1990). *Equivocal communication.* Newbury Park, CA: Sage.

Baxter, L. A. (1987). Cognition and communication in the relationship process. In P. McGhee, D. Clarke, & R. Bernett (Eds.), *Accounting for relationships: Social representations of interpersonal links* (pp. 192–212). London: Methuen.

Baxter, L. A. (1992). Forms and functions of intimate play in personal relationships. *Human Communication Research, 18,* 336–363.

Bayes, M. A. (1972). Behavioral cues of interpersonal warmth. *Journal of Consulting and Clinical Psychology, 39,* 333–339.

Bell, R. A., Buerkel-Rothfuss, N. L., & Gore, K. E. (1987). "Did you bring the yarmulke for the cabbage patch kid?" The idiomatic communication of young lovers. *Human Communication Research, 14,* 47–67.

Berscheid, E., Snyder, M., & Omato, A. M. (1989). Issues in studying close relationships: Conceptualizing and measuring closeness. In C. Hendrick (Ed.), *Review of personality and social psychology, Vol. 10. Close relationships* (pp. 63–91). Newbury Park, CA: Sage.

Bochner, A. P. (1984). The functions of human communicating in interpersonal bonding. In C. C. Arnold & J. W. Bowers (Eds.), *Handbook of rhetorical and communication theory* (pp. 544–621). Boston, MA: Allyn & Bacon.

Bowlby, J. (1969). *Attachment.* New York: Basic Books.

Bradac, J. J., Bowers, J. W., & Courtright, J. A. (1979). Three language variables in communication research: Intensity, immediacy, and diversity. *Human Communication Research, 5,* 257–269.

Brehm, S. S. (1992). *Intimate relationships* (2nd ed.). New York: McGraw-Hill.

Brown, D. E. (1991). *Human univerials.* Philadelphia, PA: Temple University Press.

Burgoon, J. K. (1978). A communication model of personal space violations: Explication and an initial test. *Human Communication Research, 4,* 129–142.

Burgoon, J. K. (1983). Nonverbal violations of expectations. In J. M. Wiemann & R. P. Harrison (Eds.), *Nonverbal interaction* (pp. 77–111). Beverly Hills, CA: Sage.

Burgoon, J. K. (1993). Interpersonal expectations, expectancy violations, and emotional communication. *Journal of Language and Social Psychology, 12,* 30–48.

Burgoon, J. K. (1994). Nonverbal signals. In M. L. Knapp & G. R. Miller (Eds.), *Handbook of interpersonal communication* (2nd ed., pp. 229–285). Newbury Park, CA: Sage.

Burgoon, J. K., & Aho, L. (1982). Three field experiments on the effects of violations of conversational distance. *Communication Monographs, 49,* 71–88.

Burgoon, J. K., Buller, D. B., & Woodall, W. G. (1996). *Nonverbal communication: The unspoken dialogue.* New York: McGraw-Hill.

Burgoon, J. K., Coker, D. A., & Coker, R. A. (1986). Communication effects of gaze behavior: A test of two contrasting explanations. *Human Communization Research, 12,* 495–524.

Burgoon, J. K., & Hale, J. L. (1988). Nonverbal expectancy violations: Model elaboration and application to immediacy behaviors. *Communication Monographs, 55,* 58–79.

Burgoon, J. K., & Newton, D. A. (1991). Applying a social meaning model to relational message interpretations of conversational involvement: Comparing observer and participant perspectives. *Southern Communication Journal, 56,* 96–113.

Burgoon, J. K., Stern, L. A., & Dillman, L. (1995). *Interpersonal adaptation: Dyadic interaction patterns.* New York: Cambridge University Press.

Burke, R. J., Weir, T., & Harrison, D. (1976). Disclosure of problems and tensions experienced by marital partners. *Psychological Reports, 38,* 531–542.

Burleson, B. R., Albrecht, T. L., Goldsmith, D. J., & Sarason, I. G. (1994). Introduction: The communication of social support. In B. R. Burleson, T. L. Albrecht, & I. G. Sarason (Eds.), *Communication of social support: Messages, interactions, relationships, and community* (pp. xi–xxx). Thousand Oaks, CA: Sage.

Buss, D. M. (1988). The evolution of human intrasexual competition: Tactics of mate attraction. *Journal of Personality and Social Psychology, 54,* 616–628.

Bryne, D., Clore, G. L., & Smeaton, G. (1986). The attraction hypothesis: Do similar attitudes affect anything? *Journal of Personality and Social Psychology, 51,* 1167–1170.

Canary, D. J., & Stafford, L. (1993). Preservation of relational characteristics: Maintenance strategies, equity, and locus of control. In P. Kalbfleisch (Ed.), *Interpersonal communication: Evolving interpersonal relationships* (pp. 237–260). Hillsdale, NJ: Erlbaum.

Canary, D. J., & Stafford, L. (1994). Maintaining relationships through strategic and routine interaction. In D. J. Canary & L. Stafford (Eds.), *Communication and relational maintenance* (pp. 3–22). San Diego, CA: Academic Press.

Cappella, J. N. (1983). Conversational involvement: Approaching and avoiding others. In J. M. Wiemann & R. P. Harrison (Eds.), *Nonverbal interaction* (113–148). Beverly Hills, CA: Sage.

Chelune, G. J., Robinson, J. T., & Kommor, M. J. (1984). A cognitive interactional model of intimate relationships. In V. J. Derlega (Ed.), *Communication, intimacy, and close relationships* (pp. 11–40). New York: Academic Press.

Cissna, K. N., & Sieburg, E. (1981). Patterns of interactional confirmation and disconfirmation. In C. Wilder-Mott & J. Weakland (Eds.), *Rigor and Imagination* (pp. 230–239). Wesport, CT: Praeger.

Cheek, J. M., & Buss, C. M. (1981). The influence of shyness on loneliness in a new situation. *Personality and Social Psychology Bulletin, 7,* 572–577.

Clarke, D. D., Allen, C. M. B., & Dickson, S. (1985). The characteristic affective tone of seven classes of interpersonal relationship. *Journal of Social and Personal Relationships, 2,* 117–120.

Clore, G. L., & Ortony, A. (1988). The semantics of the affective lexicon. In V. Hamilton, G. H. Bower, & N. H. Frijda (Eds.), *Cognitive perspectives on emotion and motivation* (pp. 367–397). Norwell, MA: Kluwer Academic.

Coker, D. A., & Burgoon, J. K. (1987). The nature of conversational involvement and nonverbal encoding patterns. *Human Communication Research, 13,* 463–494.

Conville, R. L. (1974). Linguistic nonimmediacy and communicators' anxiety. *Psychological Reports, 35,* 1107–1114.

Coutts, L. M., Schneider, F. W., & Montgomery, S. (1980). An investigation of the arousal model of interpersonal intimacy. *Journal of Experimental Social Psychology, 16,* 545–561.

Cozby, P. C. (1973). Self-disclosure: A literature review. *Psychological Bulletin, 79,* 73–91.

Cupach, W. R., & Spitzberg, B. H. (Eds). (1994). *The dark side of interpersonal communication.* Hillsdale, NJ: Erlbaum.

Dainton, M. (1991, May). *Relational maintenance revisited: The addition of physical affection measures to a maintenance typology.* Paper presented at the annual meeting of the International Communication Association, Chicago, IL.

Derlega, V. J., Barbee, A. P., & Winstead, B. A. (1994). Friendship, gender, and social support: Laboratory studies of supportive interactions. In B. R. Burleson, T. L. Albrecht, & I. G. Sarason (Eds.), *Communication of social support* (pp. 136–151). Thousand Oaks, CA: Sage.

Derlega, V. J., Metts, S., Petronio, S., & Margulis, S. T. (1993). *Self-disclosure.* Thousand Oaks, CA: Sage.

Dion, K. K., Berscheid, E., & Walster, E. (1972). What is beautiful is good. *Journal of Personality and Social Psychology, 24,* 285–290.

Dosser, D. A., Jr., Balswick, J. O., & Halverson, C. F., Jr. (1986). Male inexpressiveness and relationships. *Journal of Social and Personal Relationships, 3,* 241–258.

Duck, S. W., & Miell, E. E. (1986). Charting the development of personal relationships. In R. Gilmour & S. W. Duck (Eds.), *The emerging field of personal relationships* (pp. 133–143). Hillsdale, NJ: Erlbaum.

Duck, S., & Pond, K. (1989). Friends, Romans, countrymen, lend me your retrospections: Rhetoric and reality in personal relationships. In C. Hendrick (Ed.), *Review of personality and social psychology, Vol. 10. Close relationships* (pp. 17–38). Newbury Park, CA: Sage.

Duck, S. W., Rutt, D. J., Hurst, M. H., & Strejc, H. (1991). Some evident truths about conversation in everyday relationships: All communications are not created equal. *Human Communication Research, 18,* 228–267.

Ekman, P., & Friesen, W. V. (1975). *Unmasking the face: A guide to recognizing emotions from facial clues.* Englewood Cliffs, NJ: Prentice-Hall.

Eysenck, H. J. (1967). *The biological basis of personality.* Springfield, IL: Charles Thomas Publisher.

Feeney, J. A. (1995). Adult attachment and emotional control. *Personal Relationships, 2,* 143–159.

Forgas, J. P. (1991). Affective influences on partner choice: The role of mood in social decisions. *Journal of Personality and Social Psychology, 61,* 208–220.

Frijda, N. H. (1993). Moods, emotion episodes, and emotions. In M. Lewis & J. M. Haviland (Eds.), *Handbook of emotions* (pp. 381–404). New York: Guilford.

Goldberg, J. G. (1993). *The dark side of love: The positive role of our negative feelings—anger, jealousy, and hate.* New York: G. P. Putnam's Sons.

Gottman, J., Notarius, C., Gonso, J., & Markman, H. J. (1976). *A couple's guide to communication.* Champaign, IL: Research Press.

Gottman, J. M. (1994). *Why marriages succeed or fail.* New York: Simon & Shuster.

Guerrero, L. K. (1996a, November). *Attachment-style differences in communication skills and the expression of anger and sadness.* Paper presented at the annual meeting of the Speech Communication Association, San Diego, CA.

Guerrero, L. K. (1996b). Attachment-style differences in intimacy and involvement: A test of the four-category model. *Communication Monographs, 63,* 269–293.

Guerrero, L. K. (1997). Nonverbal involvement across interactions with same-sex friends, opposite-sex friends, and romantic partners: Consistency or change? *Journal of Social and Personal Relationships, 14,* 31–59.

Guerrero, L. K., & Andersen, P. A. (1991). The waxing and waning of relational intimacy: Touch as a function of relational stage, gender and touch avoidance. *Journal of Social and Personal Relationships, 8,* 147–165.

Guerrero, L. K., & Burgoon, J. K. (1996). Attachment styles and reactions to nonverbal involvement change in romantic dyads: Patterns of reciprocity and compensation. *Human Communication Research, 22,* 335–370.

Guerrero, L. K., Eloy, S. V., & Wabnik, A. I. (1993). Linking maintenance strategies to relationship development and disengagement: A reconceptualization. *Journal of Social and Personal Relationships, 10,* 273–283.

Hale, J. L., & Burgoon, J. K. (1984). Models of reactions to changes in nonverbal immediacy. *Journal of Nonverbal Behavior, 8,* 287–314.

Hatfield, E. (1984). The dangers of intimacy. In V. J. Derlega (Ed.), *Communication, intimacy, and close relationships* (pp. 207–220). New York: Academic Press.

Hatfield, E. (1988). Passionate and companionate love. In R. J. Sternberg & M. L. Barnes (Eds.), *The psychology of love* (pp. 191–217). New Haven, CT: Yale University Press.

Hays, R. B. (1985). A longitudinal study of friendship development. *Journal of Personality and Social Psychology, 48,* 909–924.

Hazan, C., & Shaver, P. (1987). Romantic love conceptualized as an attachment process. *Journal of Personality and Social Psychology, 52,* 511–524.

Hecht, M. L., Andersen, P. A., & Ribeau, S. A. (1989). The cultural dimensions of nonverbal communication. In M. K. Asante & W. B. Gudykunst (Eds.), *Handbook of international and intercultural communication* (pp. 163–185). Newbury Park, CA: Sage.

Hendrick, S. S., & Hendrick, C. (1992). *Romantic love.* Newbury Park, CA: Sage.

Hopper, R., Knapp, M. L., & Scott, L. (1981). Couple's personal idioms: Exploring intimate talk. *Journal of Communication, 31,* 23–33.

King, S. W., & Sereno, K. K. (1984). Conversational appropriateness as a conversational imperative. *Quarterly Journal of Speech, 70,* 264–273.

Kobak, R. R., & Hazan, C. (1991). Attachment in marriage: Effects of security and accuracy of working models. *Journal of Personality and Social Psychology, 60,* 861–869.

Lustig, M. W., & Andersen, P. A. (1991). Generalizing about communication apprehension and avoidance: Multiple replications and meta-analyses. In J. W. Neuliep (Ed.), *Replication research in the social sciences* (pp. 297–328). Newbury Park, CA: Sage.

Marshall, L. L. (1994). Physical and psychological abuse. In W. R. Cupach & B. H. Spitzberg (Eds.), *The dark side of interpersonal communication* (pp. 281–311). Hillsdale, NJ: Erlbaum.

McAdams, D. P. (1988). Personal needs and personal relationships. In S. Duck (Ed.), *Handbook of personal relationships: Theory, research, and intervention* (pp. 85–105). London: Sage.

McCroskey, J. C., & McCain, T. A. (1974). The measurement of interpersonal attraction. *Speech Monographs, 41,* 261–266.

McDaniel, E. R., & Andersen, P. A. (in press). International patterns of tactile communication: A field study. *Journal of Nonverbal Behavior.*

Mehrabian, A. (1971). *Silent messages: Implicit communication of emotions and attitudes.* Belmont, CA: Wadsworth.

Mehrabian, A., & Ksionzky, S. (1970). Models for affiliative and conformity behavior. *Psychological Bulletin, 74,* 110–126.

Mikulincer, M., & Nachshon, O. (1991). Attachment styles and patterns of self-disclosure. *Journal of Personality and Social Psychology, 61,* 321–331.

Miller, L. C., Berg, J. H., & Archer, R. L. (1983). Openers: Individuals who elicit intimate self-disclosure. *Journal of Personality and Social Psychology, 44,* 1234, 1244.

Monsour, M. (1992). Meanings of intimacy in cross- and same-sex friendships. *Journal of Social and Personal Relationships, 9,* 277–295.

Montgomery, B. M. (1988). Quality communication in personal relationships. In S. W. Duck (Ed.), *Handbook of Personal Relationships* (pp. 343–359). New York: Wiley & Sons.

Montgomery, B. M. (1994). Communication in close relationships. In A. L. Weber & J. H. Harvey (Eds.), *Perspectives on close relationships* (pp. 67–87). Boston: Allyn & Bacon.

Norton, R. (1983). *Communicator style: Theory, applications, and measures.* Newbury Park, CA: Sage.

Ortony, A., Clore, G. L., & Foss, M. (1987). The referential structure of the affective lexicon. *Cognitive Science, 11,* 361–384.

Park, K. A., & Waters, E. (1988). Traits and relationships in development perspective. In S. W. Duck (Ed.), *Handbook of personal relationships* (pp. 161–176). New York: Wiley & Sons.

Parks, M. R. (1982). Ideology and interpersonal communication: Off the couch and into the world. In M. Burgoon (Ed.), *Communication yearbook 5* (pp. 79–107). New Brunswick, NJ: Transaction Books.

Parks, M. R., & Floyd, K. (1996). Meanings for closeness and intimacy in friendship. *Journal of Social and Personal Relationships, 13,* 85–107.

Patterson, M. L. (1976). An arousal model of interpersonal intimacy. *Psychological Review, 83,* 235–245.

Perlman, D., & Fehr, B. (1987). The development of intimate relationships. In D. Perlman & S. Duck (Eds.), *Intimate relationships: Development, dynamics, and deterioration* (pp. 13–42). Newbury Park, CA: Sage.

Pilkington, C. F., & Bilbro, K. G. (1993, June). *Interactions with same-sex friends, opposite-sex friends, and lovers: How different are they?* Paper presented at the annual meeting of the International Network on Personal Relationships, Milwaukee, WI.

Planalp, S. (1985). Relational schemata: A test of alternative forms of relational knowledge as guides to communication. *Human Communication Research, 12,* 3–29.

Plutchik, R. (1984). Emotions: A general psychoevolutionary theory. In K. R. Scherer & P. Ekman (Eds.), *Approaches to emotion,* (pp. 197–219). Hillsdale, NJ: Erlbaum.

Praeger, K. J. (1995). *The psychology of intimacy.* New York: Guilford Press.

Reeder, H. (1995). *The experience of intimacy, commitment, and passion in heterosexual cross-sex friendships.* Paper presented at the annual meeting of the Speech Communication Association, San Antonio, TX.

Ruch, W. (1993). Exhilaration and humor. In M. Lewis & J. M. Haviland (Eds.), *Handbook of emotions* (pp. 605–616). New York: Guilford.

Shaver, P. R., & Hazan, C. (1988). A biased overview of the study of love. *Journal of Social and Personal Relationships, 5,* 473–501.

Shaver, P., Schwartz, J., Kirson, D., & O'Connor, C. (1987). Emotion knowledge: Further exploration of a prototype approach. *Journal of Personality and Social Psychology, 52,* 1061–1086.

Simpson, J. A., Rholes, W. S., & Nelligan, J. S. (1992). Support-seeking and support-giving within couples in an anxiety-provoking situation: The role of attachment styles. *Journal of Personality and Social Psychology, 62,* 434–446.

Smyth, J., & Aron, A. (1995, June). *Love and mood: Daily variation and covariation.* Paper presented at the meeting of the International Network on Personal Relationships, Williamsburg, VA.

Sorensen, G. (1979, May). *The effects of touch on interpersonal perceptions.* Paper presented at the annual meeting of the Eastern Communication Association, Philadelphia, PA.

Spitzberg, B. H., & Bruner, C. C. (1991). Toward a theoretical integration of context and competence research. *Western Journal of Speech Communication, 55,* 28–46.

Spitzberg, B. H., & Cupach, W. R. (Eds.). (in press). *The dark side of relationships.* Hillsdale, NJ: Erlbaum.

Spitzberg, B. H., & Hecht, M. L. (1984). Component model of relational competence. *Human Communication Research, 10,* 575–599.

Spitzberg, B. H., & Hurt, H. T. (1987). The assessment of interpersonal skills in an instructional context. *Communication Education, 36,* 28–45.

Stafford, L., & Canary, D. J. (1991). Maintenance strategies and romantic relationship type, gender and relational characteristics. *Journal of Social and Personal Relationships, 8,* 217–242.

Stearns, P. N. (1989). *Jealousy: The evolution of an emotion in American history.* New York: New York University Press.

Sternberg, R. J. (1986). A triangular theory of love. *Psychological Review, 93,* 119–135.

Sternberg, R. J. (1988). *The triangular of love: Intimacy, passion, and commitment.* New York: Basic Books.

Sunnafrank, M. (1992). On debunking the attitude similarity myth. *Communication Monographs, 59,* 164–179.

Tangney, J. P., & Fischer, K. W. (Eds.), (1995). *Self-conscious emotions: The psychology of shame, guilt, embarrassment, and pride.* New York: Guilford.

Tarvis, C. (1982). *Anger: The misunderstood emotion.* New York: Simon & Schuster.

Walster, E., & Walster, G. W. (1978). *A new look at love.* Reading, MA: Addison-Wesley.

Watzlawick, P., Beavin, J., & Jackson, D. D. (1967). *Pragmatics of human communication.* New York: W. W. Norton.

Wertin, L., & Andersen, P. A. (1996, February). *Sexual harassment and cognitive schemata: A test of cognitive valence theory.* Paper presented at the annual meeting of the Western States Communication Association, Pasadena, CA.

White, G. L. & Mullen, P. E. (1989). *Jealousy: Theory, research and clinical strategies.* New York: Guilford Press.

Wiener, M., & Mehrabian, A. (1968). *Language within language: Immediacy, a channel in verbal communication.* New York: Appleton-Century-Crofts.

Wood, J. T., & Duck, S. (1995). Off the beaten track: New shores for relationship research. In J. T. Wood & S. Duck (Eds.), *Under-studied relationships: Off the beaten track* (pp. 1–21). Thousand Oaks, CA: Sage.

Zuckerman, M., & Driver, R. E. (1989). What sounds beautiful is good: The vocal attractiveness stereotype. *Journal of Nonverbal Behavior, 13,* 67–82.

CHAPTER 12

Loving and Liking

Carolyn B. Taraban, Susan S. Hendrick, and Clyde Hendrick

Texas Tech University
Lubbock, Texas

"How do I love you; let me count the ways." This statement is one of the most famous in the English language. "How do I *tell* you that I love you" is not a famous saying, however. The lack of emphasis on *telling*, as compared to *counting*, may indicate an underlying problem people have in the communication of their most powerful emotional experiences. Consider the following vignette:

> Laura waited for him in eager anticipation. They had been dating for three months, and thoughts of Tom increasingly filled her waking hours. Within the last few days, Laura realized that she had fallen in love with Tom, and she hoped fervently that he had fallen in love with her. She vowed to somehow tell him how she felt, on their date tonight. She heard his car stop in front of her townhouse and felt her stomach start to flutter and her face flush. Tom bounded up the steps and opened the door. Her heart began to pound, and she felt a throbbing sensation in her left temple. Tom was so handsome, it took her breath away. She wanted to yell out her love to him. Instead, she said, "Hi." He said, "How've you been?" She said, "Great." He asked, "Hungry?" She replied, "Yeah." He said, "Good, let's go." As they drove away, Laura had a sinking feeling that the moment had passed. How would she ever be able to let him know the depth of her love for him?

Liking and loving other people appear to be part of our emotional heritage, the potential for which is built into the very fabric of our genetic structure (Mellen, 1981). The sophisticated communication of these emotions is not so readily achieved, however, because communication is a complex and variegated achievement of social life that takes time to master. Communication can occur indirectly via subtle nonverbal cues, directly by dramatic overt behavior, and both directly and indirectly through the complexities of language. In general, the possibilities for both verbal and nonverbal communication become more sophisticated as the individual matures. The normal individual becomes increasingly skilled at sending and receiving communication over time. In fact, one defining aspect of maturation might well be the exhibition of a high level of skilled communication.

Emotional communication is no exception, especially when the emotions, such as loving and liking, implicate the individual in interdependent relationships with others. The emotions themselves may be more or less "given." The communication of the emotions, however, is far from completely predictable.

LOVING AND LIKING AS EMOTIONS

Love and liking are among the strongest positive emotions we experience in our lives. A number of emotion theorists have included love, in particular, on their lists of basic emotions (Epstein, 1984; Fehr & Russell, 1984; Shaver, Schwartz, Kirson, & O'Connor, 1987). These basic emotions are the ones with which both adults and children identify most strongly and select frequently as "true" emotions. Bretherton and Beeghly (1982) reported that when children as young as 28 months were asked to name the emotions they knew, "love" and "like" were among the most frequently mentioned (along with "mad," "scared," "happy," and "sad").

We can safely conclude that liking and loving play a central role in the day-to-day lives of every person who has or desires a close relationship with another. When it comes to *communicating* these emotions, however, it seems that we often run into problems. Classical drama such as the story of Cyrano de Bergerac, popular songs, soap opera plots, and even the production of "secret admirer" greeting cards attest to the fact that although it may be easy to experience emotions of positive regard, it is often quite difficult to communicate them. The opening vignette represents several such communicational difficulties.

This chapter will focus on theoretical and empirical work that has explored the effective communication of liking and loving, in situations ranging from initial encounters to long-term relationships. Many emotions have more of an *intra*personal focus, so they are primarily relevant to what individuals feel, and only secondarily relevant to how those feelings are expressed. However, liking and loving clearly also have an *inter*personal focus. They are emotions that have another person as their object and are expressed in the context of a close relationship.

LIKING

Liking for another begins in initial interactions and develops somewhat mysteriously over time, through repeated interactions. How does one let another know that she or he feels positively about that other? What cues are used to communicate attraction to another in an initial meeting? Both verbal and nonverbal modes of communication must be used to communicate liking. One of the most important means of communicating liking to a potential friend or romantic partner is through the process of self-disclosure, or revealing information about oneself to another.

Self-Disclosure and Liking in Initial Encounters

Jourard's (1959) pioneering work spawned dozens of research programs aimed at understanding the relationship between self-disclosure and liking for others. The bottom-line finding from much of this research is that, particularly in initial encounters, we tend to like others who disclose to us, and we tend to disclose to others whom we like. This conclusion rests on a vast research tradition.

Collins and Miller (1994) conducted an extensive meta-analysis of the research linking self-disclosure to liking. Their analysis of more than 70 published studies supports three conclusions about disclosure and attraction. The first is that we do, indeed, like others who disclose to us. The second effect for which Collins and Miller found support is that we tend to disclose more to those whom we like, and the third self-disclosure/liking effect is that once we have self-disclosed to others, we tend to like them more. We will discuss each of the three effects in some detail.

The first effect, that we like others who communicate about themselves, was investigated with a meta-analysis of 50 studies that manipulated or measured a target person's disclosure and measured a participant's liking of the target person. Both correlational and experimental studies supported the existence of a relationship between self-disclosure and liking in initial encounters. Furthermore, the ample number of controlled experiments in the sample allowed the authors to infer a causal relationship: "In first encounters, higher disclosure leads to increased liking" (Collins & Miller, 1994, p. 462).

Through what processes does self-disclosure from one person lead to liking by another? One possible answer lies in uncertainty reduction theory (Berger & Calabrese, 1975) and subsequent research by Douglas (1990, 1991, 1994). These scholars argued that the central goal of an initial interaction between two people is to reduce uncertainty and to come to a point of being able to predict the behavior of the conversational partner. Self-disclosure and question asking are the primary means of reducing uncertainty, according to the theory. Thus, conversational partners will try to elicit as much information as possible from one another in order to predict the other's reactions. Douglas (1990) proposed that uncertainty and liking are inversely related in initial interactions. Empirical support for the claim was obtained in a study in which unacquainted dyads completed written measures of uncertainty and interpersonal attraction after a 2-, 4-, or 6-min conversation. In all three conditions, partners' uncertainty scores were negatively correlated with liking. A conceptual replication of this study (Douglas, 1994) yielded similar results. These two studies supported Douglas's idea that even in brief conversations with a stranger, people attempt to disclose and to elicit disclosures in order to reduce uncertainty about the situation. This uncertainty reduction is directly related to increases in one's confidence about the partner and the situation, and to increase liking for the partner.

The second conclusion noted by Collins and Miller (1994) is that we disclose to others whom we like. Twenty-two studies that measured both a subject's liking for and self-disclosure toward a target person were included in the meta-analysis. Strong evidence indicated that we do indeed disclose to those whom we like. In fact, support for this conclusion was the strongest of the three relationships studied in the meta-analysis. Possible reasons mentioned by Collins and Miller included self-disclosure as a means of providing a reward (in the form of self-revelation) to the liked other or as a means of eliciting reciprocal self-disclosure. As Collins and Miller noted, not much empirical work has addressed the issue of why we disclose to those whom we like, but it does seem clear that disclosure is an effective way of communicating liking toward another individual in initial encounters.

The third issue examined by Collins and Miller (1994) was whether we tend to like others more *after* we have disclosed to them. Only five studies met the authors' criteria of manipulating subjects' disclosure to a target person and subsequently measuring liking for the target prior to any opportunity for reciprocal disclosure from the target. Although the sample of studies was small, all five of them were true experiments, which allowed for the conclusion of a causal inference that "more intimate disclosures lead the discloser to have greater liking for the recipient of the disclosure" (Collins & Miller, 1994, p. 470).

Collins and Miller's (1994) work ties together and makes sense of several decades of sometimes conflicting research dealing with the links between self-disclosure and liking, at least for early encounters between people. The authors made these links very clear: We like others who self-disclose to us; we self-disclose to others whom we like; if we self-disclose to others we like them. In the communication of liking toward another, the importance of self-disclosure cannot be emphasized enough.

A cautionary note should be added, however. It is not the case that the disclosure of personal information by one partner will unequivocally bring about positive regard by the other. Some researchers (Altman & Taylor, 1973; Derlega & Grzelak, 1979) have suggested that both the timing and the intimacy of the disclosure may affect liking. Each of us can recall a time when we were held captive by someone who insisted on revealing intimate details of her or his life. These experiences are generally not positive ones, and they do not serve to increase our liking of the other person.

Collins and Miller (1994) considered some of the factors that could mediate disclosure-liking effects. They hoped to draw conclusions about whether variables such as relational stage, disclosure content (positive or negative), personality, or cultural factors might enhance or limit the effects of disclosure on liking. Unfortunately, there were not enough studies that included these types of variables to provide any definite answers. Still, it stands to reason that the context and content of one's disclosure to another will mediate the effects on liking that have been described.

Communication of emotions such as liking in initial interactions would seem to depend on more than just appropriate self-disclosure. Self-disclosure is just one piece (albeit a large one) of the larger puzzle of communication quality. "Communication quality" includes factors such as the ease, efficiency, depth, and importance of both verbal and nonverbal communication as well as the participants' general feeling of satisfaction with their interactions. It may also be the case that a person's *perceptions* of communication quality may be as important as actual communication quality in determining liking for an interaction partner, a result suggested by Sprecher and Duck (1994).

Self-Disclosure and Liking in Established Friendships

Considerable research has explored the ways in which friends communicate positive regard for one another. Hale, Lundy, and Mongeau (1989) investigated the perceived message content of relationships varying in intensity. The study was based upon prior research by Burgoon and Hale (1987) that validated a schema of eight relational themes or dimensions on which interactions between partners might vary: immediacy/affection, similarity/depth, receptivity/trust, composure, formality, dominance, equality, and task orientation. Hale et al. (1989) hypothesized that relationships varying in intimacy would also vary in the intensity of expression of each of the relational themes. Participants in the study were asked to recall a recent conversation with another person whom they could classify as an acquaintance, colleague, pal, friend, best friend, or lover and then rate the conversation on each of the eight relational message dimensions. As expected, the authors found that there was a near-linear relationship between perceived message content and the intimacy of the relationship, with the exceptions of task orientation and formality, neither of which differed as a function of intimacy. What was surprising, however, was that for four of the eight dimensions (immediacy/affection, similarity/depth, composure, and equality), the highest ratings were made in the "best friend" condition, with a slight drop-off in the scores for the lover condition, even though lovers are generally considered to have a more intimate relationship than are best friends. This sort of "nonlinearity" of intimate behaviors across increasingly intimate relational stages has been reported by others as well (Duck & Miell, 1986; Emmers & Dindia, 1995; Guerrero & Anderson, 1991). Burgoon and Hale speculated that participants may have distinguished relationships marked by intimate physical closeness from those marked by intimate psychological closeness, with psychologically close best friends communicating more intimately on a conversational level, and physically close lovers communicating more intimately on a sexual level. This research provides evidence that close friendships are marked by conversations that clearly communicate positive regard. Conversations high in affection, depth, trust, composure, and equality are certainly evidence of liking between friends.

Another way in which friends communicate liking for one another is through the use of idioms, or phrases and gestures, which have a special meaning only for the friends (see also Andersen & Guerrero, Chapter 11, this volume). Bell and Healy (1992) investigated the link between friendship closeness and friends' use of personal idioms. College students provided a functional description of each of the idioms used in their relationship along with a measure of relationship strength. The idioms were classified into one of 13 categories, based on prior research (Bell, Buerkel-Rothfuss, & Gore, 1987). The most commonly identified categories in Bell and Healey's study were: (a) labels for other people (i.e., "rabbit woman" for a vegetarian acquaintance), (b) nicknames for the friend, (c) nicknames for the self, (d) terms of affection, and (e) sexual references. A finding of particular interest was the strong, positive correlation between the measure of friendship closeness and both the number and breadth of idioms used by the friends. There is a strong link between the strength of a friendship (and presumably liking for the friend) and the use of highly personal communication in the relationship.

It is apparent that a number of variables are related to the communication of liking, first in initial interactions and then in established friendships. But what about the communication of romantic interest? Is it similar or different from the communication of liking?

ROMANTIC INTEREST

How does one communicate to a dating partner that one is either interested or disinterested in continuing the relationship? How is the desire to strengthen a casual romantic relationship communicated? What effects do these types of communication have on those who receive them? These messages are critical in moving a relationship to a deeper level. Being able to communicate and decode such messages effectively is important in the initiation of successful, stable romantic relationships.

Communicating Interest

Recent research (Fichpen, Taglakis, Judd, Wright, & Amsel, 1992) investigated verbal and nonverbal interest and lack-of-interest cues in a variety of communication contexts (only findings related to a dating context are reported here). Both men and women took part in a structured interview in which interviewers inquired about cues they used to communicate interest or lack of interest to a partner. Responses were grouped into six categories: verbal, nonverbal, paralinguistic, touch, unclassifiable, and intangible. A sampling of interest and disinterest cues frequently mentioned in each category included:

> Verbal interest—ask detailed questions, add to conversation, compliment
> Nonverbal interest—make eye contact, move closer, smile

Touch interest—touch other, put arm around other
Unclassifiable interest—hang around other, phone often
Intangible interest—pay attention to other, be friendly, flirt
Verbal disinterest—state that one already has a partner, lie, make excuses
Nonverbal disinterest—look away, stand far away
Paralinguistic disinterest—make short utterances, be silent
Unclassifiable disinterest—avoid or ignore the other
Intangible disinterest—be unfriendly, shy away

Some intriguing findings emerged. Participants reported more interest than disinterest cues, and interest cues tended to be more behaviorally specific than disinterest cues. Furthermore, the authors reported that when disinterest cues were reported, they tended to be attributed to a partner rather than to the self—that is, others were perceived as exhibiting more disinterest cues than were the participants themselves. The authors also found that certain cues were used only in a dating context (and not, for example, in daily conversations). Most of these dating-only cues were nonverbal cues such as staring at the other, looking the other over, using (unspecified) hand gestures to indicate interest, and standing far away from the other to indicate disinterest. Finally, Fichten et al. (1992) noted that certain categories of cues were used solely to indicate interest or disinterest, but not both (for example, touch was an interest-only communication cue). What is striking about these results is the fine-tuned ability of the participants to recognize their own and others' cues and to provide interpretations of the meanings of these cues. Those wishing to express their romantic interest (or disinterest) to a partner indirectly seem to have a full range of options from which to choose. Granted, the authors have no data on the accuracy of the expressions or interpretations of these cues, and it may be the case that the cues are inappropriately expressed or inaccurately perceived. Even when these cues are misused or misperceived, however, they are still acted upon, and thus play a vital role in determining whether and how a romantic relationship might begin or progress.

Within the realm of romantic disinterest, some recent research attention has focused on the perils of unrequited love. Baumeister, Wotman, and Stillwell (1993; see also Baumeister & Wotman, 1992) collected accounts assessing unrequited love from the perspectives of both the lover and the "lovee" or rejector. In the first study, participants wrote of one experience as lover and one experience as rejector. In the second study, participants were told to recount an experience *either* as a lover or as a rejector. Not surprisingly, Baumeister found that both sides of these failed relationships are fraught with miscommunication and emotional distress. A majority of the would-be lovers reported that the rejector had led them on or had, in some way, communicated love to the would-be lover. On the other hand, a majority of the rejectors' accounts included statements indicating that the would-be lovers had persisted in their pursuit even after an explicit rejection of the lover had been communicated.

Both the would-be lovers and the rejectors reported experiencing positive and negative emotions associated with the unrequited love experience, although, as could be expected, the nature of these emotions differed for the two groups. Would-be lovers reported experiencing feelings that they had "something to live for" in pursuing the other and also periods of intense happiness when they perceived that the relationship might be progressing. Rejectors, on the other hand, reported that they had felt friendship toward the would-be lovers and that they felt flattered by the lovers' attention (at least initially).

Negative emotions included heartbreak, pain, disappointment, anger, and jealousy on the part of the would-be lovers and feelings of guilt, annoyance, and anger on the part of the rejectors. Overall, would-be lovers reported more positive than negative emotions associated with the experience, while rejectors experienced more negative than positive emotions.

Traditionally, the would-be lover has been seen as the victim of the unrequited love relationship. The research of Baumeister and his colleagues (1993), however, underscores the idea that both the lover *and* the rejector suffer from the misperceptions, miscommunications, and misunderstandings that fuel unrequited love.

Intensifying Relationships

To this point, we have considered the success or failure of a romantic relationship at its earliest stage—that of communicating interest in another. What about a romantic relationship that already exists at a "casual" level? What sorts of strategies are used to move the relationship to a more serious level? Tolhuizen (1989) examined relationship intensification strategies as well as gender differences in the use of these strategies and whether the strategies would differ according to whether one or both partners desired the relationship intensification. Women and men who had been involved in at least one serious dating relationship were asked to describe the things that were said or the actions which were taken to transform a casual dating to a serious dating relationship. Participants were also asked to indicate whether they, their partner, or the two of them together had primarily desired the relationship change. The participants' written responses were analyzed, and 15 categories of intensification strategies used by more than 5% of the participants were identified. Labels, percent responses, and examples of each category are listed in Table I. Women were significantly more likely than men to use the "relationship negotiation" and "acceptance of definitional bid" strategies, whereas men were more likely to use "direct definitional bids" and "verbal expressions of affection." Not surprisingly, participants who reported that they were the ones who initially desired the relationship intensification were found to use the "direct definitional bid" strategy more frequently, and those reporting that the partner initially desired the intensification frequently reported the use of the "accept definitional bid" strategy. None of the strategies was used much more frequently than another when a bilateral or mutual

TABLE I   Strategies to Intensify Relationships[a]

---

1. Increased contact (39.2%)—seeing or calling partner more often
2. Relationship negotiation (29.1%)—openly discussing the relationship and feelings for one another
3. Social support and assistance (26.1%)—asking friend or parent for advice
4. Increase rewards (17.6%)—cleaning partner's apartment, doing favors
5. Direct definitional bid (16.6%)—asking partner to make a definite commitment
6. Tokens of affection (16.1%)—sending flowers, cards, or gifts
7. Personalized communication (15.1%)—empathic listening, idiomatic communication
8. Verbal expressions of affection (14.1%)—saying "I love you"
9. Suggestive actions (13.1%)—flirting, playing "hard to get"
10. Nonverbal expressions of affection (12.1%)—looking at, touching partner more frequently
11. Social enmeshment (11.6%)—getting to know partner's friends and family
12. Accept definitional bid (9.5%)—saying "yes" when partner makes a definitional bid
13. Personal appearance (9.5%)—changing hair or weight to please partner
14. Sexual intimacy (8%)—engaging in more intimate sexual behavior
15. Behavioral adaptation (7.5%)—acting in a manner pleasing to partner

---

[a]This table is based on data from Tolhuizen (1989).

decision to intensify the relationship was made. Overall, these findings indicate that there are many and varied ways to move a relationship from casual to serious. Of course, deciding which strategy, or set of strategies, to use in a particular relationship depends upon the unique dynamics of that relationship.

Both Tolhuizen (1989) and Fichten et al. (1992) indicated that nonverbal expressions of romantic interest are quite important. Increased proximity, eye contact, and nonverbal gestures such as playing with one's hair or stroking one's chin are all known to be methods of communicating interest to a member of the opposite sex (Richmond, McCroskey, & Payne, 1987).

One of the clearest ways of communicating romantic interest without words is through touch. Touch is a powerful communication tool, used to send messages of warmth, intimacy, sexual arousal, and status differences (Andersen, 1985; Burgoon, 1991). One can scarcely imagine a developing romantic relationship in which touch does not serve a communicative function.

Touching one's partner seems to be important in all phases of a developing romantic relationship. However, recent studies have shown that the amount of interpersonal touching, and possibly the meaning of touching, changes across the course of the relationship. Guerrero and Andersen (1991) had coders unobtrusively rate the initiation, duration, and location of interpersonal touch by opposite-sex pairs waiting in lines at the zoo or movie theaters. Couples were then asked to assess their relational stage, from nondating through casual and serious dating to marriage-bound or married. The most striking finding from the study was that relational stage and touch were curvilinearly related, with less touching occurring in the initial stage (first date or casually dating) and the stable stage (married couples) than in the intermediate relational stage (seriously dating or marriage-bound couples). Guerrero and Andersen considered a number of possibilities for the curvilinear relationship. Perhaps the intimate form of communication that touch serves in a developing relationship is superfluous in a stable relationship. Perhaps public touch is seen as a "reward" in a developing relationship, a means of publicly reinforcing a partner's likableness. Many explanations are possible.

Guerrero and Andersen's (1991) findings have been extended in at least two further studies. Emmers and Dindia (1995) investigated the hypothesis that whereas public touching might show a curvilinear pattern, *private* touch could increase linearly across relational stages, with married couples touching more when alone than casual, serious, or engaged couples. Relying on self-reports of perceived frequency of private touch, however, Emmers and Dindia reported a near-replication of Guerrero and Andersen's (1991) findings. (Emmers and Dindia found that the relationship between stage and touch increased and then leveled off, rather than becoming curvilinear). A plausible explanation for these findings comes from another extension of Guerrero and Anderson's study (Guerrero & Andersen, 1994). In the 1994 work, Guerrero and Andersen found that, among married couples, matching of the frequency of touch occurred. Although married couples touched less frequently than did seriously dating couples, the amount of touch between spouses was more closely related than that of dating partners. Although the frequency of touch in a developing relationship may serve to escalate intimacy and indicate approval of one's partner, perhaps the matching of touch in stable or married couples might indicate the partners' mutual comfort with touching behavior and communicate a feeling of bondedness.

Certainly, nonverbal messages of romantic interest, such as touching one's partner, are important in a developing relationship, but the verbal communication of interest has a central role as well. In fact, one three-word sentence has been credited by some (King & Christensen, 1983; Owen, 1987) with being among the most critical events for intensifying a romantic relationship. The sentence, of course, is "I love you."

Owen (1987) analyzed the diaries of a sample of 18 volunteers who had written about speaking or hearing the words "I love you" in a dating relationship. The study was undertaken in order to determine how the phrase was interpreted by partners as well as to explore gender differences in use of the phrase. Of the 18 participants (nine men and nine women, not involved with one another), only one woman appeared to be the first to say "I love you." This finding is consistent with Tolhuizen (1989), who found that men were more likely than women to use the "verbal expressions of affection" strategy. Owen speculated that one reason why men might predominate in saying these words is that men see "I love you" as a means of persuading their female partners to commit to the relationship. At least one man specifically admitted to using the words for this end: "The trouble is, she's not as serious [about the relationship] as me, and I just know she'll walk out eventually. Maybe if I told her how much I love her, she'd do the same and everything would be great. Girls like that . . ." (Owen, 1987, p. 19). Furthermore, several of the women participants reported feeling pressured or pushed into a premature commitment to the relationship by men who said "I love you" too soon.

Another reason that men tended to say "I love you" first, according to Owen, is that they were less able than women to withhold emotional expression. This interpretation fits well with previous findings (Hendrick, Hendrick, Foote, & Slapion-Foote, 1984) that women are more practical in love, whereas men are more passionate or likely to experience intense emotions in a romantic relationship. Women may be more controlled in their verbal expression of emotion as evidenced by the excerpt from the diary of a female participant: "I suppose I love him, but he's so emotional, I dare not tell him I love him first . . . It's just a big deal saying 'I love you.' I want to be ready when I do." (Owen, 1987, p. 19) Owen's research is also consistent with Rubin's (1970) finding that women were better able than men to distinguish love from other emotions such as caring or liking. Thus women may be more discriminating than men about saying "I love you."

Finally, Owen speculated that women may not be as likely as men to be the first to use the "three little words" because women see their relationship roles as ones of *reacting* to critical events rather than creating them. The one woman in the sample who did say "I love you" first received a rather unenthusiastic reception from her partner and wrote, "I wished I'd waited longer. I really should have just kept my mouth shut and sat on my feelings. My mother was right—always let the man lead" (p. 21). Several other women in the sample made similar remarks in which they reported that they were tired of waiting for their partners to come out and say "I love you." Owen concluded that societal pressure on men to be the proactive partner in romantic relationships is the driving force behind their dominance in expressing love first. Males may feel pressured to move the relationship along and may feel that they will be ridiculed if they do not take the lead. This interpretation is, of course, open to debate. Someone else reading the same sample of diaries might draw different inferences than Owen did. The strength of Owen's exploratory study is that it opens the door to more rigorous research into the antecedents and consequences of specific verbal communications in developing romantic relationships.

The ability to accurately communicate and decode messages of romantic interest is of critical importance to the initiation and continuation of romantic relationships. However, it is equally important in communicating love.

LOVE

As we noted earlier, even though love is an *intra*personal emotion, the communication of love is intensely *inter*personal. And to communicate effectively in a close relationship context, some basic tenets of intimate communication articulated by

Montgomery (1988) are applicable. In discussing "quality" communication, Montgomery agreed that close relationships should include high levels of intimate communication, *with some qualifications.* We apply these qualifications to the communication of love.

Communicating Love

The first of these qualifications is that nonverbal expression seems to be more highly related to relationship quality than is verbal expression, perhaps because "nonverbal behaviors are viewed as less strategic, more spontaneous, and, therefore, more honest than verbal behaviors" (Montgomery, 1988, p. 348). Such a statement would seem to imply that as important as verbal expressions of love might be, nonverbal expressions (ranging from kisses and hugs to willingness to listen and time spent together) may be even more convincing.

Montgomery's second qualification notes the ebb and flow of communication (and relationship quality) over time, thereby embodying the dialectical nature of relationships. As Baxter (1988, 1990) ably showed, basic "contradictions" in humans and their relationships include autonomy-connection, novelty-predictability, and openness-closedness. Partners who can manage these contradictions are likely to remain satisfied and stay together. In love terms, it is important to understand that love can be expressed by giving a partner "breathing room" as well as by being close, that love relationships need trust and security—but also surprise and whimsy, and that love will predictably flow in a roaring torrent at times, just as at other times it will seem to barely trickle. The greatest wisdom of love may be in accepting this ebb and flow.

A third qualification regarding communication (Montgomery, 1988) addresses the fact that partners seldom contribute equally to relationship communication. Women have typically been assigned the role of emotional maintenance in a romantic relationship, and indeed women are typically more disclosing in relationships (Derlega, Metts, Petronio, & Margulis, 1993). Thus women may tend to do more verbal and nonverbal communicating about love, particularly in established relationships, though it is important to remember that individual differences such as introversion–extroversion also influence communication of emotions such as love.

Montgomery's fourth qualification is that the style of conveying intimacy (or love) may be as or more important than specific words or behaviors (i.e., the "how" is more important than the "what"). Responsiveness is a key quality in emotional communication, so that when the response to a partner's pronouncement of love is direct eye contact and an unequivocal "I love you, too," a very special moment is created in that relationship. "Style" is a global construct composed of verbal and nonverbal expressiveness as well as timing, emotional tone, and other qualities.

Montgomery's final qualification to the simplistic "more is better" notion of the communication of intimacy and love is that the style or way in which love is expressed is critical to relationship quality. The fact is that partners are happier in the relationship when they talk about positive rather than negative things (e.g., Levinger & Senn, 1967). More is definitely not better when it concerns the problems of love rather than the pleasures of love.

Communicating love is an important and sensitive enterprise. High levels of communication that manifest love are desirable—in certain situations, under certain conditions, and subject to the qualifications outlined above.

Specifics of Love Communication

Love is a complex phenomenon. It is an emotion, as we maintain in this chapter, and as Duck (1992) pointed out, it can be viewed as "an attitude, a set of beliefs, a set of communication devices, or all of these" (p. 41). And all of these aspects are intertwined in the "process" of loving. Attempting to comprehend love's complexity as manifested in the subjective experience of lovers, Marston, Hecht, and Robers (1987) employed a series of studies. Early on, these scholars underlined the singular importance of communication by stating: "Further, we seek to understand the manners in which love is communicated, for it is our belief that communication is the fundamental action which both expresses and determines the subjective experience of romantic love . . . the importance of communication in determining and altering relationships is paramount" (Marston et al., 1987, p. 392). Using qualitative analysis to derive categories from interview data, Marston and his colleagues isolated categories representing both communication *to* one's partner and communication *from* one's partner. Most commonly mentioned communication strategies toward a partner included (a) telling the partner "I love you"; (b) doing things for the partner; (c) being understanding and supportive; (d) touching; and (e) just being together. Strategies that were coded but that seemed to be somewhat less important were talking things out, committing to each other for the future, writing cards and notes, having sex, engaging in intimate nonverbal behavior, and displaying high eye contact (Marston et al., 1987, p. 396).

This research found that the most commonly mentioned communication strategies from the partner to the self were hearing "I love you" from partner, touching, supportiveness, partner doing things for self, togetherness, communicating emotion, and eye contact, followed by the less frequently reported making a commitment for the future, facial expression (e.g., smile), sound of partner's voice, and talking about intimate topics. What is perhaps most interesting about these communication behaviors, in addition to their breadth, is the extent to which love is communicated nonverbally, both physically (e.g., touching, eye contact) and by just sharing time and space (e.g., being together, giving support).

Marston et al. (1987) employed the categories described above as well as additional ones to construct a typology of different ways of experiencing and communicating love. These included collaborative, active, secure, intuitive, committed, and traditional romantic love. Communication of love was represented by reciprocal supportiveness (collaborative love); discussion of emotions (active love); talk about intimate topics (secure love); nonverbal communication of love (intuitive love); being together and talking about future commitment (committed love); and saying "I love you" and doing romantic things for each other (traditional romantic love). These love ways were largely substantiated in additional analyses (exceptions included the emergence of expressive love as a component of traditional romantic love, and little empirical support for secure love).

Based on this research, Hecht, Marston, and Larkey (1994) designed items representing the various love ways detailed above. Factor analyses resulted in five factors or scaled love ways that included intuitive love, secure love, traditional romantic love, committed love, and companionate love (combining elements of collaborative, active and expressive love). Characteristics of the love ways were similar to love way characteristics found in the authors' previous research (Marston et al., 1987). Hecht et al. (1994) concluded that the love ways most associated with relational quality among the couples in their research were also the ways that contained several items relating to communication. Thus, communication, particularly verbal communication, is central to both love and relational quality.

Talk

Although the communication of love is central to an intimate relationship, it is clear from the Marston et al. (1987) research that love can be communicated in a variety of ways. It is also likely that lovingness or a more generalized positive affect can be communicated through other kinds of talk besides "love talk." Acitelli (1988) explored the topic of "talking about the relationship itself" with 42 married couples. Participants read scenarios of married couples in both pleasant and unpleasant situations, who both did and did not talk about their relationships. Extensive analyses revealed that talking about the relationship (and the relational awareness that the behavior of talking seemed to imply) were perceived as crucial when partners were experiencing relationship conflict (i.e., relationship talk was especially important in the unpleasant situation). The potential for relationship talk to create a more loving atmosphere (even when the talk is not about love at all) is indeed great.

Research by Duck and his colleagues (e.g., Duck, Rutt, Hurst, & Strejc, 1991) seems consistent with the idea that talk can have "loving" properties, even when the talk is not about love, and even when the talk is not heavily affective (as relationship talk is often likely to be). Even small talk or daily talk, characterized by everyday conversation rather than protestations of love or intense relationship talk, is important in relationships. In speaking of the communicative forces that can foster relationship positiveness, Duck noted that "everyday chit-chat seems to be one of the most important and overlooked of these forces" (Duck, 1992, p. 83).

Different Loves, Different Communication

Just as love can be communicated in different ways, so also might we expect different kinds of love to be communicated differently. The view of love as multidimensional has been shaped to a large extent by the work of Sternberg (1986, 1987). Initial work focused on the nature of love (i.e., whether love is a unidimensional construct; a set of cognitions, affects, and motivations that are highly related to one another; or a set of equally important affects, cognitions and motivations only moderately related to each other) (Sternberg & Grajek, 1984).

The findings of a large, unidimensional general factor of love that could be broken down into smaller clusters or components provided a basis for Sternberg's development of a Triangular Theory of Love (Sternberg, 1986, 1987). Within this approach, love can best be construed in terms of three different components; Intimacy (closeness, emotional investment component), Passion (physical involvement, motivational investment component), and Commitment (decision to stay together, cognitive component). According to Sternberg, these three components in differing proportions are core ingredients of several types of love, which vary across and within categories of intimate relationships (e.g., dating partners vs. siblings). The types of love (detailed in Table II) include nonlove, liking, infatuated love, empty love, romantic love, companionate love, fatuous love, and consummate love. One would expect different types of love to be manifested in different communication patterns. For example, infatuated love might involve passionate nonverbal communication (and little else) whereas companionate love would likely include verbal sharing as well as reciprocal support.

It is quite reasonable to anticipate different communication strategies for different love types. For example, basing their work on the attachment approach, Mikulincer and Nachshon (1991) found that persons who described themselves differently in terms of attachment (i.e., secure, anxious–ambivalent, avoidant) man-

TABLE II   Sternberg's Types of Love

Nonlove	*Absence* of all three components
Liking	Intimacy (no passion or commitment)
Infatuated love	Passion (no intimacy or commitment)
Empty love	Commitment (no intimacy or passion)
Romantic love	Intimacy and Passion (no commitment)
Companionate love	Intimacy and Commitment (no passion)
Fatuous love	Passion and Commitment (no intimacy)
Consummate love	Passion and Commitment and Intimacy

[a]These types of love are based on Sternberg's (1986) descriptions.

TABLE III   The Love Styles[a]

Eros	Passionate, involved love characterized by esteem of self and partner
Ludus	Game-playing love, characterized by playfulness and avoidance of commitment
Storge	Friendship-based love, characterized by companionability and shared values
Pragma	Practical love, characterized by a common-sense, problem-solving approach to life and love
Mania	Possessive, dependent love, characterized by jealousy and emotional ups and downs
Agape	Altruistic or "gift" love, characterized by intense concern for the partner's welfare

[a]Definitions are from Hendrick and Hendrick (1986).

ifested difference in self-disclosure. Specifically, secure and anxious–ambivalent participants engaged in more intimate disclosure than avoidant participants, and avoidants liked disclosing partners less (see Andersen & Guerrero, Chapter 3, this volume; and Feeney, Noller, & Roberts, Chapter 18, this volume for more on attachment style differences in intimacy and emotion.)

Such findings are consistent with other work on self-disclosure and love. John Alan Lee (1973) developed a typology of six major approaches to love or "love styles." A scale measuring the six styles was developed by Hendrick and Hendrick (1986) and represents the following six styles: Eros (passionate love), Storge (friendship love), Ludus (game-playing love), Pragma (practical love), Mania (possessive, dependent love), and Agape (altruistic love). The love styles (shown in Table III) have been correlated with a number of variables, including the communication variable of self-disclosure. Using measures of both self-disclosure and one's ability to elicit disclosure from others (Miller, Berg, & Archer, 1983), Hendrick and Hendrick (1987) found some interesting relationships between disclosure and love styles.

Passionate love (Eros) was strongly and positively related to both disclosure and ability to elicit disclosure, consistent with characterizations of Eros as an intense communicator. Game-playing love (Ludus) was negatively related to disclosure and unrelated to the ability to elicit disclosure, unsurprising given Ludus's need for emotional distance. Storge, or friendship love, was similar to practical love (Pragma) and possessive, dependent love (Mania) in that all three were positively related to the ability to elicit disclosure from others. Mania was also related to the giving of self-disclosure. Apparently, trying to elicit disclosure from others and being a good, responsive listener are important for many different types of lovers. Finally, altruistic love (Agape) was related to both disclosure and the ability to elicit disclosure (similar to Eros). Although self-disclosure is only one aspect of interpersonal communication, as noted previously, it is an important aspect.

Indeed, other research, comparing dating couples who stayed together with dating couples who broke up (Hendrick, Hendrick, & Adler, 1988), found that couples who stayed together were more disclosing as well as higher in Eros (passion) and lower in Ludus (game playing) than were couples who broke up. Although there has not been extensive research specifically focusing on the communication of love, it is clear that the topic is important.

If different types of love are related differentially to self-disclosure, one can be creative in imagining how different types of lovers might communicate love, using as examples the six love styles just presented. For example, a passionate Eros lover would probably communicate love verbally (e.g., saying "I love you") as well as non-verbally (e.g., intense kissing and touching), whereas a cool, game-playing ludic lover would be unlikely to communicate love either verbally or nonverbally and would most probably expect that her or his mere presence in the relationship would be all that the partner could rightfully expect. The Storge lover, oriented toward a stable friendship, might "communicate" best by simply being a good listener for the partner, or perhaps holding the partner's hand or offering a hug.

The practical Pragma lover would be likely to communicate in a problem-solving mode, possibly by offering practical help on some matter. On the other hand, the possessive, dependent Mania lover would probably offer dramatic and eloquent statements of love, both verbal and nonverbal. But there might be more than a hint of desperation in the assurances of undying love, and disclosure might be excessive, making it difficult for the partner to reciprocate. Finally, the all-giving Agape lover would probably voice quiet, sincere statements of affection, followed by a hug or a comforting pat. In fact, a study of gift giving by college students (Belk & Coon, 1993) found that giving gifts was often an expression of agapic love (here agapic love encompasses romantic, familial, and spiritual love) bestowed on a significant other.

Although a detailed integration of the several multidimensional love approaches discussed earlier is beyond the scope of this chapter, it is not difficult to draw parallels between them. For example, passionate Eros (Hendrick & Hendrick, 1986) has many of the elements of consummate love (Sternberg, 1986) as well as aspects of committed, traditional romantic, and companionate love ways (Hecht et al., 1994). And friendship-based Storge (Hendrick & Hendrick, 1986) is similar to companionate love (Sternberg, 1986) as well as to secure and companionate love ways (Hecht et al., 1994). The awareness that is perhaps most important is that there are different types of loving, and different ways of communicating love. And whatever ways are chosen, the very act of communicating love is probably the centrally important concern.

CONCLUSIONS

Communication is indispensable to the establishment and maintenance of intimate relationships. Whether in initial acquaintance or a well-developed relationship, communication processes establish the emotional tone of the interactions. The emotional tone of an interaction has direct communication value because it signals inner emotional states and it has indirect communication value because the emotional tone is a continuous correlate of other types of communication (e.g., verbal statements). The communication of emotion is carried via verbal statements and by a host of nonverbal behaviors, including facial expression, touch, movement style, and so forth.

With regard to communication of liking and loving, multiple avenues of disclosure are important. Our previous discussion suggests that both verbal and nonverbal communications are important in the many ways of expressing liking and loving. Depending on the context, nonverbal expression may be more important at one time and verbal expression may be more important at another time.

The expression of liking or loving for another is an act of emotional disclosure. The liking and loving per se, when reciprocated, is a relationship between two people. The expression of the emotion, however, is an act of self-disclosure which may be performed either verbally or nonverbally. The exact mode of self-disclosure will depend upon the stage of the relationship, whether liking in initial acquaintances, feelings of friendship in established friendships, or growth of love in romantic relationships.

Self-disclosure may be construed, most generally, as the sharing or giving of the self to another. This act of giving can be performed by words or by the "conversation of gestures." One's self (or self-concept) is, for most people, their most prized "possession." To give intimate aspects of that most valued attribute is to engage in an almost sacred act. As the other person recognizes the specialness of disclosure, that very recognition draws forth reciprocal disclosure from the partner. In this way, ideally, the two people in interaction begin to create a bond between them, that, in the beginning of a relationship, carries the emotional tone that we call liking. If the liking deepens sufficiently and the communication becomes more verbally and nonverbally intimate, we call it love.

This joint disclosure of self to each other creates a new dyadic system of meaning, a point noted by Duck (1994). The very act of mutual giving of the self is the vehicle that launches the joint sphere of meaning that is the relationship. Such disclosure provides the initial context for future growth of the relationship.

Once a relationship is well established, people communicate about an increasing array of topics, including the relationship itself (i.e., relationship talk). The hedonic tone waxes and wanes, depending on the situation and points of agreement and conflict. The feedback links between communication and the emotional tone of the relationship are continuous. As a relationship becomes more complex, the possibilities for *mis*communication increase. Miscommunication often generates intense emotions that are usually negative. Then communication "repair work" is in order to restore a positive emotional tone to the relationship. In this way, emotional expression and communication in satisfying relationships jointly create a system that moves toward a positive balance point. Communication can create emotional feelings and expression, but emotional expression can also lead to communication (see Andersen & Guerrero, Chapter 3, this volume).

In view of the importance of communication for satisfying interpersonal relationships, it is amazing how learning to communicate well to a relationship partner is left completely to chance. We teach youngsters explicitly how to ride a bike or drive a car. Why can't we also teach them the skills and etiquette of effective communication? Perhaps as we continue to discover just how important the communication of liking and love is in the building of intimate relationships, "education" for emotional communication will become one of our priorities.

REFERENCES

Acitelli, L. K. (1988). When spouses talk to each other about their relationship. *Journal of Social and Personal Relationships, 5,* 185–199.

Altman, I., & Taylor, D. A. (1973). *Social penetration: The development of interpersonal relationships.* New York: Holt, Rinehart, & Winston.

Andersen, P. A. (1985). Nonverbal immediacy in interpersonal communication. In A. W. Siegman & S. Feldstein (Eds.). *Multichannel integrations of nonverbal behavior.* Hillsdale, NJ: Erlbaum.

Baumeister, R. F., & Wotman, S. (1992). *Breaking hearts: The two side of unrequited love.* New York: Guilford.

Baumeister, R. F., Wotman, S. R., & Stillwell, M. A. (1993). Unrequited love: On heartbreak, anger, guilt, scriptlessness, and humiliation. *Journal of Personality and Social Psychology, 64,* 377–394.

Baxter, L. A. (1988). A dialectical perspective on communication strategies in relationship development. In S. Duck (Ed.), *Handbook of personal relationships: Theory, research, and interventions.* New York, Wiley.

Baxter, L. A. (1990). Dialectical contradictions in relationship development. *Journal of Social and Personal Relationships, 7,* 69–88.

Belk, R. W., & Coon, G. S. (1993). Gift giving as agapic love: An alternative to the exchange paradigm based on dating experiences. *Journal of Consumer Research, 20,* 393–417.

Bell, R. R., Buerkel-Rothfuss, N. L., & Gore, K. E. (1987). "Did you bring the yarmulke for the cabbage-patch kid?": The idiomatic communication of young lovers. *Human Communication Research, 14,* 47–67.

Bell, R. A., & Healey, J. G. (1992). Idiomatic communication and interpersonal solidarity in friends' relational cultures. *Human Communication Research, 18,* 307–335.

Berger, C. R., & Calabrese, R. J. (1975). Some explorations in initial interaction and beyond: Toward a developmental theory of interpersonal communication. *Human Communication Research, 1,* 99–112.

Bretherton, I., & Beeghly, M. (1982). Talking about internal states: The acquisition of an explicit theory of mind. *Developmental Psychology, 18,* 906–912.

Burgoon, J. K. (1991). Relational message interpretations of touch, conversational distance, and posture. *Journal of Nonverbal Behavior, 15,* 233–259.

Burgoon, J. K., & Hale, J. L. (1987). Validation and measurement of the fundamental themes of relational communication. *Communication Monographs, 54,* 19–41.

Collins, N. L., & Miller, L. C. (1994). Self-disclosure and liking: A meta-analytic review. *Psychological Bulletin, 116,* 457–475.

Derlega, V. J., & Grzelak, J. (1979). Appropriateness of self-disclosure. In G. J. Chelune (Ed.), *Self-disclosure: Origins, patterns and implications of openness in interpersonal relationships* (pp. 151–176). San Francisco: Jossey-Bass.

Derlega, V. J., Metts, S., Petronio, S., & Margulis, S. T. (1993). *Self-disclosure.* Thousand Oaks, CA: Sage.

Douglas, W. (1990). Uncertainty, information-seeking, and liking during initial interaction. *Western Journal of Speech Communication, 54,* 66–81.

Douglas, W. (1991). Expectations about initial interaction: An examination of the effects of global uncertainty. *Human Communication Research, 17,* 355–384.

Douglas, W. (1994). The acquaintanceship process: An examination of uncertainty, information-seeking, and social attraction during initial conversation. *Communication Research, 21,* 154–176.

Duck, S. (1992). *Human relationships* (2nd ed.). Thousand Oaks, CA: Sage.

Duck, S. (1994). *Meaningful relationships: Talking, sense, and relating.* Thousand Oaks, CA: Sage.

Duck, S. W., & Miell, E. E. (1986). Charting the development of personal relationships. In R. Gilmour and S. W. Duck (Eds.) *The emerging field of personal relationships* (pp. 133–143). Hillsdale, NJ: Erlbaum.

Duck, S., Rutt, D. J., Hurst, M. H., & Strejc, H. (1991). Some evident truths about conversation in everyday relationships: All communications are not created equal. *Human Communication Research, 18,* 228–267.

Emmers, T. M., & Dindia, K. (1995). The effect of relational stage and intimacy on touch: An extension of Guerrero and Andersen. *Personal Relationships, 2,* 225–236.

Epstein, S. (1984). Controversial issues in emotion theory. In P. Shaver (Ed.), *Review of personality and social psychology* (Vol. 5, pp. 64–88). Thousand Oaks, CA: Sage.

Fehr, B., & Russell, J. A. (1984). Concept of emotion viewed from a prototype perspective. *Journal of Experimental Psychology: General, 113,* 464–486.

Fichten, C. S., Taglakis, V., Judd, D., Wright, J., & Amsel, R. (1992). Verbal and nonverbal communication cues in daily conversations and dating. *The Journal of Social Psychology, 132,* 751–769.

Guerrero, L. K., & Andersen, P. A. (1991). The waxing and waning of relational intimacy: Touch as a function of relational stage, gender and touch avoidance. *Journal of Social and Personal Relationships, 8,* 147–165.

Guerrero, L. K., & Andersen, P. A. (1994). Patterns of matching and initiation: Touch behavior and touch avoidance across romantic relationship stages. *Journal of Nonverbal Behavior, 18,* 137–153.

Hale, J. L., Lundy, J. C., & Mongeau, P. A. (1989). Perceived relational intimacy and relational message content. *Communication Research Reports, 6,* 94–99.

Hecht, M. L., Marston, P. J., & Larkey, L. K. (1994). Love ways and relationship quality in heterosexual relationships. *Journal of Social and Personal Relationships, 11,* 25–43.

Hendrick, C., & Hendrick, S. S. (1986). A theory and method of love. *Journal of Personality and Social Psychology, 50,* 392–402.

Hendrick, C., Hendrick, S., Foote, F. H., & Slapion-Foote, M. J. (1984). Do men and women love differently? *Journal of Social and Personal Relationships, 1,* 177–195.

Hendrick, S. S., & Hendrick, C. (1987). Love and sexual attitudes, self-disclosure, and sensation seeking. *Journal of Social and Personal Relationships, 4,* 281–297.

Hendrick, S. S., Hendrick, C., & Adler, N. L. (1988). Romantic relationships: Love, satisfaction, and staying together. *Journal of Personality and Social Psychology, 54,* 980–988.

Jourard, S. M. (1959). Self-disclosure and other-cathexis. *Journal of Abnormal and Social Psychology, 59,* 428–431.

King, C. E. & Christensen, A. (1983). The relationship events scale: A Guttman scaling of progress in courtship. *Journal of Marriage and the Family, 45,* 671–678.

Lee, J. A. (1973). *The colors of love: An exploration of the ways of loving.* Don Mills, Ontario: New Press.

Levinger, G., & Senn, D. J. (1967). Disclosure of feelings in marriage. *Merrill-Palmer Quarterly, 13,* 237–249.

Marston, P. J., Hecht, M. L., & Robers, T. (1987). 'True love ways': The subjective experience and communication of romantic love. *Journal of Social and Personal Relationships, 4,* 387–407.

Mellen, S. L. W. (1981). *The evolution of love.* San Francisco: Freeman.

Mikulincer, M., & Nachshon, O. (1991). Attachment styles and patterns of self-disclosure. *Journal of Personality and Social Psychology, 61,* 321–331.

Miller, L. C., Berg, J. H., & Archer, R. L. (1983). Openers: Individuals who elicit intimate self-disclosure. *Journal of Personality and Social Psychology, 44,* 1234–1244.

Montgomery, B. (1988). Quality communication in personal relationships. In S. Duck (Ed.), *Handbook of personal relationships: Theory, research, and interventions* (pp. 343–359). New York: Wiley.

Owen, W. F. (1987). The verbal expression of love by women and men as a critical communication event in personal relationships. *Women's Studies in Communication, 10,* 15–24.

Richmond, V. P., McCroskey, J. C., & Payne, S. K. (1987). *Nonverbal behavior in interpersonal relationships.* Englewood Cliffs, NJ: Prentice-Hall.

Rubin, Z. (1970). Measurement of romantic love. *Journal of Personality and Social Psychology, 16,* 265–273.

Shaver, P., Schwartz, J., Kirson, D., & O'Connor, C. (1987). Emotion knowledge: Further exploration of a prototype approach. *Journal of Personality and Social Psychology, 52,* 1061–1086.

Sprecher, S., & Duck, S. (1994). Sweet talk: The importance of perceived communication for romantic and friendship attraction experienced during a get-acquainted date. *Personality and Social Psychology Bulletin, 20,* 391–400.

Sternberg, R. J. (1986). A triangular theory of love. *Psychological Review, 93,* 119–135.

Sternberg, R. J. (1987). Liking versus loving: A comparative evaluation of theories. *Psychological Bulletin, 102,* 331–345.

Sternberg, R. J., & Grajek, S. (1984). The nature of love. *Journal of Personality and Social Psychology, 47,* 312–329.

Tolhuizen, J. H. (1989). Communication strategies for intensifying dating relationships: Identification, use and structure. *Journal of Social and Personal Relationships, 6,* 413–434.

CHAPTER 13

Communication and Sexual Desire

Sandra Metts and Susan Sprecher

Illinois State University
Normal, Illinois

Pamela C. Regan

California State University—Los Angeles
Los Angeles, California

For most people, particularly in Western societies, the phenomenological experience of sexual desire is inextricably linked to a complex array of emotions and communicative expression. Popular music, fiction, television, and film provide depictions of sexually passionate and emotionally volatile romantic relationships, popular magazines provide instructions for achieving and sustaining sexual satisfaction, and advice columns provide forums for sanctioning sexual infidelity and/or for coping with sexual moral dilemmas. The drive to reproduce may be innate, but the evolution of social systems that regulate procreation has infused both the experience and expression of sexual desire with values, norms, constraints, contingencies, and secondary emotions that make it as much a symbolic, interpersonal, and social construction as a physiological fact.

As might be expected, scholarship investigating the associations among sexual desire, emotion, and communication reflects a diversity of perspectives, distinguished largely on the basis of how sexual desire and emotion are defined. The central focus of this chapter is the elaboration of two prominent approaches, which we have termed the *biological or reproductive perspective* and the *relational perspective*. The former is characterized by an orientation to sexual desire as a biological drive with a corresponding view of emotion as a finite set of innate, primary affects that function both as signals to coordinate sexual behavior and as response patterns that promote pair bonding. The latter perspective is characterized by a view of sexual desire as a subjective psychological state influenced as much by interpersonal and social influences as by perceptions of physiological arousal. The corresponding view of emotion is a complex psychological state, generated from interpretations of situational cues, and manifested as behaviors that are consistent with this interpretation. Communication assumes a more central position, not only as the means of expressing sexual desire and complicated emotional states, but also as the mechanism for negotiating the relational implications of sexual activity and emotional meanings.

In order to frame the perspectives discussed in this chapter, we begin by providing a working definition of sexual desire. We then consider briefly the complicated question of whether sexual desire is an emotion.

CONCEPTUALIZING SEXUAL DESIRE

What Is Sexual Desire?

Traditional approaches to sexual desire tend to limit the concept to its physiological component, viewing it simply as a state of arousal or a biological drive that is reduced through such instrumental actions as masturbation or intercourse (e.g., Teevan & Smith, 1967). Although neurochemical/genital arousal is generally considered one aspect of sexual desire, it is no longer thought to be sufficient for, nor isomorphic with, this sexual experience. Rather, sexual desire is considered to be a multifaceted construct, experienced as a unitary subjective state, but varying in intensity and quality as a result of the interaction of intrapsychic, interpersonal, and situational influences.

Illustrative of this more integrated view of sexual desire is the description offered by Levine (1984, 1987). He defines sexual desire as a "propensity to behave sexually" resulting from the interaction among biological *drive,* cognitions that generate the *wish* to behave sexually, and psychological processes that yield a *willingness* (motivation) to behave sexually. Changes in any of these three aspects influence the likelihood that sexual desire will be experienced and the intensity with which it will be felt. Thus, the spontaneous manifestations of genital excitement associated with sexual drive can be diminished by such factors as age, grief, illness, or medication. The wish to behave sexually (even in the absence of drive) can be stimulated by the motivation to feel loved or valued, to feel masculine or feminine, to please one's partner, and so forth. The wish not to have sex (even in the presence of drive) may stem from the conviction that it would be morally wrong, or from the fear of pregnancy or disease. Finally, although the willingness to have sex can be induced by such factors as one's own sexual drive, the verbal and nonverbal behavior of a partner, voyeuristic experiences, and attraction, these inducements are subject to modification from the broader interpersonal contexts in which they are embedded. According to Levine, these contexts might include the quality of the nonsexual relationship, the reasons for engaging in sexual episodes (self-regulating or partner-regulating), and transference from past attachments that can increase or diminish sexual motivation.

Defining sexual desire as a subjective psychological state not only distinguishes it from the physiological state of sexual arousal but also from the behaviors of sexual activity. Research indicates that young adult men and women report having engaged in sexual activity without feeling sexual desire (e.g., Beck, Bozman, & Qualtrough, 1991). Indeed, people may engage in sexual activity for a number of reasons other than for the satiation of their own desire. They may do so to avoid rejecting their partner's advances and hurting their partner's feelings, to prove that they care for their partner and find him or her attractive, to assure themselves of their own virility or attractiveness, to conceive offspring, or to express feelings of closeness, warmth, commitment, and intimacy. Conversely, the absence of sexual activity does not necessarily reflect a lack of sexual desire, even among romantically involved couples. For example, fatigue, travel schedules, and the demands of children may diminish sexual activity. Some relationship partners may abstain from sexual intercourse during times of menstruation or pregnancy due more to cultural proscriptions than to personal inclinations (e.g., Kenny, 1973).

In sum, sexual desire is considered by most contemporary sex researchers to be a psychological, subjective state. It is considered to be distinct from physiological/genital arousal, subjective sexual arousal (i.e., the awareness that one is genitally and physiologically aroused), and sexual activity, although in actual practice sexual desire usually precedes, sometimes accompanies, and may even follow, sexual arousal and activity. Sexual desire is experienced as an interest in sexual objects or activities, and/or as a wish, intention, or willingness to seek out sexual partners and/or to engage in sexual activities (e.g., Bancroft, 1988; Kaplan, 1979; Regan & Berscheid, 1995). When directed toward a specific other person, desire is manifested as sexual attraction.

Interestingly, common interpretations of the term *sexual desire* among young adults are quite consistent with the current scholarly discussion. When Regan and Berscheid (1996) asked college students to define sexual desire in open-ended responses, very few defined it in terms of psychological arousal (4.4%) or sexual activity (2.2%). Most (86.8%) referred to sexual desire as a motivational state (e.g., longing, urge, need, or attraction). In addition, many respondents (28.6%) referred to it specifically as an emotional state (e.g., emotional attraction, or a feeling) or as part of an emotional syndrome (love or passion).

It appears, then, that the notion of sexual desire, both in current scholarship and in the phenomenological experiences of men and women, is a much broader construct than the physiological arousal or sexual activity associated with reproduction. Whether it is, strictly speaking, an emotional state or not depends upon how one defines emotion.

Is Sexual Desire an Emotion?

Emotion is perhaps one of the most difficult constructs to define (Metts & Bowers, 1994). Definitions are shaped not only by the disciplinary lens of the scholars investigating it, but also by the cultural and historic assumptions that prevail during any particular period of analysis (Averill, 1992; Solomon, 1993; Stearns, 1993). Therefore, we should not be surprised to find that some scholars consider sexual desire to be an emotion whereas others do not.

For scholars who consider psychological motivational states to be emotions, sexual desire constitutes an emotion (Everaerd, 1988). For example, the sex researcher Bertocci (1988) coined the term "lust-sex" to represent "the emotion experienced by a person as a qualitative impetus whose meaning-objective is usually a member of the opposite sex deemed attractive in ways that facilitate sexual advances and intercourse" (p. 222). Similarly, DeLamater (1991) classified sexual desire as an emotion based on three features that it shares with classical definitions of emotion: (a) the presence of characteristic patterns of physiological arousal, (b) the interpretation of this arousal as sexual, and (c) the activation of cognitive schema that contain learned response tendencies (typically sexual actions when the situation allows).

By contrast, conservative views of emotion tend to exclude sexual desire, more or less explicitly. For example, scholars who distinguish between the drive and affect systems consider sexual desire to be among the biological drives (e.g., Izard, 1990, 1993) rather than among the affects. Likewise, scholars who distinguish between motivational states (i.e., goal-directed intentions) and the consequences or outcomes of motivational states, consider sexual desire to be the antecedent condition of emotion rather than an emotion *per se*. By implication, if the motivation to seek sexual activity were satisfied, positive emotions would result; if not satisfied, negative emotions would result (Harris, 1993; McIntosh & Martin, 1992; see also Lazarus, Coyne, & Folkman, 1984; Roseman, 1984, for a discussion of motivation and affect). The various definitions of emotion known collectively as appraisal theories would also probably not consider sexual desire to be an emotion because no particular pattern of appraisal has been found to generate the experience of sexual desire (Frijda, Kuipers, & ter Schure, 1989). On the other hand, it is not inconsistent with appraisal theory to speculate that if arousal in the presence of another person were attended to (attentional activity), perceived to be a pleasant stimulus (valence), and considered relevant to an individual's goals (relevance appraisal), the state of sexual attraction or lust might be considered a positive emotional state (Ellsworth & Smith, 1989; Smith & Ellsworth, 1985).

Finally, for scholars who take the position that emotions are essentially social constructions (Epstein, 1984; Oatley, 1993), sexual desire might be considered an emotion in any culture that recognizes it as such. In contemporary Western society, although sexual desire is typically considered to be an emotional state, attitudes toward its legitimacy are complicated by the fact that sexual meanings are deeply embedded within relational interpretive frames. Thus, to feel sexual desire for another person in the absence of other emotions renders it base (e.g., "merely lust"), whereas to feel sexual desire as part of the romantic love complex renders it transformative and almost spiritual. In fact, although sexual desire exists independently of romantic or passionate love, these affective states, at least in contemporary Western society, take their very character from the presence of sexual desire (see Aron & Aron, 1991; Hatfield & Rapson, 1993 for reviews). As Oatley (1993) states: "What we see when we or an acquaintance falls in love, what we imagine in such circumstances, or what we resonate to when read a love story is a complex of parts, including sexual desire, the aesthetic attraction to the other, and the altruism" (p. 346). In a similar vein is the now famous quote by Berscheid (1988), who remarked that if forced to define romantic love by "a firing squad who would shoot if not given the correct answer," she would have to say, "It's about 90 percent sexual desire as yet not sated" (p. 373).

Empirical support for the association between sexual desire and love is evident in the prototypical analyses of emotion terms conducted by Shaver and his colleagues (Shaver, Schwartz, Kirson, & O'Connor, 1987; Shaver, Wu, & Schwartz, 1992). In both Italian and American samples, Shaver et al. (1992) found that the love prototype contained some element of sexual desire, expressed variously as arousal, lust, passion, desire, infatuation, and longing. It should be no surprise that the presence of sexual desire for another person is often experienced as romantic love. Nor should it be a surprise that retrospective accounts often recast the very same emotional experience as nothing more than lust in the wake of a failed relationship (Harvey, Weber, & Orbuch, 1990; White, Fishbein, & Rutstein, 1981).

For the purposes of this chapter, it is not necessary to resolve the definitional question of whether sexual desire is or is not an emotion. In reality, there are probably occasions when sexual desire is experienced as a diffuse, unfocused sense of longing for sexual contact that is no more emotional than a fantasy or a daydream. On other occasions, sexual desire may be intense, focused, and experienced as a passion that most people would consider emotional, and that some would label lust and some would label love. Indeed, there may be individual differences in intensity of subjective arousal and responses to feelings of sexual desire (Christopher & Roosa, 1991; Simpson & Gangestad, 1991) as well as in the tendency to orient to sexual desire as the defining parameter of love as is evident in individual differences in love styles (see Taraban, Hendrick & Hendrick, Chapter 12, this volume).

For the purposes here, it is simply important to acknowledge that any perspective on the association among sexual desire, emotion, and communication is strongly influenced by definitional assumptions. For that reason, we have divided the remainder of this chapter into two general sections. The first is a summary of approaches to sexual desire, emotion, and communication that coalesce under the general rubric of reproduction. The second, and more elaborated, section is a summary of approaches to sexual desire that recognize the psychological quality of sexual desire and situate it within sociological, relational, and communicative systems.

BIOLOGICAL OR REPRODUCTIVE PERSPECTIVES

The recognition that sexual desire, emotion, and communication are functionally interdependent is not new. However, traditional biological discussions tend to view reproduction as the nexus where interest in all three constructs converge. In particular, sexual desire is viewed as a biological drive or state of arousal that may lead to some form of sexual expression (e.g., sexual intercourse). Emotion and communication are incorporated into the discussion by virtue of their role in coordinating mating and facilitating pair bonding.

Coordinating Mating

One long-standing conceptualization of emotion is as patterned states of physiological arousal manifested in universally recognized facial expressions (e.g., Ekman, 1984; Ekman, Levenson, & Friesen, 1983). Although there is continued dispute over whether emotional states correspond to distinctive patterns of arousal in the visceral system (i.e., internal organs) (Buck, 1980, 1984) or to patterns of change in neural firing (i.e., suddenness and intensity) (Tomkins, 1984), there is agreement that arousal is experienced as a component of the primary emotions (e.g., interest, fear, anger, disgust, sadness, happiness, and surprise). Emotion is presumed to occur without the need for cognitive appraisal and therefore is considered to be one of the earliest and most fundamental forms of communication through facial displays. As Ekman (1984) argues, "If there is no distinctive universal facial expression associated with a given state, which functions as a signal, I propose that we not call that state an emotion" (p. 330).

In this characterization, emotions are linked to human reproduction by virtue of their communicative potential. For example, Buck (1984) argues that, unlike the mating of rudimentary organisms that was accomplished without the need for social organization, human mating required extended coordination. Emotional expression facilitated this goal by providing visible manifestations of internal states and intentions. Although humans eventually evolved a number of socially regulative emotions (e.g., jealousy, shame, guilt) and higher levels of symbolic communication (e.g., verbal language), Buck maintained that "perhaps the most basic motivational/emotional system that went beyond a solitary, virtually automatic process involved sexual reproduction" (p. 31). Thus, sexual contact was facilitated by visible expressions of interest and positive affect that signaled the desire to approach as well as to be approached.

Buck (1984) notes that the legacy of this fundamental signaling function is still evident in modern-day flirtation rituals. Despite cultural variation in display rules, he contends that across cultures, flirtation rituals still function to indicate sexual readiness, or alternatively, to indicate sexual nonavailability. Observations of female nonverbal solicitation cues conducted by Moore and her colleagues (Moore, 1985;

Moore & Butler, 1989) provide support for this contention. Not only was Moore able to categorize types of nonverbal behaviors most likely to precede the approach of a male to a female in a bar setting, but she also demonstrated that these behaviors were largely absent in settings where men were absent (e.g., a library and a women's club). Moore concludes that although men appear to initiate courtship because they make the first overt approach, women actually trigger the advance through nonverbal displays of readiness, such as extended eye gaze, smiling, and open posture.

Facilitating Pair Bonding

Other theorists have argued that the function of emotion displays to signal reproductive intentions may have facilitated sexual contact, but it does not explain the evolution of pair bonding. For these theorists (e.g., Izard, 1990; Plutchik, 1984; Tomkins, 1980, 1984), the drive system (including sexual desire) functions like the cognitive, behavioral, and perceptual systems do—as a source of survival-relevant information for the affect system. The affect system then provides the impetus for adaptive action. According to Tomkins (1984), the drives are inert without the amplification of the affects, whereas "the affects are sufficient motivators in the absence of drives" (p. 165). In terms of reproduction, the biological drive to copulate provided humans with the motivation to engage in sexual activity, but provided no "instructions" for the pair-bonding behavior necessary for the survival of the offspring. Only when framed by the behavioral response patterns associated with the positive emotions of joy and affection could sexual pleasure lead to intimacy behaviors between partners and caregiving behaviors toward offspring. As described by Izard (1993):

> The joy experience is different from sensory pleasure, but the latter often leads to the former, as when the culmination of sexual or postprandial pleasure increases intimacy and leads to enjoyable social interaction. Openness is often heightened in such situations, and openness can contribute to the strengthening of social bonds. Social bonds and the social support they provide contribute a highly adaptive mechanism that can easily be conceived as an advantage in evolution and development. (p. 634)

Although this characterization tends to be advanced by emotion theorists, it is consistent with discussions of human sexuality in other fields. For example, in his sociological theory of human sexuality, Reiss (1986, 1989) contends that the importance placed on sexuality across cultures is due less to its reproductive function than to its role in facilitating pleasure and self-disclosure. Pleasure and self-disclosure are integrally related in sexual experience: "Experiencing intense physical pleasure in the presence of another person reveals parts of oneself which are not generally known even by one's close friends. Sexual partners thus reveal their emotions and responses in their sexual interactions and thereby learn more about each other" (1989, p. 10). Reiss maintains that, all things being equal, such disclosure is likely to lead to additional revelation in other aspects of one's life. The result is the development and strengthening of intimate pair bonds.

In sum, traditional biological approaches to linking sexual desire, emotion, and communication as they relate to reproductive advantages and cultural universals tend to emphasize emotion's communicative function in signaling interest and coordinating mating, and emotion's facilitative function in stimulating intimate communication, self-disclosure, and ultimately the attachment patterns of pair bonding. Relational approaches are not necessarily incompatible with this perspective, but are more sensitive to the systemic nature of sexual desire, emerging as it does at the vortex of psychological, relational, and sociological forces. The contingent and emergent quality of sexual desire that is characteristic of this perspective necessarily means a more complicated role for communication.

RELATIONAL PERSPECTIVES

The diverse body of research referred to here as relational perspectives share a view of sexual desire as a psychological subjective state, reflecting not simply arousal, but also the desire to have sex, the willingness to have sex, and the motivation to seek out sexual activity, whether or not such activity occurs. Implicit in this definition is the argument that the experience of sexual desire, its recognition, meaning, and consequences are largely constructed by individuals in response to situational cues. In this respect, it shares much in common with a constructionist view of emotions.

The constructionist view broadens the definition of emotion beyond a small set of universal primary emotions to include complex secondary emotions that are manifested through socially determined patterns of action and interpretation (e.g., Averill, 1980, 1992). These complex structures, also called syndromes, prototypes, and transitory social roles, have their distant origin in the fundamental response patterns present at birth, but are qualitatively different phenomena as a result of socialization and learning (Saarni, 1993). For these theorists, the experience and expression of emotion are social constructions both because knowledge of what makes a situation "emotional" is socially determined and because the enactment of emotional sequences is mediated by social norms and feeling rules understood at an intuitive level (Averill, 1992; Hochschild, 1979, 1983).

According to Leventhal (1979, 1980, 1984), the construction process begins at birth when the primary emotions experienced directly by the infant's "perceptual motor system" are contextualized through interactions with caregivers. As infants experience the sequences of responses likely to follow their emotional displays, they learn when their displays are encouraged or discouraged, as well as the reactions they are expected to display in response to others' emotion actions. Thus, emotions take on an episodic quality as they become embedded within situations and eventually become organized and differentiated along situational dimensions. This process yields relatively coherent knowledge structures or prototypes called "emotional schemata" which can then be categorized according to ordinary language labels (see Guerrero, Andersen, & Trost, Chapter 1, this volume, for a discussion of prototypes). Like all schemata, emotional schemata are perceptual templates that organize social information, direct attention to salient situational cues, and provide a model of potential responses. However, the automatic responses of the schemata system are subject to control and direction from the "conceptual system" that contains the cognitions that people hold about their emotional states, their understandings of causes and consequences, and their knowledge of social rules. Because this level includes a language component to represent emotional experience to oneself and to others and a performance component to enact emotion behaviors, it is more sequential and volitional than the schemata.

Although adults do occasionally react from the schemata level, the more typical response is one mediated by the conceptual system. Indeed, it is impossible to explain the so-called social emotions (e.g., guilt, embarrassment, shame) without recourse to socially derived cognitive structures. And, in fact, other than unmediated responses to a startling noise, a sudden pain, and so forth, even the primary emotions are to some degree social constructions (see Andersen & Guerrero, Chapter 3, this volume). As Averill (1980) explains,

> I may be angry at John for insulting me, when in actuality John was only trying to be helpful by correctly pointing out a mistake I had made. John's insult is based on my appraisal of the situation; it is as much a part of my anger as is my feeling of hurt. (p. 310)

Thus, in the constructivist account of emotion situations are not simply appraised for the degree to which they are beneficial or harmful, goal promoting or inhibiting. They are appraised for their meaning in the broadest sense and for instructions as to how to experience and enact that meaning within the constraints established by one's culture.

Similar themes are evident in the writings of scholars interested in the social construction of sexuality. For example, Blumstein and Schwartz (1990) argued that "fundamental categorical desire may not even exist. Rather, it is culture that creates understandings about how people are sexual" (p. 373). The implications of this view for the study of sexual desire are significant. Culture is fundamentally and inevitably an historical juncture, and the values, attitudes, rituals, and norms that constitute a culture are negotiated agreements. Despite the apparent inherence, timelessness, and rightness of a culture's sexual and emotional mandates, they are, in fact and in practice, social contracts that are subject to negotiation and change.

As noted previously, in contemporary Western society sexual desire is a construct linked closely with the romantic love complex (e.g., see Aron & Aron, 1994). So familiar is this association that its relatively recent appearance is forgotten. However, emotion historians are quick to point out that sexual desire, sexual activity, and romantic love have been "packaged" together only in fairly recent history. Stearns (1993), for example, describes the consequence of the shift away from arranged marriages in Europe during the 18th century:

The 18th century decline of arranged marriages cut into the group-oriented experience of premarital excitement; this shift soon led to an unprecedented association of love with privacy and with one-on-one intensity. Finally, expressions of love pulled away from a traditional range of vigorous bodily manifestations. Suitors in Wales stopped urinating on their fiancees' robes as a sign of affection; kissing became gentler, biting far less common. The relationship of love and the body, in other words, changed substantially. (p. 21)

In contemporary American society, the relationship between love and sex is facilitated by the popular media and social structures. Sex and love are frequent fare in the media, although the association is often depicted paradoxically, as both inevitable and yet separable. That is, people in the media who are in love (although not typically married, or married to each other) have sex, and people who have sex are not necessarily in love, although they are inevitably highly aroused (Metts & Cupach, 1989). One-on-one privacy is easily achieved (e.g., young adults maintain their own apartments and automobiles provide mobility, independence, and privacy), and sex outside of marriage is no longer culturally condemned or tightly regulated, although it may be condemned by religious institutions and avoided by individuals as a matter of choice. Finally, as the period of adolescent dating is extended through initiation at younger ages and marriage at later ages, the association between the subjective state of sexual desire and sexual activity becomes further removed from the traditional stage of premarital courtship (Reed & Weinberg, 1984). Thus, it falls to each couple to negotiate the meaning of sexual desire in a particular relationship at a particular point in time. Hence, communication becomes extremely important for expressing sexual desire, interpreting its meaning, and negotiating the appropriateness of various sexual behaviors in a given relationship.

This process of expression, interpretation, and negotiation is guided by a set of norms and expectations known as sexual scripts (Gagnon, 1990; Gagnon & Simon, 1973; Laws & Schwartz, 1977; Reed & Weinberg, 1984; Simon & Gagnon, 1986, 1987). For example, Simon and Gagnon (1986, 1987) argue that what may appear to be a spontaneous sexual episode is actually the manifestation of three levels of "scripted" behaviors. The *intrapsychic sexual script* is a person's understanding of what creates and sustains her or his own sexual arousal and maximizes her or his sexual satisfaction. The *interpersonal sexual script* is a person's understanding of the behaviors, expectations, and interpretations that facilitate the fulfillment of the intrapsychic level script with another person. Importantly, both of these scripts are derived from the meanings, images, and messages conveyed by the larger *cultural sexual script*.

The suggestion that sexual desire is experienced and expressed within the constraints of larger cultural scripts does not exclude the possibility of interpersonal adaptation of the cultural script. Indeed, this is the heart of the argument that sexual desire is a socially constructed emotion. For example, the prevailing sex role expectations for men to seek sex and women to resist, and for men to be sexually experienced and women to be sexually naive, are influenced by the level of relationship involvement and the presence or absence of love. Women may inhibit feelings and expressions of sexual desire in a noncommitted relationship for fear of impugning their reputation; in a committed relationship or when feeling overcome by the power of love, however, they may more freely experience and express sexual desire without the fear of negative consequences (McCabe & Collins, 1984; O'Sullivan & Byers, 1993; Roche, 1986). Nevertheless, without some coordination in the early phases of relational and sexual involvement, couples are not likely to reach more advanced stages. Sexual scripts help coordinate the early stages when uncertainty is high and idiosyncratic practices have not yet emerged. We turn now to a discussion of these initial, socially scripted phases of sexual negotiation. We set the stage for this discussion by first exploring the association between sex role expectations and the experience and expression of sexual desire.

Sex Role Expectations and Sexual Desire

The notion that men have stronger and more frequent sexual desires than women has been a pervasive theme in contemporary Western culture (see Richgels, 1992; Tolman, 1991), and at least two relatively recent surveys of high school and college students indicate that men report experiencing sexual desire with greater frequency than women (Beck et al., 1991; Useche, Villegas, & Alzate, 1990). However, this finding may reflect the greater willingness of men to report sexual feelings on a self-report instrument. In addition, women may be less likely than men to label particular experiences or feelings as sexual desire. For example, in an early study of sexual desire and the menstrual cycle, Cavanagh (1969) found it necessary to teach his female participants how to recognize sexual desire and how to make the connection between that term and specific subjective sexual feelings they could expect to experience. Finally, the assumption that men experience more sexual desire than women may stem from the common practice of using college samples in research. Sprague and Quadagno (1989) found in a sample of adults between the ages of 22 and 57 that as women get older they are more likely to report physical arousal and less likely to report love as their motivation for sexual intercourse, whereas the reverse pattern was true for men.

Robust gender differences do, however, appear to exist with respect to *perceptions* and *beliefs* about sexual desire. Men generally perceive people to be more interested in sex, and impute more sexual meaning to female behavior during heterosexual interactions, than do women (e.g., Abbey & Melby, 1986; Koeppel, Montagne-Miller, O'Hair, & Cody, 1993; Shotland & Craig, 1988). In addition, Beck et al. (1991) investigated the indices college students use to gauge their level of sexual desire, and reported that significantly more men than women indicated that they used cognitive events (e.g., dreams with sexual content, sexual fantasies) to index their level of sexual desire, and significantly more women than men said that they used behavioral or physiological events (e.g., frequency of intercourse, genital arousal). Similarly, Knoth, Boyd, and Singer (1988) found that males were more likely than females to find visual stimuli arousing, whereas females were more likely than males to find romantic/relational stimuli arousing.

More recently, Regan and Berscheid (1995) asked young adults to answer a series of free-response questions exploring their beliefs about the causes of male and female sexual desire. The majority of both men and women agreed that male and female desire have different causes. In addition, both viewed female sexual desire as heavily dependent upon relationship factors (e.g., love) and romantic environmental factors (e.g., romantic settings):

> *From a male respondent:* Thoughts of love and romance. Women tend to be more romantic . . . Women do have sexual desires brought on by suggestive surroundings but not to the extent of men. Quiet, romantic surroundings and events seem to play a large role in sexual desire.

> *From a female respondent:* Often the words "I love you" will cause sexual desire in a woman. I think that if a man showers positive attention on a woman and makes her feel desirable that causes sexual desire.

Men and women both believed that male sexual desire is strongly influenced by intraindividual (e.g., "maleness," hormones, fantasies) and erotic environmental factors (e.g., pornographic or erotic media):

> *From a male respondent:* Men have what I call a "defective gene" on their DNA ladder. This "defective gene" causes sexual desire in men. I label it as defective because it sometimes interferes with a man's way of thinking and decision making. It seems that from my experience and listening to friends that guys constantly strive for their sexual desires. These same desires don't seem to be in women, thus, my conclusion that it has something to do with our DNA structure.

> *From a female respondent:* I'm not exactly sure what causes sexual desire in a man. I would say just about anything does . . . In general, any man romantically involved or not tends to always have a sexual desire (or just about always). Anything seems to be able to set men off.

Although these respondents are providing anecdotal evidence from their own experience, their observations are consistent with research findings from the evolutionary perspective. Greer and Buss (1994), for example, summarize the results of their study on tactics used by college students to promote sexual encounters as follows: "Women often need to do nothing to promote a sexual encounter. Simply existing in time and space and being naked under their clothes is often enough to trigger approach attempts by men" (p. 197). More will be said about tactics for expressing sexual desire and promoting sexual involvement in the next section.

Expressing Sexual Desire in Developing Relationships

Before discussing the manifestation of sexual desire in sexual episodes, it is important to underscore the fact that sexual desire may be felt and may be communicated to a partner, but may not necessarily result in sexual involvement or intercourse. As Levine (1984, 1987) noted, the presence of sexual desire is not a sufficient index to determine a person's response to a sexually evocative situation. In a study of college virgins, Sprecher and Regan (1996a) found that "lack of sexual desire" was not a reason male and female virgins gave for their virginity. Most were abstaining because they had not experienced enough love for someone or because of fear of negative outcomes (e.g., pregnancy, AIDS). Similarly, research on premarital sexual standards indicates that many young adults, especially females, believe sexual expression should not begin until there is a certain level of emotional commitment in the relationship (Sprecher, 1989; Sprecher, McKinney, Walsh, & Anderson, 1988). As a consequence, couples vary considerably in the stage of relationship development where they engage in sexual activity. According to Christopher and Cate (1985), some couples are *rapid involvement couples* who begin sexual expression early in the relationship, often on their first date, and are strongly influenced by feelings of physical arousal. Other couples are *gradual involvement couples* who increase their sexual expression gradually over the four stages of dating (i.e., first date, casually dating, becoming a couple, and established as a couple). *Delayed involvement couples* delay sexual expression until they consider themselves to have become a couple. Finally, *low involvement couples* do not engage in sexual expression during courtship and usually wait until marriage. Similarly, Peplau, Rubin, and Hill (1977) distinguished among "early-sex" couples, "late sex" couples, and "abstaining" couples.

In those instances where sexual involvement does occur, how might the interaction unfold? Several reviews of the scholarly literature on sexuality and communication (e.g., Cupach & Metts, 1991; Edgar & Fitzpatrick, 1990; Metts & Cupach, 1989; Metts & Spitzberg, 1996) point to communicative patterns that characterize initial sexual involvement in developing relationships. Although most of the research in the area does not distinguish among sexual attraction, sexual interest, sexual intent, and sexual desire as the affective motivator, we can infer that at least much of the time, the sequence is prompted or promoted by sexual desire.

This research suggests that men are more likely than women to make the overt moves that initiate the sexual episode, perhaps because they have more sexual desire or perhaps because they are less inhibited by social norms from expressing their desire, are more sensitive to their own subjective arousal, or simply are responding to the prevailing interpersonal script that casts them as the initiator (see Taraban et al., Chapter 12, this volume, for a discussion of loving behaviors commonly initiated by men). In summarizing the features of sexual initiation among American heterosexual couples drawn from several decades of research, Metts and Spitzberg (1996) list a number of general conclusions. Among these are the following: (a) Despite an extensive potential repertoire of sexual pursuit tactics, only a relatively small subset is considered highly normative; (b) men are inclined to engage in the more direct forms of these tactics, and may have a larger repertoire of such direct tactics; (c) when women do employ such tactics, they are inclined to use the more indirect forms of these tactics; (d) any tactics employed by women are perceived to be effective, given men's proclivities to pursue sex; and (e) for better or worse, men are cast in the role of proactive initiator and pursuer of sex, and women are cast in the role of reactive regulator and sexual gatekeeper.

Studies also suggest that when women offer refusals, the refusals tend to be verbal and relatively direct. When female refusals are not complied with by males, stronger more direct refusals are offered, but most refusals are respected by males (Byers, 1988; Murnen, Perot, & Byrne, 1989). However, evidence from college women's descriptions of how they would reject unwanted sexual advances from a man indicate that nonverbal actions are also used. Perper and Weis (1987) content analyzed women's essays describing sexual influence episodes. Rejection themes included such techniques as simple rejection, avoiding proceptivity, avoiding intimate situations, creating distractions, making excuses, physical resistance, departure, hinting, express disapproval of man, arguments to delay, and so forth. These indirect strategies, while less face threatening, tend to invite the unfortunate attribution from men that a woman's refusal is merely "token resistance" (Muehlenhard, 1988), when it is in fact legitimate refusal (see Metts & Spitzberg, 1996, for an extended discussion of token resistance). Clearly, communicative competence in both sending refusal messages and interpreting refusal messages is critical in the negotiation of sexual involvement, regardless of intensity of sexual desire.

Communicative competence continues to be important in more developed sexual relationships as well. Not only is it necessary for negotiating the frequency and extent of sexual involvement, but also for maintaining the quality of sexual relations in the face of habituation over time and stress in other areas of the relationship. We turn now to these issues.

Expressing Sexual Desire in Established Relationships

Research on sexual initiation and refusal in long-term, heterosexual relationships (cohabiting and married) suggests that although women may initiate somewhat more often after marriage than before (e.g., Brown & Auerback, 1981), men generally continue to initiate sex more often than women and women continue to regulate the frequency of sexual intercourse (e.g., Blumstein & Schwartz, 1983). However, disagreements over whether to have sex or not tend to be resolved simply by agreeing to have sex at some other time (Byers & Heinlein, 1989). Long-term sexual partners also seem willing to engage in sex for a variety of reasons even if they do not initially feel sexual desire (Levine, 1984).

Whether initiation and refusal patterns, engaging in sexual activity in the absence of sexual desire, and related sexual circumstances influence satisfaction with the sexual relationship depends in large measure on the communicative skill of the partners. As D'Augelli and D'Augelli (1985) described in some detail, sexual partners need to have skill in two types of communication: expressive and receptive.

That is, people need to be able to express their needs and desires, describe activities that increase or inhibit their arousal, and indicate to their partner when those behaviors are being successfully enacted. People also need to be able to solicit and accept without defensiveness the same type of information from their partners. This level of talk is, in a very real sense, self-disclosure. As such, its occurrence and its effects depend on high levels of trust and acceptance. Apparently, the benefits are worth the effort, given the strong association between satisfaction with communication about sex and relationship satisfaction in general (Cupach & Comstock, 1990).

Research suggests that couples do express some aspects of their sexual feelings. The item "my feelings about our sexual relationship" was included in the self-disclosure scale completed by the 231 college dating couples in the Boston Dating Couples Study (Rubin, Hill, Peplau, & Dunkel-Schetter, 1980). The majority of the respondents (74% of the women and 73% of the men) indicated they had "full" disclosure on this topic, and most of the others reported "some" disclosure. In a study of emotion expression in relationships, Sprecher and Sedikides (1993) found that members of dating, cohabiting, and newly married couples reported expressing sexual excitement, through "display" or "disclosure," frequently within the past month. Men reported expressing sexual excitement to a greater degree than the women. This is noteworthy because only one other emotion—ambivalence—was expressed more by men than women (out of 25 positive and negative emotions measured), whereas women reported expressing 11 emotions to a greater degree than men.

Whether couples are as open about specific sexual preferences and needs is less clear. Despite the advice of clinicians and Dr. Ruth, couples may still find such personal disclosure uncomfortable. At present, little research is available on how frequently or in what manner partners communicate their preferences. What we do know is that verbal communication may be especially necessary in those circumstances where nonverbal sexual behaviors are perceived differently. Specifically, explicit communication may be needed when one person's assumption about the types of behavior most likely to arouse her or his partner are not accurate. Because men and women do not find the same sexual behaviors equally arousing (Geer & Broussard, 1990), communication between partners about what is arousing is critically important. According to research conducted by Masters and Johnson (1979; as described in Brehm, 1992), homosexual couples report greater satisfaction with their sexual experiences than do heterosexual couples in part because they find the same behaviors arousing but also because they talk more openly and easily about what they desire and what is pleasurable. Masters and Johnson (1979) described heterosexual couples as having a "persistent neglect of the vital communicative exchange" (p. 219).

We also know that if problems in communicating about sexual desire are not resolved, other aspects of the relationship are affected as well (Sprecher, Metts, Burleson, Hatfield, & Thompson, 1995). Reciprocally, problems in other areas of a relationship can affect the frequency and intensity of sexual desire and/or a partner's willingness to communicate desire when experienced. Many sex therapy programs encourage couples to focus on relationship issues, including the development of communication skills (e.g., Kaplan, 1974; Masters, Johnson, & Kolodny, 1982). Thus, in the clinical literature, it is recognized that sexual desire and communication are reciprocally linked.

Fading of Sexual Desire and Sexual Expression over Time

Research on sexual frequency in marriage indicates that sexual activity declines over the duration of marriage and with the increase in spouses' ages. Evidence of decline has been found consistently across studies, including cross-sectional research (e.g., Call, Sprecher, & Schwartz, 1995; Laumann, Gagnon, Michael, & Michaels, 1994), retrospective research (Greenblat, 1983), and longitudinal research (James, 1981; James, 1983; Udry, 1980). Decline has also been found in cohabiting, heterosexual couples and in gay and lesbian couples (e.g., Blumstein & Schwartz, 1983). The rate of decline may be greater early in the marriage than later. For example, James (1981) hypothesized that the rate declines by approximately one-half across the first year of marriage and then takes another 20 years to half again. The decline in the first year of marriage has been called "the honeymoon effect." As evidence of this decline, James (1981) analyzed diaries kept by newlyweds and found that the median frequency of sex in the first month of marriage was over 17 times, but declined to approximately eight times per month by the end of the first year. Evidence that sexual expression continues to decline after the first year of marriage was found in Greenblat's (1983) interview study with married respondents who were in their first five years of marriage. Greenblatt found that 69% of men and women married for more than a year reported that their current rate was lower than their first year rate (only 6% reported an increase).

The various explanations offered for the decline in sexual frequency do not generally make a distinction between factors affecting sexual desire and factors affecting the expression or enactment of sexual desire. The rapid drop in frequency of marital sex that occurs shortly after marriage is probably due to habituation or a decreased interest in sex with one's regular partner because of an increase in predictability. The arousal stemming from uncertainty and novelty that was experienced during early sexual exploration eventually subsides. To the extent that this generalized arousal amplified, or was perhaps experienced as, sexual desire, its decline would reduce the motivation to initiate sexual activity. Later in marriage, sexual expression can decline further because of increases in role and time demands due to children, employment, caring for elderly parents, and other obligations that may reduce the opportunity for the expression or enactment of sexual desire, even if the desire has not dissipated. Once sexual expression declines, couples are likely to modify their relationship's sexual script to include a lower level of sexual activity (Call et al., 1995). Finally, later in life, biological or health factors may decrease the ability to express one's sexual desire. Furthermore, negative attitudes in society about sexuality among older adults can lead to decline in both sexual desire and sexual expression among the elderly (Riportella-Muller, 1989).

More subjective measures of desire have also shown a decline over time in marriages or other long-term relationships. Although passion (e.g., Hatfield & Rapson, 1987, 1990) is not synonymous with sexual desire, sexual desire does appear to be an important component of passion or passionate love. Subjective measures of passion and passionate love have been found to be negatively associated with length of relationship (Acker & Davis, 1992; Hatfield & Sprecher, 1986; Sprecher & Regan, 1996b; Tucker & Aron, 1993), which suggests that verbal and nonverbal expression of passion or subjective sexual desire would also decline over time.

Although sexual expression declines over time in most long-term relationships, considerable variation exists across couples in the rate of decline. Some couples remain at a high level of sexual desire and expression until late in life. Some couples are not sexually expressive even early in their marriage. Some couples replace genital-focused sex with nongenital touching. The degree to which sexual expression declines over time in a relationship is likely to depend on how satisfied the couple is and the degree to which they experience passionate love, which helps to fuel sexual excitement and desire (Aron & Henkemeyer, 1995; Hatfield & Rapson, 1987; Sprecher & Regan, 1996b).

To some degree, then, a couple might expect changes in their sexual desire and sexual activity over the course of their relationship, although the specifics of this change will vary across couples. In many cases, these changes are not salient to a couple and go largely unmarked, particularly when communication is open and other aspects of the relationship are satisfying. In other cases, however, these changes are noticed and problematized.

Problems in Sexual Desire and Other Aspects of the Relationship

In some long-term relationships, problems of low sexual desire and/or difficulty expressing sexual desire develop for one or both partners (Spector & Carey, 1990). Sometimes, the problem is a discrepancy in sexual desire; one partner wants sex less frequently or more frequently than the other. A problem in sexual desire and expression may be due to a number of nonrelational factors, including illness, anxiety, and a history of sexual assault. However, in many cases, diminished sexual desire or unwillingness to express sexual desire may be indicative of other relationship problems (Stuart, Hammond, & Pett, 1987). For example, relationship conflict and arguments can dampen sexual desire and expression, particularly for women (e.g., Blumstein & Schwartz, 1983). Indeed, "emotional conflict with partner" was cited as the most common cause of inhibited sexual desire among married men and women in a survey of 400 physicians (Pietropinto, 1986). Moreover, even when relational climate is not overtly hostile, if it is not conducive to open communication, sexual desire may be affected. In a longitudinal study of married and cohabiting women, Hallstrom and Samuelsson (1990) found that those who reported a decrease over time in sexual desire tended to perceive insufficient emotional support and lack of a confiding relationship with their spouse. Likewise, couples who believe their relationships to be inequitable are less likely to want to have sex (Hatfield, Greenberger, Traupmann, & Lambert, 1982; Traupmann, Hatfield, & Wexler, 1983). It is no surprise that many clinicians now focus on the dynamic of the couple's relationship in seeking to treat sexual desire disorders (e.g., Regas & Sprenkle, 1984; Trudel, 1991).

Importantly, even in couples with relatively healthy sexual relationships, sexual desire and sexual expression are related to the quality of other aspects of the relationship. In general, frequency and intimacy of sexual expression are positively associated with relationship satisfaction (Blumstein & Schwartz, 1983; Call et al., 1995; Sprecher et al., 1995). Couples who are happy have more sex, presumably because they have more sexual desire for each other. However, clinical studies and case reports suggest that marital partners often use sexual desire as a "thermometer" to overall relationship adjustment. Specifically, a marked decrease or absence of sexual desire experienced by one or both partners is interpreted as a "problem" that requires correction, usually through some form of therapeutic intervention (e.g., Kaplan, 1979; Leiblum & Rosen, 1988; Levine, 1987; Talmadge & Talmadge, 1986). In addition, some clinicians posit that sexual desire may serve to regulate emotional distance between a couple; that is, sexual desire may increase or decrease as an individual's need to be close to the partner waxes and wanes (e.g., Verhulst & Heiman, 1979; Zilbergeld & Ellison, 1980).

In sum, the association between sexual desire and other relationship properties appears to be systemic. What occurs in the couple's bedroom is likely to be affected by what happens in the rest of their relationship; conversely, the activity (or lack of) in the bedroom is likely to affect the rest of the relationship. No doubt some couples may be able to punctuate the cycle by pointing to sexual problems as the cause and relationship problems as the effect, or vice versa. In reality, isolating the direction of causality is very difficult to do. As Blumstein and Schwartz (1983) describe the dilemma:

> It is hard to know whether an unsatisfactory relationship leads to less frequent sexual activity and reduced sexual pleasure or whether the problems begin in the bedroom and eventually corrode the entire relationship. From our vantage point it looks as if other problems come into the bedroom and make it less likely that the couple will want to have sex together. The low frequency then becomes a source of dissatisfaction in and of itself. (p. 201)

CONCLUSION

This chapter has explored the complex associations among communication, emotion, and sexual desire. Two views evident in the scholarly literature were discussed.

The biological or reproductive view tends to characterize sexual desire as a biological drive that is signaled through emotion displays, thereby facilitating mating; or is manifested through copulation that leads to emotional responses, which in turn lead to intimate communication and pair bonding. This view is not incompatible with the relational view, though it is more linear than systemic. The relational view tends to characterize sexual desire more broadly, noting that, although it is experienced as a unitary psychological state, it is in fact composed of several features: biological drive, cognitions that generate the wish or desire to behave sexually, and psychological processes that yield a willingness to behave sexually. This characterization places cognition (though perhaps not conscious processing) as the mediating factor between physiological arousal and sexual activity. Communication then enters the model as the vehicle to stimulate arousal, express cognitions relevant to arousal (i.e., the desire to behave sexually and the willingness to behave sexually), and to process sexual meanings and intentions with partner. Emotion may or may not be the defining feature of sexual episodes. We might speculate that for persons who construct emotions from social situations according to prevailing Western stereotypes (particularly those that define gender expectations), the presence of sexual desire is probably experienced as various shadings of the romantic love complex (e.g., infatuation, attraction, love, affection). For many people, when no relationship potential exists or when relationship affection has dissipated, sexual desire might be constructed simply as sexual need, horniness, or lust. Perhaps the distinction lies in the solitary nature of the latter situation. As several emotion theorists have noted (e.g., de Rivera, 1984), emotions are essentially social responses—the self interacting with the social environment. In the absence of any concern beyond self, arousal might be perceived as no more emotional than a state of hunger or fatigue.

In our discussion of the relational perspective, we touched on several important issues that merit additional research. Because sexual desire is often experienced and expressed within emotionally close relationships, sexual desire is related to many other relationship phenomena, including satisfaction, love, equity, and relationship duration. Unfortunately, however, there has been a dearth of research that considers both the experience and expression of sexual desire within a relational context. Other emotions related to sexuality, such as sexual satisfaction, have received more empirical and theoretical attention. More research is needed on how sexual desire and its communication are related to other sexual feelings (sexual satisfaction, sexual guilt), to sexual behaviors (frequency of sexual activity, likelihood of engaging in extradyadic sex), and to aspects of the larger relationship (e.g., satisfaction).

In particular, research needs to be directed toward understanding how sexual desire changes over time in a relationship and how its association with other relationship phenomena (e.g., relationship quality) change as well. Western culture has so embued romantic love with sexual overtones that distinguishing the two emotions in everyday life is difficult. Couples who read the arousal of sexual desire as the arousal of romantic love, may use communication to celebrate and maintain the mystery rather than to understand each other. Consequently, decreases in arousal are likely to be perceived as relational decline unless partners are able to voice their concerns and negotiate new relational meanings. Research focused on these processes in dating and married couples and in homosexual couples is essential, not only for scholars but for clinicians as well. In sum, the centrality of sexual desire to how couples define and enact their relationships necessitates further research, especially with longitudinal designs and creative methodologies.

REFERENCES

Abbey, A., & Melby, C. (1986). The effects of nonverbal cues on gender differences in perceptions of sexual intent. *Sex Roles, 15,* 283–298.

Acker, M., & Davis, M. H. (1992). Intimacy, passion, and commitment in adult romantic relationships: A test of the triangular theory of love. *Journal of Social and Personal Relationships, 9,* 21–50.

Aron, A., & Aron, E. N. (1991). Love and sexuality. In K. McKinney & S. Sprecher (Eds.), *Sexuality in close relationships* (pp. 25–48). Hillsdale, NJ: Erlbaum.

Aron, A., & Aron, E. N. (1994). Love. In A. L. Weber & J. H. Harvey (Eds.), *Perspectives on close relationships* (pp. 131–152). Boston: Allyn & Bacon.

Aron, A., & Henkemeyer, L. (1995). Marital satisfaction and passionate love. *Journal of Social and Personal Relationships, 12,* 139–146.

Averill, J. R. (1980). A constructivist view of emotion. In R. Plutchik & H. Kellerman (Eds.), *Emotion: Theory, research, and experience* (pp. 305–339). New York: Academic Press.

Averill, J. R. (1992). The structural bases of emotional behavior: A metatheoretical analysis. In M. S. Clark (Ed.), *Emotion* (pp. 1–24). Newbury Park, CA: Sage.

Bancroft, J. (1988). Sexual desire and the brain. *Sexual and Marital Therapy, 3,* 11–27.

Beck, J. G., Bozman, A. W., & Qualtrough, T. (1991). The experience of sexual desire: Psychological correlates in a college sample. *The Journal of Sex Research, 28,* 443–456.

Berscheid, E. (1988). Some comments on love's anatomy: Or, whatever happened to old-fashioned lust? In J. Sternberg & M. Barnes (Eds.), *The psychology of love* (pp. 359–374). New Haven, CT: Yale University Press.

Berscheid, E., & Walster, E. (1974). A little bit about love. In T. L. Huston (Ed.), *Foundations of interpersonal attraction* (pp. 355–381). New York: Academic Press.

Bertocci, P. A. (1988). *The person and primary emotions.* New York: Springer-Verlag.

Blumstein, P., & Schwartz, P. (1983). *American couples.* New York: Morrow.

Blumstein, P., & Schwartz, P. (1990). Intimate relationships and the creation of sexuality. In D. P. McWhirter, S. A. Sanders, & J. M. Reinisch (Eds.), *Homosexuality/heterosexuality: Concepts of sexual orientation.* New York: Oxford University Press.

Brehm, S. S. (1992). *Intimate relationships* (2nd ed.). New York: McGraw-Hill.

Brown, M., & Auerback, A. (1981). Communication patterns in initiation of marital sex. *Medical Aspects of Human Sexuality, 15,* 105–117.

Buck, R. (1980). Nonverbal behavior and the theory of emotion: The facial feedback hypothesis. *Journal of Personality and Social Psychology, 38,* 811–824.

Buck, R. (1984). *The communication of emotion.* New York: Guilford.

Byers, E. S. (1988). Effects of sexual arousal on men's and women's behavior in sexual disagreement situations. *Journal of Sex Research, 25,* 235–254.

Byers, E. S., & Heinlein, L. (1989). Predicting initiations and refusals of sexual activities in married and cohabiting heterosexual couples. *Journal of Sex Research, 26,* 210–231.

Call, V., Sprecher, S., & Schwartz, P. (1995). The incidence and frequency of marital sex in a national sample. *Journal of Marriage and the Family, 57,* 639–652.

Cavanagh, J. R. (1969). Rhythm of sexual desire in women. *Medical Aspects of Human Sexuality, 3,* 29–39.

Christopher, F. S., & Cate, R. M. (1985). Premarital sexual pathways and relationship development. *Journal of Social and Personal Relationships, 2,* 271–288.

Christopher, F. S., & Roosa, M. W. (1991). Factors affecting sexual decisions in the premarital relationships of adolescents and young adults. In K. McKinney & S. Sprecher (Eds.), *Sexuality in close relationships* (pp. 111–133). Hillsdale, NJ: Erlbaum.

Cupach, W. R., & Comstock, J. (1990). Satisfaction with sexual communication in marriage: Links to sexual satisfaction and dyadic adjustment. *Journal of Social and Personal Relationships, 7,* 179–186.

Cupach, W. R., & Metts, S. (1991). Sexuality and communication in close relationships. In K. McKinney & S. Sprecher (Eds.), *Sexuality in close relationships* (pp. 93–107). Hillsdale, NJ: Erlbaum.

D'Augelli, A., & D'Augelli, J. F. (1985). The enhancement of sexual skills and competence: Promoting lifelong sexual unfolding. In L. L'Abate & M. A. Milan (Eds.), *Handbook of social skills training and research* (pp. 170–191). New York: Wiley.

DeLamater, J. (1991). Emotions and sexuality. In K. McKinney & S. Sprecher (Eds.), *Sexuality in close relationships* (pp. 49–70). Hillsdale, NJ: Erlbaum.

DeLamater, J. (1989). The social control of human sexuality. In K. McKinney, & S. Sprecher (Eds.), *Human sexuality: The societal and interpersonal context* (pp. 30–62). Norwood, NJ: Ablex.

de Rivera, J. (1984). Development and the full range of emotional experience. In C. Z. Malatesta & C. E. Izard (Eds.), *Emotion in adult development* (pp. 45–63). Beverly Hills, CA: Sage.

Edgar, T., & Fitzpatrick, M. A. (1990). Communicating sexual desire: Message tactics for having and avoiding intercourse. In J. P. Dillard (Ed.), *Seeking compliance: The production of interpersonal influence messages* (pp. 107–122). Scottsdale, AZ: Gorsuch Scarisbrick.

Ekman, P. (1984). Expression and the nature of emotion. In K. R. Scherer & P. Ekman (Eds.), *Approaches to emotion* (pp. 319–344). Hillsdale, NJ: Erlbaum.

Ekman, P., Levenson, R. W., & Friesen, W. V. (1983). Autonomic nervous system activity distinguishes among emotions. *Science, 221,* 1208–1210.

Ellsworth, P. C., & Smith, C. A. (1989). From appraisal to emotion: Differences among unpleasant feelings. *Motivation and Emotion, 12,* 271–302.

Epstein, S. (1984). Controversial issues in emotion theory. In P. Shaver (Ed.), *Review of personality and social psychology: Emotions, relationships, and health* (pp. 64–88). Beverly Hills, CA: Sage.

Everaerd, W. (1988). Commentary on sex research: Sex as an emotion. *Journal of Psychology and Human Sexuality, 1,* 3–15.

Frijda, N. H., Kuipers, P., & ter Schure, E. (1989). Relations between emotion, appraisal, and emotional action readiness. *Journal of Personality and Social Psychology, 57,* 212–228.

Gagnon, J. H. (1990). The explicit and implicit use of the scripting perspective in sex research. In J. Bancroft (Ed.), *Annual review of sex research* (Vol. 1, pp. 1–44). Lake Mills, IA: Society for the Scientific Study of Sex.

Gagnon, J. H., & Simon, W. (1973). *Sexual conduct: The social sources of human sexuality.* Chicago: Aldine.

Geer, J. H., & Broussard, D. B. (1990). Scaling heterosexual behavior and arousal: Consistency and sex differences. *Journal of Personality and Social Psychology, 58,* 664–671.

Greenblat, C. S. (1983). The salience of sexuality in the early years of marriage. *Journal of Marriage and the Family, 45,* 289–299.

Greer, A. E., & Buss, D. M. (1994). Tactics for promoting sexual encounters. *Journal of Sex Research, 31,* 185–201.

Hallstrom, T., & Samuelsson, S. (1990). Changes in women's sexual desire in middle life: The longitudinal study of women in Gothenburg. *Archives of Sexual Behavior, 19,* 259–268.

Harris, P. L. (1993). Understanding emotion. In M. Lewis & J. M. Haviland (Eds.), *Handbook of emotion* (pp. 237–246). New York: Guilford.

Harvey, J. H., Weber, A. L., & Orbuch, T. L. (1990). *Interpersonal accounts: A social psychological perspective.* Cambridge, MA: Basil Blackwell, Inc.

Hatfield, E., Greenberger, D., Traupmann, J., & Lambert, P. (1982). Equity and sexual satisfaction in recently married couples. *Journal of Sex Research, 18,* 18–32.

Hatfield, E., & Rapson, R. (1987). Passionate love/sexual desire: Can the same paradigm explain both? *Archives of Sexual Behavior, 16,* 259–278.

Hatfield, E., & Rapson, R. L. (1990). Passionate love in intimate relationships. In B. S. Moore & A. Isen (Eds.), *Affect and social behavior* (pp. 126–152). Cambridge, UK: Cambridge University Press.

Hatfield, E., & Rapson, R. (1993). Love and attachment processes. In M. Lewis & J. M. Haviland (Eds.), *Handbook of emotion* (pp. 595–604). New York: Guilford.

Hatfield, E., & Sprecher, S. (1986). Measuring passionate love in intimate relations. *Journal of Adolescence, 9,* 383–410.

Hochschild, A. (1979). Emotion work, feeling rules and social structure. *American Journal of Sociology, 75,* 551–575.

Hochschild, A. R. (1983). *The managed heart.* Berkeley: University of California Press.

Izard, C. E. (1990). Facial expressions and the regulation of emotions. *Journal of Personality and Social Psychology, 58,* 87–498.

Izard, C. E. (1993). Organizational and motivational functions of discrete emotions. In M. Lewis & J. M. Haviland (Eds.), *Handbook of emotion* (pp. 631–642). New York: Guilford.

James, W. H. (1981). The honeymoon effect on marital coitus. *The Journal of Sex Researech, 17,* 114–123.

James, W. H. (1983). Decline in coital rates with spouses' ages and duration of marriage. *Journal of Bioscience, 15,* 83–87.

Kaplan, H. S. (1974). *The new sex therapy: Active treatment of sexual dysfunction.* New York: Brunner/Mazel.

Kaplan, H. S. (1977). Hypoactive sexual desire. *Journal of Sex and Marital Therapy, 3,* 3–9.

Kaplan, H. S. (1979). *Disorders of sexual desire and other new concepts and techniques in sex therapy.* New York: Simon & Schuster.

Kenny, J. A. (1973). Sexuality of pregnant and breastfeeding women. *Archives of Sexual Behavior, 2,* 215–229.

Knoth, R., Boyd, K., & Singer, B. (1988). Empirical tests of sexual selection theory: Predictions of sex differences in onset, intensity, and time course of sexual arousal. *Journal of Sex Research, 24,* 73–89.

Koeppel, L. B., Montagne-Miller, Y., O'Hair, D., & Cody, M. J. (1993). Friendly? Flirting? Wrong? In P. J. Kalbfleisch (Ed.), *Interpersonal communication: Evolving interpersonal relationships* (pp. 13–32). Hillsdale, NJ: Erlbaum.

Laumann, E. O., Gagnon, J. H., Michael, R. T., & Michaels, S. (1994). *The social organization of sexuality: Sexual practices in the United States.* Chicago: University of Chicago Press.

Laws, J. L., & Schwartz, P. (1977). *Sexual scripts: The social construction of female sexuality.* Hinsdale, IL: Dryden.

Lazarus, R. S., Coyne, J. C., & Folkman, S. (1984). Cognition, emotion and motivation: The doctoring of Humpty-Dumpty. In K. R. Scherer & P. Ekman (Eds.), *Approaches to emotion* (pp. 221–238). Hillsdale, NJ: Erlbaum.

Leiblum, S. R., & Rosen, R. C. (1988). Introduction: Changing perspectives on sexual desire. In S. R. Leiblum & R. C. Rosen (Eds.), *Sexual desire disorders* (pp. 1–17). New York: Guilford Press.

Leventhal, H. (1979). A perceptual motor processing model of emotion. In P. Pliner, K. R. Blankstein, & I. M. Spigel (Eds.), *Perception of emotion in self and others: Advances in the study of communication and affect, Vol. 5* (pp. 1–46). New York: Plenum.

Leventhal, H. (1980). Toward a comprehensive theory of emotion. In L. Berkowitz (Eds.), *Advances in experimental social psychology, Vol. 13* (pp. 139–207). New York: Academic Press.

Leventhal, H. (1984). A perceptual motor theory of emotion. In K. R. Scherer & P. Ekman (Eds.), *Approaches to emotion* (pp. 271–292). Hillsdale, NJ: Erlbaum.

Levine, S. B. (1984). An essay on the nature of sexual desire. *Journal of Sex & Marital Therapy, 10,* 83–96.

Levine, S. B. (1987). More on the nature of sexual desire. *Journal of Sex & Marital Therapy, 13,* 35–44.

Masters, W. H., & Johnson, V. (1979). *Homosexuality in perspective.* Boston: Little, Brown.

Masters, W. H., Johnson, V. E., & Kolodny, R. C. (1982). *Human sexuality.* Boston, MA: Little, Brown and Company.

McCabe, M. P., & Collins, J. K. (1984). Measurement of depth of desired and experienced sexual involvement at different stages of dating. *Journal of Sex Research, 20,* 377–390.

McIntosh, W. D., & Martin, L. L. (1992). The cybernetics of happiness: The relation of goal attainment, rumination, and affect. In M. S. Clark (Ed.), *Emotion and social behavior* (pp. 222–246). Newbury Park, CA: Sage.

Metts, S., & Bowers, J. W. (1994). Emotion in interpersonal communication. In M. L. Knapp & G. R. Miller (Eds.), *Handbook of interpersonal communication* (second edition) (pp. 508–541). Thousand Oaks, CA: Sage.

Metts, S., & Cupach, W. R. (1989). The role of communication in human sexuality. In K. McKinney & S. Sprecher (Eds.), *Human sexuality: The societal and interpersonal context* (pp. 193–161). Norwood, NJ: Ablex.

Metts, S., & Spitzberg, B. H. (1996). Sexual communication in interpersonal contexts: A script-based approach. In B. R. Burleson (Ed.), *Communication yearbook 19* (pp. 49–92). Thousand Oaks, CA: Sage.

Moore, M. M. (1985). Nonverbal courtship patterns in women: Context and consequences. *Ethology and Sociobiology, 6,* 237–247.

Moore, M. M., & Butler, D. L. (1989). Predictive aspects of nonverbal courtship behavior in women. *Semiotica, 76,* 205–215.

Muehlenhard, C. L. (1988). "Nice women" don't say yes and "real men" don't say no: How miscommunication and the double standard can cause sexual problems. *Women and Therapy, 7,* 96–108.

Murnen, S. K., Perot, A., & Byrne, D. (1989). Coping with unwanted sexual activity: Normative responses, situational determinants, and individual differences. *The Journal of Sex Research, 26,* 85–106.

Oatley, K. (1993). Social construction in emotion. In M. Lewis & J. M. Haviland (Ed.), *Handbook of emotions* (pp. 341–352). New York: Guilford.

O'Sullivan, L. F., & Byers, E. S. (1993). Eroding stereotypes: College women's attempts to influence reluctant male sexual partners. *The Journal of Sex Research, 30,* 270–282.

Peplau, L. A., Rubin, Z., & Hill, C. T. (1977). Sexual intimacy in dating relationships. *Journal of Social Issues, 33,* 86–109.

Perper, T., & Weis, D. L. (1987). Proceptive and rejective strategies of U.S. and Canadian college women. *Journal of Sex Research, 23,* 455–480.

Pietropinto, A. (1986). Inhibited sexual desire. *Medical Aspects of Human Sexuality, 20*(10), 46–49.

Plutchik, R. (1984). Emotions: A general psychoevolutionary theory. In K. R. Scherer & P. Ekman (Eds.), *Approaches to emotion* (pp. 197–219). Hillsdale, NJ: Erlbaum.

Reed, D., & Weinberg, M. S. (1984). Premarital coitus: Developing and established sexual scripts. *Social Psychology Quarterly, 47,* 129–138.

Regan, P. C., & Berscheid, E. (1995). Gender differences in beliefs about the causes of male and female sexual desire. *Personal Relationships, 2,* 345–358.

Regan, P. C., & Berscheid, E. (1996). Beliefs about the state, goals, and objects of sexual desire. *Journal of Sex & Marital Therapy, 22,* 110–120.

Regas, S. J., & Sprenkle, D. H. (1984). Functional family therapy and the treatment of inhibited sexual desire. *Journal of Marital and Family Therapy, 10,* 63–72.

Reiss, I. L. (1986). *Journey into sexuality: An exploratory voyage.* New York: Prentice-Hall.

Reiss, I. L. (1989). Society and sexuality: A sociological explanation. In K. McKinney & S. Sprecher (Eds.), *Human sexuality: The societal and interpersonal context* (pp. 3–29). Norwood, NJ: Ablex.

Richgels, P. B. (1992). Hypoactive sexual desire in heterosexual women: A feminist analysis. *Women and Therapy, 12,* 123–135.

Riportella-Muller, R. (1989). Sexuality in the elderly: A review. In K. McKinney & S. Sprecher (Eds.), *Human sexuality: The societal and interpersonal context* (pp. 210–236). Norwood, NJ: Ablex.

Roche, J. P. (1986). Premarital sex: Attitudes and behavior by dating stage. *Adolescence, 21,* 107–121.

Roseman, I. J. (1984). Cognitive determinants of emotion: A structural theory. In P. Shaver (Ed.), *Re-*

view of personality and social psychology: Emotions, relationships, and health (pp. 11–36). Beverly Hills, CA: Sage.

Rubin, Z., Hill, C. T., Peplau, L. A., Dunkel-Schetter, C. (1980). Self-disclosure in dating couples: Sex roles and the ethic of openness. *Journal of Marriage and the Family, 42,* 305–317.

Saarni, C. (1993). Socialization of emotion. In M. Lewis & J. M. Haviland (Eds.), *Handbook of emotion* (pp. 435–446). New York: Guilford.

Shaver, P. R., Schwartz, J. C., Kirson, D., & O'Connor, C. (1987). Emotion knowledge: Further explorations of a prototype approach. *Journal of Personality and Social Psychology, 52,* 1061–1086.

Shaver, P. R., Wu, S., & Schwartz, J. C. (1992). Cross-cultural similarities and differences in emotion and its representation: A prototype approach. In M. S. Clark (Ed.), *Emotion* (pp. 175–212). Newbury Park, CA: Sage.

Shotland, R. L., & Craig, J. M. (1988). Can men and women differentiate between friendly and sexually interested behavior? *Social Psychology Quarterly, 51,* 66–73.

Simon, W., & Gagnon, J. H. (1986). Sexual scripts: Permanence and change. *Archives of Sexual Behavior, 15,* 97–120.

Simon, W., & Gagnon, J. H. (1987). A sexual scripts approach. In J. H. Geer & W. O'Donohue (Eds.), *Theories of human sexuality* (pp. 363–383). New York: Plenum.

Simpson, J. A., & Gangestad, S. W. (1991). Personality and sexuality: Empirical relations and an integrative theoretical model. In K. McKinney & S. Sprecher (Eds.), *Sexuality in close relationships* (pp. 71–92). Hillsdale, NJ: Erlbaum.

Smith, C. A., & Ellsworth, P. C. (1985). Patterns of cognitive appraisal in emotion. *Journal of Personality and Social Psychology, 48,* 813–838.

Solomon, R. C. (1993). The philosophy of emotions. In M. Lewis & J. M. Haviland (Eds.), *Handbook of emotions* (pp. 3–16). New York: Guilford.

Spector, I. P., & Carey, M. P. (1990). Incidence and prevalence of the sexual dysfunctions: A critical review of the empirical literature. *Archives of Sexual Behavior, 19,* 389–408.

Sprague, J., & Quadagno, D. (1989). Gender and sexual motivation: An exploration of two assumptions. *Journal of Psychology and Human Sexuality, 2,* 57–76.

Sprecher, S. (1989). Premarital sexual standards for different categories of individuals. *The Journal of Sex Research, 26,* 232–248.

Sprecher, S., McKinney, K., Walsh, R., & Anderson, C. (1988). A revision of the Reiss premarital sexual permissiveness scale. *Journal of Marriage and the Family, 50,* 821–828.

Sprecher, S., Metts, S., Burleson, B., Hatfield, E., & Thompson, A. (1995). Domains of expressive interaction in intimate relationships: Associations with satisfaction and commitment. *Family Relations, 44,* 203–210.

Sprecher, S., & Regan, P. C. (1996a). College virgins: How men and women perceive their sexual status. *The Journal of Sex Reseaerch, 33,* 3–15.

Sprecher, S., & Regan, P. C. (1996b). *Passionate love vs. companionate love: Are there any differences?* Manuscript submitted for publication.

Sprecher, S., & Sedikides, C. (1993). Gender differences in perceptions of emotionality: The case of close heterosexual relationships. *Sex Roles, 28,* 511–530.

Stearns, P. N. (1993). History of emotions: The issue of change. In M. Lewis & J. M. Haviland (Eds.), *Handbook of emotions* (pp. 17–28). New York: Guilford.

Stuart, F. M., Hammond, D. C., & Pett, M. A. (1987). Inhibited sexual desire in women. *Archives of Sexual Behavior, 16,* 91–106.

Talmadge, L. D., & Talmadge, W. C. (1986). Relational sexuality: An understanding of low sexual desire. *Journal of Sex & Marital Therapy, 12,* 3–21.

Teevan, R. C., & Smith, B. D. (1967). *Motivation.* New York: McGraw-Hill.

Tolman, D. L. (1991). Adolescent girls, women and sexuality: Discerning dilemmas of desire. *Women and Therapy, 11,* 55–69.

Tomkins, S. S. (1980). Affect as amplification: Some modifications in theory. *Perceptual and Motor Skills, 18,* 119–158.

Tomkins, S. S. (1984). Affect theory. In K. R. Scherer & P. Ekman (Eds.), *Approaches to emotion* (pp. 163–196). Hillsdale, NJ: Erlbaum.

Traupmann, J., Hatfield, E., & Wexler, P. (1983). Equity and sexual satisfaction in dating couples. *British Journal of Social Psychology, 22,* 33–40.

Trudel, G. (1991). Review of psychological factors in low sexual desire. *Sexual and Marital Therapy, 6,* 261–272.

Tucker, P., & Aron, A. (1993). Passionate love and marital satisfaction at key transition points in the family life cycle. *Journal of Social and Clinical Psychology, 12,* 135–147.

Udry, J. R. (1980). Changes in the frequency of marital intercourse from panel data. *Archives of Sexual Behavior, 9,* 319–325.

Useche, B., Villegas, M., & Alzate, H. (1990). Sexual behavior of Colombian high school students. *Adolescence, 25,* 291–304.

Verhulst, J., & Heiman, J. R. (1979). An interactional approach to sexual dysfunctions. *American Journal of Family Therapy, 7,* 19–36.

White, G. L., Fishbein, S., & Rutstein, J. (1981). Passionate love and the misattribution of arousal. *Journal of Personality and Social Psychology, 41,* 56–62.

Zilbergeld, B., & Ellison, C. R. (1980). Desire discrepancies and arousal problems in sex therapy. In S. R. Leiblum & L. A. Pervin (Eds.), *Principles and practice of sex therapy* (pp. 65–101). New York: Guilford.

PART IV

Applications and Contexts

Emotional Expression in the Deception Process

David B. Buller

Judee K. Burgoon

University of Arizona
Tucson, Arizona

Deception is emotional. Emotions provoke deception, and deception provokes emotions: The desire to avoid unpleasant feelings or the thrill of "pulling the wool over someone's eyes" can lead to deceit, and lying can make deceivers feel guilty, fearful, or gleeful. Deceit can be *about* emotions, and emotions can *be* deceitful: People dissemble about how they are feeling and they can feign unfelt emotions. Emotions also accompany deceptive messages: Emotional displays may mask or reveal lies. Targets of deceit are also part of the deceit–emotion process. Their suspicions may activate emotions, and they may use emotions to cover those suspicions. Finally, the consequences of deceit entail emotions: Communicators may be worried, relieved, or delighted when deception succeeds; receivers may be hurt, angry, contemptuous, or smug when it is discovered. It is not surprising, then, that emotional processes are incorporated in every explanation of deceptive communication.

Deception, defined as a *message knowingly transmitted by a sender to foster a false belief or conclusion by the receiver,* is a very common form of information management in human interaction (DePaulo, Kashy, Kirkendol, Wyer, & Epstein, 1994; Turner, Edgley, & Olmstead, 1975). Scholars in communication and social psychology have studied this communicative phenomenon intensively; however, their theories differ on whether they emphasize the biological or social nature of emotions. Social psychologists approach emotion in deception as biological signals of cognitive experiences and are interested mainly in inadvertent emotional reactions to the act of deception and telltale expressions of these emotions (see e.g., Ekman & Friesen, 1969; Zuckerman, DePaulo, & Rosenthal, 1981). By contrast, communication scholars, such as ourselves, consider the social nature of emotion and focus on how emotions motivate deception, how emotional expressions are used to create deceptive messages, and how receivers react emotionally to deception (see e.g., Buller & Burgoon, 1994, 1996; Camden, Motley, & Wilson, 1984). Combined, these approaches reveal the multifaceted role of emotion in deception.

We begin this chapter by defining emotion and its related components. We then turn to where and how emotion enters the deception process. We frame our discussion within Interpersonal Deception Theory (IDT), a new theory we are developing that highlights the communication between sender and receiver rather than the intrapsychic processes of the actors (Buller & Burgoon, 1996). We move from considering relevant preinteraction factors that instigate deception and deception-related emotional displays, to considering deceptive and emotional messages during interaction, the iterative interaction process between senders and receivers, and the emotion-relevant consequences of such interactions. From the sender's vantage point, emotions are discussed as motivators of deception, as purposive and inadvertent parts of the deceptive message, and as signals of deceptive intent. Also examined is how successful deception depends on the sender's skill at encoding emotion. On the receiver side of the equation, the chapter describes how suspicion of deception provokes emotions and considers receivers' ability to detect deception-related emotion cues and deceptive messages about emotions. Throughout, we focus primarily on how emotion is communicated, rather than on how it is experienced psychologically.

THE NATURE OF EMOTIONS AND EMOTIONAL EXPRESSION

Emotion is an *innate reaction to a stimulus that motivates the organism to behave adaptively with respect to a stimulus.* It is a primary motivator of human cognition, organizes human consciousness, and precipitates many human actions (Andersen & Guerrero, Chapter 3, this volume; Burgoon, Buller, & Woodall, 1996; Darwin, 1965; Izard, 1971, 1972, 1977; Tomkins, 1962, 1963). To understand how emotion functions in deception requires knowing how psychological components of emotion are linked with overt emotional expression, how affect and arousal are related, and how and for what purpose communicators control emotional displays.

Components of Emotion

Emotion is comprised of three interrelated psychological, physiological, and behavioral processes—the subjective experience of emotion, arousal, and overt behavioral expression. Emotional experiences and arousal are internal events, whereas emotional expressions refer to the external behavioral manifestations that are presumed to signal the internal events.

The internal subjective experience of emotion arises from neurochemical changes in certain brain regions activated by internal and external stimuli that bring with them associated psychological labels such as joy or rage (Buck, 1984, 1991). Emotions are often thought of in these categorical terms—happiness, sadness, anger, disgust, fear, surprise (see, e.g., Ekman, 1971)—but also can be viewed as falling along dimensions of positivity, arousal/activation, and possibly intensity (Apple & Hecht, 1982; Burgoon, Kelly, Newton, & Keeley-Dyreson, 1989; Daly, Lancee, & Polivy, 1983; Plutchik, 1962, 1980; Russell, 1978, 1980, 1983; Russell & Bullock, 1985; Russell & Steiger, 1982; Schlosberg, 1952, 1954; see also Guerrero, Andersen, & Trost, Chapter 1, this volume), among others. Sometimes the terms *affect* and *feelings* are used synonymously with emotion (a practice we will follow), but sometimes they refer to the general positivity or evaluative dimension without arousal. By contrast, the term *emotion* always implicates some change in physiological arousal.

Arousal refers to various forms of autonomic, limbic, and central nervous system activation. These forms of arousal can occur with or without the presence of emotion per se (Burgoon et al., 1996; Leibowitz, 1983). For example, arousal may take the form of exhilaration, concentration, anxiety, or frustration, all internal experiences that are not typically viewed as basic emotions. These forms of arousal and their overt manifestations can also be conceptualized as falling along two dimensions: intensity (the state of physiological, psychic, and behavioral activation) and valence (whether the arousal is experienced as pleasant or unpleasant) (Burgoon et al., 1996).

Applied to deception, this means that communicators perpetrating deceit may experience arousal alone, which can vary from high to low activation and positive to negative, or emotional states such as fear or joy that themselves vary from highly aroused to nonaroused and pleasant to unpleasant. Similarly, targets of deception may experience varying degrees and types of arousal and emotions. The result can be a highly complex behavioral display, as discussed shortly.

Because both true emotional states and more generalized arousal may precede, accompany, or follow deception and instigate behavioral displays, because emotions necessarily entail arousal, and because the distinctions between emotions and arousal often become blurred (for example, between fear and apprehension), we take the broad view here in including arousal displays as part of our analysis of emotion and deception.

INTERPERSONAL DECEPTION THEORY

For the last decade, we have been pursuing an expanded approach to deceptive communication. In contrast to past approaches that often have focused on individual actors' cognitions and independent, static behavior patterns in which senders deliver messages to receivers whom they do not know over mediated channels (in writing, on audiotape, or on film or videotape) (Burgoon, 1989; DePaulo, Stone, & Lassiter, 1985; Krauss, 1981), our approach focuses squarely on the communication process and on the features of interpersonal relationships and interactions that produce conjoint patterns of dynamic action. With this conceptual shift has come a concomitant shift from a noninteractive to an interactive research paradigm.

Our perspective, instantiated in IDT, approaches deception as a relational, dyadic, and dialogic activity. Drawing upon the literature on interpersonal communication, IDT assumes that deception entails the active participation of both sender and receiver and is characterized by mutual influence. Communicative behavior is dynamic, multifunctional, multidimensional, and multimodal. Because deception is goal-directed and deliberate, senders encode strategic behaviors; however, along with purposive actions, senders also exhibit unintentional, often unconscious cues. Interactive behavior is influenced by several cognitive and behavioral factors (e.g., goals, familiarity, expectations, interpretations, social skills, contextual, and relationship features). Among the most proximal are the behaviors of the interaction partner and the perceptual, cognitive, and behavioral tasks that occur concurrently in the interaction. In addition, normative expectations are foundational organizing principles that shape interpretations and evaluations of communicators and messages, with a fundamental judgment being communicator and message credibility. The most influential expectations are the anticipation that interpersonal exchanges are veridical and that social interactants follow the norm of reciprocity. The inherence of expectations suggests that expectations can be violated and that violations have implications for interpretations of communicators and their messages.

IDT is also predicated on common assumptions from the literature on deception. Deception is conceptualized as a form of information management, something that is fundamental to human communication. Deception is also multifunctional. It can be used to achieve all of the same goals for which truthful messages are encoded (e.g., impression management, relational communication, social influence), including the expression of emotion. It is especially likely to heighten surveillance and attention to feedback so that senders can assess their success and make alterations, and receivers can attempt to detect deception, evaluate their detection strategies, and assess sender awareness of suspicion. Deception produces several cognitive and emotional responses, most notably arousal and negative affect (Ekman & Friesen, 1969; Zuckerman, DePaulo et al., 1981). Also, deception requires more cognitive resources and effort than telling the truth and may therefore produce overt indicators of cognitive arousal.

Among the 18 propositions that have been generated in IDT, many are germane to the role of emotion in deception, beginning with preinteraction factors, through initial behavioral displays and the interaction process, to outcomes. We take each of these up in turn. To preview, in the following sections we consider, from the sender's perspective, four roles that emotion and emotional expression can play in deceptive exchanges. Emotions can motivate deception. They can be the content of decep-tive messages. They can be expressed inadvertently as biological signals of arousal. And they can be expressed independently and intentionally as social code units that bolster the credibility of the deceptive message. From the receiver's perspective, we consider how deception can also activate suspicion and accompanying messages, which in turn may serve as feedback to senders. Finally, we consider how the iter-ative process of senders adapting to receiver feedback may ultimately determine re-ceivers' success in accurately interpreting emotional and deceptive messages.

EMOTION AS A MOTIVATOR OF DECEPTION

In IDT, expectations, goals, intentions, motivations, and knowledge possessed by communicators determine the interaction patterns that occur in deceptive ex-changes. Emotions play a large part in senders' goals that precipitate deception. Among senders' goals that may be accomplished through deception are creating pleasant emotions for themselves or targets of deception, avoiding unpleasant emo-tional experiences for themselves or their targets, or creating unpleasant emotion-al experiences for the target (Camden et al., 1984; Lindskold & Walters, 1983; Metts, 1989; Saarni & von Salisch, 1993; Turner et al., 1975). So, for example, communi-cators may deceive to guarantee continued love and affection from others, to escape punishment, disapproval, or embarrassment, or to prevent unpleasant repetitive re-lational episodes. They may deceive to assure targets' happiness, to minimize part-ner worry, hurt, or shame, or to avoid relational tension and trauma. Or they may lie to inflict pain intentionally on another.

Communicators also possess information about the ways in which people react emotionally. We have distinguished between three forms of familiarity or knowl-edge relevant to deception—informational, relational, and behavioral familiarity (Buller & Burgoon, 1996). Within informational familiarity is knowledge of the so-cial circumstances and environmental features that typically evoke particular emo-tions in most communicators. For instance, people generally know that certain vio-lations of social conventions create shame and embarrassment. Senders may rely on this knowledge by enacting shame to cover their deception (e.g., they appear con-trite about forgetting to honor a promise when they actually decided not to fulfill it). When past interactional experience gives someone knowledge of how a partic-ular person typically expresses emotions or how certain emotions are generally ex-pressed by others in particular situations, behavioral familiarity is operating. For ex-ample, police investigators (so-called experts at deception detection) in the O. J. Simpson trial argued that one clue that Mr. Simpson was being dishonest when he denied his culpability was that he failed to show intense negative emotion. The po-lice investigators expected to see a former husband whose wife had been brutally murdered express negative affect. This expectation presumably arose from their pri-or experiences interviewing spouses of murder victims. A more mundane example is when a communicator agrees to do something that a relational partner wants to do, despite not being interested in doing it. In this circumstance, the communicator is often called upon to show sufficiently intense positive affect toward the action to avoid being accused of disinterest and the conflict that is likely to ensue over the feigned agreement. People learn through experience with a relational partner how much positive affect must be displayed to convince the partner that they are willing participants.

Thus, communicators bring to interchanges desires to experience and avoid certain emotions, knowledge of cues that provoke emotion, and familiarity with the emotional processes of their interaction partners. In IDT, these emotion-related preinteraction factors help determine the nature of emotional displays in the subsequent interchange.

EMOTIONAL EXPRESSION DURING DECEPTIVE EPISODES

Enacted deception contains three messages: the central deceptive message (typically verbal), ancillary messages (both verbal and nonverbal) that bolster the believability of the deceptive message and safeguard the sender if the deceit is discovered, and unintentional behaviors that reveal deceptive intent and/or the honest information (mostly nonverbal "leakage" and "deception" cues as defined by Ekman & Friesen, 1969).

Emotions as Deceptive Message Content

Emotions themselves are frequently the central content of deceptive messages (i.e., people dissemble about their emotions; Saarni & von Salisch, 1993). People learn to follow culturally, relationally, and personally prescribed *display rules* that make certain emotions appropriate or inappropriate depending on the context in which the emotion is felt and the individuals to whom the emotion is expressed (K. S. Aune, Aune, & Buller, 1994; K. S. Aune, Buller, & Aune, 1996; Ekman, 1971; Oster & Ekman, 1978; Saarni, 1993). For example, cultural display rules are conventions that aid social exchange (Saarni & von Salisch, 1993; see also Andersen & Guerrero, Chapter 3, this volume). In collectivistic cultures like Japan, display rules proscribe expressing negative emotions to a member of one's in-group but permit their expression to members of another group to maintain harmonious in-group relationships and clear boundaries between in-groups and out-groups. Patterns are reversed in individualistic cultures such as the United States where in-group–out-group distinctions are less important and maintaining harmony with strangers and out-group members is valued. Relationally prescribed displays rules are negotiated by partners to maintain and to reflect relational intimacy. Thus, it is common to find that intimate partners in the United States follow display rules idiosyncratic to their relationship and are more likely to express negative emotions, whereas strangers rely more on culturally prescribed display rules (K. S. Aune et al., 1994, 1996). Finally, personal display rules help individuals cope with emotionally taxing circumstances (Saarni & von Salisch, 1993). A socially insecure individual might adopt a gruff, unpleasant demeanor to keep people at "arm's length" and avoid the possibility of social rejection. The implication of these display rules for deception is that the felt emotion is frequently the content of deceptive messages (i.e., people often fabricate their emotions).

However, these prior circumstances represent emotional deception that is governed by norms or conventions. Saarni and von Salisch (1993) pointed out that sometimes people deceive about emotions to gain positive outcomes or avoid unpleasant outcomes. In these cases, deceptive emotional expressions are not prescribed by social consensus but instead are motivated by individual goals and consequently are less predictable than those instigated by display rules.

People also use emotional expressions as elements in symbolic communication codes. That is, communicators enact certain emotional displays or parts of displays as iconically derived units that carry shared symbolic meaning in the social group. The key here is that emotional expressions are used regularly, purposively, and predictably to send a particular message that may contain meaning that is not emotional. Moreover, receivers recognize these expressions as usually intentional and decode them in similar ways (see Burgoon et al., 1996, and Wiener, Devoe, Rubinow, & Geller, 1972), for characteristics of nonverbal communication codes). These emotional expressions are not considered deceptive (Chovil & Fridlund, 1991). For example, in some cultural groups a smile can be used to communicate agreement with another person's statement or opinion just as nodding and the statement "I agree" do. Smiling can also be used as a greeting in the same way "hi" is. The felt emotion is not the content of the message nor is it spontaneous; rather, emotional expression is used symbolically to convey meaning to the interaction partner. Emotional expressions, then, can be used purposely in deception to communicate symbolically information that has very little to do with the communicators' felt emotions.

Emotions in Strategic and Nonstrategic Displays

Other times, emotions are the by-product of the act of deceiving. Many theories of deception assume that the decision to violate the expectation for truth in human interaction provokes emotion and this emotional reaction is expressed by the communicators during deception. For example, Ekman and Friesen (1969) in their *leakage hypothesis* surmised that senders would reveal their intent to deceive in cues provoked by mainly unpleasant emotions such as guilt and fear of detection. They proposed that cues signaling arousal and affect would be most apparent in communication channels with lower sending capacity (i.e., fewer discriminable behavioral units, less internal and external feedback, slower behavioral changes). In Ekman and Friesen's hierarchy, the body has the lowest sending capacity and consequently emits the most leakage. The facial and verbal channels have the highest sending capacity and the least leakage. The voice, interestingly, is also "leaky," even though it has characteristics of a high-sending capacity channel. Zuckerman, DePaulo et al. (1981) retained affect and arousal as two influences on deceptive performances in their expanded *four-factor theory* of deception. They added attempted control and complex cognitive processing as additional psychological processes that produce cues to deception.

At the heart of these two explanations is the idea that senders unintentionally, and uncontrollably, signal their emotional reactions to deception. These authors approach emotion as a *biological signal system* in which overt expressions are spontaneous, unfettered indices of internal neurochemical emotional experiences (Buck, 1984, 1991; Cacioppo, Bush, & Tassinary, 1992).

However, humans are quite capable of controlling and managing many of their emotional displays. Consequently, emotional expressions also form a *social signal system.* They are used intentionally to communicate information and fulfill a variety of functions in social interaction, beyond simply revealing one's internal emotional reactions (Buck, 1991; Buck, Losow, Murphy, & Costanzo, 1992; Chovil, 1991; Chovil & Fridlund, 1991; Fridlund, Sabini, Hedlund, Schaut, Shenker, & Knauer, 1990; Heise & O'Brien, 1993; Jones, Collins, & Hong, 1991). Individuals purposely exaggerate, minimize, and withhold expressions of felt emotions, and they enact expressions of emotions they do not feel during social interaction (Andersen & Guerrero, Chapter 3, this volume; Ekman & Friesen, 1975; Saarni, 1993; Saarni & von Salisch, 1993). Hence, in IDT, we believe that emotional expressions inadvertently signal information about the emotional state of communicators *or* are used purposively to establish the credibility of communicators and their messages, or *both.* That is, they may reflect both nonstrategic and strategic displays.

Strategic behavior refers to those portions of people's behavioral repertoires that are purposive and goal-directed. Such behaviors reflect large-scale plans but may vary in intentionality and cognitive awareness (in this we adopt perspectives forwarded by Kellermann, 1992, and Stamp & Knapp, 1990). Strategically, deceivers manage information, image, and behavior (Buller & Burgoon, 1994, 1996). Information management includes behaviors that convey uncertainty and vagueness, withhold information, express nonimmediacy, and indicate insincerity to modify or manipulate the completeness, veridicality, and relevance of the message content. Emotions are relevant here when they are the content of the central deception message (i.e., when people lie about emotional reactions). Image management is an effort to maximize communicator credibility by displaying a poised, pleasant, and controlled demeanor. Obviously, emotional displays are instrumental in projecting a pleasant front. Finally, behavior management refers to actions designed to prevent leakage and deception cues. Since several of these cues arise from emotional processes, behavior management requires emotion management.

Strategic Emotional Behavior

In our research program testing IDT, we have identified several cues of emotion that appear to be enacted strategically by partners to bolster the credibility of the deceptive message (see Figure 1 for some examples). Pleasant emotional cues and more emotional expressiveness appear to be enacted to create a positive image (Buller, Burgoon, White, & Ebesu, 1994). In fact, it appears that smiling may be a simple, all-purpose strategy enacted to cover up deceit (Buller, Burgoon, White, & Buslig, 1995). Our data are corroborated by noninteractive studies that have reported more smiles, nods, and pleasant faces by deceivers, particularly if they are not nervous (Ekman, Friesen, & Scherer, 1976; Mehrabian, 1971, 1972). However, subtle differences between false and felt smiles can be recognized. False smiles often (a) do not contain raised cheeks, narrowed eyes, bagged skin below the eyes, and crows-feet wrinkles, (b) are assymetrically encoded on the face with the left side of the expression being stronger than the right side in right-handed people, (c) are encoded too early or too late, (d) have longer apex duration, shorter onset time, and abrupt offset, and (e) contain vestiges of negative emotions when the false smile is masking a negative reaction or dampening a positive one (Ekman & Friesen, 1982). Negative emotions usually persist in upper eyelids, eye brows, and forehead and, if they are strong, in the lower face, too (i.e., lips are pressed, lower lip is pushed up, and lip corners are tightened). Positive emotions are usually dampened by pressing lips, pushing up the lower lip, and tightening the lip corners (Ekman & Friesen, 1982).

Likewise, behavior management has been evident in the reduction in anxiety cues. For example, Buller and R. K. Aune (1987) showed that brief head and face adaptors and brief body adaptors were lower among deceivers than truthtellers. Moreover, brief head and face adaptors were more stable and brief body adaptors and long body adaptors decreased over time. There is also a natural tendency for deceivers to reduce their overall kinesic or gestural animation (Buller & R. K. Aune, 1987; Buller et al., 1994), possibly in an attempt to avoid displaying arousal.

These results, though, stand in opposition to several other studies that show increased *negative* affect and arousal cues. The inconsistent results suggest that attempts at image and behavior management are not entirely successful. Competing unpleasant emotional reactions and detection apprehension caused by violating the conversational expectation for truth sometimes may be too intense to entirely mask them. Or, as IDT holds, image and behavior management are skilled activities, requiring senders to carefully negotiate between appearing naturally expressive, involved, engaged, and relaxed while trying to closely control their presentation. If senders err by overcontrolling the presentation, their strategic image and behavior management backfires.

Nonstrategic Emotional Leakage

The behavioral repertoire also includes behaviors that unintentionally signal arousal, negative and dampened affect, noninvolvement, and performance decrements (Figure 1). Negative affect and arousal have been considered important causes of behavioral patterns in deception since the earliest theoretical formulations by Ekman and Friesen (1969) and Zuckerman et al. (1981). According to these early theories, senders experience guilt when violating the conversational expectation for truth. They also are fearful or apprehensive about being detected, which produces arousal. (Ekman and Friesen also claimed that successful deception can produce positive emotions, but this "duping delight" has not been empirically examined.) Similar emotional reactions may arise in receivers who suspect or confirm deception, such as arousal, resentment, disappointment, and anger (Bok, 1978; Burgoon, Buller, Dillman, & Walther, 1995; McCornack & Levine, 1990). Emotional reactions also may reduce senders' involvement in the conversation and create performance decrements, especially if communicators overcontrol their performance to mask their emotional reactions. The lack of sufficient emotional expressiveness can make a communicator appear removed from the conversation and less competent.

Several studies examining overt manifestations of emotion and arousal confirm that deception is laden with negative emotional expressions in the form of fewer smiles, less pleasant faces, and more negative affect in the voice (Buller & R. K. Aune, 1987; Ekman & Friesen, 1974; Feldman, Devin-Sheehan, & Allen, 1978; Hocking & Leathers, 1980; Kraut, 1978, 1980; Mehrabian, 1972; Zuckerman, De-Paulo et al., 1981; Zuckerman & Driver, 1985). Senders also encode more negative

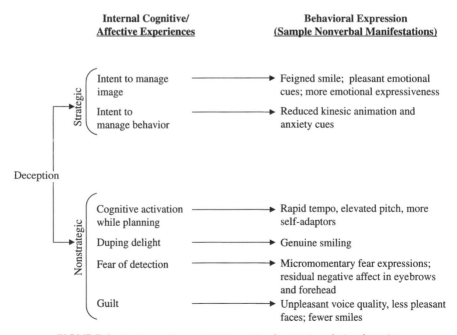

FIGURE 1   Strategic and nonstrategic emotional expressions during deception.

statements when they deceive than when they tell the truth (Knapp et al., 1974; Zuckerman, DePaulo, & Rosenthal, 1981; Zuckerman & Driver, 1985). Our research using interactive designs shows that deceivers encode unpleasant emotions, particularly in their voice tones (Buller & R. K. Aune, 1987; Buller et al., 1994).

Arousal cues also abound in deceptive performances, including more blinking and pupil dilation or instability, more self- and object-adaptors, less gesturing, higher voice pitch, and more vocal nervousness, speech errors, hesitations, and word repetitions (Berrien & Huntington, 1943; Ekman, Friesen, O'Sullivan, & Scherer, 1980; Ekman et al., 1976; Hocking & Leathers, 1980; Knapp et al., 1974; Streeter, Krauss, Geller, Olson, & Apple, 1977; Zuckerman, DePaulo et al., 1981; Zuckerman & Driver, 1985). Some arousal cues, like postural shifting, random leg, foot, and head movement, and gestural activity are less consistently displayed (Buller & R. K. Aune, 1987; Buller, Comstock, R. K. Aune, & Strzyzewski, 1989; Ekman & Friesen, 1974; Ekman et al., 1976; Knapp et al., 1974; Hocking & Leathers, 1980; Mehrabian, 1972).

The inconsistency in some arousal cues may stem from senders' strategic attempts to suppress or mask arousal. Our interactive studies show that senders try to reduce their arousal cues (e.g., Buller & R. K. Aune, 1987). Still, most of the evidence shows that they are not able to avoid or mask all arousal cues completely and that arousal cues are most likely to be displayed in less controllable nonverbal channels such as the face and voice (Buller & R. K. Aune, 1987; DePaulo et al., 1985; DePaulo, Zuckerman, & Rosenthal, 1980; Ekman & Friesen, 1969; Zuckerman & Driver, 1985).

Emotional Encoding Ability and Deception Success

Given that emotions and emotional expressions are implicated in strategic and nonstrategic performance, interactants' competence at expressing, managing, and interpreting emotions will determine the patterns of emotional expression actually witnessed in deceptive exchanges. More skilled deceivers should have a knack for encoding emotions that project a favorable image, convey adequate involvement, and cover unpleasant emotional reactions linked to anxiety and guilt.

Research confirms this, although with a few qualifications. In two studies, Riggio and his colleagues reported that social skills were associated with greater believability. The first study found that skill at emotional encoding was related to honesty judgments only when deceivers were being truthful or discussing an irrelevant point, not when deceiving (Riggio, Tucker, & Throckmorton, 1987). The second showed that more skillful communicators were more fluent and therefore more believable (Riggio, Tucker, & Widaman, 1987).

Our own research has also shown that more socially skilled senders are most successful at misleading receivers (Burgoon, Buller, & Guerrero, 1995; Burgoon, Buller, Guerrero, & Feldman, 1994). Their ability to be expressive verbally *and* to control their verbal expressions is generally important for increasing believability, but skill in encoding emotions nonverbally is especially helpful when senders conceal truthful information (as opposed to deceiving through equivocation or falsification). In order to conceal convincingly, deceivers must be able to remain emotionally expressive while withholding information. Our analysis of deceivers' actual behavior showed, as expected, that skilled deceivers were more successful at deception because they displayed higher involvement, positive affect, and hesitancy—behaviors that together connoted honesty. Thus, senders may need a combination of social skills to carry off deception, which should not be surprising, given the assumption that deception is a more difficult task than telling the truth (Buller & Burgoon, 1994, 1996; Ekman & Friesen, 1969; Zuckerman, DePaulo et al., 1981).

Effect of Interaction Features on Emotional Expression during Deception

In IDT, senders' behavioral repertoire and skills combine to determine initial interaction behavior. However, features within the interaction—including type of deception enacted, interaction behavior, receiver perceptions of suspicion, and deceiver judgments of deception success—become increasingly influential as the conversation iterates back and forth between the conversational partners. In particular, receiver suspicion is a critical interaction feature that determines the course of deceptive conversations. According to IDT, senders monitor receiver reactions to their deceptive (and truthful) statements. When receivers appear to accept deceptive messages, senders feel more successful and make fewer adjustments in their performance. By contrast, when receivers appear to be suspicious of deceptive messages, senders respond by altering their behavior to enhance their credibility. Thus, deceptive conversations are comprised of a series of moves and countermoves by senders and deceivers.

Receiver Suspicion

Emotion plays an important role in this interactive process. Skepticism and suspicion are likely to provoke emotional reactions within receivers, some of which receivers may not want to reveal to senders. For example, receivers who discover deception feel distressed, angry, aroused, resentful, disappointed, and wary of the sender (Bok, 1978; McCornack & Levine, 1990). These emotional reactions are more intense as relational involvement, information importance, and lie importance increase (McCornack & Levine, 1990). Moreover, suspicion prior to the discovery of a lie actually may provoke more intense emotional reactions than if discovery occurs without prior suspicion (McCornack & Levine, 1990). Initial suspicion about the dishonesty of an important piece of information or message may cause individuals to "stew" about the possibility of dishonesty and become upset and aroused by the thought that the partner may be lying. By the time dishonesty is confirmed, this anger and arousal have built to an intense negative level. By contrast, receivers who unexpectedly discover deception do not have this storehouse of anger and arousal; therefore, their emotional reactions to deception discovery may not be as intense.

Receivers may be particularly strategic in managing their behavior and image so as not to tip off senders, at least until they verify their suspicions. However, the negative emotional reactions to the possibility that one is being lied to may be difficult to hide completely. Consequently, receivers' actions during deceptive conversations should contain a mix of strategic behavior and nonstrategic leakage, similar to the actions of senders.

Our research has confirmed that suspicion alters receivers' performance, especially their expression of emotion. In one study, receivers followed up senders' answers with additional probing questions. When suspicious, receivers apparently tried to conceal their doubts by using accepting rather than skeptical probing questions and laughing more. Receivers also talked faster and were less fluent when probing than when not probing (Buller, Strzyzewski, & Comstock, 1991). The accepting probes and laughter appeared to be strategic emotional cues that conceal suspicion, whereas faster speaking tempo and the disfluencies were likely signs of arousal, induced by the unpleasant reactions to the possibility that senders were deceiving. In a second study on receiver suspicion, we found that receivers reacted differently to various levels of suspicion. Specifically, highly suspicious receivers were more pleasant and suppressed self-adaptors, but moderately suspicious receivers were less pleasant and more aroused (Burgoon, Buller, Dillman et al., 1995). High suspicion may have provoked strategic maneuvers on the receiver's part to project a positive image and repress arousal. Moderate suspicion may have provoked only leakage in the form of negative affect and arousal, because receivers were not certain enough about senders' deception to deploy strategies to mask their skepticism.

Senders adjust their demeanor when they perceive receiver suspicion, and this includes altering emotional expressions. Our research (Buller, Strzyzewski, et al., 1991; Burgoon, Buller, Dillman et al., 1995) shows that when they perceive suspicion, senders reduce physical and gestural movement and appear more kinesically composed, perhaps in an intentional move to mask arousal cues. They also try harder to project a favorable image and to cover negative affect by smiling and laughing more. They also were more fluent when suspected, in both studies.

Our research also confirmed the assertion that suspicion disrupts conjoint emotional patterns, as well as each interactant's emotional expressions. Suspicion reduced the natural tendency for senders and receivers to reciprocate or match emotional expressions during interaction. For instance, suspicion reduced (but did not completely eliminate) reciprocity of kinesic relaxation and kinesic pleasantness and produced compensation of kinesic relaxation (Burgoon, Buller, Dillman et al., 1995). The disruption of reciprocity patterns may come about, in part, because suspicion increases kinesic indicators of negative affect and arousal by receivers. In turn, senders who perceive suspicion react by trying to look more pleasant and less aroused. These opposing changes produce less matching or reciprocity of pleasantness and relaxation.

Finally, senders whose deception has been discovered can employ strategies to reduce receivers' negative emotional reactions. However, some strategies may work better than others. Senders who told the truth, discussed the lie and its effect on the relationship, apologized, soothed receivers' hurt feelings, invoked the relationship as a reason for why the receiver should forgive them, and made efforts to strengthen or confirm the relational bonds successfully reduced receivers' negative reactions to discovered deception (R. K. Aune, Metts, & Ebesu, 1991). Giving gifts, flowers, and cards also worked! However, providing excuses, justifying the deception, refusing to explain it, denying its occurrence, and avoiding the issue on which the sender deceived were not effective ways of eliminating the receivers' negative feelings.

To summarize, emotional expression can be the object of deception. Emotional messages also are unintentionally altered by the negative affect and arousal experienced during deception. Communicators can intentionally encode emotional expressions to manage their image and behavior during deception and often adjust these expressions based on feedback from receivers to enhance their credibility. Not surprisingly, senders who are better able to manage emotional expressions are more skillful deceivers. Suspicion and the discovery of deception provoke negative emotional reactions.

INTERPRETING EMOTIONAL EXPRESSION DURING INTERPERSONAL DECEPTION

The course of deceptive conversations depends greatly on receivers' evaluations of truthful and deceptive messages. The process by which receivers evaluate messages and detect deception has been the principle topic of investigation for most of the research on deception. Emotion expression is relevant to deception detection in two ways. First, receivers expect deception to alter emotion expression and base some of their evaluation of sender honesty on the sender's emotional expressions. Second, receivers often must judge the veracity of emotional expressions, particularly when sender emotions are the object of deceit.

Emotional Cues Associated with Deception Judgments

Stereotypes, Attributions, and Accuracy

Receivers hold beliefs or stereotypes about how deceivers act. Among them are several expressions that convey emotion and arousal. Receivers consistently believe that deceivers smile more but that these smiles are unnatural. They also believe that deceivers display more arousal cues: nervous hand gestures, postural shifts, adaptors, blinking, foot and leg movements, trembling and fidgeting, extraneous movements, speech disfluencies and hesitations, faster speech rates, and higher pitch (Hemsley, 1977; Hocking, Miller, & Fontes, 1978; Zuckerman, Koestner, & Driver, 1981). Receivers may realize that senders try to restrict their body movement when deceiving in order to avoid arousal cues, because they predict that deceivers will have tight facial movements, be tense, and be stiffer in their nonverbal display (Hocking et al., 1978).

Receiver stereotypes about how deceivers will behave, however, do not always translate into attributions of deceit. Receivers actually rely on a very small number of cues when attributing deceit to another communicator. They are most likely to attribute deception when senders enact arousal cues—postural shifts, speech disfluencies and hesitation, and higher pitch. By contrast, they actually respond positively (i.e., make attributions of honesty) when senders smile (although Stiff & Miller, 1986, report the opposite relationship) and talk faster, contrary to receiver stereotypes. The other stereotypical cues have been largely unrelated to deception judgments (Miller & Burgoon, 1982; Riggio & Friedman, 1983; Riggio, Tucker et al., 1987; Zuckerman, DePaulo et al., 1981; Zuckerman & Driver, 1985).

Receivers may attribute deception to senders who show arousal cues and do not smile because these behaviors are conspicuous and violate conversational expectations. Fiedler and Walka (1993) recently reported that receivers are more likely to judge a message as deceptive if the sender engages in nonverbal behavior that is conspicuous. A close examination of their description of conspicuous nonverbal behavior reveals that it can also be described as unexpected behavior. Bond et al. (1992) showed that unexpected behavior produced judgments of dishonesty. Consequently, we have included the violation of conversational expectations in IDT as a causal mechanism that explains the interactive process of deceptive conversations. Specifically, communicators hold normative expectations for behavior and they recognize and interpret behavior that violates these expectations. Such violations produce judgments of dishonesty (and of receiver suspicion for that matter). Research on normal (truthful) face-to-face interaction shows that communicators are expected to, and actually do, display moderate arousal, positive affect, and fluent, smooth performances (Brown & Levinson, 1987; Buller & Burgoon, 1996; Burgoon & LePoire, 1993; Burgoon, Stern, & Dillman, 1995; Cappella, 1983; Grice, 1989). Thus, senders who look highly aroused and smile less may conspicuously violate these conversational expectations and lead receivers to evaluate them as less honest.

It should also be apparent from our earlier discussion of the behavioral repertoire of deceivers that receivers hold faulty theories of deceptive performances (Burgoon et al., 1996; Miller & Burgoon, 1982; Riggio & Friedman, 1983). Hocking and Leathers (1980) speculated that these faulty stereotypes exist because senders know these stereotypes and attempt to inhibit or mask stereotypical deception behaviors. Although our own research has not borne out that senders always avoid stereotypical behaviors (see e.g., Buller, Strzyzewski et al., 1991), we too believe that the mistakes can be attributed in part to senders' strategic control of the information in their messages and of their behavior and image during the conversation which makes them appear truthful while deceiving (e.g., senders project a pleasant image when deceiving and reduce their bodily and gestural activity; Buller & Burgoon, 1994, 1996; Burgoon & Buller, 1994).

Another reason why receivers are misled is that they focus on channels that senders are most likely to control well in conversations. In two analyses comparing conversational participants to observers of conversations, we showed that conversational participants are biased toward focusing on visual, particularly facial, cues, as compared to vocal cues. Observers pay more attention to vocal cues (Buller & Hunsaker, 1995; Buller, Strzyzewski, & Hunsaker, 1991). Several studies supporting Ekman and Friesen's leakage hierarchy demonstrated that deceivers control facial cues much better than vocal cues (DePaulo et al., 1985; DePaulo et al., 1980; Ekman & Friesen, 1969, 1974; Zuckerman & Driver, 1985), so receivers who are engaged in conversation may be misled by facial expressions, such as smiling. The bias for visual and facial cues may occur because the multiple tasks required to carry on conversation (e.g., creating and interpreting messages, managing turn taking, adapting messages) take more cognitive effort than the responsibilities of being an observer of conversation. This effort may interfere with receivers' abilities to focus on a large number of behaviors, so, they rely on the common strategy of focusing on the face (Buller & Hunsaker, 1995; Buller, Strzyzewski et al., 1991).

Accuracy at Detecting Deceptive Emotional Expressions

Emotional content can also be the subject of deception. People try to put on a happy face when feeling sad, or they mime disappointment or humility when winning a prize to avoid rubbing it in to the losers. Senders actually may be more successful at deceiving about emotional content than factual information. Emotion is subjective and consequently nearly impossible to objectively verify. To do so, requires asking senders—the source of the potential deception—to confirm their internal feelings. Fiedler and Walka (1993) reported that when receivers feel it is *impossible* to verify a message's information objectively, they tend to err on the side of believing the statement. By contrast, when it is *possible* to objectively verify the information, they are more likely to err on the side of dishonesty. Interestingly, receivers show this bias even if they do not actually try to objectively verify the information. Merely knowing that one can or cannot objectively verify the information is enough to produce the judgment biases. Consistent with this speculation, Hocking, Bauchner, Kaminski, and Miller (1979) reported slightly lower accuracy scores for receivers judging emotional lies than factual lies.

Receivers also may encounter difficulty judging the veracity of emotional expressions if they rely primarily on head and face behavior. Hocking et al. (1979) reported that detection accuracy was lower when receivers judged honesty from head and face cues only compared to from audio or body cues only. This may be particularly problematic when receivers interact with deceivers, because conversational participants focus more on head and face cues than observers when judging honesty (Buller & Hunsaker, 1995; Buller, Strzyzewski et al., 1991).

Consequently, senders may be adept at perpetrating deceptions designed to convey a fake emotion. However, senders' apparent skill may be in part the result of receivers' difficulty at judging the honesty of subjective, emotional content than senders' actual capability to display deceptive emotional expressions. There is some suggestion, though, that senders do find it easier to deceive about an emotion they do not actually feel (i.e., to create a false emotion when they are not experiencing an emotional reaction) rather than to mask an emotion they actually are experiencing. Speaking about false smiles, Ekman and Friesen (1982) speculated that when an emotional reaction is present, expressions of this "true" reaction persist when senders try to mask them with a smile. Such conflicting emotional cues are not likely to be present when the sender is experiencing an emotional reaction but tries to look like they are experiencing a positive one. This implies that successfully deceiving about one's own internal emotional state is a skilled activity and does not entirely depend on receivers' inabilities to detect dishonest emotional content.

Receivers hold expectations for the behavior of deceivers that contain several emotional cues. However, they do not always rely on these stereotypes when attributing deception to others and these behaviors are not always reliable indicators of deception. It appears that violations of expectations for moderate arousal and positive affect in conversation produce attributions of dishonesty. Receivers also may focus on the wrong channels and senders may strategically manipulate behavior to avoid displaying some stereotypical cues. When emotion is the content of the central deception message, it is usually believed.

SUMMARY

Emotion permeates deceptive communication. Emotion is a biological precursor of deception, acts as a biological signal of psychological processes provoked by deception, and functions as a social signal that is used to manage the information in messages and one's behavior and image during deception. People frequently lie because they want to create, avoid, or mask an emotion. Communicators also expect certain emotions in particular communication situations. Thus, violations of conversational expectations for emotion and arousal cues affect receivers' veracity judgments and their behavioral reactions to truthful and deceptive messages. In turn, senders monitor emotional reactions by the receiver and adjust their performances, including making changes in emotion and arousal cues, to bolster their credibility. Smiling and positive emotional expressions may be a common receiver strategy aimed at projecting a favorable image. Also, deceivers seem to reduce their kinesic expressivity in an attempt to reduce the number of arousal cues they emit. However, senders often find it difficult to manage all spontaneous emotional reactions that accompany deception, so some emotion cues are exhibited unintentionally during deceptive conversations, especially in the body and tone of voice. Thus, it should come as no surprise that senders who are skilled at emotion expression enjoy greater deception success and receivers who can competently manage their emotional reactions associated with suspicion and keep deceivers off guard are better deception detectors. To manage emotion cues in deceptive conversations also requires the ability to adjust to the conversational partner and create expected conjoint behavioral patterns, such as reciprocity of arousal and pleasantness. Finally, receivers seem to be less skilled at establishing the validity of messages when the content is emotion rather than factual information. Subjective information, like senders' internal emotional reactions, is hard to verify, so receivers may simply assume it is truthful, unless they have strong reasons to suspect otherwise. All in all, emotion and emotion expression present many challenges to senders and receivers engaged in deceptive conversations. Hence, emotion is an important aspect of any explanation for this common communication phenomenon.

REFERENCES

Apple, W., & Hecht, K. (1982). Speaking emotionally: The relation between verbal and vocal communication of affect. *Journal of Personality and Social Psychology, 42,* 864–875.

Aune, K. S., Aune, R. K., & Buller, D. B. (1994). The experience, expression, and perceived appropriateness of emotions across levels of relationship development. *Journal of Social Psychology, 134,* 141–150.

Aune, K. S., Buller, D. B., & Aune, R. K. (1996). Display rule development in romantic relationships: Emotion management and perceived appropriateness of emotions across relationship stages. *Human Communication Research, 23,* 115–145.

Aune, R. K., Metts, S., & Ebesu, A. S. (1991, November). *Managing the outcomes of discovered deception.* Paper presented at the annual meeting of the Speech Communication Association, Atlanta.

Berrien, F. K., & Huntington, G. H. (1943). An exploratory study of pupillary responses during deception. *Journal of Experimental Psychology, 32,* 443–449.

Bok, S. (1978). *Lying: Moral choice in public and private life.* New York: Random House.

Bond, C. R., Omar, A., Pitre, U., Lashley, B. R., Skaggs, L. M., & Kirk, C. T. (1992). Fishy-looking liars: Deception judgment from expectancy violation. *Journal of Personality and Social Psychology, 63,* 969–977.

Brown, S. C., & Levinson, P. (1987). *Politeness: Some universals in language usage.* Cambridge: Cambridge University Press.

Buck, R. (1984). *The communication of emotion.* New York: Guilford Press.

Buck, R. (1991). Social factors in facial display and communication: A reply to Chovil and others. *Journal of Nonverbal Behavior, 15,* 155–162.

Buck, R., Losow, J. I., Murphy, M. M., & Costanzo, P. (1992). Social facilitation and inhibition of emotional expression and communication. *Journal of Personality and Social Psychology, 63,* 926–968.

Buller, D. B., & Aune, R. K. (1987). Nonverbal cues to deception among intimates, friends, and strangers. *Journal of Nonverbal Behavior, 11,* 269–290.

Buller, D. B., & Burgoon, J. K. (1994). Deception: Strategic and nonstrategic communication. In J. A. Daly & J. M. Wiemann (Eds.), *Strategic interpersonal communication* (pp. 191–223). Hillsdale, NJ: Erlbaum.

Buller, D. B., & Burgoon, J. K. (1996). Interpersonal deception theory. *Communication Theory, 6,* 203–242.

Buller, D. B., Burgoon, J. K., White, C., & Buslig, A. (1995, November). *Interpersonal deception: XIV. The effects of planning.* Paper presented at the annual meeting of the Speech Communication Association, San Antonio.

Buller, D. B., Burgoon, J. K., White, C., & Ebesu, A. S. (1994). Interpersonal deception: VII. Behavioral profiles of falsification, equivocation, and concealment. *Journal of Language and Social Psychology, 13,* 366–396.

Buller, D. B., Comstock, J., Aune, R. K., & Strzyzewski, K. D. (1989). The effect of probing on deceivers and truthtellers. *Journal of Nonverbal Behavior, 13,* 155–169.

Buller, D. B., & Hunsaker, F. (1995). Interpersonal deception: XIII. Suspicion and the truth-bias of conversational participants. In J. Aitken (Ed.), *Intrapersonal communication processes reader* (pp. 239–251). Westland, MI: McNeil.

Buller, D. B., Strzyzewski, K. D., & Comstock, J. (1991). Interpersonal deception: I. Deceivers' reactions to receivers suspicions and probing. *Communication Monographs, 58,* 1–24.

Buller, D. B., Strzyzewski, K. D., & Hunsaker, F. G. (1991). Interpersonal deception: II. The inferiority of conversational participants as deception detectors. *Communication Monographs, 58,* 25–40.

Burgoon, J. K. (1989, May). *Toward a processual view of interpersonal deception.* Paper presented at the annual convention of the International Communication Association, San Francisco.

Burgoon, J. K., & Buller, D. B. (1994). Interpersonal deception: III. Effects of deceit on perceived communication and nonverbal behavior dynamics. *Journal of Nonverbal Behavior, 18,* 155–184.

Burgoon, J. K., Buller, D. B., Dillman, L., & Walther, J. B. (1995). Interpersonal deception: IV. Effects of suspicion on perceived communication and nonverbal behavior dynamics. *Human Communication Research, 22,* 163–196.

Burgoon, J. K., Buller, D. B., & Guerrero, L. K. (1995). Interpersonal deception: IX. Effects of social skill and nonverbal communication on deception success and detection accuracy. *Journal of Language and Social Psychology, 14,* 289–311.

Burgoon, J. K., Buller, D. B., Guerrero, L. K., & Feldman, C. M. (1994). Interpersonal deception: VI. Effects of preinteractional and interactional factors on deceiver and observer perceptions of deception success. *Communication Studies, 3–4,* 263–280.

Burgoon, J. K., Buller, D. B., & Woodall, W. G. (1996). *Nonverbal communication: The unspoken dialogue* (2nd ed.). New York: McGraw-Hill.

Burgoon, J. K., Kelly, D. L., Newton, D. A., & Keeley-Dyreson, M. P. (1989). The nature of arousal and nonverbal indices. *Human Communication Research, 16,* 217–255.

Burgoon, J. K., & Le Poire, B. A. (1993). Effects of communication expectancies, actual communication, and expectancy disconfirmation on evaluations of communicators and their communication behavior. *Human Communication Research, 20,* 75–107.

Burgoon, J. K., Stern, L. A., & Dillman, L. (1995). *Interpersonal adaptation: Dyadic interaction patterns.* New York: Cambridge University Press.

Cacioppo, J. T., Bush, L. K., & Tassinary, L. G. (1992). Microexpressive facial actions as a function of affective stimuli: Replication and extension. *Personality and Social Psychology Bulletin, 18,* 515–526.

Camden, C., Motley, M. T., & Wilson, A. (1984). White lies in interpersonal communication: A taxonomy and preliminary investigation of social motivations. *Western Journal of Speech Communication, 48,* 309–325.

Cappella, J. N. (1983). Conversational involvement: Approaching and avoiding others. In J. M. Wiemann & R. P. Harrison (Eds.), *Nonverbal interaction* (pp. 113–148). Beverly Hills, CA: Sage.

Chovil, N. (1991). Social determinants of facial displays. *Journal of Nonverbal Behavior, 15,* 141–154.

Chovil, N., & Fridlund, A. J. (1991). Why emotionality cannot equal sociality: Reply to Buck. *Journal of Nonverbal Behavior, 15,* 163–168.

Daly, E. M., Lancee, W. J., & Polivy, J. (1983). A conical model for the taxonomy of emotional experience. *Journal of Personality and Social Psychology, 45,* 443–457.

Darwin, C. (1965). *The expression of emotions in man and animals.* Chicago: University of Chicago Press. (Originally published in 1872.)

DePaulo, B. M., Kashy, D. A., Kirkendol, S. E., Wyer, M. M., & Epstein, J. A. (1994). *Lying in everyday life.* Unpublished manuscript.

DePaulo, B. M., Stone, J. I., & Lassiter, G. D. (1985). Deceiving and detecting deceit. In B. R. Schlenker (Ed.), *The self and social life* (pp. 323–370). New York: McGraw Hill.

DePaulo, B. M., Zuckerman, M., & Rosenthal, R. (1980). Detecting deception: Modality effects. In L. Wheeler (Ed.), *Review of personality and social psychology* (pp. 125–162). Beverly Hills, CA: Sage.

Ekman, P. (1971). Universal and cultural differences in facial expressions of emotion. In J. K. Cole (Ed.), *Nebraska symposium on motivation* (pp. 169–222). New York: Academic Press.

Ekman, P., & Friesen, W. V. (1969). Nonverbal leakage and clues to deception. *Psychiatry, 32,* 88–105.

Ekman, P., & Friesen, W. V. (1974). Detecting deception from body or face. *Journal of Personality and Social Psychology, 29,* 288–298.

Ekman, P., & Friesen, W. V. (1975). *Unmasking the face.* Englewood Cliffs, NJ: Prentice-Hall.

Ekman, P., & Friesen, W. V. (1982). Felt, false, and miserable smiles. *Journal of Nonverbal Behavior, 6,* 238–252.

Ekman, P., Friesen, W. V., O'Sullivan, M., & Scherer, K. (1980). Relative importance of face, body and speech in judgments of personality and affect. *Journal of Personality and Social Psychology, 38,* 270–277.

Ekman, P., Friesen, W. V., & Scherer, K. (1976). Body movement and voice pitch in deceptive interaction. *Semiotica, 16,* 23–27.

Feldman, R. S., Devin-Sheehan, L., & Allen, V. L. (1978). Nonverbal cues as indicators of verbal dissembling. *American Educational Research Journal, 15,* 217–231.

Fiedler, K., & Walka, I. (1993). Training lie detectors to use nonverbal cues instead of global heuristics. *Human Communication Research, 20,* 199–223.

Fridlund, A. J., Sabini, J. P., Hedlund, L. E., Schaut, J. A., Shenker, J. I., & Knauer, M. J. (1990). Audience effects on solitary faces during imagery: Displaying to the people in your head. *Journal of Nonverbal Behavior, 14,* 113–137.

Grice, H. P. (1989). *Studies in the way of words.* Cambridge, MA: Harvard University Press.

Heise, D. R., & O'Brien, J. (1993). Emotion expression in groups. In M. Lewis & J. M. Haviland (Eds.), *Handbook of emotions* (pp. 489–497). New York: Guilford Press.

Hemsley, G. D. (1977). *Experimental studies in the behavioral indicants of deception.* Unpublished doctoral dissertation, University of Toronto.

Hocking, J. E., Bauchner, J., Kaminski, E. P., & Miller, G. R. (1979). Detecting deceptive communication from verbal, visual, and paralinguistic cues. *Human Communication Research, 6,* 33–46.

Hocking, J. E., & Leathers, D. G. (1980). Nonverbal indicators of deception: A new theoretical perspective. *Communication Monographs, 47,* 120–131.

Hocking, J. E., Miller, G. R., & Fontes, N. E. (1978). Videotape in the courtroom. *Trial, 14,* 52–55.

Izard, C. E. (1971). *The face of emotion.* Englewood Cliffs, NJ: Prentice-Hall.

Izard, C. E. (1972). *Patterns of emotion: A new analysis of anxiety and depression.* New York: Academic Press.

Izard, C. E. (1977). *Human emotions.* New York: Plenum.

Jones, S. S., Collins, K., & Hong, H. (1991). An audience effect on smile production in 10-month-old infants. *Psychological Science, 2,* 45–49.

Kellermann, K. (1992). Communication: Inherently strategic and primarily automatic. *Communication Monographs, 59,* 288–300.

Knapp, M. L., Hart, R. P., & Dennis, H. S. (1974). An exploration of deception as a communication construct. *Human Communication Research, 1,* 15–29.

Krauss, R. M. (1981). Impression formation, impression management, and nonverbal behaviors. In E. T. Higgins, C. P. Herman, & M. P. Zanna (Eds.), *Social cognition: The Ontario symposium* (Vol. 1, pp. 323–341). Hillsdale, NJ: Erlbaum.

Kraut, R. (1978). Verbal and nonverbal cues in the perception of lying. *Journal of Personality and Social Psychology, 36,* 380–391.

Kraut, R. (1980). Humans as lie detectors: Some second thoughts. *Journal of Communication, 30,* 209–216.

Leibowitz, M. R. (1983). *The chemistry of love.* Boston: Little, Brown.

Lindskold, S., & Walters, P. S. (1983). Categories for acceptability of lies. *Journal of Social Psychology, 120,* 129–136.

McCornack, S. A., & Levine, T. R. (1990). When lies are uncovered: Emotional and relational outcomes of discovered deception. *Communication Monographs, 57,* 119–138.

Mehrabian, A. (1971). Nonverbal betrayal of feeling. *Journal of Experimental Research in Personality, 5,* 64–73.

Mehrabian, A. (1972). *Nonverbal communication.* Chicago: Aldine.

Metts, S. (1989). An exploratory investigation of deception in close relationships. *Journal of Social and Personal Relationships, 6,* 159–179.

Miller, G. R., & Burgoon, J. K. (1982). Factors affecting witness credibility. In N. L. Kerr & R. M. Bray (Eds.), *The psychology of the courtroom* (pp. 169–194). New York: Academic Press.

Oster, H., & Ekman, P. (1978). Facial behavior in child development. In W. A. Collins (Ed.), *Minnesota symposia on child psychology* (pp. 231–276). Hillsdale, NJ: Erlbaum.

Plutchik, R. (1962). *The emotions: Facts, theories, and a new model.* New York: Random House.

Plutchik, R. (1980). *Emotion: A psychoevolutionary synthesis.* New York: Harper & Row.

Riggio, R. E., & Friedman, H. S. (1983). Individual differences and cues to deception. *Journal of Personality and Social Psychology, 45,* 899–915.

Riggio, R. E., Tucker, J., & Throckmorton, D. (1987). Social skills and deception ability. *Personality and Social Psychology Bulletin, 13,* 568–577.

Riggio, R. E., Tucker, J., & Widaman, K. F. (1987). Verbal and nonverbal cues as mediators of deception ability. *Journal of Nonverbal Behavior, 11,* 126–145.

Russell, J. A. (1978). Evidence of convergent validity on the dimensions of affect. *Journal of Personality and Social Psychology, 36,* 1152–1168.

Russell, J. A. (1980). A circumplex model of affect. *Journal of Personality and Social Psychology, 39,* 1161–1178.

Russell, J. A. (1983). Pancultural aspects of the human conceptual organization of emotions. *Journal of Personality and Social Psychology, 45,* 1281–1288.

Russell, J. A., & Bullock, M. (1985). Multidimensional scaling of emotional facial expressions: Similarity from preschoolers to adults. *Journal of Personality and Social Psychology, 48,* 1290–1298.

Russell, J. A., & Steiger, J. H. (1982). The structure in persons' implicit taxonomy of emotions. *Journal of Research in Personality, 16,* 447–469.

Saarni, C. (1993). Socialization of emotion. In M. Lewis & J. M. Haviland (Eds.), *Handbook of emotions* (pp. 435–446). New York: Guilford Press.

Saarni, C., & von Salisch, M. (1993). The socialization of emotional dissembling. In M. Lewis & C. Saarni (Eds.), *Lying and deception in everyday life* (pp. 106–126). New York: Guilford Press.

Schlosberg, H. (1952). The description of facial expressions in terms of two dimensions. *Journal of Experimental Psychology, 44,* 229–237.

Schlosberg, H. (1954). Three dimensions of emotions. *Psychological Review, 61,* 81–88.

Stamp, G. H., & Knapp, M. L. (1990). The construct of intent in interpersonal communication. *Quarterly Journal of Speech, 76,* 282–299.

Stiff, J. B., & Miller, G. R. (1986). "Come to think of it . . .": Interrogative probes, deceptive communication, and deception detection. *Human Communication Research, 12,* 339–358.

Streeter, L. A., Krauss, R. M., Geller, V., Olson, C., & Apple, W. (1977). Pitch changes during attempted deception. *Journal of Personality and Social Psychology, 35,* 345–350.

Tomkins, S. S. (1962). *Affect, imagery, consciousness: Vol. 1. The positive affects.* New York: Springer-Verlag.

Tomkins, S. S. (1963). *Affect, imagery, consciousness: Vol. 2. The negative affects.* New York: Springer-Verlag.

Turner, R. E., Edgley, C., & Olmstead, G. (1975). Information control in conversations: Honesty is not always the best policy. *Kansas Journal of Speech, 11,* 69–89.

Wiener, M., Devoe, S., Rubinow, S., & Geller, J. (1972). Nonverbal behavior and nonverbal communication. *Psychological Review, 79,* 185–214.

Zuckerman, M., DePaulo, B. M., & Rosenthal, R. (1981). Verbal and nonverbal communication of deception. In L. Berkowitz (Ed.), *Advances in experimental social psychology* (Vol. 14, pp. 1–59). New York: Academic Press.

Zuckerman, M., & Driver, R. E. (1985). Telling lies: Verbal and nonverbal correlates of deception. In A. W. Siegman & S. Feldstein (Eds.), *Multichannel integrations of nonverbal behavior* (pp. 129–148). Hillsdale, NJ: Erlbaum.

Zuckerman, M., Koestner, R., & Driver, R. E. (1981). Beliefs about cues associated with deception. *Journal of Nonverbal Behavior, 6,* 105–114.

CHAPTER 15

Affect, Persuasion, and Communication Processes

Peter F. Jorgensen
Western Illinois University
Macomb, Illinois

In the battle between reason and emotion, reason NEVER wins.
—Anonymous

Traditionally, the means for producing successful persuasion attempts were articulated by Aristotle and were conceptualized as consisting of three interrelated dimensions: logos, ethos, and pathos. Logos consists of a logical appeal to argument and sound reasoning, where the persuasive force is gained from the applied forms of deductive and inductive logic. Ethos is the equivalent to the modern construct of source credibility, and depends on the audience's perceptions of the speaker's expertise, dynamism, and trustworthiness to carry its persuasive force. Finally, pathos, the dimension of emotionality, is the third and final dimension whereby speakers can seek to persuade their audiences by playing upon their feelings (Wisse, 1989).

Emotionality is perhaps the least well understood of the persuasive dimensions identified long ago by Aristotle. This may appear odd, especially considering the relative ease by which emotion has been found to sway opinions and reinforce existing attitudes (Lulofs, 1991). Certainly, everyday persuasion attempts rely heavily upon the use of emotional appeals to achieve persuasive ends, and the use of emotion is an important resource in realizing these persuasive goals. Supposedly, logic is a superior dimension that has always been favored as the ideal means by which to secure persuasive ends; yet a perfectly constructed logical appeal may appear dull and cold and, despite flawless logic, may fail to significantly alter the attitude of the receiver simply because the message fails to reach the receiver on an emotional level. Indeed, persuasive messages have been found to be more likely to achieve their persuasive goals if a receiver's emotions are aroused (Arnold, 1985).

When compared to the relatively large amounts of literature produced on message design factors and source characteristics, the lack of literature focusing on emotional appeals—especially from a communication perspective—is lamentable. As noted by Sypher and Sypher (1988), although considerable research has been done in the area of nonverbal communication and emotion, the relationship between verbal communication and affect continues to be ignored. Additional research clearly needs to focus on providing a better conceptual and theoretical understanding of the role emotional appeals play in the persuasion process.

This chapter takes a decidedly receiver-oriented view of emotion and persuasion. That is, this chapter primarily focuses on how emotion affects the processing of persuasive messages in the mind of the receiver rather than looking at sender emotions in the message-generation process. This bias should not be taken to mean that such issues are not of theoretical import; indeed, such concerns as how emotions are best encoded and communicated to others is of paramount importance in gaining a full understanding of the communication process. However, this chapter focuses on how emotional appeals influence the feelings of receivers.

The chapter begins by addressing a number of conceptually "gray areas" surrounding the use and definitions of emotional appeals and affect. Emotion plays a crucial role in the formation of attitudes. Thus, by understanding the role of affect in the structure of attitudes, a better conceptualization of how affect may be effectively used in promoting and resisting persuasion may be realized. The chapter then turns to a review of models of attitude change in order to establish a better understanding of how emotional appeals are processed, and with what kinds of consequences. Next, the chapter reviews findings relevant to the communication of emotion, and finally concludes with some thoughts about how adopting a communication perspective on emotional appeals in persuasive contexts may help researchers gain a better understanding of this facet of persuasion.

DEFINITIONAL ISSUES AND GENERAL BACKGROUND

Emotion and Emotional Appeals

In truth, few claims to knowledge can be made with any degree of empirical consensus with regard to the study of emotional appeals. The study of emotion is in itself ambiguous; some emotions are defined cognitively, others physiologically, and some are defined as being a mixture of both (Bowers, Metts, & Duncanson, 1985). This difficulty in defining exactly what constitutes an emotional appeal creates further uncertainty when attempting to understand this phenomenon in relation to the influence process. Andersen and Guerrero (Chapter 3, this volume) maintain that emotions are inherently communicative. But Clark (1984), for instance, argues that emotions are an internal state with no inherent message component. Additionally, it is difficult to distinguish between an emotional appeal and a logical appeal, as the effect of one is purported to influence the other. For instance, a student may perceive a purely factual statement made by an instructor ("You are not doing as well in this class as you might be!") to be an implicit threat to devote more time to studying. Hence, the identification of emotional appeals is made more difficult by having to distinguish between emotional appeals and the emotional effects of persuasive appeals.

The study of how emotion relates to social influence is guided by competing assumptions and is usually undertaken in one of two ways. First, some researchers argue that emotion is a by-product of the persuasive process, not an integral part of the process itself. Such positions hold that cognitive reactions to the message form the underlying basis for evaluating the potential consequences and effectiveness of the message (e.g., Beck & Frankel, 1981; Sutton & Hallett, 1988, 1989). This is consistent with Clark's (1984) view that emotions are internal states, thus forming in reaction to the persuasive message and not directly attributable to the message itself. However, other researchers (e.g., Hovland, Janis, & Kelley, 1953) argue that emotional appeals such as fear are causally linked to attitude change and are an active part of persuasive messages. This discrepancy may be due in large part to the orientation adopted by the researchers in examining this phenomenon. The view of emotional appeals as epitomized by Clark (1984) appears to adopt a receiver orientation to emotional appeals, where the effectiveness or experience of emotion is of central concern; the view championed by Hovland et al. (1953) appears to adopt a source orientation to communication.

A further complication in conceptualizing affect revolves around the traditional (and possibly false) dichotomy of the dimensions of persuasion. A number of researchers have conceptualized affect as being the diametric opposite of logic; hence, the use of logic is a "rational" means to persuasion, whereas the use of emotion relies upon "irrational" appeals. Indeed, recent research into attitude formation and structure has suggested that attitudes are constructed of both affect-based and cognition-based components, which implies that efforts to change such attitudes cannot be explained well by taking a purely cognition versus affect approach (e.g., Breckler & Wiggins, 1989a; Edwards, 1990).

Clearly, a means of distinguishing between the concepts of emotional appeals, emotion, affect, and emotional effects would be of value in assessing the role of emotional appeals in facilitating or inhibiting persuasion. First, emotional (or affective) appeals are implicitly components of persuasive messages. In this sense, emotional appeals are used as a primary means to achieve persuasive ends. Not all persuasive messages utilize emotional appeals, although it could be argued that all persuasive messages have an emotional dimension to them. From a source-oriented perspective on communication, emotional appeals are intentionally used by a source in order to ultimately produce some change in the values, beliefs, opinions, attitudes, or behaviors of a receiver. Similarly, the receiver orientation would view perceived emotional appeals as elements of the message signifying or conveying intensity, concern, or need. Emotional messages geared to appeal to feelings of power, fear, humor, isolation, self-esteem, guilt, love, anger, pity, and sex are common (Chang & Gruner, 1981; Gruner, 1967; Gruner & Lampton, 1972; Lulofs, 1991; Moog, 1991).

As a message component, an emotional appeal may constitute the entirety of the message, or may be interwoven with other logical and/or heuristic appeals. Emotional appeals may be either verbal or nonverbal in nature; they may consist of photographs, videos, or objects, or they may consist of the more traditional language-based appeals such as verbal fear appeals and/or intense language. Emotional appeals may act as an *emotional contagion,* where a target experiences emotions parallel to those of the source, or as a more diffuse sense of *empathic concern* where the receiver of the message experiences a nonparallel affective response, such as feeling sympathy in response to an emotional plea for help (Andersen & Guerrero, Chapter 3, this volume; Miller, Stiff, & Ellis, 1988; Stiff, Dillard, Somera, Kim, & Sleight, 1988).

It would seem, then, that perhaps the best conceptualization of an emotional appeal is that such strategies are both a conscious and a strategic choice, in that the emotional appeal is intentionally included in the persuasive message with the goal of changing or reinforcing the attitudes of the receiver. This "direct effect" perspective on emotional appeals is echoed by Dillard and Wilson (1993) with what they term *message-induced affect.* Message-induced affect is an emotion (or emotional state) that occurs in direct response to a given message. Hence, if humor is used in an advertisement, and the recipient of the ad chuckles in response and is put into a more lighthearted frame of mind, message-induced affect has occurred. In contrast, Dillard and Wilson offer the term *message-irrelevant affect* to describe the emotional state existing prior to the reception of a particular persuasive message. The affective state is not irrelevant in and of itself, and in fact bears important consequences for the processing of the message; however, the impact of emotion on the processing of the persuasive message is due to a preexisting state rather than a feature of the message itself. For instance, a student who is feeling frustration and stress due to the approaching deadline for a term paper may react with anger to a roommate's request to help keep the apartment clean. In this case, it was not the persuasive message itself (i.e., to help keep the apartment clean) that prompted the anger, but rather that the reaction was due to the procrastinating student's mood state prior to the reception of the message. The feelings of stress and frustration experienced by the student would be an example of message-irrelevant affect.

In addition to the ambiguity associated with the conceptualization of emotional appeals, there is also a discrepancy in the ways that emotional appeals have been operationalized. This discrepancy may be due in part to the two distinct ways of conceptualizing and defining variations in emotional appeals, and is exemplified in the controversy surrounding the measurement of fear appeals in particular. As noted by O'Keefe (1990), there are two fundamentally different ways of conceiving the variations in fear appeal messages. The first method is to define the strength of the fear appeal by the properties of the message itself. In essence, a high fear appeal message "is one containing explicit, vivid depictions of negative consequences, while a 'low fear appeal message' is a tamer, toned down version" (O'Keefe, 1990, p. 165). Because this approach to fear appeals adopts a message orientation, it is important to note that the classification of high versus low fear appeals may or may not yield qualitatively different levels of arousal in the minds of the listeners. It is probable that the same problematic implications hold true for other emotional appeals as well, for the common problem remains the same: the reliable manipulation of emotional arousal.

The second approach to defining fear appeals involves the measurement of the levels of fear provoked in the audience. This second method differentiates the strength of the messages on the basis of the comparative levels of fear experienced by the audience, with a high fear appeal generating greater levels of anxiety than a low fear appeal (O'Keefe, 1990). Hence, it has proven difficult to reliably manipulate fear appeals using a message orientation (Boster & Mongeau, 1984). It would seem, then, that a carefully composed message using emotional appeals may be designed to arouse a particular emotion and yet fail to do so in any meaningful manner. The desired effects of the manipulation of the message must be confirmed in a post hoc fashion, yielding an approach that is both theoretically tentative and conceptually inelegant. Simply put, the study of emotional appeals begins with a method of trial and error, with no reliable control over what kinds of messages are actually being produced. This concern is not limited to fear appeals alone, but is a problem shared by research designs that rely on textual or verbal manipulations of emotion that have been divorced from the accompanying nonverbal messages. In essence, by focusing on one element (i.e., verbal) of the emotional appeal at the exclusion of the other dimensions of the message (i.e., nonverbal), researchers are no longer studying valid communication processes, but rather disassociated parts of the whole.

Emotions, on the other hand, may be viewed as the end product of an emotional appeal. Generally, they are conceived to be the results of evaluative judgment processes usually stimulated by increases in arousal (e.g., Buck, 1984), although whether emotions are best conceptualized as interrelated dimensions (Daly, Lancee, & Polivy, 1983; Russell, 1980; Watson & Tellegen, 1985), prototypes existing in loosely bounded regions within a multidimensional space (e.g., Shaver, Schwartz, Kirson, & O'Connor, 1987; Shaver, Wu, & Schwartz, 1992), or as qualitatively different states (e.g., Ortony, Clore, & Collins, 1988) is still a matter of some debate (see Guerrero, Andersen, & Trost, Chapter 1, this volume). Emotions are generally defined to be fairly unique and specific responses to eliciting stimuli (Isen, 1984; Morris, 1989), whereas emotional states, moods, and affective states may be thought of as being more global in nature (Isen, 1984). However, one constant through these varied conceptualizations of emotion and related constructs (e.g., affect, mood) is the central role of valence in defining the emotional experience (Dillard & Wilson, 1993).

From a receiver perspective, then, emotional appeals precede the experience and onset of emotion. What the emotional appeal engenders might be considered the emotional effects of the appeal. Whereas an emotional appeal is a quality of a message, an emotion (or mood, or affective state) is a feeling generated in the receiver as a result of emotional appeals. But how is it that the induction of desired affective states in the minds of our listeners can facilitate persuasion? The answer lies in understanding the nature and construction of attitudes.

Affect and the Structure of Attitudes

The vast majority of social influence research is concerned with engineering changes in attitudes, if not ultimately behaviors. An attitude is generally defined as a "learned predisposition to respond in a consistently favorable or unfavorable manner with respect to a given object" (Fishbein & Ajzen, 1975, p. 6). The definition of an attitude as consisting of positive and negative feelings about an attitude object is central to many definitions of attitudes (e.g., Petty & Cacioppo, 1981) and underscores the importance of emotion in the construction of attitudes (Breckler, 1993).

Attitudes have traditionally been defined as consisting of three interrelated components: affect, cognition, and behavior (e.g., Breckler, 1984; McGuire, 1989; Rosenberg & Hovland, 1960). The cognitive component represents the thoughts, beliefs, and judgments about an attitude object, whereas the affective component represents the feelings associated with the object (Breckler & Berman, 1991). The behavioral component of an attitude consists of predispositions toward action with regard to the attitude object. This tripartite model of attitude has been well supported by the available research (Breckler, 1984, 1993). Some studies, rather than focusing on all three components simultaneously, have focused instead on the relationships that cognition and affect share in relation to behavior (Breckler & Wiggins, 1989b; Millar & Tesser, 1986, 1989) as well as investigating the unique roles that affect and cognition play in the social influence process (Breckler & Wiggins, 1991; Millar & Millar, 1990).

Recent research in social psychology has attempted to identify the relationship between cognition and affect. One school of thought argues that the two processes occur conjointly; as Zajonc (1980) notes, "In nearly all cases . . . , feeling is not free from thought, nor is thought free from feelings" (p. 154). However, some scholars hold that the two do not always have to occur together; in fact, affect may be experienced independently from cognitive thought (Moreland & Zajonc, 1977; Zajonc, 1980; Zajonc & Markus, 1982, 1984). Indeed, Swann, Griffin, Predmore, and Gaines (1987) argued for the conceptualization of affect and cognition as "relatively independent systems with distinct capabilities and agendas" (p. 887). From this view, affective experience does not necessarily depend on cognition (Breckler & Wiggins, 1989a; Buck, 1985).

Even when cognition and affect are experienced together, affect often dominates cognition (Edell & Burke, 1987; Holbrook & Batra, 1987). Katz and Stotland (1959) argued that inconsistency between the affective and cognitive components of an attitude is most readily resolved by changes in cognition rather than affect. This finding suggests not only that affect is at least as capable as cognition in generating attitudinal change, but that affect may hold a position of primacy over cognition under certain conditions. Edwards (1990) found that predominantly affect-based attitudes exhibited greater change under affective means of persuasion than under cognitive means of persuasion, and that predominantly cognition-based attitudes exhibited equal amounts of change under both forms of persuasive appeals. Regardless of the ordering of these processes, it is clear that emotional experiences can, and do, significantly influence the persuasion process (e.g., Isen & Daubman, 1984; Isen & Means, 1983; Sypher & Sypher, 1988).

EMOTION AND PERSUASION: EXPLANATORY FRAMEWORKS

Models of "Message-Relevant" Effects

Elaboration Likelihood Model

The elaboration likelihood model (ELM) proposed by Petty and Cacioppo (1986a, 1986b) stipulates that certain variables can affect the amount and direction of attitude change in one of three ways: either by serving as a persuasive argument; serving as a peripheral cue; and/or affecting the extent or direction of issue and argument elaboration. The key hypothesis of this model is that argument elaboration mediates the route to persuasion, whether it be by the central route (conscious processing of logical argument quality) or by the peripheral route (where cues other than logic and argument quality are processed). The model predicts that as argument scrutiny and motivation to process arguments go down, peripheral cues (such as emotion and emotional appeals) become more important determinants of persuasion (Petty & Cacioppo, 1986b).

From a general standpoint, the ELM suggests that emotional appeals act as a peripheral cue—meaning that emotional appeals are most effectively processed when the receiver's motivation or ability to process the message is low. Given that message cues are either processed centrally or peripherally—not both—emotional appeals appear only to operate as peripheral cues according to the ELM. Although the goal of attitude change may be realized through the use of the peripheral route, research suggests that such changes are more fleeting and less enduring than changes brought about by central route processing (e.g., Petty, Wegener, Fabrigar, Priester, & Cacioppo, 1993; Petty & Cacioppo, 1986b). Furthermore, affective responses may serve alternately as information, a prompt for further issue- or message-centered elaboration, or as simple peripheral cues (Cacioppo & Petty, 1989; Petty, Cacioppo, & Kasmer, 1988; Petty, Cacioppo, Sedikides, & Strathman, 1988; Petty, Gleicher, & Baker, 1991). Hence, emotional appeals would appear to be most effective in situations where the receiver is unable or unwilling to process the cognitive aspects of the message, and only attitude change in the short term is initially desired.

Despite the important contributions of distinguishing between central cues and peripheral cues and posing two distinct paths of message processing, the ELM is not without its critics. One criticism is that although the ELM is best considered a model of process, it does not appear to be able to address the separate phases of influence that are inherent in complex persuasive messages. For instance, the creation of emotion via the use of emotional appeals followed by a strong issue-oriented argument may be an effective means for changing attitudes, but the ELM would typically focus on the argument structure rather than the effectiveness of the emotional appeals or the effect of the generated emotional state. The interactions between sequential, embedded persuasive strategies and/or multiple message strategies are too complex to be adequately explained by the ELM; indeed, there appears to be no research that attempts to use the ELM to explain the effectiveness of complex, sequential persuasive messages.

The debate over the ELM now goes back over a decade, and is fueled by the difficulty in testing the model empirically due to an insufficient specification of the theory. A number of researchers have focused on definitional, methodological, conceptual, and theoretical problems with the ELM in an effort to test the model (Allen & Reynolds, 1993; Hamilton, Hunter, & Boster, 1993; Mongeau & Stiff, 1993; Stiff, 1986; Stiff & Boster, 1987). As of yet, there is no clear victor in the ongoing debates, and the ELM continues to generate research, criticism, and alternative theories in the ongoing effort to better understand emotion and persuasion processes.

Heuristic–Systematic Processing Model

Another popular model that explains the processing of persuasive messages is the heuristic–systematic processing model (HSM). According to the model forwarded by Chaiken and her colleagues (Chaiken, 1980; Chaiken, Liberman, & Eagly, 1989), receivers of a message will reach some kind of attitude judgment about a message in one of two ways: via systematic processing that relies on a content-oriented, critical examination of the message; or via heuristic processing that occurs when the receiver develops judgments about the message based on cues external to the message itself, such as perceived source credibility, use of emotional appeals, or attractiveness (Chaiken, 1980; Chaiken et al., 1989). Furthermore, Chaiken (1980, 1987) argued for a validity-centered assessment approach as a means of explaining the motivation to process messages. This approach stipulates that a person's primary goal is to hold accurate attitudes, with attitudinal accuracy defined as a measure of consistency with relevant facts (Eagly & Chaiken, 1993).

Although similar in many respects to the ELM, the HSM model differs from the ELM in a number of ways. The primary difference is that messages may be processed simultaneously using both heuristic and systematic processes, whereas message processing as described by the ELM is limited to either central or peripheral processing at any given time. Eagly and Chaiken (1993) referred to this activity as "concurrent processing" (p. 328). Hence, according to the HSM, the multidimensional nature of messages suggests that emotional appeals may be primarily processed heuristically, although parts of the message may be processed systematically (see Pallak, Murroni, & Koch, 1983).

The HSM predicts that heuristic cues (such as mood) may bias the systematic processing of an argument (Chaiken et al., 1989; Eagly & Chaiken, 1993). For instance, an argument that is made to an audience that is currently in a good mood may be viewed more positively than a message made to an audience in a bad mood. However, this bias hypothesis is presumed only to apply in situations in which the persuasive message is ambiguous (Chaiken et al., 1989; Chaiken & Maheswaran, as cited in Eagly & Chaiken, 1993), although other lines of research have found mood to have a substantial effect on argument processing.

Cognitive Appraisal Theories

Cognitive appraisal theories consist of a group of related theories with common assumptions about the experience of emotion. Recent research by Dillard and his colleagues (Dillard & Kinney, 1994; Dillard, Kinney & Cruz, 1996) support the usefulness of cognitive appraisal theories as a means to better understand communication processes, especially where emotions and persuasion are concerned. Appraisal theorists stipulate that emotions arise as a result of a simple causal sequence (e.g., Fridja, 1986; Ortony, Clore, & Collins, 1988; Roseman, Spindel, & Jose, 1990; Scherer, 1984). Primarily, the sequence begins with the individual's perception of some event in her or his environment. The individual will then make some kind of judgment about the event with respect to the potential harmfulness or benefit that the event represents to the individual. To the extent that a given event is seen to be threatening or beneficial, an emotion arises in response to the appraisal process.

The significance of this approach for communication scholars lies in the description of the causal sequence. According to cognitive appraisal theories, emotional persuasive messages cannot have a direct effect on attitude change. Any change experienced by the individual is due to the appraisal of the message and the resulting judgment about the potential harms or benefits confronting the receiver, not to the message itself. The message is merely a stimulus to prompt a reaction, and the experience of emotion is a result of the appraisal process. Hence, to speak of an *emotional message* is incompatible with cognitive appraisal theories; rather, a given message may engender emotions as a result of the judgments about the message, or the message may fail to generate any emotion at all.

MODELS OF "MESSAGE-IRRELEVANT" EFFECTS

The previous frameworks discussed in this chapter so far have generally adopted a "direct effect," or message-relevant, approach to studying the impact of emotion on the persuasion process. In the direct-effects models, emotional appeals themselves are processed or judged and result in either increased or decreased persuasiveness, depending on the particular model, context, and circumstances. Another related body of research, but one that proceeds from a message-irrelevant approach to studying affect, seeks to explore the impact of the receiver's mood on the effectiveness of persuasive attempts as well as the associations between emotional states and perceptions of products.

The Effect of Mood on the Persuasion Process

Typically, mood research has been somewhat removed from the more specific study of emotional appeals. Mood is usually studied as a precursor to the processing of persuasive information, and is assumed to be in existence prior to the reception of the persuasive message. Yet the commonality that ties these two conceptual areas together lies in the fact that the use of emotional appeals may create, interrupt, diffuse, or intensify a specific mood-state, which in turn affects the influence process. Indeed, an extensive amount of research conducted on the effect of mood on the persuasion process has yielded significant results (Bless, Bohner, Schwarz, & Strack, 1990; Hsu & Price, 1993; Isen, 1984; Schwarz, 1990). From this view, emotional appeals are an antecedent in creating mood rather than having a direct impact on persuasion itself.

Schwartz, Bless, and Bohner (1991) posited five ways in which a recipient's mood might influence the persuasion process within this framework. Each of these possibilities uses a slightly different set of assumptions regarding the implications of attitude change and the point whereby affective states impact the persuasive process. A test of these competing frameworks found that two of these theories seem to be supported by the available research, whereas the others have failed to garner sufficient supporting evidence as to their veracity (Bless, Bohner, Schwarz, & Strack, 1990). Hence, the two most viable theoretical perspectives will be reviewed.

The first of these theoretical perspectives, *the motivational hypothesis,* posits that recipients' affective states may influence their motivation to elaborate on the content of the message (Schwarz et al., 1991). In other words, depending on whether people are in good or bad moods, they may be more or less predisposed to process the message consciously and actively (systematically) or rely upon peripheral cues (heuristically) to make judgments about the message. Moreover, if a person is in a bad mood, they are more likely to perceive the world as a threatening place and therefore would be more likely to carefully process messages in an attempt to avoid making costly judgments about the state of the world. As summarized by Frijda (1988), "emotions exist for the sake of signaling states of the world that have to be responded to, or that no longer need response and action" (p. 354). Good moods (or positive affective states), on the other hand, would be indicative of a relatively safe environment in which the need to process information critically is reduced (Schwarz et al., 1991). Furthermore, research conducted by Isen (1984) suggests that individuals experiencing positive affective states are less likely to elaborate on the messages in an effort to maintain the positive mood.

Given these explanations of positive and negative affective states, the motivational hypothesis predicts an interaction effect for affective state and argument quality. Specifically, when strong arguments are used, recipients of the argument should be more persuaded when they are in a bad mood rather than a good mood, as they should be elaborating on the strengths of the message. Conversely, recipients of weak arguments should be more persuaded when they are experiencing a positive affective state, as the weaknesses of the argument should not be apparent due to the failure to elaborate on the message (Schwarz et al., 1991).

The second hypothesis forwarded by Schwarz and his colleagues is labeled the *cognitive capacity hypothesis.* This hypothesis is in some ways an extension of the motivational hypothesis, in that it too maintains that mood will impact the recipient's ability to elaborate on messages. However, the cognitive capacity hypothesis asserts that the presence of positive or negative affective states will interfere with the information–processing capacity of the individual, although it is unclear as to whether good moods or bad moods are more likely to cause this interference in the cognitive processing.

On the one hand, previous research has suggested that positive moods increase the accessibility of positive material, which in turn leads to a predisposition to focus on positively related thoughts (Isen, Means, Patrick, & Nowicki, 1982). Hence, as the individual becomes preoccupied with reexperiencing these positive thoughts, the positive affective state interferes with the processing of the message. However, negative events that result in negative affective states "may be more likely to stimulate a search for explanations" (Schwarz et al., 1991, p. 167). In this way, the search for explanations may inhibit the elaboration of the message, thus interfering with the cognitive processing.

In general, the cognitive capacity hypothesis predicts an interaction effect between argument quality and affective state, such that individuals whose cognitive capacity is reduced by their current affective state should be more persuaded by weak arguments rather than by strong arguments. This hypothesis is differentiated from the motivational hypothesis in that cognitive capacity limitations may be overridden by time factors, as well as other factors that impact the capacity to process the information. Although the two are very similar in terms of outcomes, the explanatory framework of each differs slightly. In the case of the motivational hypothesis, effective persuasion occurs with regard to the recipient's view of the world as threatening or nonthreatening at the time, thus increasing or decreasing the need for critical examination of the message. In contrast, the cognitive capacity hypothesis maintains that it is not so much perceptions of danger in the world that determine the level of cognitive processing given to an incoming message, but rather the capacity of the individual to process the information while remaining free from distractions generated by her or his current affective state.

As previously noted, there is some empirical support for both of these hypotheses, but the findings are mixed. Schwarz et al. (1991) concluded that individuals in positive affective states were able to process the content of the message if explicitly instructed to do so. However, this finding in itself does not go far in establishing the primacy of one explanation over the other, due in large part to the difficulty of measuring cognitive capacity independently from motivational attributions. Similarly, Petty, Schumann, Richman, and Strathman (1993) found that positive mood had a direct impact on attitude change, but only under low-elaboration conditions.

Classical Conditioning Approaches

A review of the effects of emotional appeals in the communication process would be notably incomplete without the consideration of the vast array of research conducted on emotional appeals in advertising. Advertising, from a classical conditioning perspective, does not so much seek to persuade its audiences with a coherent argument, but rather relies on classical conditioning approaches that capitalize on the learned association between stimulated emotions and specific products.

Classical conditioning approaches generally seek to foster affective associations between an emotional stimulus and an attitude object. Commercial advertising is replete with examples of consumer products being paired with pleasant scenery, attractive members of the opposite sex, sports heroes, nostalgia, restful or exciting music, and socially desirable behaviors. Research tends to support the effectiveness of pairing products with positive emotional stimuli (e.g., Allen & Madden, 1985; Batra & Ray, 1986; Cohen & Areni, 1991; Gardner, 1985; Gorn, 1982). Lang and Friestad (1993) reported research showing that the association between television messages and emotions tended to grow in strength over time, and that when television messages changed in valence, so did the emotions experienced by the viewers. Stuart, Shimp, and Engle (1987) found that the desired associative state between the positive emotion and the advertisement was achieved rather quickly, with a substantial amount of conditioning having occurred after only a single trial. Edell and Burke (1987) found that positive and negative feelings were predictive not only of the advertisement's success, but that feelings contribute uniquely to attitude formation toward the advertisement itself, beliefs about the brand's attributes, and attitude toward the brand.

THE COMMUNICATION OF EMOTIONS

Understanding that emotional appeals play an important and legitimate role in the process of persuasion is an important first step for communication researchers. Yet a question even more central to the discipline of communication is the manner in which emotional messages are constructed and communicated. One of the foundations of communication research as a viable discipline is the focus on message design and structure. Arguably, an adequate explanatory framework on emotional communication should allow communication researchers to reliably and consistently design verbal and nonverbal emotional appeals that accomplish specific goals. Clearly, our knowledge of emotional appeals has not yet evolved to the point that we can design and manipulate emotional appeals with a great degree of confidence in a given context. By far, the greatest amount of literature has been generated in the attempt to understand fear appeals, and even there our ability to consistently generate fear appeals without relying on post hoc analyses of engendering "fearfulness" is severely limited (Boster & Mongeau, 1984; O'Keefe, 1990; see also Witte, Chapter 16, this volume).

Previous language-based research on emotional appeals has been plagued by inconsistent or unreliable instantiations of textual or verbal messages. Surprisingly, little research has examined the structural differences in conveying emotions through a verbal- or text-based format versus a "full-channel" approach that incorporates both verbal and nonverbal messages (or, alternatively, visual and verbal elements). Messages that lack the nonverbal or visual channels must compensate by trying to arouse the receiver through text or verbal channels alone. Donohew (1981, 1982) found that narrative forms of writing were more effective at increasing reader arousal, whereas the traditional style of reporting used by newspapers tended to decrease arousal. The experienced affect seemed to vary in the same general direction as arousal. Similarly, Kopfman, Smith, Yun, and Hodges (1994) found that narrative persuasive messages tended to produce greater results in terms of affective reactions, whereas logical arguments produced greater results in cognitive reactions to the message.

Although considerable research has looked at the role of language in communicating emotion, there is no doubt that emotion is most effectively conveyed through nonverbal channels (see Andersen, in press). It is difficult, if not impossible, to gain a thorough understanding of the relationship between emotion and persuasion by looking at only language-based behavior. Adopting a functional approach to nonverbal communication may lead to a better understanding of the influential role of emotion in persuasion processes. The functional approach stipulates that nonverbal communication is often strategic, goal-driven, and employed in the pursuit of achieving communication objectives, and is governed by three assumptions (Burgoon, Buller, & Woodall, 1996; Leathers, 1992). First, nonverbal communication utilizes multiple channels simultaneously to effectively convey meaning and serve a diverse array of communication functions (such as persuasion, intimacy, or impression management). Second, individual channels may contribute to the overall understanding of a message, but the "message" itself is a combination of multiple channels acting in concert. Third, a given nonverbal behavior may take on different meanings depending on the context of the behavior (e.g., eye contact can signal intimacy in one situation and dominance in another), and hence a single behavior is capable of accomplishing a number of different functions. The primary argument for adopting the functional approach is that it offers a more realistic view of communication processes than would a perspective that adopts a solely language-based perspective.

Available research strongly suggests that increases in nonverbal immediacy behaviors significantly enhance persuasive effectiveness (J. Andersen, 1979; P. Andersen, in press; 1985; Burgoon, Coker, & Coker, 1986; Burgoon, Manusov, Mineo, & Hale, 1985; Segrin, 1993). Emotion is primarily communicated through facial expressions and tone of voice (Ekman, 1989; Fridlund, Ekman, & Oster, 1986). Nonverbal behaviors such as posture, kinesic behavior, and gestures also aid in the expression of emotion, but their importance in the display of emotion is less well established than is the role of facial expression (Dillard & Wilson, 1993). Lang and Friestad (1993) provided additional support to the working premise that emotion is best expressed in a visual (i.e., nonverbal) mode by examining differences in verbal and visual memory for positively and negatively valenced television advertisements. Lang and Friestad's findings generally support the primacy of visual rather than verbal elements in messages, suggesting a reliance on the visual medium for assessing emotion.

DIRECTIONS FOR FUTURE RESEARCH

The continued study of emotional appeals is paramount if the persuasion process is to be fully understood. As it would happen, adopting a communication perspective in the investigation of emotional appeals would begin to address many of the deficient areas of knowledge associated with the uses of emotion and lead to a better understanding of the uses and consequences of emotional appeals. Toward these ends, a general program of communication research will be outlined in an effort to address perceived shortcomings in the emotional appeal literature.

The first and most notable lack of knowledge lies in the relatively small amount of descriptive work associated with emotional appeals. What, for instance, qualifies as an emotional appeal? Past research has conceptualized emotional appeals as one-sentence statements, multiple statements, appeals to mood, and appeals to preexisting emotions (as opposed to generating a desired emotion). Furthermore, in some cases emotional appeals are generated solely by utilizing the verbal medium, whereas other forms of emotional appeals are generated through primarily nonverbal channels and situational characteristics (Bowers et al., 1985). Some emotional appeals may be more effective if portrayed through a visual medium; others may be most effective when restricted to a verbal format, and yet others may work most effectively when combining verbal and nonverbal messages.

Furthermore, with the realization that messages are complex, understanding how multiple, sequential emotional appeals work to achieve desired ends, or how different emotional appeals work in conjunction with each other, is an area ripe for research. As with sequential compliance-gaining strategies (see Dillard, Hunter, & Burgoon, 1984) or deception detection strategies (Buller & Burgoon, Chapter 14, this volume), it might prove interesting to explore the effects of sequential uses of various emotional appeals. Conceptually, messages could vary between consisting of single emotional "notes" to emotional "compositions." It is conceivable that single-sentence instantiations of emotional appeals may not be effective due to their brevity, whereas a message overly reliant on emotional appeals may be regarded as being fallacious. Additionally, comparing the effectiveness of different types of emotional appeals can lend needed insight into how certain classes of emotions and emotional appeals work similarly or differently (see Brooker, 1981). Future research may wish to explore the overall effect of using multidimensional emotional messages in facilitating attitude change, as well as the effects of certain kinds of combinations of emotional appeals.

Perhaps the single greatest contribution that communication scholars can make to the study of emotion in persuasive attempts involves determining what types of emotional messages are most effective in establishing desired moods and/or effectively conveying specific emotions. Such strategies would no doubt be imminently practical to our understanding of how mood can be created verbally, nonverbally, and situationally. With few exceptions (see Vangelisti, Daly, & Rudnick, 1991), most communication research focuses on the persuasive effects of emotional appeals rather than trying to understand how emotional appeals are constructed. Knowing that emotion can influence the persuasion process does not necessarily contribute to our understanding of *how* a desirable affective state in a receiver is best achieved communicatively, nor does it inform us as to the specific functions served by emotional appeals in a persuasive message.

Finally, current research efforts aimed at gaining an understanding of emotional appeals focus predominantly on the persuasive effects of emotional appeals (i.e., physiological, psychological) while ignoring the functions of emotional appeals. Such approaches, which assume a single function of emotional appeals (i.e., to facilitate persuasion), may be overly simplistic. Jorgensen (1994) argued that emotional appeals may serve up to five different functions for the potential persuader: (a) to serve as evidence for an argument; (b) to heighten a source's credibility; (c) to call attention to the message, as well as to hold attention; (d) to act as an alternative to logic; and finally, (e) to create a mood state. Additionally, Jorgensen suggested that there are two "metafunctions" that emotional appeals may serve in conjunction with the other functions: to heighten involvement with the issue, and to facilitate attitude formation, change, or reinforcement. If, in fact, emotional appeals are capable of performing a number of different functions in addition to facilitating persuasion, then it behooves researchers to analyze multiple functions simultaneously in an effort to better grasp how emotional appeals may be most effectively used in communication situations.

CONCLUSION

The power of emotion to influence behavior and change attitudes is well known, but the processes whereby this occurs and the limitations inherent in these processes are not as clearly understood. Emotional appeals and the responses to such emotional messages can be intense or subtle, predictable or chaotic. Gaining a better understanding of the role of emotion in persuasion processes serves a valuable purpose in educating our future leaders and future followers about the manipulative power of emotional appeals. Emotional appeals, used ethically, have the potential to realize great change for the betterment of society; however, such knowledge can also be abused for selfish gain. Decisions made on the basis of emotion rather than logic are seldom the preferred alternatives, and yet such occurrences are all too common. It falls to scholars and students of communication to gain an understanding of such processes in order to recognize and resist undue or unethical influence attempts which capitalize on the use of emotional appeals.

REFERENCES

Allen, C. T., & Madden, T. J. (1985). A closer look at classical conditioning. *Journal of Consumer Research, 12,* 301–315.

Allen, M., & Reynolds, R. (1993). The elaboration likelihood model and the sleeper effect: An assessment of attitude change over time. *Communication Theory, 3,* 73–82.

Andersen, J. F. (1979). Teacher immediacy as a predictor of teaching effectiveness. In D. Nimmo (Ed.), *Communication yearbook 3* (pp. 543–559). New Brunswick, NJ: Transaction Books.

Andersen, P. A. (in press). *Beside language: Nonverbal communication in interpersonal interaction.* Mountain View, CA: Mayfield.

Andersen, P. A. (1985). Nonverbal immediacy in interpersonal communication. In A. W. Seigman & S. Feldstein (Eds.), *Multichannel integrations of nonverbal behavior* (pp. 1–29). Hillsdale, NJ: Erlbaum.

Arnold, V. D. (1985). The importance of pathos in persuasive appeals. *The Bulletin,* 26–27.

Batra, R., & Ray, M. L. (1986). Affective responses mediating acceptance of advertising. *Journal of Consumer Research, 13,* 234–249.

Beck, K. H., & Frankel, A. (1981). A conceptualization of threat communications and protective health behavior. *Social Psychology Quarterly, 44,* 204–217.

Bless, H., Bohner, G., Schwarz, N., & Strack, F. (1990). Mood and persuasion: A cognitive response analysis. *Personality and Social Psychology Bulletin, 16,* 331–345.

Boster, F. J., & Mongeau, P. (1984). Fear arousing persuasive messages. In R. N. Bostrom (Ed.), *Communication yearbook 8* (pp. 330–375). Beverly Hills, CA: Sage.

Bowers, J. W., Metts, S. M., & Duncanson, W. T. (1985). Emotion and interpersonal communication. In M. L. Knapp & G. R. Miller (Eds.), *Handbook of interpersonal communication* (pp. 500–550). Beverly Hills, CA: Sage.

Breckler, S. J. (1984). Empirical validation of affect, behavior, and cognition as distinct components of attitude. *Journal of Personality and Social Psychology, 47,* 1191–1205.

Breckler, S. J. (1993). Emotion and attitude change. In M. Lewis & J. M. Haviland (Eds.), *Handbook of emotions* (pp. 461–473). New York: Guilford.

Breckler, S. J., & Berman, J. S. (1991). Affective responses to attitude objects: Measurement and validation. *Journal of Social Behavior and Personality, 6,* 529–544.

Breckler, S. J., & Wiggins, E. C. (1989a). On defining attitudes and attitude theory: Once more with feeling. In A. R. Pratkanis, S. J. Breckler, & A. G. Greenwald (Eds.), *Attitude structure and function* (pp. 407–427). Hillsdale, NJ: Erlbaum.

Breckler, S. J., & Wiggins, E. C. (1989b). Affect versus evaluation in the structure of attitudes. *Journal of Experimental Social Psychology, 25,* 253–271.

Breckler, S. J., & Wiggins, E. C. (1991). Cognitive responses in persuasion: Affective and evaluative determinants. *Journal of Experimental Social Psychology, 27,* 180–200.

Brooker, G. W. (1981). A comparison of the persuasive effects of mild humor and mild fear appeals. *Journal of Advertising, 10,* 29–40.

Buck, R. (1984). *The communication of emotion.* New York: Guilford.

Buck, R. (1985). Prime theory: An integrated view of motivation and emotion. *Psychological Review, 92,* 389–413.

Burgoon, J. K., Buller, D. B., & Woodall, W. G. (1996). *Nonverbal communication: The unspoken dialogue* (2nd ed.). New York: Harper Collins.

Burgoon, J. K., Coker, D. A., & Coker, R. A. (1986). Communicative effects of gaze behavior: A test of two contrasting explanations. *Human Communication Research, 12,* 495–524.

Burgoon, J. K., Manusov, V., Mineo, P., & Hale, J. L. (1985). Effects of gaze on hiring, credibility, attraction, and relational message interpretation. *Journal of Nonverbal Behavior, 9,* 133–146.

Cacioppo, J. T., & Petty, R. E. (1989). The elaboration likelihood model: The role of affect and affect-laden information processing in persuasion. In P. Cafferata & A. Tybout (Eds.), *Cognitive and affective responses to advertising* (pp. 69–89). Lexington, MA: Lexington Books.

Chaiken, S. (1980). Heuristic versus systematic information processing and the use of source versus message cues in persuasion. *Journal of Personality and Social Psychology, 39,* 752–766.

Chaiken, S. (1987). The heuristic model of persuasion. In M. P. Zanna, J. M. Olson, & C. P. Herman (Eds.), *Social influence: The Ontario Symposium* (Vol. 5, pp. 3–39). Hillsdale, NJ: Erlbaum.

Chaiken, S., Liberman, A., & Eagly, A. H. (1989). Heuristic and systematic information processing within and beyond the persuasion context. In J. S. Uleman & J. A. Bargh (Eds.), *Unintended thought: Limits of awareness, intention, and control* (pp. 212–252). New York: Guilford.

Chang, M. J., & Gruner, C. R. (1981). Audience reaction to self-disparaging humor. *Southern Speech Communication Journal, 46,* 419–426.

Clark, R. A. (1984). *Persuasive messages.* New York: Harper & Row.

Cohen, J. B., & Areni, C. S. (1991). Affect and consumer behavior. In T. S. Robertson & H. H. Kassarjian (Eds.), *Handbook of consumer behavior* (pp. 188–240). New York: Prentice Hall.

Daly, E. M., Lancee, W. J., & Polivy, J. (1983). A conical model for the taxonomy of emotional experience. *Journal of Personality and Social Psychology, 45,* 443–457.

Dillard, J. P., Hunter, J. E., & Burgoon, M. (1984). Sequential-request persuasive strategies: Meta-analysis of foot-in-the-door and door-in-the-face. *Human Communication Research, 10,* 461–488.

Dillard, J. P., & Kinney, T. A. (1994). Experiential and physiological responses to interpersonal influence. *Human Communication Research, 20,* 502–528.

Dillard, J. P., Kinney, T. A., & Cruz, M. G. (1996). Influence, appraisals, and emotions in close relationships. *Communication Monographs, 63,* 105–130.

Dillard, J. P., & Wilson, B. J. (1993). Communication and affect: Thoughts, feelings, and issues for the future. *Communication Research, 20,* 637–646.

Donohew, L. (1981). Arousal and affective responses to writing styles. *Journal of Applied Communication Research, 9,* 109–119.

Donohew, L. (1982). Newswriting styles: What arouses the readers? *Newspaper Research Journal, 3,* 3–6.

Eagly, A. H., & Chaiken, S. (1993). *The psychology of attitudes.* New York: Harcourt Brace Jovanovich.

Edell, J. A., & Burke, M. C. (1987). The power of feelings in understanding advertising effects. *Journal of Consumer Research, 14,* 421–433.

Edwards, K. (1990). The interplay of affect and cognition in attitude formation and change. *Journal of Personality and Social Psychology, 59,* 202–216.

Ekman, P. (1989). The argument and evidence about universals in facial expressions of emotion. In H. Wagner & A. Manstead (Eds.), *Handbook of social psychophysiology* (pp. 143–163). New York: Wiley.

Fishbein, M., & Ajzen, I. (1975). *Belief, attitude, intention, and behavior: An introduction to theory and research.* Reading, MA: Addison-Wesley.

Fridlund, A. J., Ekman, P., & Oster, H. (1986). Facial expressions of emotion: Review of literature 1970–1983. In A. Siegman & S. Feldstein (Eds.), *Nonverbal behavior and communication* (pp. 143–223). Hillsdale, NJ: Erlbaum.

Frijda, N. H. (1986). *The emotions.* Cambridge, UK: Cambridge University Press.

Frijda, N. H. (1988). The laws of emotion. *American Psychologist, 43,* 349–358.

Gardner, M. P. (1985). Mood states and consumer behavior. *Journal of Consumer Research, 12,* 281–300.

Gorn, G. J. (1982). The effects of music in advertising on choice behavior: A classical conditioning approach. *Journal of Marketing, 46,* 94–101.

Gruner, C. R. (1967). Effect of humor on speaker ethos and audience information gain. *Journal of Communication, 17,* 228–233.

Gruner, C. R., & Lampton, W. E. (1972). Effects of including humorous material in a persuasive sermon. *Southern Speech Communication Journal, 38,* 188–196.

Hamilton, M. A., Hunter, J. E., & Boster, F. J. (1993). The elaboration likelihood model as a theory of attitude formation: A mathematical analysis. *Communication Theory, 3,* 50–65.

Holbrook, M. B., & Batra, R. (1987). Assessing the role of emotions as mediators of consumer responses to advertising. *Journal of Consumer Research, 14,* 404–420.

Hovland, C. I., Janis, I. L., & Kelley, H. H. (1953). *Communication and persuasion.* New Haven, CT: Yale University Press.

Hsu, M., & Price, V. (1993). Political expertise and affect: Effects on news processing. *Communication Research, 20,* 671–695.

Isen, A. M. (1984). Toward understanding the role of affect in cognition. In R. S. Wyer, Jr., & T. K. Srull (Eds.), *Handbook of social cognition* (vol. 3, pp. 179–236). Hillsdale, NJ: Erlbaum.

Isen, A. M., & Daubman, K. A. (1984). The influence of affect on categorization. *Journal of Personality and Social Psychology, 47,* 1206–1217.

Isen, A. M., & Means, B. (1983). Positive affect as a variable in decision making. *Social Cognition, 2,* 18–31.

Isen, A. M., Means, B., Patrick, R., & Nowicki, G. (1982). Some factors influencing decision making strategy and risk-taking. In M. S. Clark & S. T. Fiske (Eds.), *Affect and cognition.* Hillsdale, NJ: Erlbaum.

Jorgensen, P. F. (1994, November). *Capturing the mind and the heart: An exploration of the functions and roles of emotional appeals in the persuasion process.* Paper presented at the Speech Communication Association annual convention, New Orleans, LA.

Katz, D., & Stotland, E. (1959). A preliminary statement to a theory of attitude structure and change. In S. Koch (Ed.), *Psychology: A study of science* (Vol. 3, pp. 423–475). New York: McGraw-Hill.

Kopfman, J. E., Smith, S. W., Yun, J. K., & Hodges, A. (1994, November). *Affective and cognitive reactions to narrative versus logical argument organ donation strategies.* Paper presented at the Speech Communication Association annual convention, New Orleans, LA.

Lang, A., & Friestad, M. (1993). Emotion, hemispheric specialization, and visual and verbal memory for television messages. *Communication Research, 20,* 647–670.

Leathers, D. G. (1992). *Successful nonverbal communication: Principles and applications* (2nd ed.). New York: Macmillan.

Lulofs, R. S. (1991). *Persuasion: Contexts, people, and messages.* Scottsdale, AZ: Gorsuch-Scarisbrick.

McGuire, W. J. (1989). The structure of individual attitudes and attitude systems. In A. R. Pratkanis, S. J. Breckler, & A. G. Greenwald (Eds.), *Attitude structure and function* (pp. 37–69). Hillsdale, NJ: Erlbaum.

Millar, M. G., & Millar, K. U. (1990). Attitude change as a function of attitude type and argument type. *Journal of Personality and Social Psychology, 59,* 217–228.

Millar, M. G., & Tesser, A. (1986). Effects of affective and cognitive focus on the attitude–behavior relation. *Journal of Personality and Social Psychology, 51,* 270–276.

Millar, M. G., & Tesser, A. (1989). The effects of affective-cognitive consistency and thought on the attitude-behavior relation. *Journal of Experimental Social Psychology, 25,* 189–202.

Miller, K. I., Stiff, J. B., & Ellis, B. H. (1988). Communication and empathy as precursors to burnout among human service workers. *Communication Monographs, 55,* 250–265.

Mongeau, P. A., & Stiff, J. B. (1993). Specifying the causal relationships in the elaboration likelihood model. *Communication theory, 3,* 65–73.

Moog, C. (1991). *Are they selling her lips? Advertising and identity.* New York: Morrow & Co.

Moreland, R. L., & Zajonc, R. B. (1977). Is stimulus recognition a necessary condition for the occurrence of exposure effects? *Journal of Personality and Social Psychology, 35,* 191–199.

Morris, W. N. (1989). *Mood: The frame of mind.* New York: Springer Verlag.

O'Keefe, D. J. (1990). *Persuasion.* Newbury Park, CA: Sage.

Ortony, A., Clore, G. L., & Collins, A. (1988). *The cognitive structure of emotions.* Cambridge: Cambridge University Press.

Pallak, S. R., Murroni, E., & Koch, J. (1983). Communicator attractiveness and expertise, emotional versus rational appeals, and persuasion: A heuristic versus systematic processing interpretation. *Social Cognition, 2,* 122–141.

Petty, R. E., & Cacioppo, J. T. (1981). *Attitudes and persuasion: Classic and contemporary approaches.* Dubuque, IA: William C. Brown.

Petty, R. E., & Cacioppo, J. T. (1986a). *Communication and persuasion: Central and peripheral routes to attitude change.* New York: Springer-Verlag.

Petty, R. E., & Cacioppo, J. T. (1986b). The elaboration likelihood model of persuasion. In L. Berkowitz (Ed.), *Advances in experimental social psychology* (Vol. 19, pp. 123–205). San Diego, CA: Academic Press.

Petty, R. E., Cacioppo, J. T., & Kasmer, J. A. (1988). The role of affect in the Elaboration Likelihood Model of persuasion. In L. Donohew, H. E. Sypher, & E. T. Higgins (Eds.), *Communication, social cognition, and affect* (pp. 117–146). Hillsdale, NJ: Erlbaum.

Petty, R. E., Cacioppo, J. T., Sedikides, C., & Strathman, A. J. (1988). Affect and persuasion: A contemporary perspective. *American Behavior Scientist, 31,* 355–371.

Petty, R. E., Gleicher, F., & Baker, S. M. (1991). Multiple roles for affect in persuasion. In J. P. Forgas (Ed.), *Emotion and social judgments* (pp. 181–200). Oxford: Pergamon Press.

Petty, R. E., Schumann, D. W., Richman, S. A., & Strathman, A. J. (1993). Positive mood and persuasion: Different roles for affect under high- and low-elaboration conditions. *Journal of Personality and Social Psychology, 64,* 5–20.

Petty, R. E., Wegener, D. T., Fabrigar, L. R., Priester, J. R., & Cacioppo, J. T. (1993) Conceptual and methodological issues in the Elaboration Likelihood Model of persuasion: A reply to the Michigan State Critics. *Communication Theory, 3,* 336–362.

Roseman, I. J., Spindel, M. S., & Jose, P. E. (1990). Appraisals of emotion-eliciting events: Testing a theory of discrete emotions. *Journal of Personality and Social Psychology, 59,* 899–915.

Rosenberg, M. J., & Hovland, C. I. (1960). Cognitive, affective, and behavioral components of attitude. In M. J. Rosenberg, C. I. Hovlan, W. J. McGuire, R. P. Abelson, & J. W. Brehm (Eds.), *Attitude organization and change: An analysis of consistency among attitude components* (pp. 1–14). New Haven, CT: Yale University Press.

Russell, J. A. (1980). A circumplex model of affect. *Journal of Personality and Social Psychology, 39,* 1161–1178.

Scherer, K. R. (1984). Emotion as a multi-component process: A model and some cross-cultural data. In P. Shaver (Ed.), *Review of personality and social psychology* (Vol. 5, pp. 37–63). Beverly Hills, CA: Sage.

Schwarz, N. (1990). Feelings as information: Informational and motivational functions of affective states. In E. T. Higgins & R. M. Sorrentino (Eds.), *Handbook of motivation and cognition: Foundations of social behavior* (Vol. 2, pp. 527–561). New York: Guilford.

Schwarz, N., Bless, H., & Bohner, G. (1991). Mood and persuasion: Affective states influence the processing of persuasive communications. In M. P. Zanna (Ed.), *Advances in experimental social psychology* (Vol. 24, pp. 161–199). San Diego: Academic Press.

Segrin, C. (1993). The effects of nonverbal behavior on outcomes of compliance gaining attempts. *Communication Studies, 44,* 169–187.

Shaver, P., Schwartz, J., Kirson, D., & O'Connor, C. (1987). Emotion knowledge: Further explorations of a prototype approach. *Journal of Personality and Social Psychology, 52,* 1061–1086.

Shaver, P. R., Wu, S., & Schwartz, J. C. (1992). Cross-cultural similarities and differences in emotion and its representation: A prototype approach. In M. S. Clark (Ed.), *Emotion: Review of personality and social psychology* (Vol. 13, pp. 175–212). Thousand Oaks, CA: Sage.

Stiff, J. B. (1986). Cognitive processing of persuasive message cues: A meta-analytic review of the effects of supporting information on attitudes. *Communication Monographs, 53,* 75–89.

Stiff, J. B., & Boster, F. J. (1987). Cognitive processing: Additional thoughts and a reply to Petty, Kasmer, Haugtvedt, and Cacioppo. *Communication Monographs, 54,* 250–256.

Stiff, J. B., Dillard, J. P., Somera, L., Kim, H., & Sleight, C. (1988). Empathy, communication, and prosocial behavior. *Communication Monographs, 55,* 198–213.

Stuart, E. W., Shimp. T. A., & Engle, R. W. (1987). Classical conditioning of consumer attitudes: Four experiments in an advertising context. *Journal of Consumer Research, 14,* 334–349.

Sutton, S. R., & Hallett, R. (1988). Understanding the effects of fear arousing communications: The role of cognitive factors and the amount of fear aroused. *Journal of Behavioral Medicine, 11,* 353–360.

Sutton, S. R., & Hallett, R. (1989). The contribution of fear and cognitive factors in mediating the effects of fear-arousing communications. *Social Behavior, 4,* 83–98.

Swann, Jr., W. B., Griffon, Jr., J. J., Predmore, S. C., & Gaines, B. (1987). The cognitive-affective crossfire: When self-consistency confronts self-enhancement. *Journal of Personality and Social Psychology, 52,* 881–889.

Sypher, H. E., & Sypher, B. D. (1988). Affect and message generation. In L. Donohew, H. E. Sypher, & E. T. Higgins (Eds.), *Communication, social cognition, and affect* (pp. 81–92). Hillsdale, NJ: Erlbaum.

Vangelisti, A. L., Daly, J. A., & Rudnick, J. R. (1991). Making people feel guilty in conversations: Techniques and correlates. *Human Communication Research, 18,* 3–39.

Watson, D., & Tellegen, A. (1985). Toward a consensual structure of mood. *Psychological Bulletin, 98,* 219–235.

Wisse, J. (1989). *Ethos and pathos: From Aristotle to Cicero.* Amsterdam, The Netherlands: Hakkert.

Zajonc, R. B. (1980). Feeling and thinking: Preferences need no inferences. *American Psychologist, 35,* 151–175.

Zajonc, R. B., & Markus, H. (1982). Affective and cognitive factors in preferences. *Journal of Consumer Research, 9,* 123–131.

Zajonc, R. B., & Markus, H. (1984). Affect and cognition: The hard interface. In C. E. Izard, J. Kagan, & R. B. Zajonc (Eds.), *Emotions, cognitions, and behavior* (pp. 73–102). Cambridge, UK: Cambridge University Press.

CHAPTER 16

Fear as Motivator, Fear as Inhibitor: Using the Extended Parallel Process Model to Explain Fear Appeal Successes and Failures

Kim Witte

Michigan State University
East Lansing, Michigan

Is It PMS—Or Ovarian Cancer? The Symptoms You Shouldn't Ignore
—*Redbook,* March 1995

Beat the New Killer Viruses: A Rogues Gallery of Deadly Diseases
—*FIRST Magazine,* September 1995

When Hospitals Are Hazardous to Your Health: How to Protect Yourself
—*Family Circle,* October 1995

Terrifying diseases and physical destruction lurk around every corner if we are to believe the headlines in today's media. Fear-arousing communication messages such as these are some of the most common and popular persuasive strategies in use today. Public health specialists, politicians, physicians, teachers, parents, police officers, and many others often try to gain compliance by scaring individuals into a certain course of action or behavior. However, do fear-arousing messages work? This question has been the focus of considerable research during the last 40 years.

The purpose of this chapter is to discuss the most recent theoretical and empirical research on the topic of fear appeals. First, a brief discussion on the nature of fear will be given. Then, the historical origins of fear appeals will be discussed. Third, the most recent fear appeal model, the extended parallel process model (EPPM), will be presented, followed by a section examining the research testing this model. Finally, modifications to the EPPM and future research directions will be suggested.

THE NATURE OF FEAR

Fear is one of the basic human emotions (Ortony & Turner, 1990). Definitionally, it is a negatively valenced emotion, accompanied by a high level of arousal, and is elicited by a threat that is perceived to be significant and personally relevant (Easterling & Leventhal, 1989; Lang, 1984; Ortony & Turner, 1990). The elicitation of fear may occur following an appraisal of a threatening situation or stimulus with or without an individual's conscious intention or awareness (Bargh, 1989; Lazarus, 1991a, 1991b). Fear may be expressed physiologically (as arousal), through language behavior (verbal self-reports), or through overt acts (facial expressions) (Lang, 1984). Dillard (1994) noted that fear is expressed by "raised eyebrows that are pulled together, by raised upper eyelid and tightened lower eyelid, and by horizontal stretching of the lips" (p. 309). He also noted that fear is physiologically manifested by elevated heart rates and respirations, tension in the muscles, trembling, cortical arousal, decreased skin temperature, and lower blood flow to the extremities (Dillard, 1994).

In fear appeal studies, fear is typically measured by having participants rate the degree to which they feel frightened, tense, nervous, anxious, uncomfortable, and nauseated. These items usually yield scale reliabilities in excess of .80. These items also have been shown to correlate positively with physiological measures of fear arousal (Mewborn & Rogers, 1979). For example, Mewborn and Rogers (1979) found that a high-fear film produced accelerated heart rates, greater skin conductance, and higher self-ratings of fear (as measured by the items listed above) when compared to a low fear film.[1] Rogers (1983) concluded self-ratings may be preferable to physiological measures in measuring fear because self-ratings represent the overall emotional state, whereas physiological arousal fluctuates substantially.

HISTORICAL ORIGINS OF FEAR APPEALS

Fear was first viewed as an inhibitor to message acceptance in the now classic Janis and Feshbach (1953) study because a negative relationship was found between

---

[1]Mewborn and Rogers (1979) were interested in the *pattern* of findings for physiological arousal and self-rated fear (e.g., the high-fear condition yields a consistent pattern that is different from the low-fear condition). The actual correlation between self-ratings and physiological arousal was modest.

strength of the fear appeal (low, medium, high) and conformity with recommendations to brush one's teeth carefully. Since that time, virtually every relationship possible has been proposed as an explanation for fear appeal effects. For example, Janis (1967) and McGuire (1968) suggested a curvilinear relationship between strength of fear appeals and attitude change. Alternatively, Rogers (1975, 1983) proposed a positive linear relationship between strength of fear appeals and behaviors. Which approach is the most accurate? A close examination of the literature suggests each of these approaches explains part of the story. Before explaining my perspective, however, I will briefly review the three major theoretical perspectives that have dominated much of the fear appeal literature—the fear-as-acquired drive model, the parallel process model, and protection motivation theory (PMT).[2]

Fear-as-Acquired Drive Model

The fear-as-acquired drive model, developed by Janis and others in the Yale Communication Research program (Hovland, Janis, & Kelly, 1953; Janis, 1967), adopted a learning theory perspective and argued that fear-arousing messages produce a negative drive state that motivates people to take action. They claimed that anything reducing the negative drive would become the preferred, habitual response to a threat because it was rewarding to eliminate the negative drive. Hovland, Janis, and Kelly (1953) proposed that "reassuring recommendations" included in a fear appeal would act as drive-reduction mechanisms if they were attended to and adopted. However, they also noted that if the reassuring recommendations did not reduce the negative drive state, then other strategies such as defensive avoidance or perceived manipulation would be tried (e.g., people would avoid thinking about the threat or they would lash out in anger because of a perception of manipulation). If defensive avoidance or perceived manipulation reduced the drive before the reassuring recommendations did, then they would become the preferred and habitual response to the threat.

Janis concluded that moderate fear appeals worked best. He maintained that some fear was needed to motivate people to reach a negative drive state (which was needed to motivate action). However, he argued that the fear had to be able to be reduced (drive reduction). He stated that only when fear and the corresponding drive were reduced did attitudes or behaviors change. Janis (1967) claimed that if fear could not be reduced by a message's recommendations, then maladaptive outcomes would occur (e.g., defensive avoidance or perceived manipulative intent). Thus, he predicted a curvilinear or inverted-U shaped relation between fear and message acceptance.

---

[2]Other fear appeal models exist but these three have been the main focus of most fear appeal research. See Witte (1992b), for a complete review of all theoretical perspectives.

Parallel Process Model

Leventhal's work in the 1960s ran counter to Janis's work, showing that strong fear appeals appeared to work best. He found no evidence for a curvilinear relationship. He proposed the parallel process model (Leventhal, Safer, & Panagis, 1983; originally called the parallel response model, Leventhal, 1970, 1971), which stated that there were two distinct reactions to fear appeals. First, Leventhal (1970) posited that there was a primarily cognitive process, called the danger control process, as a result of which people thought about the threat and ways to avert it (e.g., they tried to control the danger). Second, he said there was a primarily emotional process, called the fear control process, during which people reacted to their fear and engaged in coping strategies to control their fear. Although the model was not explicitly tested nor well delineated, it offered a useful way to view people's responses to fear appeals.

Protection Motivation Theory

Rogers (1975) picked up where Leventhal left off and focused on the danger control side of the parallel process model. He was interested in people's cognitive reactions to fear appeals and how these cognitions influenced attitude or behavior changes. In his protection motivation theory (PMT), Rogers (1975, 1983) was the first to isolate the components of fear appeals. Originally, PMT stated that a fear appeal needed to contain arguments about: (a) the probability of occurrence for a threat, (b) the magnitude of noxiousness of a threat, and (c) effectiveness of the recommended response in averting the threat. Later, a fourth message component was added to PMT: (d) information about one's ability to perform a recommended response (Rogers, 1983). Rogers (1975, 1983) said that these four message components produced corresponding cognitive mediating processes resulting in perceptions of (a) vulnerability (e.g., "Am I at-risk for experiencing the threat?"), (b) severity (e.g., "Is the threat severe?"), (c) response efficacy (e.g., "Is the recommended response effective in averting the threat?"), and (d) self-efficacy (e.g., "Am I able to perform the recommended response to avert the threat?"). He maintained that if all of these cognitive mediators were at high levels, then the maximum amount of protection motivation (an intervening variable that acts as a drive) would be elicited, resulting in the maximum amount of attitude or behavior change.

The revised version of PMT, introduced in 1983, is substantially more complicated. It differentiates between maladaptive threat appraisal processes and adaptive coping appraisal processes. In the revised PMT, Rogers argued that in the threat appraisal process, perceptions of severity and vulnerability are subtracted from any rewards of conducting an unhealthy behavior. Thus, if rewards are greater than perceptions of severity and vulnerability, then maladaptive responses to the threat ensue, resulting in a lack of self-protective behavior. Alternatively, in the coping appraisal process, Rogers (1983; Maddux & Rogers, 1983) said that perceptions of the costs of performing a recommended behavior are subtracted from perceptions of response and self-efficacy. Thus, when people hold strong response and self-efficacy beliefs, and perceive low costs to performing a recommended action, they engage in adaptive, self-protective responses to a health threat.

The predictions from the revised PMT model are difficult to discern. Rogers (1983) stated,

> The motivation to protect oneself from danger is a positive linear function of four beliefs: (1) the threat is severe, (2) one is personally vulnerable to the threat, (3) one has the ability to perform the coping response, and (4) the coping response is effective in averting the threat. Furthermore, the motivation is a negative linear function of (1) the reinforcements associated with the maladaptive response, and (2) the response costs. (p. 170)

This prediction is clear and straightforward. However, Rogers also stated, "The additive model holds within each appraisal process. When combining components between the two processes, second-order interaction effects occur" (p. 170). This latter statement appears inconsistent with the former quotation. Specifically, each of the variables listed in the first quotation are said to add together to form either positive or negative linear functions. Yet, Rogers (1983) stated that the threat appraisal variables (i.e., rewards, severity, vulnerability) and the coping appraisal variables (i.e., response costs, response efficacy, self-efficacy) combine multiplicatively. It is unclear how the six variables listed actually work together based on the model illustrations and text.

Overall, the original PMT does a good job predicting the conditions under which fear appeals work. Specifically, when perceptions of severity, susceptibility, response efficacy, and self-efficacy are high, then people appear to accept message recommendations and make attitude, intention, and behavior changes. However, both versions of PMT fail to account for when and why people reject message recommendations. Additionally, in both versions, fear plays only a tangential role (i.e., it was said to relate to perceptions of severity only).

Summary

Each of these theories explains some aspect of reactions to fear appeals (for critique of each model see Witte, 1992b). Leventhal's work (1970) offered insights into the mechanisms underlying reactions to fear appeals. Janis's (1967) theorizing provided explanations as to why fear appeals sometimes failed. Rogers' (1975, 1983) research demonstrated the conditions under which fear appeals worked. However, each theory by itself failed to explain in an integrated, thorough manner, the conditions under which fear appeals worked and the conditions under which they failed. The EPPM attempts to do just this.

THE EXTENDED PARALLEL PROCESS MODEL

The EPPM integrates and expands on previous perspectives to explain when and why fear appeals work and when and why they fail (Witte, 1992b, 1994a). It adopts Leventhal's parallel process model as the overall explanatory framework and then adapts portions of Janis's fear-as-acquired drive model into the fear control side and Rogers's PMT into the danger control side of the model. Prior to a complete explanation of the model it is useful to have clear definitions of each term. Table I presents precise definitions for each component of the model.

Overview

According to the EPPM, fear-arousing messages may initiate two appraisals—appraisal of the threat and appraisal of the efficacy of the recommended response. These appraisals, in turn, produce one of three responses to the message: no response, acceptance, or rejection. Specifically, individuals first appraise the severity of the threat (e.g., "How harmful is skin cancer?") and their susceptibility to the threat (e.g., "Am I at-risk for getting skin cancer?") in an additive manner (i.e., perceived severity + perceived susceptibility = perceived threat) when exposed to a fear appeal. If people do not believe themselves to be at-risk for experiencing a health threat (low susceptibility) and/or believe the health threat to be trivial (low severity), they will simply not respond to the message because they are not motivated to do so. For example, college students exposed to skin cancer fear appeals often state, "I won't get skin cancer because I have naturally dark skin [low perceived susceptibility] and besides, even if I do get it the dermatologist will just burn it off [low perceived severity]." Thus, if people have low threat perceptions (i.e., low perceived severity and/or susceptibility), they ignore a fear appeal, do not process any information about the efficacy of a recommended response, and make no attitude, intention, or behavior changes.

If perceptions of threat reach a certain threshold level, then people are motivated to begin the second appraisal, where the efficacy of the recommended response is evaluated and weighed against the perceived strength of the threat. Thus, when people believe themselves to be at-risk for a significant and terrible threat (e.g., "I'm susceptible to contracting a terrible disease")—thus reaching the threshold level—they become scared. Their fear, in turn, may cause them to perceive a threat to be greater than they originally thought, which may further increase their fear, which may again increase their perception of threat, and so on. This heightened level of fear and threat motivates people to take some kind of action—any action. There are two general paths people take when they become frightened from a perceived threat. People can become motivated to *control the danger* of the threat or people can become motivated to *control their fear* about the threat.

Perceived efficacy determines whether or not people will engage in danger control

TABLE I   Key Fear Appeal Constructs

Fear	Fear is an internal emotional reaction composed of psychological and physiological dimensions that may be aroused when a serious and personally relevant threat is perceived.
Threat	A threat is a danger or harm that exists in the environment whether we know it or not. Perceived threat is cognitions or thoughts about that danger or harm. Perceived threat is composed of two underlying dimensions, severity susceptibility.
Perceived susceptibility	Beliefs about one's risk of experiencing the threat (e.g., "I'm at risk for skin cancer because I don't use sunscreen").
Perceived severity	Beliefs about the significance or magnitude of the threat (e.g., "Skin cancer leads to death").
Efficacy	Efficacy pertains to the effectiveness, feasibility, and ease with which a recommended response impedes or averts a threat. Perceived efficacy is thoughts or cognitions about its underlying dimensions, response efficacy, and self-efficacy.
Response efficacy	Beliefs about the effectiveness of the recommended response in deterring the threat (e.g., "Using sunscreen consistently will prevent my getting skin cancer").
Self-efficacy	Beliefs about one's ability to perform the recommended response to avert the threat (e.g., "I am able to use sunscreen consistently to prevent my getting skin cancer").
Danger control	A cognitive process eliciting protection motivation that occurs when one believes she or he is able to effectively avert a significant and relevant threat through self-protective changes. When in danger control, people think of strategies to avert a threat.
Danger control responses	Belief, attitude, intention, and behavior changes in accordance with a message's recommendations.
Fear control	An emotional process eliciting defensive motivation that occurs when people are faced with a significant and relevant threat but believe themselves to be unable to perform a recommended response and/or they believe the response to be ineffective. The high levels of fear caused by this condition produce defensive motivation resulting in coping responses that reduce fear and prevent danger control responses from occurring.
Fear control responses	Coping responses that diminish fear such as defensive avoidance, denial, and reactance (including issue and message derogation and perceived manipulative intent).

or fear control processes. Perceived efficacy refers to response efficacy, defined as individuals' beliefs about the effectiveness of a recommended response (e.g., "Does wearing my seatbelt prevent harm in a car accident?"), and self-efficacy, defined as individuals' beliefs about their ability to perform the recommended response (e.g., "Am I able to wear a seatbelt consistently?"). (Each of the efficacy dimensions is perceived in an additive manner as well; i.e., perceived response efficacy + perceived self-efficacy = perceived efficacy.)

In this secondary appraisal process, people evaluate the efficacy of the recommended response in light of the strength of the perceived threat to determine the ease, feasibility, and practicality of performing the recommended response. As long as perceived efficacy is stronger than perceived threat, individuals will engage in danger control processes. High perceived efficacy (i.e., people feel able to perform an effective recommended response) coupled with high perceived threat (i.e., people believe they are vulnerable to a significant threat) promotes protection motivation and danger control responses where people think carefully about the recommended responses advocated in a persuasive message and adopt those as a means to control the danger (e.g., "I know I can use condoms every time I have sex to prevent AIDS. I'm going to keep some in my purse"). The emotion fear has a somewhat tangential role in danger control processes. Although fear is not directly related to danger control responses such as attitude, intention, or behavior change, it can be indirectly related when it causes individuals to upgrade their estimates of perceived threat. Thus, perceived threat may mediate the relationship between fear and danger control responses.

At some critical point, however, perceptions of threat may begin to exceed perceptions of efficacy. At this critical point, where perceived threat begins to exceed perceived efficacy, people will shift into fear control processes (bypassing all thoughts about threat and efficacy), and begin focusing on how to manage their fear instead of thinking about the threat. People engage in fear control processes when they do not think they are able to adopt an effective response to avert a serious and relevant threat because the response is too hard, too costly, takes too much time, or they think it will not work (i.e., low perceived response and self-efficacy). Thus, low perceived efficacy (i.e., people feel *un*able to perform response and/or believe the response to be ineffective) coupled with high perceived threat (i.e., people believe they are vulnerable to a significant threat) promotes defensive motivation and fear control responses where people focus on how frightened they feel and try to get rid of their fear through denial (e.g., "I'm not at-risk for AIDS, I'm special"), defensive avoidance (e.g., "This is just too scary, I'm simply not going to think about it"), or reactance (e.g., "They're just trying to manipulate me. I'm going to ignore them"). Fear plays a critical role in fear control processes as it is the direct cause of defensive avoidance, reactance, and other fear control responses. Cognitions about the recommended response play little part in fear control processes because people have given up on thinking about the danger and are attempting instead to control their fear.

Overall, the EPPM suggests that individuals implicitly weigh perceived threat against perceived efficacy in a multiplicative manner in their cognitive appraisal. Therefore, an interaction between threat and efficacy would be expected.

Individual differences, such as worldviews, trait variables (e.g., locus of control, anxiety), or prior experiences do not directly influence outcomes (e.g., attitudes, intentions, behaviors, defensive avoidance, reactance, etc.), according to the EPPM. Instead, individual differences are posited to influence perceptions of threat and efficacy only, which then influence outcomes. For example, if an individual is highly anxious by nature, then she or he is likely to perceive threats and the efficacy of a recommended response differently than an individual who is low in trait anxiety by nature. High- and low-anxiety individuals are likely to combine their perceptions of threat and efficacy in different manners and may end up undergoing different parallel processes. For example, highly anxious people tend to see threats as worse than they really are and recommended responses as more difficult to undertake than they really are. Thus, highly anxious people may be more likely to reach the critical point where perceived threat exceeds perceived efficacy (resulting in fear control processes) sooner than low-anxiety people. Thus, the EPPM suggests that individual differences *indirectly* influence outcomes, as mediated by perceptions of threat and efficacy.

In sum, the EPPM suggests that two appraisal processes (i.e., threat appraisal and efficacy appraisal) lead to one of three outcomes: (a) no response when perceived threat is low; (b) primarily cognitive danger control processes leading to acceptance of fear-arousing messages when perceived threat and perceived efficacy are high; and (c) primarily emotional fear control processes leading to rejection of fear-arousing messages when perceived threat is high but perceived efficacy is low. Perceived threat determines the strength or how much of a response there is to a fear appeal, whereas perceived efficacy determines the nature of the response—whether a fear appeal induces danger control or fear control processes. Fear directly causes fear control responses but can indirectly influence danger control responses when mediated by perceptions of threat. Individual differences can indirectly influence outcomes when they influence perceptions of threat and efficacy.

The Depiction of the Model

The EPPM is depicted in Figure 1. This figure is an imperfect attempt to represent the model pictorially in a parsimonious manner. It is difficult to graphically represent the message-processing aspects of the model because of the complex relationships (e.g., interactions, indirect effects, appraisals, etc.) between threat, efficacy, fear, and individual differences. In addition, figures often fail to capture the longitudinal nature of message processing. Henceforth, the text above should be used to generate precise predictions. The figure should be used for heuristic and pedagogical purposes only.

Briefly, the figure shows that external stimuli influence message processing, which then produce outcomes. The message-processing aspects of the model (which focus on perceived threat, perceived efficacy, and fear arousal) include threat and efficacy appraisals, the relationship between threat and fear, and the relationship between individual differences and perceptions of threat, efficacy, and fear arousal. Either danger control or fear control processes act as outcomes to message processing. If danger control processes dominate, then protection motivation is elicited, re-

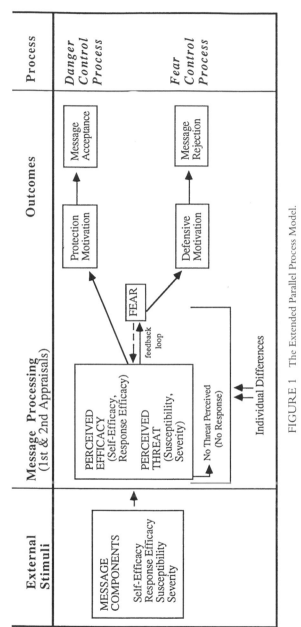

FIGURE 1   The Extended Parallel Process Model.

sulting in danger control responses (e.g., attitude change, behavior change), and the acceptance of message recommendations. If fear control processes dominate, then defensive motivation is elicited, resulting in fear control responses (e.g., defensive avoidance, reactance), and the rejection of message recommendations.

I have presented the model in text and graphically without reference to the supporting literature explaining why certain claims are made. Additionally, I have not stated what makes the EPPM unique from other models. Following is a discussion of these issues.

Appraisals

In previous fear appeal models, no distinction was made as to how people initially process fear appeals. It was assumed that people exposed to a fear appeal would process it all at once. For example, in PMT the four components of a fear appeal apparently automatically induced four corresponding cognitive mediators (i.e., susceptibility, severity, response efficacy, self-efficacy). In contrast, the EPPM suggests that the two appraisals operate sequentially. First, the threat appraisal must produce a certain threshold level of perceived threat before people will even consider thinking about the recommended response in the efficacy appraisal. Once the threshold is reached, then the second appraisal of the efficacy of the recommended response occurs. The appraisal processes occur at lightning-fast speed, which make experimental study a challenge.

The coping literature has found support for two appraisals such as those outlined in the EPPM. For example, the threat and efficacy appraisals in the EPPM are similar to Folkman's (1984) primary and secondary appraisals (see McKeon, 1995, for a discussion of the similarities and differences). Folkman (1984) stated that in the primary appraisal process an individual evaluates a certain behavior in terms of its impact as a harm or loss, threat, or challenge. During the secondary appraisal process, individuals evaluate coping options and resources (Folkman, 1984). McKeon (1995) noted that Folkman's primary appraisal is similar to the EPPM's threat appraisal because people evaluate how much harm or loss will occur and how threatening and challenging a certain situation is perceived to be. She also pointed out that Folkman's secondary appraisal is similar to the EPPM's efficacy appraisal because people evaluate the environment and situation in an attempt to determine whether or not something can be done in the face of a stressful situation.

Two studies have specifically assessed whether or not the order of threat and efficacy messages influences reactions to fear appeals. Skilbeck, Tulips, and Ley (1977) found that recommendations (including efficacy information) immediately following a fear appeal were clearly superior when compared to recommendations given first or recommendations given much later. Leventhal and Singer (1966) also gave recommendations before, during, or after the presentation of a high or low fear appeal. Their results indicated that those people receiving the fear appeal first, followed by the recommendations message, had the highest level of acceptance toward the recommendations, when compared to those receiving the recommendations message before or during the fear appeal. These results suggest that effective fear appeals induce threat appraisal first and then offer recommendations to induce efficacy appraisal, where the recommendations are evaluated in light of the threat. More research is needed before the threat and efficacy appraisals will be fully understood.

Distinction between Threat and Fear

Threat and fear, though highly correlated and influencing each other at lightning-quick speed, are distinct concepts resulting in fundamentally different outcomes (see Table I for definitions). In general, fear directly causes fear control responses and is unrelated to danger control responses. Cognitions about the threat and especially about the recommended response directly cause danger control responses. Thus, fear dominates in the primarily emotional fear control processes and cognitions about the threat and efficacy of the recommended responses dominate in the primarily cognitive danger control processes.

However, if the EPPM is correct, then why did Boster and Mongeau's (1984; see also Mongeau, 1991, and Sutton, 1982) meta-analysis reveal small correlations between fear and attitudes ($r = .21$), and fear and behaviors ($r = .10$)? The EPPM suggests that the reason for these small correlations is that fear can be *indirectly* related to danger control responses, such as attitudes and behaviors under certain conditions—namely *when perceived efficacy is high* (indicating danger control processes are dominating). Specifically, the EPPM maintains that when people believe they can effectively deter the threat (i.e., perceived efficacy is greater than perceived threat), then (a) the emotion fear can be cognitively appraised, (b) the cognitive appraisal of the emotion fear can cause one to upgrade her or his perceptions of threat, and (c) these upgraded perceptions of threat can positively influence message acceptance (see Figure 1, feedback loop; i.e., fear → perceived threat → danger control response). Other scientists support this view that fear can be cognitively appraised under certain conditions. For example, Janis and Mann (1977) noted, "every physical symptom a person notices in himself [or herself] constitutes a warning signal" (p. 66).

The research evidence supports this position. Specifically, Witte (1994a) found that, with a general population (including individuals with both high- and low-efficacy perceptions), fear was neither directly nor indirectly related to behaviors. However, when only those people with high-efficacy perceptions were included in the analyses (indicating danger control dominance), fear still had no direct effect on behaviors but had a significant indirect effect of .15 on behaviors when mediated by perceived threat (i.e., fear → perceived threat → behaviors). Thus, it appears that, in general, fear is not directly related to danger control responses, but when perceived efficacy is high and danger control processes are dominating, then fear can indirectly influence danger control responses by first influencing perceptions of threat. Other researchers have offered the same point-of-view. Specifically, Rogers (1983) and Beck and Frankel (1981) suggested that cognitions about a threat coupled with perceptions of efficacy toward the recommended response are what lead to attitude or behavior change. In contrast, the research evidence suggests that fear is the direct cause of fear control responses such as defensive avoidance (Witte, 1994a).

The biggest problem with this portion of the model is one of measurement. How does one measure the emotion fear separate from cognitions about threat? Traditionally, fear has been measured with a series of adjectives (e.g., "[THREAT] makes me feel . . . scared/fearful/anxious/etc."), which have rough approximation to physiological indices of fear (Mewborn & Rogers, 1979). Threat has been measured with questions assessing thoughts about one's susceptibility to a threat (e.g., "I'm at-risk for contracting HIV") and thoughts about the severity of a health threat (e.g., "Skin cancer is deadly"). However, much more research is needed to isolate independent measures of fear and threat, which will help to isolate the independent effects of these two variables.

Dillard (1994) and Stephenson (1992) offered excellent analyses on how to conceptualize and measure fear. Based on a thorough review of the emotion and affect literature, Stephenson (1992) suggested that fear is associated with increased heart rate, decreased blood flow, lower skin temperature, and increased perspiration resulting in higher levels of galvanic skin response. Dillard (1994) concurred with these physiological expressions in his review, as outlined at the beginning of this chapter. These findings offer starting points for those interested in developing measures of fear arousal. Until we develop more sophisticated measures of fear arousal, testing some aspects of the EPPM will remain difficult.

Threat and Efficacy: Interaction Effects

The EPPM suggests that threat and efficacy interact multiplicatively to influence outcomes. Additionally, the EPPM states that both the threat and efficacy constructs are made up of two distinct dimensions each (i.e., threat = susceptibility to the threat + severity of the threat; efficacy = response efficacy + self-efficacy). Interaction effects are now new in the fear appeal literature. What is new is the notion that perceived threat is an overall construct including the conceptually distinct dimensions of susceptibility and severity and that perceived efficacy is an overall construct including the conceptually distinct dimensions of response efficacy and self-efficacy.

Many researchers have attempted to manipulate the threat dimensions separately but "attempts to manipulate these conceptually distinguishable factors independently have not been particularly successful" (Eagly & Chaiken, 1993, p. 443). Furthermore, many using a PMT framework have tried to test the efficacy and threat dimensions separately within a four-way interaction framework (i.e., severity × susceptibility × response efficacy × self-efficacy). Although the data do not support four-way interactions, they do show that at least one threat variable always seems to interact with at least one efficacy variable to influence outcomes. For example, Mulilis and Lippa (1990) found interactions between the following variables: susceptibility × response efficacy, susceptibility × response efficacy × self-efficacy, and susceptibility × response efficacy × severity. Similarly, Rogers and Mewborn (1976) found susceptibility × response efficacy and severity × response efficacy interactions. In addition, Maddux and Rogers (1983) also detected a susceptibility × response efficacy × self-efficacy interaction. This pattern of at least one threat variable interacting with at least one efficacy variable is consistent across other studies as well (e.g., Kleinot & Rogers, 1982; Wurtele & Maddux, 1987).

Two measurement studies utilizing confirmatory factor analyses procedures have found support for the proposition that threat and efficacy are composed of two dimensions each. Both studies found that severity, susceptibility, response efficacy, and self-efficacy formed unique and reliable dimensions that worked together in a predictable manner to make up second-order unidimensional factors of threat and efficacy (Witte, Cameron, McKeon, & Berkowitz, 1995; Witte & Morrison, 1995a). Given this pattern of findings across studies, it appears that severity and susceptibility should be combined into a higher order factor of threat, and response efficacy and self-efficacy should be combined into a higher order factor of efficacy.

Defining the Threat

Researchers typically choose a health topic and assume the threat is obvious. For example, in an HIV/AIDS campaign, death and sickness from AIDS is usually described as the threat in a fear appeal. In a skin cancer campaign, physical harm from the skin cancer is typically described as the threat. However, researchers may define certain negative consequences as threats when their target audience does not. For example, Witte (1997) discovered in focus group research that teen girls did not view "getting pregnant" as a threat or negative consequence of sexual intercourse. According to these teens, far greater threats were "getting fat" or "losing friends." Thus, the teens suggested that an effective pregnancy prevention fear appeal should threaten loss of friendship or weight gain as a consequence of sexual intercourse leading to pregnancy. Overall, to develop effective fear appeals, researchers must determine carefully what is scary or threatening about a defined topic for a specific target audience.

Three Possible Outcomes

Heretofore, most fear appeal researchers have simply measured attitude, intention, and behavior changes. Fear appeals were thought to work if attitudes, intentions, and behaviors changed in the direction advocated, and were thought to fail if no change or changes counter to those predicted were discovered. The original fear appeal work by Hovland, Janis, and Kelly (1953) assessed multiple and diverse responses to fear appeals. However, this practice was not continued by other researchers. The EPPM adopts their multiple response approach, although suggesting that fear appeals may fail for two reasons. First, fear appeals may fail because people simply did not process the message or react to it—a null response. Second, fear appeals may fail because people engage in certain strategies that prevent or interfere with attitude, intention, or behavior change. Fear control responses, such as defensive avoidance, denial, and reactance are *qualitatively* different responses that occur in reaction to a fear appeal and interfere with and prevent attitude, intention, and behavior change. For example, if a person denies being at risk for HIV infection, he or she is unlikely to use a condom.

Danger Control Responses

When individuals perceive high threat and high efficacy, they are motivated to control the danger of the threat. Thus, the danger control outcomes are the traditional persuasion outcomes of attitude, intention, and behavior change. Danger control responses are typically seen as adaptive responses to a significant threat because they protect an individual against harm. Danger control responses have been the focus of most of Rogers's (1975; 1983) work (Rippetoe & Rogers, 1987, is a notable exception).

Fear Control Responses

When individuals perceive high threat and low efficacy, they are motivated to control their fear. Thus, fear control responses are typically seen as maladaptive responses to a significant threat because the individual fails to protect him- or herself from harm. Instead, the individual ignores the threat and recommended responses and instead engages in coping responses that reduce fear. The fear control responses in the EPPM are borrowed from Hovland, Janis, and Kelly's (1953; Janis, 1967; Janis & Feshbach, 1953) research. Hovland, Janis, and Kelly (1953) suggested three alternative reactions to fear appeals that interfere with attitude change: (a) aggression toward the communicator; (b) defensive avoidance; and (c) inattentiveness to the communication.

First, aggression toward the communicator refers to a perception by the audience of manipulative intent on the part of the communicator and/or communication. This perceived manipulation prompts individuals to either reject the message outright or to get angry about the communicator's intent, instead of thinking about the message. Aggression toward the communicator may be exhibited by defiance, derogation, or contempt toward the speaker and is similar to the construct of reactance (Brehm, 1966; Janis & Feshbach, 1953). In one study we did on radon awareness, we found that when focus group participants felt threatened by risks of radon exposure and believed there was little they could do to prevent harm from exposure, they then began to question whether the whole issue of radon was a government plot and subsequently began to convince themselves that radon was probably made up to scare people. In the EPPM, aggression has been measured through perceived manipulation and issue or message derogation measures.

Second, defensive avoidance is defined by Hovland, Janis, and Kelly (1953) as a motivated resistance to a fear appeal where people avoid subsequent thoughts about the message. Expanding on this fear control response, the EPPM interprets defensive avoidance as a form of perceptual defense (see Witte, 1994a, for full discussion). Perceptual defense is where "anxiety-provoking stimuli are defended against in perception or prevented from coming to awareness" (Maddi, 1989, p. 199). When defensive avoidance occurs, individuals distort or ignore any incoming information about a threat. Selective attention and exposure, where people avoid exposing themselves to information about the threat, may occur. For example, those individuals with high-threat and low-efficacy perceptions toward HIV and AIDS may flip the television channel or skip through a magazine article on HIV and AIDS to avoid having to think about it. To measure defensive avoidance, one must have a delayed measure to assess whether information about a threat or recommended response has been blocked by some unconscious defensive processes.

A third fear control response suggested by Hovland, Janis, and Kelly (1953) is inattentiveness to the communication, where individuals attempt "to change the subject of conversation to a less disturbing topic" (Janis & Feshbach, 1953, p. 78). For example, not listening, blocking of associations, or evasiveness all characterize inattention to the communication (Janis & Feshbach, 1953). This type of fear control response is similar to defensive avoidance, except that it happens immediately instead of over time. It has been operationalized in the EPPM as denial, where people deny they are at-risk for a certain threat.

Modifications to the Original EPPM

The 12 propositions contained in Table II summarize the theoretical statements made here. These propositions differ from the 11 published in Witte (1992b) in three ways. First, it appears that Witte's (1992b) original proposition 5, "Maladaptive responses will be inversely related to adaptive responses," is definitional in nature and not propositional. That is, by definition, if one is controlling one's fear through defensive avoidance, reactance, or denial, one is not making appropriate attitude, intention, and behavior changes. Thus, this proposition has been dropped.

Second, a new proposition specifying how threat and efficacy operate together to influence outcomes has been added (proposition 11). And third, a new proposition specifying the relationship between individual differences and outcomes has been added (proposition 12).

TABLE II   Propositions for the Extended Parallel Process Model

Proposition 1	When perceived threat is low, regardless of perceived efficacy level, there will be no further processing of the message.
Proposition 2	As perceived threat increases when perceived efficacy is high, so will message acceptance.
Proposition 3	Cognitions about the threat and efficacy cause attitude, intention, or behavior changes (i.e., danger control responses).
Proposition 4	As perceived threat increases when perceived efficacy is low, people will do the opposite of what is advocated.
Proposition 5[a]	As perceived threat increases when perceived efficacy is moderate, message acceptance will first increase, and then decrease, resulting in an inverted U-shaped function.
Proposition 6	Fear causes fear control responses.
Proposition 7	When perceived efficacy is high, fear indirectly influences danger control outcomes, as mediated by perceived threat.
Proposition 8	When perceived efficacy is high, there is a reciprocal relationship between perceived threat and fear.
Proposition 9	Cognitions about efficacy are unrelated to fear control responses.
Proposition 10	Cognitions about threat are indirectly related to fear control responses.
Proposition 11	Perceived threat determines the intensity of a response (how strong the response) and perceived efficacy determines the nature of the response (either fear or danger control).
Proposition 12	Individual differences influence outcomes indirectly, as mediated by perceived threat and efficacy.

[a]Proposition 5 formerly said, "Maladaptive responses will be inversely related to adaptive responses." However, this statement appears to be definitional in nature and not propositional. Two new propositions have been added. One specifies how threat and efficacy operate in influencing outcomes (proposition 11). The other specifies the relationship between individual differences and outcomes (proposition 12). Also, adaptive responses are now called danger control responses (i.e., attitude, intention, behaviors) and maladaptive responses are now called fear control responses (i.e., defensive avoidance, denial, reactance).

One other modification has been made to the original EPPM. Originally, the EPPM referred to danger control responses as adaptive and fear control responses as maladaptive. This distinction has been dropped because in some cases fear control responses may be adaptive (as when a threat is unavoidable and defensive avoidance is the best way to cope). Thus, in the current version of the EPPM, danger control responses refer to message acceptance in the form of positive attitude, intention, or behavior changes, and fear control responses refer to message rejection in the form of defensive avoidance, reactance, or denial.

DISTINGUISHING THE EXTENDED PARALLEL PROCESS MODEL FROM OTHER FEAR APPEAL MODELS

The EPPM draws heavily on other fear appeal models and may be seen as an integration of previous perspectives. Following are brief discussions on how the EPPM differs from prominent fear appeal models.

Fear-as-Acquired Drive Model

The EPPM expands on the Fear-as-Acquired Drive Model to explain fear control processes, in particular focusing on the variables fear and fear control responses. Specifically, the EPPM reinstates fear to a central role by stating that if fear gets too high, then people will engage in responses such as defensive avoidance or reactance (similar to the drive model). However, it differs from the drive model in that the drive model says little about the cognitive processes underlying people's reactions to fear appeals and does not carefully distinguish between message variables (i.e., the components of a fear appeal) or information-processing variables (e.g., threat, efficacy, fear arousal).

Parallel Process Model

The EPPM adopts the parallel process model as the overall organizing framework for explaining reactions to fear appeals. It improves on the original model by offering specific propositions and predictions as to the conditions under which fear appeals succeed and fail. In the original model, Leventhal (1970) viewed the parallel processes as working together in mutually interfering or mutually facilitating ways. The EPPM departs from the original model by saying that only one process will dominate at a time; that fear may either interfere (in fear control processes) or facilitate (in danger control processes) behavior change, but it cannot do both. (Again, by definition, if one is defensively avoiding a health issue or denying she or he is at-risk, then one is not engaging in self-protective behaviors.) Furthermore, the original model states that fear arousal can cause either danger or fear control, whereas the EPPM specifies that fear causes fear control all of the time and only indirectly relates to danger control when mediated by perceptions of threat (under high-efficacy conditions). Also, the original parallel process model does not distinguish between threat and fear, does not address the variable efficacy, and fails to specify exactly when people switch from danger to fear control, as does the EPPM.

Protection Motivation Theory

PMT explains the danger control side of the EPPM. Thus, both theories state that fear appeals should be made up of four basic components and both maintain that cognition leads to message acceptance. The EPPM expands on PMT by reincorporating fear as a central variable, adding fear control processes to the model, and including fear control outcomes such as defensive avoidance, denial, or reactance. The EPPM suggests first a threat appraisal followed by an efficacy appraisal, whereas PMT suggests threat and coping appraisals (including rewards and costs) that occur simultaneously. Finally, the EPPM introduces the notion of a "critical point" to isolate when people shift from danger to fear control processes.

Other Health Behavior Models

The origins of fear appeal research coincided with the development of many health behavior change models. The health belief model (HBM) originated in the same era as Hovland, Janis, and Kelly's (1953) fear appeal theory (Rosenstock, 1974). Some scholars have even suggested that fear appeal theories are experimental variants of the health belief model (Prentice-Dunn & Rogers, 1986). Both the EPPM and the HBM focus on how certain stimuli (fear appeals—EPPM, cues to action—HBM) influence perceptions of susceptibility and severity to influence behaviors. The differences between the two models are that the HBM focuses on how benefits and barriers to performing recommended responses influence behavior. Furthermore, the HBM does not address how fear arousal or any other emotion influences behaviors. HBM's benefits component and barriers component may be seen as subsets of the EPPM's response efficacy and self-efficacy components. Specifically, the EPPM's response efficacy component addresses perceptions about performing certain actions—both the benefits and the drawbacks. Similarly, the EPPM's self-efficacy component addresses any perceptions about one's ability to perform a recommended response, both positive (i.e., "I know how to do breast self-examinations; I am capable of doing them") and negative (e.g., "I'm not able to take prenatal vitamins because they cost too much," "I'm not able to get a mammogram because I don't have transportation to get to the clinic," "I'm not able to use condoms because I'm too embarrassed to bring up the issue with a partner"). Negative perceptions about self-efficacy appear to be identical to the HBM's barriers variable (e.g., cost, transportation). In sum, the EPPM's definitions of response and self-efficacy are broader than and include the HBM's definitions of benefits and barriers.

Bandura's (1977) social learning theory plays a central role in the EPPM, as self-efficacy is one of the central concepts in the model. Furthermore, the variable Bandura calls outcome expectations (if I perform behavior X what do I expect the outcome to be?) may be seen as loosely related to response efficacy (if I perform behavior X what will the outcome regarding the threat be?). Perceived susceptibility, severity, and fear arousal are not addressed in Bandura's model, because it focuses on a broader set of behaviors.

Dillard (1994; Dillard, Plotnick, Godbold, Freimuth, & Edgar, 1996) has begun new work assessing the multiple emotions induced from fear appeals. His work shows that fear is the strongest emotion emerging from fear appeals accounting for the strongest relationship to outcomes. However, anger also appears to result from exposure to fear appeals. It is unclear, however, whether or not fear comes first and whether or not anger can be seen as an outcome related to reactance. What is clear is that multiple emotions (e.g., sadness, anger, disgust) are elicited from fear appeals, but fear appears to be the force driving the action (given its influence on outcomes).

RESEARCH ON THE EXTENDED PARALLEL PROCESS MODEL TO DATE

The EPPM follows a long line of health behavior models and attempts to integrate them in a manner that is parsimonious with high explanatory power. What follows is a review of research to date on the EPPM.

Table III shows a summary of work thus far testing the EPPM. Across a variety of topics, populations, and methods, it appears that threat and efficacy interact to influence attitudes, intentions, and behaviors (see also Witte & Allen, 1996). Also, it appears that fear directly influences fear control responses and only indirectly influences danger control responses for those with high perceived efficacy (indicating danger control dominance) (see Rodriguez, 1995, for an exception). Across these studies, fear appeals reliably increased fear and perceptions of threat. However, little is known about how the specific attributes of fear-arousing messages lead to increases in fear, threat, and efficacy perceptions. Witte (1993) suggested that, by definition, strong fear appeals are those that are vivid, personalistic, specific, and contain intense language. Rodriguez (1995) argued that argument quality also influences how people respond to fear appeals. More research is needed in this area.

Across these studies it appears that fear-arousing messages produce relatively immediate and short-lived increases in perceived threat and fear. In addition, fear arousal seems to increase the degree or intensity of message acceptance or rejection. Efficacy messages appear to be thought about, pondered, and considered over longer periods of time. As such, the effect of efficacy messages takes longer to emerge. However, although threat and fear produce immediate outcomes, perceived efficacy appears to produce the long-term, stable influence on individuals' behaviors. For example, the survey studies that measured perceptions of threat and efficacy discovered that existing perceptions of efficacy explained people's entrenched behaviors, not existing perceptions of threat. Thus, it appears that threat and fear trigger actions but efficacy determines exactly what those actions are and how long they last.

TABLE III Summary of Research on the Extended Parallel Process Model to Date

Study	Topic	Population[a]	Method	Findings[b]
Casey, 1995	HIV/AIDS	N/A	Theoretical	Modified the extended parallel process model to include fatalistic mentality as an intervening variable between appraisal of threat and perception of threat.
Kline, 1995	Breast cancer	N/A	Content analysis	"Pamphlets contained appropriate severity and susceptibility messages but they did not contain appropriate response efficacy and self-efficacy messages for breast-self examination."
Rodriguez, 1995	Bicycle helmets Tetanus Drunk driving	College students (Michigan)	Experiment	Did not find support for PMT, EPPM, or the Elaboration Likelihood Model. Found that fear-arousing content causes greater perceived argument quality and may be a confound in fear appeals.
Stephenson, 1993	Skin cancer	College students (Texas)	Experiment	Found that fear-arousing pictures could be manipulated supraliminally and subliminally. Discovered that supraliminal pictures produced stronger fear control responses, and subliminal embeds produced stronger danger control responses.
Witte, 1992b	Fear appeals in general	N/A	Theoretical	Presented the extended parallel process model; discussed past literature, integrated previous perspectives, offered propositions.
Witte, 1992c	HIV/AIDS	College students (California)	Experiment	Found Threat $\times$ Efficacy interaction for attitude change and behaviors.
Witte, 1993	Fear appeals in general	N/A	Theoretical	Examined the message attributes of fear appeals to determine what made high- and low-fear appeals; assessed potential confounds in the fear appeal literature; made recommendations for those conducting fear appeal studies.

(continues)

TABLE III (*continued*)

Study	Topic	Population[a]	Method	Findings[b]
Witte, 1994a	HIV/AIDS	College students (California)	Experiment	Found that fear directly caused fear control responses and was unrelated to danger control responses, except when mediated by perceived threat under high-efficacy conditions.
Witte, 1994b	HIV/AIDS	College students (California—2 samples)	Survey	Described and tested a formula to distinguish between those in fear and danger control for applied settings.
Wille, 1997	Teen pregnancy	African-American, Hispanic, & Native American teen mothers (Michigan)	Focus groups	Learned that teens did not view pregnancy as a threat; gaining weight and losing friends were seen as threats. Teens recommended "reality-based" fear appeals focusing on these threats.
Witte, Berkowitz, Cameron, McKeon, 1995	Genital warts	College students (Michigan)	Experiment	Showed that fear appeal campaigns appear to fail if efficacy perceptions are not addressed. Showed that fear appeals work when people have high efficacy perceptions; the fear appeal triggered action but efficacy determined what the action was.
Witte et al., 1996	Radon awareness	African-American smokers and mothers (Michigan)	Focus groups	Discovered that this population had high threat perceptions regarding radon and low-efficacy perceptions toward recommended responses. Little self-protective behaviors evident.
Witte, Cameron, McKeon, Berkowitz, 1996	Genital warts	College students (Michigan)	Mail survey	Developed a "risk behavior diagnosis scale" in order to assess whether clients or audiences were in danger or fear control in order to develop effective health communications.
Witte, Cameron, & Nzyuko, 1995	HIV/AIDS	Commercial sex workers Truck drivers/assistants Adolescents (Kenya)	Focus groups	Discovered that participants had high threat perceptions toward HIV/AIDS but low-efficacy perceptions toward condom use. Fear control responses appeared to be the dominant response to the threat of AIDS

Witte & Morrison, 1995a	HIV/AIDS	College students (California)	Experiment	Determined that trait anxiety had neither a direct, indirect, or interactive effect on danger or fear control responses (defensive avoidance was an exception).
Witte & Morrison, 1995b	Culture and fear appeals	N/A	Theoretical	Examined medical systems around the world and proposed a modified version of the EPPM including family values, fatalistic outlook, and barriers to explain culturally diverse individuals' health-related behaviors.
Witte & Morrison, 1995c	HIV/AIDS	Juvenile delinquents/ high school students (Texas)	Experiment	Found that low sensation seekers were more persuaded by a fear appeal than high sensation seekers, who were not persuaded by any presentation.
Witte et al., 1993	Tractor safety	Farmers (Texas)	Telephone and mail surveys, face-to-face interviews	Conducted a formative evaluation for a campaign. Found that farmers had strong efficacy perceptions toward recommended safety practices, but lacked sufficient motivation to use them (needed threat/fear arousal). Perceived efficacy was strongest predictor of outcomes.
Witte, Sampson, Liu, & Morrison, 1995 1995	HIV/AIDS	Jr. high students (California)	Experiment	Examined the target of a threat in a fear appeal and found that fear appeals threatening one's family produced more fear for members of collectivist cultures than fear appeals threatening the individual, which produced more fear for members of individualist cultures.
Wunsch, J. M., 1996	Diet (fruit and vegetable intake)	WIC program participants (Federal program—women, infants, and children)	Survey	Assessed whether participants were in fear or danger control for future persuasive nutrition messages. Examined differences between those in fear and danger control.

[a]N/A, not applicable
[b]EPPM, extended parallel process model; PMT, protection motivation theory.

The relationship between individual differences and reactions to fear appeals is unclear. In some cases, individual differences appear to be completely unrelated to outcomes, whereas in other cases individual differences appear to increase explanatory power. For example, Witte and Morrison (1995a) found that trait anxiety was unrelated to any danger control responses, such as attitudes, intentions, and behaviors. However, Witte and Morrison (1995c) found that sensation seeking was related to danger control outcomes. Some scholars have suggested addressing other individual variables such as fatalism (Casey, 1995) or cultural worldviews (Witte & Morrison, 1995b). Much more work is needed to find out which individual differences influence reactions to fear appeals.

The EPPM has proved useful in applied health settings in isolating why some campaign materials fail and why others work. For example, Kline (1995) analyzed breast cancer prevention posters and found that some would be more likely to produce counterproductive boomerang responses (where people do the opposite of what is advocated) because they promoted high threat and low efficacy perceptions. For example, she noted that, "A poster I saw at a health center stated this in no uncertain terms: it depicted a woman with her hand on her breast (apparently engaging in breast self-examination) with a caption that said something like 'This woman just missed the cancer that will take her life.'" (p. 24). The EPPM would suggest that this type of poster does far more harm than good as it is likely to promote fear control responses and may even cause boomerang behavioral responses where individuals do the exact opposite of what is advocated—in this case avoid any kind of breast examinations. Overall, the EPPM may be useful for guiding campaign material development as well as for evaluating the effectiveness of existing public health campaigns (see Witte, 1997; Witte, Cameron, & Nzyuko, 1995). For example, the EPPM framework was used to develop tractor safety messages in Texas and is currently being used to develop targeted messages in HIV counseling and testing sessions.

FUTURE DIRECTIONS

Several issues need research attention in the fear appeal literature. First, the nature of threat and efficacy appraisals need to be explored. Do they occur in the sequential order suggested by the EPPM, in reverse order, or simultaneously? Does it matter in what order they are appraised? One problem in evaluating the order question is that information-processing mechanisms occur at such rapid speed that it is difficult to discern order effects.

Second, the link between messages, physiological responses of fear, and perceived threat and perceived efficacy needs to be explored. Do perceptions of threat lead to fear arousal, which in turn lead to upgrades of perceptions of threat? How exactly does the feedback loop operate? Again, it is difficult to adequately test the feedback loop given the swift nature of the threat–fear relationship. New and clever methodologies are needed to adequately test our theories.

Third, research on what exactly constitutes a fear appeal is needed. O'Keefe (1990) noted that fear appeals can be defined in terms of their content (specific message attributes) and/or by the reaction they produce in an audience. Most fear appeal researchers combine these definitions and vary the content of their message (e.g., gruesome pictures, vivid language) in order to produce fear in their audience (assessed by manipulation checks). However, little has been done to establish the specific message attributes leading to fear, threat, or efficacy. What is it exactly about fear appeals that promotes fear, threat, or efficacy?

Fourth, cognitive and emotional response research needs to be conducted to develop valid and reliable measures of fear appeal constructs. Currently, social scientists lack sensitive measures for many cognitive and emotional constructs. For example, fear control responses can be tricky to measure. For example, if one is truly defensively avoiding an issue, then how can one self-report this information? Because fear control responses cannot be directly observed (they are defensive mechanisms occurring in someone's head), they must be inferred from self-report measures. Eagly and Chaiken (1993) call for more thought listing, argument recall, and other cognitive response measures in order to better understand how people respond to fear appeals. Indeed, this type of information has proven very useful when measuring fear control responses. For example, Witte (1994a) was able to validate a defensive avoidance measure by assessing memory and recall of a fear appeal as well as examining thoughts listed.

Fifth, a greater range of fear needs to be induced and examined in fear appeal studies. For example, Eagly and Chaiken (1993) noted that curvilinear relationships should not be dismissed simply because they are rare in the literature. They noted that researchers may not have produced an adequate range of threat and fear arousal to test whether or not there is a curvilinear relationship between threat and fear and attitude change. Indeed, even though three or more levels of threat and fear are needed to test a curvilinear hypothesis, this type of study is rarely seen in the literature.

Finally, an examination of the effects of fear appeals in natural settings is desperately needed. Most fear appeal studies occur in laboratory settings where exposure to a fear appeal is forced on participants. However, what happens in real life? If a fear-arousing public service announcement appears on television, do people process it in the same manner as they do in a laboratory or do they quickly change channels? Issues of selective exposure, attention, and comprehension need to be studied with fear appeals in natural settings.

CONCLUSION

In sum, to answer the question first asked at the beginning of this chapter (i.e., "do fear-arousing messages work?"), yes, they work when people have strong efficacy perceptions. However, they can and do fail when people have low-efficacy perceptions. In short, one can arouse fear to gain compliance, but only if individuals see themselves as able to perform an effective recommended response.

Many social scientists are excited about what they think is "new" and "innovative" research (myself included!). It is humbling, therefore, to realize that our "new" research is merely confirming what ancient philosophers have always known. For example, the EPPM was succinctly summarized by Aristotle over 2,000 years ago (cited in Mongeau, 1991):

> If there is to be the anguish of uncertainty, there must be some lurking hope of deliverance; and that this is so would appear from the fact that fear sets [people] deliberating— but no one deliberates about things that are hopeless. (pp. 101–102)

ACKNOWLEDGMENTS

Kenzie Cameron's comments on this chapter improved it substantially and I am grateful for her contribution.

REFERENCES

Bandura, A. (1977). Self-efficacy: Toward a unifying theory of behavioral change. *Psychological Review, 84,* 191–215.

Bargh, J. A. (1989). Conditional automaticity: Varieties of automatic influence in social perception and cognition. In J. S. Uleman & J. A. Bargh (Eds.), *Unintended thought* (pp. 3–51). New York: Guilford.

Beck, K. H., & Frankel, A. (1981). A conceptualization of threat communications and protective health behavior. *Social Psychology Quarterly, 44,* 204–217.

Boster, F. J., & Mongeau, P. (1984). Fear-arousing persuasive messages. In R. N. Bostrom, & B. H. Westley (Eds.), *Communication Yearbook 8* (pp. 330–375). Newbury Park, CA: Sage.

Brehm, J. W. (1966). *A theory of reactance.* New York: Academic Press.

Casey, M. K. (1995, November). *Fatalism and the modification of the extended parallel process model.* Paper presented at the annual meeting of the Speech Communication Association, San Antonio, Texas.

Dillard, J. P. (1994). Rethinking the study of fear appeals: An emotional perspective. *Communication Theory, 4,* 295–323.

Dillard, J. P., Plotnick, C. A., Godbold, L. C., Freimuth, V. S., & Edgar, T. (1996). The multiple affective outcomes of AIDS PSAs: Fear appeals do more than scare people. *Communication Research.*

Eagly, A. H., & Chaiken, S. (1993). *The psychology of attitudes.* Fort Worth, TX: Harcourt Brace Jovanovich.

Easterling, D. V., & Leventhal, H. (1989). Contribution of concrete cognition to emotion: Neutral symptoms as elicitors of worry about cancer. *Journal of Applied Psychology, 74,* 787–796.

Folkman, S. (1984). Personal control and stress and coping processes: A theoretical approach. *Journal of Personality and Social Psychology, 46,* 839–852.

Hovland, C., Janis, I., & Kelly, H. (1953). *Communication and persuasion.* New Haven, CT: Yale University.

Janis, I. L. (1967). Effects of fear arousal on attitude change: Recent developments in theory and experimental research. In L. Berkowitz (Ed.), *Advances in experimental social psychology* (Vol. 3, pp. 166–225). New York: Academic Press.

Janis, I. L., & Feshbach, S. (1953). Effects of fear-arousing communications. *The Journal of Abnormal and Social Psychology, 48,* 78–92.

Janis, I. L., & Mann, L. (1977). *Decision making: A psychological analysis of conflict, choice, and commitment.* New York: The Free Press.

Kleinot, M. C., & Rogers, R. W. (1982). Identifying effective components of alcohol misuse prevention programs. *Journal of Studies on Alcohol, 43,* 802–811.

Kline, K. N. (1995, November). *Applying Witte's extended parallel process model to pamphlets urging women to engage in BSE: Where are the efficacy messages?* Paper presented at the annual meeting of the Speech Communication Association, San Antonio, Texas.

Lang, P. J. (1984). Cognition and emotion: Concept and action. In C. E. Izard, J. Kagan, & R. B. Zajonc (Eds.), *Emotions, cognition, and behavior* (pp. 192–226). Cambridge: Cambridge University Press.

Lazarus, R. S. (1991a). Cognition and motivation in emotion. *American Psychologist, 46,* 352–367.

Lazarus, R. S. (1991b). Progress on a cognitive-motivational-relational theory of emotion. *American Psychologist, 46,* 819–834.

Leventhal, H. (1970). Findings and theory in the study of fear communications. In L. Berkowitz (Ed.), *Advances in experimental social psychology* (Vol. 5, pp. 119–186). New York: Academic Press.

Leventhal, H. (1971). Fear appeals and persuasion: The differentiation of a motivational construct. *American Journal of Public Health, 61,* 1208–1224.

Leventhal, H., Safer, M. A., & Panagis, D. M. (1983). The impact of communications on the self-regulation of health beliefs, decisions, and behavior. *Health Education Quarterly, 10,* 3–29.

Leventhal, H., & Singer, R. P. (1966). Affect arousal and positioning of recommendations in persuasive communications. *Journal of Personality and Social Psychology, 4,* 137–146.

Maddi, S. R. (1989). *Personality theories: A comparative analysis* (5th ed.). Chicago, IL: Dorsey.

Maddux, J. E., & Rogers, R. W. (1983). Protection motivation and self-efficacy: A revised theory of fear appeals and attitude change. *Journal of Experimental Social Psychology, 19,* 469–479.

McGuire, W. J. (1968). Personality and susceptibility to social influence. In E. Borgatta & W. Lambert (Eds.), *Handbook of personality theory and research* (pp. 1130–1187). Chicago: Rand McNally.

McKeon, J. K. (1995). *Comparing the extended parallel process model to coping responses: A look at negotiating condom usage.* Unpublished manuscript, Michigan State University, East Lansing, MI.

Mewborn, C. R., & Rogers, R. W. (1979). Effects of threatening and reassuring components of fear appeals on physiological and verbal measures of emotion and attitudes. *Journal of Experimental Social Psychology, 15,* 242–253.

Mongeau, P. (1991, February). *Fear-arousing persuasive messages: A meta-analysis revisited.* Paper presented at the annual meeting of the Western States Communication Association, Phoenix, Arizona.

Mulilis, J. P., Lippa, R. (1990). Behavioral change in earthquake preparedness due to negative threat appeals: A test of protection motivation theory. *Journal of Applied Social Psychology, 20,* 619–638.

O'Keefe, D. J. (1990). *Persuasion: Theory and research.* Newbury Park, CA: Sage.

Ortony, A., & Turner, T. J. (1990). What's basic about basic emotions? *Psychological Review, 97,* 315–331.

Prentice-Dunn, S., & Rogers, R. W. (1986). Protection motivation theory and preventive health: Beyond the health belief model. *Health Education Research, 1,* 153–161.

Rippetoe, P. A., & Rogers, R. W. (1987). Effects of components of protection-motivation theory on adaptive and maladaptive coping with a health threat. *Journal of Personality and Social Psychology, 52,* 596–604.

Rodriguez, J. I. (1995). *Confounds in fear arousing persuasive messages: Do the paths less traveled make all the difference?* Unpublished doctoral dissertation, Michigan State, East Lansing, MI.

Rogers, R. W. (1975). A protection motivation theory of fear appeals and attitude change. *Journal of Psychology, 91,* 93–114.

Rogers, R. W. (1983). Cognitive and physiological processes in fear appeals and attitude change: A revised theory of protection motivation. In J. Cacioppo & R. Petty (Eds.), *Social psychophysiology* (pp. 153–176). New York: Guilford.

Rogers, R. W., & Mewborn, C. R. (1976). Fear appeals and attitude change: Effects of a threat's noxiousness, probability of occurrence, and the efficacy of the coping responses. *Journal of Personality and Social Psychology, 34,* 54–61.

Rosenstock, I. M. (1974). The health belief model and preventive health behavior. *Health Education Monographs, 2,* 354–386.

Skilbeck, C., Tulips, J., & Ley, P. (1977). The effects of fear arousal, fear position, fear exposure, and sidedness on compliance with dietary instructions. *European Journal of Psychology, 7,* 221–239.

Stephenson, M. (1992). *Physiological responses to fear: Explicating fear and danger control in the EPPM*. Unpublished manuscript, Texas A&M University, College Station, TX.

Stephenson, M. T. (1993). *A subliminal manipulation of the extended parallel process model*. Unpublished master's thesis, Texas A&M University.

Sutton, S. R. (1982). Fear-arousing communications: A critical examination of theory and research. In Eiser, J. R. (Ed.), *Social psychology and behavioral medicine* (pp. 303–337). London: Wiley.

Witte, K. (1992). Putting the fear back into fear appeals: The extended parallel process model. *Communication Monographs, 59,* 329–349.

Witte, K. (1992c). The role of threat and efficacy in AIDS prevention. *International Quarterly of Community Health Education, 12,* 225–249.

Witte, K. (1993). Message and conceptual confounds in fear appeals: The role of threat, fear, and efficacy. *Southern Communication Journal, 58,* 147–155.

Witte, K. (1994a). Fear control and danger control: A test of the Extended Parallel Process Model (EPPM). *Communication Monographs, 61,* 113–134.

Witte, K. (1994b). Generating effective risk messages: How scary should your risk communication be? *Communication Yearbook, 18,* 229–254.

Witte, K., & Allen, M. (1996, November). *When do scare tactics work? A meta-analysis of fear appeals*. Paper presented at the annual meeting of the Speech Communication Association, San Diego, California.

Witte, K., Berkowitz, J., Cameron, K., & McKeon, J. (1995, November). *Preventing the spread of genital warts: Using fear appeals to promote self-protective behaviors*. Paper presented at the annual meeting of the Speech Communication Association, San Antonio, Texas.

Witte, K., Berkowitz, J., McKeon, J., Cameron, K., Lapinski, M. K., & Liu, W. Y. (1996, November). *Radon Awareness and Reduction Campaigns for African-Americans: A Theoretically-Based Formative and Summative Evaluation*. Paper presented at the annual meeting of the Speech Communication Association, San Diego, California.

Witte, K. (1997). *Preventing teen pregnancy through persuasive communications: Realities, myths, and the hard-fact truths*. Journal of Community Health, 22, 137–154.

Witte, K., Cameron, K. A., McKeon, J., & Berkowitz, J. (1996). Predicting risk behaviors: Development and validation of a diagnostic scale. *Journal of Health Communication, 1,* 317–341.

Witte, K., Cameron, K., & Nzyuko, S. (1995). *HIV/AIDS along the Trans-Africa Highway in Kenya: Examining risk perceptions, recommended responses, and campaign materials*. Report submitted to the All-University Research Initiative Grant program, Michigan State University, East Lansing, MI.

Witte, K., & Morrison, K. (1995a). *Examining the influence of trait anxiety/repression-sensitization on individuals' reactions to fear appeals*. Unpublished manuscript.

Witte, K., & Morrison, K. (1995c). The use of scare tactics in AIDS prevention: The case of juvenile detention and high school youth. *Journal of Applied Communication Research, 23,* 128–142.

Witte, K., & Morrison, K. (1995b). Intercultural and cross-cultural health communication: Understanding people and motivating healthy behaviors. *International and Intercultural Communication Annual, 19,* 216–246.

Witte, K., Peterson, T. R., Vallabhan, S., Stephenson, M. T., Plugge, C. D., Givens, V. K., Todd, J. D., Becktold, M. G., Hyde, M. K., Jarrett, R. (1993). Preventing tractor-related injuries and deaths in rural populations: Using a Persuasive Health Message (PHM) framework in formative evaluation research. *International Quarterly of Community Health Education, 13,* 219–251.

Witte, K., Sampson, J., Liu, W. Y., & Morrison, K. (1995). *Addressing cultural orientations in fear appeals: Promoting AIDS-protective behaviors among Hispanic immigrant and African-American adolescents*. Unpublished manuscript.

Wunsch, J. M. (1996). Perceived threat of cancer and perceived efficacy of fruit and vegetable intake in reducing cancer risk by participants in a WIC program. Manuscript under review.

Wurtele, S. K., & Maddux, J. E. (1987). Relative contributions of protection motivation theory components in predicting exercise intentions and behavior. *Health Psychology, 6,* 453–466.

CHAPTER 17

Cultural Influences on Emotional Expression: Implications for Intercultural Communication

Richard E. Porter

California State University, Long Beach
Long Beach, California

Larry A. Samovar

San Diego State University
San Diego, California

Intercultural communication examines the situation in which a message is encoded in one culture for consumption in another culture. The correct interpretation of verbal and nonverbal messages encoded in another culture is largely dependent upon one's proficiency in social perception and experience in intercultural communication. Cultural diversity in social perception adds to the complexity of intercultural communication because the meanings that we give to messages and the sense that we make of our social environments depend largely upon the influence of our own culture.

One of the ongoing dynamics of interpersonal communication involves each participant attempting to "read" other participants' emotional states. Without question, emotion is expressed continuously during interaction. But, how that emotion is perceived, interpreted, and reacted to becomes more complex when we move into the realm of intercultural communication. In large measure, culture affects the display and recognition of emotion by specifying how, when, in what social context, and by whom emotion is being displayed and recognized.

In this chapter, our primary concern is to explore the relationship between culture and the communication of emotional states during intercultural communication. Specifically, we address both the degree to which emotional display and recognition are universal attributes of humankind and the extent to which such display and recognition are mediated by culture. Before we turn to the concerns of emotions in intercultural communication, however, we begin with a brief look at the nature of emotions.

THE NATURE OF EMOTIONS

Because the nature of emotions and their expression and recognition has been dealt with extensively in earlier chapters in this book, we will give only a brief overview of the general nature of emotions to establish a continuity of thought. Emotions originate in communication (Duncan, 1968; Andersen & Guerrero, Chapter 3, this volume, Planalp, Chapter 2, this volume). When we are born, we are unaware of shame, envy, pride, disgust, remorse, and the myriad feelings we experience as we interact with others or reflect upon our own behavior. As Duncan (1968) suggested, we learn "social feelings" through communication with others by observing their responses to us and learning what our acts mean to them, and subsequently to ourselves as we act out our roles in the community and culture. It is these "feelings" that become "complex, feeling-state[s] involving conscious experience and internal and overt physical responses that tend to facilitate or inhibit motivational behavior" (Dworetsky, 1985, p. 301).

Research indicates that there are at least six primary emotions—anger, fear, surprise, sadness, disgust, and happiness—which are usually considered to be physiologically based and expressed similarly across cultures (Ekman & Friesen, 1975, 1986). Secondary emotions, such as pride, guilt, and shame arise culturally through participation in the sociocultural environment and tend to vary based on age, gender, and culture (Izard, 1985; Labouvie-Vief, Hakim-Larson, Devoe, & Schoeberlein, 1989). Although there is general recognition of both the physiological and cultural bases of primary and secondary emotions, there has been an ongoing debate about whether the communication of emotional states is universal or culturally relative.

THE INFLUENCE OF CULTURE ON EMOTIONAL EXPRESSION AND RECOGNITION

As noted above, emotions or social feelings are learned through communication with others. Because this learning occurs within a cultural context, it follows that culture influences the expression and recognition of emotions. But, just what is culture? Although there are numerous definitions of culture, we prefer the following:

> Culture is shared learned behavior which is transmitted from one generation to another for purposes of promoting individual and social survival, adaptation, and growth and development. Culture has both external (e.g., artifacts, roles, institutions) and internal rep-

resentations (e.g., values, attitudes, beliefs, cognitive/affective/sensory styles, conscious-ness patterns, and epistemologies. (Marsella, 1994, pp. 166–167)

Because emotions have a reality within ourselves, we tend to believe them to be natural. From our own experiences, we think it is natural when mothers love their children, when people envy the success of others, or when we are sad when some-one dies. Seeing human emotions as natural permits us to see them as causes for certain types of behavior. We explain war as natural aggression, marriage as the re-sult of love, and motherhood as an expression of maternal instincts. We consider our emotional responses to be "natural" and responses that differ from ours as "un-natural." Although this approach may seem logically consistent, it overlooks the role of culture and its impact on the human psyche.

Universalism versus Relativism

Interest in emotions and emotional expression in communication has been of con-cern for well over 2,500 years. In the *Rhetoric,* Aristotle (1954) analyzed emotions in terms of their constituent meanings (Turski, 1991). He, for instance, assigned "anger" a prominent role when he said, "anger may be defined as an impulse, ac-companied by a pain, to a conspicuous revenge for a conspicuous slight directed without justification toward what concerns oneself or towards what concerns one's friends" (Turski, 1991, p. 92). Scientists argued for well over 100 years whether fa-cial expressions of emotion are universal or culture-specific. Darwin (1872) was among the first to believe that emotional expressions were biological and had evo-lutionary adaptive value. Those who shared Darwin's view were labeled universal-ists (e.g. Eibl-Eibesfeldt; 1972, Lorenz, 1965; Tomkins, 1962). Others, who con-tended that emotional expression was culture-specific, took a cultural relative perspective (e.g., Birdwhistell, 1970; Kleinberg, 1940; LaBarre, 1947; Leach, 1972; Mead, 1975).

Convincing research from the past 20 years has provided evidence of both uni-versal and culture-specific influences on the expression and perception of emotion (Matsumoto, 1991; see also Andersen & Guerrero, Chapter 3, this volume). Many current scholars interested in emotion have embraced both universalism and differ-entialism positions. Universalism posits that emotion, just like perception, cogni-tion, or learning, is a basic mechanism of human functioning that is relatively in-variant over races and cultures. Differentialism, on the other hand, posits that emotions, as identified by different language labels, are differentiated with respect to physiological symptoms, expressive behavior, motivation, and subjective feeling (Scherer & Wallbott, 1994).

Universalism

Universalists argue that there is an innate or universally learned relationship between emotions and specific facial behaviors. Their argument is based on numerous cross-cultural studies that have shown emotional communicative behavior posed by members of one culture can be identified by members of another culture (Boucher & Ekman, 1975). Although this universalist position has been challenged by cultural relativists, a consistent body of evidence has emerged to reveal a pan-cultural element in the association of facial behavior with emotion (Ekman, Friesen, & Ellsworth, 1972).

Certain facial expressions of emotion, in particular, seem to be universal across cultures. Subjects from various literate cultures associate the same facial expressions with the emotional states of happiness, fear, surprise, anger, disgust, and sadness or equivalent emotion words in their own language (Ekman, 1973; Ekman & Friesen, 1971). "The same emotions were judged for the same facial behaviors by observers from different cultures in experiments that had many different stimuli of many different stimulus persons and many different groups of observers from 14 cultures or nations" (Ekman, Friesen, & Ellsworth, 1982, p. 141). Similar results were also obtained with isolated, preliterate subjects (Ekman & Friesen, 1971).

In studying facial displays, researchers have found that the face provides multiple signals to convey more than one kind of message. These include static (e.g., skin color), slow (e.g., permanent wrinkles), and rapid (e.g., raising the eyebrows) signals (Ekman & Friesen, 1975). Of greatest import in the study of emotions are the rapid signals that result in temporary changes in facial appearance, such as shifts in the location and shape of the facial features that flash on the face for a matter of seconds or fractions of a second. Transitory feelings, such as fear, anger, or surprise, lead to facial muscle contraction, and there are visible changes in the appearance of the face. Wrinkles appear or disappear, the eyebrows, eyes, eyelids, nostrils, lips, cheeks, and chin temporarily change. Research has shown that accurate judgments of emotion can be made from these rapid face signals. (Ekman & Friesen, 1975, p. 11).

Although emotional messages are not transmitted primarily by either the slow or static facial signals, it is important to note that these signals may affect the implications of an emotional message. If a person has a fat or thin face, a smooth or wrinkled face, an old or young face, a male or a female face, that in of itself does not convey happiness, anger, or sadness. But these signals may affect attributions about the emotion and subsequent impression formation. For instance, if rapid facial signals tell you that a person is happy, your impression of why the person is happy and what he or she is likely to do while happy may depend in part upon the information gleaned from the static and slow facial signals about the person's age, sex, personality, and character (Ekman & Friesen, 1975).

Evidence that there is a cross-cultural universality in the facial expressions used to convey happiness, surprise, fear, anger, disgust, and sadness raises the issue of whether these expressions may have a biological basis (see Guerrero, Andersen, & Trost, Chapter 1, this volume; Planalp, Chapter 2, this volume). Ekman et al. (1987) concluded that "the evidence now for universality is overwhelming, whereas that for cultural differences is sparse" (p. 171).

Relativism

Despite considerable evidence for universality in expression, there are some indications of cross-cultural differences, particularly in rates of recognition and in the frequencies with which emotional expressions are displayed or mentioned in self-reports. At the same time it is equally clear that culture and past experience have a strong effect on facial expression and bodily movement. For example, some emotions, like contempt, seem to have culturally specific facial expressions. In other cases, the importance of masking emotions will affect all facial movement in the presence of other people. Where people are taught to be polite and sensitive to the feelings of others, as in Japan, this will affect the facial movements used in the presence of others. In the same situation, Japanese smile more, for example, than Americans do (Mirowsky & Ross, 1984).

Research on facial expressions has shown how they are simultaneously universal and culturally specific, effectively resolving the debate concerning the universality of emotion. These differences are accounted for by Ekman and Friesen (1971), who suggested that facial prototypes of each of the universal emotions are stored in a biologically based facial affect program. Facial expressions convey discrete emotions, making them a most specific and precise nonverbal signal system. Facial expressions also illustrate speech, regulate conversation, and provide social impressions (Matsumoto, 1991).

Despite the biologically based facial affect program, there seem to be relatively clear cultural expectations as to how appropriate particular emotions and particular intensities of emotion are in certain situations, as well as which type of emotional expression seems to be legitimate and which methods of managing emotion are to be preferred at any one time (Scherer, Summerfield & Wallbott, 1983).

Cultural differences have been found in the absolute intensity levels of the emotions attributed to facial expressions (Ekman et al., 1987). In a cross-cultural study involving Asian and American subjects, intensity ratings of happiness, surprise, and fear were found to vary significantly across cultures. Asian subjects gave lower intensity ratings than the non-Asian subjects (Besquita & Frijda, 1992). Matsumoto (1991) suggested that differences in "decoding rules" might account for cultural dissimilarity in intensity ratings. He correlated the ratings of seven countries on cultural value dimensions (as had been measured by Hofstede, 1980) with the emotional intensity ratings of these countries as obtained by Ekman et al. (1987). The cultural variation questionnaire measured four dimensions. Significant correlations were established between emotional expression and two of these dimensions—Power Distance and Individualism correlated with the intensity ratings of anger, fear, and sadness expressions such that people from individualistic cultures were more likely to communicate a wider variety of emotional behaviors than were members of collective cultures. Members of high power-distance cultures tend to display emotions that emphasize and preserve status differences, whereas members of low power-difference cultures tend to display emotions that minimize power and status differences.

Research has shown cultures exert considerable influence over emotion. Ekman and Friesen's (1971) early study on emotional expressions documented how the display of emotion differs across cultures, depending on social situation. In their study, Japanese and American subjects viewed highly stressful films first alone and then again in the presence of a higher status experimenter. When alone, members of both cultures displayed similar facial expressions of disgust, anger, sadness, and fear. When in the presence of the experimenter, however, their expressions differed dramatically, with the Japanese invariably smiling rather than displaying their true negative feelings (Matsumoto, 1993, p. 108). This research provides compelling evidence that although the private experience and expression of a particular emotion is similar across cultures, public emotional expression is dependent on cultural display rules.

Matsumoto (1991) found cultural differences between Americans and Japanese in appropriateness ratings for facial expressions of six universal emotions in five social situations—alone, with ingroups, with outgroups, with higher-status others, and with lower-status others. Japanese rated anger and fear more appropriate to outgroups, and anger more appropriate to lower-status others than did the Americans. The Americans, however, rated disgust and sadness more appropriate to ingroups (Matsumoto, 1993, p. 108).

CULTURAL DYNAMICS AFFECTING EMOTION

In the remainder of this chapter, we examine several significant cultural dynamics that affect the display of emotion and ultimately intercultural communication. These diverse aspects of culture are (1) display rules, (2) antecedent events, (3) individual-collectivism and power distance, (4) context, (5) nonverbal communication, and (6) language. These aspects are included here because their cultural diversity impacts the expression of emotions in intercultural settings.

Display Rules

Ekman and Friesen (1975) have coined the term "display rules" to describe cultural influences on what people learn about the need to manage the appearance of particular emotions in various situations. This management and supression of emotional expressions follow five culturally learned display rules (Andersen & Guerrero, Chapter 3, this volume; Ekman, 1978; Shennum & Bugental, 1982), which include *simulation, intensification, neutralization* (or inhibition), *deintensification* (or miniaturization), and *masking* (see also Guerrero et al., Chapter 1, this volume). Simulation involves showing nonexisting feelings. Intensification is to give the appearance of more feelings than actually felt. Neutralization or inhibition involves giving the appearance of having no feelings when you really have a feeling. Deintensification of miniaturization is the act of appearing to have less feelings than you actually possess. Finally, masking involves covering one's true feeling by expressing a feeling that is not being felt (Andersen, Andersen, & Landgraf, 1985). For example, urban, white, adult males in the United States tend to follow the display rule that prohibits the showing of fear in public. Their young female counterparts tend to follow a display rule that prohibits displaying anger in public.

Culture imposes display rules as children are taught what they may and may not do, often through unconscious observation, imitation of peers and adults, and/or through parental reinforcement (see Andersen & Guerrero, Chapter 3, this volume). Once learned, cultural display rules become habitual, and people do not need to think about what they are doing unless they make a mistake and display the wrong emotion in the wrong situation. Ekman and Friesen (1975) revealed that people only pause to think about display rules if they are in a strange or unique situation or if they are unable to interpret the social situation and need to determine their role and what is expected of them.

Display rules govern which emotions may be displayed in various social circumstances, and they specify the intensity of the emotional display. In many Asian countries such as China, Japan, Taiwan, or Korea, display rules are derived from Confucian principles and strong collective social relationships. In such an orientation, it is important to maintain proper social relationships (Yun, 1994). Accordingly, it is normally improper to display emotions such as anger, disagreement, or contempt in public situations. Instead, a smile may emerge that functions to mask real feelings and to maintain appropriate social relationships. In other cultures, such as those of the Middle East, display rules prescribe loud, prolonged, and often anguishing behaviors when expressing anger or grief.

Although culture is predominant in determining the rules that prescribe emotional expression, it also tends to specify which antecedent, external events lead to emotional displays.

Antecedent Events and Emotion Appraisal

What external events cause emotional experiences? There is conflicting evidence concerning antecedent events that arouse various emotions and the appraisal of those emotions. Mesquita and Frijda (1992) claimed that certain kinds of events elicit emotions in widely different cultures and that these events tend to elicit the same emotions in these different cultures. Studies by Boucher and Brandt (1981, 1985) suggest cross-cultural similarities of the antecedents of anger, fear, joy, sadness, and surprise among Americans, Malaysians, Koreans, and Samoans. Cultural similarity in antecedents has also been established in a series of studies on sadness, anger, fear, and happiness (Scherer, Summerfield, & Walbott, 1983; Scherer, Wallbott, Matsumoto, & Kudoh, 1988; Scherer, Walbott, & Summerfield, 1986).

There is also, however, evidence of cultural diversity in antecedent events. Mesquita and Frijda (1992), for instance, suggest that in instances of antecedent diversity, emotions may differ between cultures, but the appraisals of these antecedents frequently remain the same. For example, the appraisal of self-blame is seen as a general antecedent of guilt. The actual antecedents leading to guilt may, however, be very specific. A husband's infidelity may be a reason for self-blame among Japanese women, but women elsewhere may accept little or no blame for their husband's actions. Mesquita and Frijda also suggested that antecedent differences are manifested by distinctions in the nature as well as the frequency of particular emotion-eliciting events. In other words, members of different cultures may see the same stimuli differently. For example, a kangaroo is likely to elicit different emotions in Canada and Australia because of sensitization and frequency of exposure. In addition, Mesquita and Frijda suggested that differences may exist in the propensity of different cultures to appraise emotionally relevant situations in a particular manner so that some groups may tend to avoid particular modes of appraisal. For instance, in one culture anger might be elicited by events that appear innocuous or barely disturbing to members of a different culture. Such differences also may be due to cultural diversity in regulation processes that suppress undesirable appraisals.

Cultural diversity in antecedent events and the effect it has on various emotional states may be seen by looking at the emotions of joy and happiness, sadness and grief, fear and anxiety, and anger and rage.

Joy and Happiness

Scherer and Wallbott (1994), for instance, specify differences in the nature and patterns of antecedent events across European, Japanese, and U.S. cultures with the greatest differences being found between the Japanese and Western cultures. They found that among Europeans and Americans, the birth of a new family member and body-centered pleasures were important antecedent events eliciting joy. But, among Japanese, these events were less frequent antecedents for joy. Scherer et al. (1994) speculated that

> the relative insignificance of bodily pleasure seems to underline the stereotypical notion of the Japanese as a sober, hardworking, and at times somewhat ascetic people. Our finding that the birth of a new family member was less a source of joy for the Japanese may be related to the observation that to older children, the birth of younger siblings threatens an already strong parent–child bond. Thus in Japanese society the birth of a younger sibling may represent an event that separates older children from their parents' care and love, much more so than in other cultures. (p. 11)

Achievement-related joy situations were found more frequently in the United States and Europe than in Japan. Although achievement seems to be equally important in both the United States and Japan, there is often more pressure for achievement and possibly higher expectations for success—both by the person and the social environment in Japanese culture. Among the Japanese there also are implicit and subtle rules that inhibit joy reactions to personal success while supporting such reactions to group-oriented achievements (Scherer & Wallbott, 1994).

Sadness and Grief

Scherer and Wallbott (1994) found significant differences among cultures for almost all classes of antecedent events leading to sadness and grief. The most striking difference was the sadness experiences provoked by the death of a family member or close friend. In both Europe and the United States, such events caused approximately 1 in 5 of all sadness experiences. Yet in Japan, the same antecedent led to only 1 in 20 sadness situations. Scherer et al. suggest that this difference might be explained by religious differences due to Shinto–Buddhist rules of ancestor veneration and the different connotations for death found in Japanese culture. Although Japanese mourn the loss of loved ones in much the same way as other people, In Japanese culture a belief exists that the dead person's soul always remains with and is protected by her or his family leading to a consciousness that the deceased is still and will always be with the family (Scherer et al., 1994).

Fear/Anxiety

In examining fear and anxiety, Scherer and Wallbott (1994) found several interesting cultural differences. Among Americans, stranger fear was the most frequent category followed by fear of failure in achievement situations. Among the Europeans, stranger fear was predominant followed by the fear of traffic accidents. Among the Japanese, however, fear of strangers is almost insignificant since it is dwarfed by fear of novel situations, fear of failure in achievement situations, and fear of traffic. Scherer et al. (1994) speculated that these differences are probably related to the differential incidence of threatening events in each of the cultures. Crime is likely to be a more frequent occurrence in U.S. urban areas than in many European countries or Japan. Realizing the relatively low incidence of crime and stranger aggression among the Japanese, it seems plausible to expect this antecedent to cause less fear than in the United States or Europe (Scherer & Wallbott, 1994).

A fear-producing antecedent that causes greater anxiety among Japanese is relationship produced—the fear of hurting or angering one's parents or lover. Because the Japanese have strong concern for the people around them, they tend to monitor and regulate their social relationships constantly, particularly when social transgressions could potentially occur. This concern with appropriate relational communication seems likely to be a much stronger antecedent of fear in Japan than in the United States or Europe (Scherer & Wallbott, 1994).

Anger/Rage

Again, the Japanese are quite different than Europeans and Americans in their anger antecedents. Where Americans and Europeans found anger induced by problems with known others, the Japanese are much more angered by strangers. Among a sample of U.S. students, almost 60% of their anger situations were due to some problem in their interpersonal relationships. Anger induced by interpersonal strangers was limited to about 15% for Americans and about 20% for Europeans. In Japan, however, more than half of the anger situations were produced by antecedent experiences with strangers. Again, the cultural diversity found between the Japanese and their American and European counterparts probably accounts for the differences in anger-inducing antecedents. In Japan, the social norms for communication in relationships are more highly structured and readily obeyed, which makes it less likely that a breach of these norms occurs to induce angry outbursts. Even in a situation where a social transgression has occurred, the situation often dictates that one should not become angry or at least not show her or his anger (Scherer & Wallbott, 1994).

Individualism and Collectivism and Power Distance

Individuals readily learn to control their behavior on the basis of the social differences that exist within their cultures. The effect of culture on social differences stems, in part, from where a culture is located along independence–collectivism (I-C) and power distance (PD) dimensions (Hofstede, 1980). The five most independent or individualistic cultures are the United States, Australia, Great Britain, Canada, and the Netherlands, whereas the five cultures at the collectivistic end of the dimension include Venezuela, Colombia, Pakistan, Peru, and Taiwan (Hofstede, 1980).

The influence of these cultural dynamics may be understood in terms of social roles and structures knows as *ingroups/outgroups* and *status* respectively. Self or ingroup relations provide the safety and comfort requisite for free emotional expression and tolerate a broad spectrum of emotional behavior. Self or outgroup relationships do not provide this flexibility and tolerance. People are more comfortable in expressing emotions to their families than to strangers in public. Family histories of familiarity, intimacy, and tolerance provide an environment in which emotions may be expressed in ways that could not be understood or perhaps tolerated by strangers. Part of one's emotional development involves the learning of just who are ingroup and outgroup members and the behaviors appropriate in their presence (Matsumoto, 1991, p. 131).

Independence and Collectivism

The meanings of self and ingroup and self and outgroup relationships are culturally diverse and lead to cultural differences in emotional behavior (Triandis, Botempo, Vilareal, Asai, & Lucca, 1988). Cultures with an individualistic orientation have more ingroups, and their members have little attachment to any single ingroup because there are numerous such groups to which they may attach. Societal survival of individualistic cultures is dependent in large measure upon individual efficiency and striving rather than upon groups within the society. In collective cultures, people belong to fewer ingroups, and their commitment to those groups is much greater than in individualistic cultures. In collectivist cultures, societal survival is much more dependent upon the effective functioning of groups rather than upon individual achievement (Matsumoto, 1991).

Individualistic and collectivist cultures produce ingroups with differing degrees of harmony, cohesion, cooperation, and conformity between the self and the group (Matsumoto, 1991). In collective cultures, a greater degree of conformity is found within ingroups, and severe sanctions may exist for lack of conformity. Commitment to conformity helps ensure group identification and bonding that permits groups to function maximally. Such collectivism necessarily leads to the subjugation of personal goals in deference to collective goals. Less conformity is found within groups among individualistic cultures because they rely less on group identification and effective group operations because societal survival is not dependent upon groups (Matsumoto, 1991).

Because of the differences in group relationships brought about by cultural differences in individualism–collectivism, Matsumoto (1991) argued that collective cultures will foster emotional displays that maintain and facilitate group cohesion, harmony, and cooperation to a greater degree than individualistic cultures. He suggested that the degree to which emotions are communicated in a culture varies according to how well they facilitate or hinder group cohesion. Collectivist cultures, consequently, exhibit more cohesion-producing emotions than individualistic cultures. Japanese, therefore, are more likely than Americans to suppress negative emotions because their collective culture demands a greater degree of harmony within its ingroups. Yet, Japanese would be more inclined than Americans to express negative emotions if it would facilitate group cohesion (Matsumoto, 1991).

Compared to Japanese, Americans more often display positive harmony-producing emotions to strangers, casual acquaintances, or new ingroup members because they consider interactions with other individuals on an individual basis (Triandis, et al., 1987) Japanese, on the other hand, do not hesitate to communicate less positive emotions to outgroup members because there is little or no need to form cohesive bonds.

A wide variety of emotional behaviors is found within individualistic cultures than within collectivist cultures. Although variety is valued in individualistic cultures, it is frowned upon in collective cultures, and wide ranges of individual variation are discouraged (Matsumoto, 1991).

Differences in the amount of emotional behavior displayed between ingroups and outgroups in individualistic cultures will be quite large. In collective cultures, however, the amount of emotional behavior displayed between ingroups and outgroups will be smaller because collective cultures discourage the display of emotional behavior directed to those outside the ingroup. Consequently, the emotional behavior of Americans and Japanese generally differs depending on whether they are interacting with close friends or with strangers in public.

Power Distance

Power distance, or differentiated social status, is another cultural variable that causes people to modify their emotional displays according to self–other relationships. Power distance refers to the extent to which a society accepts that power in relationships, institutions, and organizations is distributed unequally. According to Hofstede (1980), countries that prefer high power distances include the Philippines, Mexico, Venezuela, India, and Yugoslavia. At the other extreme of the dimension are found such countries as Austria, Israel, Denmark, New Zealand, and Ireland.

This cultural orientation helps determine the way in which personal relationships form and develop when power differences are present or at least perceived to be present. Having more power in social relationships is not the same as being dominant in actual behavior. Power may be defined as a potential for exercising influence over other people's actions, decisions, and thoughts (Marsella, 1994, pp. 83–84).

Cultures differ considerably in how social status is defined and differentiated. In free market societies such as the United States, for example, power and status are often related to money or to the ability to perform behaviors that most others cannot (e.g., striking out batters in the National League or scoring three-point baskets in the National Basketball Association). Yet in other cultures it may be related to social position, hereditary nobility, occupation, or caste systems. As with individualism-collectivism, emotional socialization requires learning appropriate emotional responses according to the self–other status differences (Matsumoto, 1991).

Cultural diversity in power distance has been shown to affect emotional behavior. High power-distance cultures foster emotional behaviors that maintain status differences. This, for example, could involve displaying positive emotions to persons of higher status and negative emotions to persons of lower status (Collins, 1984). This power distance display rule serves to maintain the power and status differences between individuals because a transgression of the rule would threaten power distance (Matsumoto, 1991).

In low power-distance cultures, emotional behaviors that minimize power and status differences are encouraged. People who live in low power-distance cultures tend to communicate more positive emotions to lower-status others and more negative emotions to high-status others. People in low power-distance cultures are freer to display negative emotions to social superiors without fear of repercussion. Moreover, the importance of suppressing status-threatening emotions is minimized because status differences are small (Matsumoto, 1991).

Matsumoto (1991) offered as an example of power distance behavior by comparing status differences among retail clerks, department managers, store managers, and regional directors in retail businesses in both Japanese and American cultures. In Japan, department managers would routinely display negative emotions to their lower status retail clerks. These clerks, however, would refrain from displaying negative emotions to the manager. These social conventions clearly maintain status differences between the department manager and the clerks. In American businesses, however, status is much less differentiated, and department managers would tend to treat their clerks as equals, minimizing status differences and attempting to reduce friction.

The degree of difference between perceiving oneself as occupying a high or low status during interactions also differs according to power-distance diversity. In high power-distance cultures, status should have a considerable effect on emotional behavior. For instance, the difference in behavior between the Japanese department manager and the retail clerks and the difference in behavior between the same manager and the store manager would be quite large. In low power-distance cultures, however, the same interactions would yield much less difference in communicative behavior.

Context Diversity

Ekman, Friesen, and Ellsworth (1989) pointed out that people seldom perceive faces alone without any context, and that when they do they tend not to make inferences about emotion. Context is the social and physical environment in which communication occurs and includes the preceding and consequent facial behaviors as well as body positions and movements, words and vocal tones, the nature of the setting, what has been happening previously, and who else is present. Ekman et al. (1989) concluded that although facial expressions dominate emotion judgments, context information becomes important when facial expressions are ambiguous or the emotion portrayed is low in intensity. In real-life situations, however, we rarely confront a static face. "Real-life" observers receive information not only from facial expressions but from other behaviors such as gestures, vocal qualities, or body position, as well as the situational context in which a given facial expression occurs (Walbott, 1994; see also Planalp, Chapter 2, this volume).

The notion of context has two dimensions. First, the *social* context influences the interpretation of emotions. This notion of context is reflected by the environment in which communication occurs: the workplace, church or temple, dinner with friends, a court of law, a wedding, a baseball game, or family gathering. In all of these contexts, the social environment helps determine which emotions may be displayed and aids in the interpretation of those emotions.

The second dimension of context refers to Hall's (1976) concept of *high- and low-context cultures*. Hall (1976) specified: "One of the functions of culture is to provide a highly selective screen between [humans] and the outside world. In its many forms, culture therefore designates what we pay attention to and what we ignore" (1976, p. 74). He categorized cultures as being either high or low context depending on how much meaning their members attach to settings. Context is defined as "the information that surrounds an event; it is inextricably bound up with the meaning of the event" (Hall & Hall, 1990, p. 6). The high- and low-context of cultures affects the types of messages that are created within those cultures.

> A high context (HC) communication or message is one in which most of the information is already in the person, while very little is in the coded, explicitly transmitted part of the message. A low context (LC) communication is just the opposite; i.e., the mass of the information is vested in the explicit code (Hall, 1976, p. 79).

Hall is suggesting that in high-context cultures such as the Japanese, Chinese, and Korean, people are very homogeneous with regard to experiences, information networks, and the like. High-context cultures, because of tradition and history, change very little over time. These cultures enjoy a consistency of messages that produce consistent responses to the environment. "For most normal transactions in daily life they do not require, nor do they expect, much in-depth, background information" (Hall & Hall, 1990, p. 6).

In low-context cultures such as the German, Canadian, and American, the population is less homogeneous and tends to compartmentalize interpersonal contacts. They lack a large pool of common experiences, which means that whenever they interact with others then need detailed background information (Hall & Hall, 1990).

Contextual differences lead to cultural diversity in expression. In high-context cultures relatively little information is actually contained in verbal messages or facial expressions. In low-context cultures, most of the information is contained in the verbal message or in facial and bodily movements. A traditional wife, in a high-context culture, for instance, might show anger with her husband not by verbal or facial expressions but by making a flower arrangement in which a single flower is slightly out of place. When perceived by the husband, he will be aware of his wife's anger. In a low-context culture, however, anger will more likely be displayed by both verbal and nonverbal expressions.

In addition to the culturally diverse dimensions we have discussed above, there are two aspects of emotional communication that are also subject to cultural diversity in on of themselves. These are (1) nonverbal behavior and (2) verbal or linguistic behavior.

Nonverbal Communication

It is well established that culture can affect nonverbal communication (Samovar & Porter, 1995). Tsunoda (1979) has shown how cultures transform simple behaviors into many different messages. In our interactions with people from different cultures, we encounter nonverbal displays with unique meanings to their culture or subculture (Tsunoda, 1979). Scherer and Wallbott (1994), for instance, have reported that Japanese students employ fewer body part motions (mostly hand and arm gestures) and whole-body reactions than Europeans or Americans when expressing all forms of emotion. This indicates that the Japanese are less expressive in terms of their gross motor activity and gesturing behaviors.

Cultural differences in the unmasking of the face are important enough for us to discuss in detail. In many Mediterranean cultures, people exaggerate signs of grief or sadness. It is not uncommon in this region of the world to see men crying in public. Yet in the United States, males tend to suppress the desire to show these emotions. Japanese men even go so far as to hide expressions of anger, sorrow, or disgust by laughing or smiling. The Chinese also do not readily show emotion for reasons that are rooted deeply in their culture—the Chinese concept of saving face being one of the most important. For the Chinese, displaying emotion violates face-saving norms by disrupting harmony and causing conflict (Wenzhong & Grove, 1991).

In North America, a smile can be a sign of happiness or friendly affirmation. Although these same meanings are found among the Japanese, the smile is also used to mask emotions more frequently in Japan than in North America (McDaniel, 1993).

Linguistic Diversity

Culture impacts emotional expression by determining how such feelings as happiness, sadness, and anger should be expressed (McConatha, Lightner, & Deaner, 1994). Ekman (1972) coined the terms "feeling rules," which are held to determine individuals' interpretations of their environments, and "display rules," which determine the circumstances under which emotions are expressed or inhibited.

It is not surprising that language affects judgments of emotion given the close connection between language and culture and between culture and emotion judgment. All languages derive from and represent the cultures from which they originate (Matsumoto & Assar, 1992).

The connection between language and culture may be observed by a comparison of American English and Japanese. American English is a relatively complex, rather idiosyncratic language that involves rules of grammar and syntax but contains many exceptions to these rules. American culture is less structured, places little emphasis on social positions, and permits significant individual variation in adhering to the rules of the culture. Thus, American English tends to be relatively independent of social context and varies little despite differences in the social positions of the persons interacting. Japanese, on the other hand, is a rigid, highly structured language that also employs rules of grammar and syntax but allows very few exceptions to those rules. Because Japanese culture and society is bound by rigid rules that govern social relationships and social status in all aspects of life, the Japanese language differs substantially in various social situations. If a Japanese is speaking to someone of lower social position, then he or she is permitted to speak in a particular way. If a person is speaking to someone of higher status, however, the person must adapt her or his language usage accordingly even though the message content is identical (Matsumoto & Assar, 1992).

Language serves as a guide to deriving emotions. Hints about the various emotions may be gleaned from various languages. Kundra (1980), for instance, revealed that

> *Litost* is a Czech word with no exact translation into any other language. It designates a feeling as infinite as an open accordion, a feeling that is the synthesis of many others: grief, sympathy, remorse, and an indefinable longing. . . . Under certain circumstances, however, it can have a very narrow meaning, a meaning as definite, precise, and sharp as a well-honed cutting edge. I have never found an equivalent in other languages for this sense of the word either, though I do not see how anyone can understand the human soul without it. . . . *Litost* is a state of torment caused by a sudden insight into one's miserable self. . . . *Litost* works like a two-stroke motor. First comes a feeling of torment, then the desire for revenge. (pp. 121–122)

Russell (1991) provided additional examples of linguistic diversity where there are words that reflect an emotion within a culture that have no translation into English. The German word *schadenfreude,* which refers to pleasure derived from another's displeasure, has no direct English translation. Similarly, the German word *angst* has no English translation. And from the Japanese language is the word *itoshii,* which refers to a feeling associatied with observing someone praiseworthy overcoming an obstacle. From Bengalis is the word *obhiman,* which refers to sorrow caused by the insensitivity of a loved one.

Just as there is a lack of direct English translations for emotion words from other languages, some English words have no equivalent in some other language. Arabic, for instance, does not contain a lexical equivalent for the English word "frustration." And, although English appears to distinguish between such words as "terror," "horror," "dread," "apprehension," and "timidity" as types or degrees of fear, in the Gidjingali language a single word, *gurakadj,* suffices (Hiatt, 1978).

Not only is there the difficulty of not having lexical equivalents for emotions across various cultures, some languages fail to distinguish clearly what English separates into basic level emotional categories (Russell, 1991). Leff (1973), for instance, has shown how some African languages use the same word to convey what English would distinguish as anger and sadness. In addition, Orly (1970, p. 3) provides an example from the Luganda language, which is spoken by the Buganda of Uganda, Africa:

> The difference between anger and sorrow is not stressed to the same extent as in English, and it is not uncommon to hear an interpreter using [the word] *okusunguwals* (to get angry) as a translation of *to get sad,* nor would he really feel he had made a mistake even when "corrected." If one wishes to speak specifically about the grief of mourning or of a friend's departure, then the verb *okusaalirwa* is used, but even then I have heard of men mourning at a funeral being said to be *basunguwadde* (angry).

Another example of culturally based linguistic diversity in emotional communication is found in an examination of the emotion *shame.* In English, the word shame is associated with a desire not to be seen. Izard (1969) stated that "when subjects are asked how they feel or what they do when they experience shame, they very frequently indicate that they want to disappear; they want very badly not to be seen" (p. 275).

In the Australian language Gidjingali, however, the closest lexical equivalent does not seem to reveal an association with the desire not to be seen. Hiatt (1978) claimed the Gidjingali word associates the feeling of shame with a desire to retreat or run away. Consequently, the Gidjingali word can appropriately be used as an equivalent of the English words "shame" or "fear." It would appear that to the speakers of Gidjingali, shame and fear are essentially the same feeling because they are both seen in terms of the same impulse to retreat or to avoid. But, from an English speaker's point of view, shame and fear are two different emotions.

The American English distinction between shame and embarrassment is not made by the Japanese (Lebra, 1983), Tahitians (Levy, 1973), Ifalukians (Lutz, 1980), or Indonesians (Keeler, 1983). Among the Ilongot, one word is used to cover shame, timidity, awe, embarrassment, obedience, and respect (Rosalodo, 1983), whereas the Javanese use the word *isin* to name shame, guilt, shyness, and embarrassment (Geertz, 1959).

Another culturally diverse linguistic device is the framing of communicative behavior. To ensure the success of emotional communication, there must be a large reduction of uncertainty in terms of the possible interpretations that can be made. When affect is conveyed unsuccessfully, the reason generally is that the cognitive frame for the interpretation of the behavior was insufficiently established (Beeman, 1988). The Persian language contains a rich set of idiomatic expressions that help individuals convey their feelings. The Persian culture provides basic frames that inform individuals about appropriate language behavior for any given situation.

The Persian language contains a number of stylistic devices that help individuals signal each other concerning many aspects of their assessment of their relationship. These devices deal with contrasts between relationships that are status differentiated and those that are status undifferentiated (Beeman, 1988).

Although hierarchial differentiation is nearly a universal feature of human interaction, in some societies such as India, Japan, and Iran, it takes on a special symbolic significance. Few societies take the obligations of status as seriously as the Iranians. Because the Iranian basic pattern of interaction represents stability within the system of social life, it is a system of high-pattern congruity. Conformity to the basic patterns during interaction represents predictability for interactants (Beeman, 1988).

Iranians value inside situations and orientations far more than outside situations. Beeman (1988) provided an interesting example of how these interaction patterns operate in ordinary conversation.

> A man is arguing with an army official over a petition for a military service waiver for his son. The discussion proceeds, the man making himself more and more abject in his petition, to no avail. Finally he breaks down in tears and begins to address the officer in familiar terms. The officer's mood immediately changes, and he quiets the man, telling him he will do what he can for the boy. When asked why he changed his mind, the officer said, "Well, it was obvious he was sincere; he was speaking from the bottom of his heart." (p. 21)

In an outside situation, the petitioner conformed to the basic interaction pattern for a long while, and then "flooded out" into inside behavior. His message was then clearly read as prompted by sincere emotion and was valued positively (Beeman, 1988).

Another Iranian cultural dynamic that affects emotional expression and recognition occurs when two people are so angry with each other that they cannot reach an agreement on their differences. In this instance they withdraw and refuse to interact on any level. This action is known in Persia as being *gahr* with someone. Being *gahr* with another person is an extreme expression of affect and a control mechanism that lies outside basic Iranian interaction patterns. In fact, it is so far removed from normal interaction that it is immediately noticed by others.

The irony in this position is that one cannot be in a state of *gahr* with someone for whom one does not feel some affection. The state of *gahr* represents a break in an ongoing relationship, which signals a disturbance in a normal emotional relationship. As a control mechanism, a state of *gahr* will eventually lead to a reconciliation of the problem that caused the breach in the relationship. Such reconciliation normally occurs through an intermediary who tries to get the two parties to reconcile their differences simultaneously in order to avoid the prospect of one party having to give into the other (Beeman, 1988).

SUMMARY AND CONCLUSION

In this chapter we have briefly described the nature of emotions and discussed the manner in which culture affects how we learn to have feelings and express them in manners that are consistent with our culture. We revealed that there are both universal and culturally relative aspects to the communication of emotions. For the most part, the specific communicative behaviors that reflect various emotions are universal, but culture determines who may express emotions as well as both the circumstances under which they may be expressed and the degree to which they may be expressed.

Culture was shown to affect the expression and recognition of emotions across a variety of cultural dimensions that included display rules, antecedent events, individualism, collectivism and power distance, communication context, nonverbal communication, and linguistic diversity. Five displays rules involving intensification, simulation, inhibition, deintensification, and masking were shown to affect the manner in which emotions are expressed. Antecedent events were discussed in the context of the emotions of joy and happiness, fear and anxiety, and anger and rage and the effect these events have in eliciting emotional behavior. Hofstede's (1980) cultural dimensions of individualism and collectivism and power distance were shown to exert an influence on ingroup and outgroup relationships and on how emotional displays are mediated to maintain the integrity of the ingroup. Next, cultural influences on both the social context in which communication occurs as well as the contextual form of the culture (i.e., Hall & Hall's high- and low-context cultures) were also found to affect both the manner in which emotions may be expressed as well as the need for emotional expression. Cultural diversity in nonverbal communication behavior was also found to affect emotional communication. And, finally, linguistic diversity was found to affect emotional communication in terms of language structure. In fact, some cultures lack the appropriate word to express an emotion that is readily expressed in other cultures.

Success in intercultural communication requires that participants be able to interpret each other's emotional states. To some degree, emotional behavior is both universal and culturally specific. To the extent that culture influences emotional communication, intercultural communicators must be aware of and understand the cultural dynamics that produce this behavior. In addition, they must develop a facility that permits them not only to interpret the behavior, but also to be (or at least appear to be) comfortable with the ambiguity that can come from emotional expressions that seem out of place or inappropriate to a particular situation.

By reviewing the material in this chapter, we have attempted to provide readers with a referential background from which to draw upon and develop an understanding of cultural diversity in emotional communication. From a richer understanding of cultural diversity, improved intercultural communication facility may emerge.

REFERENCES

Alabas, D. C., McCluskey, K. W., & Albas, C. A. (1976). Perception of the emotional content of speech: A comparison of two Canadian groups. *Journal of Cross-Cultural Psychology, 7,* 481–490.

Andersen, J. F., Andersen, P. A., & Landgraf, J. (1985, May). *The development of nonverbal communication competence in childhood.* Paper presented at the annual convention of the International Communication Association, Honolulu, HI.

Aristotle (1954). *Rhetoric.* (W. R. Roberts, Trans.). New York: The Modern Library.

Beeman, W. O. (1988). Affectivity in Persian language use. *Culture, Medicine and Psychiatry, 12,* 9–30.

Besquita, B., & Frijda, N. H. (1992). Cultural variations in emotions: A review. *Psychological Bulletin, 112,* 179–204.

Birdwhistell, R. L. (1970). *Kinesics and context.* Philadelphia: University of Pennsylvania Press.

Brandt, M. E., & Boucher, J. D. (1985). Judgments of emotions from the antecedent situations in three cultures. In I. R. Lagunes & Y. H. Poortinga (Eds.), *From a different perspective: Studies of behavior across cultures* (pp. 348–362). Lisse, The Netherlands: Swets & Zeitlinger.

Brandt, M. E., & Boucher, J. D. (1986). Concepts of depression in emotion lexicons of eight cultures. *International Journal of Intercultural Relations, 10,* 321–346.

Boucher, J. D., & Carlson, G. E. (1980). Recognition of expression in three cultures. *Journal of Cross-Cultural Psychology, 11,* 263–280.

Boucher, J. D., & Ekman, P. (1975). Facial areas and emotional information. *Journal of Communication, 25,* 21–29.

Boucher, J. D. & Brandt, M. E. (1981). Judgement of emotion: American and Malay antecedents. *Journal of Cross-Cultural Psychology, 12,* 272–283.

Campos, J. J., Mumme, D. L., Kermoian, R., & Campos, R. G. (1994). A functionalist perspective on the nature of emotion. *Monographs of the Society for Research in Child Development, 59,* 284–303.

Collins, R. (1984). The role of emotion in social structure. In K. Scherer & P. Ekman (Eds.), *Approaches to emotion* (pp. 385–396). New York: Erlbaum.

Darwin, G. (1872). *The expression of emotion in man and animals.* New York: Philosophical Library.

Dillard, J. P. (1993). Epilogue. *Journal of Language and Social Psychology, 12,* 153–161.

Ducci, L., Arcuri, L., W/ Georgis, T., & Sineshaw, T. (1982). Emotion recognition in Ethiopia: The effect of familiarity with Western culture on accuracy of recognition. *Journal of Cross-Cultural Psychology, 13,* 340–351.

Duncan, H. D. (1968). *Symbols in society.* New York: Oxford University Press.

Dworetsky, J. P. (1985). *Psychology.* St. Paul, MN: West.

Efron, D. (1972). *Gesture, race and culture.* The Hague: Mouton.

Eibl-Eibesfeldt, I. (1972) Similarities and differences between cultures in expressive movements. In R. A. Hinde (Ed.), *Nonverbal communication.* Cambridge, UK: Cambridge University Press.

Ekman, P. (1978). Facial expression. In A. W. Siegman & S. Feldstein (Eds.), *Nonverbal behavior and communication* (pp. 96–116). Hillsdale, NJ: Erlbaum.

Ekman, P., & Friesen, W. V. (1971). Constants across cultures in face and emotion. *Journal of Personality and Social Psychology, 17,* 124–129.

Ekman, P., & Friesen, W. V. (1975). *Unmasking the face: A guide to recognizing emotions from facial clues.* Englewood Cliffs, NJ: Prentice-Hall.

Ekman, P., & Friesen, W. V. (1986). A new pan-cultural facial expression of emotion. *Motivation and Emotion, 10,* 159–165.

Ekman, P., Friesen, W. V., & Ellsworth, P. (1972). *Emotions in the human face: Guidelines for research and an integration of findings.* New York: Pergamon Press.

Ekman, P., Friesen, W. V., & Ellsworth, P. (1982). What are the relative contributions of facial behavior and contextual information to the judgment of emotion? In P. Ekman (Ed.), *Emotions in the human face* (2nd ed., pp. 111–127). New York: Cambridge University Press.

Ekman, P., Friesen, W., & Ellsworth, P. (1989). *Emotion in the human face: Guidelines for research and an integration of findings* (2nd ed.). New York: Pergamon.

Ekman, P., Friesen, W. V., O'Sullivan, M., Diacoayanni-Tarlatzis, I., Krause, R., Pitcairn, T., Scherer, K., Chan, A., Heider, K., Ayan LeCompte, W., Ricci-Bitti, P. E., & Tomita, M. (1987). Universals and cultural differences in the judgments of facial expressions of emotion. *Journal of Personality and Social Psychology, 53,* 712–717.

Geertz, H. (1959). The vocabulary of emotion: A study of Javanese socialization processes. *Psychiatry, 22,* 225–237.

Hall, E. T. (1976). *Beyond culture.* Garden City, NY: Doubleday.

Hall, E. T. & Hall, M. R. (1990). *Understanding cultural differences: Germans, French and Americans.* Yarmouth, ME: Intercultural Press.

Hiatt, L. R. (1978). Classification of the emotions. In L. R. Hiatt (Ed.), *Australian aboriginal concepts* (pp. 182–187). Princeton, NJ: Humanities Press.

Hofstede, G. (1980). *Culture's Consequences: International Differences in Work-Related Values.* Beverly Hills, CA: Sage.

Izard, C. (1969). *The face of emotion.* New York: Appleton Century-Crofts.

Izard, C. E. (1985) Emotions in personality and culture. *Ethos, 11,* 305–312.

Ishii, S. (1990). Japanese and Americans compared on the affect orientation construct. *Psychological Reports, 66,* 985–986.

Keeler, W. (1983). Shame and stage fright in Java. *Ethos, 11,* 152–165.

Klineberg, O. (1940). *Social psychology.* New York: Henry Holt.

Kundera, M. (1980). *The book of laughter and forgetting* (M. H. Heim, Trans.) New York: Knopf.

LaBarre, W. (1947). The cultural basis of emotion and gestures. *Journal of Personality, 16,* 19–68.

Labouvie-Vief, G., Hakim-Larson, J., DeVoe, M., & Schoeberiein, S. (1989). Emotions and self-regulation: A life span view. *Human Development, 32,* 279–299.

Leach, E. (1972). The influence of cultural context on nonverbal communication in man. In R. A. Hinbde (Ed.), *Nonverbal communication* (pp. 315–347). Cambridge: Cambridge University Press.

Lebra, T. S. (1983). Shame and guilt: A psychocultural view of the Japanese self. *Ethos, 11,* 192–231.

Leff, J. (1973). Culture and the differentiation of emotional states. *British Journal of Psychiatry, 123,* 299–306.

Levy, R. I. (1973). *Tahitians.* Chicago: University of Chicago Press.

Lorenz, K. (1965). *Evolution and modification of behavior.* Chicago: University of Chicago Press.

Lutz, C. (1980). *Emotion words and emotional development on Ifaluk Atoll.* Unpublished doctoral dissertation, Harvard University, Cambridge, MA.

Marsella, A. J. (1994). The measurement of emotional reactions to work: Methodological and research issues. *Work and Stress. 8,* 153–176.

Matsumoto, D. (1991). Cultural influences on facial expressions of emotion. *The Southern Communication Journal, 56,* 128–137.

Matsumoto, D., & Assar, M. (1992). The effects of language on judgments of universal facial expressions of emotion. *Journal of Nonverbal Behavior, 16,* 85–99.

Matsumoto, D. (1993). Ethnic differences in affect intensity, emotion judgments, display rule attitudes, and self-reported emotional expression in an American sample. *Motivation and Emotion, 17,* 107–123.

McConatha, J. T., Lightner, E., & Deaner, S. L. (1994). Culture, age, and gender as variables in the expression of emotions. *Journal of Social Behavior and Personality, 9,* 481–488.

McDaniel, E. R. (1993, November). *Japanese nonverbal communication: A review and critique of literature.* Paper presented at the annual convention of the Speech Communication Association, Miami Beach, FL.

Mead, M. (1975). Review of Darwin and facial expression. *Journal of Communication, 25,* 209–213.

Mesquita, B., & Frijda, N. H. (1992). Cultural variations in emotions: A review. *Psychological Bulletin, 112,* 179–204.

Mirowsky, J., & Ross, C. E. (1984). Mexican culture and its emotional contradictions. *Journal of Health and Social Behavior, 25,* 2–13.

Orly, J. H. (1970). *Culture and mental illness.* Nairobi, Kenya: East Africa.

Rosaldo, M. Z. (1983). The shame of headhunters and the autonomy of self. *Ethos, 11,* 135–151.

Russell, J. A. (1991). Culture and the categorization of emotions. *Psychological Bulletin, 110,* 426–450.

Samovar, L. A., & Porter, R. E. (1995). *Communication between cultures.* Belmont, CA: Wadsworth.

Scheflen, A. E., & Scheflen, A. (1972). *Body language and social order: Communication as behavioral control.* Englewood Cliffs, NJ: Prentice-Hall.

Scherer, K. R., Summerfield, A. B., & Wallbott, H. G. (1983). Cross-national research on antecedents and components of emotion: A progress report. *Social Science Information, 22,* 355–385.

Scherer, K. R., Wallbott, H. G., Matsumoto, D., & Kudoh, T. (1988). Emotional experience in cultural context: A comparison between Europe, Japan, and the United States in K. R. Klaus (Ed.), *Facets of emotion: Recent Research* (pp. 5–30). Hillsdale, NJ: Erlbaum.

Scherer, K. R., & Wallbott, H. G. (1994). Evidence for universality and cultural variation of differential emotion response patterning. *Journal of Personality and Social Psychology, 66,* 310–328.

Scherer, K. R., Wallbott, H. G., & Summerfield, A. B. (Eds.). (1986). *Experiencing emotion: A cross-cultural study.* Cambridge, England: Cambridge University Press.

Shennum, W. A., & Bugental, D. B. (1982). The development of control over affective expression in nonverbal behavior. In R. S. Feldman (Ed.), *Development of nonverbal behavior in children* (pp. 101–112). New York: Springer-Verlag.

Tomkins, S. S. (1962). *Affect, Imagery, Consciousness Vol. I. The Positive Affects.* New York: Springer.

Triandis, H. C., Botempo, R., Villareal, M. J., Asai, M., & Lucca, N. (1988). Individualism and collectivism: Cross-cultural perspectives on self-ingroup relationship. *Journal of Personality and Social Psychology, 4,* 323–338.

Tsunoda, T. (1979). Difference in the mechanism of emotion in Japanese and Westerner. *Psychotherapy and Psychosomatics, 31,* 367–372.

Turski, G. (1991). Experience and expression: The moral linguistic constitution of emotions. *Journal for the Theory of Social Behavior, 21,* 373–392.

Walbott, H. G. (1994). Faces in context: The relative importance of facial expression and context information in determining emotion attributions. In K. R. Scherer (Ed.), *Facets of emotion: Recent research* (pp. 139–160). Hillsdale, NJ: Erlbaum.

Wallbott, H. G., & Scherer, K. R. (1994). How universal and specific is emotional experience? Evidence from 27 countries on five continents. In K. R. Scherer (Ed.), *Facets of emotion: Recent research* (pp. 31–56). Hillsdale, NJ: Erlbaum.

Wenzhong, H. & Grove, C. L. (1991). *Encountering the Chinese.* Yarmouth, ME: Intercultural Press.

Yun, J. O. (1994). The impact of Confucianism on interpersonal relationships and communication patterns in East Asia. In L. A. Samovar & R. E. Porter (Eds.), *Intercultural communication: A reader* (7th ed., pp. 75–86). Belmont, CA: Wadsworth.

Zajonc, R. B. & McIntosh, D. N. (1992). Some promising questions and some questionable promises. *Psychological Sciences, 3,* 70–74.

CHAPTER 18

Emotion, Attachment, and Satisfaction in Close Relationships

Judith A. Feeney, Patricia Noller, and Nigel Roberts

University of Queensland
Queensland, Australia

As Fitness and Fletcher (1993) pointed out, "The notion that intimate sexual relationships are inextricably intertwined with strong feelings and emotions is a truism in romantic novels and commonsense thinking alike" (p. 942). It would seem clear that emotions, both positive and negative, play an important part in close romantic relationships like marriage. It is also true that we learn about emotions in the context of our very early family relationships (Buck, 1989). Moreover, our most intense emotional reactions, at any stage of life, occur in the context of our close affectional bonds, particularly if those bonds are at risk (Bowlby, 1973).

In this chapter, we discuss theoretical and empirical approaches to the study of emotion in close relationships, and the impact of the experience and the expression of emotion on relationship satisfaction. As was noted by Andersen and Guerrero in Chapter 3, this volume, recent research and theorizing has emphasized the interrelatedness of affect and cognition (Bradbury & Fincham, 1987, 1991). This interrelatedness may be seen at its best in the attachment perspective, which emphasizes the emotional bonds that are fueled between people by mental models of self and other. In later sections, we report two studies exploring the links between attachment style, emotion, and relationship satisfaction. Study 1 examines emotional *expression* (and emotional control), based on dating couples' self-reports of responses to partic-

Handbook of Communication and Emotion: Research, Theory, Applications, and Contexts
Copyright © 1998 by Academic Press. All rights of reproduction in any form reserved.

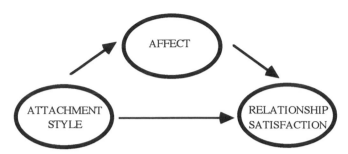

FIGURE 1   Hypothesized association between attachment style and relationship satisfaction, which is mediated by affect.

ular negative emotions. In Study 2, we explore the *experience* of emotion during relationship conflict, using a variety of self-report and physiological measures. In both studies, we test whether the experience or expression of emotion mediates the link between attachment style and relationship satisfaction (see Figure 1).

GENERAL THEORIES OF EMOTION IN CLOSE RELATIONSHIPS

Several theories provide a general framework for studying emotion in close relationships. One of the earliest of these theories was proposed by Mandler (1975), who posited that emotion follows from the interruption of an organized action sequence (which may be a sequence of behaviors, or an activity). Berscheid (1983) extended Mandler's theory to apply to close relationships. According to Berscheid, emotion in relationships is likely to occur when a behavior of Partner A interrupts a highly organized action sequence of Partner B. Given that close relationships tend to be characterized by strong emotional investment (that is, the members of the dyad are highly interdependent), there is considerable potential for emotional events to occur. Which emotion is aroused by the interruption will depend on how the interruption is appraised and interpreted by Partner B (see Andersen & Guerrero, Chapter 3, this volume). Mandler argued that interruption is a necessary and possibly sufficient condition for emotion to occur, and that neither positive nor negative stimuli produce much emotion, unless they are interrupting.

It is important to note that Scherer (1984) argued against Mandler's interruption theory, mainly because it focuses predominantly on negative emotion. Scherer argued for a more general theory in which emotion involves the cognitive appraisal of an event or some aspect of one's environment, the development of behavioral plans, physiological activation that provides energy for a response, and behavioral expression of the emotion. Specifically, Scherer (1984) argued that there is a general consensus in the literature that the psychological construct of emotion involves five components (Averill, 1980; Izard, 1977; Plutchik, 1980): (a) subjective feeling state, (b) cognitive appraisal, (c) a motivational component (behavioral intentions), (d) motor expression, and (e) activation or arousal.

To understand emotion fully, especially in the context of relationships, it is important to study both the *experience* and the *expression* of emotion. Zajonc (1984) discussed two classes of theories about emotion: Those that emphasize cognition as a necessary component (Lazarus, 1966; Mandler, 1975; Schachter & Singer, 1962), and those that put more emphasis on the somatic and motor aspects of emotion (Gottman, 1994). The first class of theories focuses particularly on the experience of emotion, whereas the second class places more emphasis on the expression of emotion. As already noted, the studies to be reported here address both these aspects of emotion.

Just as emotional experience and expression are related processes, so are affect and cognition. In fact, Bradbury and Fincham (1987) argued that affect and cognition are closely intertwined in close relationships, and that creating an artificial distinction between these two processes prevents a full understanding of emotional experience and expression. To counteract this artificial separation, Bradbury and Fincham (1987, 1990, 1991) developed a detailed model in which affect and cognition work together, particularly in the context of conflict, to produce selective attention and recall of negative relationship events. In turn, selective attention and recall are associated with high negative arousal and reduced capacity for effective problem solving. This model removes the distinction between affect and cognition; both are seen as aspects of internal mental processing, which can be either primary (that is, the immediate reaction) or secondary (that is, following the primary processing) (see also Andersen & Guerrero, Chapter 3, this volume).

Proximal and distal context variables are other important components of Bradbury and Fincham's model, as also noted by Andersen and Guerrero (Chapter 3, this volume). The proximal context includes elements that are actually happening in the current interaction, such as partner's transient thoughts, their emotional reactions, and their appraisals of the other's intention. The distal context includes each partner's stable personality characteristics, their ideas about relationships in general, and their evaluation of the quality of their own relationship in particular. As we shall see later, attachment styles are an important part of the distal context, which may also include aspects of partners' relationship histories and recent events, such as the argument they had earlier in the day. Proximal and distal contexts affect the current interaction, but are also affected by it.

EMOTION AND RELATIONSHIP SATISFACTION

As Berscheid (1983) noted, events can be identified as emotional in three ways: through individuals reporting verbally on their own emotional experience, through outsiders observing their nonverbal communication, and through assessment of physiological responses. Research on emotion in relationships has examined all three aspects of emotion, using a wide variety of methodologies.

Own and Partner's Emotional Experience

In a diary study, Kirchler (1988, 1989) had spouses report on their own and partners' affect at randomly selected times over a period of several weeks. Spouses whose relationships were generally satisfying reported more positive affect in the presence of their partner than when the partner was absent. It is interesting to note that spouses were better able to assess the partner's current mood during times of agreement than during times of conflict. It seems that one's own emotional state is likely to get in the way of being sensitive to the emotions of one's partner.

In a unique study of emotional experience in families, Larson and Richards (1994) provided family members (mother, father, and teenage child) with beepers and paged them simultaneously at various times during the day. In this way the researchers were able to explore the immediate emotional reactions of these family members, sometimes when they were in the same context (such as at home watching television in the evening) and at other times when they were in quite different contexts. Some husbands and wives showed an imbalance in terms of their emotional experience between the work and family spheres. These men reported more negative emotion at work, but more positive emotion at home; the women tended to report the opposite pattern, with more negative emotion at home and more positive emotion when at work or with friends. In such families, negative emotion and hostility were particularly likely to be experienced during the six o'clock "crash," when one or both parents were returning home from work.

In healthier families, on the other hand, both men and women were able to maintain more balance between their emotional lives inside the family, and their involvement outside. Fathers in these families were less likely to arrive home "emotional wrecks," and the mothers had rewarding activities outside of the home. These mothers also allowed themselves time to relax and attend to their own needs at home. The results of this better balance were that neither husbands nor wives felt like victims at home, they did not arrive home with a lot of unmet emotional needs, they did not have to leave home in order to have their emotional needs met, and they were "less dependent on the family for emotional sustenance" (p. 214). In addition, they were better able to meet the emotional needs of their children, and the emotional state of one family member was less likely to be passed on to the rest of the family, and hence to create cycles of negativity and hostility.

The accuracy with which spouses understand each other's emotional expression has also been studied by having spouses engage in a videotaped interaction, and then report on both their own and their partners' affect during replay of that interaction. For example, Gaelick, Bodenhausen, and Wyer (1985) and Noller and Ruzzene

(1991) videotaped couples during discussion of a conflict, and then had spouses report on the affect they were experiencing during that interaction. Gaelick et al. showed that spouses tended to reciprocate whichever emotion (in this case, love or hostility) they thought their partner was conveying. However, because spouses were not as accurate at decoding their partners' expressions of love as they were at decoding their hostility, they were more likely to reciprocate the negative emotion. In addition, they saw their partners as reciprocating their own affect.

Noller and Ruzzene (1991) similarly showed that distressed spouses had particular problems in accurately identifying the affect experienced by their partners during conflict episodes, and lacked rapport with their partners. It seems that one reason distressed spouses tend to reciprocate negative, but not positive, interaction (Gottman, Markman, & Notarius, 1977) is that they fail to accurately encode or decode positive affect. Findings from Noller's (1984) study of marital misunderstandings suggest that husbands' difficulty in encoding positive messages is likely to contribute to this problem.

There is also evidence of a link between marital satisfaction and depression, which increases in magnitude over the first few years of marriage (e.g., Beach & O'Leary, 1993; Schaefer & Burnett, 1987, Segrin, Chapter 8, this volume). How does negative affect in marriage come to be increasingly linked with depression over time? There is considerable stability in individuals' levels of positive and negative affect over time (Schuerger, Zarrella, & Hotz, 1989), with emotional experience tending to be trait-like. Those chronically high in negative affectivity tend to experience high levels of anxiety, tension, anger, feelings of rejection, sadness, and possibly more intense reactions to negative stimuli (Larsen & Ketelaar, 1991; see also Segrin, Chapter 8, this volume). Conversely, those high in positive affectivity are likely to experience high levels of well-being, social dominance, energy, and adventurousness (Clark & Watson, 1991), and may also be more responsive to positive stimuli (Larsen & Ketelaar, 1991). High levels of positive affectivity are also related to interest in social interaction, sex, and achievement.

Given that variables such as anger, feelings of rejection, and interest in social interaction and sex are relevant to marital interaction, it seems reasonable to expect a link between levels of positive and negative affect on the one hand, and relationship satisfaction on the other. In addition, premarital depression in either husbands or wives is a predictor of lower marital satisfaction longitudinally (Markman, Duncan, Storaasli, & Howes, 1987), but the psychopathology of husbands seems to have a stronger effect on marital satisfaction over the long term. Beach and O'Leary (1993) also reported that premarital depression predicts a subsequent decline in marital satisfaction. Conversely, low marital satisfaction early in marriage predicts later increases in depression, particularly for persons with a dysphoric affective style (Beach & O'Leary, 1993; Segrin, Chapter 8, this volume). Accordingly, it appears that marital health and level of depressive symptomatology are related in important ways, with some persons being at greater risk than others of developing marital problems and of responding to marital problems with increased depression.

As noted earlier, affect and cognition in close relationships are inextricably linked, hence it is important to consider cognitive processes that are likely to impact emotional experience and expression. Differences between distressed and nondistressed couples have been documented across a wide range of cognitive phenomena, including assumptions and beliefs about relationships, expectancies about relationship behaviors, and attributions about why events occur (Bradbury & Fincham, 1990; Eidelson & Epstein, 1982; Fincham & Bradbury, 1988; Fitzpatrick, 1988). Some of these cognitive variables are likely to form part of the proximal context (e.g., appraisals of partner intention in the immediate situation), whereas others are more relevant to the distal context (e.g., attributions about causes of problems, expectations).

How events and situations are appraised or evaluated by individuals is crucial to their experience of emotion. According to Lazarus and Smith (1988), if one appraises a situation as having direct implications for one's well-being, emotion will result. These researchers have shown that such appraisals are closely related to emotion, and account for more of the variance in emotion than do causal attributions. In fact, these researchers found that once appraisals were taken into account, causal attributions added very little to the prediction of emotion.

The relations between marital satisfaction and perceptions of marital partners' intentions were explored by Guthrie and Noller (1988). These researchers studied communication in married couples in three different affective situations: when angry with the partner, when depressed about the relationship, and when feeling affectionate. Spouses low in marital adjustment were less accurate than other spouses at perceiving their partners' intentions, and attributed more negative intentions to their partners than did those high in marital adjustment for both the depression and the affection situations. There were no differences between distressed and nondistressed couples for the anger situation, with all spouses tending to assume a negative intention when they or their partners were angry.

These findings suggest that distressed couples, in particular, are likely to have problems in understanding each other's affect and intentions. For example, a husband who thinks that his wife is angry with him for being late, when she is really anxious about his safety, is likely to respond in ways that make the situation worse, rather than better. Hence, it may be important in programs of prevention, enrichment, and therapy, to teach couples how to check that they have understood their partners' emotion and/or intention.

Other evidence suggests that perception and cognitive processing affect marital satisfaction. Bradbury and Fincham (1987) argued that the high levels of negative affect and behavior generally found in distressed couples are due, at least in part, to the ways in which negative behavior by the partner is processed. In distressed couples, negative spouse behavior is viewed as global, enduring and intentional, and as highly meaningful and relevant to the self. In contrast, nondistressed couples tend to discount negative partner behavior by attributing it to specific, situational, and unstable factors, and are therefore less likely to keep deliberating about the implications of the behavior.

There is a considerable literature linking attributional style and marital distress. A number of cross-sectional investigations demonstrate a link between attributional style and marital distress (Bradbury & Fincham, 1990), and several longitudinal studies support the proposition that certain attributions cause marital distress (Fincham & Bradbury, 1987). In addition, studies have shown that attributional style affects the way spouses behave towards one another (e.g., Byrne & Arias, in press; Fincham & Bradbury, 1988; Holtzworth-Munroe & Hutchinson, 1993; Sillars, 1985).

It appears that early in a relationship, partners begin to form stable attributions regarding the nature of their relationship conflict. Distressed couples appear to be quite willing to attribute blame to one another, and to do so with a high level of certainty (Noller & Ruzzene, 1991). Noller and Ruzzene found that distressed spouses, especially wives, tended to see problem-related behavior as pervasive and unlikely to change, and partner behavior as selfish and blameworthy; they approached problem discussions from this perspective. For spouses who make these negative responsibility attributions, the propensity for negative interaction will be intensified. On the other hand, making more benign attributions of responsibility for conflict should lead to spouses having healthier patterns of interaction over time.

Nonverbal Communication

Nonverbal communication has generally been studied through observing couples' interactions (e.g., Gottman, 1994; Gottman et al., 1977; Noller, 1984; see Weiss & Heyman, 1990, for a review of studies to that time). Both conflict interactions and positive interactions have been studied in this way.

Affect in marriage has been most frequently studied in the context of conflict, with couples being asked to discuss salient issues in their relationships, and these discussions being videotaped. It is important to remember that only the participants themselves can know about their own *experience* of emotion (unless physiological measures are taken), although others, including spouses, may pick up behavioral cues to that emotion as *expressed* (Noller & Guthrie, 1991).

Using observation, emotion in relationships can be studied in terms of how it is expressed, and how that expression is responded to by the partner. It seems clear that spouses high in relationship satisfaction deal with conflict, and the associated emotion, rather differently from those low in satisfaction. Overall, satisfied spouses are more positive in their interactions with their partners (Birchler, Clopton & Adams, 1984; Noller, 1982; Revenstorf, Hahlweg, Schindler & Vogel, 1984; Schaap & Jansen-Nawas, 1987), and express more agreement and more humor (Revenstorf et al., 1984; Schaap, 1984) more approval and caring (Birchler et al., 1984: Schaap,

1984) and more empathy (Birchler et al., 1984). Spouses low in satisfaction tend to be more negative overall in their interactions with one another (Notarius, Benson & Sloane, 1989), to be more critical (Hooley & Hahlweg, 1989), to complain more (Revenstorf et al., 1984), especially with negative affect (Alberts, 1988), and to express more displeasure and hostility (Roberts & Krokoff, 1990).

Responses to the spouse's expression of emotion are usually studied in terms of sequences of behavior. An important concept here is that of reciprocity, or one partner responding to the other's expression of affect with a similar affective tone. Findings on reciprocity are mixed, although in general they suggest that negative affect reciprocity is more consistently related to low levels of relationship satisfaction (Gottman, 1994). There is some evidence that wives are more likely to reciprocate their husbands' affect, both positive and negative (Notarius & Johnson, 1982), although Schaap (1984) found evidence for negative affect reciprocity for both husbands and wives in satisfied couples only, with satisfied husbands also reciprocating wives' positive affect. For dissatisfied couples in Schaap's study, aversive behavior by wives tended to be followed by acquiescence or less negative behavior on the part of husbands. This pattern of husband acquiescence may be similar to the withdrawal reported in other studies, such as that of Roberts and Krokoff (1990). These researchers found some evidence for negative affect reciprocity (wife displeasure–husband displeasure), but also found that husbands were inclined to withdraw from conflict, and that wives responded to this withdrawal with hostility. On this basis, they argued that demand–withdraw interaction may begin with the husband withdrawing from a conflict interaction and the wife becoming angry in response.

The demand–withdraw pattern of dealing with conflict has been studied extensively by Christensen and his colleagues (Christensen & Heavey, 1990; Christensen & Shenk, 1991; Heavey, Layne & Christensen, 1993). They have shown that this pattern of interaction is highly related to marital satisfaction, and that wives are more likely to be in the demanding role and husbands more likely to be in the withdrawing role, particularly when discussing issues raised by the wife. In this situation, wives seem to become distressed or angry in their attempts to get husbands to deal with issues, while husbands seem to avoid dealing with them. This pattern of interaction is inversely related to both concurrent and later marital satisfaction (Feeney, Noller & Callan, 1994a; Heavey et al., 1993; Noller, Feeney, Bonnell & Callan, 1994). As we will see later, Gottman and Levenson (1988) argued that men withdraw from conflict to deal with their high levels of emotional arousal.

Positive interaction is also important to marital quality. Maritally satisfied couples not only handle the emotions involved in conflict better than distressed couples, but also report much higher rates of positive behavior in daily interactions with their partners (Broderick & O'Leary, 1986). In addition, recent work has demonstrated that the development of a sense of shared positive marital history is an important predictor of long-term marital satisfaction (Buehlman, Gottman & Katz, 1992).

Furthermore, when long-term happily married couples are asked about how they keep their relationships satisfying, they tend to focus on the role of positive affect (Osgarby & Halford, 1996). More than three-quarters of the couples in this study identified positive intimate behaviors as crucial to maintaining satisfaction in their relationships, and only around 10% focused on the management of conflict. These couples talked about such positive behaviors as spending enjoyable time together, and sharing verbal intimacy, as creating a climate of positive affect.

Despite couples' reports of the importance they attach to positive affect, only a few studies have been able to identify positive, intimate behaviors that are observed during interactions and covary with marital satisfaction. For example, when Halford and Sanders (1990) asked couples to discuss the previous day's activities in a relaxed setting, differences between distressed and nondistressed couples related primarily to higher rates of negative behavior in the distressed couples, with few differences in positive behavior. Similarly, studies of distressed and nondistressed couples consistently find negative behaviors to be a better discriminator of marital distress than positive behaviors (Weiss & Heyman, 1990). This effect may reflect the nature of the task used, rather than a lack of influence of positive behaviors on marital satisfaction. As we noted earlier, researchers typically ask couples to discuss conflictual topics, which are unlikely to elicit positive intimacy skills. On the other hand, when couples are asked to discuss a nonconflictual topic, and to provide social support for a problem experienced by the spouse, marital satisfaction is correlated with positive, prosocial behavior (Julien & Markman, 1991; Julien, 1992).

Osgarby and Halford (1996) developed a task designed to directly assess couples' positive intimacy skills. It involved each partner identifying a very positive experience in their relationship history, and then the partners discussing its significance with each other. As expected, this task resulted in maritally happy couples showing higher rates of positive behaviors (both speaker and listener skills), higher rates of positive affect arousal, and higher rates of positive cognitions than distressed couples. Happy couples also showed significantly higher levels of "conversational meshing" than distressed couples; that is, they engaged in a series of communication behaviors in which they positively presented a conjoint story about a relationship event.

Physiological Responding

The finding that affect, particularly negative affect and negative affect reciprocity, discriminates between distressed and nondistressed couples, led Levenson and Gottman (1983, 1985) to explore the physiological concomitants of negative affect in marital interaction. In their initial study, Levenson and Gottman (1983) assessed the extent to which both partners became highly physiologically aroused together (labeled "physiological linkage"), suggesting that they are both reacting negatively. Husbands and wives in distressed marriages showed higher physiological linkage, and the researchers claimed that 60% of the variance in marital satisfaction was accounted for by this variable.

Furthermore, other indices of physiological arousal explained significant variance in current marital satisfaction, beyond that accounted for by physiological linkage. In particular, lower marital satisfaction was related to husbands' skin conductance levels and heart rate (interbeat interval) during marital interaction. However, individual correlations revealed a contradictory pattern: The skin conductance predictors suggested that unhappy marriages were characterized by an underaroused husband, whereas the results for heart rate suggested greater arousal for unhappy husbands.

When these couples were reassessed 3 years later, the researchers found that the physiological arousal of couples during the original assessment very accurately predicted their later marital satisfaction. In fact, the physiological variables accounted for almost 90% of the change in marital satisfaction over the 3-year period (Gottman, 1990). In contrast to their initial study, the pattern of results was very consistent. Higher levels of physiological arousal for husbands and wives were strongly related to decrements in marital satisfaction. In contrast to their cross-sectional findings, physiological linkage was unrelated to marital satisfaction.

In a later study reported by Gottman (1994), physiological linkage was the only variable (out of 11 physiological variables tested) that discriminated between conflict engagers and conflict avoiders, although there is no indication of whether this variable discriminated between regulated couples (those who had higher levels of positive than negative affect, and were more satisfied and less likely to divorce) and unregulated couples (who had much more negativity). Regulated and unregulated couples differed in terms of the wife's heart rate (interbeat interval) and the wife's pulse amplitude, with regulated wives having higher scores on these variables, indicating that the wives in distressed relationships were more physiologically aroused.

Gottman and Levenson (1988) expounded a theory of gender differences in marital interaction, focusing on differences between husbands and wives in their ability to function in the context of high negative affect. They reviewed a body of literature that suggests that males display larger autonomic nervous system responses to stress than females. They argued that men are able to play a reconciling role during low levels of marital conflict, but that due to the stress associated with high levels of marital conflict, they are likely to withdraw in these situations. Gottman and Levenson saw this withdrawal as being particularly likely for distressed husbands. It is possible that this physiological responding and the accompanying withdrawal are related to the demand–withdraw interaction pattern described earlier.

Gottman (1994) expounded a new process model of marital interaction in which physiological arousal is seen as crucial. Data assessing the prediction of divorce from physiological responses of couples followed up after 8 years showed that only 1 variable out of 10 baseline physiological measures and 1 out of the 10 physiological measures taken during the interaction were predictive of divorce, and only 1 out of 20 was significantly related to separation. In all three cases, the relevant variable was wife's heart rate. These data do not provide strong support for the idea that diffuse physiological arousal plays a crucial role in the progression towards divorce.

ATTACHMENT STYLE AND EMOTION

Attachment theory has recently provided a new approach to the study of emotion in adults' close relationships, and one which is consistent with earlier work on the link between emotion and assumptions and beliefs about the social world. Although attachment theory was originally formulated by Bowlby (1969, 1973) to describe the processes by which infants bond with their caregivers, it has been applied more recently to adults' romantic relationships by Hazan and Shaver (1987). Since their pioneering work, the application of attachment theory to adult relationships has been widespread (e.g., Collins & Read, 1990; Feeney & Noller, 1990, 1991; Levy & Davis, 1988).

Researchers have used a variety of techniques to measure attachment style. However, there is considerable evidence that adult attachment style can be adequately represented in terms of two underlying dimensions (Feeney, Noller, & Callan, 1994a; Simpson, 1990; Strahan, 1991). These dimensions reflect the degree to which an individual feels comfortable in close romantic relationships (labeled comfort with closeness), and the degree to which he or she fears abandonment from romantic partners (anxiety over relationships). Low comfort with closeness involves a belief that attachment figures are untrustworthy and cannot be relied upon to provide assistance in times of need. In contrast, high anxiety over relationships involves a belief that one is unlovable and unworthy of help from attachment figures in times of need. Another common way of viewing attachment has been by way of four discrete categories: preoccupied, fearful avoidant, dismissing avoidant, and secure (Bartholomew, 1990; Bartholomew & Horowitz, 1991). However, these four categories are easily conceptualized in terms of the two underlying dimensions of attachment style. Fearful and dismissing individuals report lower comfort with closeness, whereas preoccupied and fearful individuals report higher anxiety over relationships (Feeney, 1995).

The behavior of individuals low in comfort with closeness is characterized by two related features. First, they are reluctant to form intimate relationships; they deny the importance of attachment figures and emphasize emotional self-sufficiency (Bartholomew, 1990; Bartholomew & Horowitz, 1991). Second, they tend to suppress displays of emotion, particularly negative emotion (Hazan & Shaver, 1994), having learned that negative emotions do not elicit "contingent responses" from attachment figures (Kobak & Hazan, 1991).

The behavior associated with high anxiety over relationships reflects a reluctance to face life alone. People with high anxiety over relationships gain a sense of worth through their relationships with their attachment figures (Bartholomew, 1990). However, inconsistent treatment from attachment figures has led such individuals to develop a heightened sensitivity to their potential abandonment by relationship partners (Simpson, Rholes, & Nelligan, 1992). Distress is dealt with in a hypervigilant way and through the formation of possessive, clinging relationships (Collins & Read, 1994; Kobak & Sceery, 1988).

Attachment Style and Emotional Control

Attachment theorists have proposed that attachment style is closely linked to the regulation of negative affect. Attachment styles are thought to reflect rules and strategies that, by a process of generalization, come to guide responses to any distressing situation (Sroufe & Waters, 1977). Secure attachment develops from sensitive and responsive caregiving, and reflects rules that allow the individual to acknowledge distress and to turn to others for support and comfort; avoidant attachment develops in the face of distancing and rejection from caregivers, and reflects rules that restrict the acknowledgment of distress and the seeking of support; anxious/ambivalent (preoccupied) attachment stems from insensitive or inconsistent caregiving, and is marked by the tendency to express distress in a heightened manner and to focus on the signs and symptoms of distress (Kobak & Sceery, 1988).

Given this theoretical base, researchers into adult attachment have used the concept of affect regulation to explain differences between attachment groups on variables as diverse as fear of personal death (Mikulincer, Florian, & Tolmacz, 1990), illness behaviors (Feeney & Ryan, 1994), and responses to relationship breakups (Feeney & Noller, 1992). Nevertheless, there has been little empirical research directly assessing the expression and control of negative emotion in interactions with current attachment figures. A study indirectly relevant to this issue is the work of Simpson et al. (1992), which examined the influence of attachment style on couples' behavior in a stressful situation. These researchers informed each female subject that she was soon to participate in a stressful experiment: Following this stress-induction procedure, the couple's interactions were videotaped without their knowledge. Whereas securely attached women turned to their partners for support as their anxiety increased, avoidant women retreated from their partners physically and emotionally. Similarly, avoidant men showed a decline in overall supportiveness of their partners as partner anxiety increased.

The study by Simpson et al. (1992) was noteworthy in supporting the link between attachment style and affect regulation. This research focused, however, on support seeking and support giving rather than on the expression or the control of negative emotions. In addition to that study, there has been some research linking adult attachment style to the experience of emotion within couple relationships; this research has focused primarily on global ratings of positive and negative affect, and suggests that secure attachment is associated with more positive and less negative emotion (Fuller & Fincham, 1995; Simpson, 1990). Feeney (1995) was the first study to relate adult attachment style explicitly to the expression and control of *particular negative emotions* within couple relationships.

This study was driven, in part, by concerns over the simplicity of the theoretical formulation relating avoidant attachment to the control of negative affect, and anxious/ambivalent attachment to extreme displays of negative affect. First, this formulation does not distinguish between dismissing and fearful avoidance, although these two styles may differ in terms of emotional regulation. Dismissing avoidants tend to avoid attachment-related situations that may elicit anxiety and to exclude negative emotions from conscious awareness; fearful avoidants are likely to experience high levels of attachment-related distress, but may inhibit the expression of such distress for fear of alienating others (Bartholomew, 1990).

Second, the link between attachment style and responses to negative affect may depend on the particular negative emotion under consideration. Although the basic negative emotions of anger, sadness, and anxiety (Chance, 1980; Shaver, Schwartz, Kirson & O'Connor, 1987) are all rated as negative in hedonic tone (or low in pleasantness), they differ in important ways. For example, the experience of anger is associated with tension and with a tendency for destructive behavior; hence social norms tend to discourage the expression of anger (Canary, Spitzberg, & Semic, Chapter 7, this volume; Wallbott & Scherer, 1988). By contrast, the experience of sadness is characterized by less tension than most negative emotions, and is usually regarded as more tolerable. The experience of anxiety is associated with uncertainty, tension, and lack of control, but also with low impulsiveness (Izard, 1991).

The possible implications of these differences between particular negative emotions can be seen in the following example. Recall that preoccupied (anxious/ambivalent) individuals are supposed to display heightened expressions of negative emotion. However, both preoccupied and fearful individuals experience a great deal of anxiety about their relationships and, in particular, about possible abandonment by relationship partners. Because of this anxiety, these attachment groups may inhibit the expression of emotions that they see as a potential threat to their relationships. Anger may have negative consequences for close relationships and, as noted above, tends to be discouraged by social norms; hence preoccupied subjects may actually *inhibit* their expression of anger to attachment figures.

The research reported by Feeney (1995) explored the link between adult attachment style and control of emotional expression in long-term dating relationships. Seventy-two couples who had been in their current relationship for a minimum of 12 months completed questionnaire measures of attachment and emotional control. Specifically, control of three negative emotions (anger, sadness, and anxiety) was assessed. Subjects were asked to report not only on their *own* control of negative emotion within the relationship, but also on their *partners'* control of anger, sadness and anxiety, and the extent to which partners *wanted* them (the subjects) to control these emotions. In each case, emotional control was defined in terms of suppressing and 'bottling up' emotions, based on self-report items developed by Watson and Greer (1983).

As expected, the results supported the link between attachment style and emotional control. Securely attached individuals reported a tendency *not* to control their own expression of negative affect, and to perceive their partners as doing the same. In addition, securely attached individuals perceived their partners as *not wanting* them (the subjects) to control their own expression of negative affect. In terms of the link between attachment dimensions and reports of their own emotional control, comfort with closeness was inversely related to subjects' control of all three negative emotions. This finding fits with the proposition that avoidant subjects (those low in comfort with closeness) have a general tendency to avoid acknowledging distress and seeking support from attachment figures.

Other aspects of the results, however, indicated the importance of distinguishing between the different negative emotions. First, the perception that partners controlled their sadness was associated with high anxiety over relationships, and the perception that partners wanted subjects to control their sadness was associated with high anxiety over relationships and with low comfort with closeness. These findings suggest that insecure attachment is linked with the belief that relationship partners should project a happy and untroubled image. Such a belief may have serious consequences for the individual and the relationship, because it may prevent the insecure individual from using the partner as a "safe haven" when feeling sad.

Second, overall, subjects reported controlling anger more than sadness, and sadness more than anxiety; they also perceived their partners as behaving in this manner, and as wanting them to do the same. These findings highlight the fact that anger is subject to high levels of social control, partly because of its potential impact on close relationships. Open-ended descriptions of responses to anger supported this proposition. Subjects low in comfort with closeness tended to report avoidant and aggressive responses to anger, rather than the use of direct and bilateral strategies. Those high in anxiety over relationships reported avoidant and indirect responses (showing anger nonverbally and by 'not speaking'), suggesting a fear of confronting the partner about the situation.

In summary, the results pointed to relatively complex relations between attachment dimensions and emotional control, with the effects being dependent on gender, target, and emotion. It appears that the theoretical formulation that links avoidant attachment (low comfort with closeness) to a general tendency to control negative affect may be overly simplistic. Similarly, the results did not completely support the notion that anxious/ambivalent attachment (anxiety over relationships) is linked with exaggerated expression of attachment-related emotion; in fact for males, anxiety over relationships seemed to inhibit the expression of anger.

ATTACHMENT STYLE, EMOTION, AND RELATIONSHIP SATISFACTION

The association between adult attachment style and relationship satisfaction is very robust, regardless of the method used to assess attachment style (Collins & Read, 1990; Feeney, Noller, & Callan, 1994; Levy & Davis, 1988; Simpson, 1990). However, there is some evidence that the attachment dimension predicting partners' relationship satisfaction is different for husbands and wives: for husbands, comfort with closeness is the most important dimension and for wives, anxiety over relationships is the important dimension (Collins & Read, 1990; Kirkpatrick & Davis, 1994). In addition, there is a wealth of literature linking relationship satisfaction with partners' open expression of thoughts and feelings (e.g., Cahn, 1990; Davidson, Balswick, & Halverson, 1983; Kirchler, 1989; Noller & Fitzpatrick, 1990).

In this chapter, we report two studies exploring the links between attachment style, emotion, and relationship satisfaction. As noted earlier, Study 1 examines emotional *expression* (and emotional control) based on dating couples' self-reports of responses to particular negative emotions. In Study 2, we explore the *experience* of emotion during relationship conflict, using a variety of self-report and physiological measures. In both studies, we test whether the experience or expression of emotion mediates the link between attachment style and relationship satisfaction (again, see Figure 1).

STUDY 1: ATTACHMENT STYLE AND EMOTIONAL CONTROL

In the first study, the work reported by Feeney (1995) is extended by exploring the implications of attachment style and emotional control for relationship satisfaction, using the same sample of dating couples. This development was possible because these couples also completed the Quality Marriage Index (Norton, 1983), an evaluative measure of relationship satisfaction. The research to be described here focused on attachment style and emotional control as predictors of relationship satisfaction. The central research question was whether emotional control variables added to the prediction of relationship satisfaction, after controlling for the attachment characteristics of both partners.

This research question was addressed using hierarchical regression analyses, in which one's own and partner's attachment dimensions were entered at Step 1, and measures of emotional control were entered at Step 2. In conducting these analyses, three specific issues were of interest. The first issue concerned whether better prediction of relationship satisfaction is provided by a *global* measure of emotional control, or by *separate* measures of the control of anger, sadness, and anxiety. Recall that the results reported by Feeney (1995) suggest the importance of distinguishing between the various negative emotions, particularly with regard to the implications of attachment style for emotional control. Given these results, it was expected that better prediction would be afforded by separate measures of the three negative emotions.

The second issue concerned whether better prediction of one's own relationship satisfaction is provided by measures of one's *own* control of negative emotion, or by measures of the *partner's* emotional control. Given that an individual can engage in as much or as little emotional control (suppression of negative feelings) as he or she likes, but generally has little influence over the partner's behavior in this regard, we expected that relationship satisfaction would be more strongly associated with partner's emotional control than with own emotional control. For example, a husband's failure to express his feelings is likely to have more of an impact on his wife's satisfaction than on his own.

As noted above, relationship satisfaction has been linked both with attachment style and with the expression (or control) of feelings. In view of these associations, a third issue explored in this research was whether the effects of attachment on relationship satisfaction may be *mediated* by emotional control; that is, whether the link between security of attachment and greater relationship satisfaction may be explained, in part, by the tendency of secure individuals to express their negative feelings more openly.[1]

In order to address these questions, four pairs of regression analyses were conducted. Within each pair, a separate regression analysis was conducted for males and females. In each case, as noted above, own and partner's attachment dimensions were entered at the first step. These dimensions provided potent prediction of relationship satisfaction, explaining 24% of the variance in both males' and females' satisfaction. In each case, the best predictor was own comfort with closeness ($\beta = .34$ for males and .39 for females; $p < .005$); that is, own comfort with closeness was positively related to satisfaction. Partner's comfort with closeness was also associated with greater satisfaction ($\beta = .26$ for males and .25 for females; $p < .05$ in each case). The observed link between relationship satisfaction and own and partner's security of attachment (comfort with closeness) is consistent with previous research (e.g. Feeney, Noller, & Callan, 1994; Feeney, 1994), although we also expected an association between satisfaction and anxiety over relationships.

In the first pair of analyses, the global measure of own emotional control was entered at the second step. This measure failed to add significantly to the explained variance in relationship satisfaction (however, there was a weak but significant bivariate correlation between own emotional control and relationship satisfaction, $r = -.18$ for both males and females). The second pair of analyses involved entering the global measure of partner's emotional control at Step 2. This measure also failed to add to the explained variance in relationship satisfaction; moreover, the bivariate correlation between relationship satisfaction and partner's overall emotional control was nonsignificant. Together, the results from these analyses suggest that relationship satisfaction is only weakly and negatively related to own and partner's control of negative emotion, as assessed by *global* measures.

In the third pair of analyses, separate measures of own control of anger, sadness, and anxiety were entered at Step 2. As a block, these measures did not provide a significant increase in explained variance (however, the bivariate correlation between satisfaction and own control of anxiety was significant for both males and females, $r = -.27$ and $-.22$ respectively).

The final pair of analyses involved entering separate measures of partner's control of anger, sadness, and anxiety at Step 2. As for all previous analyses, the results

---

[1]Four conditions are necessary to demonstrate that the relation between attachment style and relationship satisfaction is mediated by affect (Baron & Kenny, 1986): attachment style must be related to relationship satisfaction; affect must be related to relationship satisfaction; attachment style must be related to affect; and the association between attachment style and relationship satisfaction must be reduced in significance when affect is statistically controlled.

were remarkably similar for the two genders. In each case, the three measures of partner's emotional control accounted for additional variance in relationship satisfaction, beyond that explained by attachment dimensions (an additional 18% for males, and 8% for females). Hence, satisfaction was not associated with the extent to which individuals controlled their own emotion, but was associated with how much their partners controlled *particular* negative emotions.

Specifically, satisfaction was *inversely* related to partner's control of sadness ($\beta =$ $-.42$ for males and $-.29$ for females). Note that this result is consistent with previous research linking relationship satisfaction with the open expression of feelings. Interestingly, however, satisfaction was *directly* related to partner's control of anger ($\beta = .49$ for males and .32 for females). In other words, both males and females reported greater relationship satisfaction when their partners "bottled up" their anger, but expressed their sadness. This finding was not expected, but fits with the notion that anger is a potentially destructive emotion, and one which people think should generally be controlled.

In summary, these analyses provide evidence that emotional control variables add to the prediction of relationship satisfaction, beyond that explained by attachment dimensions. However, such prediction is afforded only by measures of the partner's emotional control, and only by measures that distinguish between the various negative emotions. Specifically, the important predictors were the extent to which the relationship partner controlled her or his sadness and anger; control of sadness appears to be detrimental to relationships, whereas control of anger seems to be beneficial. In interpreting the latter finding, it should not be concluded that individuals should always suppress anger within their relationships. Rather, anger should be expressed in ways that do not attack the partner or invalidate her or his point of view; by expressing anger in a nonblaming way, partners are then able to discuss issues constructively and are more likely to resolve the conflict (see also Canary, Spitzberg, & Semic, Chapter 7, this volume).

The final pair of analyses provided little evidence that measures of partner's control of specific emotions mediated the relationship between attachment dimensions and relationship satisfaction. In predicting males' relationship satisfaction, the importance of both partners' comfort with closeness was unaffected by the addition of the measures of partner's emotional control. Thus it appears that own and partner's attachment security and partner's emotional control exert separate effects on males' evaluations of their relationships.

In predicting females' satisfaction, the importance of females' comfort with closeness was not affected by the addition of the emotional control variables, but the importance of males' comfort with closeness was reduced somewhat (from $\beta = .25, p < .05$, to $\beta = .18$, n.s.). In other words, females' relationship satisfaction seems to be linked with own comfort with closeness, independent of emotional control measures; on the other hand, the link between females' satisfaction and their male partner's comfort with closeness seems to be explained, at least in part, by the patterns of emotional control associated with males' comfort. Specifically, Feeney

(1995) showed that males who were comfortable with closeness reported less control of their sadness and anxiety.

STUDY 2: ATTACHMENT AND THE EXPERIENCE OF AFFECT DURING MARITAL CONFLICT

Attachment and Affect

In the previous study, we focused on the expression (or control) of emotion, and the implications for relationship satisfaction; we now move on to consider couples' experience of emotion during conflict. The second study seeks to bring together two extremely robust findings from the relationship literature. The first finding is that distressed couples experience higher levels of negative affect during marital interaction than happy couples (see Noller & Fitzpatrick, 1990; Weiss & Heyman, 1990 for reviews), and the second is that there is a strong association between attachment style and relationship satisfaction (as already noted). More specifically, the issue under investigation is whether the relation between attachment style and marital satisfaction is mediated by the affect that couples experience during marital conflict.

From a theoretical standpoint, there is good reason to expect anxiety over relationships to affect the way that individuals experience and deal with marital conflict. Displays of anxiety and anger are natural processes used to protest the inaccessibility of an attachment figure (Bowlby, 1988). As we saw earlier, however, anxiety over relationships is associated with high emotional expressivity and with preoccupation over distress and conflict. Consequently, in the case of an individual with high anxiety over relationships, displays of anger in response to the inaccessibility of the attachment figure may become exaggerated to the extent of being dysfunctional or even murderous (Bowlby, 1988).

Given that attachment processes are concerned with the availability of attachment figures, and that conflict can be seen as a threat to the partner's availability (Pistole, 1989), it is easy to see why anxiety over relationships would be associated with heightened anxiety and arousal during marital conflict. However, it is also suggested, somewhat paradoxically, that conflict may offer the opportunity for increased intimacy, through the sharing of feelings and airing of grievances (Straus, 1979; Vuchinich, 1987). Therefore it might be expected that individuals who are either low on comfort with closeness *or* high on anxiety over relationships might *experience* heightened negative affect during conflict interaction with their spouse.

Although theoretically there is some support for anxiety over relationships and comfort with closeness being related to levels of negative affect during marital conflict, empirical support is very limited. Research has tended to focus either on the overall emotional climate of relationships (e.g., Simpson, 1990), or on the strategies used during conflict and other stressful interactions (e.g., Feeney, Noller, & Callan,

1994; Kobak & Hazan, 1991; Pistole, 1989; Simpson et al., 1992). The literature has failed to provide a specific investigation into whether adult attachment style is related to levels of emotion *experienced* during marital conflict.

Arousal and Marital Conflict

Unlike most studies of marital interaction, the present study employs psychophysiological measures to gauge emotion. Other than the work of Gottman and his colleagues (Buehlman, Gottman & Katz, 1992; Levenson & Gottman, 1983; 1985), there is little published work of this type, despite calls for the greater use of psychophysiological approaches to assess social interaction in general (e.g., Notarius & Herrick, 1989; Wagner & Calam, 1988), and to replicate and extend Levenson and Gottman's initial work, in particular (e.g., O'Leary & Smith, 1991).

The findings of Levenson and Gottman (1983, 1985) are doubtless very important, and have been influential over the last 10 years. However, there is a need to replicate these studies for two reasons. First, the small sample size and large number of variables involved in these studies may make the data analyses relatively unstable (two subjects for each predictor variable, in one analysis). Second, as noted by O'Leary and Smith (1991), many of the findings were quite unexpected, with measures originally intended as baseline measures being used as predictors, and with different results for longitudinal and cross-sectional analyses, and for males and females.

As mentioned earlier, Gottman and Levenson (1986, 1988, Gottman, 1990) suggested that females and males may experience different levels of autonomic nervous system arousal in response to stress, and that these differences help explain gender differences in marital interaction. However, research by Christensen and his colleagues suggests that although males may withdraw more than females during discussion of conflict issues in which females are seeking change, the pattern is not as consistent when males are seeking change. Thus it might be expected that husbands should be more physiologically aroused than their wives during discussion of conflict issues, but particularly so when the wives are seeking change. Such physiological results should also be paralleled by self-reports of affect.

The above possibilities are investigated in Study 2, which had three aims. The primary aim was to test the hypothesized mediational model, in which the relation between attachment style and marital satisfaction is mediated by the affect that couples experience during marital conflict. Second, in testing this model, a partial replication of Levenson and Gottman's (1983) work was undertaken. It was hypothesized that happy and unhappy couples would differ in terms of levels of physiological arousal and the amount of "physiological linkage" in their interactions. The third aim was to test Gottman and Levenson's (1986, 1988) suggestion that "diffuse physiological arousal" can explain some gender differences in marital interaction. More specifically, the study sought to examine whether males are more physiologically aroused than females during marital conflict, and whether this effect is especially marked for unhappy couples, or during discussion of an issue for which the wife is seeking change.

A total of 48 married or cohabiting couples participated in the study. Each couple engaged in four 10-min marital interactions (only two reported here). Each individual chose an issue that involved a change he or she would like to make in the relationship, and with which the partner disagreed. During these interactions, partners' skin conductance levels and interbeat intervals were measured continuously. Skin conductance levels and interbeat intervals were also monitored during four 5-min closed-eye baselines that preceded each interaction. Following the interactions, couples watched their discussions on videotape and supplied a continuous measure of their anxiety using a handheld dial.

Before the interactions, couples completed measures of relationship satisfaction using the Quality Marriage Index (Norton, 1983) and attachment dimensions (anxiety over relationships and comfort with closeness, cf. Study 1). Following each interaction, partners rated their overall affect using a paper-and-pencil version of the self-assessment manikin (SAM; Hodes, Cook, & Lang, 1985; Lang, 1980), which is a simple instrument for obtaining ratings on the three primary dimensions underlying human emotion (Osgood, May, & Miron, 1975): evaluation (negativity), activity (arousal), and potency (power), on 5-point scales.

To understand the communication process using the physiological and anxiety ratings, we used a time series analysis that provided measures of the degree to which each person's emotion could be predicted from her or his partner's emotion across the course of the interaction.[2] In testing whether affect mediates the association between attachment and relationship satisfaction, it was necessary to create a smaller number of summary variables, because of the relatively small number of subjects and large number of variables. Each subject's scores for the measures of affect were averaged across the two conflict interactions. In addition, the physiological arousal variables were collapsed across gender.[3]

The relation between attachment style and relationship satisfaction was investi-

---

[2]The physiological measures and anxiety ratings were converted to 10-sec averages. To control for individual differences in baseline physiological arousal, the 10-sec averages for skin conductance levels and interbeat interval were then expressed as z-scores, using the mean and standard deviation from each individual's baseline periods. Bivariate time series analysis was conducted on these data streams. Prior to conducting the time series analyses, all appropriate treatment of the data was carried out, as outlined by Gottman (1981). The Gottman-Williams (Williams & Gottman, 1981) BIVAR program was then used to detect for lead-lag relationships between couples' data streams (i.e., skin conductance levels, interbeat interval, and anxiety ratings). Essentially, this program determines the degree to which each of the cross-regressive models are predictive beyond the autoregressive models and expresses this as two z-scores. These z-scores were then used as dependent variables in subsequent analyses.

[3]Collapsing these variables across gender may seem unusual. However, all the MANOVAs that were conducted failed to reveal any main effects for gender, or any interactions involving gender, suggesting that little information was lost. Furthermore, male and female scores on the physiological arousal measures were correlated.

TABLE I   Summary Statistics for the Multiple Regression Analyses Predicting Relationship Satisfaction from the Four Attachment Dimensions.

Predictors	Male satisfaction		Female satisfaction	
	r	β	r	β
Male anxiety over relationships	−.33*	−.27*	−.38**	−.33**
Male comfort with closeness	.44**	.42**	.42**	.38**
Female anxiety over relationships	−.11	−.11	−.02	−.02
Female comfort with closeness	.21	.11	.18	.08

*p < .05.
**p < .01.

gated using multiple regression to predict satisfaction from husbands' and wives' anxiety over relationships and comfort with closeness. This relation was significant for both males ($R = .55$, $F(4,43) = 4.77$, $p < .005$) and females ($R = .55$, $F(4,43) = 4.63$, $p < .005$). However, examination of the correlations and standardized regression weights (Table I) reveals that both partners' satisfaction was related only to males' attachment style. Therefore, in all further analyses involving attachment style, only males' attachment dimensions were considered.

To assess whether affect mediates the association between attachment and relationship satisfaction, we used multiple regression analyses conducted separately for female and male satisfaction. First, males' attachment dimensions were related to the affect variables, separately for anxiety over relationships and comfort with closeness. We then related the affect variables to relationship satisfaction. Finally, we tested whether males' attachment dimensions continued to predict relationship satisfaction after controlling for affect.

Several clear findings emerged (see Tables II and III for summaries of these results). First, as expected, there was a relation between satisfaction and the levels of negative affect experienced during conflict, with couples high in satisfaction experiencing lower levels of affect. However, we did not replicate Levenson and Gottman's (1983) finding of a strong association between physiological linkage and satisfaction; emotional linkage variables were the only measures of affect that did *not* relate to the satisfaction of either males or females.

Second, there was no evidence that levels of affect during conflict mediated the link between attachment style and satisfaction. This finding was due mainly to the failure of the affect variables to relate to attachment style. The only significant association between attachment style and affect was between males' comfort with closeness and the emotional linkage measures. Furthermore, the strongest predictor of attachment among the emotional linkage measures was the extent to which males' interbeat intervals were linked to those of their partners. Although we expected comfort with closeness to be associated with low levels of emotional link-

TABLE II Summary of Regression Analyses Testing Whether Affect Mediates the Association between Attachment and Males' Relationship Satisfaction[a,b]

Measure	Attachment and affect	Affect and satisfaction	Attachment and satisfaction	Attachment and satisfaction (affect controlled)
Emotional linkage	Comfort[a] $R = .54$, $F_{(6,35)} = 2.42$*	n.s.	Comfort[a] $\beta = .40$** Anxiety[a] $\beta = -.24$ n.s.	Comfort[a] $\beta = .44$** Anxiety[a] $\beta = -.34$*
Physiological arousal	n.s.	$R = .52$, $F_{(4,38)} = 3.47$*	Comfort[a] $\beta = .40$** Anxiety[a] $\beta = -.24$ n.s.	Comfort[a] $\beta = .33$* Anxiety[a] $\beta = -.23$ n.s.
Anxiety ratings	n.s.	$R = .39$, $F_{(2,44)} = 3.94$*	Comfort[a] $\beta = .40$** Anxiety[a] $\beta = -.26$†	Comfort[a] $\beta = .35$* Anxiety[a] $\beta = -.20$ n.s.
Self-assessment manikin ratings	n.s.	$R = .64$, $F_{(6,41)} = 4.74$**	Comfort[a] $\beta = .41$** Anxiety[a] $\beta = -.29$*	Comfort[a] $\beta = .33$** Anxiety[a] $\beta = -.15$ n.s.

[a] n.s. nonsignificant; † $p < .06$; * $p < .05$; ** $p < .01$.

[b] β weights for the attachment dimensions vary slightly across the affect measures because of missing data. Anxiety[a], Anxiety over relationships; comfort[a], Comfort with closeness.

TABLE III   Summary of Regression Analyses Testing Whether Affect Mediates
the Association between Attachment and Females' Relationship Satisfaction[a,b]

Measure	Attachment and affect	Affect and satisfaction	Attachment and satisfaction	Attachment and satisfaction (affect controlled)
Emotional Linkage	n.s.	n.s.	Comfort[a] $\beta = .42$** Anxiety[a] $\beta = -.30$*	Comfort[a] $\beta = .54$** Anxiety[a] $\beta = -.37$**
Physiological Arousal	n.s.	n.s.	Comfort[a] $\beta = .42$** Anxiety[a] $\beta = -.31$*	Comfort[a] $\beta = .36$** Anxiety[a] $\beta = -.36$*
Anxiety Ratings	n.s.	$R = .44$, $F_{(2,44)} = 5.33$**	Comfort[a] $\beta = .38$** Anxiety[a] $\beta = -.35$**	Comfort[a] $\beta = .29$* Anxiety[a] $\beta = -.29$*
Self-assessment manikin ratings	n.s.	$R = .56$, $F_{(6,41)} = 3.17$**	Comfort[a] $\beta = .38$** Anxiety[a] $\beta = -.35$**	Comfort[a] $\beta = .33$** Anxiety[a] $\beta = -.23$ n.s.

[a] n.s. nonsignificant; *$p < .05$; **$p < .01$.
[b] β weights for the attachment dimensions vary slightly across the affect measures because of missing data. Anxiety[a], Anxiety over relationships; Comfort[a], Comfort with closeness.

age, we actually found a positive association. In addition, as noted earlier, emotional linkage was unrelated to satisfaction.

The strongest overall result was that attachment style and levels of affect were independent predictors of satisfaction. That is, in the main, males' attachment dimensions continued to predict both partners' satisfaction, after controlling for levels of affect experienced by couples during conflict (females' attachment dimensions were unrelated to relationship satisfaction).

To further assess the relation between affect experienced during conflict and relationship satisfaction, and to test our hypotheses regarding gender differences and affect during conflict interaction, a series of multivariate analyses of variance (MANOVA) was also conducted. The first analysis used the emotional linkage variables (predictability of skin conductance levels from the partner's, predictability of interbeat interval from the partner's, and predictability of anxiety ratings from the partner's) as the dependent variables. The second analysis used the SAM ratings (power, negativity, and arousal) as dependent variables. For both analyses, the between-subjects variable was relationship satisfaction (satisfied and dissatisfied), with dissatisfied defined as either partner having a score on the Quality Marriage Index ≤ 37. Based on this criterion, 19 couples were defined as dissatisfied and 29 couples as satisfied. The within-subjects variables were gender and topic (male's issue, female's issue).

The first MANOVA revealed no significant main effects or interactions. Thus none of the variables, including satisfaction, had an effect on the degree to which couples' physiological and anxiety levels were temporally linked. This finding again stands in contrast to that of Levenson and Gottman (1983), who found a very strong relationship (60% shared variance) between physiological linkage and marital satisfaction.

For the SAM variables, only the multivariate main effect of satisfaction was significant ($F(3,44) = 5.65$, $p < .005$). Table IV displays the means and standard deviations for all of the variables as a function of satisfaction. The SAM ratings suggest that unhappy couples feel more aroused, less powerful, and more negative during conflict discussions. The univariate tests for satisfaction were significant for all three dependent variables: arousal ($F(1,46) = 4.60$, $p < .05$), power ($F(1,46) = 6.02$, $p < .05$), and negativity ($F(1,46) = 17.34$, $p < .001$).

A third MANOVA included the additional within-subjects variable of interaction stage, which previous research has suggested as important (e.g., Margolin, Burman, & John, 1989). Each of the 10-min interactions was simply divided into three segments of equal duration. The dependent variables for this analysis were the four measures of physiological arousal (mean skin conductance level, variability in skin conductance, mean interbeat interval, and variability in interbeat interval). Multivariate main effects were found for satisfaction ($F(4.37) = 4.11$, $p < .01$) and for interaction stage ($F(4,37) = 6.79$, $p < .05$). Univariate results showed that the main effect of satisfaction was significant for mean skin conductance levels ($F(1.40) = 5.73$, $p < .05$) and interbeat interval variability ($F(1.40) = 7.29$, $p < .05$). Univariate results also showed that the main effect of stage was significant for all four dependent variables.

TABLE IV   Means and Standard Deviations of Summary Variables for Satisfied and Dissatisfied Couples[a]

	Satisfied couples		Dissatisfied couples	
	Mean	Standard deviation	Mean	Standard deviation
a. Linkage variables				
Linkage in skin conductance levels	0.80	0.75	1.06	0.89
Linkage in interbeat intervals	0.74	0.46	0.63	0.68
Linkage in anxiety ratings	1.24	1.18	1.33	1.06
b. Self-assessment manikin ratings				
Power	3.20	0.53	2.76	0.69
Arousal	2.41	0.68	2.84	0.67
Negativity	2.55	0.64	3.38	0.73
c. Physiological arousal				
Mean skin conductance level	1.92	1.59	3.14	1.63
Mean interbeat interval	−0.41	0.51	−0.36	0.82
Skin conductance level variability	1.69	1.16	2.72	1.45
Interbeat interval variability	0.97	0.20	1.15	0.22
d. Anxiety ratings				
Female anxiety ratings	2.59	1.88	3.62	1.25
Male anxiety ratings	2.36	1.47	3.20	1.67

[a]Physiological measures were standardized according to subjects' baseline levels.

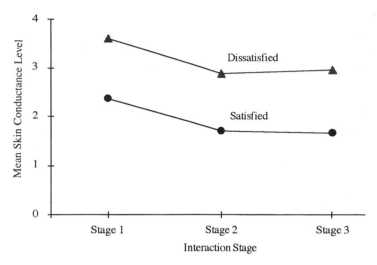

FIGURE 2   Mean skin conductance level, collapsed across gender and topic, as a function of relationship satisfaction and interaction stage.

Figures 2 and 3 depict the mean level of skin conductance and the variability of interbeat interval respectively, as a function of satisfaction and interaction stage. These figures illustrate the main effects of satisfaction and interaction stage. In both cases, the significant difference between happy and unhappy couples can be seen across the interaction, with unhappy couples being more aroused. The effect of in-

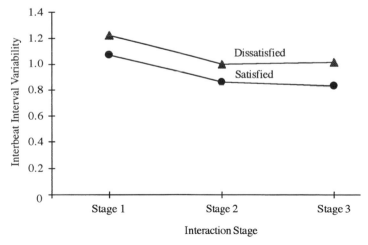

FIGURE 3   Variability in interbeat interval (standard deviation), collapsed across gender and topic, as a function of relationship satisfaction and interaction stage.

teraction stage showed that all couples were more physiologically aroused during the initial stage of the interaction.

Finally, an analysis of variance was performed using the same independent variables as the above analyses, but using mean anxiety ratings as the dependent variable. Main effects were found for satisfaction ($F(1,45) = 5.97$, $p < .05$) and for stage ($F(2,44) = 10.4$, $p < .001$). A significant two-way interaction was also found between satisfaction and stage ($F(2,44) = 3.55$, $p < .05$). No other main effects or interactions were obtained. Figure 4 shows that satisfied and dissatisfied couples differed in mean anxiety ratings only in the final two-thirds of the discussion. Thus it appears that happy and unhappy couples enter the interaction with the same level of subjective anxiety, but differ as the interaction progresses. Maybe the escalating anxiety experienced by unhappy couples is the result of the distress that they experience as the issue fails to be resolved, due to a lack of problem-solving skills.

However, the results for physiological arousal suggest a somewhat different picture. To the extent that higher levels of skin conductance and greater variability in interbeat interval indicate greater physiological arousal, unhappy couples had *consistently* higher arousal levels than happy couples across the course of their interactions. The discrepancy between self-report and physiological measures may simply reflect the fact that these methods provide separate, but complementary, information about couples' experiences of conflict. Together, however, the results provide a picture of unhappy dyads struggling through their disagreements, experiencing greater negativity, higher physiological and subjective arousal, more self-reported anxiety, and a greater sense of powerlessness.

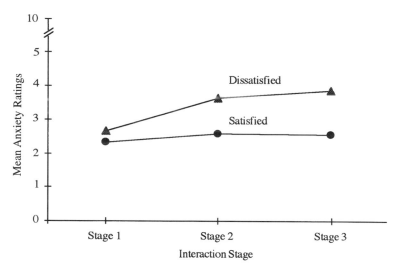

FIGURE 4   Mean anxiety ratings collapsed across gender and topic, as a function of relationship satisfaction and interaction stage.

The current study failed to support Levenson and Gottman's (1983) major findings. First, physiological linkage did not relate to concurrent satisfaction. Second, the finding that concurrent dissatisfaction was related to physiological arousal (as shown by higher mean skin conductance levels and greater variability in heart rate) is difficult to integrate with their results; Levenson and Gottman found no consistent relation between physiological arousal and concurrent satisfaction. More recently, Gottman (1994) also failed to find consistent links between these variables. Perhaps earlier expectations of the ability of psychophysiological techniques to shed light on marital interaction were overly optimistic. Although it is acknowledged that psychophysiological techniques do offer additional information beyond self-report measures, the present results also caution against perceptions that they provide a "window to the soul." It is also important to note that there are no published replications of Levenson and Gottman's findings.

The present analyses also consistently fail to support Gottman and Levenson's suggestions (1986, 1988) regarding males' greater levels of diffuse physiological activity during dyadic conflict. Males and females did not differ in their levels of physiological arousal or self-reported affect. Nor were there any significant interactions between gender and topic, in contrast to Christensen et al.'s findings concerning withdrawal. Thus no support was obtained for Gottman and Levenson's hypothesis that males' heightened levels of autonomic nervous system arousal explain their tendency to withdraw more from marital conflict than females. Finally, no interactions between gender and satisfaction were obtained, contrary to their suggestions that gender differences in autonomic nervous system arousal are particularly strong in unhappy marriages.

GENERAL DISCUSSION

Both studies presented here supported the link between emotion and relationship satisfaction, whether the *expression* or the *experience* of emotion was the focus. This result is consistent with the large body of research reviewed earlier, showing that satisfied and dissatisfied couples differ in the emotional climate of their relationships.

In the second study, which focused on the *experience* of emotion, there was no support for the hypothesis that affect mediates the link between attachment and satisfaction. In contrast, there was some support for the mediational model in the first study, where the *expression* (vs. control) of emotion was the focus. Specifically, the link between males' comfort with closeness and females' satisfaction seems to reflect, in part, the fact that males who are high in comfort tend to express feelings such as sadness in a direct and open manner. The failure to support the mediational hypothesis in Study 2 was due primarily to the fact that there was no link between attachment dimensions and the experience of emotion, in contrast to the link between attachment dimensions and the control of emotional expression in

Study 1. The mixed findings concerning the mediational hypothesis highlight the importance of maintaining the distinction between the experience and the expression of emotion in studying close relationships.

It is important to note that, of the three negative emotions assessed in Study 1, only sadness and anger (but not anxiety) were associated with relationship satisfaction, in terms of the control of emotional expression. The measures of emotion in Study 2 focused either on anxiety, or on the dimensions underlying emotional experience in general. Hence, an alternative explanation for the lack of support for the mediational model in that study centers on the different emotions explored. Specifically, to detect a relation between attachment style and emotion (whether the experience *or* the expression), researchers may need to focus clearly on specific emotions, rather than on the general dimensions underlying affect.

As noted earlier, in both studies we found associations between affect and relationship satisfaction. Thus, it appears that a dimensional approach to studying emotion (e.g., Osgood et al., 1975) is adequate for detecting global relationship differences between happy and unhappy couples. However, greater specificity seems to be required when trying to isolate differences between attachment styles. It is noted that previous researchers have suggested that although there is only one way to be secure, there may be many ways of being insecure (Feeney, Noller, & Hanrahan, 1994b).

It is also important to remember that the data for Study 2 were based solely on conflict interactions. By contrast, couples in Study 1 were asked to describe their typical responses to a range of negative emotions, which did not necessarily stem from negative partner behavior. Other research has suggested that, in conflict interactions, most couples are likely to be angry and to perceive their partners in a negative way (Guthrie & Noller, 1988). It is possible that attachment style differences in experienced affect are more likely to occur in situations other than conflict. We know that attachment groups differ in the ways they deal with conflict; for example, Feeney, Noller, and Callan (1994) found that those who were anxious about relationships reported higher levels of coercion, domination, and demand–withdraw during conflict. However, they may not differ markedly in the levels of emotion experienced during conflict.

Further research is needed to explore the relations among attachment, gender, and the experience and expression of emotion, and we are currently investigating some of the issues outlined above. For example, we plan to analyze the interactions of the couples in Study 2 for two other contexts: trivial disagreements and self-disclosures of negative events. We also plan to use time series analysis to assess whether individuals differ in what they express during dyadic interaction when they report feeling anxious. Thus we will be able to see how these individuals behave when they experience anxiety.

In summary, these studies support the well-established link between emotion and relationship satisfaction. On the other hand, they point to very complex links among attachment, gender, and the experience and expression of emotion, an area that has so far received little attention. Our results suggest that *emotional expression* is linked with attachment style, and that attachment style and emotional expression generally exert independent effects on couples' relationship satisfaction. In predicting females' satisfaction, however, there was evidence that the effect of males' comfort with closeness was mediated by their expression of negative emotion, in accordance with the model presented in Figure 1. In other words, the high satisfaction reported by partners of males high in comfort with closeness seems to stem from the fact that these males are prepared to openly express feelings such as sadness. In terms of *emotional experience,* however, our results did not suggest that affect mediates the association between attachment style and relationship satisfaction. In fact, measures of emotional experience were largely unrelated to attachment style, at least for this sample of married and cohabiting couples. Our results point to the importance of measuring a range of emotions and using a range of methods of assessing affect, in order to increase our understanding of the role of affect in close personal relationships.

REFERENCES

Alberts, J. K. (1988). An analysis of couples' conversational complaints. *Communication Monographs, 55,* 184–197.

Averill, J. R. (1980). A Constructivist view of emotion. In R. Plutchik & H. Kellerman (Eds.), *Emotion: Theory, research, and experience: Vol. 1.* New York: Academic Press.

Baron, R. M., & Kenny, D. A. (1986). The moderator-mediator variable distinction in social psychological research: Conceptual, strategic and statistical considerations. *Journal of Personality and Social Psychology, 51,* 1173–1182.

Bartholomew, K. (1990). Avoidance of intimacy: An attachment perspective. *Journal of Social and Personal Relationships, 7,* 147–178.

Bartholomew, K., & Horowitz, L. M. (1991). Attachment styles among young adults: A test of a four-category model. *Journal of Personality and Social Psychology, 61,* 226–244.

Beach, S. R. H., & O'Leary, K. D. (1993). Dysphoria and marital discord: Are dysphoric individuals at risk for marital maladjustment? *Journal of Marital and Family Therapy, 19,* 355–368.

Berscheid, E. (1983). Emotion. In H. H. Kelley, E. Berscheid, A. Christensen, J. H. Harvey, T. L. Juston, G. Levinger, E. McClintock, L. A. Peplau, & D. R. Peterson (Eds.), *Close relationships* (pp. 110–168). New York: Freeman.

Birchler, G. R., Clopton, P. L., & Adams, N. L. (1984). Marital conflict resolution: Factors influencing concordance between partners and trained coders. *American Journal of Family Therapy, 12,* 15–28.

Bowlby, J. (1969). *Attachment and loss: Vol. 1. Attachment.* New York: Basic Books.

Bowlby, J. (1973). *Attachment and loss: Vol. 2. Separation: Anxiety and anger.* New York: Basic Books.

Bowlby, J. (1988). *A secure base.* New York: Basic Books.

Bradbury, T. N., & Fincham, F. D. (1987). Affect and cognition in close relationships: Toward an integrative model. *Cognition and Emotion, 1,* 59–87.

Bradbury, T. N., & Fincham, F. D. (1990). Attributions in marriage: Review and critique. *Psychological Bulletin, 107,* 3–33.

Bradbury, T. N., & Fincham, F. D. (1991). A contextual model for advancing the study of marriage. In G. J. O. Fletcher & F. D. Fincham (Eds.), *Cognition in close relationships* (pp. 127–147). Hillsdale, NJ: Erlbaum.

Broderick, J. E., & O'Leary, K. D. (1986). Contributions of affect, attitude and behavior to marital satisfaction. *Journal of Consulting and Clinical Psychology, 54,* 514–517.

Buck, R. (1989). Emotional communication in personal relationships: A developmental-interactionist view. In C. Hendrick (Ed.), *Close relationships* (pp. 144–163). Newbury Park, CA: Sage.

Buehlman, K. T., Gottman, J. M., & Katz, L. (1992). How a couple views their past predicts their future: Predicting divorce from an oral history interview. *Journal of Family Psychology, 5,* 295–318.

Byrne, C. A., & Arias, I. (in press). Marital satisfaction and marital violence: Moderating effects of attributional processes. *Journal of Family Psychology.*

Cahn, D. D. (1990). Confrontation behaviors, perceived understanding and relationship growth. In D. Cahn (Ed.), *Intimates in conflict* (pp. 153–165). Hillsdale, NJ: Erlbaum.

Chance, M. R. A. (1980). An ethological assessment of emotion. In R. Plutchik & H. Kellerman (Eds.), *Emotion: Theory, research, and experience* (pp. 81–111). New York: Academic Press.

Christensen, A., & Heavey, C. L. (1990). Gender and social structure in the demand/withdraw pattern of marital conflict. *Journal of Personality and Social Psychology, 59,* 73–81.

Christensen, A., & Shenk, J. L. (1991). Communication, conflict and psychological distance in nondistressed, clinic and divorcing couples. *Journal of Consulting and Clinical Psychology, 59,* 458–463.

Clark, L. A., & Watson, D. (1991). General affective dispositions in physical and psychological health. In C. R. Snyder & D. R. Forsyth (Eds.), *Handbook of social and clinical psychology* (pp. 221–245). New York: Pergamon.

Collins, N. S., & Read, S. J. (1990). Adult attachment, working models, and relationship quality in dating couples. *Journal of Personality and Social Psychology, 58,* 644–663.

Collins, N. S., & Read, S. J. (1994). Cognitive representations of attachment: The structure and function of working models. *Advances in Personal Relationships, 5,* 53–90.

Davidson, B. J., Balswick, J., & Halverson, C. (1983). Affective self-disclosure and marital adjustment: A test of equity theory. *Journal of Marriage and the Family, 45,* 93–102.

Eidelson, R. J., & Epstein, N. (1982). Cognition and relationship maladjustment: Development of a measure of dysfunctional relationship beliefs. *Journal of Consulting and Clinical Psychology, 50,* 715–720.

Feeney, J. A. (1994). Attachment style, communication patterns and satisfaction across the life cycle of marriage. *Personal Relationships, 1,* 333–348.

Feeney, J. A. (1995). Adult attachment and emotional control. *Personal Relationships, 2,* 143–159.

Feeney, J. A., & Noller, P. (1990). Attachment style as a predictor of adult romantic relationships. *Journal of Personality and Social Psycholgy, 58,* 281–291.

Feeney, J. A., & Noller, P. (1991). Attachment style and verbal descriptions of romantic partners. *Journal of Social and Personal Relationships, 8,* 187–215.

Feeney, J. A., & Noller, P. (1992). Attachment style and romantic love: Relationship dissolution. *Australian Journal of Psychology, 44,* 69–74.

Feeney, J. A., Noller, P., & Callan, V. J. (1994). Attachment style, communication and satisfaction in the early years of marriage. *Advances in Personal Relationships, 5,* 269–308.

Feeney, J. A., Noller, P., & Hanrahan, M. (1994). Assessing adult attachment. In M. B. Sperling and W. H. Berman (Eds.), *Attachment in adults: Clinical and developmental perspectives* (pp. 128–152). New York: Guilford.

Feeney, J. A., & Ryan, S. M. (1994). Attachment style and affect regulation: Relationships with health behavior and family experiences of illness in a student sample. *Health Psychology, 13,* 334–345.

Fincham, F. D., & Bradbury, T. N. (1987). The impact of attributions in marriage: A longitudinal analysis. *Journal of Personality and Social Psychology, 53,* 510–517.

Fincham, F. D., & Bradbury, T. N. (1988). The impact of attributions in marriage: Empirical and conceptual foundations. *British Journal of Clinical Psychology, 27,* 77–90.

Fitness, J., & Fletcher, G. J. O. (1993). Love, hate, anger, and jealousy in close relationships: A prototype and cognitive appraisal analysis. *Journal of Personality and Social Psychology, 65,* 942–958.

Fitzpatrick, M. A. (1988). *Between husbands and wives.* Newbury Park, CA: Sage.

Fuller, T. L., & Fincham, F. D. (1995). Attachment style in married couples: Relation to current marital functioning, stability over time, and method of assessment. *Personal Relationships, 2,* 17–34.

Gaelick, L., Bodenhausen, G., & Wyer, R. S. (1985). Emotional communication in close relationships. *Journal of Personality and Social Psychology, 49,* 1246–1265.

Gottman, J. M. (1981). *Time-series analysis: A comprehensive introduction for social scientists.* Cambridge: Cambridge University Press.

Gottman, J. M. (1990). How marriages change. In G. R. Patterson (Ed.), *Depression and aggression in family interaction* (pp. 75–101). Hillsdale, NJ: Lawrence Erlbaum.

Gottman, J. M. (1994). *What predicts divorce? The relationship between marital processes and marital outcomes.* Hillsdale, NJ: Lawrence Erlbaum.

Gottman, J. M., & Levenson, R. W. (1986). Assessing the role of emotion in marriage. *Behavioral Assessment, 8,* 31–48.

Gottman, J. M., & Levenson, R. W. (1988). The social psychophysiology of marriage. In P. Noller & M. A. Fitzpatrick (Eds.), *Perspectives on marital interaction* (pp. 182–200). Clevedon & Philadelphia: Multilingual Matters.

Gottman, J., Markman, H., & Notarius, C. (1977). The topography of marital conflict: A study of verbal and nonverbal behavior. *Journal of Marriage and the Family, 39,* 461–477.

Guthrie, D. M., & Noller, P. (1988). Spouses' perceptions of one another in emotional situations. In P. Noller & M. A. Fitzpatrick (Eds.), *Perspectives on marital interaction* (pp. 153–181). Clevedon & Philadelphia: Multilingual Matters.

Halford, W. K., & Sanders, M. (1990). The relationship of cognition and behavior during marital interaction. *Journal of Social and Clinical Psychology, 9,* 489–510.

Hazan, C., & Shaver, P. R. (1987). Romantic love conceptualized as an attachment process. *Journal of Personality and Social Psychology, 52,* 511–524.

Hazan, C., & Shaver, P. R. (1994). Attachment as an organizational framework for research on close relationships. *Psychological Inquiry, 5(4),* 1–22.

Heavey, C. L., Layne, C., & Christensen, A. (1993). Gender and conflict structure in marital interaction: A replication and extension. *Journal of Consulting and Clinical Psychology, 61,* 16–27.

Hodes, R. L., Cook, E. W., & Lang, P. J. (1985). Individual differences in autonomic response: Conditioned association or conditioned fear? *Psychophysiology, 22(5),* 545–560.

Holtzworth-Munroe, A., & Hutchinson, G. (1993). Attributing negative intent to wife behavior: The attributions of maritally violent versus nonviolent men. *Journal of Abnormal Psychology, 102,* 206–211.

Hooley, J. M., & Hahlweg, K. (1989). Marital satisfaction and marital communication in German and English couples. *Behavioral Assessment, 11,* 119–133.

Izard, C. E. (1977). *Human emotions.* New York: Plenum Press.

Izard, C. E. (1991). *The psychology of emotions.* New York: Plenum Press.

Julien, D. (1992, July). *Expanding marital adjustment theories: What if marriage was fun?* Paper presented at the Fourth World Congress on Behavior Therapy, Gold Coast, Australia.

Julien, D., & Markman, H. J. (1991). Social support networks as determinants of individual and marital outcomes. *Journal of Social and Personal Relationships, 8,* 549–568.

Kirchler, E. (1988). Marital happiness and interaction in everyday surroundings: A time-sample diary approach for couples. *Journal of Social and Personal Relationships, 5,* 375–382.

Kirchler, E. (1989). Everyday life experiences at home: An interaction diary approach to assess marital relationships. *Journal of Family Psychology, 2,* 311–336.

Kirkpatrick, L. A., & Davis, K. E. (1994). Attachment style, gender, and relationship stability: A longitudinal analysis. *Journal of Personality and Social Psychology, 66(3),* 502–512.

Kobak, R. R., & Hazan, C. (1991). Attachment in marriage: Effects of security and accuracy of working models. *Journal of Personality and Social Psychology, 60,* 861–869.

Kobak, R. R., & Sceery, A. (1988). Attachment in late adolescence: Working models, affect regulation, and representations of self and others. *Child Development, 59,* 135–146.

Lang, P. J. (1980). Behavioral treatment and bio-behavioral assessment: Computer applications. In J. B. Sidowski, J. H. Johnson, & T. A. Williams (Eds.), *Technology in mental health care delivery systems* (pp. 129–139). Norwood, NJ: Ablex.

Larsen, R. J., & Ketelaar, T. (1991). Personality and susceptibility to positive and negative emotional states. *Journal of Personality and Social Psychology, 61,* 132–140.

Larson, R., & Richards, M. (1994). *Divergent realities: The emotional lives of mothers, fathers and adolescents.* New York: Basic Books.

Lazarus, R. S. (1966). Psychological stress and the coping process. New York: McGraw-Hill.

Lazarus, R., & Smith, C. (1988). Knowledge and appraisal in the cognition-emotion relationship. *Cognition and Emotion, 2,* 281–300.

Levenson, R. W., & Gottman, J. M. (1983). Marital interaction: Physiological linkage and affective exchange. *Journal of Personality and Social Psychology, 45,* 587–597.

Levenson, R. W., & Gottman, J. M. (1985). Physiological and affective predictors of change in relationship satisfaction. *Journal of Personality and Social Psychology, 49,* 85–94.

Levy, M. B., & Davis, K. D. (1988). Love styles and attachment styles compared: Their relations to each other and to various relationship characteristics. *Journal of Social and Personal Relationships, 5,* 439–471.

Mandler, G. (1975). *Mind and emotion.* New York: Wiley.

Margolin, G., Burman, B., & John, R. S. (1989). Home observations of married couples reenacting naturalistic conflicts. *Behavioral Assessment, 11,* 101–118.

Markman, H. J., Duncan, S. W., Storaasli, R. D., & Howes, P. W. (1987). The prediction of marital distress: A longitudinal investigation. In K. Hahlweg & M. Goldstein (Eds.), *Understanding major mental disorder: The contribution of family interaction research* (pp. 266–289). New York: Family Process Press.

Mikulincer, M., Florian, V., & Tolmacz, R. (1990). Attachment styles and fear of personal death: A case study of affect regulation. *Journal of Personality and Social Psychology, 58,* 273–280.

Noller, P. (1982). Channel consistency and inconsistency in the communication of married couples. *Journal of Personality and Social Psychology, 43,* 732–741.

Noller, P. (1984). *Nonverbal communication and marital interaction.* Oxford: Pergamon.

Noller, P., Feeney, J. A., Bonnell, D., & Callan, V. J. (1994). A longitudinal study of conflict in early marriage. *Journal of Social and Personal Relationships, 11,* 233–252.

Noller, P., & Fitzpatrick, M. A. (1990). Marital communication in the eighties. *Journal of Marriage and the Family, 52,* 832–843.

Noller, P., & Guthrie, D. M. (1991). Methodological issues in studying communication in close relationships. In W. H. Jones & D. M. Perlman (Eds.), *Advances in personal relationships.* London: Jessica Kingsley.

Noller, P., & Ruzzene, M. (1991). The effects of cognition and affect on marital communication. In G. Fletcher & F. D. Fincham (Eds.), *Cognition in close relationships* (pp. 203–233). New York: Lawrence Erlbaum.

Norton, R. (1983). Measuring marital quality: A critical look at the dependent variable. *Journal of Marriage and the Family, 45,* 141–151.

Notarius, C. I., Benson, P. R., & Sloane, D. (1989). Exploring the interface between perception and behavior: An analysis of marital interaction in distressed and nondistressed couples. *Behavioral Assessment, 11,* 39–64.

Notarius, C. I., & Herrick, L. R. (1989). The psychophysiology of dyadic interaction. In H. Wagner & A. Manstead (Eds.), *Handbook of social psychophysiology* (pp. 393–419). Chichester: John Wiley & Sons.

Notarius, C. I., & Johnson, J. S. (1982). Emotional expression in husbands and wives. *Journal of Marriage and the Family, 44,* 483–389.

O'Leary, K. D., & Smith, D. A. (1991). Marital interactions. *Annual Review of Psychology, 42,* 191–212.

Osgarby, S. M., & Halford, W. K. (1996). *Being positive does matter: Behaviour, cognition, affect and physiology of couples during problem solving and positive reminiscence discussions.* Unpublished manuscript, Psychiatry Department, the University of Queensland, Australia.

Osgood, C. E., May, W. H., & Miron, M. S. (1975). *Cross-cultural universals of affective meaning.* Urbana: University of Illinois Press.

Pistole, M. (1989). Attachment in adult romantic relationships: Style of conflict resolution and relationship satisfaction. *Journal of Social and Personal Relationships, 6,* 505–510.

Plutchik, R. (1980). *Emotions: A psychoevolutionary synthesis.* New York: Harper Row.

Revenstorf, D., Hahlweg, K., Schindler, L., & Vogel, B. (1984). Interaction analysis of marital conflict. In K. Hahlweg & N. S. Jacobson (Eds.), *Marital interaction: Analysis and modification* (pp. 159–181). New York: Guilford.

Roberts, L. J., & Krokoff, L. J. (1990). A time-series analysis of withdrawal, hostility, and displeasure in satisfied and dissatisfied marriages. *Journal of Marriage and the Family, 52,* 95–105.

Schaap, C. (1984). A comparison of the interaction of distressed and nondistressed married couples in a laboratory situation: Literature survey, methodological issues, and an empirical investigation. In K. Hahlweg & N. S. Jacobson (Eds.), *Marital interaction: Analysis and modification* (pp. 133–158). New York: Guilford.

Schaap, C., & Jansen-Nawas, C. (1987). Marital interaction, affect and conflict resolution. *Sexual and Marital Therapy, 2,* 35–51.

Schachter, S., & Singer, J. E. (1962). Cognitive, social and physiological determinants of emotional state. *Psychological Review, 69,* 379–399.

Schaefer, E. S., & Burnett, C. K. (1987). Stability and predictability of quality of women's marital relationships and demoralization. *Journal of Personality and Social Psychology, 53,* 1129–1136.

Shaver, P. R., Schwartz, J., Kirson, D., & O'Connor, C. (1987). Emotion knowledge: Further exploration of a prototype approach. *Journal of Personality and Social Psychology, 52,* 1061–1086.

Scherer, K. R. (1984). On the nature and function of emotion: A component process approach. In K. R. Scherer & P. Ekman (Eds.), *Approaches to emotion* (pp. 293–317). Hillsdale, NJ: Erlbaum.

Schuerger, J. M., Zarrella, K. L., & Hotz, A. S. (1989). Factors that influence the temporal stability of personality by questionnaire. *Journal of Personality and Social Psychology, 56,* 777–783.

Sillars, A. L. (1985). Interpersonal perception in relationships. In W. Ickes (Ed.), *Compatible and incompatible relationships* (pp. 277–305). New York: Springer-Verlag.

Simpson, J. (1990). Influence of attachment styles on romantic relationships. *Journal of Personality and Social Psychology, 59,* 971–980.

Simpson, J. A., Rholes, W. S., & Nelligan, J. S. (1992). Support seeking and support giving within couples in an anxiety-provoking situation: The role of attachment styles. *Journal of Personality and Social Psychology, 62(3),* 434–446.

Sroufe, L. A., & Waters, E. (1977). Attachment as an organizational construct. *Child Development, 48,* 1184–1199.

Strahan, B. J. (1991). Attachment theory and family functioning: Expectations and congruencies. *Australian Journal of Marriage and Family, 12,* 12–26.

Straus, M. A. (1979). Measuring intrafamily conflict and violence: The conflict tactics (CT) scales. *Journal of Marriage and the Family, 41,* 75–86.

Vuchinich, S. (1987). Starting and stopping spontaneous family conflict. *Journal of Marriage and the Family, 49,* 591–601.

Wagner, H. L., & Callam, R. M. (1988). Interpersonal psychophysiology and the study of the family. In H. Wagner (Ed.), *Social psychophysiology and emotion: Theory and clinical applications* (pp. 211–229) Chichester: John Wiley & Sons.

Wallbott, H. G., & Scherer, K. R. (1988). How universal and specific is emotional experience? In K. R. Scherer (Ed.), *Facets of emotion* (pp. 31–56). Hillsdale, NJ: Erlbaum.

Watson, M., & Greer, S. (1983). Development of a questionnaire measure of emotional control. *Journal of Psychosomatic Research, 27,* 299–305.

Weiss, R. L., & Heyman, R. E. (1990). Observation of marital interaction. In F. D. Fincham & T. N. Bradbury (Eds.), *The psychology of marriage* (pp. 87–117). New York: Guilford.

Williams, E. A., & Gottman, J. M. (1981). *The Gottman–Williams computer programs for social scientists.* University of Illinois, Urbana, IL.

Zajonc, R. B. (1984). On primacy of affect. In K. R. Scherer & P. Ekman (Eds.), *Approaches to emotion* (pp. 259–270). Hillsdale, NJ: Erlbaum.

CHAPTER 19

Communication of Emotions in Friendships

Stanley O. Gaines, Jr.

Pomona College
Claremont, California

with

Katrina L. Bledsoe, Karlyn R. Farris, Michael C. Henderson, Gregory J. Kurland, Jodie K. Lara, William D. Marelich, Mary S. Page, Laura J. Palucki, W. Neil Steers, and Ann M. West

The Claremont Graduate School[1]
Claremont, California

> *Throughout our lives, . . . we have friends and "just" friends, old friends and new friends, good friends and best friends—each relationship meeting some part of ourselves that cries out for expression. One friend taps our intellectual capacities more deeply than others, another connects most profoundly to our emotional side. One calls upon our nurturant, caretaking qualities, another permits our dependency needs to surface. One friend touches our fun-loving side, another our more serious part. One friend is the sister we wish we had, another offers the mothering we missed.*
> —Lillian Rubin, *Just Friends* (1985, p. 56)

Unlike siblings, friends choose to be related to each other. Unlike spouses, friends can renew their relationships instantly with a timely phone call, letter, or e-mail message—even after years without having seen or heard from each other. As the above quote from Lillian Rubin (1985) attested, friends often develop bonds of emotional intimacy that are unparalleled in individuals' relational lives. Thus, even if individuals cannot express their emotions within their families of origin or their families of procreation, they usually can let their guard down when in the company of one or more friends.

This chapter addresses the ways in which individuals communicate various emotions toward their friends. We define *friendships* as nonkin peer relationships that are

---

[1] The second through eleventh authors contributed equally to this chapter.

voluntary and are characterized by relatively high levels of emotional (but not physical) intimacy (see Nardi, 1992; O'Connor, 1992; Swain, 1992). We used Plutchik's (1980b) circular or circumplex model as the basis for identifying the universe of emotions that might be communicated by individuals toward their friends, partly because of the model's conceptual elegance and partly because Plutchik (1962, 1980a, 1983) viewed chronic emotions as the precursors of interpersonal traits and, ultimately, of patterns of communication in personal relationships (for a comprehensive critique of circumplex models of emotions, see Larsen & Diener, 1992). Plutchik's (1980b) model is illustrated in Figure 1.

According to Plutchik (1980a, 1980b), four pairs of opposing emotions (i.e., joy versus sadness, acceptance versus disgust, fear versus anger, and surprise versus anticipation) comprise the domain of primary emotions. An additional four pairs of opposing emotions (i.e., love versus remorse, submission versus contempt, awe ver-

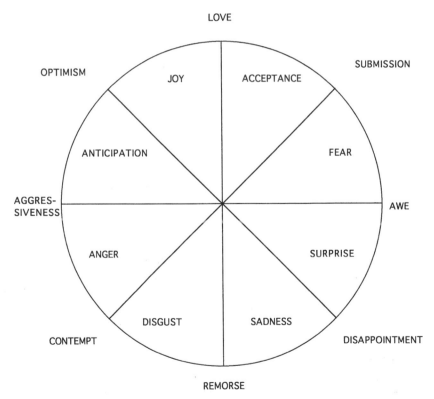

FIGURE 1   Initial adaptation of Plutchik's (1980b) Model of Emotions. Reprinted with permission from *Psychology Today* magazine, copyright © 1980 (Sussex Publishers, Inc.).

sus aggressiveness, and optimism versus disappointment) comprise the domain of secondary emotions (i.e., blends of the primary emotions). The corresponding emotions are defined as follows.

Among the primary emotions, *joy* is a positive, transitory emotion characterized by the establishment or gain of attachment, whereas *sadness* is a negative, transitory emotion characterized by the decline or loss of attachment. *Acceptance* is a positive, transitory emotion characterized by incorporation of concern with another person's psychological well-being into oneself, whereas *disgust* is a negative, transitory emotion characterized by rejection of concern with another person's psychological well-being from oneself. *Fear* is a negative, transitory emotion characterized by avoidance of a potentially pain-inducing stimulus, whereas *anger* is a negative, transitory emotion characterized by approach toward a potentially pain-inducing stimulus. Finally, *surprise* is a positive or negative, transitory emotion characterized by approach toward a novel stimulus, whereas *anticipation* is a positive, transitory emotion characterized by approach toward a familiar stimulus.

Regarding secondary emotions, *love* (a blend of joy and acceptance) is a positive, long-lasting emotion characterized by the establishment or gain of attachment, whereas *remorse* (a blend of sadness and disgust) is a negative, long-lasting emotion characterized by decline or loss of attachment. *Submission* (a blend of acceptance and fear) is a negative, long-lasting emotion characterized by incorporation of concern with another person's psychological well-being into oneself, whereas *contempt* (a blend of anger and disgust) is a negative, long-lasting emotion characterized by rejection of concern with another person's psychological well-being from oneself. *Awe* (a blend of fear and surprise) is a positive, long-lasting emotion characterized by approach toward a potentially pleasure-inducing stimulus, whereas *aggressiveness* (a blend of anger and anticipation) is a negative, long-lasting emotion characterized by approach toward a potentially pain-inducing stimulus. Finally, *optimism* (a blend of joy and anticipation) is a positive, long-lasting emotion characterized by approach toward a novel stimulus, whereas *disappointment* (a blend of surprise and sadness) is a negative, long-lasting emotion characterized by avoidance of a familiar stimulus.

But which, if any, of the aforementioned emotions (whether primary or secondary) have been examined within the context of individuals' communication with friends? In the following sections, we shall consider each of the pairs of opposing emotions in greater detail. We are interested particularly in distinguishing between those emotions that have received at least some attention in past studies of communication in friendships and those emotions that have not received such attention in the empirical literature. By identifying those emotions that have been studied within the context of friendships, we might be able to ascertain which current social-psychological theories are most likely to explain substantial individual differences in friends' communication of emotion. Conversely, by identifying those emotions that have *not* been studied within the context of friendships, we might be able to suggest fruitful areas for future theorization and research.

COMMUNICATION OF PRIMARY EMOTIONS IN FRIENDSHIPS

Joy versus Sadness

Most research on the communication of joy and sadness has focused on gender differences in frequency of expression. Females tend to be more adept at recognizing and expressing emotions in general (Allen & Haccoun, 1976; Sogon & Izard, 1987; Stapley & Haviland, 1989) and sadness in particular (Sogon & Izard, 1987) than are males. Both males and females are more likely to express joy and sadness to opposite-sex than to same-sex targets (Allen & Haccoun, 1976); and females tend to score higher in self-reported sadness than do males, regardless of the gender of the target person (Blier & Blier-Wilson, 1989).

The expressions of joy and sadness in friendships seem to be contingent upon individuals' age as well as gender. Although the propensity toward expressing joy and sadness remains constant, individuals' *expression* of joy and sadness may become more muted as they develop and presumably succumb to societal norms (Fabes & Martin, 1991). For example, when a toddler is sad, he or she is likely to cry anywhere and toward anyone; an adult, however, is likely to suppress outward expressions of sadness until he or she has found a relatively safe interpersonal context (e.g., when with one's best friend) in which to express that emotion openly. Interestingly, Stapley and Haviland (1989) have posited a curvilinear relationship between emotional concealment and age, whereby adolescents feel greater pressure to refrain from expressing sadness than either children or adults.

Perhaps the most obvious nonverbal manner in which adults communicate sadness to their friends is by frowning. In fact, individuals asked to manipulate their facial muscles so as to *simulate* sadness actually *feel* sad after they have stopped frowning (Hatfield, Cacioppo, & Rapson, 1992). Similar nonverbal expressions, such as pouting and sulking, also convey sadness and, within the context of friendships as well as romantic relationships, collectively may be described as *neglect* behaviors (i.e., passive, potentially relationship-threatening responses to relationship partners' dissatisfaction; Rusbult, Drigotas, & Verette, 1994). When individuals respond to their friends' anger or criticism by silently pouting or sulking, they have succeeded in communicating sadness toward their friends by disengaging themselves temporarily from their friends. However, if this social withdrawal persists over time, friendships may gradually disintegrate, leaving former friends to come to terms with the fact that they must have hurt each other some time ago (Rusbult, Drigotas, & Verette, 1994; see also LaFrance & Banaji, 1992; Rawlins, 1994; Vangelisti & Sprague, Chapter 5, this volume).

Relationship type also appears to influence individuals' expression of joy and sadness. In a study of exchange relationships (i.e., relationships characterized by explicit norms regarding reciprocity, such as acquaintances and business relationships) and communal relationships (i.e., relationships *not* characterized by such explicit

norms, such as friendships and relationships with family members), Clark and Taraban (1991) found that sadness was expressed significantly more often in communal
than in exchange relationships. However, individuals' expressions of joy were not
influenced significantly by relationship type. Thus, it appears that societal perceptions of sadness actually hinder its expression in relationships until appropriate levels of trust are established in those relationships (Zammuner & Frijda, 1994).

Overall, sadness has received greater attention in the literature on friends' communication of emotions than has joy. One potential problem in assessing joy and
sadness as dichotomous emotional states in friendships is that they may not be polar opposites after all. As Wierzbicka (1992) noted, *joy* (which by definition is interpersonal in nature; Kemper, 1990) typically is experienced positively as well as
actively by individuals, whereas *sadness* (which may reflect a more generalized state
of depression or loneliness) typically is experienced negatively as well as passively
by individuals (see Segrin, Chapter 8, this volume). Unfortunately, no studies have
employed the friendship dyad (rather than the individual) as the unit of analysis for
examining the expression of joy or sadness, whether in same-sex or opposite-sex
friendships. Perhaps the safest assumption to be made regarding the communication
of joy and sadness in friendships is that joy is likely to be expressed in a variety of
friendships, whereas sadness is likely to be expressed only in the closest of friendships.

Acceptance versus Disgust

Research on the communication of acceptance in friendships has focused primarily upon peer relationships among elementary school children and adolescents. In
contrast, research on the communication of the opposing emotion of disgust in
friendships virtually has been nonexistent. Therefore, the bulk of the literature reviewed in this section will be devoted to research on the communication of acceptance, rather than disgust, in friendships.

Of all the emotions, acceptance may be most likely to be interpreted by relationship partners as signaling friendship (Plutchik, 1980a). Studies of children's and
adolescents' peer relationships frequently employ sociometric evaluations of peers
as measures of acceptance (Inderbitzen-Pisaruk & Foster, 1990). Using this approach, researchers typically ask participants to indicate which peers they like most
and which peers they like least. Contrary to the acceptance or disgust dimension
posited by Plutchik (1980a, 1980b), the sociometric evaluation procedure yields a
range of responses influencing acceptance, including neglect and rejection. These
relationship status dimensions have received considerable attention within developmental and clinical psychology (Inderbitzen-Pisaruk & Foster, 1990).

In a study explicitly examining individuals' communication skills as influenced
by individuals' acceptance by their peers, Burleson et al. (1986) found that children
who were neglected by their peers generally displayed less well-developed com-

munication skills, including persuasion and comforting skills (e.g., saying "It's OK," patting peer on the shoulder). In addition, peers who come to be regarded as generally less accepted by others are more likely to rate their friendships as lower in quality (Parker & Asher, 1993), experience a greater sense of loneliness (Parker & Asher, 1993; Renshaw & Brown, 1993; see Segrin, Chapter 8, this volume), and develop a greater propensity toward alcohol and drug abuse as well as low achievement later in life (Burleson, 1986) than do peers who come to be regarded as generally accepted by others. Furthermore, once peers come to be accepted or rejected by others, they often continue to be viewed as such over time (Bukowski & Newcomb, 1984).

Several investigators have assessed the importance of acceptance in friendships among different demographic groups. Regarding age, Tesch and Martin (1983) concluded that college students tended to emphasize acceptance to a lesser extent in their descriptions of friendships than did older university alumni (even though the alumni were only 5 years older, on average, than were college students). Regarding gender, Parham and Tinsley (1980) reported that female college students valued acceptance in friendships to a greater extent than did male college students. However, Rose (1985) indicated that gender *per se* did not affect the degree to which individuals valued friendships; rather, importance of acceptance differed as a function of gender only with regard to cross-sex friendships (i.e., women tended to indicate that opposite-sex friendships provided less acceptance than did men). Regardless of gender, however, individuals often communicate acceptance by "beckoning a friend in welcome" (Sogon & Masutani, 1989, p. 46) and by comforting their friends when distressed (see Burleson & Goldsmith, Chapter 9, this volume; Konstantareas & Homatidis, 1984).

Fear versus Anger

Most of the research on the communication of fear versus anger in friendships has focused on anger rather than fear. Thus, it is difficult to determine whether fear and anger (Plutchik, 1980a, 1980b) can be viewed correctly as opposing emotions. Anger expression resembles another emotion, sadness, in terms of the presence of a frown; unlike sadness, though, an angry frown typically is accompanied by a "clenched jaw" and "red face" (Canary, Spitzberg, & Semic, Chapter 7, this volume; Tomkins, 1980). Nevertheless, anger and sadness both may be communicated via individuals' temporary (and, in time, permanent) social withdrawal from their friends (Rusbult, Drigotas, & Verette, 1994; see also LaFrance & Banaji, 1992; Rawlins, 1994; Canary et al., Chapter 7, this volume) following their friends' expressed dissatisfaction or as a response to a negative emotion felt in the presence of friends.

In a study of black adolescents' communication of anger in personal relationships, Jones, Peacock, and Christopher (1992) found that individuals often express anger toward their friends as well as toward their family members (although family members, particularly mothers, are targets of individuals' anger more often than are friends). Girls were more likely to display anger via crying and maintaining silence than were boys. Conversely, boys were more likely to display anger via outward aggression than were girls.

Gender differences regarding the communication of anger in same-sex friendships also surfaced in a study by Windle (1994), who analyzed videotaped interactions among second-grade, sixth-grade, and tenth-grade pairs of best friends. When asked to choose mutually interesting topics to discuss during interaction, female pairs tried more often to avoid danger or disagreement at all (and thus were more successful at reaching consensus as to which topics they would discuss) than did male pairs. In contrast, male pairs experienced greater discomfort as well as greater difficulty agreeing on which topics they would discuss than did female pairs.

Windle (1994) also reported that among adolescents' friendships in particular, greater frequencies of covert and overt hostility displayed toward best friends were positively associated with individuals' levels of alcohol consumption, percentage of friends who drink, frequency of delinquent activity, severity of depressive symptoms, and frequency of suicidal behaviors. Based on these results, Windle concluded that adolescents who do an inadequate job at expressing themselves in general and who resort to covert and overt displays of anger in particular, when communicating with their best friends, are at risk for developing an array of self-destructive behaviors over time (e.g., hitting teachers or parents, skipping school, stealing). Thus, it appears that having a best friend in and of itself does not necessarily promote psychological well-being. In fact, being unable to express oneself constructively toward one's closest friend carries negative implications for one's psychosocial development.

Surprise versus Anticipation

Rarely has the emotion of surprise been examined, except in experimental situations involving subjects reactions to novel stimuli (Hupka & Eshett, 1988; McFalls, Roe, & Blick, 1980). Surprise has been considered primarily as a reaction to being "caught off guard" in certain situations, such as those involving unexpected humor or even electric shock (Decker, 1993). Virtually the only research specifically addressing the emotion of surprise has been Ekman's (1984) study of the communication of surprise and other emotions via facial expressions (e.g., arched eyebrows, lips open yet silent). Part of the problem, according to Ervin and Martin (1986), is that "surprise, as a 'pure' emotion, is a short-lived phenomenon, leading to some other state" (p. 164).

Anticipation has been studied primarily with regard to gender differences in role expectations and corresponding behavior (Abrahams, Feldman, & Nash, 1978; Petronio, Martin, & Littlefield, 1984). With regard to friendships, anticipation may be communicated by handshakes in male-only friendships (thus making such friendships difficult to distinguish from more emotionally distant acquaintanceships) and by hugs in female-only friendships (as well as male–female friendships; see Batgos & Leadbeater, 1994; Berman, Marcus, & Raynes Berman, 1994; Fiske & Taylor, 1991). Nevertheless, anticipation—which may be a cause as well as a consequence of friendship maintenance (Buck, 1989)—allows friends in general to experience varying degrees of emotional intimacy while simultaneously limiting the boundaries of physical intimacy. In contrast, romantic relationships may be characterized by greater novelty as well as greater long-term uncertainty than friendships.

At least one additional construct bearing some resemblance to anticipation has received some attention in the literature on communicating emotions in friendships. Specifically, *predictability* (i.e., an aspect of interpersonal trust reflecting one's confidence that his or her relationship partner has behaved in a consistent manner and will continue to do so in the future; Rempel, Holmes, & Zanna, 1985) might serve as a proxy for anticipation. Viewed in this way, individuals clearly let their friends know that they expect each other to behave consistently (e.g., by saying "I'm counting on you") over time. Conversely, individuals sometimes warn their friends *not* to behave inconsistently (e.g., by saying "Please don't let me down"), which might be construed as indicating that they do not want to be surprised.

Overall, individuals' professed belief in their friends' predictability might be taken as communication of anticipation toward their friends. Such a link, however, may be tenuous at best. Furthermore, the opposing emotion of surprise does not necessarily constitute a *lack* of belief in friends' predictability (see Fiske & Taylor, 1991).

COMMUNICATION OF MIXED EMOTIONS IN FRIENDSHIPS

Love versus Remorse

In theory (Plutchik, 1980a, 1980b), love and remorse are mirror images of each other. The emotion of love results from a *gain* of someone special in one's life, consisting of euphoric feelings and positive future expectations for the relationship. In contrast, the emotion of remorse results from a *loss* of someone special in one's life, consisting of ambivalent feelings and no future expectations for the relationship. In practice, however, studies of communication in friendships are much more likely to emphasize love than remorse.

As emotional intimacy grows in personal relationships, both verbal and nonverbal communication increase (Rands & Levinger, 1979). Verbal statements of love (e.g., "I love you") often serve to communicate emotional intimacy in personal relationships. Indeed, language is a primary vehicle by which individuals express a variety of everyday observations, feelings, and thoughts (Berger & Luckman, 1966). In addition to verbal communication, physical acts (e.g., holding hands, hugging, caressing) can serve to communicate love in personal relationships (see Taraban, Hendrick, & Hendrick, Chapter 12, this volume). In looking at the meanings associated with receiving physical contact (e.g., touching) from an opposite-sex friend, Nguyen, Heslin, and Nguyen (1975) concluded that stroking (as distinct from patting, squeezing, or brushing) is interpreted as communicating warmth and love in a friendship.

Although the aforementioned behaviors might be used quite often in communicating love in female–female (and, perhaps, male–female) friendships, such is not the case with regard to men's friendships. According to R. Lewis (1978), the communication of love in males' friendships is discouraged in American society. Lewis identified four primary barriers to communicating love in men's friendships: (a) *Competition* (i.e., the emphasis placed upon competition among men allows little room for emotional intimacy); (b) *homophobia* (i.e., verbal and nonverbal expressions of love among men typically are interpreted by onlookers as manifestations of homosexuality); (c) *aversion to vulnerability and openness* (i.e., societal stereotypes regarding males' stoic and unemotional nature serve as self-fulfilling prophecies, inhibiting males' communication of love to same-sex friends); and (4) *lack of role models* (i.e., positive role models for men regarding the expression of emotional intimacy in general are hard to find in popular culture). Consistent with R. Lewis's (1978) assertions, Small, Gross, Erdwins, and Gessner (1979) reported that women tended to view their same-sex friendships as higher in love than did men. No gender difference was obtained regarding men's and women's perspectives on cross-sex friendships (see Z. Rubin, 1970). Furthermore, in investigating love disclosures of married couples toward spouses and friends, Balswick (1988) found that: (a) Love disclosure is higher toward one's spouse than toward one's friend; and (b) females tend to disclose love at higher levels than do males toward either same-sex or opposite-sex friends.

Although the communication of the opposing emotion of remorse, which involves negative emotions regarding the end of intimate relationships that have been addressed elsewhere (e.g., Brehm, 1992), few studies have examined the communication of remorse in friendships. Part of the problem in studying remorse in friendships is that, unlike other relationships outside of individuals' families of origin (e.g., marital relationships), friendships in American society typically are not signified by specific rites of entrance or dissolution. Thus, it is more common for friendships to decline via gradual, often imperceptible atrophy (e.g., losing touch because one or both friends have moved to different locations) than to end with a sudden, mutually acknowledged event (e.g., divorce) that would cause individuals to discuss their regrets directly to each other. Interestingly, though, this does not necessarily prevent friends from communicating remorse *indirectly* (e.g., by expressing regrets to third parties familiar with one or both friends; see Tannen, 1990; see also Kalbfleisch, 1993).

Submission versus Contempt

Although Plutchik (1980a, 1980b) unequivocally viewed submission (and its polar opposite, contempt) as an emotional state, not all emotion theorists would agree that submission in itself qualifies as an emotion. Gilbert, Pehl, and Allan (1994) suggested that behaviors commonly regarded as "submissive" actually reflect feelings of shame. Moreover, according to Gilbert et al. (1994), submissive behavior is correlated significantly with "feelings of helplessness, anger at others, anger at self, inferiority, and self-consciousness that arise in shaming situations" (p. 31). Nevertheless, some studies have addressed the communication and/or consequences of submission as an emotion in friendships.

In a study of victimization and submission among 6- and 8-year-old boys, Schwartz, Dodge, and Coie (1993) reported that chronic victims in peer relationships tended to display fewer assertive behaviors (e.g., persuasion attempts, social conversation initiatives) and more nonassertive behaviors (e.g., giving in to peers' social initiatives) than did individuals who were not chronic victims. In turn, children who communicate submission to their peers often are socially rejected or ostracized. Especially noteworthy is the fact that children who are rejected by peers due to submission appear to suffer greater psychosocial hardships than do children who are rejected by peers due to aggression (e.g., children who have communicated submission to their peers are lonelier, worry more about their relations with others, and report less positive beliefs about peers than do children who have communicated aggression toward their peers; Parkhurst & Asher, 1992; Rabiner, Keane, & Mackinnon-Lewis, 1993).

Most of the research on the communication of submission in friendships focuses on children's peer relationships and casts aggression (rather than contempt *per se*) as the polar opposite of submission. For example, Rabiner and Gordon (1992) compared the intellectual and goal coordination deficits of submissive and aggressive boys who had been rejected by their peers. Unlike submissive rejected boys, aggressive rejected boys experienced greater difficulty integrating or balancing goals, regardless of whether the goals were individually or interpersonally oriented. Thus, although the communication of submission in friendships might carry negative implications for individuals' *emotional* functioning, such is not necessarily the case for individuals' *cognitive* functioning.

Regarding the communication of contempt in general, some studies (e.g., Ekman & Friesen, 1986; Matsumoto, 1992) have suggested that a tightened, curled lip is the most universal sign of contempt experienced by one person toward another. However, other studies either have failed to support such a conclusion (e.g., Russell, 1991a; Russell, Suzuki, & Ishida, 1993) or have raised questions regarding methodological flaws in research on facial expressions of contempt (e.g., Ekman, O'Sullivan, & Matsumoto, 1991a, 1991b; Russell, 1991b, 1991c; Russell, 1993). Given the hotly contested nature of findings regarding the communication of contempt as a whole, perhaps it is not surprising that studies of the communication of contempt in friendships (or, for that matter in *any* personal relationships) virtually are nonexistent.

Awe versus Aggressiveness

Awe and aggressiveness are not often considered as opposite ends of the same dimension in theories or research on emotions (e.g., Fromme & O'Brien, 1982). It does make sense, however, to construe them as such within the domain of personal relationships. Awe has been conceptualized broadly as similar to wonder, which is the feeling that one's true self and the world are one (Keen, 1969). This feeling typically is experienced as mysterious, unusual, and sudden. Fromm (1956) went so far as to suggest that awe is a natural result of becoming one with another human being in a personal relationship. In contrast, aggressiveness may be viewed as a feeling of alienation following the decline of relationship closeness (Fromm, 1956; Wallace, 1985). Of the two emotions, aggressiveness has been examined more often as an emotion communicated in friendships than has awe.

In adolescent and adult friendships, individuals may feel aggressive and act accordingly when they expect to be made angry by their peers (Kubany, Richard, Bauer, & Muraoka, 1992a,b). Aggressive feelings often are communicated through accusatory "you" statements (e.g., "You're making me angry"), which clearly convey such an expectation. Such statements, in turn, may create psychological distance within friendships to the extent that they evoke alienation as well as relationship-threatening, aggressive verbal and nonverbal responses from the recipients of those statements.

According to Baxter (1992), hostile feelings are elicited in adult friendships by playful behaviors such as engaging in mock fights with, wrestling with, and stealing from friends. In turn, Bell and Healey (1992) reported that friends often use idioms (e.g., "You are hurting my *peelings*") as a relatively safe way to communicate the impact of each other's potentially hurtful behavior. Confrontational idioms also may be used as taunts and insults in their own right. Neither playful behaviors nor idiomatic communication are believed to emerge until friendships are well established in order to prevent the destructive consequences that would probably result had they emerged earlier. Thus, these tend to be safer ways of communicating hurt and hostility than accusatory statements.

Unfortunately, neither awe nor aggressiveness have been investigated as emotions communicated specifically in cross-sex friendships. Tannen's (1990) overview of social interaction among male–male, female–female, and male–female friendships suggests that verbal communication patterns evident in male–male friendships (e.g., verbal put-downs as signs of aggressiveness) also would be expected in male–female friendships (see also Gaines, 1994). However, it is doubtful that *nonverbal* communication of aggressiveness (e.g., wrestling, mock fighting) would be as prevalent in male–female friendships as in male–male friendships, due to prevailing social norms discouraging males' physical aggressiveness toward females (see Konstantareas & Homatidis, 1984).

Optimism versus Disappointment

Assuming that optimism and disappointment are polar opposites as proposed by Plutchik (1980a, 1980b), the manner in which these two emotions are communicated in friendships might be expected to contrast sharply. In general, positive emotions directed toward the listener are disclosed more frequently by the speaker than are negative emotions directed toward the listener. Therefore, we might expect optimism to be communicated directly from one friend to another, given its positive nature (Shimanoff, 1983; cf. Winton, 1990). Conversely, we might expect disappointment, a negative emotion, to be communicated in a nonverbal manner (Winton, 1990).

Studies of optimism in personal relationships have tended to focus primarily upon the development (rather than the communication) of optimism (Carnelley & Janoff-Bulman, 1992). Optimism reflects the manner in which individuals view the long-term prospects of their personal relationships. Moreover, optimism generally is brought about in part by past experiences (or, more precisely, the manner in which individuals interpret the results of past relationship experiences). Thus, when prior relationships are remembered as rewarding, relationship optimism will prevail. When relationships have been hurtful, pessimism is more likely. Although the literature on the communication of optimism in personal relationships is concerned primarily with romantic relationships (Carnelley & Janoff-Bulman, 1992), one might reason that optimism in friendships may develop similarly.

One aspect of personal relationships in which optimism might be manifested is *faith* (conceptualized as a component of interpersonal trust reflecting the belief that one's hopes and desires about the relationship will be realized; Rempel, Holmes, & Zanna, 1985). In this sense, faith can be considered analogous to optimism since both are developed from the notion that the relationship will survive over time. As its name implies, faith can take on an almost religious quality, in that friends' (as opposed to romantic partners') commitment to each other is based largely on the hope that friends always will be there for each other.

Like optimism, disappointment in friendships and other current personal relationships develops largely in response to individuals' past relationship experiences. For example, children whose parents are divorced are more likely to expect future disappointment in their interpersonal lives than are children whose parents are still married (Wallerstein, 1987). In general, however, disappointment has been studied more extensively than optimism as an emotion communicated in personal relationships. Regarding friendships in particular, adolescents apparently want to be able to communicate disappointment overtly to their friends but instead tend to express disappointment by distancing themselves passively from their peers (Mitchell, 1976).

Thus, disappointment often is communicated via non-behaviors or *lack* of overt communication. Avoiding communication may lead to further social isolation from their peers, in turn leading to greater disappointment.

RECONSIDERING THE ACCEPTANCE–DISGUST DICHOTOMY IN PLUTCHIK'S MODEL

So far, we have presented Plutchik's (1980b) circumplex model of emotions in an uncritical manner. However, further inspection of the circumplex reveals certain logical inconsistencies. Perhaps the most obvious inconsistency concerns the acceptance–disgust dichotomy proposed by Plutchik. These terms lack face validity as conceptual opposites. The logical opposite of acceptance is *rejection* rather than disgust, whereas the logical opposite of disgust is *delight* rather than acceptance. How are we to reconcile these logical opposites with Plutchik's (1980b) model?

One solution is to propose two clusters of emotions (i.e., acceptance and delight, rejection and disgust), with the two clusters conceptualized as logical opposites. Van de Ven (1995) described delight as subsuming acceptance, contentment, satisfaction, encouragement, enlightenment, happiness, and pride. In addition, Plutchik (1962) described rejection as subsuming disgust, loathing, dislike, boredom, and tiresomeness. Foa and Foa (1974) depicted socioemotional acceptance (affection-giving and respect-giving behavior) as inversely related to socioemotional rejection (affection-denying and respect-denying behavior; see also Gaines, 1994), whereas Bridges (1930) depicted experiences of delight as inversely related to experiences of disgust (which, in turn, is a form of distress). By integrating rejection (which is similar to disgust and dissimilar to acceptance) and delight (which is similar to acceptance and dissimilar to disgust) into Plutchik's model, we can account for a number of additional studies of the communication of emotion in friendships that otherwise would not fit neatly into the model. Our proposed revision of Plutchik's model is presented in Figure 2.

According to Bridges (1930), delight is communicated in children's friendships by behaviors such as laughing, giggling, hand clapping, exclamations, jumping up and down, and speaking in a loud and quick manner. Although the communication of delight in adult friendships is subdued in contrast, several expressions of delight persist from childhood to adulthood, such as smiles (Fleming & Darley, 1989) and outbursts of laughter (McAdams & Powers, 1981). Interestingly, in an experiment on reactions to horror films within the context of opposite-sex acquaintanceships (Zillmann, Weaver, Mundorf, & Aust, 1986), men expressed the *greatest* delight when paired with women who were highly distressed, whereas women expressed the *least* delight when paired with men who were highly distressed.

Consistent with Allport's (1954/1979) typology of forms of outgroup rejection, several studies have identified verbal threats, avoidance or withdrawal, and physical attacks as rejecting behaviors (Frude, 1993). Although in many instances the targets

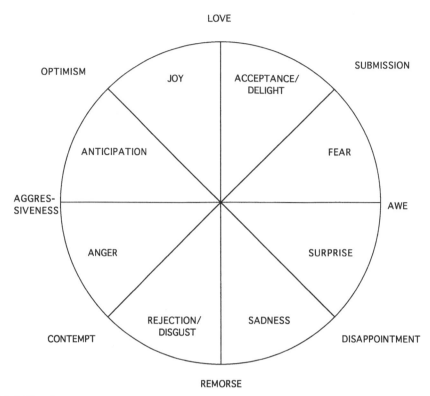

LOVE

OPTIMISM   SUBMISSION

JOY   ACCEPTANCE/
DELIGHT

ANTICIPATION   FEAR

AGGRES-
SIVENESS   AWE

ANGER   SURPRISE

REJECTION/   SADNESS
DISGUST
CONTEMPT   DISAPPOINTMENT

REMORSE

FIGURE 2   Revised adaptation of Plutchik's (1980b) Model of Emotions. Reprinted with permission from *Psychology Today* magazine, copyright © 1980 (Sussex Publishers, Inc.).

of rejection have brought social isolation upon themselves through prior aggressive behavior (Coie, Belding, & Underwood, 1988), several studies of peer rejection have shown that simply being a member of a stigmatized group (e.g., racial and ethnic minorities, physically or mentally handicapped persons) is sufficient to elicit rejection from other children (Frude, 1993; see also Goffman, 1963). Furthermore, rejection due to ingroup–outgroup bias is by no means limited to children's friendships. Even among adults, "normal" individuals sometimes passively (if not actively) reject their stigmatized friends, especially when stigmatizing occurs after friendships already have been established (e.g., when gay men and lesbians reveal their sexual preference to heterosexual friends, or when previously "normal" friends become stigmatized due to paralysis following traffic accidents; de Sales French, 1984).

Most studies of peer rejection have been conducted under the assumption that a lack of peer nominations within social networks equals peer rejection (e.g., Cillessen, van IJzendoorn, van Lieshout, & Hartup, 1992; Coie, Dodge, Terry, & Wright, 1991; Malik & Furman, 1993; Volling, Mackinnon-Lewis, Rabiner, &

Baradaran, 1993). Rarely, if ever, are patterns of communication of rejection among dyads or pairs of friends explicitly examined. One problem with defining peer rejection solely in terms of a lack of peer nominations is that approximately 50% of all children thus labeled as "unaccepted" nonetheless have one or more close friends; moreover, approximately 20% of all children labeled as "accepted" do not have *any* close friends (Malik & Furman, 1993; see also Cairns, Cairns, & Neckerman, 1988). In addition, research on peer rejection almost invariably focuses on the social networks of boys rather than of girls. Finally, research on peer rejection virtually always examines children who are disliked by their classmates; very little is known about the nature of peer rejection by children's neighbors.

According to Volling, Mackinnon-Lewis, Rabiner, and Baradaran (1993), peer rejection may develop along one of two developmental pathways: (a) Peers react to aggressive and assertive child behaviors by refusing to play with them (thus communicating rejection); and (b) inhibited and shy children who shun social interaction eventually are viewed by peers as deviant, which then leads the peers to withdraw (thus communicating rejection). Peer rejection (which by definition occurs within a social or interpersonal context) also tends to covary with academic failure (which generally is believed to occur within a personal or intrapersonal context), although it is not clear whether peer rejection *causes* academic failure or vice versa (Kimmel, 1976; Patterson, de Barsyshe, & Ramsay, 1989). Finally, despite the problems associated with using peer nominations as the basis for determining peer rejection, peer rejection thus defined during childhood appears to be a reliable predictor of psychosocial problems during adulthood (Bierman, 1985; Landau, Millich, & Whitten, 1984).

DIALECTICS WITHIN PLUTCHIK'S MODEL

Moving beyond the more obvious reasons for criticizing Plutchik's (1980b) model, we now turn to the apparent dichotomies within the model that actually represent *dialectics* (see Andersen, 1993). One such dichotomy is the distinction between fear and anger. As biologists will attest, humans and other animals have two primary modes of response when confronted with potentially threatening stimuli, namely to fight (a manifestation of anger) or to flee (a manifestation of fear). In fact, Plutchik (1962) contended that fear results from activation of the sympathetic nervous system, whereas anger results from activation of the parasympathetic nervous system. However, as biologists will attest, Plutchik's description of the links between emotions and the autonomous nervous system is incorrect. Both fear *and* anger reflect sympathetic arousal, as illustrated by similar physiological patterns of heightened pulse rate, hyperventilating, and sweat (Bridges, 1930; Fromme & O'Brien, 1982). Together with distress or disgust, fear and anger can evoke *anxiety* (as opposed to security) and, consequently, threats to individuals' self-esteem (Sullivan, 1953).

Another ostensibly straightforward dichotomy in Plutchik's (1980b) model pits surprise against anticipation. According to Plutchik (1962), "That which is surprising cannot have been expected. An organism cannot be both surprised and expectant about the same thing at the same time" (p. 106). Indeed, multidimensional scaling analyses of laypersons' sorting of emotion terms (Haslam, 1995a) lend support to Plutchik's account of surprise and anticipation as mutually exclusive emotions. However, a relationship-based account of surprise and anticipation yields a markedly different conclusion. Specifically, both surprise *and* anticipation, together with novelty, may expand the boundaries of friendships and other personal relationships. Predictability, on the other hand, creates comfortable certainty and clear boundaries (Andersen, 1993).

In the relational maintenance literature, both predictability and novelty have been found to create positive relational climates. Thus, these emotions may play a more central role in friendships (as well as other personal relationships) than much of the literature suggests. Andersen (1993) examined the resulting dialectic between novelty and predictability in relationships:

> Certainly an abundance of theory and research has shown that relationships, particularly in their early stages, are driven by a need to reduce uncertainty. . . . But too much certainty can produce boredom, mundane interaction, and a lack of spontaneity and adventure. . . . Relationships are energized by cognitive uncertainty, a state that produces arousal and enhances feelings of emotion. But too much uncertainty is frightening, and too much spontaneity and arousal can easily become fear or stress. Cognitively and emotionally we walk a fine line in our relationships between stressful excitement and boring predictability. (p. 11)

Consistent with Andersen (1993), M. Lewis (1994) noted that surprise can reflect a reaction to "violations of expected events" but also can reflect a reaction to "discovery, as in 'Aha!' experience" (p. 76). Ironically, Plutchik's own changes in his conceptualizations of surprise from the 1960s to the 1980s lend support to Andersen's (1993) analysis. In particular, Plutchik initially placed surprise midway between fear and the positive emotion of *acceptance* (Plutchik, 1962) but subsequently placed surprise midway between fear and the negative emotion of *sadness* (Plutchik, 1980b) along the emotion circumplex. Perhaps it would be most accurate to conclude that Plutchik's (1980b) model is a dynamic, evolving characterization of the links among emotions rather than as static or complete.

THEORETICAL IMPLICATIONS

Now that we have discussed the emotional communication of friends within the circumplex model, we turn to some theoretical explanations for emotional communication in friendships. To some extent, the portions of Plutchik's (1980b) circumplex that are represented in the literature on communication of emotions in friendships are instructive in themselves. For example, the primary emotion of acceptance and the secondary emotions derived from it (i.e., love and submission)—

all of which were examined in one or more of the studies that we cited—form the nucleus of *resource exchange theory* (Foa & Foa, 1974; see also Blieszner & Adams, 1992; Foa, 1961; Foa, Tornblom, Foa, Converse, 1991; Gaines, 1994, 1995, 1996; Haslam, 1995b; Wiggins, 1979, 1991). According to resource exchange theory, *affection* (i.e., love, or emotional acceptance of another person) and *respect* (i.e., submission, or social acceptance of another person) are intangible commodities or resources that constitute much of the basis for interpersonal behavior, especially within personal (as opposed to impersonal or role) relationships. In a study of same-sex and opposite-sex adult friendships, Gaines (1994) found that affectionate behaviors (e.g., trying to please one's partner and doing the things one's partner likes, sharing things with one's partner, showing trust in one's partner) and respectful behaviors (e.g., showing admiration for what one's partner does, showing pride in what one's partner can do, praising whatever one's partner does) are given more often than not. However, the only significant pattern of *reciprocity* of interpersonal resources observed among friends was with regard to *disrespectful* behavior (e.g., treating partner with disrespect, looking down on partner's abilities, criticizing partner)—and then, only among male–female friendships.

Another primary emotion within Plutchik's (1980a, 1980b) circumplex that has been investigated in the literature on communicating emotion in friendships is sadness, along with one of the secondary emotions, disappointment, derived from it. According to Higgins's (1987) *self-discrepancy theory,* "When people believe that they have lost or will never obtain some desired goal, they feel sad or disappointed. When people believe that something terrible is going to happen they feel apprehensive or threatened" (p. 322). That is, Higgins distinguished between *dejection-related* emotions and *agitation-related* emotions. The former emotions reflect the discrepancy between the attributes that individuals perceive themselves as having and the attributes that those individuals would like to possess, such as sadness and disappointment. Agitation-related emotions, on the other hand, reflect the discrepancy between the attributes that individuals perceive themselves as having and the attributes that significant others believe that those individuals should possess (see also Scott & O'Hara, 1993), such as fear and awe. Unfortunately, surprise, which is one of the primary emotions constituting the dejection-related emotion of disappointment *and* the agitation-related emotion of awe, does not fit neatly within Higgins's dichotomy. Our review of the literature suggests that research on communicating emotion in friendships has tended to focus on dejection-related emotions, which result from an absence of positive outcomes, rather than agitation-related emotions, which result from a presence of negative outcomes. Dejection-related emotions such as sadness and disappointment appear to be manifested in individuals' withdrawal of "touch, caress, embrace, and body contact" (Mitchell, 1976, p. 278) from friends—particularly those of the opposite gender—who have rejected them. Actual-ideal self-discrepancies are particularly likely to result in dejection-related emotions among firstborn and only children often "fight, nag, interrupt, criticize, and make unceasing demands to obtain cooperation" (Hoopes & Harper, 1987, p. 38) from friends in goal-oriented situations that do not appear to be going well (see also Drewry & Clark, 1985).

The final cluster of emotions in Plutchik's (1980a, 1980b) model that has received attention within the literature on communicating emotion in friendships consists of the primary emotions of anger and anticipation, as well as the secondary emotion, aggressiveness, that is derived from them. Not coincidentally, Bandura's *social learning theory* (Bandura, 1969, 1973, 1978; Bandura & Walters, 1959, 1967) posits that when aversive stimuli simultaneously arouse anger in individuals and lead those individuals to anticipate that they will not be punished, and perhaps will be *rewarded,* for retaliating against aversive stimuli, aggressiveness is likely to result (see also Okey, 1992). Furthermore, anticipating negative behavior from a peer often serves as the aversive stimulus that triggers anger in the first place (Konstantareas & Homatidis, 1984; see also Weiner & Handel, 1985). Social learning theory suggests that when an individual manifests anger (e.g., by expressing indignation upon being insulted by one's friend; Sogon & Masutani, 1989) *and* manifests anticipation (e.g., by looking at one's friend closely; Sogon & Masutani, 1989) toward a friend, the individual is likely to communicate aggressiveness. Aggressiveness is often expressed through verbal communication such as "swearing, screaming, name-calling, teasing and threatening" (Konstantareas & Homatidis, 1984, p. 612) and/or through physically violent behaviors such as "hitting, kicking, pulling, pushing and shoving"; Konstantareas & Homatidis, 1984, p. 612; see also Canary et al., Chapter 7, this volume). Consistent with the predictions generated by social learning theory, Konstantareas and Homatidis (1984) reported that "conflict-disordered children" were significantly more likely to interpret their peers' ambiguous intentions as malevolent and stable—and, in turn, to communicate unambiguous aggressiveness toward their peers—than were nondisordered children.

SUMMARY AND CONCLUDING THOUGHTS

In this chapter, we have seen that among the emotions identified by Plutchik (1962, 1980a, 1980b, 1983), (a) sadness has been emphasized over joy, (b) anticipation has been emphasized over surprise, (c) anger has been emphasized over fear, (d) acceptance has been emphasized over disgust, (e) love has been emphasized over remorse, (f) disappointment has been emphasized over optimism, (g) aggressiveness has been emphasized over awe, and (h) submission has been emphasized over contempt within the literature on communicating emotions in friendships. A disproportionately large number of studies that we reviewed operationalized friendship in terms of children's peer relationships. Overall, relatively few studies dealt specifically with emotions as communicated in friendships.

The present review of research on friends' communication suggests several intriguing possibilities regarding future research. For example, it is clear that a number of primary and secondary emotions are not captured by prevailing social-psychological theories such as resource exchange theory (Foa & Foa, 1974), self-discrepancy theory (Higgins, 1987), or social learning theory (Bandura & Walters, 1959). Perhaps general social-psychological theories can be developed to account for primarily positive emotions (optimism and joy), primarily negative emotions (fear, contempt, remorse, and disgust), and ambivalent emotions (awe and surprise) that are integral to circumplex models of emotions but that have not been integral to previous research on the communication of emotion in friendships (see Duck, 1994). Or, perhaps new theories specifically within the field of personal relationships (and possibly drawing upon social psychology, communication studies, and/or other neighboring disciplines) will be needed in order to do justice to these understudied emotions (see Berscheid, 1985).

Future research also might profitably focus on Plutchik's (1962) assertion that "persisting situations which produce mixed emotions produce personality traits" (p. 121). Taken together with Sullivan's (1953) pronouncement that "personality is the relatively enduring pattern of recurrent interpersonal situations which characterize a human life" (p. 110–111), Plutchik's assertion regarding emotions and traits implies that friendships (or "chumships," as Sullivan [1953] put it; see Gaines, 1994) serve as important interpersonal contexts in which relatively unstable emotions are communicated *and* in which relatively stable traits are formed (see also Wiggins, 1979). Circumplex models of interpersonal traits (Conte & Plutchik, 1981), emotions (Plutchik, 1980a, 1980b), moods (Fisher, Heise, Bohrnstedt, & Lucke, 1985), and interpersonal behavior (Gifford & O'Connor, 1987) all potentially could contribute to relationship researchers' understanding of the processes by which friends communicate emotions to each other. However, to date, attempts at integrating the respective circumplex models have been relatively rare and limited largely to clinical settings (e.g., Schaefer & Plutchik, 1966). It is hoped that researchers in the field of personal relationships increasingly will utilize circumplex models of traits, emotions, moods, and behavior simultaneously in predicting the degree to which personality—in all its complexity—is revealed in ordinary processes of communication in friendships.

In closing, we return to the functions of friendships described so vividly by Lillian Rubin in *Just Friends* (1985). Regarding the effect of friends on children's socioemotional development, some authors have concluded that peers are good (e.g., Attili, 1986), whereas other authors have concluded that peers are bad (e.g., Sants, 1986). However, friendships—whether between children or between adults—do not conform well to a simple good–bad dichotomy. Perhaps relationship theorists and researchers increasingly will profit from examining the ways in which friendships make it possible for individuals to communicate the entire range of human emotions, not just the ways in which friendships bolster or batter individuals' self-esteem. It is hoped that the circumplex model of emotions developed by Plutchik (1962, 1980a, 1980b), combined with the empirical results reported in the present chapter, will encourage theorists and researchers to address the processes as well as the outcomes of friendship establishment, maintenance, or dissolution.

REFERENCES

Abrahams, B., Feldman, S. S., & Nash, S. C. (1978). Sex role self-concept and sex-role attitudes: Enduring personality characteristics or adaptations to changing life situations? *Developmental Psychology, 14,* 393–400.

Allen, J. G., & Haccoun, D. M. (1976). Sex differences in emotionality: A multidimensional approach. *Human Relations, 29,* 711–722.

Allport, G. W. (1954/1979). *The nature of prejudice.* Reading, MA: Addison-Wesley.

Andersen, P. A. (1993). Cognitive schemata in personal relationships. In S. Duck (Ed.), *Individuals in relationships* (pp. 1–29). Newbury Park, CA: Sage.

Attili, G. (1986). The development of preferred relationships in preschool children: Child–child and child–adult relationships. In R. Gilmour & S. Duck (Eds.), *The emerging field of personal relationships* (pp. 173–185). Hillsdale, NJ: Erlbaum.

Balswick, J. (1988). *The inexpressive male.* Lexington, MA: Lexington Books.

Bandura, A. (1969). *Principles of behavior modification.* New York: Holt, Rinehart, & Winston.

Bandura, A. (1973). *Aggression: A social learning analysis.* Englewood Cliffs, NJ: Prentice-Hall.

Bandura, A. (1978). Social learning theory of aggression. *Journal of Communication, 28,* 12–29.

Bandura, A., & Walters, R. H. (1959). *Adolescent aggression: A study of the influence of child-training practices and family interrelationships.* New York: Ronald Press.

Bandura, A., & Walters, R. H. (1967). *Social learning and personality development.* New York: Holt, Rinehart, & Winston.

Batgos, J., & Leadbeater, B. J. (1994). Parental attachment, peer relations, and dysphoria in adolescence. In M. B. Sperling & W. H. Berman (Eds.), *Attachment in adults: Clinical and developmental perspectives* (pp. 155–178). New York: Guilford.

Baxter, L. A. (1992). Forms and functions of intimate play in personal relationships. *Human Communication Research, 18,* 336–363.

Bell, R. A., & Healey, J. G. (1992). Idiomatic communication and interpersonal solidarity in friends' relational cultures. *Human Communication Research, 18,* 307–335.

Berger, P. L., & Luckman, T. (1966). *The social construction of reality: A treatise in the sociology of knowledge.* New York: Anchor Books.

Berman, W. H., Marcus, L., & Raynes Berman, E. (1994). Attachment in marital relations. In M. B. Sperling & W. H. Berman (Eds.), *Attachment in adults: Clinical and developmental perspectives* (pp. 204–231). New York: Guilford.

Berscheid, E. (1985). Interpersonal attraction. In G. Lindzey & E. Aronson (Eds.), *Handbook of social psychology: Vol. 2* (3rd ed., pp. 413–484). New York: Random House.

Bierman, K. (1985). The clinical significance and assessment of poor peer relations: Peer neglect vs. peer rejection. *Journal of Developmental and Behavioral Pediatrics, 8,* 233–240.

Blier, M. J., & Blier-Wilson, L. A. (1989). Gender differences in self-rated emotional expressiveness. *Sex Roles, 21,* 287–295.

Blieszner, R., & Adams, R. G. (1992). *Adult friendship.* Newbury Park, CA: Sage.

Brehm, S. (1992). *Intimate relationships,* 2nd ed. New York: McGraw-Hill.

Bridges, K. M. B. (1930). A genetic theory of the emotions. *Journal of Genetic Psychology, 37,* 514–527.

Bukowski, W. M., & Newcomb, A. F. (1984). Stability and determinants of sociometric status and friendship choice: A longitudinal perspective. *Developmental Psychology, 20,* 941–952.

Buck, R. (1989). Emotional communication in personal relationships: A developmental-interactionist view. In C. Hendrick (Ed.), *Close relationships* (pp. 144–163). Newbury Park, CA: Sage.

Burleson, B. R. (1986). Communication skills and childhood and peer relationships: An overview. In M. L. McLaughlin (Ed.), *Communication yearbook 9* (pp. 143–180). Beverly Hills, CA: Sage.

Burleson, B. R., Applegate, J. L., Burke, J. A., Clark, R. A., Delia, J. G., & Kline, S. L. (1986). Communicative correlates of peer acceptance in childhood. *Communication Education, 35,* 349–367.

Cairns, R. D., Cairns, B. D., & Neckerman, H. J. (1988). Social networks and aggressive behavior: Peer support or peer rejection. *Developmental Psychology, 24,* 815–823.

Carnelley, K. B., & Janoff-Bulman, R. (1992). Optimism about love relationships: General versus specific lessons from one's personal experiences. *Journal of Social and Personal Relationships, 9,* 5–20.

Cillessen, A., van IJzendoorn, H., van Lieshout, C., & Hartup, W. (1992). Heterogeneity among peer-rejected boys: Subtypes and stabilities. *Child Development, 63,* 893–905.

Clark, M. S., & Taraban, C. (1991). Reactions to and willingness to express emotions in communal and exchange relationships. *Journal of Experimental Social Psychology, 27,* 324–336.

Coie, J. D., Belding, M., & Underwood, M. (1988). Aggression and peer rejection in childhood. *Advances in Clinical Child Psychology, 11,* 125–158.

Coie, J., Dodge, K., Terry, R., & Wright, V. (1991). The role of aggression in peer relations: An analysis of regression episodes in boys' play groups. *Child Development, 62,* 812–826.

Conte, H. R., & Plutchik, R. (1981). A circumplex model for interpersonal personality traits. *Journal of Personality and Social Psychology, 40,* 701–711.

Decker, L. R. (1993). Beliefs, post-traumatic stress disorder, and mysticism. *Journal of Humanistic Psychology, 33,* 15–37.

de Sales French, R. (1984). The long-term relationships of marked people. In E. E. Jones, A. Farina, A. H. Hastorf, H. Markus, D. T. Miller, & R. A. Scott (Eds.), *Social stigma: The psychology of marked relationships* (pp. 254–294). New York: Freeman.

Drewry, D. L., & Clark, M. L. (1985). Factors important in the formation of preschoolers' friendships. *Journal of Genetic Psychology, 146,* 37–44.

Duck, S. (1994). *Meaningful relationships: Talking, sense, and relating.* Thousand Oaks, CA: Sage.

Ekman, P. (1984). Expression and the nature of emotion. In K. Scherer & P. Ekman (Eds.), *Approaches to emotion* (pp. 319–343). Hillsdale, NJ: Erlbaum.

Ekman, P., & Friesen, W. V. (1986). A new pan-cultural facial expression of emotion. *Motivation and Emotion, 10,* 159–168.

Ekman, P., O'Sullivan, M., & Matsumoto, D. (1991a). Confusions about context in the judgment of facial expression: A reply to "The contempt expression and the relativity thesis." *Motivation and Emotion, 15,* 169–176.

Ekman, P., O'Sullivan, M., & Matsumoto, D. (1991b). Contradictions in the study of contempt: What's it all about? Reply to Russell. *Motivation and Emotion, 15,* 293–296.

Ervin, F. R., & Martin, J. (1986). Neurophysiological bases of the primary emotions. In R. Plutchik & H. Kellerman (Eds.), *Emotion: Theory, research, and experience: Vol. 3* (pp. 145–170). Orlando, FL: Academic Press.

Fabes, R. A., & Martin, C. L. (1991). Gender and age stereotypes of emotionality. *Personality and Social Psychology Bulletin, 17,* 532–540.

Fisher, G. A., Heise, D. R., Bohrnstedt, G. W., & Lucke, J. F. (1985). Evidence for extending the circumplex model of personality trait language to self-reported moods. *Journal of Personality and Social Psychology, 49,* 233–242.

Fiske, S. T., & Taylor, S. E. (1991). *Social cognition* (2nd ed.). New York: McGraw-Hill.

Fleming, J. H., & Darley, J. M. (1989). Perceiving choice and constraint: The effects of contextual and behavioral cues on attitude attribution. *Journal of Personality and Social Psychology, 56,* 27–40.

Foa, U. G. (1961). Convergencies in the analysis of the structure of interpersonal behavior. *Psychological Review, 68,* 341–353.

Foa, U. G., & Foa, E. B. (1974). *Societal structures of the mind.* Springfield, IL: Thomas.

Foa, U. G., Tornblom, K. Y., Foa, E. B., & Converse, J., Jr. (1991). Introduction: Resource theory in social psychology. In U. G. Foa, J. Converse, Jr., Tornblom, & E. B. Foa (Eds.), *Resource theory: Explorations and applications* (pp. 1–10). San Diego, CA: Academic Press.

Fromm, E. (1956). *The art of loving.* New York: Harper and Brothers.

Fromme, D. K., & O'Brien, C. S. (1982). A dimensional approach to the circular ordering of the emotions. *Motivation and Emotion, 6,* 337–363.

Frude, N. (1993). Hatred between children. In N. Varma (Ed.), *How and why children hate: A study of conscious and unconscious sources* (pp. 72–93). London: Kingsley.

Gaines, S. O., Jr. (1994). Exchange of respect-denying behaviors among male–female friendships. *Journal of Social and Personal Relationships, 11,* 5–24.

Gaines, S. O., Jr. (1995). Classifying dating couples: Gender as reflected in traits, roles, and resulting behavior. *Basic and Applied Social Psychology, 16,* 75–94.

Gaines, S. O., Jr. (1996). Impact of interpersonal traits and gender-role compliance on interpersonal resource exchange among dating and engaged/married couples. *Journal of Social and Personal Relationships, 13,* 241–261.

Gifford, R., & O'Connor, B. (1987). The interpersonal circumplex as a behavior map. *Journal of Personality and Social Psychology, 52,* 1019–1026.

Gilbert, P., Pehl, J., & Allen, S. (1994). The phenomenology of shame and guilt: An empirical investigation. *British Journal of Medical Psychology, 67,* 23–36.

Goffman, E. (1963). *Stigma: Notes on the management of spoiled identity.* Englewood Cliffs, NJ: Prentice-Hall.

Haslam, N. (1995a). The discreteness of emotion concepts: Categorical structure in the affective circumplex. *Personality and Social Psychology Bulletin, 21,* 1012–1019.

Haslam, N. (1995b). Factor structure of social relationships: An examination of relational models and resource exchange theories. *Journal of Social and Personal Relationships, 12,* 217–227.

Hatfield, E., Cacioppo, J. T., & Rapson, R. L. (1992). Primitive emotional contagion. In M. S. Clark (Ed.), *Emotion and social behavior* (pp. 151–177). Newbury Park, CA: Sage.

Higgins, E. T. (1987). Self-discrepancy: A theory relating self and affect. *Psychological Review, 94,* 319–340.

Hoopes, M. M., & Harper, J. M. (1987). *Birth order roles and sibling patterns in individual and family therapy.* Rockville, MD: Aspen.

Hupka, R. B., & Eshett, C. (1988). Cognitive organization of emotion: Differences between labels and descriptors of emotion in jealousy situations. *Perceptual and Motor Skills, 66,* 935–949.

Inderbitzen-Pisaruk, H., & Foster, S. L. (1990). Adolescent friendships and peer acceptance: Implications for social skills training. *Clinical Psychology Review, 10,* 425–439.

Jones, M. B., Peacock, M. K., & Christopher, J. (1992). Self-reported anger in Black high school adolescents. *Journal of Adolescent Health, 13,* 461–465.

Kalbfleisch, P. J. (1993). Public portrayals of enduring friendships. In P. J. Kalbfleisch (Ed.), *Interpersonal communication: Evolving interpersonal relationships* (pp. 189–212). Hillsdale, NJ: Erlbaum.

Keen, S. (1969). *Apology for wonder.* New York: Harper & Row.

Kemper, T. (1990). Social relations and emotions: A structural approach. In T. Kemper (Ed.), *Research agendas in the sociology of emotion* (pp. 207–237). Albany, NY: SUNY Press.

Kimmel, J. (1976). The rational barb in the treatment of social rejection. *Rational Living, 11,* 23–25.

Konstantareas, M. M., & Homatidis, S. (1984). Aggressive and prosocial behaviours before and after treatment in conduct-disordered children and in matched controls. *Journal of Child Psychology and Psychiatry, 25,* 607–620.

Kubany, E. S., Richard, D. C., Bauer, G. B., & Muraoka, M. Y. (1992a). Impact of assertive and accusatory communication of distress and anger: A verbal component analysis. *Aggressive Behavior, 18,* 337–347.

Kubany, E. S., Richard, D. C., Bauer, G. B., & Muraoka, M. Y. (1992b). Verbalized anger and accusatory "you" messages as cues for anger and antagonism among adolescents. *Adolescence, 27,* 505–516.

LaFrance, M., & Banaji, M. (1992). Toward a reconsideration of the gender-emotion relationship. In M. S. Clark (Ed.), *Emotion and social behavior* (pp. 178–201). Newbury Park, CA: Sage.

Landau, S., Millich, R., & Whitten, P. (1984). A comparison of teacher and peer assessment of social status. *Journal of Clinical Child Psychology, 13,* 44–49.

Larsen, R. J., & Diener, E. (1992). Promises and problems with the circumplex model of emotion. In M. S. Clark (Ed.), *Emotion* (pp. 25–59). Newbury Park, CA: Sage.

Lewis, M. (1994). Self-conscious emotions. *American Scientist, 83,* 68–78.

Lewis, R. A. (1978). Emotional intimacy among men. *Journal of Social Issues, 34,* 108–121.

Malik, N., & Furman, W. (1993). Practitioner review: Problems in children's peer relations: What can the clinician do? *Journal of Child Psychology, 34,* 1303–1326.

Matsumoto, D. (1992). More evidence for the universality of a contempt expression. *Motivation and Emotion, 16,* 363–368.

McAdams, D. P., & Powers, J. (1981). Themes of intimacy in behavior and thought. *Journal of Personality and Social Psychology, 40,* 573–587.

McFalls, H. M., Roe, K. E., & Blick, K. A. (1980). Intensity of emotional content in dreams recalled by college students. *Perceptual and Motor Skills, 51,* 654.

Mitchell, J. J. (1976). Adolescent intimacy. *Adolescence, 11,* 275–280.

Nardi, P. M. (1992). "Seamless souls": An introduction to men's friendships. In P. M. Nardi (Ed.), *Men's friendships* (pp. 1–14). Newbury Park, CA: Sage.

Newman, L. S., Higgins, E. T., & Vookles, J. (1992). Self-guide strength and emotional vulnerability: Birth order as a moderator of self-affect relations. *Personality and Social Psychology Bulletin, 18,* 402–411.

Nguyen, T., Heslin, R., & Nguyen, M. L. (1975). The meanings of touch: Sex differences. *Journal of Communication, 25,* 92–103.

O'Connor, P. (1992). *Friendships between women: A critical review.* New York: Guilford.

Okey, J. L. (1992). Human aggression: The etiology of individual differences. *Journal of Humanistic Psychology, 32,* 51–64.

Parham, W. D., & Tinsley, H. E. A. (1980). What are friends for? Students' expectations of the friendship encounter. *Journal of Counseling Psychology, 27,* 524–527.

Parker, J. G., & Asher, S. R. (1993). Friendship and friendship quality in middle childhood: Links with peer group acceptance and feelings of loneliness and social dissatisfaction. *Developmental Psychology, 29,* 611–621.

Parkhurst, J. T., & Asher, S. R. (1992). Peer rejection in middle school: Subgroup differences in behavior, loneliness and interpersonal concerns. *Developmental Psychology, 28,* 231–241.

Patterson, C. R., de Barsyshe, B. D., & Ramsay, E. (1989). A developmental perspective on antisocial behavior. *American Psychologist, 44,* 328–336.

Petronio, S., Martin, J., & Littlefield, R. (1984). Prerequisite conditions for self-disclosing: A gender issue. *Communication Monographs, 51,* 268–273.

Plutchik, R. (1962). *The emotions: Facts, theories, and a new model.* New York: Random House.

Plutchik, R. (1980a). A general psychoevolutionary theory of emotion. In R. Plutchik & H. Kellerman (Eds.), *Emotion: Theory, research, and experience: Vol. 1* (pp. 3–33). Orlando, FL: Academic Press.

Plutchik, R. (1980b). A language for the emotions. *Psychology Today, 13(9),* 68–78.

Plutchik, R. (1983). Emotions in early development: A psychoevolutionary approach. In R. Plutchik & H. Kellerman (Eds.), *Emotion: Theory, research, and experience: Vol. 2* (pp. 221–257). Orlando, FL: Academic Press.

Rabiner, D. L., & Gordon, L. V. (1992). The coordination of conflicting social goals: Differences between rejected and nonrejected boys. *Child Development, 63,* 1344–1350.

Rabiner, D. L., Keane, S. P., & Mackinnon Lewis, C. (1993). Children's beliefs about familiar and unfamiliar peers in relation to their sociometric status. *Developmental Psychology, 29,* 236–243.

Rands, M., & Levinger, G. (1979). Implicit theories of relationship: An intergenerational study. *Journal of Personality and Social Psychology, 37,* 645–661.

Rawlins, W. K. (1994). Being there and growing apart: Sustaining friendships during adulthood. In D. J. Canary & L. Stafford (Eds.), *Communication and relational maintenance* (pp. 275–294). San Diego, CA: Academic Press.

Rempel, J. K., Holmes, J. G., & Zanna, M. P. (1985). Trust in close relationships. *Journal of Personality and Social Psychology, 49,* 95–112.

Renshaw, P. D., & Brown, P. J. (1993). Loneliness in middle childhood: Concurrent and longitudinal predictors. *Child Development, 64,* 1271–1284.

Rose, S. M. (1985). Same- and cross-sex friendships and the psychology of homosociality. *Sex Roles, 12,* 63–74.

Rubin, L. B. (1985). *Just friends: The role of friendship in our lives.* New York: Harper & Row.

Rubin, Z. (1970). Measurement of romantic love. *Journal of Personality and Social Psychology, 16,* 265–273.

Rusbult, C. E., Drigotas, S. M., & Verette, J. (1994). The investment model: An interdependence analysis of commitment processes and relationship maintenance phenomena. In D. J. Canary & L. Stafford (Eds.), *Communication and relational maintenance* (pp. 115–139). San Diego, CA: Academic Press.

Russell, J. A. (1991a). Confusions about context in the judgment of facial expression: A reply to "The contempt expression and the relativity thesis." *Motivation and Emotion, 15,* 177–184.

Russell, J. A. (1991b). The contempt expression and the relativity thesis. *Motivation and Emotion, 15,* 149–168.

Russell, J. A. (1991c). Negative results on a reported facial expression of contempt. *Motivation and Emotion, 15,* 281–291.

Russell, J. A. (1993). Forced-choice response format in the study of facial expression. *Motivation and Emotion, 17,* 41–51.

Russell, J. A., Suzuki, N., & Ishida, N. (1993). Canadian, Greek, and Japanese freely produced emotion labels for facial expressions. *Motivation and Emotion, 17,* 337–351.

Sants, H. K. A. (1986). The relation between patterns of friendship, self-concept, and conceptions of friendship in six-year-olds. In R. Gilmour & S. Duck (Eds.), *The emerging field of personal relationships* (pp. 161–172). Hillsdale, NJ: Erlbaum.

Schaefer, K. S., & Plutchik, R. (1966). Interrelationships of emotions, traits, and diagnostic constructs. *Psychological Reports, 18,* 399–410.

Schwartz, D., Dodge, K. A., & Coie, J. D. (1993). The emergence of chronic peer victimization in boys' play groups. *Child Development, 64,* 1755–1772.

Scott, L., & O'Hara, M. W. (1993). Self-discrepancies in clinically anxious and depressed university students. *Journal of Abnormal Psychology, 102,* 282–287.

Shimanoff, S. (1983). The role of gender in linguistic reference to emotive states. *Communication Quarterly, 30,* 174–179.

Small, A., Gross, R., Erdwins, C., & Gessner, T. (1979). Social attitude correlates of sex role. *Journal of Psychology, 101,* 115–121.

Sogon, S., & Izard, C. E. (1987). Sex differences in emotion recognition by observing body movements: A case of American students. *Japanese Psychological Research, 29,* 89–93.

Sogon, S., & Masutani, M. (1989). Identification of emotion from body movements: A cross-cultural study of Americans and Japanese. *Psychological Reports, 65,* 35–46.

Stapley, J. C., & Haviland, J. M. (1989). Beyond depression: Gender differences in normal adolescents' emotional experiences. *Sex Roles, 20,* 295–308.

Sullivan, H. S. (1953). *The interpersonal theory of psychiatry.* New York: Norton.

Swain, S. O. (1992). Men's friendships with women: Intimacy, sexual boundaries, and the informant role. In P. M. Nardi (Ed.), *Men's friendships* (pp. 153–171). Newbury Park, CA: Sage.

Tannen, D. (1990). *You just don't understand: Women and men in communication.* New York: Ballantine.

Tesch, S. A., & Martin, R. R. (1983). Friendship concepts of young adults in two age groups. *Journal of Psychology, 115,* 7–12.

Tomkins, S. S. (1980). Affect as amplification: Some modifications in theory. In R. Plutchik & H. Kellerman (Eds.), *Emotion: Theory, research, and experience: Vol. 1* (pp. 141–164). Orlando, FL: Academic Press.

van de Ven, P. (1995). A comparison of two teaching modules for reducing homophobia in young offenders. *Journal of Applied Social Psychology, 25,* 632–649.

Volling, B., Mackinnon-Lewis, C., Rabiner, D., & Baradaran, L. (1993). Children's social competence and sociometric status: Further exploration of aggression, social withdrawal, and peer rejection. *Development and Psychopathology, 5,* 459–483.

Wallace, A. T. (1985). Ongoing marriage: Maintaining the awe. *Studies in Formative Spirituality, 6,* 271–281.

Wallerstein, J. S. (1987). Children of Divorce: Report of a ten year follow up of early latency age children. *American Journal of Orthopsychiatry, 57,* 199–211.

Weiner, B., & Handel, S. J. (1985). A cognition-emotion-action sequence: Anticipated emotional consequences of causal attributions and reported communication strategy. *Developmental Psychology, 21,* 102–107.

Wierzbicka, A. (1992). Defining emotion concepts. *Cognitive Science, 16,* 539–581.

Wiggins, J. S. (1979). A psychological taxonomy of trait-descriptive terms: The interpersonal domain. *Journal of Personality and Social Psychology, 37,* 395–412.

Wiggins, J. S. (1991). Agency and communion as conceptual coordinates for the understanding and measurement of interpersonal behavior. In W. M. Grove and D. Cicchetti (Eds.), *Thinking clearly about psychology: Vol. 2* (pp. 89–113). Minneapolis, MN: University of Minnesota Press.

Windle, M. (1994). A study of friendship characteristics and problem behaviors among middle adolescents. *Child Development, 65,* 1764–1777.

Winton, J. (1990). Language and emotion. In H. Giles and W. P. Robinson (Eds.), *Handbook of language and social psychology* (pp. 33–49). Chichester, UK: Wiley.

Zammuner, V. L., & Frijda, N. H. (1994). Felt and communicated emotions: Sadness and jealousy. *Cognition and Emotion, 8,* 37–53.

Zillmann, D., Weaver, J. B., Mundorf, N., & Aust, C. F. (1986). Effects of an opposite-gender companion's affective response to horror on distress, delight, and attraction. *Journal of Personality and Social Psychology, 51,* 586–594.

CHAPTER 20

Children's Responses to Emotional Portrayals on Television

Barbara J. Wilson and Stacy L. Smith

University of California, Santa Barbara
Santa Barbara, California

Television presents a myriad of emotions and emotional situations to young viewers. Characters in fictional programs fall in love, fight with family members, experience sadness when someone dies, and feel angry when they are cheated. People are shown coping with natural disasters, violent crime, and war in television news as well as reality-based shows like *Cops.* Not only is the content of television often emotional, but so is its form. Production techniques such as close-ups, slow motion, and music are used to heighten the suspense and realism of emotional portrayals. In addition, camera angle and sound effects can increase a viewer's feeling of personal involvement in a depicted event.

Children may be especially vulnerable to such emotional portrayals given the sheer amount of time they devote to television. Estimates suggest that children in the United States spend an average of 2 to 3 hours a day watching television (Children Now, 1995). In fact, by age 17 the average American young person will have spent more time watching television than attending school (Comstock & Paik, 1991). Given these statistics, it seems reasonable to assume that young children encounter certain emotions and affective situations on television long before they experience these same phenomena in real life. Indeed, several researchers have argued that television plays a central role in children's beliefs about emotions, their own emotional experiences, and their overall emotional development (Dorr, Doubleday, & Kovaric, 1983; Huston et al., 1992).

The purpose of this chapter is to review comprehensively the research on children's responses to emotional portrayals on television. In an early review, Dorr (1982) described the amount of research on this topic as "minuscule" and to some extent, the state of our knowledge is still somewhat limited. For decades, media researchers have focused primarily on negative or antisocial effects of television on children such as its impact on aggressive behavior and academic functioning (see Comstock & Paik, 1991). Only recently have scholars begun to pay attention to more subtle, and arguably more pervasive, outcomes of children's interaction with television. After all, television is more likely to produce diverse emotional reactions in a wide range of children than it is to cause these same children to act aggressively.

We have divided this chapter into five broad areas. The first section concentrates on developmental differences in children's processing of television. This explanatory framework is essential because much of the research reviewed below reveals differences in children's responses to emotional content as a function of level of cognitive development, often indexed broadly by age. The second section focuses on children's understanding of emotional portrayals on television. As will be shown, there are developmental differences in children's ability to recognize and comprehend characters' emotional experiences. The third section deals with more generalized learning from television. For many children, television is a rich source of information about the nature and causes of emotion in real life. The fourth section focuses on how children react emotionally themselves to television portrayals. Much attention has been devoted to how different types of content, such as violence and horror, impact children's emotions. The final section will deal with more long-term consequences of children's exposure to affective portrayals on television, such as desensitization and the development of parasocial relationships.

DEVELOPMENTAL DIFFERENCES IN CHILDREN'S PROCESSING OF TELEVISION

The television experience cannot be fully understood without taking into account the complex interactions among the viewer, the type of content viewed, and the environment within which television is viewed. For children, one of the most important considerations is their level of cognitive functioning (Dorr, 1986; Van Evra, 1990). A growing body of evidence indicates that younger children often attend to and interpret the same television program in a slightly different way than do their older counterparts (see Collins, 1983; Dorr, 1986). Several influential perspectives on child development such as Piaget's (1952, 1960) theory of cognitive development and more recent models of information processing (e.g., Flavell, 1985; Siegler, 1991) support this idea. Because of the tremendous variation in how and when children develop, there are no precise age markers associated with these changes. However, most research reveals pronounced differences between preschoolers and early elementary schoolers on the one hand and older elementary school children on the other in terms of the strategies that are used to make sense of the world (see Siegler, 1991).

What cognitive skills are entailed in television viewing? One of the first things a child must do is allocate attention to the multitude of auditory and visual signals that are presented. Studies suggest that younger children are more likely to attend to perceptually salient features on television such as animation, lively music, and sound effects (Anderson & Levin, 1976; Calvert & Gersh, 1987). In contrast, older children tend to be more selective in their attention, searching for cues that have information value as opposed to features that are merely salient (Calvert, Huston, Watkins, & Wright, 1982). As an example, Hoffner and Cantor (1985) found that younger children were more likely to focus on physical appearance when evaluating a television character, whereas older children were able to discount misleading appearances and focus instead on the character's behavior. This shift from perceptual to conceptual processing has implications for children's responses to emotional portrayals, as will be seen below.

The next step for a child is to integrate or make sense of the information that is perceived. The television world presents some unique interpretive challenges because information is presented auditorially and visually, and it is not always presented in a continuous or chronological fashion. Amidst this complex and changing set of signals, younger children often struggle to differentiate peripheral information from information that is more central or crucial to the plot (Collins, Wellman, Keniston, & Westby, 1978). Consequently, younger children typically show less understanding of the key elements in a television story line than do their older counterparts (Watkins, Calvert, Huston-Stein, & Wright, 1980).

Comprehension of the plot not only involves understanding explicit program content but also implicit information in the unfolding storyline. Television programs often jump from one scene to the next and require the viewer to "read between the lines" to make sense of the story. For instance, in one scene a character may describe his fear of the neighborhood bully to his mother, and in the next scene he may be shown crying over a black eye. The viewer must deduce that the bully hit the boy even though this is not portrayed explicitly. Studies indicate that younger children are less able than older children to draw different types of inferences from verbally presented passages (Ackerman, 1988; Thompson & Meyers, 1985). The same developmental difference shows up in the context of television viewing; younger children are less able to link scenes together and infer connections among characters' motives, behaviors, and consequences of their actions (see Collins, 1983).

In addition to comprehending the content of television, children also need to understand its form. Production techniques like cuts, fades, and sound effects are used to signal shifts in time, changes in setting, and other structural aspects of content. These formal features have been described as the syntax or grammar of television (Huston & Wright, 1989). Research suggests that even preschoolers can comprehend conventional production techniques such close-ups and zooms (Abelman, 1989; Smith, Anderson, & Fischer, 1985), in part because they simulate real-world perceptual events. However, specialized techniques that have no real-world analog require more conceptual reasoning. Studies indicate that older children are able to comprehend formal features such as flashbacks and instant replays, whereas younger children are likely to interpret such cues literally as the repetition of action (Calvert, 1988; Rice, Huston, & Wright, 1986). In addition to conceptual reasoning skills, increased experience with television helps children comprehend these techniques (Abelman, 1989, 1990).

Another important aspect of comprehending television is the ability to distinguish reality from fantasy. Perceived reality of television is a multidimensional construct that is influenced by the genre or type of program, production cues, and the social realism or similarity of the content to real life (Hawkins, 1977; Wright, Huston, Reitz, & Piemyat, 1994). Regardless of what aspect of reality is measured, however, most studies demonstrate strong developmental differences in children's perceptions (Dorr, 1983; Wright et al., 1994). Very young 2- and 3-year-olds perceive no boundaries between television and the real world (Jaglom & Gardner, 1981), and may even talk and wave to characters on the screen (Noble, 1975). Preschool children begin to appreciate the representational nature of television, but tend to assume that anything that *looks* real on television is real (Brown, Skeen, & Osborn, 1979; Dorr, 1983). This literal approach has been called the "magic window" perspective, and is consistent with younger children's tendency to be swayed by how things appear rather than how things really are (see Flavell, 1986). Preschoolers may be able to report that cartoons are "not real," but their perceptual and emotional reactions to animated characters often fail to reflect this distinction (Wright et al., 1994). As children mature, they increasingly judge television in terms of whether the people and events *possibly* could happen in real life (Dorr, 1983; Morison, Kelly, & Gardner, 1981; Wright et al., 1994). By adolescence, such judgments more often are based on the *probability* of events occurring in real life rather than the mere possibility (Dorr, 1983; Morison, Kelly, & Gardner, 1981).

Another cognitive skill that is used in making sense of television is perspective taking. Although there are exceptions (e.g., Kevin on *Wonder Years*), characters on television seldom narrate the story so their thoughts and feelings may not be explicitly identified. Viewers often need to role take or imagine themselves in a character's situation to fully grasp the depicted emotion or behavior in a scene. Like perceived reality, role taking is conceptualized as a multidimensional construct involving perceptual, cognitive, and affective components (see Higgins, 1981). In general, the ability to adopt another's perspective has been shown to increase developmentally (Chandler & Greenspan, 1972; Kurdek, 1977). Therefore, older children should be better able to adopt the role of a television character and imagine themselves in that character's situation.

One final point should be made regarding the processing of television. Older children not only utilize more advanced cognitive strategies, but they also are able to consider more information at one time when applying such strategies to television content. Research has documented a steady improvement with age in memory span or the amount of information that can be held in working memory (see Dempster, 1978; Kail, 1990). Thus, older television viewers are better able than younger viewers to consider multiple cues, including emotional signals, within a scene or across several scenes when interpreting a portrayal (Collins, Berndt, & Hess, 1974; Hoffner, Cantor, & Thorson, 1989).

To summarize, watching television is an active process that requires a number of cognitive skills. Children must learn to allocate attention selectively so as not to be misled by perceptually salient cues in a scene. They also need to be able to distinguish central plot information from peripheral details, and they must be able to link scenes together and draw inferences about implicit plot information. Comprehension also requires some understanding of the production techniques used in the medium. Lastly, children's interpretations are influenced by their ability to distinguish reality from fantasy and their capacity to role take with characters. All of these skills together with working memory capacity improve with development such that older children typically evidence a fuller and richer understanding of television when compared to younger children.

UNDERSTANDING EMOTIONAL PORTRAYALS ON TELEVISION

Many television programs prominently feature the emotional experiences of main characters. As an example, a recent episode of *Fresh Prince of Bel Air* features two teens, Will and his cousin Carlton, being robbed at gunpoint. The robber shoots Will and the remainder of the episode focuses on people trying to cope with the tragedy. Will lies in pain at the hospital as his distressed family watches over him. Traumatized by the robbery, Carlton decides to carry a gun everywhere he goes. The episode ends as Will emotionally pleads with Carlton to give up the gun. A child viewer watching this program conceivably could learn something about the nature of fear and anger, about violent events that cause these emotions, about how to cope with such feelings, and about how family members can help in emotional situations. However, these benefits are possible only if the child understands the emotional depictions in the program.

How well do children comprehend emotional content on television? Most of the research to date has concentrated on whether children are able to recognize the affective experiences of others. In general, studies indicate that by age 5, most children can correctly identify the emotions of happiness, sadness, anger, and fear from pictures of facial expressions (Izard, 1971; Odom & Lemond, 1972). Younger children also are able to listen to stories and match these basic emotions to typical situations that cause them (Borke, 1973; Camras & Allison, 1985). The same level of accuracy has been found when videotaped or televised vignettes are used as stimuli. Although the tendency to spontaneously label the specific affect improves with age (Cantor & Wilson, 1984; Wilson & Cantor, 1985), preschoolers generally are able to identify and differentiate the basic emotions experienced by characters (e.g., Deutsch, 1974; Strayer, 1989).

Yet emotions on television often are more complex than feelings like sadness or fear, which are associated with distinct facial expressions and prototypical situational events. Several studies indicate that younger children are less able to comprehend intricate emotions like shame, guilt, and contempt (Izard, 1971; Odom & Lemond, 1972; Harter & Whitesell, 1989). For example, Thompson (1989) found that younger children attributed feelings of pride and guilt to all types of situations involving success and failure, whereas older children recognized that these complex feelings are tied to personal effort and responsibility as well as to others' reactions in a situation.

Not only are certain emotions more complicated, but so too are certain situations. At times, a person's facial and bodily movements may appear to be inconsistent with the emotional event occurring (e.g., a person exhibits sadness while opening birthday presents). Several studies have presented children with such conflicting cues in narrated stories or in videotape vignettes (e.g., Gnepp, 1983; Hoffner & Badzinski, 1989; Wiggers & van Lieshout, 1985). Generally, preschool and younger elementary school children are more strongly influenced by facial expressions in such conflicting scenarios. In contrast, older elementary schoolers give more weight to situational cues, and show an increased ability to consider personal information and prior events that led up to the situation when trying to reconcile the cues.

Another example of a complicated emotional portrayal is when a person experiences two different feelings at once. Harter and her colleagues (Harter & Buddin, 1987; Harter & Whitesell, 1989) have found that children show a clear developmental progression in their ability to understand conflicting emotions. Very young children deny that people can experience two emotions simultaneously. By around age 6, children recognize that two emotions can occur at once, but only if they are of the same valence (e.g., sad and mad). By around age 10, children begin to realize that people can experience two emotions of opposite valence at once, such as feeling happy and mad.

Collectively, this research suggests that children acquire a more differentiated understanding of emotions as they develop (see Harris & Saarni, 1989). When applied to television, we can expect that preschoolers will understand simple portrayals in which characters experience basic emotions like happiness and sadness. During the school years, children increasingly should comprehend portrayals involving complex emotions, simultaneous emotional experiences, and idiosyncratic affective reactions to equivocal situations. As outlined in the previous section, these developmental improvements are consistent with the older child's increasing ability to (a) attend to conceptual information like a character's personal history and personality, (b) consider and integrate multiple pieces of information at one time, (c) role take with characters, and (d) draw inferences from emotional information that is not overtly depicted. Unfortunately, most of these conclusions are drawn from studies that do not involve television at all or that simply use television as a vehicle for testing children's responses. Such a focus neglects the possibility that television itself might contribute to children's beliefs and expectations about emotion, the topic of the next section.

LEARNING ABOUT EMOTIONS FROM TELEVISION

According to social learning theory, children can acquire knowledge, attitudes, and behaviors through the observation of models (Bandura, 1986). Bandura (1994) proposed a multiprocess view of social learning. An observer first must *attend* to the modeled event. Studies suggest that children pay more attention to models who are attractive (see Bandura, 1986) and who are perceived as similar to the self (Bandura, Ross, & Ross, 1963a). Next, the observer must *retain* or encode the observed events into memory. Finally, the observer must possess the personal ability and the motivation to *perform* what has been learned. In general, children are more likely to imitate a modeled event if they anticipate positive outcomes or rewards for such performance (e.g., Bandura, 1965; Bandura, Ross, & Ross, 1963b).

Although parents, peers, and teachers often function as models in children's immediate environment, Bandura (1994) noted that "the accelerated growth of video delivery technologies has vastly expanded the range of models to which members of society are exposed day in and day out" (p. 67). Indeed, a large body of work has accumulated on children's social learning from television. Studies indicate that children can acquire stereotyped attitudes (see Graves, 1993), aggressive behaviors (see Paik & Comstock, 1994), and even prosocial actions like cooperation (see Hearold, 1986) from watching TV. Yet almost no systematic research has been conducted on children's learning about emotions from television. Two exceptions are the following: research on educational programming and a set of recent studies on family TV series.

Educational Programming

Both *Sesame Street* and *Mister Rogers' Neighborhood* have made concerted efforts to teach preschoolers about emotions. *Sesame Street,* the older and arguably more successful series, was created by Children's Television Workshop (CTW) in 1969. The program is viewed by over five million preschoolers each week in the United States (Nielsen, 1995), and has been shown in over 130 countries around the world (Children's Television Workshop, 1995). One of the recurring goals of this program is to teach preschoolers to recognize and label feelings such as love and anger, to recall situations that made them feel these emotions, and to be aware of these feelings in others. In the last few years, a more specific goal of *Sesame Street* has been to improve race relations by showing that children with different skin colors share the same types of needs and emotions, and can be close friends (Lovelace, Scheiner, Segui, & Black, 1994).

What does the research say about the impact of such educational programming? Consistent with findings cited above, studies show that preschoolers can learn about simple emotions like anger and fear from watching *Sesame Street* episodes, but that segments featuring complex emotions like pride are more difficult for this age group (Lasker & Bernath, 1974). Longitudinal research indicates that preschoolers who regularly watch *Sesame Street* learn more about the emotions that children typically feel than do infrequent viewers (Bogatz & Ball, 1971). Studies also suggest that *Sesame Street* can teach children to feel more positively about people from different racial backgrounds (Bogatz & Ball, 1971; Gorn, Goldberg, & Kanungo, 1976), and that exposure to *Mister Rogers' Neighborhood* can increase children's giving of positive reinforcement, sympathy, and affection toward others (Coates, Pusser, & Goodman, 1976).

Such findings are encouraging because they demonstrate that programming can be specifically designed to teach children about the nature of emotions experienced by the self and by others. One obvious limitation is that most of these efforts have been targeted to preschoolers rather than older children. Furthermore, educational programming that is carefully designed and tested to nurture children's emotional growth has been limited primarily to public broadcasting.

Family Series

Family TV series have been a regular part of television's history, from *Leave It to Beaver* and *I Love Lucy* to the *Cosby Show* and *Full House*. Such programming is extremely popular among children (Dorr, 1986; Weiss & Wilson, 1993). A recent phone survey of parents revealed that *Full House* was mentioned most often as a favorite program among elementary schoolers (Cantor, in press). Furthermore, 1995 Nielsen ratings indicate that 7 of the 10 most watched programs among 2- to 11-year-olds were family series, including *Step by Step, Home Improvement,* and *Family Matters* (Stipp, 1995).

In addition to their sheer popularity, there are at least two reasons why children are likely to learn about emotions from family TV series. First, family sitcoms prominently feature common, everyday problems and emotional reactions to these situations in the main story line (Weiss & Wilson, 1996). Second, both younger and older children perceive the events and particularly the feelings in family sitcoms as very similar to those experienced by real-life families (Dorr, Kovaric, & Doubleday, 1990; Weiss & Wilson, 1993). Research suggests that viewers are more likely to learn from content that is seen as realistic (Feshbach, 1972; Greenberg, 1974).

Several content analyses have examined the emotional portrayals contained in family programs (Heintz, 1992; Hoffner & Cantor, 1991c; Kovaric, Doubleday, &

Dorr, 1991; Larson, 1993). In general, these studies show that families on television grapple with simple emotions like anger and happiness more often than complex feelings like guilt or shame. This research also shows that most interactions among family members are positive or affiliative rather than conflictual. However, characters who experience negative emotions like fear and anger frequently are ignored by other family members.

In a recent study, Weiss and Wilson (1996) took a closer look at how emotions are contextualized in five popular family sitcoms. The researchers found that the main plot in such programming typically features a child experiencing a negative emotional situation. Usually, the negative situation is resolved happily by the end of the half-hour program. In addition, most family sitcoms include a secondary storyline or subplot that is interspersed throughout the main plot and that revolves around a more positive, often humorous event.

In a subsequent study, Weiss and Wilson (in press) were interested in whether such a subplot might influence children's learning about emotions. Children from two grade levels (K-2 vs. 3-5) viewed one of two episodes of *Full House* that featured a negative emotion, either fear of an earthquake or anger over a bike accident, in the main plot. Additionally, half the children saw a humorous subplot that was interwoven throughout the main plot, and half saw no such subplot. Regardless of which emotional episode was viewed, younger children showed less understanding of the events in the main plot than did older children. Moreover, the inclusion of the subplot reduced younger children's comprehension of the main story line even further. These findings are consistent with developmental differences in children's ability to draw inferences across disjointed scenes. Older viewers were better able to make sense of the main plot in spite of an interwoven subplot.

Though the subplot had no impact on older children's comprehension, it did affect *both* age groups' perceptions of emotion in the program. Children who viewed the humorous subplot rated the main character as feeling less negative (either less frightened by earthquakes or less angry over a bike accident) than did those who did not view the subplot. Moreover, exposure to the subplot had some impact on perceptions of emotions in real life. Among those who saw the earthquake episode, children who viewed the humorous subplot judged earthquakes in real life as significantly less severe than did those who did not see the subplot. This pattern was especially strong among those who rated *Full House* as highly realistic.

The latter finding is consistent with the idea that televised depictions can impact a viewer's mental representation or schema for an emotional event. A schema is conceptualized as an organized structure of knowledge about a concept or stimulus that helps a person anticipate and assimilate new information (Fiske & Taylor, 1991). Scholars have theorized that people possess schemata or prototypes for emotions, which include information about expressive signals, situational causes, and display rules typically associated with each affect (e.g., Campos & Barret, 1984; Gordon, 1989). Studies suggest that children utilize various schemata to help organize and interpret television (Meadowcroft & Reeves, 1989; Rabin & Dorr, 1995; Wilson,

1991). In turn, the schemata that children bring to television may be altered by the very experience of viewing. As an example of this interplay, one recent study found that children who perceived television to be realistic held schemata for occupations, like nursing and policing, that were similar to TV images of such jobs (Wright et al., 1995).

Schematic processing can be applied to children's learning from family sitcoms. In the Weiss and Wilson (in press) study, exposure to one humorous subplot within an emotional episode altered children's perceptions of the main characters' feelings. Perhaps repeated exposure to the routine juxtaposition of humorous subplots in such programming teaches children that such negative emotions are not very significant or painful in real life. This type of transfer is illustrated by the fact that the humorous subplot also caused children who viewed the fear episode to downplay the seriousness of earthquakes in real life. Thus, children's beliefs about emotional events in the real world can be influenced by television.

Family series may result in other types of emotional learning, especially among those who perceive the programs to be highly realistic. Child viewers may acquire norms for expressing emotions like anger and fear from watching the everyday problems featured in family sitcoms. Viewers also may learn valuable coping strategies since many of the characters are shown solving their own problems. Moreover, family sitcoms could help children to adopt a positive outlook on emotional problems since families on television routinely resolve their crises. And even though negative emotions often are ignored in such programming, television families generally are affiliative and supportive of each other, providing strong models of prosocial interaction for young viewers (Buerkel-Rothfuss, Greenberg, Atkin, & Neuendorf, 1982).

To summarize, educational programs as well as popular family series like *Fresh Prince of Bel Air, Full House,* and *Step by Step* have the potential to influence children's emotional development. Yet most of the work to date has focused on children's processing of and short-term learning from particular portrayals. Researchers have yet to explore the long-term messages acquired from regular viewing of these shows, and the consequences of this learning for children's interpersonal relationships. Moreover, very little attention has been paid to family series involving more caustic humor like *Roseanne* and the *Simpsons* (Larson, 1993), or to other genres of programming like talk shows, which also might affect children's beliefs about emotion. The importance of this research is underscored by the strong interdependencies between children's comprehension of emotions on television and their understanding of emotional events in real life.

EMOTIONAL REACTIONS TO TELEVISION

It is difficult to imagine a child who has not laughed at a humorous scene in a sitcom or felt frightened by a tragedy depicted in a movie. The very existence of television depends in part on engaging the audience and evoking viewers' emotions. To declare, however, that television often causes children to feel happy or scared is not very enlightening. The real questions of interest are when and why such emotional experiences occur. As with children's understanding of emotional portrayals, affective responses are a function of multiple factors. In this section, we consider three types of factors that have been shown to influence children's emotions: the type of program viewed, the type of viewer involved, and the environment within which the program is viewed.

Program Characteristics

Traditionally, society has tried to shield children from emotional experiences like death and danger, but in many ways television threatens that control (Gordon, 1989). With the advent of new technologies like cable television and videocassette recorders, children now have increased access to portrayals of horror, violent anger, and destruction that often are not intended for younger viewers. As a result, most of the research in this area has focused on potentially problematic portrayals that can elicit negative reactions in young viewers. By comparison, very little research has investigated children's affective reactions to potentially prosocial or positive content such as educational programs and situation comedies. In this section, we will review research on four different types of content that have been shown to produce emotions in child viewers. We will conclude with a brief discussion of how the forms or production techniques of television also may influence children's affective responding.

Horror

Horror-filled presentations have received considerable attention in recent years as they proliferate in number and increase in graphicness (Sharkey, 1994). Obvious examples are films like *Friday the 13th, Nightmare on Elm Street,* and their numerous sequels, many of which eventually make their way to television. But even Disney movies like *The Lion King* have caused concern because of scenes depicting parental death and scary creatures (Lachnit, 1994). In addition to films, some television series are devoted entirely to frightening events. For instance, the Fox network recently has adapted the popular children's book series *Goosebumps* into a live-action show featuring ghost stories and monsters (Graham, 1995).

Studies show that a majority of preschool and elementary school children have experienced fear reactions to horror-filled content (Cantor & Reilly, 1982; Cantor & Sparks, 1984; Lyle & Hoffman, 1972; Sparks, 1986; Wilson, Hoffner, & Cantor, 1987). Many of these fright reactions have persisted beyond the viewing experience, resulting in bad dreams, sleep disturbances, and regret over seeing the program (Palmer, Hockett, & Dean, 1983; see also, Cantor, 1991).

Cantor (1994) offered a stimulus-generalization explanation for why fictional portrayals cause fear when, objectively speaking, the viewer is not in any immediate danger. The basis for the explanation is that certain stimuli are automatically associated with fear (e.g., snakes) or are conditioned to produce fear in the real world. According to the notion of stimulus generalization, television portrayals that are perceptually similar to these real-life fear stimuli will evoke a similar, albeit less intense, fright response in viewers. Cantor has outlined three categories of stimuli frequently featured in horror portrayals that also commonly evoke real-world fear: (a) distorted natural forms (e.g., monster, supernatural creature), (b) dangerous events that cause injury (e.g., natural disaster, murder), and (c) the experience of endangerment and fear by characters.

The first two categories illustrate cases in which viewers respond directly to the fear-evoking stimuli, whereas the last category involves responding indirectly through the emotional experiences of characters. Though all three classes of stimuli can produce fear, research suggests there are developmental differences in the types of portrayals that upset children the most (see Cantor, 1991; Wilson, Linz, & Randall, 1990). For example, younger children are more frightened than older children by characters and events that are visually grotesque or scary looking, examples of the first category. In one survey, Cantor and Sparks (1984) found that parents of preschoolers most often mentioned programs involving grotesque-looking characters, such as *The Incredible Hulk* and *The Wizard of Oz,* as those that caused fear in their children. In contrast, parents of older children more often mentioned programs that involve nonvisual threats or threats that require more imagination, such as *Poltergeist* and *Amityville Horror.* Such findings have been replicated in a subsequent survey of children themselves (Sparks, 1986), and in an experiment involving scenes from *The Incredible Hulk* (Sparks & Cantor, 1986). This pattern regarding visual threats can be explained by the developmental shift from perceptual to conceptual processing outlined in the first section of this chapter.

Regarding the second category, dangerous events that cause injury, several surveys indicate that younger children are more frightened than older children by programs that feature fantastic or impossible incidents (Cantor & Sparks, 1984; Sparks, 1986). In contrast, older children are more upset by portrayals of realistic threats or events that could possibly occur in real life. Such findings are consistent with developmental differences in the ability to distinguish reality from fantasy, as discussed in the first part of this chapter.

Another feature related to dangerous events is the degree to which the threat is abstract in nature. In a random survey of parents, Cantor, Wilson, and Hoffner (1986) assessed children's reactions to the television movie *The Day After,* which depicted the aftermath of nuclear war. Because the movie focused primarily on abstract consequences like radiation sickness rather than graphic scenes of bombing and destruction, the researchers predicted that fear reactions would increase with age. Consistent with developmental differences in abstract reasoning, children over 12 years of age were more frightened by the movie than were younger viewers.

The final category deals with the degree to which a program focuses on the victim's emotion. Many programs seem to emphasize a character's terror more than the actual event or creature that is responsible for this fear. Researchers have posited that when a viewer vicariously shares a character's emotion, the process of empathy is involved (Strayer, 1987; Zillmann, 1991). Although the precise definition and nature of this construct have been hotly debated, most scholars seem to agree that empathy entails some cognitive awareness of the other's emotion as well as some affective response (see Eisenberg & Strayer, 1987).

A developmental continuum for empathy has been proposed by Strayer (1989), based on progressively more complex levels of cognitive involvement. The earliest precursor to empathy is the facial mimicry and automatic emotional responding to others' emotions often observed among infants and very young children (see Hoffman, 1987). Eventually, the child is able to distinguish the self from others and to accurately identify others' emotions. When sharing a concordant emotion, however, the younger child responds primarily to situational events impinging on the other person rather than attending to the person's internal psychological experience. The most sophisticated level of empathy emerges in late childhood and involves affective sharing based on role taking or imagining the self in another's place.

Consistent with Strayer's (1989) model, research indicates that there are developmental differences in the tendency to empathize with a television character's fear. In one experiment (Wilson & Cantor, 1985), preschool and older elementary school children were exposed to a film clip of either a large menacing killer bee or a character's fear response to this frightening stimulus. Younger children were less emotionally aroused by the character's fear than by the frightening stimulus itself, whereas older children responded emotionally to both versions. This pattern is congruent with developmental improvements in role-taking ability as outlined earlier in the chapter. Thus, programs that focus primarily on the terrorized reactions of a threatened victim should be more frightening for older children than for younger children.

Taken together, this research suggests that fear reactions to horror are quite common and are often developmental in nature. Younger children are more likely to be frightened by programs featuring visually grotesque characters who may be fantastic in nature. Older children are more likely to be upset by programs that feature events that could possibly occur in real life, abstract threats, and scenes of a victim's terror reactions. But this focus on fear neglects one other important and somewhat paradoxical finding that runs throughout the literature—many children report that they like scary programs (Sparks, 1986). For example, Palmer et al. (1983) found that 40% of second graders and 65% of sixth graders reported that they liked scary shows. In another study, over 75% of the preschool and elementary school children interviewed said they liked scary programs (Wilson et al., 1987).

How can children both fear and enjoy horror? Zillmann (1991) has proposed an explanation for why people enjoy suspense based on the process of excitation transfer. According to excitation transfer (Zillmann, 1971), physiological arousal from a stimulating event decays slowly and thus can serve to elevate a subsequent emotional experience. Based on this idea, Zillmann has argued that residual arousal from earlier frightening scenes can intensify the relief and euphoria that is typically experienced when a threat is eliminated and a happy resolution occurs. Therefore, the more intensely frightening a program is, the more relief and potential enjoyment a viewer can experience once the threat is resolved. In support of this reasoning, one experiment found that children who were exposed to a highly suspenseful program exhibited more facial fear and reported more enjoyment than did those who viewed a less suspenseful version of the same plot (Zillmann, Hay, & Bryant, 1975). In another experiment (Hoffner & Cantor, 1991a), children's ratings of enjoyment were positively correlated with negative affect during a scary program, though children enjoyed the show regardless of whether a successful resolution was presented. Clearly, there are complex relations between positive and negative reactions to horror that depend on the nature of the threat, the resolution, and as we will see in the next section, the characters involved. More research is needed on these program features as they interact with each other.

Violence

Another type of TV content that has been the focus of a great deal of public attention is violence. Admittedly, some of the programs described in the previous section contain violence, but the primary goal of the horror genre is to scare the audience. In this section we will concentrate on entertainment programming that contains violent action and adventure, and is designed primarily to excite rather than to scare. A recent content analysis of a week of American television across 23 channels indicates that nearly 60% of programs contain some form of physical violence directed against animate beings (Wilson et al., 1996). Furthermore, almost 70% of programs targeted specifically to children contain violence.

There are literally hundreds of studies on the impact of media violence, but much of this research has concentrated on whether such content causes aggression in viewers (see Comstock & Paik, 1991; Paik & Comstock, 1994). Consequently, we know very little about children's emotional reactions to violent portrayals. The tremendous popularity of *Mighty Morphin Power Rangers* and before it, *Teenage Mutant Ninja Turtles,* seems to suggest that at a minimum children enjoy TV violence. In 1994, the *Power Rangers* reached an astounding 57% of the 6- to 11-year-old viewing audience and was responsible for over $1 billion in sales of Ranger toys and merchandise (Meyer & Tsiantar, 1994).

Yet the success of individual programs does not demonstrate conclusively that violence is enjoyable, nor does it tell us much about why such a show might be popular. Social science research on children's liking of violent programs has yielded mixed results. Some studies have found that children prefer violent programs to nonviolent ones (Surbeck & Endsley, 1979; Greenberg & Gordon, 1972), whereas at least one investigation has found the opposite results (Osborn & Endsley, 1971).

In all of these studies, however, children viewed violent and nonviolent programs that differed on a variety of dimensions. Using this type of methodology, it is impossible to detect precisely what it is about the programs that children did or did not like. To date, no published study has ever systematically assessed whether the addition of violence, while holding all other content features constant, increases or decreases children's liking of a program (for review, see Cantor, in press).

In spite of the lack of controlled studies, it is difficult to deny the widespread popularity of TV violence among children. Recent Nielsen ratings indicate that the majority of children's favorite programs on Saturday morning are action-adventure shows featuring violent heroes, with *Spiderman, X-Men, Power Rangers,* and *Ninja Turtles* routinely among the top 10 (Stipp, 1995). Nevertheless, children from different age groups do seem to show preferences for different types of violent genres. In a survey of parents, Cantor (in press) found that interest in action cartoons like *Ninja Turtles* decreased between kindergarten and sixth grade, whereas interest in reality shows like *Cops* increased with age. Consistent with this pattern, preschoolers have been shown to exhibit more facial enjoyment during cartoon violence than during nonanimated TV violence (Lagerspetz, Wahlroos, & Wendelin, 1978). In contrast, older elementary school children have been shown to prefer *Johnny Quest* over more unrealistic programs like *Popeye* or *Tom and Jerry* (Cramer & Mechem, 1982). This increasing preference for more realistic content is consistent with developmental improvements in children's ability to distinguish reality and fantasy on television.

In spite of changing preferences, why are children of all ages so attracted to TV violence? One possible explanation is that viewers enjoy violence because it is exciting or arousing (Cantor, in press). In a survey by Bruce (1995a), self-reported feelings of excitement while watching television violence were correlated strongly with children's liking of this content. As additional support, research on adults has established that exposure to media violence does increase physiological arousal (see Zillmann, 1991), and several studies of children have shown similar results (e.g., Osborn & Endsley, 1971; Zillmann et al., 1975).

An explanation based on generalized arousal, however, does not take into account the particular content of violent programming. An alternative reason for attraction to violence is that children may like the characters featured in such programs. Research indicates that viewers are attracted to and identify with characters who act prosocially or helpful toward others (see Hoffner & Cantor, 1991b). Moreover, children as young as 4 years of age can distinguish between prototypically good and bad characters on television (Berndt & Berndt, 1975; Liss, Reinhardt, & Fredricksen, 1983). A common formula in violent shows is the "good guy" or hero who is forced to do battle against evil to save the world (Potter & Ware, 1987). Part of the satisfaction of such programs may come from seeing good characters triumph and bad characters fail.

In support of this idea, Jose and Brewer (1984) found that overall liking of a story was a joint function of character valence (good or bad) and valence of the outcome, particularly for older children. In particular, older elementary schoolers liked positive endings for good characters and negative endings for bad characters. Although kindergartners also preferred good characters over bad ones, they tended to like happy endings regardless of the valence of the character, consistent with the idea that they may have more difficulty integrating multiple cues in a story. These findings suggest that violent programs will be most appealing when they feature heroes or good characters who prevail in the end (Zillmann, 1991).

That said, we still know very little about children's liking of television violence. More systematic efforts need to be undertaken to assess how the addition of violence to a scene or throughout an entire program might influence affective responding. Additionally, scholars need to examine how children's enjoyment of media violence may vary as a function of the types of characters involved as well as other contextual features such as the amount of pain and harm depicted, and whether humor is involved.

Other emotional reactions to violence should be studied as well. For example, several of the studies cited above suggest that realistic portrayals of violence can be frightening for children (Osborn & Endsley, 1971; Lagerspetz et al., 1978; Surbeck & Endsley, 1979), though again this research suffers from a lack of controlled comparisons of content. Like horror, violent entertainment on television can be enjoyed and/or feared depending on the nature of the portrayal. More attention should be paid to such contrasting emotional responses to TV violence, which in turn may increase our understanding of the conditions under which children imitate or learn aggressive behaviors from this type of content (Ekman et al., 1972; Lagerspetz & Engbolm, 1979).

News

The previous two sections have concentrated on children's affective reactions to fictional television content such as horror and violence. Far less attention has been given to more realistic programming such as television news. Perhaps this neglect is due in part to the assumption that children do not regularly watch news programming. But recent evidence suggests that this assumption simply is not true. In one national poll, 65% of 11- to 16-year-olds reportedly had watched a TV news program during the previous day (Children Now, 1994). Recent Nielsen ratings indicate that almost one million American children between the ages of 2 and 11 view the evening network news on a given day (Stipp, 1995). And even if some do not routinely watch such programming, the bombing of the Federal Building in Oklahoma City reminds us that children can be exposed inadvertently to graphic coverage of national tragedies (Cimons, 1995).

Most of the efforts to assess children's emotional reactions to TV news have focused on major catastrophic events on the same scale as the Oklahoma City bombing or the TWA flight 800 crash. In one of the earliest of such studies, Siegel (1965) examined children's reactions to the Kennedy assassination and found that more than two-thirds of those surveyed reportedly felt sad, worried, and angry after the event. Many children also reported suffering from headaches, loss of appetite, and sleeping difficulties.

Like the Kennedy assassination, the explosion of the space shuttle *Challenger* caused a great deal of national concern, especially because many school children watched the live TV coverage of what was supposed to be the first teacher-astronaut in orbit. Wright, Kunkel, Pinon, and Huston (1989) interviewed elementary schoolers and found that the explosion aroused strong negative feelings in many children. Furthermore, those who expressed more personal involvement with the teacher and her family expressed more emotional upset.

A number of researchers examined children's reactions to media coverage of the Persian Gulf War (see Greenberg & Gantz, 1993). In one survey, Cantor, Mares, and Oliver (1993) found that nearly half the parents of first through eleventh graders reported that TV coverage of the war had upset their child. The researchers also documented developmental differences in the aspects of the coverage that caused this upset. Younger children reportedly were most disturbed by graphic visual images of the war and by concrete stories about dangers to people in the Gulf region, whereas older children were more concerned about abstract aspects of the coverage such as terrorism and possible nuclear war. In a survey of children themselves, Hoffner and Haefner (1993) found that over 90% reported feeling sadness in response to televised coverage of the war, and similarly high percentages also reported anger and fear. Hoffner and Haefner also found that greater exposure to TV news coverage of the war increased children's emotional upset and their concern for their own and others' safety.

More recently, scholars have begun to examine children's emotional reactions to typical or everyday news programming. In one study, Cantor and Nathanson (1996) interviewed a random sample of parents from Madison, Wisconsin, about their elementary schoolers' fright reactions to TV news. At roughly the same time in Santa Barbara, California, we interviewed a sample of elementary school children about their reactions to daily news programming (Wilson & Smith, 1995). The results from these two investigations are strikingly similar. Both studies found that older children were significantly more likely to be frightened by television news than were younger children. This finding is consistent with the fact that older children are more likely to watch TV news (Atkin & Gantz, 1978; Wilson & Smith, 1995), and are more capable of comprehending the abstract information that is often featured in such programming. Age differences also were found in the types of new stories that caused fear. Younger children were more frightened by stories involving natural disasters and accidents, which often feature graphic scenes of destruction as well as scenes of the actual event as it is occurring. On the other hand, older children were more upset by crime stories like murders or kidnappings, which seldom are overtly depicted but instead focus on the aftermath and consequences for the family. Such age differences are congruent with developmental differences in perceptual versus conceptual processing of television as outlined earlier.

To summarize, the handful of studies that have explored children's reactions to TV news indicate that such programming can result in feelings such as fear and sadness, and that such reactions vary as a function of the type of news story and age of the viewer. More controlled studies need to assess specific features of a news story that might elevate or reduce emotional responses. For example, the research on catastrophic events suggests that at least for younger children, visual footage of destruction may be particularly upsetting. Other studies indicate that the proximity of a news event to a child's hometown may affect fear reactions (Cantor & Hoffner, 1990; Cohen, Wigand, & Harrison, 1977). Experimental studies of such factors would help us to understand better children's fright reactions, and might have practical implications for designing "family sensitive news" during early evening hours ("Family Sensitive News," 1994). In addition, research should explore children's affective responses to tabloid news shows like *Hard Copy* and *A Current Affair,* which are popular among younger viewers and often confused with regular news programming (Wilson & Smith, 1995).

Other Types of Content

Because media researchers have tended to focus on portrayals that might upset children or that might encourage antisocial behavior, other types of content that do not have such serious societal implications have been neglected. Yet children experience a multitude of feelings when watching programs that do not necessarily contain horror or violence. Studies suggest that younger children laugh and report enjoyment during educational programs like *Sesame Street* (Sproull, 1973), and older children find programs like *Ghostwriter* appealing (Williams, Hall, & Schiro, 1995). Moreover, experimental studies indicate that children enjoy instructional episodes more when they include humorous inserts than when they are devoid of humor (Wakshlag, Day, & Zillmann, 1981; Zillmann, Williams, Bryant, Boynton, & Wolf, 1980).

When different types of content are compared directly, younger children report that programs containing humor and action are most likely to make them feel happy, and they show a preference for cartoons over other genres of programming (Argenta, Stoneman, & Brody, 1986; Cantor & Hoffner, 1991; Prawat & Prawat, 1975). Older children reportedly experience happiness when programs feature either the resolution of an unhappy situation or other people succeeding (Cantor & Hoffner, 1991), reflecting their increased ability to comprehend others' emotional experiences and to role take. Yet these generalizations are based on survey data or on uncontrolled studies of programs that differ on a variety of dimensions. More systematic research is needed on sitcoms, dramas, and nonviolent cartoons because children may experience many of their first feelings of joy and sadness while watching such programming.

Production Techniques

Children not only respond emotionally to the content of a program, but also to its formal features or production techniques. In one experiment, children who were exposed to production cues suggesting that the upcoming scene was only a dream were less frightened by the scary scene than were those who saw no such dream cues (Wilson, 1991). Production conventions also may affect children's enjoyment or liking of a program. Potts, Huston, and Wright (1986) found that regardless of the amount of violence, preschool boys paid more attention to a portrayal that contained a high amount of action than one that was slow in place. A variety of formal features like camera angle, music, and visual effects should be examined for their impact on children's emotions. Some formal features may detract attention or confuse children and therefore interfere with affective reactions, whereas others are likely to signal dramatic content and thus heighten emotional responding.

Viewer Characteristics

The research we have reviewed thus far clearly demonstrates that television is capable of eliciting emotional reactions in young viewers. Yet not all children are affected in uniform ways. Instead, their emotional reactions are mediated to some degree by certain characteristics they bring to the viewing environment. One important characteristic we have covered extensively throughout the preceding section is the child's level of cognitive development. We will now describe three other viewer attributes that affect emotional responding: sex, dispositional or personality differences, and prior affective state.

Sex

Research consistently shows that boys respond to emotional portrayals differently than do girls. In particular, young males enjoy both horror and violence on television more than do young females (Cantor, in press; Donohue, 1975; Lyle & Hoffman, 1972). Furthermore, boys typically experience less fear and emotional upset in response to these types of portrayals (Cantor, Sparks, & Hoffner, 1988; Cantor & Wilson, 1987; Palmer et al., 1983; Wilson, 1987, 1989; Wilson & Smith, 1995). Such findings often are explained in terms of differences in sex-role socialization. Congruent with this explanation, Wright et al. (1989) found that girls exhibited an emotional orientation toward the *Challenger* disaster that focused on the personal aspects of the tragedy, whereas boys reacted with a more detached, cognitive orientation. Sex differences also have been attributed to the availability of role models on TV. Most violent programs feature male characters as perpetrators, so that boys may find it easier to identify with and enjoy such content.

Dispositional Differences

Individual differences in personality or disposition also can influence a child's emotional reactions to affect-laden events on TV. One such dispositional characteristic is a person's overall level of anxiousness. In a study of college students, highly anxious subjects who viewed 6 weeks of violent programming in which the evildoers went unpunished showed a significant increase in their anxiety levels (Bryant, Carveth, & Brown, 1981). Similarly, fifth graders scoring high in trait anxiety reported significantly more fear in response to scary scenes in a play than did those low in trait anxiety, though this pattern was found only for girls (Kase, Sikes, & Spielberger, 1978). Highly anxious children, then, may intentionally avoid scary or arousing content in an effort to protect themselves from further anxiety (Bruce, 1995b).

Alternatively, some theorists have argued that individuals who are overly anxious actually may seek out violent or frightening media portrayals in an effort to overcome or desensitize themselves to their real-world fears (see Cantor, in press; Zillmann, 1980). The study involving college students also supports this idea. In contrast to those who viewed injustice, highly anxious subjects who viewed violent programs with "just" endings showed a significant *decrease* in anxiety levels after 6 weeks of viewing. Thus, some emotional portrayals on television may be reassuring for anxious children, whereas others may leave them feeling more distressed.

Another dispositional attribute that can mediate affective responding is a child's coping style (Hoffner, 1993a, 1995; Spirek, 1992; Spirek & Sparks, 1993). Like adults, some children can be classified as "monitors" because they have a need to seek out and attend to information in threatening situations, whereas others can be described as "blunters" because they prefer to avoid or distract themselves from such information (Hoffner, 1993a; Spirek, 1992). In general, high blunters experience more negative affect when they are forewarned about the events in an upcoming scary scene than when they are given no such information, whereas monitors feel the greatest anxiety when prior information is not available (Sparks, 1989; Spirek & Sparks, 1993).

A final dispositional trait that can mediate emotional responses to television is empathy. In a previous section, we reviewed evidence suggesting that empathy is a developmental skill. Research also suggests that there are individual differences in the tendency to be sensitive and responsive to the feelings of others (see Barnett, 1987). Children who are highly empathic are more likely to react emotionally to the affective experiences of fictional TV characters and to people featured in more realistic programs. For example, Hoffner and Haefner (1993) found that elementary school children who scored high on empathy experienced more negative affect and enduring upset in response to news coverage of the Gulf War. Parental affection and comforting skills seem to promote the development of empathy in children (Burleson & Kunkel, 1995; Eisenberg & Strayer, 1987), but children also can learn emotional sensitivity from television role models (Coates et al., 1976).

Prior Affective State

A child's prior mood or affective state also can affect emotional responding to television. Zillmann (1991) argued that individuals selectively seek out particular entertainment fare as a function of their emotional state. Viewers who are bored or understimulated should prefer entertainment fare that is exciting. On the other hand, viewers who are upset or angry should seek out programs that are calming or distracting. These mood-dependent efforts at selective exposure have been documented extensively with adult viewers (see Zillmann & Bryant, 1994). Such preferences have been partially replicated with preschoolers. In an experiment by Master, Ford, and Arend (1983), preschool boys who were treated in a hostile manner were significantly more likely to prefer nurturing segments from *Mister Rogers' Neighborhood* than were boys who were treated in a positive fashion. Unexpectedly, preschool girls showed no such preferences as a function of prior mood.

In addition to affecting selective exposure, children's prior affective state may influence emotional reactions to television content. As described above, Zillmann's (1971) excitation transfer paradigm indicates that individuals who are aroused prior to viewing will respond more intensely to emotional scenes than will those who are not previously stimulated. Although no systematic research exists with children, we can reason that prior arousal from physically aggressive play can heighten a child's subsequent enjoyment of a violent program. Likewise, arousal left over from being disciplined by a parent may serve to accentuate a young viewer's fear reactions to a horror film.

Environmental Characteristics

Emotional reactions to television are not only a function of children's own personal characteristics but also the nature of the viewing environment itself. One of the most important environmental mediators of affective responding is whether a child watches TV with someone else. Research indicates that at least half of children's television viewing is in the context of family or friends (Kubey & Larson, 1990; Rubin, 1986), and that coviewing is most common during adult-oriented programs like drama and news (St. Peters, Fitch, Huston, Wright, & Eakins, 1991).

Of particular interest is children's coviewing with family members. Watching television with a parent or other adult can help children comprehend the central plot of a program (Watkins et al., 1980), draw inferences about implicit program content (Collins, Sobol, & Westby, 1981), and distinguish reality from fantasy on TV (Austin, Roberts, & Nass, 1990). Research suggests that parent coviewers also frequently explain characters' emotions and behaviors to their children (Stoneman & Brody, 1982), and can influence their emotional responding. In one study, viewing with a parent significantly increased preschoolers' enjoyment of *Sesame Street* (Salmon, 1977). In another study, mothers' verbalizations about characters' emotions were positively correlated with children's feelings of sadness and distress during a sympathy-inducing film (Eisenberg et al., 1992). Siblings also can affect children's emotions. One recent study found that preschoolers who watched a scary program with an older sibling were less frightened and liked the program more than did those who viewed alone (Wilson & Weiss, 1993).

Taken together, these findings suggest that a coviewer can directly influence a child's affective reaction to television, especially when explicit mediation is used. If a parent or sibling encourages a child to empathize with a character, the child's emotions are likely to be intensified. On the other hand, if a coviewer provides verbal and nonverbal reassurance, as did the older siblings in the Wilson and Weiss study, a child's emotions are likely to be diminished. Another possibility is that a coviewer's emotions rather than overt behaviors can affect a child. Studies suggest that children's affective reactions are frequently correlated with their parents' own emotional responses to an arousing program (Cantor et al., 1993; Eisenberg et al., 1992; van der Voort, van Lil, & Vooijs, 1993). This pattern is consistent with the fact that children frequently monitor or look at a coviewer while watching TV (Anderson, Lorch, Smith, Bradford, & Levin, 1981; Wilson & Weiss, 1993), presumably searching for cues on how to respond. This social referencing process is discussed in Chapter 1 (see Guerrero, Andersen, & Trost, this volume).

AFFECTIVE SOCIALIZATION

The literature reviewed thus far has dealt primarily with immediate or short-term reactions children have when viewing television. Children may misinterpret an emotional event in a sitcom, or they may experience transitory feelings of excitement or fear when watching a violent program. Such reactions constitute part of a child's daily experiences so they are important in their own right. But beyond these short-term responses, children also can experience more enduring reactions to television. In this section, we turn to the question of whether repeated exposure to television or to particular types of programming can have more long-term effects on a child's affective development and socialization. The research on television's contribution to children's emotional development is in its infancy, and has been limited largely to four areas: the development of emotional disturbances, cultivation, desensitization, and the formation of parasocial relationships.

Emotional Disturbances

In a previous section, we established that a majority of children report having experienced short-term fear responses to a frightening portrayal, and that such reactions often persist beyond the viewing experience. Less common, but more serious, are those cases when more intense emotional disturbances develop as a result of exposure to a scary scene or program. Most of the evidence for such reactions comes from case studies of children exhibiting traumatic responses or from clinical studies of phobias. For example, in a book on the fears of childhood, Sarafino (1986) reported that many children he interviewed were anxious and worried because of monsters, witches, and violence they had seen on TV. Sarafino (1986) concluded that frightening television portrayals are capable of not only hindering but also impairing children's psychological and emotional development.

Clinicians also have documented the long-term psychological effects of television on children. Simons and Silveria (1994) diagnosed two 10-year-old boys as suffering from "post-traumatic stress disorder" after watching the program *Ghostwatch* on television. For several months after viewing this show, the boys experienced panic attacks, recurring nightmares, and maladaptive behaviors like clinging to their parents. Similar emotional disturbances over frightening programs also have been observed among adults (Horowitz, 1976; Johnson, 1980).

Together, these studies reveal that under some circumstances television can produce intense and persistent emotions that interfere with normal functioning. Because most of this research is based on case studies and in-depth interviews with troubled children, we have no idea how pervasive such responses are, nor do we know much about their long-term implications for adolescence and adulthood.

Cultivation

A second way in which television can contribute to affective socialization is through cultivation. Advanced by Gerbner and his colleagues (for recent summary, see Gerbner, Gross, Morgan, & Signorielli, 1994), cultivation refers to television's impact on perceptions of social reality. According to cultivation theory, heavy exposure to television can alter a person's view of social reality in a way that matches the TV world. Gerbner and his colleagues first tested this theory in terms of television messages about violence (e.g., Gerbner & Gross, 1976; Gerbner, Gross, Morgan, & Signorielli, 1980). In numerous studies involving samples of all age groups, these researchers consistently found that frequent viewers of television see the world as a more dangerous place and are more frightened of being a victim of violence than are infrequent viewers (see Signorielli & Morgan, 1990).

Cultivation theory has been critiqued methodologically because much of the evidence for it is correlational (e.g., Doob & Macdonald, 1979; Hirsch, 1980). However, more recent experimental evidence has shown that heavy exposure to media violence under controlled conditions can cause fear and anxiety in viewers (Bryant et al., 1981; Ogles & Hoffner, 1987). Researchers also have identified conceptual weaknesses in the theory (e.g., Potter, 1993), resulting in efforts to delineate mediating factors and underlying psychological processes involved in cultivation (e.g., Hawkins & Pingree, 1990). For example, studies indicate that cultivation is more likely to occur among those who perceive television as realistic (e.g., Potter, 1986). Cultivation also may depend to some extent on the developmental or cognitive abilities of the viewer (Van Evra, 1990). Given that younger viewers possess less real-world experience and have a more limited knowledge base, their attitudes and emotions may be influenced more by media messages (Hawkins & Pingree, 1980). In support of this idea, children who are more integrated into peer groups or have closer ties with family have been shown to be less susceptible to cultivation (Rothschild, 1984), presumably because these interpersonal relationships provide alternative sources of information about the world.

Research suggests that television can impact other social beliefs besides those involving violence and crime. Studies have found that cumulative exposure to television contributes to sex-role beliefs (Morgan, 1982), beliefs about marriage (Signorielli, 1991), and even beliefs about physicians and the medical profession (Pfau, Mullen, & Garrow, 1995). Thus, it seems reasonable to expect that heavy exposure to television can influence a child's beliefs about emotions. In an earlier section of this chapter, we posited that viewing of sitcoms, for example, can contribute to children's schemata or expectations about affect and affective experiences in families. With extensive viewing, this short-term learning may be reinforced to such an extent that it becomes a stable part of a child's belief system. Indeed, Shrum (1995) offered an explanation of cultivation based on information processing and the availability heuristic. He argued that heavy viewers have vivid and repeated television examples stored in memory, and that these exemplars are easily retrieved when such viewers make social judgments about the real world.

Desensitization

Another potential long-term effect of television on emotions is desensitization. Desensitization refers to the process by which repeated exposure to a stimulus can result in reduced emotional responsiveness to it. One of the primary concerns regarding desensitization is the impact of extensive exposure to TV violence. For example, research has demonstrated that physiological responses can be dampened by prolonged exposure to media violence. One study found that boys who were heavy viewers of television violence exhibited less physiological arousal to a film clip containing violence than did light viewers (Cline, Croft, & Courrier, 1973). Other studies involving adults have documented that heart rate and skin conductance decrease over time during exposure to a prolonged violent program (Lazarus & Alfert, 1964; Speisman, Lazarus, Mordkoff, & Davidson, 1964).

If extensive exposure merely resulted in decreased arousal to fictional portrayals of violence, there might be little cause for concern. However, desensitization also can influence reactions to real-life violence. One study found that children who were exposed to dramatized violence on television subsequently showed less arousal to a real-life incident involving a fight between two preschoolers (Thomas, Horton, Lippincott, & Drabman, 1977). Additionally, desensitization can result in callous attitudes toward real aggression. In an experiment by Thomas and Drabman (1975), first and third graders viewed either a violent or a neutral television program and then were asked to monitor the behavior of two preschoolers at play. Older children who had been exposed to the violent TV program were significantly slower in getting help when the preschoolers broke into a fight. In fact, over half of the older children in the violent TV condition never left the room to warn an adult about the ensuing real-life aggression. Such unresponsiveness to real violence has been replicated in two other studies involving children (Drabman & Thomas, 1974; Hirsch & Molitor, 1994).

Desensitization is clearly problematic with regard to television violence, but it can have beneficial effects for other types of content such as frightening portrayals. Consistent with clinical uses of desensitization on phobias, several studies have employed gradual exposure techniques to help prepare children for an upcoming scary program (Weiss, Imrich, & Wilson, 1993; Wilson, 1987, 1989; Wilson & Cantor, 1987). In these studies, children typically are exposed to a fear stimulus like a lizard or a realistic replica of a tarantula before watching a frightening scene involving the stimulus. This research consistently demonstrates that such exposure strategies can be effective in reducing children's fright reactions to television portrayals.

The results from all these studies demonstrate that repeated exposure to different types of portrayals can desensitize children. This emotional numbing can be harmful if it spills over and affects a child's reactions to real-life events, especially those involving interpersonal violence. On the other hand, desensitization can be beneficial if it helps children to cope with fictional television portrayals that may be frightening. Future research should be conducted on the conditions that facilitate desensitization and on how long such unresponsiveness persists (Mullin & Linz, 1995).

Parasocial Relationships

One final long-term effect of television exposure that has been examined is the development of parasocial relationships. Parasocial relationships are feelings of attachment or perceived friendship that individuals form with certain television characters and personalities (Hoffner, 1993b; Noble, 1975). Research indicates that children form these relationships with characters who are perceived as attractive and as similar to the self in terms of demographics, personal experiences, and emotions (Hoffner, 1993b).

Although we know very little about children's parasocial relationships, several scholars have speculated that these attachments contribute to social learning (Dorr, 1982; Hoffner, 1993b). Like real-life relationships, parasocial interactions may provide children with opportunities to imagine how they would behave or feel in different situations, and viewers may even model a favorite character's appearance, emotional responses, and other mannerisms. Indeed, Hoffner (1993b) found that children's parasocial attachment to characters was positively correlated with watching TV to learn about the self in social contexts.

Parasocial relationships also may provide children with feelings of affiliation and intimacy. Consistent with this idea, Hoffner (1993b) found that children's parasocial interaction was correlated positively with watching television for companionship. Such relationships may be especially comforting to lonely children, though in extreme cases they could become substitutes for interactions with family and friends. Very little is known about the parameters of children's parasocial relationships with television characters.

SUMMARY AND IMPLICATIONS

Our goal in this chapter has been to provide a framework for understanding children's reactions to emotional portrayals on television. This review clearly demonstrates that learning from and responding to television is a complex process, influenced by a multitude of factors. Figure 1 outlines some of the factors that have been examined by researchers. Television programming, represented on the left side, interacts with both viewer characteristics and environmental factors such that certain types of children in particular settings will selectively seek out and be affected by different types of content, characters, and formal features. The type of portrayal, the unique features of the child, and the environment in turn affect how information from television is processed and stored in memory. For example, an anxious child who frequently watches a lot of graphic horror alone is likely to interpret a scary scene differently than a happy child who seldom watches this type of content except in the company of parents. All of these factors ultimately influence the three outcomes of emotional portrayals: short-term learning, immediate emotional reactions, and affective socialization. It should be noted that most of the relationships in the model are bidirectional because interactions with television are likely to alter how a child responds to future encounters with this medium. We will now discuss the various components of the model in more detail, pointing out directions for future research.

The middle part of the diagram arguably is the most important because it represents what a child *does* with television. One of the core assumptions of this chapter is that children actively process and make sense of television, employing information-processing skills like attention, integration, and inferential reasoning to interpret programming. As we have pointed out, many of these skills are developmentally acquired and improved upon during childhood. In addition, children rely on a set of stored knowledge structures or schemata to interpret television, and maturation contributes to the sheer amount and richness of such information available in memory. Consequently, older viewers are better able than younger viewers to comprehend complex emotional scenes, draw inferences across scenes in a program, role take and empathize with characters, and differentiate fantastic depictions from more realistic content. Any model or theory of children's reactions to television must incorporate such developmental differences.

In this review, we noted that most of the research to date deals with only a limited part of the process identified in Figure 1. By far, the majority of studies have concentrated on the types of television content (e.g., horror, violence) that produce

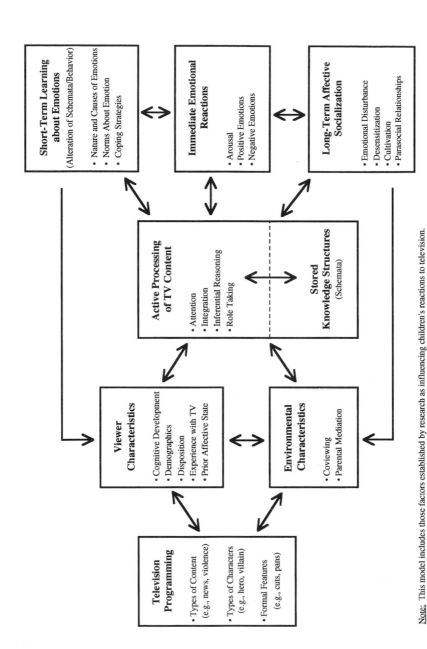

FIGURE 1   Factors involved in children's responses to emotional portrayals on television.

Note: This model includes those factors established by research as influencing children's reactions to television.

negative emotional reactions in children. This preoccupation has been due in part to public concern about the potential harmful effects of viewing certain programming. A growing body of literature indicates that children do experience fright reactions to different types of content, and that these reactions often are a function of the child's level of cognitive development. Yet these same types of programs that cause fear and upset are frequently enjoyed by children as well. This paradoxical relationship between negative and positive emotions deserves further exploration. We also know very little about other types of programming that are less controversial and may in fact be prosocial. How do situation comedies, after-school specials, and prime-time dramas make children feel? Surely there are programs that are capable of producing feelings of joy, anger, sorrow, and even contempt. Moreover, what types of characters and production conventions elicit such emotions?

Another notable gap in the literature concerns the diversity of children who make up the viewing audience. In contrast to developmental level, there is very little research on how individual characteristics like prior mood, ethnicity, and personality traits affect reactions to a program. Furthermore, much of the experimental research does not take into account the child's environment. For instance, a child who spends long hours alone presumably will respond differently to a movie featuring a lonely character than will a gregarious child watching with friends. A child whose parents continually argue and fight may respond more intensely to an emotional scene about divorce than will a child in a more secure environment.

The concentration on emotional reactions to television also ignores two other types of outcomes: short-term learning and long-term socialization. The research on educational programs like *Sesame Street* indicates that children can learn about the nature and causes of emotions, and about how to respond emotionally to others from watching television. Furthermore, the studies of family sitcoms indicate that television is capable of distorting some perceptions about emotion. Such short-term learning is likely to be most pervasive among children who perceive television as realistic and who strongly identify with certain characters. The possibility that children may view a character like Bart Simpson as a role model may concern some parents because of the potential consequences for social learning. As we have argued, more research in this arena is critical given the time children spend with this medium and the multitude of messages about emotion that are available to a young viewer with limited real-world knowledge.

Ultimately, what may be most critical is how television contributes to children's emotional developmental and socialization. Preliminary studies suggest that there can be long-term consequences of exposure to programming such as emotional disturbances and desensitization. Additionally, the research on cultivation indicates that a child's belief system and perceptions of the real world can be shaped by repeated exposure to television. Finally, children can form feelings of attachment and imaginary relationships with television characters. What are the implications of such long-term effects for children's interactions in the real world? A child who is traumatized by a television program or a news scene may become anxious and antisocial. A child who is desensitized to media violence may ignore or even enjoy inter-personal aggression at school. A child who believes that television families are real-istic may be disappointed when a parent shows less affection or gets more angry than a parental figure on TV. As these examples illustrate, such issues challenge us as researchers to ignore traditional boundaries between interpersonal and mass com-munication. Clearly, media researchers need to better integrate children's interper-sonal relationships into the television viewing experience. Moreover, scholars in-terested in family and relational communication need to consider how television plays into a child's expectations about and responses to real-life interactions.

REFERENCES

Abelman, R. (1989). From here to eternity: Children's acquisition of understanding projective size on television. *Human Communication Research, 15,* 463–481.

Abelman, R. (1990). You can't get there from here: Children's understanding of time-leaps on televi-sion. *Journal of Broadcasting & Electronic Media, 34,* 469–476.

Ackerman, B. P. (1988). Reasons inference in the story comprehension of children and adults. *Child De-velopment, 59,* 1426–1442.

Anderson, D. R., & Levin, S. R. (1976). Young children's attention to "Sesame Street." *Child Develop-ment, 47,* 806–811.

Anderson, D. R., Lorch, E. P., Smith, R. S., Bradford, R., & Levin, S. R. (1981). Effects of peer pres-ence on preschool children's television-viewing behavior. *Developmental Psychology, 17,* 446–453.

Atkin, C. K., & Gantz, W. (1978). Television news and political socialization. *The Public Opinion Quar-terly, 42*(2), 183–198.

Argenta, D. M., Stoneman, Z., & Brody, G. H. (1986). The effects of three different television programs on young children's peer interactions and toy play. *Journal of Applied Developmental Psychology, 7,* 355–371.

Austin, E. W., Roberts, D. F., & Nass, C. I. (1990). Influences of family communication on children's television interpretation processes. *Communication Research, 17,* 545–564.

Bandura, A. (1965). Influence of models' reinforcement contingencies on the acquisition of imitative responses. *Journal of Personality and Social Psychology, 1,* 589–595.

Bandura, A. (1986). *Social foundations of thought and action: A social cognitive theory.* Englewood Cliffs, NJ: Prentice-Hall.

Bandura, A. (1994). Social cognitive theory of mass communication. In J. Bryant & D. Zillmann (Eds.), *Media effects* (pp. 61–90). Hillsdale, NJ: Erlbaum.

Bandura, A., Ross, D., & Ross, S. A. (1963a). Imitation of film-mediated aggressive models. *Journal of Abnormal and Social Psychology, 66,* 3–11.

Bandura, A., Ross, D., & Ross, S. A. (1963b). Vicarious reinforcement and imitative learning. *Journal of Abnormal and Social Psychology, 67,* 601–607.

Barnett, M. A. (1987). Empathy and related responses in children. In N. Eisenberg & J. Strayer (Eds.), *Empathy and its development* (pp. 146–162). New York: Cambridge University Press.

Berndt, T. J., & Berndt, E. G. (1975). Children's use of motives and intentionality in person perceptions and moral judgment. *Child Development, 46,* 904–912.

Bogatz, G. A., & Ball, S. (1971). *The second year of Sesame Street: A continuing evaluation* (Vol. 1 & 2). Prince-ton, NJ: Educational Testing Services.

Borke, H. (1973). The development of empathy in Chinese and American children between three and six years of age: A cross-culture study. *Developmental Psychology, 9,* 102–108.

Brown, M. H., Skeen, P., & Osborn, D. K. (1979). Young children's perception of the reality of television. *Contemporary Education, 50,* 129–133.

Bruce, L. (1995a). *At the intersection of real-life and television violence: Emotional effects, cognitive effects and interpretive activities of children.* Unpublished doctoral dissertation, University of Wisconsin-Madison.

Bruce, L. (1995b, May). *Interpretive activities of traumatized children in response to violent television fare.* Paper presented at the annual conference of the International Communication Association, Albuquerque, NM.

Bryant, J., Carveth, R. A., & Brown, D. (1981). Television viewing and anxiety: An experimental examination. *Journal of Communication, 31*(1), 106–119.

Buerkel-Rothfuss, N. L., Greenberg, B. S., Atkin, C. K., & Neuendorf, K. (1982). Learning about the family from television. *Journal of Communication, 32*(3), 191–201.

Burleson, B. R., & Kunkel, A. W. (1995, May). *Parental and peer contributions to the emotional support skills of the child: From whom do children learn to express support?* Paper presented at the annual conference of the International Communication Association, Albuquerque, NM.

Calvert, S. L. (1988). Television production feature effects on children's comprehension of time. *Journal of Applied Developmental Psychology, 9,* 363–375.

Calvert, S. L., & Gersh, T. L. (1987). The selective use of sound effects and visual inserts for children's story comprehension. *Journal of Applied Developmental Psychology, 8,* 363–374.

Calvert, S. L., Huston, A. C., Watkins, B. A., & Wright, J. C. (1982). The relations between selective attention to television forms and children's comprehension of content. *Child Development, 53,* 601–610.

Campos, L. A., & Barret, K. C. (1984). Toward a new understanding of emotions and their development. In C. E. Izard & R. B. Zajonc (Eds.), *Emotion, cognition, and behavior* (pp. 229–263). Cambridge, UK: Cambridge University Press.

Camras, L. A., & Allison, K. (1985). Children's understanding of emotional facial expressions and verbal labels. *Journal of Nonverbal Behavior, 9,* 84–94.

Cantor, J. (1991). Fright responses to mass media predictions. In J. Bryant & D. Zillmann (Eds.), *Responding to the screen: Reception and reaction processes* (pp. 169–197). Hillsdale, NJ: Erlbaum.

Cantor, J. (1994). Fright reactions to mass media. In J. Bryant & D. Zillmann (Eds.), *Media effects* (pp. 213–245). Hillsdale, NJ: Erlbaum.

Cantor, J. (in press). Children's attraction to violent television programming. In J. Goldstein (Ed.), *Why We Watch.* London: Routledge.

Cantor, J., & Hoffner, C. (1990). Children's fear reactions to a televised film as a function of perceived immediacy of depicted threat. *Journal of Broadcasting and Electronic Media, 34,* 421–442.

Cantor, J., & Hoffner, C. (1991). *Children's reports of happiness and sadness induced by the mass media.* Unpublished manuscript.

Cantor, J., Mares, M. J., & Oliver, M. B. (1993). Parents' and children's emotional reactions to TV coverage of the Gulf War. In B. S. Greenberg & W. Gantz (Eds.), *Desert Storm and the mass media* (pp. 325–340). Cresskill, NJ: Hampton Press.

Cantor, J., & Nathanson, A. I. (1996). Children's fright reactions to television news. *Journal of Communication, 46*(4), 139–152.

Cantor, J., & Reilly, S. (1982). Adolescents' fright reactions to television and films. *Journal of Communication, 32*(1), 87–99.

Cantor, J., & Sparks, G. G. (1984). Children's fear responses to mass media: Testing some Piagetian predictions. *Journal of Communication, 34*(2), 90–103.

Cantor, J., Sparks, G. G., & Hoffner, C. (1988). Calming children's television fears: Mr. Rogers vs. The Incredible Hulk. *Journal of Broadcasting & Electronic Media, 32,* 271–288.

Cantor, J., & Wilson, B. J. (1984). Modifying fear responses to mass media in preschool and elementary school children. *Journal of Broadcasting, 28,* 431–443.

Cantor, J., & Wilson, B. J. (1987). Helping children cope with frightening media presentation. *Current Psychology: Research & Reviews, 7,* 58–75.

Cantor, J., Wilson, B. J., & Hoffner, C. (1986). Emotional responses to a televised nuclear holocaust film. *Communication Research, 13,* 257–277.

Chandler, M. J., & Greenspan, S. (1972). Ersatz egocentrism: A reply to Borke. *Developmental Psychology, 7,* 104–106.

Children Now. (1994). *Tuned in or tuned out? America's children speak out on the news media.* Available E-mail: Children@dnai.com.

Children Now. (1995, November). *Sending signals: Kids speak out about values in the media.* Available E-mail: Children@dnai.com.

Children's Television Workshop. (1995, February). *The Big Bag: Statement of curriculum goals and content guidelines.* (Available from Children's Television Workshop, 1 Lincoln Plaza, New York, NY, 10023).

Cimons, M. (1995, April 21). Experts weigh in on helping kids cope. *Los Angeles Times,* p. A18.

Cline, V. B., Croft, R. G., & Courrier, S. (1973). Desensitization of children to television violence. *Journal of Personality and Social Psychology, 27,* 360–365.

Coates, B., Pusser, H. E., & Goodman, I. (1976). The influence of "Sesame Street" and "Mister Rogers' Neighborhood" on children's social behavior in the preschool. *Child Development, 47,* 138–144.

Cohen, A. A., Wigand, R. T., & Harrison, R. P. (1977). The effects of emotion-arousing events on children's learning from news. *Journal Quarterly, 53,* 204–210.

Collins, W. A. (1983). Interpretation and inference in children's television viewing. In J. Bryant & D. R. Anderson (Eds.), *Children's understanding of television* (pp. 125–150). New York: Academic Press.

Collins, W. A., Berndt, T. J., & Hess, V. L. (1974). Observational learning of motives and consequences for television aggression: A developmental study. *Child Development, 45,* 799–802.

Collins, W. A., Sobol, B. L., & Westby, S. (1981). Effects of adult commentary on children's comprehension and inferences about a televised aggressive portrayal. *Child Development, 52,* 158–163.

Collins, W. A., Wellman, H., Keniston, A., & Westby, S. (1978). Age-related aspects of comprehension and inference from a televised dramatic narrative. *Child Development, 49,* 389–399.

Comstock, G., & Paik, H. (1991). *Television and the American child.* San Diego, CA: Academic Press.

Cramer, P., & Mechem, M. B. (1982). Violence in children's animated television. *Journal of Applied Developmental Psychology, 3,* 23–39.

Deutsch, F. (1974). Female preschoolers' perceptions of affective responses and interpersonal behavior in videotaped episodes. *Developmental Psychology, 10,* 773–740.

Dempster, F. N. (1978). Memory span and short-term memory capacity: A developmental study. *Journal of Experimental Child Psychology, 26,* 419–431.

Doob, A. N., & Macdonald, G. E. (1979). Television viewing and fear of victimisation: Is the relationship causal? *Journal of Personality and Social Psychology, 37,* 170–179.

Donohue, T. R. (1975). Black children's perceptions of favorite TV characters. *Journal of Broadcasting, 19,* 153–167.

Dorr, A. (1982). Television and affective development and functioning. In D. Pearl, L. Bouthilet, & J. Lazar (Eds.), *Television and behavior: Ten years of scientific progress and implications for the eighties* (Vol. 2, pp. 68–77). Washington, DC: U.S. Government Printing Office.

Dorr, A. (1983). No shortcuts to judging reality. In J. Bryant & D. R. Anderson (Eds.), *Children's understanding of television* (pp. 199–220). New York: Academic Press.

Dorr, A. (1986). *Television and children: A special medium for a special audience.* Beverly Hills, CA: Sage.

Dorr, A., Doubleday, C., & Kovaric, P. (1983). Emotions depicted on and stimulated by television programs. In M. Meyer (Ed.), *Children and the formal features of television* (pp. 97–143). New York: Saur.

Dorr, A., Kovaric, P., & Doubleday, C. (1990). Age and content influences on children's perceptions of the realism of television families. *Journal of Broadcasting and Electronic Media, 34,* 377–397.

Drabman, R. S., & Thomas, M. H. (1974). Does media violence increase children's toleration of real-life aggression? *Developmental Psychology, 10,* 418–421.

Eisenberg, N., & Strayer, J. (1987). Critical issues in the study of empathy. In N. Eisenberg & J. Strayer (Eds.), *Empathy and its development* (pp. 3–16). New York: Cambridge University Press.

Eisenberg, N., Fabes, R. A., Gustave, C., Troyer, D., Speer, A. L., Karbon, M., & Switzer, G. (1992). The relations of maternal practices and characteristics to children's vicarious emotional responsiveness. *Child Development, 63,* 583–602.

Ekman, P., Liebert, R. A., Friesen, W. V., Harrison, R., Zlatchin, C., Malmstrom, E. J., & Baron, R. A. (1972). Facial expression while watching televised violence as predictors of subsequent aggression. In G. A. Comstock, E. A. Rubinstein, & J. P. Murray, (Eds.), *Television and social behavior* (Vol. 5, pp. 22–43). Washington, DC: U.S. Government Printing Office.

Family sensitive news: A kinder, gentler newscast. (1994, Summer). *Connect, 7,* 15.

Feshbach, S. (1972). Reality and fantasy in filmed violence. In G. A. Comstock, E. A. Rubinstein, & J. P. Murray, (Eds.), *Television and social behavior* (Vol. 2, pp. 318–345). Washington, DC: U.S. Government Printing Office.

Fiske, S. T., & Taylor, S. E. (1991). *Social cognition* (2nd. ed.). New York: McGraw Hill.

Flavell, J. H. (1985). *Cognitive development* (2nd ed.). Englewood Cliffs, NJ: Prentice-Hall.

Flavell, J. H. (1986). The development of children's knowledge about the appearance-reality distinction. *American Psychologist, 41,* 418–425.

Gerbner, G., & Gross, L. (1976). Living with television: The violence profile. *Journal of Communication, 26*(2), 172–199.

Gerbner, G., Gross, L., Morgan, M., & Signorielli, N. (1980). The 'mainstreaming' of America: Violence profile no. 11. *Journal of Communication, 30*(3), 10–29.

Gerbner, G., Gross, L., Morgan, M., & Signorielli, N. (1994). Growing up with television: The cultivation perspective. In J. Bryant & D. Zillmann (Eds.), *Media effects* (pp. 17–41). Hillsdale, NJ: Erlbaum.

Gnepp, J. (1983). Children's social sensitivity: Inferring emotions from conflicting cues. *Developmental Psychology, 19,* 805–814.

Gorn, G. J., Goldberg, M. E., & Kanungo, R. N. (1976). The role of educational television in changing the intergroup attitudes of children. *Child Development, 47,* 277–280.

Gordon, S. L. (1989). The socialization of children's emotions: Emotional culture, competence and exposure. In C. Saarni & P. L. Harris (Eds.), *Children's understanding of emotion* (pp. 319–349). New York: Cambridge University Press.

Graham, J. (1995, October, 24). Fox gets "Goosebumps." *USA Today,* 3D.

Graves, S. B. (1993). Television, the portrayal of African Americans, and the development of children's attitudes. In G. L. Berry & J. K. Asamen (Eds.), *Children and television: Images in a changing sociocultural world* (pp. 179–190). Beverly Hills, CA: Sage.

Greenberg, B. S. (1974). Gratifications of television viewing and their correlates for British children. In J. G. Blumer & E. Katz (Eds.), *The uses of mass communications* (pp. 71–92). Beverly Hills, CA: Sage.

Greenberg, B. S., & Gantz, W. (Eds.). (1993). *Desert Storm and the mass media.* Cresskill, NJ: Hampton Press.

Greenberg, B. S., & Gordon, T. F. (1972). Children's perceptions of television violence: A replication. In E. A. Rubinstein, G. A. Comstock, & J. P. Murray (Eds.), *Television and social behavior* (Vol. 2, pp. 211–230). Washington, DC: U.S. Government Printing Office.

Harris, P. L., & Saarni, C. (1989). Children's understanding of emotion: An introduction. In C. Saarni & P. L. Harris (Eds.), *Children's understanding of emotion* (pp. 3–24). New York: Cambridge.

Harter, S., & Buddin, B. J. (1987). Children's understanding of the simultaneity of two emotions: A five stage developmental acquisition sequence. *Developmental Psychology, 23,* 388–399.

Harter, S., & Whitesell, N. R. (1989). Changes in understanding of emotion concepts. In C. Saarni & P. L. Harris (Eds.), *Children's understanding of emotion* (pp. 117–150). New York: Cambridge University Press.

Hawkins, R. P. (1977). The dimensional structure of children's perceptions of television reality. *Communication Research, 7,* 193–226.

Hawkins, R. P., & Pingree, S. (1980). Some processes in the cultivation effect. *Communication Research, 7,* 193–226.

Hawkins, R. P., & Pingree, S. (1990). Divergent psychological processes in constructing social reality from mass media content. In N. Signorielli & M. Morgan (Eds.), *Cultivation analysis* (pp. 35–50). Newbury Park, CA: Sage.

Hearold, S. (1986). A synthesis of 1043 effects of television on social behavior. In G. Comstock (Ed.), *Public communication and behavior* (Vol. 1, pp. 65–133). New York: Academic Press.

Heintz, K. E. (1992, May). *Children's interpretations of television families: An examination of the influence of family structure on children's perceptions of real-life and TV families and parents.* Paper presented at the annual conference of the International Communication Association, Miami, FL.

Higgins, E. T. (1981). Role taking and social judgment: Alternative developmental perspectives and processes. In J. H. Flavell & L. Ross (Eds.), *Social cognitive development.* New York: Cambridge University Press.

Hirsch, K., & Molitor, F. (1994, July). *Children's toleration of real-life aggression after exposure to media violence: A replication of the Drabman and Thomas Studies.* Paper presented at the annual conference of the International Communication Association, Sydney, Australia.

Hirsch, P. M. (1980). The 'scary world' of the nonviewer and other anomalies: A reanalysis of Gerbner et al.'s findings of cultivation analysis, part I. *Communication Research, 7,* 403–456.

Hoffman, M. L. (1987). The contribution of empathy to justice and moral judgment. In N. Eisenberg & J. Strayer (Eds.), *Empathy and its development* (pp. 47–80). New York: Cambridge University Press.

Hoffner, C. (1993a). Children's strategies for coping with stress: Blunting and monitoring. *Motivation and Emotion, 17,* 91–106.

Hoffner, C. (1993b, May). *Children's responses to television characters: Determinants and outcomes of parasocial interaction.* Paper presented at the annual conference of the International Communication Association, Washington, DC.

Hoffner, C. (1995, May). *Children's emotional reactions to a scary film: The role of prior outcome information and coping preference.* Paper presented at the annual conference of the International Communication Association, Albuquerque, NM.

Hoffner, C., & Badzinski, D. M. (1989). Children's integration of facial and situational cues to emotion. *Child Development, 60,* 411–422.

Hoffner, C., & Cantor, J. (1985). Developmental differences in responses to a television character's appearance and behavior. *Developmental Psychology, 21,* 1065–1074.

Hoffner, C., & Cantor, J. (1991a). Factors affecting children's enjoyment of a frightening scene. *Communication Monographs, 58,* 41–62.

Hoffner, C., & Cantor, J. (1991b). Perceiving and responding to mass media characters. In J. Bryant & D. Zillmann (Eds.), *Responding to the screen* (pp. 63–101). Hillsdale, NJ: Erlbaum.

Hoffner, C., & Cantor, J. (1991c). *Sex differences in emotional depictions on prime-time programs popular with children.* Paper presented at the annual conference of the International Communication Association, Atlanta, GA.

Hoffner, C., Cantor, J., & Thorson, E. (1989). Children's responses to conflicting auditory and visual features of a televised narrative. *Human Communication Research, 16,* 256–278.

Hoffner, C., & Haefner, M. J. (1993). Children's responses to news coverage of the war. In B. S. Greenberg & W. Gantz (Eds.), *Desert Storm and the mass media* (pp. 364–380). Cresskill, NJ: Hampton Press.

Horowitz, M. J. (1976). *Stress response syndromes.* New York: Appleton-Century-Crofts.

Huston, A. C., Donnerstein, E., Fairchild, H., Feshbach, N. D., Katz, P. A., Murray, J. P., Rubinstein, E. A., Wilcox, B. L., & Zuckerman, D. (1992). *Big world, small screen: The role of television in American society.* Lincoln: University of Nebraska Press.

Huston, A. C., & Wright, J. C. (1989). Forms of television and the child viewer. In G. Comstock (Ed.), *Public communication and behavior* (Vol. 2, pp. 103–158). New York: Academic Press.

Izard, C. E. (1971). *The face of emotion.* New York: Appleton-Century-Crofts.

Jaglom, L. M., & Gardner, H. (1981). The preschool television viewer as anthropologist. In H. Kelly & H. Gardner (Eds.), *New directions for child development: Viewing children through television* (pp. 9–30). San Francisco, CA: Jossey-Bass.

Johnson, B. R. (1980). General occurrence of stressful reactions to commercial motion pictures and elements in films subjectively identified as stressors. *Psychological Reports, 47,* 775–786.

Jose, P. E., & Brewer, W. F. (1984). Development of story liking: Character identification, suspense, and outcome resolution. *Developmental Psychology, 20,* 911–924.

Kail, R. (1990). *The development of memory in children.* New York: Freeman.

Kase, J., Sikes, S., & Spielberger, C. (1978). Emotional reactions to frightening and neutral scenes in story theatre. *Communication Monographs, 45,* 181–186.

Kovaric, P., Doubleday, C., & Dorr, A. (1991, May). *Conceptualizing television messages about emotion in the family.* Paper presented at the annual conference of the International Communication Association, Chicago, IL.

Kubey, R., & Larson, R. (1990). The use and experience of the new video media among children and young adolescents. *Communication Research, 17,* 107–130.

Kurdek, L. A. (1977). Structural components and intellectual correlates of cognitive perspective taking in first- through fourth-grade children. *Child Development, 48,* 1503–1511.

Lachnit, C. (1994, July 2). "Lion King" too violent for little viewers? *Los Angeles Times,* p. F4.

Lagerspetz, K. M., & Engbolm, P. (1979). Immediate reactions to TV-violence by Finnish pre-school children of different personality types. *Scandinavian Journal of Psychology, 20,* 43–53.

Lagerspetz, K. M., Wahlroos, C., & Wendelin, C. (1978). Facial expressions of pre-school children while watching televised violence. *Scandinavian Journal of Psychology, 19,* 213–222.

Larson, M. S. (1993). Family communication on prime-time television. *Journal of Broadcasting and Electronic Media, 37,* 349–357.

Lasker, H., & Bernath, N. (1974). *Comprehension study of Sesame Street affect bits.* New York: Children's Television Workshop. (ERIC Document Reproduction Service No. ED 126 866).

Lazarus, R. S., & Alfert, E. (1964). Short-circuiting of threat by experimentally altering cognitive appraisal. *Journal of Abnormal and Social Psychology, 69,* 195–205.

Liss, M. B., Reinhardt, L. C., & Fredriksen, S. (1983). TV heroes: The impact of rhetoric and deeds. *Journal of Applied Developmental Psychology, 4,* 175–187.

Lovelace, V., Scheiner, S., Sequi, I., & Black, T. (1994). Making a neighborhood the "Sesame Street" way: Developing a methodology to evaluate children's understanding of race. *Journal of Educational television, 20*(2), 69–78.

Lyle, J., & Hoffman, H. R. (1972). Children's use of television and other media. In E. A. Rubinstein, G. A. Comstock, & J. P. Murray (Eds.), *Television and social behavior* (Vol. 4, pp. 129–256). Washington, DC: U.S. Government Printing Office.

Master, J. C., Ford, M. E., & Arend, R. A. (1983). Children's strategies for controlling affective responses to aversive social experience. *Motivation and Emotion, 7,* 103–116.

Meadowcroft, J. M., & Reeves, B. (1989). Influence of story scheme development on children's attention to television. *Communication Research, 16,* 352–374.

Meyer, M., & Tsiantar, D. (1994, August 8). Ninja turtles, eat our dust. *Newsweek,* 34–35.

Morgan, M. (1982). Television and adolescent's sex role stereotypes: A longitudinal study. *Journal of Personality and Social Psychology, 43,* 947–955.

Morison, P., Kelly, H., & Gardner, H. (1981). Reasoning about the realities of television: A developmental study. *Journal of Broadcasting, 25,* 229–242.

Mullin, C. R., & Linz, D. (1995). Desensitization and resensitization to violence against women: Effects of exposure to sexually violent films on judgments of domestic violence victims. *Journal of Personality and Social Psychology, 69,* 449–459.

Nielsen Media Research. (1995). *National television index.* Northbrook, IL: Author.

Noble, G. (1975). *Children in front of a small screen.* Beverly Hills, CA: Sage.

Odom, R. D., & Lemond, C. M. (1972). Developmental differences in the perception and production of facial expression. *Child Development, 43,* 359–369.

Ogles, R. M., & Hoffner, C. (1987). Film violence and perceptions of crime: The cultivation effect. In M. L. McLaughlin (Ed.), *Communication yearbook* (Vol. 10, pp. 384–394). Newbury Park, CA: Sage.

Osborn, D. K., & Endsley, R. C. (1971). Emotional reactions of young children to tv violence. *Child Development, 42,* 321–331.

Paik, H., & Comstock, G. (1994). The effects of television violence on antisocial behavior: A meta-analysis. *Communication Research, 21,* 516–546.

Palmer, E. L., Hockett, A. B., & Dean, W. W. (1983). The television family and children's fright reactions. *Journal of Family Issues, 4,* 279–292.

Pfau, M., Mullen, L. J., & Garrow, K. (1995). The influence of television viewing on public perceptions of physicians. *Journal of Broadcasting & Electronic Media, 39,* 441–458.

Piaget, J. (1952). *The origins of intelligence in children.* New York: International Universities Press.

Piaget, J. (1960). *The child's conception of the world.* London: Routledge.

Potter, W. J. (1986). Perceived reality and the cultivation hypothesis. *Journal of Broadcasting & Electronic Media, 30,* 159–174.

Potter, W. J. (1993). Cultivation theory and research: A conceptual critique. *Human Communication Research, 19,* 564–601.

Potter, W. J., & Ware, W. (1987). An analysis of the contexts of antisocial acts on prime-time television. *Communication Research, 14,* 664–686.

Potts, R., Huston, A. C., & Wright, J. C. (1986). The effects of television form and violent content on boys' attention and social behavior. *Journal of Experimental Child Psychology, 41,* 1–17.

Prawat, D. M., & Prawat, R. S. (1975). Preschoolers' viewing behavior while watching two types of television fare. *Perceptual and Motor Skills, 40,* 575–582.

Rabin, B. E., & Dorr, A. (1995, March). *Children's understanding of emotional events on family television series.* Paper presented at the biennial meeting of the Society for Research in Child Development, Indianapolis, IN.

Rice, M. L., Huston, A. C., & Wright, J. C. (1986). Replays as repetitions: Young children's interpretation of television forms. *Journal of Applied Developmental Psychology, 7,* 61–76.

Rothschild, N. (1984). Small group affiliation as a mediating factor in the cultivation process. In G. Melischek, K. E. Rosengren, & J. Stappers (Eds.), *Cultural indicators: An international symposium* (pp. 377–387). Vienna, Austria: Verlag der Osterreichischen Akademie der Wissenschaften.

Rubin, A. M. (1986). Age and family control influences on children's television viewing. *Southern Speech Communication Journal, 52,* 35–51.

Salmon, G. (1977). Effects of encouraging Israeli mothers to co-observe "Sesame Street" with their five-year-olds. *Child Development, 48,* 1146–1151.

Sarafino, E. P. (1986). *The fears of childhood: A guide to recognizing and reducing fearful states in children.* New York: Human Sciences Press.

Sharkey, B. (1994, October 30). Cover your eyes, quick. *New York Times,* pp. H1, 24–25.

Shrum, L. J. (1995). Assessing the social influence of television: A social cognition perspective of cultivation effects. *Communication Research, 22,* 402–429.

Siegler, R. S. (1991). *Children's thinking* (2nd ed.). Englewood Cliffs, NJ: Prentice-Hall.

Siegel, R. S. (1965). Television and the reactions of school children to the assassination. In B. S. Greenberg & E. B. Parker (Eds.), *The Kennedy assassination and the American public* (pp. 199–219). Stanford, CA: Stanford University Press.

Signoriclli, N. (1991). Adolescents and ambivalence towards marriage: A cultivation analysis. *Youth and Society, 23*(1), 121–149.

Signorielli, N., & Morgan, M. (Eds.). (1990). *Cultivation analysis: New directions in media effects research.* Newbury Park, CA: Sage.

Simons, D., & Silveira, W. R. (1994). Post-traumatic stress disorder in children after television programmes. *British Medical Journal, 308,* 389–390.

Smith, R., Anderson, D. R., & Fischer, C. (1985). Young children's comprehension of montage. *Child Development, 56,* 962–971.

Sparks, G. G. (1986). Developmental differences in children's reports of fear induced by the mass media. *Child Study Journal, 16,* 55–66.

Sparks, G. G. (1989). Understanding emotional reactions to a suspenseful movie: The interaction between forewarning and preferred coping style. *Communication Monographs, 56,* 325–340.

Sparks, G. G., & Cantor, J. (1986). Developmental differences in fright responses to a television program depicting a character transformation. *Journal of Broadcasting & Electronic Media, 30,* 309–323.

Speisman, J. C., Lazarus, R. S., Mordkoff, A., & Davidson, L. (1964). Experimental reduction of stress based on ego-defense theory. *Journal of Abnormal and Social Psychology, 68,* 367–380.

Spirek, M. (1992, May). *The children's coping measure: The development of a scale to indicate monitoring and blunting stress preferences.* Paper presented at the annual conference of the International Communication Association, Miami, FL.

Spirek, M., & Sparks, G. G. (1993, May). *The impact of children's coping style on emotional reactions to a frightening movie.* Paper presented at the annual conference of the International Communication Association, Washington, DC.

Sproull, N. (1973). Visual attention, modeling behaviors and other verbal and nonverbal meta-communication of prekindergarten children viewing Sesame Street. *American Educational Research Journal, 10*(2), 101–114.

St. Peters, M., Fitch, M., Huston, A. C., Wright, J. C., & Eakins, D. J. (1991). Television and families: What do young children watch with their parents? *Child Development, 62,* 1409–1423.

Stipp, H. (1995, May). *Children's viewing of news, reality-shows, and other programming.* Paper presented at the annual conference of the International Communication Association, Albuquerque, NM.

Stoneman, Z., & Brody, G. H. (1982). An in-home investigation of maternal teaching strategies during Sesame Street and a popular situation comedy. *Journal of Applied Developmental Psychology, 3,* 275–284.

Strayer, J. (1987). Affective and cognitive perspectives on empathy. In N. Eisenberg & J. Strayer (Eds.), *Empathy and its development* (pp. 218–244). New York: Cambridge University Press.

Strayer, J. (1989). What children know and feel in response to witnessing affective events. In C. Saarni & P. L. Harris (Eds.), *Children's understanding of emotion* (pp. 259–289). New York: Cambridge University Press.

Surbeck, E., & Endsley, R. C. (1979). Children's emotional reactions to TV violence: Effects of film character, reassurance, age and sex. *The Journal of Social Psychology, 109,* 269–281.

Thomas, M. H., & Drabman, R. S. (1975). Toleration of real life aggression as a function of exposure to televised violence and age of subject. *Merrill-Palmer Quarterly, 21,* 227–232.

Thomas, M. H., Horton, R. W., Lippencott, E. C., & Drabman, R. S. (1977). Desensitization to portrayals of real-life aggression as a function of exposure to television violence. *Journal of Personality and Social Psychology, 35,* 450–458.

Thompson, R. A. (1989). Casual attributions and children's emotional understanding. In C. Saarni & P. L. Harris (Eds.), *Children's understanding of emotion* (pp. 117–150). New York: Cambridge University Press.

Thompson, J. G., & Myers, N. A. (1985). Inferences and recall at ages four and seven. *Child Development, 56,* 1134–1144.

van der Voort, T. H. A., van Lil, J. E., & Vooijs, M. W. (1993). Parent and child emotional involvement in the Netherlands. In B. S. Greenberg & W. Gantz (Eds.), *Desert Storm and the mass media* (pp. 341–352). Cresskill, NJ: Hampton Press.

Van Evra, J. (1990). *Television and child development.* Hillsdale, NJ: Erlbaum.

Wakshlag, J. J., Day, K. D., & Zillmann, D. (1981). Selective exposure to educational television programs as a function of differently paced humorous inserts. *Journal of Educational Psychology, 73,* 27–32.

Watkins, B. A., Calvert, S. L., Huston-Stein, A. C., & Wright, J. C. (1980). Children's recall of television material: Effects of presentation mode and adult labeling. *Developmental Psychology, 16,* 672–674.

Weiss, A. J., Imrich, D., & Wilson, B. J. (1993). Prior exposure to creatures from a horror film. *Human Communication Research, 20,* 41–66.

Weiss, A. J., & Wilson, B. J. (1993, March). *Developmental differences in children's understanding of emotions and emotional storylines in family-formatted situation comedies.* Paper presented at the biennial meeting of the Society for Research in Child Development, New Orleans, LA.

Weiss, A. J., & Wilson, B. J. (in press). Children's cognitive and emotional responses to the portrayals of negative emotions in family-formatted situation comedies. *Human Communication Research.*

Weiss, A. J., & Wilson, B. J. (1996). Emotional portrayals in family television series that are popular among children. *Journal of Broadcasting & Electronic Media, 40,* 1–29.

Wiggers, M., & van Lieshout, C. F. M. (1985). Development of recognition of emotions: Children's reliance on situational and facial expressive cues. *Developmental Psychology, 21,* 338–349.

Williams, M. E., Hall, E. R. & Schiro, K. A. (1995, July). *Childrens response to fictional conflict and violence on Ghostwriter.*Paper presented at the annual conference of the International Communication Association, Albuquerque, NM.

Wilson, B. J. (1987). Reducing Children's emotional reactions to mass media through rehearsed explanation and exposure to a replica of a fear object. *Human Communication Research, 14,* 3–26.

Wilson, B. J. (1989). Desensitizing children's emotional reactions to the mass media. *Communication Research, 16,* 723–745.

Wilson, B. J. (1991). Chidren's reactions to dreams conveyed in mass programming. *Communication Research, 18,* 283–305.

Wilson, B. J., & Cantor, J. (1985). Developmental differences in empathy with a television protagonist's fear. *Journal of Experimental Child Psychology, 39,* 284–299.

Wilson, B. J., & Cantor, J. (1987). Reducing fear reactions to mass media: Effects of visual exposure and verbal explanation. In M. McLaughlin (Ed.), *Communication yearbook 10* (pp. 553–573). Newbury Park, CA: Sage.

Wilson, B. J., Hoffner, C. & Cantor, J. (1987). Children's perceptions of the effectivness of techniques to reduce fear from mass media. *Journal of Applied Developmental Psychology, 8,* 39–52.

Wilson, B. J., Kunkel, D., Linz, D., Potter, J., Donnerstein, E., Smith, S. L., Blumenthal, E., & Gray, T. (1996, February). Violence in television programming overall: University of California, Santa Barbara study. *National television violence study: Executive summary.* Studio City, CA: Mediascope.

Wilson, B. J., Linz, D., & Randall, B. (1990). Applying social science research to film ratings: A shift from offensiveness to harmful effects. *Journal of Broadcasting & Electronic Media, 34,* 443–468.

Wilson, B. J., & Smith, S. L. (1995), May). *Children's comprehension of and emotional reactions to TV news.* Paper presented at the annual conference of the International Communication Association, Albuquerque, NM.

Wilson, B. J., & Weiss, A. J. (1993). The effects of co-viewing with a sibling on preschoolers' reactions to a suspenseful movie scene. *Communication Research, 20,* 214–248.

Wright, J. C., Huston, A. C., Reitz, A. L. & Piemyat, S. (1994). Young children's perceptions of television reality: Determinants and developmental differences. *Developmental Psychology, 30,* 299–239.

Wright, J. C., Huston, A. C., Truglio, R., Fitch, M., Smith, E., & Piemyat, S. (1995). Occupational portrayals on television: Children's role schemata, career aspirations, and perceptions of reality. *Child Development, 66,* 1706–1718.

Wright, J. C., Kunkel, D., Pinon, M., & Huston, A. C. (1989). How children reacted to televised coverage of the space shuttle disaster. *Journal of Communication, 39*(2), 27–45.

Zillmann, D. (1971). Excitation transfer in communication-mediated aggressive behavior. *Journal of Experimental Social Psychology, 7,* 419–434.

Zillmann, D. (1980). Anatomy of suspense. In P. H. Tannenbaum (Ed.), *The entertainment functions of television* (pp. 133–163). Hillsdale, NJ: Erlbaum.

Zillmann, D. (1991). Empathy: Affect from bearing witness to the emotions of others. In J. Bryant & D. Zillmann (Eds.), *Responding to the screen* (pp. 135–167). Hillsdale, NJ: Erlbaum.

Zillmann, D., & Bryant, J. (1994). Entertainment as media effect. In D. Zillmann & J. Bryant (Eds.), *Media effects* (pp. 437–462). Hillsdale, NJ: Erlbaum.

Zillmann, H., Hay, T. A., & Bryant, J. (1975). The effect of suspense and its resolution on the appreciation of dramatic presentation. *Journal of Research in Personality, 9,* 307–323.

Zillmann, D., Williams, B. R., Bryant, J., Boynton, K. R., & Wolf, M. A. (1980). Acquisition of information from educational television programs as a function of differently paced humorous inserts. *Journal of Educational Psychology, 72,* 170–180.

Index